fourth edition

INTRODUCTION TO INTERNATIONAL RELATIONS: Power and Justice

Theodore A. Couloumbis
The University of Athens

James H. Wolfe
The University of Southern Mississippi

PRENTICE HALL, ENGLEWOOD CLIFFS, NEW JERSEY 07632

Library of Congress Cataloging-in-Publication Data

Couloumbis, Theodore A.
    Introduction to international relations : power and justice /
  Theodore A. Couloumbis, James H. Wolfe. -- 4th ed.
        p.   cm.
    Includes bibliographical references.
    ISBN 0-13-484684-2
    1. International relations.   I. Wolfe, James Hastings.
  II. Title.
  JX1391.C68   1990
  327--dc20   89-36267
                                                            CIP

Editorial/production supervision and
   interior design: Serena Hoffman
Cover design: Lundgren Graphics
Manufacturing buyer: Peter Havens
Photo research: Page Poore

Printed in the United States of America
10   9   8   7   6   5   4   3   2   1

ISBN 0-13-484684-2

PRENTICE-HALL INTERNATIONAL (UK) LIMITED, *London*
PRENTICE-HALL OF AUSTRALIA PTY. LIMITED, *Sydney*
PRENTICE-HALL CANADA INC., *Toronto*
PRENTICE-HALL HISPANOAMERICANA, S.A., *Mexico*
PRENTICE-HALL OF INDIA PRIVATE LIMITED, *New Delhi*
PRENTICE-HALL OF JAPAN, INC., *Tokyo*
SIMON & SCHUSTER ASIA PTE. LTD., *Singapore*
EDITORA PRENTICE-HALL DO BRASIL, LTDA., *Rio de Janeiro*

To Alexander and Angela, Christine and Karin

CONTENTS

v

3 THE BALANCE-OF-POWER SYSTEM AND ITS VARIATIONS   39

Part II: National Actors: Their Attributes, Interests, and Policies   59

4 THE NATION-STATE AND NATIONALISM   59

5 POWER AND CAPABILITIES OF NATION-STATES   77

6 NATIONAL INTEREST AND OTHER INTERESTS   96

7 FOREIGN-POLICY DECISION MAKING   114

Part III: International Political Processes: Civilized Actors in a Primitive System   139

8 DIPLOMACY AND STATECRAFT   139

Part IV: The Rudimentary Institutions
of the International System   245

PREFACE

The most descriptive word that comes to mind in qualifying this text is *balance*. Our book has been consciously designed to bridge gaps that have divided the study of international relations at both the teaching and the research levels. Our major shortcoming may be that those comfortably positioned on either side of our bridges may be unwilling to cross them.

Methodologically, our text seeks to juxtapose and where possible synthesize the behavioralist (scientific) and the traditionalist orientations of our discipline. As such, it presents itself as an eclectic approach to the traditionalist-versus-scientific debate.

Philosophically, the text seeks to re-create and present in simple language the timeless debate between the advocates of realism (who emphasize power and survival) and the advocates of idealism (who emphasize moral principles and justice). Here too we seek to synthesize, by arguing for an outlook of "prudent idealism" that might lead to a future world where the "justice of power" can be gradually replaced by the "power of justice." For instance, there are often debates on the merits of foreign policies rooted in general principles and policies generated only by pragmatic considerations. We suggest that in the long run, principles and pragmatism do not necessarily clash. Principled foreign policies can also be prudent foreign policies.

Pedagogically, our text attempts to bridge the division in the field of political science between the students of international politics and those of comparative politics. The latter focus normally on governmental institutions and hierarchical political processes within nation-states. They find that the rule in domestic politics is "order" achieved through methods and processes of peaceful change as legislated, adjudicated, and administered by strong, centralized, and legitimate governmental institutions. On the other hand, the students of international politics find that the international system is in a state of near anarchy. It lacks meaningful central institutions and relies on the "rules" of balanced power to attain a modicum of order. Thus, the two approaches have traditionally studied their respective subject matters without much concern for each other's research, insights, and generalizations. Our text points up the need to synthesize domestic politics, foreign policies, and the overall functioning of the international system. We assume throughout that there is a fundamental unity in all politics, whether domestic or international. We suggest that attempts to insulate domestic and international politics into separate chambers are arbitrary, artificial, and counterproductive. The unity of politics at various levels of analysis has become more evident with the rise of "new actors" in world politics (such as multinational corporations, regional economic units, producers' cartels, religious movements, and ethnic groups), which are having a potent albeit somewhat unexplored impact on world politics.

In the sphere of ideology, we do not seek to bridge the gap between well-identified ideologies such as single-party communism, democratic capitalism, and various forms of fascist or managerial authoritarianism. We just present each of these ideologies in the sense that they affect the style if not the substance of international politics. It is our view, however, that ideological differentiations despite occasional revival periods seem to be gradually declining. We suggest that with technological growth and its ecocidal by-products, most nation-states seem to be heading toward increased governmental intervention as a means of executing the regulatory and conservationist functions that are necessary in complex societies.

Our concluding chapter shows clearly that we cautiously place our faith for the future of humankind in the development of effective and legitimate institutions at the local, national, regional, and global levels. Ideally, humankind can replace war with peaceful change as the "final argument" in the settlement of disputes. We realize that the task of global institutionalization is difficult and risky, but the dangers of a do-nothing attitude and just trusting the "invisible hand" are even greater.

In the last analysis, our book is balanced in the sense that we have tried to write it from the point of view of plain citizens of our planet. We have consciously sought to transcend national, cultural, ideological, political, ethnic, and other biases. In doing so, we hope we have written a book with the interests of humanity as a totality as a guide. It is, of course, up to others to evaluate whether we have succeeded in our endeavors.

In preparing the fourth edition of this text we have continued the practice of incorporating criticisms and suggestions for improvement made by its users—professors and students across the country and overseas. We have, additionally, updated facts and introduced into the discussion insights gained from events and their analysis since 1986. More specifically, we have revised and updated various sections of the book, concentrating on the sections dealing with the evolution of the discipline of international relations, nationalism and ethnicity, national interest, war, arms control (referring to the historic development of the INF treaty), regional integration (with focus on the expanding use of regime analysis), and epidemic diseases (AIDS) as a challenge to the survival of humankind. Tables and figures have been revised, replaced, and, where appropriate, removed, and footnotes and end-of-chapter annotated bibliographies have been reinforced to reflect the latest developments in the state of our discipline.

Over the years we have accumulated a heavy intellectual debt. The previous and present editions of this book have benefited greatly by the evaluations and critical suggestions of Professors Astrid Anderson, Earl Backman, J. John Diestel, Robin Dorff, Arthur E. Dowell, Ole Holsti, Jacob Hurwitz, John Iatrides, Curtis Martin, Neil Richardson, Jerel Rosati, Fred Sondermann, Miriam Steiner, and Raymond Wylie.

We are indebted to our colleagues Glen Camp, Costas Hadjiconstantinou, William Olson, Nicholas Onuf, Abdul Said, and Larman Wilson, who were kind enough to discuss with us portions of the manuscript and to offer useful critical suggestions. Dr. Prodromos Yannas, an adjunct professor at the American University, offered us critical research support as well as his insights and wisdom throughout the taxing fourth edition preparation process. We wish to acknowledge the helpful criticism provided by the fourth edition reviewers: Walter M. Bacon, Jr., University of Nebraska; Waltraud Queiser Morales, University of Southern Florida; and Henry A. Shockley, Boston University. In addition, we would like to thank Sandra J. Wurth-Hough of East Carolina University for producing a thoughtful and practical Instructor's Manual that genuinely reflects the substance of our book while enhancing its use by professors and their associates.

Finally, we are thankful for their firm and professional guidance to the editorial staff of Prentice Hall, especially Karen Horton, Dolores Mars, and Serena Hoffman. Ann Hofstra Grogg, our superb copy editor, is indeed very high on the list of our debts.

Naturally, all the fine persons mentioned above should not be held accountable for our errors of fact, judgment, or omission, for which we are entirely responsible.

The two of us have enjoyed working together in the difficult years of this book's preparation and subsequent revisions. Both of us have worked with every chapter in the book in order to ensure that every chapter reflects our insights and knowledge of the subject matter. James Wolfe has been the primary author of Chapters 9–12, and Theodore Couloumbis has been the primary author of the remaining chapters.

Theodore A. Couloumbis
James H. Wolfe

1

APPROACHES TO THE STUDY OF POLITICS

"What is politics?"

Although answers to this question vary with one's frame of reference, two schools of thought stand in clear juxtaposition under the key words "competition" and "cooperation." Writing in essay number ten of *The Federalist Papers* (1787), James Madison described politics as a constant struggle waged by individuals or groups for economic power and advantage. Opposed to this point of view is the conviction that the cause of justice is best served by political institutions which unite society, either national or global, in a common effort to achieve an equitable distribution of resources. The ideal of the Indian independence leader Mahatma Gandhi (1869–1948) that no individual can gain spiritually while others around him or her suffer is representative of the cooperative interpretation of politics to which the goal of a world polity owes its development. In our analysis of international relations we will endeavor to assess the strengths and weaknesses of both interpretations of political life.

Politics has been defined by scholars as the "authoritative allocation of values,"[1] where *values* stands for desired conditions or commodities and where *authoritative* denotes some form of legitimate (i.e., generally acceptable, official, managerial, governmental) process through which people regulate their interre-

---

[1] David Easton, *The Political System: An Inquiry into the State of Political Science,* 2nd ed. (New York: Knopf, 1971), p. 129. Other works by the same author include *A Framework for Political Analysis* (Englewood Cliffs, N.J.: Prentice-Hall, 1965), and *A Systems Analysis of Political Life* (New York: John Wiley, 1965).

lationships with respect to the question of "who gets what, when, and how."[2] We might be tempted, therefore, to say that political activities are those activities involving people's relationships with their government—whether we are talking about the executive, legislative, or judiciary aspects of government. But some might argue that this is too restrictive a definition of politics, that political relationships exist at all levels of human interaction, provided they involve a clashing of human wills and the attempt by individuals or groups to impose their will upon others. On the basis of this latter, and considerably broader, definition of politics, a parent's attempt to discipline his or her children, the informal hierarchy among inmates in prisons, the "politics" played by faculty, students, and administrators in universities, the disciplinary procedures characteristic of neighborhood gangs, and even the interactions in large, illicit groups such as the Mafia—all these could be considered forms of politics. Politics is, therefore, a concept[3] that could be restrictive or comprehensive in its focus, depending on the definition employed by a given analyst.

Politics could also be understood as a person's *concern* with *public affairs.* Public affairs affect collective interests rather than narrow personal interests. This is approximately the way ancient Greek philosophers visualized the phenomenon of politics. Aristotle, in fact, identified man as "a political animal." Politics derived its name from the Greek word *polis,* which means city. Concern with the affairs of the city was viewed by ancient Athenians as both an honor and a duty. Athens, as a democratic society, was predicated on the existence of free, informed, and concerned citizens *participating* in the affairs of that city. Pericles,

James Madison (1751–1836), fourth president of the United States. (Copyrighted by the White House Historical Association; photograph by the National Geographic Society)

---

[2]Harold D. Lasswell, *Politics: Who Gets What, When, How* (New York: Whittlesey House, McGraw-Hill, 1936).

[3]A *concept* is an abstraction or generalization that helps us organize knowledge for purposes of theoretical inquiry. Some of the basic concepts in the field of politics are justice, power, freedom, interest, equality, security, conflict, peace, and participation.

Mahatma Gandhi (1869–1948), the father of modern India. (UPI/Bettmann Newsphotos)

in his famous funeral oration before his fellow citizens, best exemplified this attitude:

> Our citizens attend both to public and private duties, and do not allow absorption in their own various affairs to interfere with their knowledge of the city's. We differ from other states in regarding the man who holds aloof from public life not as "quiet" but as useless; we decide or debate carefully and in person all matters of policy, holding not that words and deeds go ill together, but that acts are foredoomed to failure when undertaken undiscussed.[4]

ALTERNATIVE STYLES OF POLITICS

Political activities can be categorized in a number of ways. A very common dichotomy is that between *high* and *low* politics. *High politics* is the type of politics played by leaders of countries and by other high-level government officials. High politics in international relations refers to the making of vital, large-impact decisions, such as committing a country to wars or alliances. In the case of domestic politics, high politics involves large-scale decisions and policies such as instituting pathbreaking laws in order to initiate a comprehensive social security system, to

[4]Quoted in Thucydides, *The History of the Peloponnesian War,* ed. and trans. Richard Livingstone (New York: Oxford University Press, 1960), p. 113. Quoted materials are being used here with the permission of Oxford University Press.

call for racial or ethnic integration, to nationalize private industry, or to make radical changes in the system and form of government.

Low politics, on the other hand, is the type of politics usually played by bureaucrats and administrators. It involves small-magnitude decisions that do not alter appreciably the social, political, and economic structure of a country or of the international system. It is also the politics that maintains large social systems in some form of equilibrium. Low politics has been defined additionally as bureaucratic behavior designed to implement high political decisions without disturbing the foundations of the social, political, and economic status quo. Examples of low politics at the international level are the routine replacement and rotation of diplomatic personnel, the administration of technical, economic, and military aid programs, and the facilitation of trade, tourist, and investment exchanges. Low politics at the domestic level includes activities such as passing regulatory laws on environmental pollution, deciding on increments in the minimum wage and in social security benefits, and introducing school-lunch programs.[5]

A second way of subdividing politics is in terms of the *politics of violence* versus the *politics of persuasion*. War or the threat of it, revolution, and civil disturbances of various magnitudes are forms of *violent politics*. The purpose of war—to follow von Clausewitz's reasoning—is to continue politics by violent means.[6] A person, a group, or a country fights or threatens to fight in order to change or control the behavior of an enemy. As long as violence or the threat of it is used with political objectives in mind (namely, to change or to preserve a situation in accordance with one's interests), then one cannot deny these violent acts the status of politics.

The *politics of persuasion*, in turn, could be referred to as the politics of logic, of morality, of cooperation and interdependence, and, on occasion, of bribery (unless one considers bribes and other forms of corruptive incentives as psychological forms of violence). The processes involved here include diplomacy; treaties; negotiations; deliberations; law making; collective bargaining; economic, social, cultural, and scientific cooperation; and even the politics of vigorous competition—provided this competition is carried out under widely accepted and predetermined (i.e., legitimate) rules.

There is, however, a relatively large zone of activities that bridges the politics of persuasion and the politics of violence. In this hybrid zone one finds many instances of persuasive relationships that are the result of either explicit

---

[5]At the international level, high politics has been equated, as we indicated above, with decisions that involve the risk of war. We could, with some justification, criticize this arbitrary association of conflict and war politics with the word *high,* and cooperation and regulation politics with the word *low.* Indeed, it might be high time in international politics to reverse our thinking and equate *high politics* with international cooperation and *low politics* with conflict and war.

[6]Karl von Clausewitz, *On War,* trans. O. J. Matthijs Jolles (New York: Modern Library, 1943). See also the discussion of war in Chapters 10 and 11 of the present text.

or implicit threats of force and violence. Under this heading could be classified numerous activities that are difficult to pinpoint as purely violent or purely persuasive politics. Good examples of hybrid politics are, in the case of domestic affairs, the public's submission to the dictates of a well-entrenched, oppressive, authoritarian regime and, internationally, the obedience of small satellite nations to the dictates of their great-power protectors.

A third subdivision—although somewhat difficult to establish—is between *hierarchical* and *pluralistic* politics. *Hierarchical politics* presupposes pyramidal arrangements of increasing power and authority, both domestically and internationally. Political relationships in this category involve dependencies of subordinate units on superior units. At the apex of each hierarchical society is an ultimate, if not always legitimate, authority from which powers flow to dependent tiers of authority, which in turn control more subordinate tiers, all the way down to the common citizens. Rules are dictated downward from the top parts of this pyramid, interpreted and applied by the middle parts, and absorbed (usually without overt controversy) by the populous majority at the bases.

On the other hand, *pluralistic politics* involves relationships among equal or nearly equal actors. Here, societies consist of well-informed, active, and autonomous political units (individuals, groups, or states) that are quite jealous of maintaining their own independence and well-being, but that also recognize the virtues of cooperative and regulated coexistence for their self-interest as well as for the good of the whole society. Pluralistic politics, we can assume, is practiced in societies that have enough goods and services to satisfy the demands and needs of their members. Further, pluralistic politics assumes a free and competitive system of education and information that does not rely on monopolistic control of the mass media in order to develop a feeling of artificial societal consensus through highly slanted propaganda campaigns.

All politics is to a great extent a mixture of both the hierarchical and the pluralistic types. But one can classify political systems over time as being more or less consensual or more or less hierarchical. For instance, Western-type democracies could be said to exhibit more pluralistic than hierarchical types of political behavior. Political authority in these democracies is supposed to be considerably fragmented and diffused, and policies are the outcomes of publicly waged competition among conflicting interest groups that is refereed by publicly accountable governmental institutions. In contrast, authoritarian systems or polities, whether communist or capitalist, exhibit a greater tendency toward hierarchical forms of politics.

One can also differentiate between hierarchical and pluralistic politics on the international scale. For example, alliances among unequals exhibit more frequent instances of hierarchical politics, whereas alliances among relatively equal partners must rely more heavily on pluralistic arrangements. To illustrate this with a concrete example, we encounter more pluralistic politics in the relations between the United States and Britain than in the relations between the United States and its smaller NATO allies, such as Portugal, Greece, and Turkey.

FOUR APPROACHES TO POLITICS

There is obviously no one generally accepted set of definitions and classifications of politics. We shall therefore discuss here at least four different approaches to the study of politics (whether domestic or international), based on four radically different philosophical foundations.[7] The first is the *realist* approach. This approach argues that politics *should* be played in a *realistic* fashion. Power for the realist is the essence of politics. The realist approach is normative (i.e., prescriptive) in that it recommends the use, by leaders, of amoral and power-oriented political techniques and places the highest priority on the pursuit of one's practical interests. The second approach, the *idealist,* is also normative. Unlike the realist approach, which argues that people should act in the future as they have acted in the past, the idealist approach argues that people should abandon ineffective modes of behavior and, instead, act with knowledge, reason, compassion, and self-restraint. The third approach, the *Marxist,* is at times considered to be a subtype of the idealist approach. It posits that at the basis of politics are issues of economics and that human relationships can best be explained by focusing on the struggle between the capitalists and the working class over the control of the means of production. The fourth approach is the *empirical/scientific.* The strict proponents of this approach argue that politics should merely be observed and reported for what it *is* or *has been* rather than for what it *should be.* These students of politics are especially concerned that one's biases and values not be allowed to color the detached and dispassionate observations of reality—however the chips might fall. In this respect, the fourth approach wishes to be descriptive, explanatory, and predictive but not prescriptive (normative).

Realist Politics

The realist school of thought in international politics has been associated with scholars such as Edward H. Carr, Hans Morgenthau, Arnold Wolfers, and George Kennan.[8] The realists see politics as "a struggle for power."[9] Power is loosely defined as a psychological relationship in which one actor is able to *control* the behavior of another actor. A second central concept for the realists is *interest.* A rational political actor is one who acts to promote his or her interests. The realists

---

[7]Two excellent reviews of the literature on alternative approaches to the study of international politics are contained in John A. Vasquez, *The Power of Power Politics: A Critique* (New Brunswick, N.J.: Rutgers University Press, 1983); and K. J. Holsti, *The Dividing Discipline: Hegemony and Diversity in International Theory* (Boston: Allen & Unwin, 1987).

[8]E. H. Carr, *The Twenty-Years' Crisis, 1919–1939: An Introduction to the Study of International Relations* (London: Macmillan, 1939); Hans J. Morgenthau, *Politics among Nations: The Struggle for Power and Peace,* 5th ed. (New York: Knopf, 1973), and *Scientific Man vs. Power Politics* (Chicago: University of Chicago Press, 1946); Arnold Wolfers, *Discord and Collaboration: Essays on International Politics* (Baltimore: Johns Hopkins University Press, 1962); George F. Kennan, *Realities of American Foreign Policy* (Princeton, N.J.: Princeton University Press, 1954).

[9]Morgenthau, *Politics among Nations,* p. 27.

conveniently close the definitional gap between interest and power by practically equating these two concepts. Thus, to act rationally (that is, to act in one's interest) is to seek power (that is, to have the ability and the willingness to control others).

For the realists, acting in pursuit of personal, group, and national interests is being eminently political. It is also obeying forces that are inherent in human nature. To seek power in order to promote one's interests is to follow the basic dictates of the "laws" of nature. Hence, the realists are quite impatient with the proponents of the idealist school of thought, who argue that politics should follow the highest moral and legal principles. The realists argue that the adoption of legalistic, moralistic, and even ideological behavior in politics tends to run contrary to the forces of nature and to result either in pacifism and defeatism on the one hand or a fierce, exclusivist, and crusading spirit on the other.

So, to sum up, for the realist a "good political person" is a "rational political person"—a person, that is, who understands and seeks power but who also moderates the quest for power because he or she realizes that others also understand and seek power. The rational political person's most important characteristic is *prudence*. The realist is concerned for the survival and the growth of his or her social collectivity. But such a person never risks the collectivity's survival in the pursuit of limitless growth, or in defense of ideological, moralistic, or legalistic righteousness. The rational political person is, in the last analysis, a pragmatist: understandings, bargains, and compromises are more likely to prevail than rules, adjudication, and moral righteousness. For the political realist, Niccolò Machiavelli remains the source and the inspiration of survival-oriented

Niccolò Machiavelli (1469–1527), Florentine writer, statesman, theorist, patriot.

behavior.[10] Morality, legalism, ideologies—these are luxuries that can be pursued only if they do not endanger the viability and the vital interests of the political collectivity or the government that speaks for the collectivity.

Idealist Politics

To the idealist[11] school of thought, the realist maxims appear morbid, reactionary, cynical, and quite often self-serving. The great variety of proponents of the idealist school include pacifists, world federalists, humanitarians, legalists, and moralists. This school is identified with great names such as Henri de Saint-Simon, Mahatma Gandhi, Woodrow Wilson, and Bertrand Russell.[12] The reader should note that practicing politicians, unlike political-science scholars, frequently employ idealist rhetoric. This rhetoric generally remains, however, outside the gates of practical application.

For the idealist, politics is "the art of good government" rather than the "art of the possible." A good political leader does not do what is possible; rather, he or she does what is good. Leadership provides for the good life—which involves justice, obedience to legitimate rules (that is, rules derived from universal moral principles), and respect for fellow humans, both domestically and internationally. Idealists disagree with the fatalistic orientation of the realists, who assume that "power politics" is a natural phenomenon, indeed an unchanging law of nature. For the idealists, no pattern of behavior is unchangeable. Humans have the capacity to learn and to change and control their behavior. Purely interest-motivated behavior reduces a person to the instincts of the beast. Over time, humans learn, improve, and grow. Civilization means learning to coexist in societies, operating under fair laws, and banning the laws of the jungle, which permit the survival only of the most wily, the most powerful, and the most ferocious.

For the idealist the art of the possible, as a guideline for political action, becomes a sinfully permissive type of philosophical justification. It licenses the

---

[10]A native of Florence and a descendant of an established Tuscan family, Machiavelli came to prominence in 1498 with the fall of the Medici family. He assumed at that time the position of first secretary of the Council of the Republic of Florence. He remained in that office until 1512, when the Medici family regained control and subsequently imprisoned him. Pope Leo X, however, interceded on his behalf, and Machiavelli was permitted to live out his life near Florence, where he occupied himself with historical and political writing.

[11]The term *idealist* should be clearly differentiated from the term *ideologue*. Ideologues are fervent proponents of a given ideology. They tend to promote and propagate their ideological tenets while rejecting facts and ideas that challenge their ideological preconceptions. A review of the role of ideologies as these affect and are affected by national interests is presented in Chapter 6.

[12]Bertrand Russell, *Has Man a Future?* (New York: Simon & Schuster, 1962), and *Which Way to Peace?* (London: M. Joseph, 1936); Henri de Saint-Simon, *Social Organization, the Science of Man and Other Writings,* ed. and trans. Felix Markham (New York: Harper & Row, 1964); Mahatma Gandhi, *Gandhi: Selected Writings,* ed. Ronald Duncan (New York: Harper & Row, 1971), and *Gandhi on Non-Violence,* ed. Thomas Merton (New York: New Directions, 1965); Woodrow Wilson, *A Day of Dedication: The Essential Writings and Speeches of Woodrow Wilson,* ed. Albert Fried (New York: Macmillan, 1965), *The State: Elements of Historical and Practical Politics,* rev. Edward Elliott (Boston: D. C. Heath, 1918), and *On Being Human* (New York: Harper & Brothers, 1916).

practitioners of politics to lie, cheat, burgle, kill, and torture, if necessary, in defense of personal, party, or national interests. Political action is thus reduced to a game of deadly violence rather than a game of political wits. In contrast, moral principles—which are universal among all of the world's major religions—can serve as the foundations from which fair and just laws can be derived, which in turn can be applied effectively (that is, with adequate sanctions) against those who break them. Thus, for the idealist, politics should involve the abandonment of force, the encouragement of learning, and the coexistence of societies under the leadership of adequately enlightened rulers.

The dual problem facing the idealists, as one might suspect, is to be found in the nature and in the implementation of their ideas. For example, we must ponder whether an adequate method exists for arriving at the substance of "universal ideals." Will it be possible in a multiculture world occupied by states in drastically different stages of economic development to agree on what is "good politics"? Further, how does one bring about "enlightened societies," both at the domestic and at the international levels? What does one do with the lawbreakers, especially if they become more numerous than those who scrupulously observe the laws? What happens if violence and oppression are employed by ruthless governments in the name of law, order, and justice?

The various proponents of the idealist school are divided with respect to how best to meet internal violence and external aggression by states. The pacifists feel that fighting violence with violence is merely falling into a Machiavellian/realist trap.[13] If one tries, that is, to have one's way (even if this way defends the principles of justice and peace) by using force or violence, then one fulfills the major axiom of the realists—that conflict, regardless of its purpose, is inherent in collective human affairs. The only viable alternative, according to the pacifists, is to resist nonviolently and to hope that in the long run the cultural patterns of good political behavior will displace primitive patterns characterized by "power politics." In contrast, legalists and world federalists argue that the use of centralized and legitimate force is necessary to deter individual actors in a given society from breaking the rules that guarantee collective coexistence without sacrificing fundamental individual rights.[14] These thinkers often point to Western democratic-competitive systems as models of societies that operate in accordance with idealistic principles. These principles include the respect of rules rather than rulers, peaceful and arbitrated change, progressive taxation that allows for gradual redistribution of income and property, fragmented and accountable gov-

[13]See, for example, Russell, *Which Way to Peace?*

[14]See, for example, Grenville Clark and Louis B. Sohn, *World Peace through World Law: Two Alternative Plans*, 3rd ed. (Cambridge, Mass.: Harvard University Press, 1966). For detailed discussions of world federalism, see Richard A. Falk and Saul H. Mendlovitz, "Towards a Warless World: One Legal Formula to Achieve Transition," *Yale Law Journal*, 73 (January 1964), 399–424; Vernon Nash, *The World Must Be Governed* (New York: Harper, 1949); Pittman B. Potter, "The Concept of International Government," *American Political Science Review*, 25 (August 1931), 713–17; B. R. Sen, "An Asian Views World Government," *Annals of the American Academy of Political and Social Science*, 264 (July 1949), 39–45; Quincy Wright, "Empires and World Governments before 1918," *Current History*, n.s., 39 (August 1960), 65–74.

ernmental structures, and, above all, civil rights that guarantee the freedoms of speech, worship, organization, and peaceful petitioning of the government. So, the legalists and world federalists argue, if Western states (the United States primary among them, given its ethnic diversity) can coexist within bounds of controlled violence, and under enlightened and liberal principles of behavior, then a world federation with central authority that monopolizes but does not abuse force can be instituted. Thus, the world will be freed from the scourge of international war and many of its derivative civil wars.

Marxist Politics

The Marxist approach to the analysis of human affairs, which has appeared in many variations, provides us with a combination of predictive and prescriptive maxims that pave the way to what Marxists consider an unavoidable historical route toward the attainment of world communism. The end objective and the inevitable end-state for humanity is a perpetually peaceful classless and stateless society where justice will be understood by the simple principle "from each according to his ability, to each according to his needs."

According to the philosophical fathers of Marxism, Karl Marx and Friedrich Engels, the economic system is at the foundation of every society.[15] Economic relations, therefore, help us explain and understand all social and political relations. The concept of class and the struggle of the classes for control of the means of production is at the root of social interaction. Marx considered the class struggle the most important aspect of the constantly evolving history of human society.

The theory goes on to state that in precommunist societies one privileged class (the bourgeoisie) owns and controls the means of production (tools, machines, assembly lines) as well as the banks and related financial institutions. The bourgeoisie, in turn, dominates the state (i.e., the government and all institutions connected with it) and society at large. In such a situation, the working class (the proletariat) is at the mercy of the all-powerful bourgeoisie for whom it produces a surplus of goods at very low wages. The net result is much wealth for the capitalists and subsistence wages for the debt-ridden working masses.

According to Marxist theory, the capitalist class (bourgeoisie) views labor as just another commodity subject to the laws of economic supply and demand. Hence, the capitalists make a systematic effort to maintain a surplus of labor or, in other words, a certain level of "tolerable" unemployment. A large supply of labor faced with a limited demand for it permits the bourgeoisie to keep wages artificially low, thus enlarging its own profits. The bourgeoisie seeks to perpetuate this favorable state of affairs by using the state (as an ally and an instrument)

[15]See Karl Marx and Friedrich Engels, *Manifesto of the Communist Party* (published 1848) (New York: International Publishers, 1932), and *Das Kapital,* vol. I (published 1867) and vols. II and III (published by Engels in 1885 and 1894), English translation: *Capital: A Critique of Political Economy* (New York: Random House [Modern Library], no date). For an excellent review of Marxist thought as it applies to international relations, see V. Kubálková and A. A. Cruickshank, *Marxism-Leninism and Theory of International Relations* (London: Routledge & Kegan Paul, 1980).

Karl Marx (1818–1883), revolutionist and political, economic, and social theorist, (New York Public Library Picture Collection)

in maintaining control over the working class. The state, in other words, becomes the sword and the shield with which the rich and the powerful maintain their domination over the workers, the weak, the poor, and the illiterate.

Marxist theory posits that the state (i.e., the apparatus of government) has not always existed. Early societies did not require intricate governmental mechanisms until a certain stage of economic development was reached. This stage, which was deeply affected by rapid industrialization patterns in Central and Western Europe, led societies to fragment into distinct and unequal classes (unequal in both size and power). The powerful bourgeoisie soon developed and nurtured the state, an instrument meant to guarantee that the workers would remain permanently in their subordinate place. Simultaneously, the working class was subjected to another effective weapon of the bourgeoisie—social and cultural training. This training, according to Marxist theory, was administered by the capitalists with the aid of state-controlled and state-perpetuated educational institutions and allied religious establishments. For the Marxists, there was only one credible way left to free the masses from their bondage—violent revolution.

Revolution would free the proletariat from the bourgeoisie and would allow workers to take control of the means of production. Violence was viewed as a necessary midwife of revolutionary change, and the new and just society would be forged after a transitional period during which the workers (through the Communist Party) would exercise all political control—a period referred to as the "dictatorship of the proletariat."

Marxist theory predicted that communism would eventually replace capitalism everywhere just as capitalism had replaced its inferior predecessor—feudalism. The fall of capitalism, it was argued, would be the inevitable outcome of irreconcilable contradictions separating the bourgeoisie from the working classes. Marx, writing in the second half of the nineteenth century, predicted that the first proletarian revolutions would take place in advanced capitalist states such as England, France, and Germany, where the working classes were more numerous and developed.

History, however, did not conform to Marxist predictions. Instead, beginning in 1917 communist revolutions have taken place in less industrially developed states such as Russia, China, Cuba, and Vietnam. It became the task of Vladimir Ilyich Ulyanov (Lenin), the architect of the Soviet Union's Bolshevik revolution (1917) and the theoretician of applied communism, to explain this major miscalculation in the predictive capacity of Marxist theory.[16]

Lenin claimed that the ability of advanced Western states to avoid revolution rested with their effectiveness in manipulating the capitalist-inspired international system. The advanced capitalist states, according to Lenin, were given a new lease on life by pampering and co-opting their own workers at home while exploiting the working masses in the colonial territories of the earth. In Lenin's view, imperialism (the domination of new markets and the creation of political dependencies) in what is today the Third World became the highest stage and the last phase of capitalism.[17]

Looking at the record of nation-states where Marxist-Leninist revolutions and takeovers have occurred, we note a considerable gap separating theoretical promise and practical performance. Marxist theory predicted the development of classless and stateless societies after each revolution. But instead of the "state withering away" we have witnessed among communist/socialist states a geometric rise in the size and functional responsibility of governmental authorities. As for the transition to classless societies, we have witnessed the growth of new clusters of powerful and privileged elites (usually associated with Communist Party structures) that have secured for themselves and are perpetuating positions of prominence and power. In fact, in an attempt to provide realistic incentives for production through hard work, the idealistic maxim of Marxism "from each according to his ability, to each according to his *needs*" has been changed to read, "from each according to his ability, to each according to his *work*." (See Article 15 of the Soviet Constitution of 1977.)[18]

Finally, Marxist-Leninist theory had clearly advanced the proposition that international wars had been the product of capitalist-imperialist states searching and competing aggressively for new markets and political dependencies. The logical expectation was, therefore, that wars among socialist (i.e., nonimperialist) states would be unthinkable. In fact, it was argued, once communism as a system of government had spread itself throughout the world, war as a social

---

[16]For the complete works of Lenin, see V. I. Lenin, *Collected Works,* 44 vols. (Moscow: Foreign Language Publishing House, 1963).

[17]V. I. Lenin, *Imperialism: The Highest Stage of Capitalism,* rev. ed. (New York: International Publishers, 1933).

[18]The partial return to market principles in order to generate growth and productivity in the Soviet economy is strongly advocated by Mikhail Gorbachev, *Perestroika: New Thinking for Our Century and the World* (New York: Harper and Row, 1987).

phenomenon would disappear altogether. Instead, the past two decades have been replete with inexplicable (according to Marxist doctrine) inter-communist-state quarrels such as the Soviet military interventions in Hungary (1956), Czechoslovakia (1968), Afghanistan (1979); the cold war between the USSR and the People's Republic of China; and the protracted conflicts between communist states such as China and Vietnam, and Vietnam and Kampuchea (Cambodia).

Scientific Politics

Somewhere between or perhaps altogether outside the range formed by the realists, the idealists, and the Marxists, one finds the scientists or behavioralists of politics. They argue that it is a waste of time to analyze politics from a position of "faith" and "intuition," that humans are either inherently good or evil, exploitive or exploited. Likewise, it is purposeless to make arbitrary statements about violence being either a natural/hereditary phenomenon or an acquired pattern of behavior caused by manipulable environmental conditions such as political cultures, social norms, and class confrontations. The scientists suggest, instead, that human behavior should be observed systematically and comprehensively, that only generalizations rooted in empirical evidence should be formulated, and that these generalizations should then be tested and retested in accordance with the scientific method.

The scientists challenge the unquestioned acceptance of "unscientific" definitions of politics, such as the class struggle, the struggle for power, or the search for a good life. Instead, they prefer inductive definitions (based on observation) such as, "Politics is what the behavior of humans illustrates it to be." So, for the strict scientists the root of politics is the behavior of humans.[19] For a purist proponent of the scientific approach to politics, people are engaged in political behavior when they rule, obey, persuade, compromise, promise, cooperate, bargain, coerce, represent, fight, and fear.[20] Politics is thus defined in terms of observable ranges of action and reaction rather than in terms of abstract concepts and impressions.

The pure scientist views the political person as neither good nor bad by nature, neither conflictive nor cooperative, neither prudent nor adventurist. Scientists have found that individual and collective behavior fluctuate over time and that the same person, given the proper stimuli, is capable of reacting in diametrically opposed fashions. The same person, group, or state may react cooperatively in some situations and combatively in others, depending on variables such as time, place, threat, and environmental challenge. So the guidelines for the scientifically oriented political scientist are: "Observe, observe, observe! Then proceed to offer propositions and hypotheses, but only to the extent that you can support these with observed behavior. And finally, accept your propositions

[19]See Heinz Eulau, *The Behavioral Persuasion in Politics* (New York: Random House, 1963), and *Micro-Macro Political Analysis: Accents of Inquiry* (Chicago: Aldine, 1969).
[20]See Eulau, *Behavioral Persuasion in Politics*, pp. 4–5.

as proven only to the degree to which your data samples are adequate in terms of time, space, and numbers." We find, then, that scientists will rarely advance generalizations that apply to humankind as a whole and over all time. On the contrary, they prefer to look at a few factors and their interrelationships, assuming all other factors to be out of the scope of their study.

There are some problems inherent in the scientific approach to politics, as was the case with each of the previous approaches. If an analyst argues that politics is anything that humans demonstrate it to be, then he or she equates politics with all possible cooperative and conflictive behavior—in other words, all human interaction. There is precious little interactive behavior that can be left out of this catchall definition. The problem, then, lies in the excessive permissiveness of the definition. If, for example, the label *politics* were to be attached with disinterested ease to phenomena such as assassination, bribery, hijacking, sabotage, and saturation bombing, then these violent and treacherous acts would be placed on an equal plane with benign processes such as persuasion, cooperation, compromise, arbitration, and adjudication. To say that politics is all-inclusive, from the pole of love to the pole of war, is perhaps to ignore the essence of politics, which should be peaceful and dignified coexistence, peaceful and equitable regulation of competition, peaceful and equitable redistribution of wealth and status—in short, peaceful and just change.

There is a second and subtler problem that we should be aware of. Some scientists have implicitly assumed that there are two ways of making important decisions: one way is "political" and the other way is "scientific." The argument is then made that scientific decisions are superior in quality and impact to political decisions. Scientific decisions are allegedly made on the basis of adequate information and according to rational criteria concerning the common interest. In contrast, it is argued, political decisions from the collective point of view are irrational, since they are designed to maximize the power and interests of the occasional decision maker and those groups surrounding, and attempting to influence him or her. The obvious implication of all of this argumentation is that informed scientists make better decisions than selfish politicians. But this entire argument proceeds from overambitious assumptions that political decisions regarding "who gets what, when, and how" can indeed be arrived at scientifically. Furthermore, the scientist (now turned politician) may, under a mantle of scientific expertise and scholarship, pursue policies designed to maximize personal or group interests. In the last analysis, for scientists to assume the incorruptibility of fellow scientists is for them to enter securely into the idealist school of thought.

The 1970s introduced a useful attitude of eclecticism among the four approaches discussed above. This trend has been further accelerated in the 1980s. A number of scientifically oriented scholars have abandoned their self-neutralizing role of purely unobtrusive and value-free observation. They have realized that by serving only as human cameras and tape recorders they have been fulfilling useful functions, but in no way positively affecting or changing their environment. Many scientists have, therefore, returned to the values prescribed by realist, idealist, Marxist, or other orientations. In fact, they have sought to combine their rediscovered values with the very best in rigor and accuracy that a systematic application of the scientific method can provide. Other scientists, wishing to become "policy-relevant," have become "policy scientists" and "engineers."[21] Viewed as a social engineer, the political scientist is urged to go beyond observation and explanation. Instead, he or she is urged to focus on societal variables such as population growth, gross national product (GNP) per capita, type of governmental organization, war-proneness, and other factors that are subject to manipulation and control.[22] So if the transportation engineer can build bridges and roads to avoid traffic congestion, the social engineer can recommend or implement social legislation designed to reduce social tension that would otherwise contribute to internal or international conflict. Our "engineer" in the social sciences wishes to move beyond description and explanation and into the realm of action. But at this point, we should caution social scientists to differentiate carefully between engineering projects that are socially desirable and permissible and those that may prove harmful, especially in the long run. The choice here too—ultimately—remains political.

DILEMMAS BETWEEN POWER AND JUSTICE

The central theme of our book involves the reconciliation of the reality of power with the need to evolve structures and processes capable of securing justice. Following the political theorist John Rawls, justice may be said to embody two principles.[23] The first is that each individual or, in world politics, nation-state should possess a status of equality compatible with the rights and duties of others. The second follows from the first in that the distribution of global resources should, while not being equal, be to everyone's advantage.[24] These ideals may appear unrealistic when viewed against a background of statecraft often dominated by a recourse to military force. As Willy Brandt, a leader of the Socialist International and chancellor of the Federal Republic of Germany from 1969 to 1974, has pointed out: "What do freedom, justice and dignity mean to those who go hungry to bed today, not knowing if they will eat tomorrow? In other words: social and liberal human rights go together."[25]

In his history of the Peloponnesian War (431–404 B.C.) Thucydides highlighted within the Western tradition the problem of power and justice by report-

[21]Davis Bobrow, *International Relations: New Approaches* (New York: Foreign Policy Association, 1972).

[22]See Nazli Choucri and R. C. North, "Dynamics of International Conflict: Some Policy Implications of Population, Resources, and Technology," *World Politics*, supplement 24 (Spring 1972), 80–122.

[23]John Rawls, *A Theory of Justice* (Cambridge, Mass.: Belknap Press at Harvard University Press, 1971), pp. 60–62.

[24]An engaging and readable review of the literature, identifying dilemmas involving considerations of power/interest versus collective survival in a setting of distributive justice, is Lynn H. Miller, *Global Order: Values and Power in International Politics* (Boulder, Colo.: Westview Press, 1985).

[25]For this appeal to justice rather than power, see Willy Brandt, *World Armament and World Hunger: A Call for Action* (London: Victor Gollancz, 1986), p. 193.

ing a series of contrived dialogues between the proponents of justice as a basis for international behavior and those who view power as the true guide to a successful policy. In each debate the first side would render an appeal to Hellenic law as the framework within which to secure justice within the Greek city-state system. The standards of nonintervention, adherence to alliance, and respect for human rights were the goals of this school of thought. Opposed were those who advocated, often with undisguised cynicism, the thesis that in international politics the strong take what they can and the weak surrender what they must. Thucydides left no doubt that the advocates of expediency and power invariably won out in the councils of state.

The Indian Kautilya, a keen observer of political behavior in the ancient world, contributed to the origins of realism by making power the focal point of his theoretical framework. Although little is known of Kautilya, his writings, dating from the fourth century B.C., have survived to provide us with what was probably the first systematic effort to formulate empirical rules of statecraft. As we will see in Chapter 5, he concentrated on a concept of power defined in terms of goal attainment and from that derived an intricate set of maxims whereby a "conqueror" could maintain and expand his domain. Propaganda, espionage, and even assassination were the prescribed techniques of control at home and of subversion abroad. Kautilya's work bears the title *Arthasastra* (Art of Government), that is, a description of the world as it is rather than as it should be. Although his principles may sound cynical and harsh, Kautilya would doubtlessly argue in his defense that he merely accepted the reality of the uncontrolled anarchy which is international relations. Many centuries later, a subcommittee of the U.S. Senate published a series of reports (1975–76) that raised serious questions about the compatibility of clandestine political warfare with constitutional democracy. A reading of Kautilya places the Senate findings in perspective and enhances one's appreciation of the problem of covert action as employed by democratic states.

The realistic, if somewhat pessimistic, views of human nature sketched by Thucydides and Kautilya derived from both direct observation and intuitive wisdom. Their unclouded description of the dynamics of international politics did not preclude a consideration of the question of how policy makers ought to behave. Thucydides's account of the internal political decay of Athens during a prolonged war possesses an analytical dimension worthy of recognition today. Kautilya's "conqueror" sought power not only for its own sake but also to secure the lives and property of his subjects and to provide a semblance of stability in an otherwise anarchical world. As morally questionable as subverting a neighboring government may be, it was preferable to open warfare in which innocents would perish. Kautilya conceived of an early world-order model based on a delicate balance of power, which he termed a "circle of states." His goal—certainly a prescriptive one—was a reduction in international violence. In this instance, as in others, empirical rules of political action tend over time to assume a character which is partially prescriptive.

The Thucydidean and Kautilyan emphasis on realism and power stands in contrast to the interpretation of government as an institution established to achieve justice. The Chinese philosopher Confucious (K'ung-fu-tzu, 551–478 B.C.) was perhaps the earliest proponent of this positive interpretation of human nature, which presumed a set of relations among individuals and governments as conforming to a carefully articulated set of mutual obligations. A heavenly mandate bestowed governmental authority on rulers and committed them to a policy of securing justice for their subjects. Despite continuing warfare among the dynasties of ancient China, Confucianism and its ideal of justice persisted and laid an ethical basis for the political culture of modern China.

In the Mediterranean world Plato (428–347 B.C.) interpreted the role of the Greek city-state (*polis*) as one of securing justice for individuals and society. In the *Republic* Plato portrayed his teacher Socrates as initiating a dialogue by asking the pivotal question, "What is justice?" The ensuing exchange of views established a concept of politics as a means whereby individuals join together to achieve shared goals within the framework of a society. In the wake of the Peloponnesian War, Socrates was accused of "crimes" against his native Athens and put to death. The philosopher's tragic fate is typical of that which skeptics often ascribe to idealists, yet we remember Socrates for his steadfastness in the cause of justice and have long since forgotten those who condemned him.

The unifying concept of this book is the art of politics. Politics blends the affairs of people—acting as individuals, groups, nation-states, alliances, empires, and transnational and international organizations, and seeking to maximize their individual and collective well-being. The basic challenge of all politics is to arrive at a fair and workable harmonization of conflicting individual, group, and aggregate human needs. In well-functioning societies, organized sensitive and legitimate institutions offer the necessary regulatory mechanisms for effective and equitable distribution of opportunity, income, and responsibility. The main problem with the international system when viewed as a political community has been the absence of effective and legitimate political institutions. In an atmosphere of relative international anarchy, diplomacy and war have sought to fill the globe's institutional gap. It is, therefore, an important objective of this book to discuss and analyze the existing, inadequate international system, which is founded infirmly on the risk of war. Our hope is that with increased understanding the generations of people to come will gradually but steadily transform the earth into a well-regulated community free of the scourge of war and the plight of poverty.

We shall proceed throughout this book on the assumption that international and domestic politics are not separate entities but are interrelated levels of political activity linked by a common need to reconcile the ideal of justice with the reality of power. In a world of increasing interdependence and interpenetration, domestic and international variables fuse so closely that a political analyst separates them only at his or her peril. Although the following chapters focus on discrete aspects of international relations, we enjoin our readers not to lose sight of the continuity of politics, whether domestic or international, and nowhere is that continuity more evident than in the search for a balance between power and justice.

SUGGESTIONS FOR FURTHER STUDY

The literature devoted to reconciling power and justice spans centuries. Thucydides' chronicle, *The Peloponnesian War* (431–404 B.C.) is a premier example. Kautilya, an Indian thinker of the fourth century B.C., wrote a treatise on the balance of power and statecraft—the *Arthasastra* (Art of Government), available in translation from Sanskrit by either R. Shamasastry (8th ed.; Mysore: Mysore Printing and Publishing, 1967), or R. P. Kangle (2nd ed.; Bombay: University of Bombay, 1972). The classic Chinese study of war and diplomacy is Shang Yang, *The Book of Lord Shang,* trans. J. J. L. Duyvendak (Chicago: University of Chicago Press, 1963). Nizam al-Mulk (1018–1092) laid the basis for much of contemporary international law in *The Book of Government or Rules for Kings,* trans. Hubert Darke (2nd ed.; London: Routledge & Kegan Paul, 1960). The Arab scholar Ibn Khaldûn (1332–1406) made a major contribution to the theory of the state as an international actor in *The Muqaddimah: An Introduction to History,* trans. Franz Rosenthal, 3 vols. (New York: Pantheon Books, 1958). A compendium of his thought is available in *An Arab Philosophy of History: Selections from the Prolegomena of Ibn Khaldun of Tunis,* trans. Charles Issawi (London: John Murray, 1950). The Florentine diplomat Niccolò Machiavelli (1469–1527) used an empirical and historical technique in *The Prince*—a set of guidelines for survival in the milieu of power politics. Francesco Guicciardini, a compatriot and sometime collaborator of Machiavelli, utilized historical research to advance an incomplete, yet fruitful theory of the balance of power in his *Ricordi,* as translated by Mario Domandi in *Maxims and Reflections of a Renaissance Statesman* (New York: Harper Torchbooks, 1965).

2

THE STUDY
OF INTERNATIONAL RELATIONS:
THEORY AND PRACTICE

International relations[1] as a distinct field of study has developed primarily in an Anglo-American setting.[2] It has been taught as one or more courses in departments of political science of various colleges and universities. The components of the field of international relations include international relations theory, American and comparative foreign policy analysis, international law, international organization, comparative politics and regional (or area) studies, strategic studies, international development, international communications, and peace studies and conflict resolution (including concern with arms control and disarmament).

There is some debate among international relations scholars with respect to the status of the field. Some consider it as a subdivision of the greater field of political science and emphasize the need to study political phenomena at the global level. Others view problems such as peace maintenance, arms control, population control, and development as subjects suitable only for interdisciplinary research teams drawing on the expertise of many disciplines including political science, economics, sociology, psychology, anthropology, business management,

---

[1]Frequently terms such as *international politics, world politics,* and *international affairs* have been employed as synonyms for *international relations.* For a comprehensive review of the history and development of international relations, see William Olson and Nicholas Onuf, "The Growth of a Discipline," in *International Relations: British and American Perspectives,* ed. Steve Smith (Oxford: Blackwells, 1985)

[2]The Anglo-American dominance of the field of international relations is convincingly documented in K. J. Holsti, *The Dividing Discipline: Hegemony and Diversity in International Theory* (Boston: Allen & Unwin, 1985).

public administration, engineering, physics, chemistry, medicine, cybernetics, and communication, to name a few. In the view of the authors of this book this should not be an either-or proposition. Our view is that we can proceed separately and simultaneously with both these orientations, which are mutually reinforcing rather than mutually exclusive.

Before World War I, faculties of history, law, and philosophy shared the responsibility for the teaching of international relations. Historians recorded the substance of diplomacy and strategy; jurists interpreted treaties and national legal practices; and philosophers speculated on human nature, war, peace, and justice.

World War I demonstrated to scholars the fragility and inadequacy of traditional European diplomacy as a means of securing world order. After four years of stalemated warfare in which over twenty million lives were lost, world public opinion demanded the abolition of war as an instrument of statecraft and the establishment of a global system of collective security capable of restraining the ambitions of aggressors. The outlook of that period was typified in the United States under President Woodrow Wilson, where World War I became known as the "war to end war."

The emergence of the United States as a power with global responsibilities in the 1920s stimulated the teaching of international relations as a separate discipline at American universities. As a result, in most colleges and universities, courses on the subjects of international relations, international law, and international organization were added to their political-science curriculums. Prevailing scholarship, still shocked by the memories of World War I, adopted an essentially legalistic-moralistic (i.e., *idealist*) approach, and looked upon war as both an accident and a sin. War was regarded as an accident because of the absence of international institutions effective in providing meaningful alternatives to this "ultimate argument of kings."[3] It was viewed also as a sin because it revealed the darker side of human nature and was therefore to be suppressed as vigorously as possible. The most promising antidote to war appeared to be that of a world government with adequate adjudicatory and enforcement powers to resolve disputes among states. Federalism, following its successful application in the United States, became a fashionable blueprint for well-meaning scholars seeking to substitute world order and rationality for the uncertainty and disorder of war and the international balance of power.

Unfortunately, this era of liberalism and hopefulness did not last for long. The expansionist policies of Nazi Germany and Imperial Japan in the 1930s deeply undermined the idealist search for peace through legal norms applied by supranational institutions. Soon thereafter, the interwar period's designs for a rational, legal world order lay in the ruins of the shattered cities of Asia and Europe. World War II, which left more than sixty million dead, proved no monu-

---

[3]The analogy of a busy downtown intersection without a functioning traffic light or policeman was often presented as explaining the frequency of political collisions.

ment to the rationality and orderliness of humankind. After World War II a new generation of pragmatic scholars arose, determined never again to succumb to the lure of an idealism so powerful that it had prevented their predecessors from anticipating, confronting, and neutralizing the probing tactics of Asian and European totalitarian powers in the 1930s. This new school of thought termed itself *realist* and rejected out of hand the previously dominant legalistic and moralistic guidelines for diplomacy.

In the 1950s the realists became the prevalent school of thought in international relations. Using the argument that only policies based on power could afford a semblance of global security, they had comparatively little difficulty in overcoming the remnants of the idealistic tradition associated with the popular conception of Wilsonian diplomacy. A vocal debate between realists and idealists continued, however, and commanded considerable attention in journal articles, professional conferences, and university classrooms.

Gradually, an increasing number of international relations scholars found that the dictums of "power politics" were also too imprecise and intuitive to be an effective guide for either analysis or action. They searched for a new approach, one of a scientific character and suited to the needs of a postindustrial power with global commitments and capabilities.

In the late 1950s, such an approach emerged in the form of a third school of thought, which rejected both the realist and idealist traditions in international relations. Dubbing themselves *behavioralists* in recognition of their debt to the methods and findings of such behavioral sciences as sociology, economics, and psychology, the adherents of the new approach were quick to declare the *traditionalist* view of world politics, whether idealist or realist, to be of interest only as a foundation upon which to build a genuine science of international relations.[4] The debate between the proponents of the behavioral or scientific approach and the adherents of traditional historical and legal studies has characterized the field of international relations for well over two decades. Indeed, much of the traditionalist-behavioralist dialogue concerning the relevance of international-relations theory to the policy maker centers on the relative merits of the two approaches. As we shall see shortly, beginning with the mid-1970s the debates among the idealists, realists, and behavioralists have subsided considerably. Newer, *postbehavioral* approaches, employing a more tolerant and eclectic orientation, have sought to modify and reorient the study of international relations away from traditional concerns such as diplomacy and wars between national governments and toward treating the planet earth as an endangered community that needs to develop newer global institutions in order to secure its survival well into the twenty-first century.

---

[4]Whether consciously or subconsciously, behavioralist scholars dubbed their non-quantitatively-oriented colleagues as *traditionalists,* thus raising images of scholarship that would be soon considered a "museum piece." We, on the contrary, are using the term *traditionalist* without a pejorative connotation.

THE TRADITIONALIST, SCIENTIFIC, AND POSTBEHAVIORAL SCHOOLS OF THOUGHT

Since the traditionalist scholars[5] predated the scientific school[6] by at least one generation, we shall open with their conception of the discipline of international relations. According to most traditionalists (of the idealist or realist orientation), international relations is the study of patterns of action and reaction among sovereign states. It covers a range of relationships spanning from cooperation to conflict and from peace to war. For the realist the task is to understand the clashing of interests that "inevitably" leads to war. For the idealist the task is to eliminate war by developing institutions for the peaceful settlement of disputes.

Traditionalist scholars assume that a myriad of factors (or variables) affect the behavior of diplomats and soldiers as implementers of state policy. These variables range from the climatic conditions, geographic location, and population density of a given nation-state to its literacy rates, historical and cultural traditions, economic conditions and commercial interests, religious and ideological maxims, and historical myths, as well as the capricious quirks of national leaders and their supportive elites. But an attempt to trace the reasons behind the actions of a given government to a hierarchical order among these variables—according to the traditionalist—is a hopeless task; at best, it results in highly tenuous hypotheses. The traditionalists, therefore, consider as most important the observed behavior of governments, which they explain in terms of concepts such as the *balance of power*, the *pursuit of national interest*, the quest for *world order*, and the diplomacy of *prudence*. We shall return to these concepts in some detail in later portions of this text.

There is a voluminous body of *traditional theory* (especially of the realist variety) to which we can refer. Among the leading contributors to traditional scholarship are Raymond Aron, Stanley Hoffmann, Hans Morgenthau, Reinhold Niebuhr, and Arnold Wolfers. Representative of this school is the theory of *political realism* advanced by Hans Morgenthau. According to Morgenthau, the political realist can safely predict that state behavior will reflect the rational actions of diplomats and soldiers who strive to maximize benefits for their countries within

---

[5]The citations below are only a sample of a huge body of traditional literature: Raymond Aron, *Peace and War: A Theory of International Relations* (New York: Doubleday, 1966); Inis L. Claude, Jr., *Power and International Relations* (New York: Random House, 1962); Stanley Hoffmann, *The State of War: Essays on the Theory and Practice of International Politics* (New York: Praeger, 1965); Hans J. Morgenthau, *Politics among Nations: The Struggle for Power and Peace*, 5th ed. rev. (New York: Knopf, 1978); Reinhold Niebuhr, *Moral Man and Immoral Society: A Study in Ethics and Politics* (New York: Scribner's, 1947); Frederick L. Schuman, *International Politics: The Western State System and the World Community*, 6th ed. (New York: McGraw-Hill, 1958).

[6]See, for example, the works of scientifically oriented scholars: Karl W. Deutsch et al., *Political Community and the North Atlantic Area* (Princeton, N.J.: Princeton University Press, 1957); Harold Guetzkow et al., *Simulation in International Relations* (Englewood Cliffs, N.J.: Prentice-Hall, 1963); Morton A. Kaplan, ed., *New Approaches to International Politics* (New York: St. Martin's Press, 1968); Herbert C. Kelman, ed., *International Behavior* (New York: Holt, Rinehart & Winston, 1965); James N. Rosenau, ed., *International Politics and Foreign Policy*, 2nd ed. rev. (New York: Free Press, 1969); J. D. Singer, ed., *Quantitative International Politics* (New York: Free Press, 1968).

the limits of prudence, limits established by the need for political as well as national survival. Morgenthau has elevated the concept of *power* (that is, the capability of one foreign-policy elite to dominate the thoughts and actions of another) to central importance in the analysis of international politics. But the central concept of political power often defies an operational (i.e., specific and readily quantifiable) definition, for it is a psychological relationship of dominance that may be based on factors varying from the intangible of moral persuasion to the potential reality of a nuclear-strike capability.[7]

The definitional problem regarding the concept of power characterizes other concepts fundamental to traditionalist theory. Among these are *national interest, balance of power,* and *world order,* which are often used with different meanings by the same author in a single chapter. The concept of balance of power may, for example, serve as a slogan justifying either the maintenance of the international status quo for satisfied states or the revision of the status quo for states seeking to pursue irredentist claims. Both sides argue in the interest of a given balance of power. But which is the better balance, the present or the future? The answer depends upon where one sits, how satisfied, frustrated, or ambitious one is, and what one envisions to be the future of humankind.

In summation, the traditionalists have enabled us to sketch some general propositions about international politics that serve to explain and, to a limited degree, predict the responses of foreign-policy elites in crisis situations. The historical empiricism that is the hallmark of the traditionalist approach has also made an important contribution to the field. Traditionalists generally regard international relations to be a subdivision of political science and philosophy, but a subdivision with unique features that endow it with a separate identity. Unlike political science—which they assume is primarily the study of the governance of established political communities—traditionalists treat international relations as the study of the nearly anarchic relations existent among sovereign political entities. These sovereign entities recognize no supreme international judge or referee, and they resort to threat of force or outright war in order to protect and advance what they consider to be their vital interests. Thus, whereas traditionalists view political science as the analysis of "order" in the distribution of political goods in relatively stabilized and advanced political systems, they consider international relations as the study of "disorder" in a nearly primitive and inegalitarian international system.

It is on this issue of the identity of the field that the scientific (or behavioral) school of thought first challenged the traditionalists—for the scientists generally consider international relations to be too broad and complex a field to fit within the confines of political science or any other single discipline. Most advocates of the scientific approach believe international relations to be an interdisciplinary field and emphasize "international" concepts and problems not only in political science and history, but also in the experimental social sciences and,

---

[7]Morgenthau, *Politics among Nations: The Struggle for Power and Peace,* 5th ed. (New York: Knopf, 1973), p. 28.

when appropriate, the natural sciences. It should be pointed out that both the traditionalist and the scientific schools are to varying degrees interdisciplinary. The distinction between the two lies primarily in the effort of the latter to overcome the alleged imprecision of the former by employing quantitative techniques and model building. According to the scientifically oriented scholars, international relations has reached a traditionalist plateau, and a new set of methodological tools must now be employed if the heights of theory are to be ascended.

The scientists are typically skeptical of traditionalist "theories" because they consider them to be too vague and inclusive to furnish useful explanations of international political behavior, or too impressionistic and flexible to withstand the rigorous scientific test of verification. Most scientific scholars are strong believers in the empirical method, inductive reasoning, and comprehensive testing of hypotheses; explicit rules or principles must always be confirmed by repeated observation and testing. Scientific scholars insist on the *operationalization* of concepts by the precise measurement of variables. *Operationalization* refers to a process by which one uses detailed rules for definition and coding to turn relevant facts into "data" that is quantifiable and, therefore, measurable. This allows other independent observers to repeat the observations and check their accuracy. The stress on the exact measurement of variables leads scientific scholars to recommend extensive training in statistical techniques and computer sciences to those who would enter the field.

Propositions and conclusions derived from such unstructured processes as intuition and deep but unquantifiable insight are unacceptable to the scientists, who argue that traditionalism has little to offer methodologically other than the "wisdom approach." Given the rigor of their criteria, the scientists believe that it is too early to advance general theories of international relations.[8] There are so many variables that affect the behavior of the international system that it is impossible to link them all scientifically. Therefore, most scientists concentrate on intermediate-level projects that link and relate a few selected variables at a time. By this incremental method they hope to achieve gradually a consistent set of partial or middle-range theories that will stand the test of empirical verification.

Some scientific scholars, in their attempt to study international politics in an abstract and timeless fashion, have constructed conceptual frameworks and partial models of the international system. Then, with the assistance of graduate students and colleagues, they have collected data relevant to these models in order to verify or discard their initial hypotheses. Presumably, this procedure imparts additional credibility to the general but imprecise frameworks of the traditionalist school. Some scientists, such as Deutsch, Kaplan, and Rosenau,[9] have advanced tentative hypotheses that provide sweeping analogues of political behavior in an international environment, but for the most part their colleagues

---

[8]Some scientifically oriented scholars have endeavored to formulate theories encompassing the entire international system. See especially Kaplan, ed., *New Approaches to International Relations.*
[9]For citations of their work, see note 6.

have concentrated in depth on narrower, more tangible projects—despite occasional criticisms that they are studying microscopic trivia.

Typical of middle-range investigations designed to develop clusters of theory that can later be combined into a set of descriptive, explanatory, and predictive propositions on international political behavior is the research of J. David Singer and Melvin Small, who have focused on the statistical correlation of such variables as the incidence of war and alliance policy in Europe from 1815 to 1945.[10] As a result, Singer and Small have advanced modest and careful propositions on the degree to which alliances contribute to, are irrelevant to, or prevent war. One major problem with this type of study is that too many other variables besides alliances may have contributed to the warlike behavior of a given nation-state. (Some of these variables are outlined in Chapter 10.)

Another example of microscopic and systematic analysis is Ole Holsti's exhaustive "content analysis" of the public speeches, articles, books, and communiques of John Foster Dulles, U.S. secretary of state from 1953 to 1959.[11] Holsti sought to reconstruct Dulles's "belief system" and thus explain the secretary's apparent extreme distrust of the allegedly conniving, conspiratorial, fiercely ideological, and predatory Soviet state. Although everything Dulles had written for the public record was available to Holsti for the purpose of coding and measuring, he was not allowed to see Dulles's private and classified papers. Ultimately—and this was perhaps the grand limitation—Holsti could not enter Dulles's mind to determine whether or not the secretary subordinated his diplomacy to his world view, or whether his professed image of the Soviet union and its leadership was merely a convenient political myth.

Thus far, the scientific school has produced "more promise than performance," to paraphrase J. David Singer, and more process analysis than substantive experimentation.[12] Its main contribution has been the leadership of the "methodological revolution" that the international-relations field began to experience in the early 1950s. The application of the scientific method to international relations has brought to the field not only concepts and sophisticated research tools from other social sciences, but also a body of "pretheory" that lends itself to testing and verification procedures. Although the scientists have thus far offered the political science community few fully substantiated theoretical propositions, the promise of their endeavors is worth awaiting, for its fulfillment will mean that theorists in international relations will be able to predict accurately and, by implication, to control the behavior of actors on the international scene.

---

[10]See J. David Singer and Melvin Small, "National Alliance Commitments and War Involvement, 1818–1945," in *International Politics and Foreign Policy,* ed. Rosenau, 2nd ed. rev., pp. 513–42.

[11]Ole Holsti, "The Belief System and National Images: A Case Study," *Journal of Conflict Resolution,* 6 (1962), 244–52.

[12]J. David Singer, "The Behavioral Science Approach to International Relations: Payoff and Prospects," in *ibid.,* p. 69. In a carefully researched study John Vasquez has demonstrated that only a disappointing number of 48 hypotheses out of a total of 7,158 generated by the scientific school of thought have not been falsified. See his *Power of Power Politics: A Critique* (New Brunswick, N.J.: Rutgers University Press, 1983), p. 202.

In the late 1960s and the 1970s the intensity of the debate between traditionalists and behavioralists began to subside. Both schools of thought have retreated from polemical stances such as "politics cannot be studied scientifically" or "political science without quantification and value freedom is not very useful." Instead, we are seeing more and more eclectically oriented studies (the postbehavioral orientation), often combining elements of the scientific approach with clear value objectives such as the control of nuclear weapons, the substitution for war of peaceful methods for dispute settlement, the control of population, the protection of the environment, and the eradication of poverty, disease, and human alienation.

A very good example of the postbehavioral eclectic trend can be provided by a study conducted in the mid-1980s by University of Hawaii professor Rudolph Rummel.[13] In this study Rummel, a well-known student of the behavioral/scientific orientation, using well-developed statistical methods to process his data, presented evidence confirming some of the earliest nineteenth century liberal-theory hypotheses regarding the "causes" of war. Rummel specifically tested and confirmed two hypotheses. The first of these asserts that democratically governed states with free-enterprise economies become involved in fewer wars than authoritarian states and/or states with centrally planned economies (i.e., with communist governments). The second hypothesis, startlingly, demonstrates that what Rummel calls libertarian states (free-enterprise democracies) just do not engage in wars with each other. Unlike early behavioralists, Rummel stated in this article that he saw nothing incompatible between proposing normative or even ideologically oriented hypotheses provided they are subjected to scientific testing designed to verify or falsify these hypotheses. The publication of Rummel's findings has proven quite challenging and controversial and has generated a heated academic debate between Rummel and his critics.[14]

Assessing the scholarly production of the 1980s, we observe that the field of international relations continues to be in a state of fluidity and transition involving a variety of approaches competing to secure the status of *dominant paradigm*.[15] Most books and journal articles focusing on questions of foreign policy, area studies, arms control, deterrence, and development are proceeding along the path of the traditional-realist approach outlined earlier.[16] In the more theoretically oriented journals,[17] however, there is a growing emphasis on the study

[13]R. J. Rummel, "Libertarianism and International Violence," *Journal of Conflict Resolution,* 27, no. 1 (March 1983), 27–71.

[14]See the Jack Vincent versus R. J. Rummel debate in *International Studies Quarterly,* 31, no. 1 (March 1987), 103–25.

[15]The word *paradigm* has been defined variously. Let it stand for schools of thought sharing some basic assumptions about a field of study, including its primary units of analysis and the typical modes of interactive behavior among those units. A formal treatment of scientific waves of thought can be found in Thomas Kuhn, *The Structure of Scientific Revolutions* (Chicago: University of Chicago Press, 1962).

[16]One of the most influential new voices continuing on the state-dominant realist tradition is Robert G. Gilpin, *War and Change in World Politics* (New York: Cambridge University Press, 1981). See also K. J. Holsti, *Dividing Discipline.*

[17]See for example *International Studies Quarterly, International Organization, World Politics.*

of the behavior of political actors in addition to the nation-state, such as multinational corporations, regional and global international organizations, international regimes,[18] terrorist organizations, political parties, social classes, pressure groups, and a variety of additional political actors (see the discussion in Chapter 18). These newer theoretical endeavors have been named the *dependency,* the *world-order,* and the *interdependence* schools of thought.

Dependency theorists,[19] proceeding in most instances from a Marxist perspective, argue that *class* is a much better unit of analysis than *state*. They believe that international relations divides the world horizontally (into nation-states), while the reality of political and economic life can be better understood in vertical terms by depicting the capitalist classes and their domination of the working classes.

World-order theorists—whose approaches are examined at some length in Chapter 19—represent the latest strand in idealist thought.[20] Focusing on threats facing humankind such as nuclear war, environmental pollution, finite-resource exhaustion, and overpopulation, they call for a peaceful transition from the current anarchic international system to a world order based on participatory and legitimate global institutions. Failure to make this transition will, they fear, result in the destruction of the planet either through a nuclear holocaust or through environmental collapse followed by global famine and pestilence.

The *interdependence school*[21] represents a synthesis of idealist and realist assumptions and propositions. These theorists employ the idealist tradition in forecasting the gradual development of a global system of *complex interdependence* in which economic, technological, and cultural interpenetration will render classical warfare over territorial issues obsolete. They then revert to realist premises when they focus on international clusters of specialized activity (which they call *regimes*) such as international trade, international debt, arms control and disarmament, deep-seabed exploitation, and others. Regime studies employ realist hypotheses in the sense that they relate regime stability to the existence of a single hegemonic power or a nucleus of great powers that together establish the basic rules of the game.

Having concluded this brief review of the history of international relations as a discipline, we should perhaps pause and ask ourselves this question: What is the proper outlook and training for a specialist in the field of interna-

---

[18]The most widely quoted definition of *regime* is Stephen Krasner's. It reads: regimes are "implicit or explicit principles, norms, rules and decision-making procedures around which actors' expectations converge in a given area of international relations." Given its comprehensiveness, this definition is admittedly elusive. See Stephen Krasner, "Structural Causes and Regime Consequences: Regimes as Intervening Variables," *International Organization,* 36 (Spring 1982), 185.

[19]For representative examples of dependency theory, see Fernando Cardoso and Enzo Faletto, *Dependency and Development in Latin America* (Los Angeles: University of California Press, 1979); see also Johan Galtung, "A Structural Theory of Imperialism," *Journal of Peace Research,* no. 8 (1971), 81–118.

[20]For a good example of this type of literature, see Richard Falk, *A Study of Future Worlds* (New York: Free Press, 1975).

[21]The undisputed leadership of this school of thought was established when Robert Keohane and Joseph Nye, Jr., published their influential *Power and Interdependence: World Politics in Transition* (Boston: Little, Brown, 1977).

tional relations? Students of international relations should have a grounding in law and history as well as a specialized knowledge of the politics and culture of one area of the world in addition to their own. An appreciation of a foreign culture enables one to interpret "raw data" in relativistic terms and thereby avoid the pitfalls of dogmatism and parochialism. Statistical skills and the ability to employ computerized research services are also valuable tools for the study of international relations. Additionally, the student should acquire an active ability in at least one foreign language to be honed by overseas study or residence abroad.

The standards are high, and it pays the beginning student of international relations to realize early in the game that he or she is not in a narrowly circumscribed academic specialization, but in a form of general education. Preparation for the study of international relations best begins with curriculums that combine the humanities with an appreciation of the eclectic approach to the solution of methodological problems. The acquisition of "expert" status is usually accompanied by an acute awareness that theory is not synonymous with method and by a painful realization of the relative indeterminacy of international phenomena.

THEORIES AND THEORY BUILDING
IN INTERNATIONAL RELATIONS

The word *theory* derives from the Greek Θεωρώ (pronounced *theoró*), which means "to look at." Stanley Hoffmann, a scholar of the traditionalist school, has defined contemporary theory of international relations as "a systematic study of observable phenomena that tries to discover the principal variables, to explain behavior, and to reveal the characteristic types of relations among national units."[22] But, Hoffmann argues that within the general boundaries of the scope of international-relations theory we should also include the works of normative (prescriptive) thinkers and of policy scientists. The former—scholars with a philosophical orientation—are concerned with the *evaluation* of political reality and with the generation of *prescriptions* or *remedies* leading toward a better political life. The latter—in the fashion of engineers—try to go beyond description and explanation and wish to become involved in the formulation of policy (applied theory) that will serve the interest of a given political entity.

J. David Singer, a scientifically oriented scholar, has offered a shorter and much more restrictive definition: Theory is "a body of internally consistent empirical generalizations of descriptive, predictive, and explanatory power."[23] For Singer, these generalizations should best be expressed in the form of hypotheses and propositions that are testable, verifiable, and falsifiable (hence quantifi-

---

[22]Stanley Hoffmann, "Theory and International Relations," in *International Politics and Foreign Policy*, ed. Rosenau, 2nd ed. rev., p. 30.

[23]J. David Singer, "Inter-Nation Influence: A Formal Model," in *ibid.*, p. 380.

able). The overlapping between the traditionalist and scientific definitions of theory is considerable. Both agree that the generalizations must be empirically derived, logically sound, and have the capability to describe, explain, and predict.[24] It is notable, however, that Singer denies a theoretical role to "prescription."[25] He believes that normative (prescriptive) thinkers and policy scientists may well benefit from scientific theory, but that their prescriptive maxims are not part of theory.

Units and Levels of Analysis of International Politics

Academic disciplines encompassing a respectable theoretical body of literature have devised sets of conceptual units (also referred to as taxonomies or classifications) that facilitate study, analysis, and understanding.[26] Generally accepted and utilized classifications and symbols enable scholars in the same field to collaborate with one another and to engage in cumulative learning and theory building. The field of chemistry, for example, can study micro-units (such as atoms), intermediate-sized units (such as compounds), or aggregate and complex "units" (such as industrial pollution). Economics also deals with units of increasing inclusiveness and complexity, beginning with individuals, through business firms and national economies, and extending all the way to the international economic system.

In international relations one finds a somewhat comparable state of affairs. Here, however, in addition to the term *unit of analysis* one also encounters the term *actor.* An *actor* is a unit capable of purposeful (human-produced) action. Political actors can range from individuals such as presidents and kings, to organized groups such as labor unions and political parties, to nation-states such as the United States and Soviet Union, to large geographical regions such as the European Community, all the way up to global-scale organizations such as the

---

[24]It appears that another leading student of the international-relations field, Charles A. McClelland (who would invariably accept the Singer definition), is not convinced that the field of international relations has managed to develop any theory at all. At best, it has developed a series of "conceptualizations" or generalizations, but little or no theory. McClelland argues, for instance, that "the step of conceptualization is the only one that we have taken, and there is very little in the way of existing theory to discipline and guide organized inquiry or research." *A Design for International Relations Research: Scope, Theory, Methods and Relevance,* Monograph 10, American Academy of Political and Social Science (Philadelphia, 1970), p. 72. James Rosenau frequently argues that *pre-theories,* another term for conceptualizations, are what we have achieved, at best, to date.

[25]Singer, "Behavioral Science Approach to International Relations," p. 65.

[26]On this central theoretical question of units, actors, and levels of analysis and their interrelationships, see Heinz Eulau, *Micro-Macro Political Analysis: Accents of Inquiry* (Chicago: Aldine, 1969), pp. 17–18; James N. Rosenau, "Pre-Theories and Theories of Foreign Policy," in *Approaches to Comparative and International Politics,* ed. R. Barry Farrell (Evanston, Ill.: Northwestern University Press, 1966), pp. 27–92; and J. David Singer, "The Level of Analysis Problem in International Relations," in *The International System: Theoretical Essays,* ed. Klaus Knorr and Sidney Verba (Princeton, N.J.: Princeton University Press, 1961), pp. 77–92. For a traditionalist's treatment of this same problem, see Kenneth Waltz's brilliant *Man, the State and War: A Theoretical Analysis* (New York: Columbia University Press, 1959).

United Nations. All actors can be referred to as units (units of action), but not all units can be thought of as being actors. For instance, the analytical unit of "power" in politics—which is analogous to the unit of wealth (or money) in economics—cannot be said to be an actor. Power is merely employed or perceived by actors but has no will or cognition of its own independent of its users.

The term *level of analysis* denotes the focus of attention with which scholars regard their subject matter. A scholar can study phenomena in terms of wholes (the *macro*-level), for example, or in terms of their component parts (the *micro*-level). The levels of analysis most often employed in international relations are the individual level, the nation-state level, and the international-system level. Needless to say, one studies and analyzes phenomena at the various levels of analysis by employing units and actors of one's preference.

At the microlevel, there are studies devoted to the leadership style of individual national leaders. Traditionalists usually term these studies biographies, and scientists refer to them as investigations of *elite idiosyncratic behavior* or *operational codes.*[27] The next and most popular level of analysis focuses on the nation-state and its foreign policies. The assumption is made that the nation-state, seen through the actions of its government, is a convenient unit of analysis for a field that, by definition, seeks to explain relations among nation-states. At the macro level, there is a significant body of literature that treats the international political system and its processes as a whole. The work of traditionalists such as Hans Morgenthau and Raymond Aron and scientists such as Karl Deutsch and Morton Kaplan is representative of analysis at this level. Remarkably, Thucydides, in his chronicle of the war between Athens and Sparta in the fifth century B.C., worked at all three levels. He wrote of individual leaders such as Pericles, of the politics and policies of the Athenian empire, and finally, of the balance of power among the city-states of ancient Greece.

More recently, and with the influx of the behavioral persuasion in political science and international relations, a mixture of new and intermediate analytical units and actors has been adopted. For instance, the individual has been split into subunits such as ego, id, superego, and roles. The state has been split into groups, classes, parties, firms, organizations, and anomic collectivities. The international system has been split into regions, voting blocs, transnational movements or organizations such as the Roman Catholic Church, international organizations such as the United Nations and its agencies, international regimes such as the global financial and food-distribution complexes, internationalist or revolutionist parties and movements, and multinational corporations. Additional analytical units have been developed primarily to measure or reflect transactions and relationships between and among nation-states such as events, messages,

---

[27]See, for example, David S. McLellan, "The 'Operational Code' Approach to the Study of Political Leaders: Dean Acheson's Philosophical and Instrumental Beliefs," *Canadian Journal of Political Science,* 4, no. 1 (March 1971), 52–75; and Ole Holsti, "The 'Operational Code' Approach to the Study of Political Leaders: John Foster Dulles' Philosophical and Instrumental Beliefs," *Canadian Journal of Political Science,* 3, no. 1 (March 1970), 123–57.

treaties, capabilities, conflictive interactions, cooperative interactions, and other transactional indicators that can be measured systematically.

The central problem for the theorist of international relations is to link the insights derived at the various levels and from different actors and units of analysis. If, for example, one wishes to identify the factors that contributed to the decision of President John F. Kennedy to order a naval "quarantine" around Cuba during the missile crisis of 1962, where does one begin to look?[28] At the level of microanalysis, the researcher would examine President Kennedy's personality, as well as that of those around him (if such an investigation were at all feasible). At the national level, one would study such factors as the routing and timing of information, the competing roles of bureaucratic and congressional elites, and the impact on the president of representatives of influential interest groups outside the government. At the international level, one would analyze the relationships of the principal protagonists, the United States and the Soviet Union, to each other, to their allies, and to Cuba. The constraints of geography, world opinion, the law of the sea, and international organizations at the highest level of analysis should be considered to have affected the decision.

Working at different levels of analysis, the researcher can identify different pieces of a multidimensional puzzle. But how can these pieces be put together into a general theory of interaction, a theory that has both descriptive and predictive powers?[29] What portion of the decision to order a "quarantine" derived from idiosyncratic factors, from complex forces within the state, or from characteristics of the international system?[30] At this stage of the development of the international-relations field, the most feasible research strategy appears to be the building of islands of middle-range propositions at each level of analysis, which can some day be linked together in a general theory.

The Utility of Theory in International Relations

A question that arises with regularity in courses on international relations is: How can concepts, hypotheses,[31] and theoretical constructs be used in the making and implementation of foreign policy? Our answer is that although theorizing is an aid to *understanding* international political phenomena, it is not necessarily a practical guide for the day-to-day operations of a foreign office or a defense ministry. An analogy may serve to illustrate the problem. Babe Ruth was one of the

---

[28]For a very perceptive study on this subject, see Graham T. Allison, "Conceptual Models and the Cuban Missile Crisis," *American Political Science Review,* 63 (September 1969), 689–718. See also Allison, *Essence of Decision: Explaining the Cuban Missile Crisis* (Boston: Little, Brown, 1971).

[29]For some interesting insights on this problem see James N. Rosenau, *Linkage Politics* (New York: The Free Press, 1969), pp. 1–63.

[30]See Rosenau, "Pre-Theories and Theories of Foreign Policy."

[31]A *hypothesis* is a propositional statement usually presented in an "if . . . then" type of format. A good example of a hypothesis would read: "*If* state A and state B increase their trade exchanges, *then* the probability of conflict between them decreases."

most powerful batters in the history of baseball. Yet if he had been asked to develop a *theory* of hitting home runs, he would have had to concentrate his time and energy on the study of such questions as ballistics, trajectories, wind speed, visibility, coordination of motion, crowd effects, coaching, and inputs from team-mates. By the time he had acquired the necessary knowledge and become scientifically conscious of his movements, his ability to hit home runs would have been somewhat impaired. In international relations the "batters" are national leaders and generals. Social scientists specializing in the theory of the field resemble sportscasters and commentators. They amass statistics and interpret the records of "teams" and "players."

If we are looking for the best mix between theoretical prowess and field experience, we might focus on the emerging role of the *policy scientist,* which appears to offer opportunities for effective inputs from the scope of theory to the realm of political action.[32] The policy scientist stands on the middle ground between the empiricist, who is concerned with the "what is" of international relations, and the normativist, whose concern is centered in the "what ought to be." The policy scientist is usually not content with observation, description, and prediction, but goes beyond these goals of theory building to prescribe policy guidelines. These prescriptions extend, however, beyond the abstract ideal of the common good and are designed to further the specific interests of a particular group, such as a government agency, a political party, a trade union, or a commercial enterprise. Policy scientists deliberately utilize the propositions of theory to enable their clients to play a more powerful role in international politics. The success or failure of the client provides, therefore, a measure of validation for the theory that underlies the recommendations of the policy scientist.

The policy scientist is perhaps philosophically, if not operationally, closest to Voltaire's adventuresome Candide, who, despairing of ever divining the nature of such abstractions as truth and justice, retires to cultivate his garden. Thus, too, policy scientists devote themselves to the maximization of a given group's objectives. The rest of the world is left to its own devices on the assumption that individuals and groups, in their separate efforts to maximize their own interests, will somehow provide for the common good.

The future of policy science as an attempt to link the theory and the practice of international relations remains unclear. One of the main problems is that of moral relativism. Should policy scientists have normatively defined boundaries within which they work? In the process of human engineering, should policy scientists be dependent members of private or governmental authorities bound by "superior orders," or should they be autonomous individuals responsible to a higher moral code? All too often, the former rather than the latter role predominates.

---

[32]Alexander L. George and Richard Smoke, "Theory and Policy in International Relations," *Policy Sciences,* 4, no. 4 (December 1973), 387–414. See also Sallie M. Hicks et al., "Influencing the Prince: A Role for Academicians," *Polity,* 15, no. 2 (1982), 288–93.

Limitations on Theory Building in International Relations

The theoretically oriented student of international relations faces serious problems, some of which can never be overcome because they are part of the human condition. Personal involvement, characteristics of the data, and the very nature of the process of acquiring knowledge combine to make the formulation of a rigorous, cumulative body of theory a difficult undertaking.

Personal Involvement. The theorist in international relations and other social sciences does not enjoy an abstract, impersonal relationship with the object of study, as would, for example, a chemist. Instead, the theorist approaches the subject from perspectives provided by culture, citizen loyalty, political affiliation, educational experiences, family, and friends. All these perspectives create pressures, some reinforcing and others opposing, and combine to affect the output of theoretical investigations. The dedicated theorist will, of course, make every effort to transcend conscious preconceptions—even if his or her high degree of objectivity may at times result in the forfeiting of friends and social privileges.

A second set of individual limitations that cannot be removed consists of subconscious predispositions and perceptual distortions that lead to withdrawal from certain ideas or their categorization in such a fashion as to influence the product of one's research. Such perceptual mechanisms will vitally affect the manner in which the theorist treats data. Where others saw only windmills, Don Quixote recognized giants and rushed to the attack. On the other hand, the "giant" of the missile-gap crisis between the Soviet Union and the United States in 1960 proved to be only a "windmill" after the Kennedy administration assumed power. Many similar episodes have occurred in other parts of the world.

Ambition is another aspect of personal involvement that may cloud the judgment of the theorist. As Plato became the advisor of the king of Syracuse and Aristotle the tutor of Alexander, it is natural for the theorist to seek to influence the course of events. Indeed, the Western tradition of historical empiricism in international relations has its roots in the effort of Niccolò Machiavelli in 1513 to formulate a consistent "theory of statecraft" for his prince. The temptation of the theorist to conform to popular beliefs and to compromise principles may be at times too great to resist.

The problem exists not only for individuals but also for organizations. Government agencies engaged in a bureaucratic struggle for budgetary support may seek external assistance in the form of outside advisory opinions that support the work of the agency. A new agency head, for example, may contract the services of a "think tank" so that expertise outside the hierarchy of government can be used to subject policies to a review that would be impossible within a hierarchical framework. But the question remaining is how free will such experts be in criticizing those who are funding their efforts? As Machiavelli hoped, a wise prince will listen to a detached counselor. But how many princes are indeed wise, and how many counselors can remain detached?

The scientific school of international relations appears to have developed a better defense than the traditionalists against conscious and subconscious perceptual distortions. Multiple and independent observations of the same phenomenon provide a basis for cross-checking these observations and eliminating some individual misperceptions or biases. Nevertheless, the twin engines of political socialization and professional peer pressure are often powerful enough to transform giants into windmills.

Characteristics of Data. An important limitation of international-relations theory in this category is the sheer unavailability of pertinent data. The sensitive questions of war and peace are often debated behind sealed doors. Of necessity, diplomats and soldiers hold the student of international relations at arm's length. The major European and North American governments withhold their diplomatic archives from scholarly investigation for an average of fifty years. The United States is perhaps the most liberal of the great powers in releasing documentary sources after a thirty-year period, yet exceptions are often made, especially when the interests of an ally require that documents not be released.

A related limitation is, paradoxically, the opposite of the first: Researchers are often inundated by too much information. Newspapers, periodicals, books, films, and other media are multiplying at such a rate that even the most conscientious scholar is overwhelmed with information. The problem of discriminating among various sources of information is monumental, and it is in this area that computerized information-retrieval banks are likely to prove of great value in the years to come.

In the data category, the major limitation on cumulative theory building in international relations is the difficulty with which agreement is reached on units of analysis and definitions of key terms. Although an American chemist and a Chinese chemist may readily agree on the validity of certain formulas, students of international relations from these diverse political and cultural backgrounds would find the effort to define such fundamental concepts as *democracy, justice, imperialism, political development,* and even *power,* a source of endless frustration.

To cope with this problem, scientifically oriented scholars have endeavored to develop a value-free vocabulary of terms that will endow the field with a unity of concepts. But when one tries to fit this depoliticized vocabulary to reality, the cleavages of culture and ideology again become apparent. Little is gained by referring to democracy and dictatorship as *nondirective* and *directive* political systems respectively, when there is no international agreement on the characteristics of the two forms of regime. As we indicated earlier, international relations is a subject of inquiry that has developed most prominently in an American setting, and consequently, it may be more reflective of the needs of American society than the needs of an international community of scholars.

The Process of Acquiring Knowledge.   An important limitation in the process of acquiring knowledge concerns the adequacy of the samples we use to construct hypotheses. Students of the natural sciences usually work with phenomena that they can duplicate in the laboratory; theorists of international relations enjoy no such advantage. The leadership elites of opposing powers may or may not respond in the same fashion to comparable crisis situations over a period of time. The Soviet-American engagement in and around Berlin from the blockade of 1948–49 to the Quadripartite Agreement of 1971 is a case in point. We cannot predict with certainty whether a threat such as Chairman Nikita Khrushchev's 1958 demand that West Berlin be converted into a "free" city in six months is credible or not. We can hardly be certain that the idiosyncratic or personality factor is adequately represented in empirical studies. Or, to put the matter in the form of a question: Can we assume that "what is" "will be" in the study of international relations?

An example serves to illustrate this problem. Let us suppose that we are studying the history of interactions between two nation-states. We discover that over a period of time there is a pattern of increasing communications and trade between the citizens of the states in question, and that the incidence of conflict between the two governments decreases over the same period. May we then assume that a growth in international exchanges always promotes peace and cooperation? Not necessarily so. As Karl Deutsch has pointed out, the correlation between the two trends depends upon the specific circumstances that obtain at the time and in the two states.[33] It is possible, for example, that two states are at peace because they do not relate at all, being separated by geographic, cultural, and linguistic barriers. Moreover, the rise of extensive contacts between the two previously isolated political communities might result in tensions between them that lead eventually to war.

A second limitation in the formulation of theoretical knowledge is the temptation to rely upon historical analogies as evidence of the presumed reliability of policy guidelines. Since it was first implied by Thucydides, in his chronicle of the Peloponnesian War, the *domino theory* has been paraded again and again as proof that to concede one point to a potential aggressor only encourages that aggressor to risk greater provocations and ultimately war. In retrospect, the four-nation Munich agreement of 1938, which provided for the transfer of a disputed frontier region from the Czechoslovak Republic to Germany, has been likened to a fallen domino that triggered the fall of other dominoes and led eventually to World War II. Yet are we justified in assuming that negotiated settlements in other areas of the world at other times necessarily constitute an invitation to further aggression?

---

[33]See Karl W. Deutsch, "The Impact of Communications upon International Relations Theory," in *Theories of International Relations: The Crisis of Relevance,* ed. Abdul A. Said (Englewood Cliffs, N.J.: Prentice-Hall, 1968), pp. 74–92.

A third limitation in the acquisition of knowledge is the intrusion of the researcher into the environment under study. In other words, the presence of the observer tends to alter the behavior of those being observed. Politicians being interviewed usually seek to project an image of rationality and restraint. Such an image may bear little resemblance to the conduct of the same individuals in an actual political conflict. Social scientists suggest that a good way to bypass this particular limitation is to conduct what is referred to as "unobtrusive observation" or "participant observation." In this situation, the observer does not inform the subjects that they are being observed so as not to affect their behavior. But unobtrusive observation in activities that are replete with governmental security precautions may prove quite risky for the observer who, among other things, could be accused of being a spy.

There is, however, a wider problem with experimentation in the social sciences. No one denies that experimentation under controlled conditions is possible with human subjects. But within the past fifty years, private and governmental authorities in various countries have, through the use of deception or force, carried out inhuman behavioral experiments, the scientific benefits of which are indeed dubious. To these and other criticisms, proponents of theory building through experimentation reply that the study of decision-making dynamics under laboratory conditions (using techniques such as simulation and game theory) offers no threat to the physical well-being or the personal dignity of the participants.

As learning techniques, gaming and simulation have long been used by service academies and advanced military schools, in executive training programs conducted by commercial firms, and by professors of organization theory. Although the utility of simulated experiments in decision making for teaching is generally recognized, using this method to build relevant international-relations theory remains a questionable enterprise. The difficulty with such experimental situations is that the participants playing out the contrived diplomatic and military roles are in most instances students or civil servants whose responses to international crisis may, at best, have only an accidental parallel to the reactions of the African, Chinese, or Soviet officials whose behavior they are simulating. Moreover, the gains and losses of a simulated international encounter are paper transactions, and the participants—even if they are professionals—tend to be either more adventurous or more inhibited in the compressed time circumstances of a simulated environment than they would be at the country desk of a foreign office or defense ministry. Nonetheless, our feeling is that simulation and gaming conducted within realistic limits may offer the best chance for the application of experimental techniques to the study of international relations. We must not forget, however, that our object of study involves human beings who possess the freedom to refuse to be coded and programmed merely to provide a satisfying solution to the "problem."

It is probably limitations such as those we have enumerated above that led Robert Gilpin, a prominent student of international relations, to express some frustration. He wrote in one of his major studies that we "must inquire whether or not twentieth-century students of international relations know anything that Thucydides and his fifth-century compatriots did not know about the behavior of states."[34] If we were to share this pessimistic and perhaps realistic point of view, we might well ask: Why continue to study a field so hard to define, so filled with uncertainty, and so defiant of prediction? The answer is that international relations can affect the outcome of a vast variety of human endeavors, ranging from the improvement of the quality of life in a society to the avoidance of a global thermonuclear war. To use Stanley Hoffmann's thoughtful analogy, the game of international nuclear-power roulette is currently played in a dark and fortified cellar.[35] The players crouch around the table and carefully place their bets, despite the constant jostling of an unruly crowd of spectators who insist upon giving unwanted advice. In the computation of odds between nuclear war and peace, the stakes are high and the probabilities of success uncertain. Yet with care and compassion we may not only survive, but also achieve a measure of progress in developing institutions that will reduce the likelihood of global warfare and better the human condition in a spirit of equity.

Perhaps a "simple folk story" will serve to illustrate the need for patience and skepticism in our efforts to master our subject.

> There was once a man named Nasreddin Hodza[36] who lived in a small, well-knit village community somewhere in Turkey. One day he woke up at daybreak, went out in the yard in front of his house, bent down on his knees, and began a vigorous and meticulous search—inch by inch—through his well-kept garden. Soon his neighbors and other passers-by stopped and watched him. Curious, they asked him what he was doing. He looked up momentarily and said that he had lost his precious gold coin the night before and was trying to find it. Now there were not too many such gold coins around the village, and the good neighbors, sympathizing with Nasreddin, volunteered to search with him.
>
> The search continued for hours, with increasing urgency. But the gold coin was nowhere to be found. As sundown was approaching, one frustrated neighbor asked Nasreddin, "Now see here! Help us a little! Where approximately do you think you lost this famous gold coin of yours?" Nasreddin looked him straight in the eye and said, "I am sure I lost it inside the house." "Then why in Heaven's name are we searching for it out here?" snapped the exasperated neighbor. Nasreddin shook his head knowingly and muttered, "Because there is more light out here!"

Students of international relations should remember that they too may be searching for the elusive concepts and causes of politics in areas where there is more adequate light for them to conduct the search.

---

[34]Gilpin, *War and Change in World Politics,* p. 227.

[35]Hoffmann, *State of War,* Chap. 6.

[36]For a Chinese version of the exploits of Nasreddin Hodza, see *The Effendi and the Pregnant Pot: Uygur Folk Tales from China,* trans. Primerose Gigliesi and Robert C. Friend (Beijing: New World Press, 1982).

SUGGESTIONS FOR FURTHER STUDY

Patrick M. Morgan has systematically examined the problem of rational thought and action in world politics in *Theories and Approaches to International Politics: What Are We to Think?*, 4th ed. (New Brunswick, N.J.: Transaction Books, 1987). James E. Dougherty and Robert L. Pfaltzgraff, Jr., have developed a strong case for realism in *Contending Theories of International Relations: A Comprehensive Survey*, 2nd ed. (New York: Harper & Row, 1981). K.J. Holsti has identified realism as the predominant paradigm in the study of international relations in *The Dividing Discipline: Hegemony and Diversity in International Theory* (Boston: Allen & Unwin, 1985). A review of modern schools of thought is the focus of Margot Light and A.J.R. Groom, eds., *International Relations: A Handbook of Current Theory* (London: Pinter Publishers, 1985). Realism and general systems theory are the objects of careful scrutiny in Stanley Hoffmann, "International Relations: The Long Road to Theory," *World Politics*, 11 (April 1959), 346–77. For an overview of leading interpretations, see William C. Olson, *The Theory and Practice of International Relations*, 7th ed. (Englewood Cliffs, N.J.: Prentice-Hall, 1987); as well as Abdul Aziz Said and Charles O. Lerche, Jr., *Concepts of International Politics in Global Perspective*, 3rd ed. (Englewood Cliffs, N.J.: Prentice-Hall, 1979). Dina A. Zinnes has provided directions for further investigation in "Research Frontiers in the Study of International Politics," in *Handbook of Political Science*, ed. Fred I. Greenstein and Nelson W. Polsby, 8 vols. (Reading, Mass.: Addison-Wesley, 1975), vol. VIII: *International Politics*, pp. 87–195. For a review of the major schools of thought in international-relations research, see Charles A. McClelland, *Theory and the International System* (New York: Macmillan, 1966); and Kenneth N. Waltz, *Theory of International Politics* (Reading, Mass.: Addison-Wesley, 1979). The intrusion of values in the analysis of political dynamics is discussed by Gabriel A. Almond and Stephen J. Genco in "Clouds, Clocks, and the Study of Politics," *World Politics*, 29 (July 1977), 489–522; as well as Ernest Nagel, *The Structure of Science: Problems in the Logic of Scientific Explanation* (New York: Harcourt, Brace & World, 1961).

3

THE BALANCE-OF-POWER SYSTEM AND ITS VARIATIONS

In the sixteenth year of the Peloponnesian War (431–404 B.C.), which pitted ancient Athens against Sparta, a particularly dramatic episode occurred. Mighty Athens decided to incorporate into its sphere of influence the small and defenseless island of Melos. At the beginning of the war, Melos had been a dependency of Sparta, but Sparta gradually lost interest in the island's military importance. Then, in 415 B.C., overwhelming Athenian naval and ground forces surrounded Melos. The Melians, however, wishing to maintain their independence and neutrality, refused to submit to Athenian military power.

The Athenians gave the Melians a classic choice: Either submit to Athenian rule or be destroyed. Athenian envoys and Melian magistrates then met to debate the possibility of a peaceful settlement to their dispute. The Athenians' approach was typical of the amoral, realpolitical orientation discussed in various parts of this textbook. They sought to impress upon the Melians that considerations of justice arise only between parties of equal strength and that there is no dishonor but only prudence when the weak capitulate to the strong. The Melians employed the language of idealism and sought to deter the Athenians with arguments about higher justice and with threats that other states, such as Sparta, would come to their aid. This debate, recorded in remarkably clinical fashion by Thucydides, illustrates the loneliness, the tragedy, and the ultimate constraints of decision making in a decentralized and power-regulated system.[1] But we shall let the protagonists for a moment speak for themselves:

[1]For the full text of the Melian debate, see Thucydides, *The History of the Peloponnesian War,* ed. and trans. Richard Livingstone (New York: Oxford University Press, 1960), pp. 265ff. Quoted materials are being used here with the permission of Oxford University Press.

ATHENIANS: We are seeking the safety of your state; for we wish you to become our subjects with least trouble to ourselves and we would like you to survive in our interests as well as your own.

MELIANS: It may be your interest to be our masters: how can it be ours to be your slaves?

ATHENIANS: By submitting you would avoid a terrible fate, and we should gain by not destroying you. . . .

MELIANS: Surely . . . it would be criminal cowardice in us, who are still free, not to take any and every measure before submitting to slavery.

ATHENIANS: No, if you reflect calmly; *for this is not a competition in heroism between equals,* where your honour is at stake, but a question of self-preservation, to save you from a struggle with a far stronger power. . . . The choice between war and safety is given you; do not obstinately take the worse alternative. *The most successful people are those who stand up to their equals, behave properly to their superiors, and treat their inferiors fairly.* Think it over when we withdraw, and reflect once and again that you have only one country, and that its prosperity or ruin depends on one decision.

The Melians deliberated for some time afterward and decided to refuse the Athenian "offer." Athens, in response, blockaded the island for months and eventually moved in for the kill. Thucydides described the finale as follows:

> Reinforcements were sent from Athens, and the siege was now pressed vigorously; there was some treachery in the town, and the Melians surrendered at discretion to the Athenians, who put to death all the grown men whom they took, and sold the women and children for slaves; subsequently they sent out five hundred settlers and colonized the island.

In a rudimentary way, the Melian debate illustrates most of the nuances of the realist-idealist debate within a context of the balance-of-power system and its imperfection as a protector of national security. Should the Melians have given in to the Athenians in order to avoid being destroyed? They did not know in advance the outcome of their subsequent struggle with the Athenians. Nor did they know for sure whether the Athenians were merely bluffing and whether after a victory they would spare the Melians from death. In an earlier, similar situation the Athenians had at the last moment spared the vanquished. Further, the Melians had been hoping to secure help from Sparta in order to achieve a balance-of-power situation vis-à-vis Athens. Also, they had trusted in the righteousness of their cause and had hoped that a primitive form of collective security would have acted as a restraining influence on Athens. (See Chapter 14 for a discussion of the concept and practice of collective security.) Finally, the Melians had been faced with a classic question of honor: Is it better to *live* as a slave or to *die* fighting for one's freedom?

The Athenians sought methodically to discourage sentimental, religious, wishful, or moralistic reasoning by the Melians. They counseled prudence, urged the Melians to view their situation realistically, and asserted that there can be no dishonor and for that matter no justice in relations among unequals. They also warned the Melians not to expect help from a disinterested Sparta and not to trust in the gods for help, for the latter were *indifferent* to matters of political power and justice. Perhaps what sealed the doom of the Melians was the Athenian resolve to turn them into a test case that would discourage other Athenian dependencies from rising in revolt (an early, albeit inverted, form of the domino theory). We can also note the presence of domestic factors in this unhappy episode. Prior to the fall of Melos, says Thucydides, there was treachery within the town. We also know that the Athenians, both elites and public, were bitterly divided as to the range of Athenian power and as to the proper policy vis-à-vis Melos. Internal divisiveness in both Melos and Athens increased the uncertainty besetting their respective decision makers.

If we generalize from this single case—a risky practice, as we have suggested earlier—we can reach a few conclusions about the terrible tragedy. The Melians can be faulted for not recognizing the deadly danger posed by powerful, arrogant, and determined Athens. Also, in their calculations they overemphasized intangible factors such as ideological solidarity (i.e., help from Sparta), moral righteousness, and Athenian self-restraint. The Melians proved disastrously wrong in their assessments. The Athenians, naturally, have to be blamed for brutally destroying a small and defenseless population in order to demonstrate their might.

We can learn from the study of this episode some lessons regarding political systems that rely on a balance of power to maintain a primitive form of order. The fundamental problem with such systems is their *uncertainty*. If the Melians had known in advance that their choice was between *certain* capitulation and *certain* death, they might have capitulated and thereby saved themselves. They could then have waited for a subsequent opportunity to rise up against the Athenians. But they did not know for certain the intentions of the Athenians. Nor could they calculate the impact of the assistance they might have secured from Sparta or other Greek city-states. And there was always that intangible element called hope.

THE CONCEPT OF BALANCE OF POWER

Balance of power is not a precise and easily measurable concept. It has been interpreted in several different ways by scholars and practitioners of international politics. Ernst Haas, in a seminal article, criticized it as too vague a concept for use by political scientists. He pointed out that the concept had been utilized extensively in at least eight mutually exclusive versions:

1. Equilibrium resulting from *equal* distribution of power among nation-states
2. Equilibrium resulting from *unequal* distribution of power among nation-states
3. Equilibrium resulting from the dominance of one nation-state (the balancer)

4. A system providing for relative stability and peace
5. A system characterized by instability and war
6. Another way of saying power politics
7. A universal law of history
8. A guide for policy makers[2]

Haas's criticism is well taken. Yet we cannot discard the balance-of-power concept—despite its imprecision—because it is near the very core of international politics. In Chapters 4–12, we will reflect on the workings of the balance-of-power system as it has been practiced in a number of variations since 1648. We shall use balance of power in a descriptive and analytical sense and as an aid to our understanding of the primitive mechanisms of international regulation. For our purposes, we shall assume four prerequisites for the existence of a balance-of-power system that have been suggested in the literature of international relations:

1. A multiplicity of sovereign political actors that results in the absence of a single, centralized, legitimate, and strong authority over these sovereign actors.
2. Relatively unequal distribution of power (i.e., status, wealth, size, military capability) among the political actors that make up the system. This permits the differentiation of states into at least three categories: great powers, intermediate powers, and smaller nation-states.
3. Continuous but controlled competition and conflict among sovereign political actors for what are perceived as scarce world resources and other values.
4. An implicit understanding among the rulers of the great powers that the perpetuation of the existing power distribution benefits them mutually.

We must differentiate between national and municipal "power balances" on the one hand and the international balance-of-power system on the other. Our basis for doing so is *autonomy,* a term derived from a Greek word meaning self-rule. In national and municipal systems, the political actors (individuals, corporations, municipalities, ethnic or racial groups, political parties, labor unions, and so on) are *not* autonomous, since they are subject to powerful and normally legitimate central authorities. In contrast, according to the "rules" of the international balance of power, there are no central authorities controlling the nation-states. The regulators of international intercourse are the desire of nation-states for benefits and security and their mutual fear of conflict and its consequences. (For an elaboration of this point, see Chapter 13.) Thus, stripped of all its rhetoric, the balance of power provides policy makers with the alternatives of either risking war or reaching acceptable settlements to their disputes through negotiation. Informality, the absence of binding and enforceable rules, the threat and the

---

[2]Ernst Haas, "The Balance of Power: Prescription, Concept, or Propaganda?" *World Politics,* 5 (July 1953), 442–77.

use of violence as means of settling disputes, and the absence of supranational institutions have prompted some analysts to view the balance of power as a primitive political system.[3]

The balance-of-power system can also be viewed as a halfway mark between world order and international chaos. The former would require pervasive central authorities powerful enough to impose a given order of things (whether based on premises of equality or inequality) upon the various political actors. World chaos would mean political actors restrained only by the law of the jungle. Survival of the fittest would apply here: Only strong, shrewd, and mobile actors would grow and prosper; weak, dense, and stationary actors would suffer and die.

The balance-of-power system has gradually evolved into a grand and convenient compromise between the poles of credible order and absolute chaos. The system's lack of strong global institutions safeguards the sovereignty of participants to a greater or lesser degree. (The concepts of *nationalism* and *national sovereignty* will be discussed in detail in Chapter 4.) The maintenance of each actor's autonomy works, naturally, to the advantage of the stronger and the more prosperous nation-states. Overall, however, the fragmentation of world power and the continuous competition for wealth, influence, and other values results in a certain level of security for large and small states alike against the designs of expansionist or revisionist members of the international community.

Ultimately, one is tempted to view the balance-of-power system as an informal and flexible pecking order of nation-states arranged in terms of decreasing capability and power potential. (The concepts of *power* and *capability* will be the focus of Chapter 5.) In turn, the stronger among these states agree informally to perpetuate this status quo. For the balance of power to work, the great powers must be satisfied with the existing hierarchy of power in the international system. Further, these governments must want to perpetuate their autonomy, to frustrate any attempts by a single state for world dominance, to prevent the rise of powerful international authorities, and to insulate their domestic political systems from external interference. When one or more great powers deviate and seek world dominance, when they question the internal legitimacy of the governments of other great powers, when major (rather than limited) wars break out, we can assume that the international balance of power as a regulatory system has broken down and ceases to exist.

In the remainder of this chapter, we shall briefly trace the history of the classical version of balance of power up to the "revolutionary" confrontations of the twentieth century (World War I and World War II and the cold war). Then we shall present a number of different conceptions of the international political system of the future. Finally, we shall attempt to assess the effectiveness of various decentralized systems of international regulation in maintaining world peace.

---

[3]See Roger D. Masters, "World Politics as a Primitive Political System," *World Politics,* 16 (July 1964), 595–619.

THE BALANCE OF POWER IN MODERN HISTORY

The dominant view in the literature of international relations is that the classical system of balance of power flourished in a specific international political climate.[4] The period between 1648 (the Peace of Westphalia) and 1789 (the French Revolution) may be considered the first golden age of classical balance of power. Religious conflict during that period was deemphasized, mercantilism gave way to free trade, and absolute monarchies were gradually replaced by systems of popular sovereignty. Wars between nation-states—although numerous—were quite often ritualized and limited in intensity. (The phenomenon of war is discussed in depth in Chapters 10 and 11.) Rarely did they affect the civilian populations of the major European powers.

The primary characteristic of the period 1648–1789 was the "corporate mentality" of the various aristocracies ruling the European countries. (The role of elites in the formulation of foreign policy is discussed in Chapter 7.) These elites (monarchs, princes, nobles, diplomats, and military officers) found much more in common with one another than with their own people. This period was, in short, characterized by political and economic homogeneity among states. There were no status-quo states facing revolutionary states. There were no fundamental variations among political structures or among philosophies of leaders. The values of the enlightenment bound the European ruling aristocracies together. Major wars, which could result only in mutual disadvantage to these elites, were therefore avoided.

The French Revolution radically destabilized the classical balance-of-power system. The citizen armies, the electrifying slogans ("Liberty, Equality, Fraternity!"), the fusion of nationalism with popular sovereignty—all were given a militant, messianic, and adventurist character by Napoleon Bonaparte. His romantic and expansionist military campaigns were directed to the creation of a new order, modeled after France, throughout the known world. These actions were contrary to the central rules of classical balance-of-power behavior: Wars should be kept limited, and no attempt should be made by any one great power to conquer and destroy any other great power belonging to the select club of wealthy, militarily mobile, and influential nation-states.

The reaction of strong European nation-states to Napoleon's challenge was to band together in order to defeat him and to restore principles such as legitimacy and moderation to the highly disturbed international system. After the final defeat of Napoleon at Waterloo, the great powers convened the Congress of Vienna (1815) in order to restore the European balance-of-power system. Under the diplomatic leadership of Prince Metternich of Austria and Czar Alexander I

[4]See, for example, Raymond Aron, *Peace and War: A Theory of International Relations* (New York: Doubleday, 1966); Stanley Hoffmann, *The State of War: Essays on the Theory and Practice of International Politics* (New York: Praeger, 1965); and Hans J. Morgenthau, *Politics among Nations: The Struggle for Power and Peace*, 5th ed. rev. (New York: Knopf, 1978).

of Russia, a new era of balance of power was structured.[5] It lasted until the beginning of World War I.

The nineteenth century (1815–1914) can then be called the second golden age of the classical balance of power. France under the restored Bourbon dynasty was allowed to remain in the ranks of great powers. These powers—England, France, Prussia, Austria-Hungary, and Russia—returned to the practice of stable and ideologically homogeneous international politics. This meant, first, that European governments were in ideological agreement concerning the nature of acceptable relations between rulers and ruled. A second ideological similarity was a desire for government that would not interfere in the social, economic, religious, and educational spheres of national activity—in other words, laissez-faire government. The European states also called for combined great-power action against popular, nationalist revolts. Such uprisings, they feared, could threaten the legitimacy of European monarchies and destabilize the existing distribution of political power by dissolving multinational political entities, such as the Austro-Hungarian and the Ottoman Empires.

In the nineteenth century, wars were reduced to the minor status of violent but limited politicomilitary tools for the adjustment of marginal-in-importance international disputes. Holy wars, wars of national liberation, wars for popular sovereignty—in general, wars involving mutually exclusive ideological objectives—were considered extremely dangerous by European elites. Such conflicts tended to become unlimited and to undermine the existing and "legitimate" national and international status quo (in other words, the status quo acceptable to the great-power elites). It was during the nineteenth century, then, that international law of war began to flourish. (For a discussion of theory, practice, and substantive rules of international law, see Chapter 13.) This growth stemmed from the recognition by the great powers that mutual advantages were to be derived from limiting the destructiveness and ferocity of combat. The wars of this period, being fought away from the major population centers, were romanticized by imaginative members of the European aristocracies and provided subjects for some of the world's finest literature and art.

But beginning in the 1870s, the order of Vienna began to unravel under the impact of new and challenging social forces. It could be argued that technological breakthroughs in the industrial revolution were at the bottom of these most recent major transformations in the international political system. The rise of mass nationalism; the emergence of imperial armies; the increasing differences of interest among ruling elites, who began developing strong nationalist identities and relaxing their previous ties with an international aristocracy; the production of weapons that could cause major destruction without differentiating between military forces and civilian populations—all could be viewed as by-products of the technological revolution.

[5]The classic treatment of this subject is Henry Kissinger, *A World Restored: Metternich, Castlereagh, and the Problems of Peace, 1812–1822* (New York: Grosset and Dunlap, 1964). For a portrait of Kissinger as a statesman, see Chapter 8.

Thus, the twentieth century, with its two major world wars and the psychologically intense cold war, came to be considered a revolutionary age. The destabilizing forces of the twentieth century have been unleashed primarily by imperialist nationalism rationalized by crusading and exclusivist ideologies. (For an elaboration of the theory and practice related to ideologies, see Chapter 6.) The century has witnessed at least three such movements: the fascism of Mussolini's Italy and Nazi Germany, the communism of the Soviet Union and China, and the free-enterprise capitalism of the post–World War II United States and its principal allies.

Revolutionary attitudes destroy the major conditions for the classical international balance of power, which is based on controlled competition among mutually acceptable governmental elites. In a revolutionary environment, elites and masses indulge themselves in dreams of national or international glory. They link their identities completely with the "fatherland" or with other higher causes. They believe that their brand of world order ought to prevail universally; only then can peace be ensured and human and societal goals fulfilled. Wars cannot remain limited, pragmatic, and amoral exercises in an environment of mutually exclusive and often hate-filled ideologies, antagonistic and expansionist national drives, deep popular involvement in political, economic, and military affairs, and the availability of weapons of mass destructiveness. One now fights for freedom, for truth, and for survival. Mutual perceptions (which are often misperceptions) pit the forces of "good" against the forces of "evil." Compromise or mutual accommodation is considered treason or defeatism. One destroys rather than compromises with the devil so that universal peace and universal good can prevail forever.

Since World War II, the unlimited destructiveness of nuclear weapons has contributed heavily to the containment of Soviet-American cold-war conflicts below the threshold of global nuclear war. In the aftermath of the Cuban missile crisis (1962)—which brought the United States and the Soviet Union to the brink of nuclear war—the stalemated war of attrition in Vietnam, the unfolding of a deep and uncompromising conflict between Soviet communists and Chinese communists, and the coming to power of pragmatic as well as elitist leaders, such as Richard Nixon, Henry A. Kissinger, Leonid Brezhnev, Ronald Reagan (second term), and Mikhail Gorbachev, we might be witnessing a new global attempt to restore an updated version of the classical balance-of-power system, modified to accommodate twentieth-century developments in technology, weaponry, and information management.

For the classical balance-of-power system to be restored in any form, great powers (such as the United States and the Soviet Union) and near–great powers (such as Japan, China, and a Western European entity) must accept one another's governmental legitimacy and cease interfering in one another's vital internal affairs. This requires a deemphasis of ideological differences and a tacit agreement to contain international conflicts well below the nuclear threshold. Under such a system the United Nations Security Council, no longer hampered by automatic vetoes, might become more effective and humankind might enter a new era of relative peace. (The United Nations and other international organizations are discussed in Chapters 14 and 15.) This peace, however, will not necessarily result in a just distribution of territory, wealth, and status among and within nation-states. (See Chapter 17 for a discussion of the unequal distribution of resources in the world.)

DEFINING POLITICAL SYSTEMS AND OTHER SYSTEMS

A *system* has been defined as a set of interacting units (actors) distinguished through identifiable boundaries from the environment of this set. Systems can be subdivided into *natural* (a chemical compound, the solar system, a galaxy), *mechanical* (a clock, a robot, or a computer), and *social* (a society, a polity, or an economy).[6] In this book we are concerned with social systems and more specifically with political systems. Social (including political and economic) systems can vary in size and inclusiveness. They range from small systems (a household or a family), to intermediate systems (villages and cities, social classes, political parties, labor unions, corporations, and ethnic groups), to large systems (nation-states, geographic regions, multinational corporations, international organizations, and transnational religious movements, all the way up to the largest and most inclusive system, the world political system). The international political system is the central focus of courses dealing with world politics or international relations.[7]

In all social systems, depending on the interest of the observer, there are relationships among actors of the system (referred to as *processes*), which can be classified as *social, economic,* or *political.* For example, in a social system at the nation-state level, sociologists focus on primary actors such as individuals, families, social classes, ethnic groups, and other entities that are competing, cooperating, and on occasion, coexisting within a given society. Sociologists study phenomena such as social integration, disintegration, adaptation, mobility, stasis, and so forth. Economists look at a national economic system and focus on the *functions* (i.e., tasks or roles of actors within a system) of primary actors such as individuals, firms, corporations, labor unions, economic classes, and the government, which intervenes (through legislation, for example) to regulate economic relationships in a given society. Economists study processes such as production, distribution, inflation, unemployment, recession, and depression. Political scientists who focus their attention on national political systems observe primary actors such as individuals, political parties, and pressure and interest groups as these and others interact to influence government (executive, legislative, and judiciary branches). They also analyze the way governments allocate values, that is,

---

[6]Here there may be some philosophical controversy as to whether social systems are developed by people or just naturally evolved over time. We will accept that social systems are in most instances designed by their users.

[7]For the purposes of this discussion we are treating *world politics* and *international relations* synonymously. The same applies to *world* or *planetary political system* and *international political system.*

how they go about their function of determining who pays what, when, and how (e.g., who pays what taxes), as well as who gets what, when, and how through government services and subsidies in education, medical care, and security—through fire department, police, and armed forces.

All social systems (political and economic) can be classified on the basis of how they are organized (more or less) or how they are structured. Let us give a few examples: A family can be classified on criteria of inclusiveness as *nuclear* (e.g., a family of four persons) or *extended* (includes relatives such as grandparents, uncles, aunts, and cousins). A family that is dominated in decision making by a father is referred to as patriarchical, and by a mother figure as matriarchical. Political parties that are ineffectively organized, inadequately institutionalized, and dominated by powerful charismatic leaders can be referred to as *personalistic,* while political parties with strong and highly organized and institutionalized procedures can be referred to as bureaucratized, managerial, or collective leadership parties. Nation-states, in turn, can be classified by the degree of possession of centralization of power: democracies (decentralized), dictatorships (centralized), unitary states (centralized), or federations (decentralized).

Finally, the international system can be (and has been) more or less centralized and organized in various periods of our planet's history. For example, as we have already discussed, the international system since 1648 (the Peace of Westphalia) has been described as anarchic, quasi-anarchic, primitive, and so forth. These descriptions were made on the assumption that the primary actors of the international system—sovereign states acting through their governments—recognize no higher authority and settle their disputes through negotiations (diplomacy) or war. Yet, as we know, in earlier historical eras, the world political system was much more centralized (e.g., under the aegis of a central authority during the long centuries of the Roman Empire).

Whether or not we view families, villages, cities, nation-states, regions, or the whole planet as political systems, we quickly realize that their component parts are often involved in disputes, which can lead to collisions, which in turn can threaten the very cohesiveness and existence of the system in question. For example, if disputes between father and mother in a family go out of control, the "political system" may break down by divorce or even murder. If disputes between labor and management at the level of a corporation go out of control, a workers' strike may lead to a lockout or even plant shutdown and resultant violence. At the nation-state level disputes between parties, classes, and ethnic groups may also go out of control, and then demonstrations, political violence, and repressive measures may lead to civil conflict and even destabilizing and destructive civil wars. Finally, at the international-system level, when disputes between states go out of control, then hostilities erupt, at times leading to bloody and destructive wars such as World War I and World War II.

Analysts and students of international relations, as we shall see, like to point out that in the case of systems such as families, factories, cities, and states there exist strong and effective institutions (courts, parliaments, and executive authorities) that provide effective methods for the peaceful settlement of disputes and for peaceful change. Unfortunately, the argument continues, the international political system contains no legitimate and effective global institutions that can put a stop to violence, arbitrate between and among conflicting parties, and arrest, judge, and punish the lawbreakers.

In the post–World War II era, following the development of weapons of mass (if not planetary) destruction, war and other forms of organized violence between states have become increasingly prohibitive. A total nuclear war would surely lead to the devastation of our planet and its inhabitants. Hence, with increasing urgency political scientists are pointing out the need to develop global-level institutions that will permit the global political system to maintain itself over time.

VARIATIONS OF WORLD POLITICAL SYSTEMS

Morton A. Kaplan, in an influential book reflecting the scientific orientation, presented a very useful array of real and hypothetical models of global political organization.[8] The discussion that follows is indebted to Kaplan's work. In it, we refer to some of Kaplan's models, leave others out, and include some models not discussed in his book. Kaplan's work has been criticized for presenting a series of rigid and imaginary international systems that he claims have existed in the past or may be encountered in the future. Real life probably cannot be classified according to compact models that consistently obey different rules and that possess fixed and identifiable attributes. However, we have found it quite useful to employ these models in the classroom, because they help the student recognize that the present structure of the international system is not timeless, that it has changed over time, and that it will more than likely experience a number of changes in the future.

The Oligopolar (or Classical Balance-of-Power) Model

The period from 1815 to 1914, according to Kaplan, is the historical counterpart of this model. The classical balance-of-power model operates best when the international system includes at least five major powers and no regional or universal international organizations (such as the European Community and the United Nations).[9] Alliances in this system tend to be specific and short in duration, and they tend to shift on the basis of pragmatic rather than ideological advantage. Wars between major powers tend to be limited. Wars involving minor powers are not allowed to escalate and are settled in a fashion that is compatible with

[8]Morton A. Kaplan, *System and Process in International Politics* (New York: John Wiley, 1962).
[9]There should also be an upper limit to the number of major powers—a limit somewhere between nine and fourteen. An arbitrary rule could be employed that no more than 10 percent of all independent nation-states should be allowed to attain great-power status. The rationale for the upper limit is that the balance-of-power system can best be managed by a small-in-number but powerful-in-capability group of actors who share a common interest: the perpetuation of their privileged great-power status.

the interests of the major powers. International law is quite operative (primarily in the area of law of war) because its rules, which are acceptable to the heads of the major powers, are habitually practiced. Kaplan feels that the classical balance of power was exemplified by nineteenth-century European international political behavior. By his own definition, he does not expect it to occur again as long as nuclear weapons continue to be in the possession of major powers and as long as world organizations such as the United Nations continue.[10]

We disagree with Kaplan on two counts: First, it is possible for a balance-of-power style of behavior to exist in an international environment where a limited number of great powers possess nuclear weapons and do not use them except as deterrents to total nuclear war. (The theory of nuclear deterrence will be discussed in Chapter 11.) Great-power objectives can remain cautious and marginal under a mutually neutralizing nuclear umbrella. Second, the existence of organizations such as the United Nations, its specialized agencies, and regional groupings such as the East European Council for Mutual Economic Assistance, the European Community, and the Organization of American States does not prevent the basic and informal rules of the balance-of-power system from operating.

The Loose Bipolar Model

This model, also called the cold-war model, characterizes the history of our globe from approximately 1947 to 1971.[11] The loose bipolar model operates when the international system has two superpowers. Each of these superpowers acts as an ally, protector, and even controller of a number of weaker nation-states that belong to its bloc. There are also some peripheral nation-states that are not aligned with either bloc. The major blocs tend to abide by and to transmit uncompromising and mutually exclusive ideologies and to function with drastically different governmental, social, and economic structures. In fact, the differences are of such magnitude that the adoption by one bloc of the political system of the other would call for the replacement of the ruling elites and alter the existing distribution of power, status, and wealth in the newly transformed bloc.[12] The nonaligned nation-states, in contrast, are characterized by a variety of ideologies and governmental systems.

Kaplan emphasizes the importance of nuclear weapons in this type of system. He suggests that bipolarity is a function of the possession of credible

[10]See Morton A. Kaplan, ed., *Great Issues of International Politics* (Chicago: Aldine, 1970), p. 8.

[11]These are arbitrary dates denoting the beginning and the end of the Soviet-American cold war. However, one could also argue that the cold war ended in June 1963 (the date of President John F. Kennedy's speech at the American University), for example, or that it still exists, notwithstanding occasional phases or just claims of détente.

[12]Kenneth Waltz in an influential book argues that bipolarity is a function of capability of states and not of extraneous factors such as ideological orientation, elite rhetoric, and so forth. In other words, it is possible to have bipolarity organized through the duopoly of two powerful states whose elites may be ideologically and culturally quite incompatible. See Kenneth Waltz, *Theory of International Politics* (Reading, Mass.: Addison-Wesley, 1979).

nuclear arsenals by the two bloc leaders, the United States and the Soviet Union. We, less rigid than Kaplan, argue that bipolarity after World War II would have developed regardless of nuclear weapons and that it would have been a function of the overwhelming economic, industrial, and conventional military capabilities of the two superpowers.

Unlike the classical balance-of-power model, the loose bipolar model calls for long-term, highly formal, and institutionalized alliances based on interests that are perceived as permanent and that are couched in ideological terms. Given the high level of governmentally encouraged psychological hostility, wars in this system would tend to be total and uncompromising; one politicoeconomic system would be destroyed by the other. The mutual destructiveness of the nuclear weapons available to both blocs has, however, kept hostilities below the level of total military confrontation.

The Tight Bipolar Model

There is no historical counterpart to this model, according to Kaplan, and we shall not elaborate much on it. Its major assumption is that all nonaligned nation-states are absorbed into one bloc or the other. The uncompromising hostility in regard to ideology and security is much the same as in the loose bipolar model, except that it is now extended throughout the world. The tight bipolar model can best be envisioned as a world cleanly divided into two major empires, one headed by Washington and the other by Moscow. Each metropolis seeks to maintain tight control over its allies and to sustain high-level hostility toward the other empire. This model could also develop into a less conflictive variant described as "duopoly." In this system, the two superpowers would formally *agree* to play down their ideological differences and to cooperate in the management of their respective spheres and in the maintenance of the international system, so as to serve their respective interests.

The Unit-Veto (or Nuclear Proliferation) Model

This model, fortunately up to this point, has no historical counterpart.[13] It depicts a highly unstable and potentially deadly style of international intercourse. It envisages an international system in which most states possess relatively credible nuclear-weapon capabilities, which they can use to discourage other states from pursuing unfriendly policies toward them. Thus, any one of over a hundred separate political entities could trigger nuclear warfare and cause global catastrophe. This model, if it came to pass, would create the kind of climate that would exist among a number of unfriendly and mutually suspicious people finding themselves on a large yacht, each wanting to take the vessel to different parts of the

---

[13]For an informative review of literature dealing with nuclear proliferation and its control, see George H. Quester, "The Statistical 'n' of 'nth' Nuclear Weapon States," *Journal of Conflict Resolution*, 27, no. 1 (March 1983), 161–79.

world and use it for different purposes. These people cannot ever resolve their disagreements because each of them has immediate access to a button that, if pushed, will blow the boat and all its passengers to pieces. Each can therefore threaten all the others with collective suicide unless his or her will is respected. The chances of destruction through miscalculation, irrationality, obstinacy, or accident are extremely high in such a system.

Fearing an accidental nuclear confrontation resulting from a misunderstanding, states would tend to limit their contacts in a unit-veto system, thus minimizing the exchange of goods, people, and services across national boundaries. There could be no conventional wars, because any war, once erupted, would most probably escalate to the nuclear level. The unit-veto system could assume even more dreaded proportions if subnational actors were to possess nuclear weapons and crude but effective means of delivering them. Such actors could be terrorist/liberation groups, criminal organizations (such as the Mafia), multinational corporations, ethnic or racial minorities, or demented individuals wishing to cause large-scale harm to their fellow human beings.

It should be clear by now that a unit-veto system would seriously press the leaders of nation-states to accept some form of centralized global authority— an authority with the power to appropriate all nuclear weapons or destroy totally nuclear stockpiles. The question is whether a nuclear accident will occur before national leaders become pressed enough to realize that the risk of general nuclear war has become a totally unacceptable option. (Efforts at arms control and disarmament, with special emphasis on nuclear weapons, are discussed in Chapter 12.)

The Collective-Security Model

This is an ideal model (with no historical counterpart).[14] The best way to visualize it is to think in terms of the United Nations working according to the lofty ideals of its founders. (For a discussion of the United Nations, see Chapter 14.) The collective-security model calls for a voluntary system of regulation. In this system, military force as an instrument of policy is forbidden; there are no alliances, either short-term or long-term; and aggression by one state against any other is punished by economic and military sanctions imposed collectively by all other states. Over time, therefore, this system could be a relatively peaceful one. In an environment of collective security, the United Nations or its successor could become progressively more effective in settling international disputes peacefully.

The collective-security system has been criticized as being too idealistic and impractical. It is based on a primitive structure similar to that of the balance-of-power system. Yet it expects nation-states and their governments to abide by moral and legal restrictions voluntarily, rather than out of respect or fear of cen-

---

[14]For an elaboration of the concept of collective security, see Inis L. Claude, Jr., *Power and International Relations* (New York: Random House, 1962). See especially pp. 94–190, which are devoted to a discussion and critique of the collective-security system.

tralized world authorities. It also assumes that states will agree consistently on the definition and the interpretation of aggression and that they will be willing to defend any other state being aggressed against regardless of their own national interests. The collective-security system, further, expects the United Nations to function effectively without watering down the sovereignty of individual states. Finally, a collective-security system is unrealistic because its implementation would require nation-states, which exist now in what is fundamentally a decentralized, balance-of-power system, to refrain from entering into alliances or other, less formal political arrangements.

The Multibloc (or Interregional) Model

This model, which would also fit in the oligopolar category, comes in two varieties.[15] The first portrays a world divided into five to seven mutually exclusive spheres of influence. Each of these spheres would consist of a hierarchy of countries controlled by one of the world's major powers. Major powers would institutionalize their respective spheres of influence by means of security-political organizations of the NATO and Warsaw Pact variety. Each of the major powers would refrain from interfering in the "internal affairs" of any of the other spheres of influence.

The second variant of the multibloc model would result from successful economic- and political-integration efforts within the inhabited continents of our earth. (For a discussion of regional integration, see Chapter 15.) This variant envisions a world organized into large and autonomous integrated regions, such as North America, South America, Western Europe, the Soviet Union and Eastern Europe, Africa, the Middle East, and various difficult-to-forecast regional arrangements involving South and Southeast Asia, East Asia, and Oceania. Following gradual economic and political integration within these regions, the distribution of global power will be radically affected. Mobile and transcontinental national powers will no longer exist.

The National-Fragmentation (or Multipolar) Model

Here we must imagine processes of political and territorial disintegration at work in states multiplying geometrically the units of political action. Ethnic, tribal, racial,[16] and economic separatist movements could challenge seriously the political cohesiveness of polyethnic, multilingual, multireligious, multiracial, or unevenly developed states. Contemporary separatist movements in Canada, Yugo-

---

[15]For elaboration, see Roger D. Masters, "A Multi-Bloc Model of the International System," *American Political Science Review,* 55 (December 1961), 782.

[16]The meanings of these three terms are not always clear. *Ethnic* and *tribal,* for instance, should be considered synonymous. To refer to conflict in Ulster as *ethnic* and to conflict in Nigeria as *tribal* is to exhibit a subconscious bias toward Europe, if not outright racism. Either of the two terms should be used uniformly for internal conflicts throughout the globe to eliminate the bias. For elaboration on all three terms, see our discussion in Chapter 4.

slavia, Ulster, Cyprus, Belgium, Spain, Nigeria, and Turkey could be emulated by separatist elements in many other countries, such as the United States, the USSR, China, Brazil, India, Indonesia, Sudan, and Australia. It would be plausible, then, that a process of global political and economic integration would first undergo a phase of fragmentation of the existing national states, especially those with a disproportionately large amount of power and wealth.[17] The fragmentation of nation-states presumably would eliminate the resistance to a transformation of the existing international system into a system of world government. On the other hand, it would entail imponderable—in level and intensity—civil and international conflicts.

The Post–Nuclear-War Model

Here we must visualize our earth after a catastrophic nuclear war. As many as half a billion people could perish as a result of the explosions, heat, and radiation. But that would not be all. Transportation, communications, and industrial production would grind to a halt. Entire regions of the earth would be contaminated with nuclear fallout. Diseased and maimed people would be scrambling frantically for shelter, food, and medication. The fear of contamination would drive healthy citizens to treat potentially diseased ones as vermin to be quarantined or exterminated. The sight of heaps of mangled and scalded human bodies, the debris of fallen buildings, the scorched earth, the stench of death, and the howling of the dying could all have totally unpredictable psychological consequences upon the survivors. Following the immediate effects, the deathly coldness of "nuclear winter" will set in. In such a nightmarish situation, only the most tyrannical regimes would be able to maintain enough order for the distribution of food, shelter, and medical treatment.[18] This is a system that we certainly do not wish upon our children and grandchildren. But beyond wishes, it is important that we quickly develop effective safeguards against the madness of a total nuclear war and a world in which the living will envy the dead.[19]

The Hierarchical (or Monopolar) Model

This model clearly falls outside the family of decentralized political systems (that is, systems relying on a balance of power for regulation) that we have been discussing so far in this section. As its name implies, this model describes a pyramidal system of international regulation that could best be achieved through world

---

[17]Arnold Toynbee, for example, envisioned a global community whose component parts would not be states but small, village-sized entities encouraging frequent interpersonal contact. See Arnold Toynbee, *Mankind and Mother Earth* (New York: Oxford University Press, 1976), p. 593.

[18]Another appropriate name for this model would be the nuclear-damage–control model.

[19]See Herman Kahn, *Thinking about the Unthinkable* (New York: Horizon Press, 1962), and Philip Green, *Deadly Logic: The theory of Nuclear Deterrence* (Columbus, Ohio: Ohio State University Press, 1966) for diametrically opposed views regarding a post–nuclear-war setting. Kahn finds recuperation difficult but likely. Green is much more pessimistic. We tend to agree with Green's pessimism.

government. Such a government could be based on federal and democratic principles and could evolve from the rudimentary institutions of the United Nations. It could, on the other hand, result from conquest and control of the globe by a single power. The Roman Empire, which resulted from the military conquests of the Romans, is a rough example of this type of system. Had Napoleon succeeded in his expansionist objectives, or had Adolf Hitler won World War II, the outcome might have been a worldwide version of authoritarian government. A hierarchical system could develop in the future if the United States, the Soviet Union, or a third power were to prevail upon the remaining superpowers. The hierarchical system, whether democratic or authoritarian, would not necessarily be very stable in the long run. It would undoubtedly suffer from separatist tendencies, which could degenerate into a deadly global "civil war."

THE CONFLICT QUOTIENT OF VARIOUS INTERNATIONAL SYSTEMS

Political scientists have speculated on the merits and demerits of various means of regulating the international system. They have asked a simple question: What type of international system provides for the least conflict? Implicit assumptions in this question are that a system's structure affects the incidence of war and that a system of low conflict is preferable to any system involving greater conflict. There is considerable diversity among the findings of these scholars. At times, well-known political scientists have arrived at nearly irreconcilable positions. Kenneth Waltz, for example, prefers a system of global Soviet-American bipolarity because in his opinion it would minimize international conflict.[20] Waltz expects that if most nation-states are grouped under the influence of the United States or the Soviet Union and if vigilance is maintained in an intensely adversary atmosphere, the "Munich mentality" of aggressor appeasement can be avoided. In such a system of mutual vigilance, only small and limited wars in the periphery of the great blocs would be allowed. If both blocs systematically avoid pacifism, demilitarization, disorganization, and appeasement, neither bloc will be tempted to seek dominance over the other.

Karl W. Deutsch and J. David Singer, on the other hand, argue that a multipolar balance-of-power system allows for less net conflict than the bipolar system.[21] They fear that once war breaks out in a bipolar system there is great danger that it will be fought to the very end, with catastrophic results. In a multipolar system, though, given the uncertainty created by the variety of alliances, wars are mathematically more likely to be marginal and involve only a small fraction of each belligerent's capabilities. Deutsch and Singer also feel that in a multi-

---

[20]Kenneth N. Waltz, "International Structure, National Force, and the Balance of World Power," *Journal of International Affairs,* 21 (1967), 215–31.

[21]Karl W. Deutsch and J. David Singer, "Multipolar Power Systems and International Stability," *World Politics,* 16 (1964), 390–406.

polar balance-of-power system the attention of nation-states will not be focused exclusively on a single source of threat and that in such an environment arms races are likely to be more controlled.

Richard Rosecrance has sought to bridge the differences between the models of bipolarity and multipolarity by fusing them into a single political system, which he calls bi-multipolarity.[22] He believes that this model has the highest probability of minimizing violent conflict. To restate the model, there should be bipolarity at the nuclear level of activity and multipolarity at the politicoeconomic and conventional (nonnuclear) military levels. Rosecrance argues that under conditions of multipolarity the probability of war breaking out is higher, but the wars that do erupt are limited in terms of participants and destructiveness. Under conditions of bipolarity the situation is just the opposite: There is a lower probability of war breaking out, but the destructiveness of war would be very high since it would involve the half of the world led by the United States fighting the half led by the Soviet Union. Rosecrance, fearing that the spread of nuclear weapons would turn a multipolar system into an earth-sized sphere of explosive material, wishes to see nuclear proliferation limited. Simultaneously, he finds that the political and economic fragmentation of the international system would prevent local wars from escalating rapidly into major East-West confrontations.

Despite the excitement generated by the bipolarity-multipolarity debate, we tend to become somewhat skeptical when we look at statistics of international and civil wars over time.[23] As we will see in Chapter 11, the incidence of war has been increasing steadily throughout history; fluctutations of excessive war activity occur approximately every twenty to forty years. We also know that from 1648 to the present, the world has been characterized by multipolar and/or bipolar systems of both legitimate and revolutionary nature. Yet, wars have occurred with monotonous regularity during that time. Even nation-states ruled by powerful and centralized authorities have witnessed frequent and costly civil conflicts. We should not forget, after all, that the heaviest losses the United States suffered in any war it has fought to date was its own civil war.

A PARTING WORD

The effectiveness of the balance-of-power system has rested so far on the assumption that participating nation-states are led by rational leaders who constantly strive to protect the existence of their governments and their nation-states. As a result, they have devised techniques of diplomacy and limited war to protect their interests, and they have normally operated within the limits of prudence dictated

---

[22]Richard N. Rosecrance, "Bipolarity, Multipolarity, and the Future," *Journal of Conflict Resolution,* 10 (1966), 314–27.

[23]See, for example, Melvin Small and J. David Singer, *Resort to Arms: International and Civil Wars, 1816–1980* (Beverly Hills, Calif.: Sage Publications, 1982); and Quincy Wright, *A Study of War,* 2nd ed. (Chicago: University of Chicago Press, 1965).

by the instincts of self-preservation. However, since the development of nuclear weapons by the United States and the USSR, the balance of power has become, in Winston Churchill's words, the "balance of terror." The balance of terror is based on the assumption that if both the United States and the USSR can maintain enough "invulnerable" nuclear weapons in submarines, bombers, and hardened silos, then either superpower can cause "unacceptable damage" to the other side, regardless of who strikes first. In such a situation, the "rational" thing to do would be to avoid using nuclear weapons altogether, since their usage would result in mutual suicide. But should we rest the future of humankind on primitive institutions based on assumptions of rationality that are rooted in instincts of self-preservation, self-help, and self-limitation? The following story does not leave us with much ground for optimism.

There was once a frog preparing to swim across a river. A scorpion suddenly approached him, and while the terrified frog was keeping a safe distance they began a conversation that went something like this:

SCORPION: Dear Frog. I can't swim. I need urgently to cross the river. Would you please take me on your back to the other side?

FROG: Heavens no! You are an aggressive creature. Your reputation is well known. You sting others to kill them. On top of that, you seem to enjoy it.

SCORPION: (obviously educated in logic and bargaining techniques) What you say makes sense. But listen to my cold logic. Let me jump on your back while you are in deep water. Then you know that if I sting you, you will die. If you die, you will sink. If you sink, I will also sink— since by nature I cannot swim—and I will also die. But I don't want to die, and therefore I will not sting you.

FROG: (who has a good nature and an appreciation of deterrence theory) Well, I suppose you are right. There is not much I can lose by helping you, and I might gain by having you on my good side.

So the frog and scorpion slowly start crossing the river. About halfway across, the wet and moist back of the frog begins to tempt the scorpion. There below him is inviting flesh waiting for the sting. The scorpion hesitates for one more moment and then stings the frog. The venom quickly penetrates the system of the frog. The frog loses control of his muscular motion. He begins to sink, and with him, of course, the mischievous scorpion. In a last moment of existential curiosity, the frog looks up at the scorpion.

FROG: What on earth made you do it? Now we will both die!

SCORPION: (bewildered) I couldn't help it! I suppose it's my nature to sting!

This story leaves us with a nagging question: Can we trust mass-destructive nuclear weapons in the hands of leaders who—at some time or another—might show the kind of suicidal mentality exhibited by the deadly scorpion?

SUGGESTIONS FOR FURTHER STUDY

The problem of stability and fragmentation is examined in an anthology edited by Ole R. Holsti, Randolph M. Siverson, and Alexander L. George under the title *Change in the International System* (Boulder, Colo.: Westview Press, 1980). In his introductory chapter to *Latin America in the International Political System* (New York: Free Press, 1977), G. Pope Atkins has studied systems analysis as a framework within which to organize the material in international relations. The seamless web of international relations is the thesis of Immanuel Wallerstein, *The Modern World-System* (New York: Academic Press, 1974), and *The Modern World-System II* (New York: Academic Press, 1980). Prescriptive thinking characterizes Albert Bergeson, "The Emerging Science of the World System," *International Social Science Journal,* 34 (1981), 23–36. For an overview of the background and concepts of systems analysis, see Richard Little, "A Systems Approach," in *Approaches and Theory in International Relations,* ed. Trevor Taylor (New York: Longman, 1978). Morton A. Kaplan has replied to his critics in "The Systems Approach to International Politics," in *New Approaches to International Politics,* ed. Morton A. Kaplan (New York: St. Martin's Press, 1968). Donald E. Lampert, Lawrence S. Falkowski, and Richard W. Mansbach affirm the utility of the systems theory in "Is There an International System?" *International Studies Quarterly,* 22 (March 1978), 143–66. Changes in the international system as they affect foreign policy behavior are the theme of Maurice A. East, "The International System Perspective and Foreign Policy," in *Why Nations Act: Theoretical Perspectives for Comparative Foreign Policy Studies,* ed. Maurice A. East, Stephen A. Salmore, and Charles F. Hermann (Beverly Hills, Calif.: Sage Publications, 1978). Wolfram F. Hanrieder has examined stability and systemic interaction in "The International System: Bipolar or Multibloc?" *Journal of Conflict Resolution,* 9 (September 1965), 299–308. Anton W. DePorte has evaluated the diplomacy of bipolarity in a positive light in *Europe between the Superpowers: The Enduring Balance* (New Haven: Yale University Press, 1980), in contrast to the interpretation offered by Stanley Hoffmann in *Primacy or World Order: American Foreign Policy since the Cold War* (New York: McGraw-Hill, 1978).

PART II: National Actors: Their Attributes, Interests, and Policies

4

THE NATION-STATE AND NATIONALISM

> It is certain that the greatest miracles in virtue have been produced by patriotism: This fine and lively feeling, which gives to the force of self-love all the beauty of virtue, lends it an energy which, without disfiguring it, makes it the most heroic of all passions.
>
> Jean Jacques Rousseau

In politics individuals normally do not act alone, but in connection with social groupings. Historically, the political world has been divided in terms of "we" versus "they," the latter being referred to as barbarians, foreigners, outsiders, or, more often, simply the "enemy."[1] Most of us belong to a large number of groups that reflect our work, political views, religious beliefs, and life-styles. But there is one group that pervades all others: the nation-state. National stereotypes are powerful images, and their use can induce emotional and physiological reactions, such as the primordial "fight-or-flight" syndrome. An investigation of national-ism, both as a pattern of learned group behavior and as a political institution called the nation-state, is fundamental to an understanding of global politics.

NATIONS AND STATES

The terms *nation* and *state* are quite distinct conceptually, yet they are often used interchangeably. The *nation* is a concept denoting a common ethnic and cultural

---

[1]See David J. Finlay, Ole R. Holsti, and Richard R. Fagen, *Enemies in Politics* (Chicago: Rand McNally, 1967), pp. 6–22.

identity shared by a single people; the *state* is a political unit defined in terms of territory, population, and an autonomous government that exercises effective control of the territory and its inhabitants regardless of their ethnic homogeneity or heterogeneity. The state provides a basis for political and legal jurisdiction in the form of citizenship, whereas the nation promotes an emotional relationship through which the individual gains a sense of cultural identity. Nations and states do not always share the same cultural and territorial boundaries. Therefore, the term nation-state has been used by social scientists to denote the gradual fusion that may occur between cultural and political boundaries after prolonged maintenance of political control by a central authority over a given territory and its inhabitants.

Nationalism[2] can be defined as a perceived identity of oneself with a territorially organized political collectivity such as the United States, the USSR, and other countries. The psychological need to define oneself in terms of membership in a given community is at the root of nationalist sentiment. The hallmarks of nationalism are a sense of territoriality manifested in a love of one's homeland, a written and spoken language, a tradition of achievement in the arts and literature, a narrative history (as opposed to legends or folk tales), and, frequently, the perpetuation from generation to generation of the fear of the "enemy" whose real or imagined hostility threatens the security of the nation-state.

National self-determination is the idealistic belief born of the French Revolution that the cause of peace would be well served if each nation were able to choose its own political destiny. In 1918, President Woodrow Wilson announced the Fourteen Points on the basis of which he hoped to achieve an end to World War I. Point Ten was a guarantee to the nations of the Austro-Hungarian Empire that they would be given an opportunity for autonomous political development. Subsequent generations have echoed the same demand for other nations, and Article 1(2) of the United Nations Charter commits that world organization to respect the "self-determination of peoples."[3]

ETHNIC PLURALISM AND NATION-STATES

There is no major controversy among scholars as to the definition of *nation-state*. The positivist school of international law defines a *state* as a legal and political entity with the attributes of population, territory, and an autonomous government that exercises effective control over the population and territory and is willing and able to meet fundamental international responsibilities. Additionally, a large number of governments must extend *de jure* recognition to the state before

[2]The term *patriotism* can be used as a synonym for *nationalism*, especially in states such as the United States and the Soviet Union, whose populations are characterized by considerable ethnic, linguistic, religious, and cultural diversity.

[3]Leland M. Goodrich and Edvard I. Hambro, *Charter of the United Nations: Commentary and Documents* (Boston: World Peace Foundation, 1949), pp. 95–96.

it can claim a demonstrable legal existence.[4] This approach legally equates all states as actors in the international system without regard to the prevalence of ethnic cleavages within them. The advantages of using international legal criteria for the purpose of distinguishing between state and nonstate actors in world affairs are obvious, but this distinction may be somewhat misleading, especially in the uncertain area of assessing the internal cohesiveness of these various actors.

Ethnically, nation-states can be either homogeneous or heterogeneous. Most nation-states fall into the latter category. Heterogeneous nation-states encompass a number of ethnic groups that possess either an actualized or an incipient sense of nationhood. Characteristic examples of such states are Brazil, Canada, Great Britain, India, Indonesia, Lebanon, Nigeria, Peru, the Soviet Union, Switzerland, and the United States. Expert studies have indicated that there is indeed a great disparity between ethnic and political boundaries throughout the world. Walker Connor, in an important article published in 1972, found that out of 132 nation-states included in his study only 12 (9.1 percent) could have been described as being ethnically homogeneous.[5] Twenty-five more nation-states (18.9 percent) contained an overwhelmingly large ethnic group accounting for over 90 percent of those states' population. In 25 additional nation-states Connor found that the majority ethnic group accounted for 75 to 89 percent of their population. However, he found that in 31 states (23.5 percent of his sample) the majority ethnic element represented only between 50 and 74 percent of their population. Finally, in 39 states (29.5 percent of his sample) the most populous ethnic group did not manage to reach even the 50 percent level of the total population. Connor found, further, that a multiplicity of ethnic groups were indeed living together (whether in peace or in conflict) within a large number of modern nation-states. In some cases, states included within their boundaries hundreds of diverse ethnic groups, while in 53 states out of 132 the population comprised five or more distinct and significant ethnic groups.

Since the study of international relations focuses primarily on the relations between nation-states, it is necessary to analyze in some depth the social and ethnic composition of these relatively persistent units of political action. Even if we were to assume that nation-states are transitory phenomena gradually being replaced by nonstate actors, contemporary reality is such that most individuals look to their respective nation-states for protection, identity, and direction.

There is considerable controversy regarding the best way in which to study the nation-state in its ethnic dimension and to analyze the phenomenon of nationalism. To resolve this difficulty, we suggest a distinction among three approaches. The first is the *objective* (attributive), the second is the *subjective* (attitudinal), and the third we shall call the *eclectic* (synthetic). The *objective* approach

[4]Charles G. Fenwick, *International Law,* 4th ed. rev. (New York: Appleton-Century-Crofts, 1965), pp. 124, 155–203.
[5]Walker Connor, "Nation-Building or Nation-Destroying," *World Politics,* 24 (1972), 319–55.

seeks to identify nationalism and the nation-state in terms of observable and readily quantifiable attributes, among which are linguistic, racial, and religious homogeneity.[6] The *subjective* approach views nationalism and the nation-state as a set of emotional, ideological, and patriotic feelings binding an individual and a community regardless of the ethnic structure (homogeneous/heterogeneous) of that community.[7] The *eclectic* approach, somewhat closer to the subjective than the objective premises, equates terms such as *nationalism* and *patriotism* and posits that protracted communication and exchange in an era of mass-media growth, together with practices such as interethnic marriage, mixed neighborhoods, and common (integrated) educational systems, lead to the adoption over time of a single, collective identity.[8] The United States represents the very embodiment of the principles and premises of the eclectic approach to nationalism.

Subjective and objective definitions can be misleading, however, if they are used separately. For instance, the population on both sides of a political frontier may possess a common national/ethnic identity—the objective test—and at the same time be politically and legally divided between two or more states. In this category, examples abound: the overseas Chinese of Southeast Asia, the Magyar minority of Romania, the Incas of the Andean highlands, and the Turkish cultural community, whose members are dispersed from the Balkans across western Asia and into China. On the other hand, such ethnically heterogeneous states as Belgium and Switzerland exhibit considerable diversity at the objective level, yet subjectively their citizens have a strong feeling of patriotism toward the state that provides them with security and enables their heterogeneous society to achieve its goals.

THE ROOTS OF NATIONALISM

It is to antiquity that we must turn in order to understand the forces that have evolved into contemporary nationalism. From the beginning of recorded history, humans have banded together in groups in order to face collectively the animate and inanimate challenges of nature. Consequently, throughout history we see various territorially based political organizations. The earliest of these, crude and anomic bands, eventually gave way to tribes, villages, walled cities, manors, princi-

[6]For a survey of anthropological and ethnographic studies stressing the objective approach, see Richard L. Merritt, *Nationalism and National Development: An Interdisciplinary Bibliography* (Cambridge, Mass.: MIT Press, 1970).

[7]For representative writings on the subjective approach, see Rupert Emerson, *From Empire to Nation: The Rise and Self-Assertion of Asian and African Peoples* (Boston: Beacon Press, 1960); Benedict Anderson, *Imagined Communities: Reflections on the Origin and Spread of Nationalism* (London, Verso, 1983); and especially Hans Kohn, *The Idea of Nationalism: A Study of Its Origins and Background* (New York: Macmillan, 1951) and *Prelude to Nation-States: The French and German Experience, 1789–1815,* (Princeton, N.J.: Van Nostrand, 1967).

[8]The eclectic approach is best represented by the pioneering work of Karl Deutsch. See especially his *Nationalism and Social Communication: An Inquiry into the Foundations of Nationality,* 2nd ed. rev. (Cambridge, Mass.: MIT Press, 1966), and *Nationalism and Its Alternatives* (New York: Knopf, 1969).

palities, empires and their subdivisions, and, most recently, nation-states and regional economic communities.

The recorded history of the human species is about ten thousand years old. A review of the rise and decline of ancient peoples and their cultures supports the we-versus-they phenomenon on which nationalism is based. One of the first peoples whose history has been reconstructed is the Sumerians. They lived in valleys adjacent to the Tigris and Euphrates rivers and organized themselves into an agriculturally oriented city-state system. These city-states were independent of one another, accepted no central authority, and settled their disputes through conflict or bargaining processes premised on power. The earliest known treaty was concluded between the kings of the Sumerian city-states of Umma and Lagash about 3000 B.C. This treaty called for the two rulers to submit a frontier dispute to third-party arbitration.

At the same time, and gradually thereafter, other great civilizations developed among the Egyptians, the Hittites, the Indians, the Chinese, the Hebrews, the Assyrians, the Phoenicians, the Persians, the Greeks, and the Mayas and Aztecs in what later came to be known as the New World.

The ancient Greek city-state system that was flourishing five centuries before the birth of Jesus provides us with some examples of strong albeit parochial forms of nationalism. The famous funeral oration of Pericles (495–429 B.C.), a ruler of ancient Athens, to his fellow Athenians is a model of nationalism and patriotism. As he mourned the Athenian dead after a battle with Sparta, Pericles justified the terrible sacrifice on the grounds of preserving Athens. His speech was a glorification of the city of Athens, its ancestors, and their accomplishments. Athenian culture, government, military organization, and way of life were second to none, according to Pericles. He was proud to belong to Athens, and he placed it above all other cities in ancient Greece. The distinction between "we" and "they" cannot be made more emphatically than it was in this speech. Pericles praised Athens for being an open and creative city distinguished by a unique system of government called democracy, a great love for education, leisure, and the fine arts, respect for beauty and poetry, and an unceasing commitment to improvement and growth. "In a word," he concluded, "I claim that our city as a whole is an education to Greece. . . . No other city of the present day goes out to her ordeal greater than ever men dreamed; no other is so powerful that the invader feels no bitterness when he suffers at her hands, and her subjects no shame at the indignity of their dependence."[9]

If we continue briefly to look at the history of the Western world, we see a constant ebb and flow between patterns of political integration and patterns of political fragmentation, represented by empires and city-state systems respectively. For example, the Greek city-states were united forcibly by Philip of Macedon (382–336 B.C.). His son, Alexander the Great (356–323 B.C.), led the

---

[9]Quoted in Thucydides, *The History of the Peloponnesian War*, ed. and trans. Richard Livingstone (New York: Oxford University Press, 1960), p. 114. Quoted materials are being used here with the permission of Oxford University Press.

The Parthenon on the Acropolis in Athens (built 447–438 B.C.), the finest architectural achievement of classical Greece. (Greek National Tourist Office)

Greeks to adventurous growth and empire. Alexander's empire can be understood both as an elementary form of Greek nationalist expansionism and as an early attempt at supranational integration. The Macedonian Empire gradually but steadily began to fall into fragments, and eventually it succumbed to a new and vigorous expansionist force originating in Rome.

The Roman Empire provides us with a good example of the coexistence between nationalism and multinationalism. For instance, the Romans had two systems of law—one for themselves and one for the "nations" that were under their control. In its heyday the Roman Empire extended from India to Scotland and from the Danube to the Sahara. It was a model of world government, a hierarchy controlled vigorously by Rome. After the collapse of the empire in A.D. 476, its western half disintegrated into numerous political units. Centuries later (A.D. 962), a halfhearted attempt was made to revive the empire by combining these units into the Holy Roman Empire.

The eastern and southern half of the fallen empire passed into the hands of the Byzantine and Arabic empires, which were dominated by Greeks and Arabs respectively. After many centuries of adventurous and creative existence, these two empires were also overtaken by a new and vigorous national group known as the Ottoman Turks, and the Ottoman Empire was born. This empire also flourished for centuries. Its formal "death" occurred with the breakup of the empire at the ebb of World War I and the emergence of the modern nation-state of Turkey in 1923.

The western half of the Roman Empire, unlike the eastern half, followed the road of political fragmentation rather than of empire. Small feudal states persisted in an atmosphere of continual but controlled religious and temporal warfare. Territorial rearrangements were most often the result of military conquests or marriages of convenience among rulers. It is in this atmosphere of ethnic pluralism and political fragmentation that we can trace the genesis of modern nation-states.

The first large and politically centralized entities in the West developed in Spain, England, and France between the middle of the thirteenth century and the middle of the sixteenth century. These nation-states were at first loose and pluralist agglomerations of people held together primarily by the absolute authority of monarchs. Spain, for example, emerged as a single country as a result of the fusion of Aragon and Castile evolving from the marriage of Ferdinand and Isabella.

Dynastic legitimacy rather than national and ethnic cohesiveness provided the cement that kept countries such as Spain, France, and England together. The rising merchant and professional middle classes found that the absolute power of the king was a convenient device for eroding the power of corrupt and decadent traditional aristocracies and distant imperial bonds. But for the process of modern nationalist development to be completed, supreme authority had to be transferred from kings and queens to the people.

THE RISE OF MODERN FORMS OF NATIONALISM

Seventeenth-century England is usually presented as the first modern nation-state in which nationalism and its related concept of patriotism became coequal with the idea of individual liberties and popular participation in public affairs.[10] The American Revolution (1776) and the French Revolution (1789) are landmarks in the development of heterogeneous nationalism (in the United States) and homogeneous nationalism (in France). The United States was the result of the unification of former British colonies that had fought against their metropolis to obtain political rights, tolerance of religious diversity, and individual liberties. The Declaration of Independence proclaimed a brand of nationalism based on the perpetuation of a system of liberal ideas and a pluralist and secular way of life. Certain "truths" were held to be self-evident, "that all men are created equal, that they are endowed by their Creator with certain inalienable rights, that among these are life, liberty, and the pursuit of happiness." Given the subsequent ethnic and religious diversity of Americans, the coining of the patriotic slogan *e pluribus unum* is not surprising.

French nationalism was more vigorous, romantic, and ethnically homogeneous than the verbally restrained Anglo-Saxon versions, but equally expansionist. Maximilien Robespierre (1758–94), one of the masterminds of the French Revolution, exemplified the French spirit with these words of self-sacrifice: "I am French, I am one of thy [France's] representatives. . . . Oh sublime people! Accept

[10]Hans Kohn, *Nationalism: Its Meaning in History,* rev. ed. (Princeton, N.J.: Van Nostrand, 1965), p. 17.

the sacrifices of my whole being. Happy is the man who is born in your midst; happier is he who can die for your happiness."[11] Napoleon Bonaparte transformed patriotic and nationalist sentiments such as these into an expansionist ideology. The institution of mass conscription called for deep and tangible involvement of citizens in the life of the nation-state. Napoleon's "citizen armies" carried him to victory after victory throughout Europe and the Middle East. Eventually, he was defeated by the very forces of nationalism he had helped awaken.

A third variation of nationalism is associated with the North American frontier of the eighteenth and nineteenth centuries and with the political unification of Germany (1864–71). Some of the proponents of this brand of nationalism likened the state to a living organism passing through the phases of birth, adolescence, maturity, and finally old age. Often, they claimed a dominant role for their nation because of its presumed superior biological heritage.[12] Others saw the nation-state as inspired by a divine idea and charged it with a unique historical mission.[13] Whatever the nuances of interpretation, a central idea unites what came to be known as the organic school: the state must expand or die; the conquest of living space (*Lebensraum*) is therefore vital. Germany in the 1933–45 period, under the totalitarian rule of Adolf Hitler, epitomized an extreme and reckless version of organic nationalism. Benito Mussolini (1883–1945), the *Duce* of Fascist Italy, expressed the organic view of the nation-state most graphically:

> Fascism is an historical conception, in which man is what he is only insofar as he works with the spiritual process in which he finds himself, in the family or social group, in the nation and in the history in which all nations collaborate.... Outside history man is nothing. Consequently Fascism is opposed to all the individualistic abstractions of a materialistic nature like those of the eighteenth century; ... Against individualism, the Fascist conception is for the State; and it is for the individual insofar as he coincides with the State, which is the conscience and universal will of man in his historical existence.... The nation as the State is an ethical reality which exists and lives insofar as it develops. To arrest its development is to kill it.... Thus [the State] can be likened to the human will which knows no limits to its development and realizes itself in testing its own limitlessness.[14]

The organic and mystical conception of the nation-state was built substantially on the philosophical foundations provided by Georg Wilhelm Friedrich Hegel (1770–1831), the German philosopher.[15] Hegel viewed the history of hu-

[11]Quoted in *ibid.,* p. 27.

[12]A widely read treatise on so-called biological nationalism is Joseph Arthur de Gobineau, *The Inequality of Human Races*, trans. Adrian Collins (New York: Putnam, 1915). Gobineau ascribed to the Nordic peoples of Europe a decisive role in history. See also Michael D. Biddiss, ed., *Gobineau: Selected Political Writings* (London: Cape, 1970).

[13]See Georg Wilhelm Friedrich Hegel, *Political Writings*, trans. T. M. Knox (Oxford: Clarendon Press, 1964), and *Philosophy of History*, 2nd ed., rev. and trans. J. Sibree (New York: Collier, 1905).

[14]Quoted in Michael Oakeshott, *The Social and Political Doctrines of Contemporary Europe* (London: Cambridge University Press, 1939), pp. 165–68.

[15]This brief discussion of Hegelian thought derives in large part from the interpretation of George H. Sabine, *A History of Political Theory*, 3rd ed. rev. (New York: Holt, Rinehart & Winston, 1961), pp. 620–67.

Georg W.F. Hegel (1770–1831), idealist philosopher and father of dialectical reasoning. (The Bettmann Archive)

man civilization as a succession of national cultures. For him, the national state was the highest form of political unit, the embodiment of political power. The *Volksgeist*, the genius and the spirit of a nation, imbued the nation with the qualities of a huge, collective, living, and growing organism. The parts of this organism (such as individuals, groups, regions, and political parties) were to be subordinated to the whole. A lack of such subordination would result in anarchy and chaos. True freedom could be found only within the strict disciplinary lines of the nation-state. The state (as a government) thus emerged as the embodiment of a nation's will and destiny. Finally, the state was seen as having no higher duty than to preserve and strengthen itself.

According to this conception, individuals are best understood as "means" of the state, their value to be measured in terms of their contribution to the survival of the state organism. History is seen as proceeding according to organic laws that are beyond the control of individuals. Thus, concluded Hegel, true political genius could be found among those persons who knew how to identify with higher principles such as the survival, growth, and prosperity of their nation-states.

It was in the spirit of organic nationalism that a Japanese petty officer, having chosen to die as a kamikaze pilot, could write these words to his dearest ones on October 28, 1944:

> Dear Parents:
> Please congratulate me. I have been given a splendid opportunity to die. This is my last day. The destiny of our homeland hinges on the decisive battle in the seas to the south where I shall fall like a blossom from a radiant cherry tree.
> I shall be a shield for His Majestey and die cleanly along with my squadron leader and other friends. I wish that I could be born seven times, each time to smite the enemy.

How I appreciate this chance to die like a man! I am grateful from the depths of my heart to the parents who have reared me with their constant prayers and tender love. And I am grateful as well to my squadron leader and superior officers who have looked after me as if I were their own son and given me such careful training.

Thank you, my parents, for the twenty-three years during which you have cared for me and inspired me. I hope that my present deed will in some small way repay what you have done for me. Think well of me and know that your Isao died for our country. This is my last wish, and there is nothing else that I desire.[16]

NATIONAL SOVEREIGNTY

A major characteristic of the nation-state is sovereignty. In the literature of international relations, sovereignty has been defined as supreme state authority subject to no external limitations. The French philosopher Jean Bodin (1530–96) is associated with the earliest clear definition of this concept. Bodin was concerned with the fragmentation and sectionalism that had led to frequent civil wars and chaos in France. His main object, therefore, was to strengthen the position of the monarch as the source of order and unity throughout France. Writing in 1586, Bodin defined the state as "a lawful government of several households, and their uncommon posessions, with sovereign power."[17] Citizenship became the subjection of an individual to the sovereign. Sovereignty was defined as "supreme power over citizens and subjects unrestrained by law."[18] Thus, the king was given the right to *make, interpret, and execute law unrestrained by all human authority*. He was subject only to the laws of God and to fundamental natural laws such as those requiring the keeping of agreements and respect for private property.

Thomas Hobbes (1588–1679), the famous British political philosopher, elaborated on the concept of sovereignty, subtly shifting its emphasis from the person of the king to the abstraction called government or state.[19] During the turbulent years from 1640 to 1651 in England, which were marked by factionalism and bloodshed, Hobbes wrote with the purpose of strengthening the authority of the king and of absolute government. Hobbes felt that if humans remained in a state of nature (i.e., prior to being organized politically), leading a "solitary, poor, nasty, brutish, and short" life, bloody and uncontrollable conflict would be inevitable. Thus, in order to limit conflict and to preserve the collectivity, it was necessary to concentrate all social authority in the sovereign. The sovereign, a "mortal God" on earth, was equated with the state, which in turn was equated with the government. For sovereignty to shift to its third and contemporary

---

[16]Quoted in Rikihei Inoguchi, Tadashi Nakajima, and Roger Pineau, *The Divine Wind: Japan's Kamikaze Force in World War II* (Annapolis, Md.: United States Naval Institute, 1958). Quoted with permission of the editors.

[17]Sabine, *History of Political Theory*, p. 402.

[18]*Ibid.*, p. 405.

[19]See *ibid.*, pp. 455–76.

phase, ultimate authority had to be transferred symbolically from the government to the people inhabiting the nation-state.

The French Revolution (1789) epitomizes the symbolic transfer of sovereignty from the king and the government to the people. Since it has proved difficult, however, for the people as a totality to rule in other than small-town settings,
sovereignty has remained substantially in the hands of governments who rule in
the name of their people. In such states, there is an implicit understanding that
the people will scrutinize governmental actions and as a last resort will revolt
should their government betray its implicit contract with them.

A helpful distinction should be made between *internal* and *external* sovereignty. *Internal sovereignty* concerns the supreme and lawful authority of the state
over its citizens. *External sovereignty,* on the other hand, refers to the recognition
by all states of the independence, territorial integrity, and inviolability of each
state as represented by its government. The Dutch jurist Hugo Grotius (1583–
1645), reputed to be the father of international law, defined *sovereignty* as "that
power whose acts are not subject to the control of another." For Grotius, sovereignty was manifested when a state, in dealing with its internal affairs, remained
free from the control of all other states. Thus defined, sovereignty has become
the cornerstone of the modern international system, where power and authority
remain consciously divided and decentralized.

In the final analysis, sovereignty is the ability of a nation-state, through
its government, to be master in its house, to have control over its domestic affairs,
and in its foreign affairs to have the options of entering or leaving alliances, of
going to war or remaining neutral so as to best defend its interests. In practice,
however, we find that certain countries have been "more sovereign" than others:
some of the great powers enjoy the substance as well as the letter of sovereignty,
whereas smaller countries, especially if they are strategically located, are penetrated quite often by the great powers and can be called "sovereign" only in a
relatively unauthentic sense of the word.

This discussion of sovereignty brings us to the provocative arguments of
John Herz, a thoughtful scholar of international relations, regarding the rise of
nation-states and nationalism.[20] Herz maintains that the nation-state is the kind
of political unit that, given the nature of available weapons systems, is best designed to keep a territory "impermeable" and to protect its inhabitants. He feels
that throughout history the unit which has afforded the best protection and security to human beings has also become the basic political unit. People, according
to Herz, tend to recognize in the long run the authority, any authority, which
possesses the power of *protection.*[21]

So, in Herz's view, technology and weaponry (both defensive and offen-

---

[20]See John H. Herz, "The Rise and Demise of the Territorial State," in *International Politics and Foreign
Policy,* ed. James N. Rosenau (New York: Free Press, 1961), pp. 80–86. A plethora of literature published
in the 1980s points up the inadequacy of the nation-state to cope with modern technological, environmental, and other challenges. We review this literature at some length in Chapters 18 and 19.

[21]*Ibid.,* p. 81.

sive) are directly responsible for the type of political organization of the international system. Herz maintains convincingly that the death of the feudal system and the walled city-state as units of political autonomy came only after the invention of gunpowder by the German monk Berthold Schwarz (who was also the maker of the first powder gun, used at Ghent in 1314). Gunpowder, according to Herz, was responsible for the transition from feudalism to territorial states. This transition resulted in the neutralization of castles in the interior of territorial states and the construction of elaborate fortifications along the states' borders. Once nation-states, as fundamental units of protection, had been forged, the resulting ease of economic and social interaction within them and the relative isolation of their populations from neighboring states helped solidify the different cultures, institutions, and linguistic and religious patterns of behavior that we identify with nation-states today.

According to Herz, international law from the sixteenth century on increasingly legitimized national territoriality. Each nation-state (and especially its ruling elite) was jealous of its independence and wished to maintain its political and military "impermeability." Therefore, we find that early international law focused on the delimiting of national territorial jurisdiction in order to help legitimize and safeguard the independence and sovereignty—in short, the impermeability—of nation-states. War, recognized as well as sanitized by international law, remained the ultimate means of settling disputes among sovereign territorial states whenever peaceful methods of settlement failed to bear fruit. Once established, sovereign authorities sought to perfect and strengthen their administrative control over their subjects. For their part, the people sought and in many instances gained access to the political process, either through electoral participation or through the indirect method of representation. Political democracy, especially as manifested in the extension of the franchise, became the hallmark of the conversion of the state from a dynastic to a participatory entity.

In international as well as in domestic affairs, governments have tried to endow their actions with an aura of legitimacy. Consequently, by adhering to treaties and to customary international law, different ruling elites found that they could benefit mutually. Over time, the development of a nation-state system founded upon an acceptable balance of power gave impetus to the renaissance of the international law of which Grotius was a leading spokesman. The formalization of diplomatic procedure, the establishment of collective defense systems through alliances, and the acceptance of the principle of sovereignty and its corollary of nonintervention in the domestic affairs of other states—all of these were developments that strengthened the hand of nation-state builders. But in the case of ideologically or ethnically fragmented societies, coercive means such as subversion and war were often employed to overthrow legitimate governments. Without a firm basis in a stable political community, sovereignty often proved to be an illusion.

The modern doctrine of popular sovereignty has transferred the source of absolute power from the monarch to the "people." But this transfer of power does not mean necessarily that individual citizens become more able to check the transgressions of expanding administrative states. Indeed, the popularization of sovereignty gave rise to the ideology of mass nationalism, which equates the fate of the citizenry with that of its political leadership. Mass conscription for either military or industrial service, government control of the mass media for the purpose of propagandizing foreign-policy objectives, and the centralization of educational systems to ensure an uninterrupted process of political socialization combined to spread the fever of nationalism that produced the major conflicts of the twentieth century.

CHALLENGES TO NATIONALISM

The biological and mystical conception of nationalism possesses the formidable weapon of assuring its adherents that they alone have a world historical mission to fulfill and that, by implication, their actions in world politics must be just. A typical but certainly not exclusive representative of this point of view was Senator Albert J. Beveridge, who in 1900, while arguing for the annexation of the Philippine Islands by the United States, asserted that the American nation had been chosen to "lead in the regeneration of the world. This is the divine mission of America, and it holds for us all the profit, all the glory, all the happiness possible to man. We are trustees of the world's progress, guardians of its righteous peace."[22]

Nationalism grew steadily in the last two hundred years to reinforce the identification of the individual with the state. The process of political socialization, carried out by the family, schools, and peer groups, taught the citizen the inescapable lesson that loyalty to the state fulfills not only an ideological but also a pragmatic purpose. For it is the state that, in return for obedience to its laws, provides innumerable concrete services. Thus, citizen allegiance and government efficiency in the performance of its functions are mutually supportive.

The rise of modern states that were based on a strong nationalistic sentiment was a logical historical response to the industrial revolution. But in the present-day postindustrial international setting, the idealized notion of the nation-state is coming under increasing attack from three quarters: the advance of military technology, the rise of supranational organizations, and the growing role of transnational ideological, religious, functional, and political movements. In the 1950s, many analysts pointed out the increasing military vulnerability of the state. Principal among these was John Herz, who wrote of the "demise" of the state, arguing that it was no longer capable of protecting its citizens in the event of a three-dimensional modern war involving nuclear, psychological, and economic weapons. Herz foresaw the transformation of the international system into a condition dominated by conflicting regional alliances. Some years later, seeing the impact of decolonization, Herz gradually abandoned his notion of the

---

[22]U.S. Congress, Senate, Senator Albert J. Beveridge, 56th Cong., January 9, 1900, *Congressional Record,* 33:711.

demise of the state.[23] Yet, as long as the economic and military viability of many of the new states remains in question, the image of a bipolar or tripolar international system retains some validity. In a future time, George Orwell's dreary *1984* scenario may indeed materialize, and our earth may be dominated by the three superpowers of Oceania, Eurasia, and Eastasia.[24]

Assuming that the hallmark of national sovereignty is the rigorous application of the doctrine of nonintervention in the affairs of one state by another, the development of supranational organizations poses the second problem for the future of presumably impermeable nation-states. Among the democracies of the West, notably those of Europe, supranational collaboration to achieve shared goals in the fields of economic development, health, and education is proceeding swiftly. Member states of supranational organizations with policy-making and policy-implementing powers, such as the European Community and the Nordic Council, employ the argument (or perhaps the rationalization) that their sovereignty remains unaffected because they have delegated governmental authority to the international civil servants who staff the executive bodies of these organizations. In a legal sense this argument merits respect, but the politics of interdependence have eroded the absolutist quality of the concept of sovereignty and are likely to create rivals for the nation-state as the sole focus of political loyalty.

Transnational ideological/political movements of the twentieth century, such as fascism and communism, present a third formidable challenge to nationalism. The "New Order" or the German National Socialists led by Adolf Hitler (1889–1945) castigated the liberal nineteenth-century version of the nation-state and called for the formation of a hierarchical European system dominated by what Hitler considered a biologically select race committed to an ideology of purity and power. In accordance with this objective, the Elite Guard (SS) of the Nazi movement organized non-German units throughout occupied Europe and sought to use them as a basis for a new Praetorian state whose military despotism would sound the death knell of the conventional European national communities.[25] The outcome of the Nazi assault on the traditional European nation-states was a cataclysmic war from which humankind has yet to recover materially, and from which it may never completely recover spiritually.

Marxism—from a very different angle—also sought to challenge the nation-state and nationalism. In the *Communist Manifesto* (1848) Karl Marx and Friedrich Engels rejected nationalism, viewing it as an instrument of the bourgeois class to divide workers across national frontiers. Although Joseph Stalin (1879–1953) modified this ideological doctrine by making Soviet policy in 1928 a policy of "socialism in one country" and also by appealing to the historic force of Russian nationalism during the great war with Germany, orthodox Marxists

---

[23]See Herz, "Rise and Demise of the Territorial State," and "The Territorial State Revisited: Reflections on the Future of the Nation-State," in *International Politics and Foreign Policy,* ed. James N. Rosenau, 2nd ed., rev. (New York: Free Press, 1969), pp. 80–89.

[24]George Orwell, *1984* (New York: A. M. Heath, 1949).

[25]See George Stein, *The Waffen SS: Hitler's Elite Guard at War, 1939–1945* (Ithaca, N.Y.: Cornell University Press, 1966).

continue to this day to treat the nation-state as a "category of history" that is designed to serve the interests of capitalism and that is doomed to disappearance once working classes everywhere rise to power.

On the tactical level, however, revolutionary communist movements have readily espoused the cause of nationalism and have sought to align themselves with anticolonial forces in the Third World. For instance, the support of a coalition of nationalist forces such as the Popular Movement for the Liberation of Angola (MPLA) had been an integral part of Soviet policy. Demands for political self-determination in Eastern Europe, on the other hand, tend to receive a markedly different response. Ruling Eastern European Communist parties subscribe, rather, to the doctrine of "proletarian solidarity" and accept an obligation to combat presumed counterrevolutionary tendencies within their bloc. Under the leadership of the Soviet Union, the members of the Warsaw Pact (with the exception of Romania) occupied Czechoslovakia in 1968 in order to limit revisionist Czech liberalism and by extension Czech nationalism.

The Polish events of 1980–81 reflected yet another powerful example of the gradual fusion between nationalism and communism. The attempt of Polish workers, peasants, and students (supported by the powerful Roman Catholic Church of Poland) was obviously aimed toward the objective of attaining communism with a "Polish face."

In 1976, on the occasion of the Twenty-Fifth Congress of the Communist Party of the Soviet Union (CPSU) and at a subsequent meeting of European Communist leaders in East Berlin, the hard line of "proletarian solidarity" was softened somewhat, much to the satisfaction of the leaders of Communist parties in France, Italy, and Spain, who assert that their parties must formulate policies reflecting the diversity of their national settings rather than blanket guidance from Moscow. Moreover, national communism is still in evidence in Eastern Europe: Hungarian history books continue to refer to Hungary's border with Romania as a historical injustice, and Romanian scholars continue to remind their readers of some Romanian provinces that were lost to the Soviet Union in 1945. When confronted with nationalist fervor in the form of unresolved frontier disputes, the plea of "proletarian solidarity" begins to weaken in appeal.

Despite the threat of multidimensional warfare, the rise of supranational organizations, the challenge of expansionist fascism, and the partial success of communism as a transnational political movement, nationalism remains a vibrant force in world affairs and a solid point of entry into the web of motives surrounding foreign-policy decision making. In Parts IV and V of our text, we shall consider in greater depth the question of whether or not nationalism can surmount the challenges currently posed by international organizations and by global ecological interdependency.

PROSPECTS FOR NATIONALISM

Careful researchers have found that international wars waged to regain lost territory and revolutions undertaken by an ethnic minority in the interest of national self-determination have accounted for 70 percent of all international conflicts.[26] Given the strong relationship between nationalism and war, a difficult question arises: Are nationalism and its corollary, the nation-state, useful or harmful forces in world affairs? The answer must be carefully qualified.

Nationalism can be a useful force when it provides the individual with a sense of identity and belonging. It allows the individual to unite with fellow citizens in the pursuit of the common good—a behavior pattern that may well reduce individualism and alienation. This pattern may also engender competitive and even mildly conflicting behavior in the form of national assertiveness in the face of obstacles. This type of competition and managed conflict is a key element in the process of social evolution. However, national self-actualization in this sense should not be synonymous with violence and expansionism. To the extent that social systems compete to overtake one another by improving their own quality of life, people in general benefit.

Nationalism can be a destructive force when it postulates a hierarchy of peoples and seeks to impose this world view by force. Whenever a nation ascribes to itself a superior role that can be fulfilled only at the expense of the territory and welfare of others, armed conflict becomes unavoidable. The history of the twentieth century is filled with the tragedy wrought by such nationalist-expansionist movements.

Idealists often argue that only a structural reform of the international system—a reform that eliminates sovereign and unaccountable nation-states—can provide an effective safeguard against nationalists who are prepared to accept destruction for themselves and their followers rather than the abandonment of their grandiose political goals.[27] The realists retort that the struggle for power is inherent in all political collectivities, and they point out that the total casualties from civil wars exceed those from international wars.[28] Given the staggering number of human losses resulting from internal strife, who is to say that the blight of civil conflict would not also plague a world state?

If—as Barbara Ward argues—nationalism is one of the most pervasive concepts with which the student of international relations must cope, it is important to ask whether nationalism is on the rise or on the wane.[29] Although precise quantitative measures are difficult to develop, it is notable that the membership of the United Nations has increased threefold since the organization's founding in 1945, and some states are still awaiting admission. Moreover, even in regions such as Western Europe—long held to be the prototype of successful supranational integration—the pressures of ethnic separatism appear to be growing and,

[26]See Steven Rosen, ed., *A Survey of World Conflicts* (Pittsburgh: University of Pittsburgh Center for International Studies, 1969).

[27]See Richard A. Falk, *Future Worlds,* Headline Series 229 (New York: Foreign Policy Association, 1976), pp. 38–45.

[28]See, for example, Quincy Wright, *A Study of War,* 2nd ed. (Chicago: University of Chicago Press, 1965); and Lewis F. Richardson, *Statistics of Deadly Quarrels* (Chicago: Quadrangle, 1960).

[29]Barbara Ward, *Five Ideas That Changed the World* (New York: Norton, 1959), p. 28.

in some cases, threatening established states with political fragmentation. In Great Britain, local self-government for Scotland and Wales is now a fact of political life; Belgium has amended its constitution to grant cultural autonomy to the Flemings and the Walloons; and Italy has established an autonomous provincial government for the South Tyroleans, a German-speaking minority. While the European Community continues to strive for political integration, its member states decentralize their governmental processes in order to satisfy ethnic or nationalist hopes that they have long ignored.

The processes of international politics are dynamic. The phenomena of national integration and disintegration can and often do occur simultaneously. Nationalism can be a force for either the unification or the fragmentation of a state. On the international level as well, the satisfaction of nationalist demands can have either stabilizing or destabilizing effects. In order to understand and cope with this most powerful force, social scientists representing various disciplines and approaches have employed their techniques and findings in an effort to synthesize nationalism and internationalism in such a way that humankind will not have to sacrifice cultural pluralism in the name of world order and at the same time will not have to subordinate its general welfare to the wishes of a few powerful and acquisitive nation-states.

SUGGESTIONS FOR FURTHER STUDY

In a "Special Issue on the State in Comparative and International Perspective," published by *Comparative Political Studies,* 21 (April 1988), James A. Caporaso, James N. Rosenau, Ted Robert Gurr, Stephen D. Krasner, Gregg O. Kvistad, and David Wilsford have addressed the role of the territorial state as a unit of analysis. Although the focus is largely on the European experience, the theme is universal. For a Third World view, see Kenneth J. Menkhaus and Charles W. Kegley, Jr., "The Compliant Foreign Policy of the Dependent State Revisited—Linkages and Lessons from the Case of Somalia," *Comparative Political Studies,* 21 (October 1988), 315–46. Phillip Taylor has questioned the central role of the state in *Nonstate Actors in International Politics: From Transregional to Substate Organizations* (Boulder, Colo.: Westview Press, 1984). In *Nationalism: A Religion* (New York: Macmillan, 1960), Carlton J. H. Hayes distinguished among the various types of nationalism experienced in Western societies. Giuseppe Mazzini (1805–72) linked the awakening of national consciousness with constitutional government in *The Duties of Man and Other Essays* (London: J. M. Dent & Sons, 1955). Alfred Cobban argued that nationalism and the demand for autonomy could be destabilizing forces in his analysis of *National Self-Determination* (New York: Oxford University Press, 1945). Similarly, Wolfram F. Hanrieder has questioned the nebulous contours of national identity in "Dissolving International Politics: Reflections on the Nation-State," *American Political Science Review,* 72 (December 1978), 1276–87. Mazzini and Cobban represent the idealist and the realist approaches, respectively, to nationalism. Karl W. Deutsch undertook an empirical investigation of the question in

Nationalism and Social Communication: An Inquiry into the Foundations of Nationality 2nd ed. (Cambridge, Mass.: MIT Press, 1966), and in *Patriotism and Nationalism: Their Psychological Foundations* (New Haven: Yale University Press, 1964). Leonard W. Doob examined the political dynamics of national identity in South Tyrol. Revolutionary nationalism emerges in the contemporary world both as a means of self-actualization and political development, as interpreted by Frantz Fanon in *The Wretched of the Earth,* trans. Constance Farrington (New York: Grove Press, 1968). For a historical panorama of the ideologies of nationalism, see Hans Kohn, *The Idea of Nationalism* (New York: Macmillan, 1944, 1961); and Boyd C. Shafer, *Nationalism: Myth and Reality* (New York: Harcourt, Brace & World, 1955). The social and legal dimensions of ethnic conflict are discussed in Benjamin Akzin, *States and Nations* (Garden City, N.Y.: Doubleday, Anchor Books, 1966).

5

POWER AND CAPABILITIES OF NATION-STATES

THE IMPRECISION OF POWER AS A CONCEPT

From ancient times to the present, political scientists have assumed that *power* is intimately related to political action. Yet there has been continuing debate over its definition.

One important question being debated is whether power should be viewed as a set of *attributes* of a person, a group, or a nation-state or whether it should be best understood as a *relationship* between two political actors with independent wills. Is power, for example, a measurable characteristic of nation-states, such as economic output, size, population, and military strength? Or, is it a set of subtle and changing human relationships resting on a combination of strength, reputation, and manipulative skills?

Writing in the fourth century B.C., Kautilya, the earlier-mentioned master of statecraft in ancient India, interpreted power as the "possession of strength" (an attribute) derived from three elements: knowledge, military might, and valor.[1] Writing approximately twenty-three centuries later, Hans Morgenthau—one of Kautilya's realist descendants—preferred to define power as a *relationship* between two political actors in which actor A has the ability to control the mind and actions of actor B. Thus, power, according to Morgenthau, "may comprise *anything* that establishes and maintains control of man over man [and it] covers

---

[1] *The Kautilya Arthasastra: Part II,* trans. R. P. Kangle, 2nd ed. (Bombay: University of Bombay, 1972), p. 319.

all social relationships which serve that end, from physical violence to the most subtle psychological ties by which one mind controls another."[2]

We can use a simple example to help illustrate the difference between viewing power as a set of attributes of a given actor as opposed to viewing it as a relationship between two actors. Looking only at attributes, we consider a boxer "powerful" if he is six feet tall, weighs 180 pounds, is between twenty and thirty-three years old, has strong muscles, and appears to be intelligent as well as agile. In a specific situation, however, this powerful man may prove powerless when matched against a six-foot-eight, 240-pound younger man of good health, intelligence, and considerable agility. A country like Belgium, for example, is "weak" when compared with the United States, but it is "strong" when compared with tiny Luxembourg.

A second question that has been debated from antiquity to our own day deals with the degree to which coercion (military, economic, or psychological) should be considered a central ingredient of power. Some political scientists view coercion as the primary ingredient of power, if they do not flatly equate the two terms.[3] Others, on the contrary, consider coercion to be one among many factors constituting power, which include economic capability, political cohesiveness, effectiveness of political system, leadership skills, and reputation.

For our purpose here, we believe the best way to depict the concept of *power* is to see it as a relationship of independent wills. On the other hand, the best way to operationalize and measure a state's capacity to exercise power is to concentrate on its specific attributes that lend themselves readily to measurement. With respect to whether *power* should be directly equated with *coercion/force*, we choose to view the concept *power* as an amalgam containing diverse elements of persuasion; these range from military coercion, to economic inducement, all the way to ideological solidarity and moral suasion. To equate power with coercion only is to miss the whole side of the political coin that reflects cooperation, compromise, solidarity, and mutual advantage.

Concepts such as power, influence, force, authority, freedom, oppression, love, hate, obscenity, discrimination, aggression, conflict, and peace are complex and subjective and, consequently, resistant to operational and simultaneously widely acceptable definitions. One is tempted, when dealing with complex concepts, to paraphrase Supreme Court Justice Byron White and say about power what he said about obscenity: "I cannot define it, but I know it when I see it." But we also know that a textbook on international relations cannot proceed without offering a working definition of what is perhaps the most central concept of the field.

---

[2]Hans J. Morgenthau, *Politics among Nations: The Struggle for Power and Peace,* 5th ed. (New York: Knopf, 1973), p. 9 (emphasis supplied). A classic treatment of the concept of power employing the behavioral orientation is Harold Lasswell and Abraham Kaplan, *Power and Society: A Framework for Political Inquiry* (New Haven: Yale University Press, 1950).

[3]Inis L. Claude, Jr., equates power with force in his *Power and International Relations* (New York: Random House, 1962).

Accordingly, we will define *power* as an umbrella concept that denotes anything that establishes and maintains the control of actor A over actor B. Power, in turn, can be seen as having three important ingredients. The first ingredient is *force*, which can be defined as the explicit threat or the use of military, economic, and other instruments of coercion by actor A against actor B in pursuit of A's political objectives. The second ingredient is *influence*, which we define as the use of instruments of persuasion—short of force—by actor A in order to maintain or alter the behavior of actor B in a fashion suitable to the preferences of actor A. The third ingredient of power is *authority*, which we will define as actor B's voluntary compliance with directives (prescriptions, orders) issued by actor A, nurtured by B's perceptions regarding A—such as respect, solidarity, affection, affinity, leadership, knowledge, expertise. We can depict the umbrella concept of power schematically as follows:

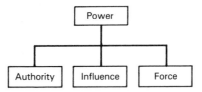

An important distinction we should make is between power as an end and power as a means. Most scholars consider power as a means—that is, as the ability to control the behavior of others in order to accomplish certain ends (higher purposes, long-range objectives, and so forth). If the long-range objectives involve values such as peace, security, national progress, economic development, the spread of democracy, or the spread of communism, then power is considered necessary as a currency with which to buy these values. Other scholars, especially students of realpolitik, prefer to see power as both a means and an end of political action.[4] Realpoliticians, in other words, consider messianic objectives such as permanent peace and endless progress as inapplicable in the short run and therefore irrelevant to the very process of politics, which is oriented to the short run. According to this thinking—which equates the ends of a state with its survival—power, which purchases security, becomes an end in itself.

Before we proceed with our discussion of more systematic attempts to measure power, we must make one final clarification: Power cannot be viewed merely as a static, one-time, and one-directional relationship. It should be viewed, rather, as a dynamic, ongoing, and feedback relationship. For example, if today A controls B's behavior over an issue, it may be that three months or three years later the balance of power will shift so that B controls A's behavior over the same issue. The situation becomes considerably more complicated when we consider

---

[4]*Realpolitik* is a power/interest–oriented approach that is recommended to national leaders by realist scholars. See Chapter 8 for a discussion of realpolitik.

that power relationships between two countries may vary widely on an issue-by-issue basis and depending on the leaders' capacity, interest (salience), and willingness to apply power and its ingredients in order to accomplish their objectives. It is important, then, for us to realize that power can be actual or potential, and that it can be subdivided into economic, political, military, moral, and other types. Actual power is power immediately available, whereas potential power is power that can be generated following situations of crisis and other degrees of need.

The greatest intangible in considering power relationships is one's *will* to employ one's power. A powerful nation-state that either does not know its power or is unwilling or unable to decide how to use it is for all practical purposes powerless.

It should be clear to us by now that the concept of power, although central to the study of international relations, is quite vague and elusive. More precise and more useful definitions are seriously needed. On the other hand, we should keep in mind that the more precise our definitions become the less they account for the plethora of this concept's ingredients.

ATTEMPTS TO OPERATIONALIZE THE DEFINITION OF POWER

Some interesting attempts have been made to operationalize definitions of power and thereby afford students of international politics an opportunity to measure it.[5] We shall deal briefly with three of the more noteworthy of these attempts.

First, Ray S. Cline—a man with a long and distinguished record both in the intelligence field and in academic research—has suggested a very useful method for the measurement of the concept of power. For him power is important in the sense that it is perceived both by its wielders and by those over whom it is exercised. He has advanced a simple formula that does not necessarily permit for the "exact" measurement of power but is amenable to quantification.[6] It is as follows:

$$Pp = (C + E + M) \times (S + W)$$

The symbols are defined thus:

Pp = Perceived Power
C = Critical Mass = Population and Territory
E = Economic capability

[5]The discussion in this section is heavily indebted to Robert J. Lieber, *Theory and World Politics* (Cambridge, Mass.: Winthrop, 1972), pp. 89–98; and Karl W. Deutsch, *The Nerves of Government: Models of Political Communication and Control* (New York: Free Press, 1966), pp. 110–27, and *The Analysis of International Relations* (Englewood Cliffs, N.J.: Prentice Hall, 1968), pp. 21–39. See also Robert Gilpin, *War and Change in World Politics* (Cambridge: Cambridge University Press, 1981).
[6]Ray S. Cline, *World Power Assessment: A Calculus of Strategic Drift* (Washington, D.C.: Georgetown University, Center for Strategic and International Studies, 1975), p. 11.

M = Military capability
S = Strategic purpose
W = Will to pursue national strategy

Ingredients of perceived power, such as population, territory, or economic and military capability, are subject to relatively exact measurement. Yet it is obvious that Cline places very important value on difficult-to-measure ingredients such as "strategic purpose" and "will to pursue one's purposes." But how does one assign a specific number to intangible concepts such as *purpose* and *will*? Cline recommends that panels of country analysts can assign values or weights to countries' ability to define their objectives and then to their capacity and willingness to pursue them without wavering. In Cline's study, for example, although the United States scores high in military and economic capability, the Soviet Union scores higher in its ability to define its strategic objectives and to pursue them systematically and with vigor.

The second approach toward the measurement of power that we will discuss belongs to political scientist Robert Dahl. Dahl has defined power as "the ability to shift the probability of outcomes."[7] In his highly sophisticated analysis, Dahl also views power as a *relationship* between political actors, such as individuals, groups, political parties, governments, and international organizations. According to Dahl, "A has power over B to the extent that he can get B to do something that B would not otherwise do." There are a number of ways of arriving at concrete values denoting power as it is defined by Dahl. One way, for example, is to calculate, using the proceedings of political bodies such as the United Nations or the U.S. Senate, the number of times that a political actor votes with the majority. The inference here is that if you are often associated with majorities, you are influential in bringing these majorities about. Such a measurement has been criticized, however, because it does not differentiate between leaders and followers of legislation—that is, between controllers of power and survival-oriented political chameleons. Therefore, this technique of measurement is improved if one calculates the success of legislators with respect to legislation that they *initiate* and heavily favor.[8]

Measurement such as the above, which involves precise mathematical and statistical procedures, may result in useful probabilistic rankings of the power or influence of various political actors, be they nation-states, political parties, or senators. Obviously, such methods may be applied only in situations where parliamentary proceedings are publicized and voting records are kept and made available to the analyst. In countries having closed hearings, where the alternative positions of participants in the decision-making process are not

---

[7]See Robert Dahl, "The Concept of Power," *Behavioral Science*, 2 (1957), 201–15.

[8]But even this technique of assessing power can be quite misleading. A powerful actor (for instance, the United States in the United Nations) can secure the agreement of a weak and dependent client (such as Nationalist China in the past) to initiate legislation. So behind the formal source of power there is an informal but substantive source, which is hard to trace even if one uses scientific techniques.

A Soviet military parade in Moscow. (Tass from Sovfoto)

known, it is quite difficult to employ Dahl-type methods to assess relative power or influence.

The third useful attempt to quantify power can be credited to Karl Deutsch.[9] Deutsch, influenced by the work of the noted sociologist Talcott Parsons, likes to view power as a form of currency that allows its holders to "buy" important values and attain objectives. There is an interesting analogy to be made here between economics and politics. For example, the economic power of an individual, company, or nation-state depends not merely on the amount of cash on hand, but also on the amount of credit available. Credit, in turn, can be secured on the basis of the reputation of borrowers and their expected capacity to repay the loan. In politics, a nation-state's power is to be understood not merely in terms of its specific military and economic capabilities but also in terms of its capacity to supplement its power base by means of techniques such as alliances, treaties, and leases of territory to foreign nation-states. Proceeding beyond this conceptualization, Deutsch suggests three specific dimensions of power that can be readily measured and that permit analysts to quantify and rank the actual and projected capabilities of nation-states. Deutsch calls these three dimensions of power *domain, range,* and *scope.*

[9]Deutsch, *Analysis of International Relations*, pp. 21–39.

Domain of Power

When we talk about *domain,* we ask the question, over whom and what is power exercised? The obvious answer is that power is usually exercised over people, territory, and wealth. Following Deutsch's logic, it might be useful to subdivide *domain* further in terms of the *internal domain* and the *external domain* of nation-states. *Internal domain* coincides with the territory and population within the boundaries of a country. Internal domain is thus easy to determine, except in the case of nation-states that are experiencing uprisings, guerrilla warfare, or territorial disputes. *External domain* is a much more elusive concept. It includes those territories and populations outside a nation-state that belong to its "sphere of influence."

The measurement of the internal domain of power and the ranking of nation-states on that basis pose relatively few problems. For example, we can rank nation-states according to the area and population over which the central government exercises its power, as depicted in Tables 5–1 and 5–2. Deutsch also suggests a third usable measure of internal domain—the gross national product (GNP). Table 5–3 ranks leading nation-states in terms of their GNP.

External domain is a less precise concept. It is extremely difficult to devise accurate and meaningful quantitative measures with which we can rank nation-states in terms of their ability to exercise power outside of their territorial limits.[10] We can only suggest, therefore, some approaches to the measurement of external domain.

**Table 5–1   The Internal Domain of National Power
in Terms of Area, 1988
(Top Ten Nation-States)**

Country	Total Area (Square Kilometers)
Soviet Union	22,402,200
Canada	9,976,140
China	9,596,960
United States	9,372,610
Brazil	8,511,970
Australia	7,686,850
India	3,287,590
Argentina	2,766,890
Sudan	2,505,810
Algeria	2,381,740

SOURCE: *The World Factbook 1988* (Washington, D.C.: Central Intelligence Agency, 1988).

[10]For an interesting study on this topic, see Charles W. Kegley, Jr., and Eugene R. Wittkopf, "Structural Characteristics of International Influence Relationships," *International Studies Quarterly,* 20, no. 2 (June 1976), 261–300.

**Table 5-2   The Internal Domain of National Power
in Terms of Population, 1987
(Top Ten Nation-States)**

Country	Population (000)	Growth Rate % 1973–85
China	1,041,094	1.4
India	765,147	2.2
Soviet Union	277,563	0.9
United States	238,780	1.0
Indonesia	162,212	2.3
Brazil	135,539	2.3
Japan	120,579	0.9
Bangladesh	100,592	2.5
Nigeria	99,669	2.8
Pakistan	94,933	3.0

SOURCE: *The World Bank Atlas - 1987* (Washington, D.C.: The World Bank, 1987).

One such approach would be to equate the spheres of influence of the great powers with their respective alliance systems and then to calculate the combined populations, territories, and GNPs of these systems. Thus, in the case of the United States, one would calculate the combined population, territory, and GNP of the countries belonging to the North Atlantic Treaty Organization (NATO), the Australia–New Zealand–United States (ANZUS) Treaty, the Organization of American States (OAS), and all other bilateral defense pacts in which the United States is a member. In the case of the Soviet Union, one would do the same with the member states of the Warsaw Treaty Organization (WTO) and with

**Table 5-3   The Internal Domain of National Power in Terms of Gross National
Product, 1987 (Top Ten Nation-States)**

Country	GNP at 1985 Prices (In Billions of U.S. Dollars)	GNP per Capita at 1985 Prices (In U.S. Dollars)
United States	$ 4,486.2	$ 18,400
Japan	2,664.0	21,820
Soviet Union	2,356.7	8,375
Federal Republic of Germany	908.3	14,890
Italy	743.0	12,955
France*	724.1	13,020
United Kingdom	556.8	9,800
Canada*	412.8	15,910
China	286.0	280
Spain	282.0	7,240

SOURCE: *The World Factbook 1988* (Washington, D.C.: Central Intelligence Agency, 1988).
*Gross Domestic Product (GDP)

all other Soviet bilateral allies. However, the closer we look at this particular "measuring device," the more complex and unsatisfactory it becomes. What do we do, for example, with former allies whose political relations have become strained? Do we include France in the external domain of the United States? And do we include Hungary and Romania in the external domain of the Soviet Union? Further, as we indicated earlier in this chapter, power is a feedback relationship rather than a static, one-time, and one-sided entity. Thus, although we can claim that West Germany is in the American sphere of influence, we can also reverse the claim and say that to a certain (and naturally lesser) extent the United States is in the West German sphere of influence.

The traditionalist literature of international politics has used terms such as *colonialism, neocolonialism, imperialism, dependency,* and *intervention* to denote concepts very similar to the concept of external domain. In another useful attempt to examine systematically the power relationships embraced by this concept, James Rosenau has devised the concept of *penetration.*[11] Rosenau defines *penetration* as a process in which "members of one polity serve as *participants* in the political processes of another."[12] We could therefore measure penetration in terms of indicators such as military presence of nation-state A in nation-state B (as demonstrated by military bases, personnel, and so on), foreign aid given (whether military, economic, or humanitarian), size of military missions abroad, economic dependency of B on A, and cultural diffusion. We could then rank nation-states in terms of their demonstrated ability to penetrate other nation-states, or, to put it differently, in terms of their capacity to demonstrate an outflow of their power. We could eventually arrive at relatively reliable but not necessarily valid measures of external domain as indicated by instances of penetration.[13]

Range of Power

Deutsch defines *range* as "the difference between the highest reward (or indulgence) and the worst punishment (or deprivation) which a power-holder can bestow (or inflict) upon some person in his domain."[14]

Range of power can also be divided into internal and external components. Within nation-states, for example, governments can exercise power over

---

[11]See James N. Rosenau, *The Scientific Study of Foreign Policy* (New York: Free Press, 1971), pp. 151–96, 275–338.

[12]*Ibid.,* p. 319.

[13]*Reliable measures* are accurate and duplicatable measures of various precisely defined properties of selected actors or elements. *Valid measures,* however, presuppose that selected quantitative indicators reflect the essence of the concept that they are supposed to measure. For example, let us assume that we wish to operationalize the definition of the concept of health. An indicator such as body temperature is both reliable—its measurement can be accurately replicated—and valid—it can be substantively related to the concept it is supposed to measure. On the other hand, if we selected the intelligence quotient (I.Q.) as an indicator of health, rather than of intelligence, we could say that it is relatively reliable, for it can be measured objectively. But it would be totally invalid as a measure of health, though it is considerably valid as a measure of intelligence.

[14]Deutsch, *Analysis of International Relations,* p. 32.

their subjects by both benign and malignant means—that is, through techniques of reward as well as of punishment. Tyrants generally prefer to rely on threats and punishments as means of securing public order. Popularly elected governments, in contrast, prefer to rely on positive incentives and rewards. The range of power of tyrants who possess only small and badly trained military-security forces is smaller than that of heavily armed tyrants. Benign governments, on the other hand, are limited by their capacity to bestow favors and other rewards—that is, by the size of their budgets.

Specific measurements of internal range can be made by using governmental budget statistics and establishing how much these governments are spending for public security purposes (punishment mechanisms) and how much for social welfare such as education and medical care (reward mechanisms).

In the external range of power of nation-states, colonialism could be considered the external analogue of tyranny. On the other hand, a mutually beneficial alliance or an equitable structure for the economic integration of nation-states is more analogous to a just and benign national government. The indicators with which one could measure the external range of power should follow logically from the discussion of internal range. For example, security-defense expenditures of governments would be a reliable and valid indicator of the punishment-oriented range of national power. By extension, a government's expenses on foreign aid and technical assistance would be reliable and valid indicators of the reward-oriented range of power.

Scope of Power

By *scope* of power, Deutsch wishes to denote "the set or collection of all the particular kinds of classes of behavior, relations and affairs that are effectively subjected to [governmental power]."[15] This "set or collection" includes all the types of activities a government seeks to regulate, internal as well as external. It is obvious that with technological and urban growth, the internal scope of governmental power has increased steadily. In the days of laissez-faire government, for example, governments were restricted to a few main functions: They collected taxes, kept internal order, and fought wars. But over time, the role of governments has expanded and their functions have increased, especially in regulatory areas such as internal and external trade, communications, transportation, education, medical services, labor-management relations, scientific research, industrial management, and environmental protection.

Scope of power can also be divided into internal and external categories. Government budgets and government organization charts can be used as evidence of the width and diversity of functions that fall under government supervision and regulation. Experience would suggest that the internal scope of power is usually narrower in countries with democratic and competitive systems of government than in countries with centrally planned economies. Generally, liberal

---

[15]*Ibid.,* p. 34.

democratic governments allow for more private initiative and enterprise in the economic, social, and cultural spheres than do socialist ones, especially those that are of the communist variety.

The external scope of power has also increased over time. Pure control relationships, in which strong nation-states demonstrate their predominance over weak ones by collecting tribute, showing their naval flag, or exacting symbolic signs of submission, have given way to complex and multifunctional systems of dependence and interdependence. Today, one country can maintain control over another without firing a shot. Countries are dependent on one another for such things as vital technologies; energy materials such as oil, uranium, and natural gas; investment capital; managerial personnel; unskilled labor; military equipment; and information-processing systems.

THE POWER PROFILES OF NATION-STATES

We could continue to list at length the various ways of defining and measuring power. We hope we have given you some ideas as to how this effort could be continued. But we must turn now to a discussion of the elements of power (or the capabilities) of nation-states. Summarizing our thoughts to this point, we could argue that the specific power of nation-state A over nation-state B is a function of the human and material capabilities of A, as well as A's ability and willingness to employ these capabilities in order to control the behavior of B. Abdul Said and Charles O. Lerche have enumerated the capabilities of nation-states in terms of *tangible* and *intangible* components.[16] We shall proceed in a similar fashion. (The following discussions of tangible and intangible elements of power should be supplemented by a careful reading of Chapter 7.)

Tangible Elements (Attributes) of Power

Population. Population can be considered a tangible element in the sense that it can be readily counted. The assumption is frequently made that populous nation-states are also powerful. To a certain extent this is true. But we can err seriously if we assume that there is a direct relationship between population and power. For example, although China is more populous than both the United States and the Soviet Union, it is still considered less powerful than either of these nation-states. On the other hand, Israel is disproportionately powerful, considering its small population of just over four million. Further, even a tangible element of power such as population has aspects of intangibility. It is obvious that all populations are not the same. A population that is healthy, well fed, unified, evenly spaced, well informed, and loyal to its governmental authorities is likely to be much more powerful than a population that is badly nourished, dis-

---

[16]See Abdul Said and Charles O. Lerche, *Concepts of International Politics in Global Perspective,* 3rd ed. (Englewood Cliffs, N.J.: Prentice Hall, 1979), pp. 66–74.

eased, overcrowded, illiterate, disunited, and disloyal. Many characteristics of populations, such as unity, literacy, and loyalty, are difficult to measure and even more difficult to assess with respect to their impact upon power. For example, do literate soldiers fight more effectively than illiterate ones? Is unity a function of open and free education or of centrally controlled and policed indoctrination? Are densely populated countries more or less likely to fight over questions of interest, prestige, or territory?

Territory. The second tangible element of power is territory. As in the case of population, we can hypothesize that larger nation-states are more powerful than smaller ones. However, the mere measurement of an area in square kilometers is not necessarily adequate even as a partial measure of power. Israel, once more, offers us a striking example of a small country that has demonstrated a disproportionately large amount of military power. On the other hand, some large countries, such as Canada, Zaire, Australia, and the Sudan are not nearly as powerful as their size might indicate.

Territory also has a dimension of intangibility, which we enter when we talk about territorial characteristics such as natural boundaries, climate, strategic or peripheral location, and number of neighbors. For example, a mountainous country would be considered more difficult to overcome militarily than a flat country situated at a large plain and lacking formidable natural boundaries. On the other hand, a country blessed with fertile and productive plains rather than mountains would contain a better-fed and more prosperous population. Further, we could assume that a country that has common borders with five or six other countries would be proportionately more vulnerable to attack than a country that has only one or two neighbors. Controversial questions could also arise as to what constitutes the best natural boundaries for the purpose of security. For example, are insular countries such as Britain and Japan more or less vulnerable than continental countries such as Germany and the Soviet Union? Is a mountainous country such as Switzerland more or less vulnerable than an archipelago such as Indonesia?

These and similar questions fall under the heading of geopolitics. This discipline, which fuses subjects such as geography, strategy, and politics, was quite popular in the late nineteenth century and early twentieth century. Two of the best-known geopolitical thinkers—Sir Halford Mackinder and Alfred T. Mahan—held fundamentally contradictory ideas.[17] Mackinder's famous *heartland theory* sought to relate power to the ability of a nation-state to control large land masses. His formula was succinct: "He who rules Eastern Europe commands the Heartland of Eurasia; who rules the Heartland commands the World Island of Europe, Asia, and Africa; and who rules the World Island commands the World."[18] Mahan, on the other hand, emphasized the importance of naval control

---

[17]See Halford Mackinder, *Democratic Ideals and Reality* (New York: Holt, 1919); and Alfred T. Mahan, *The Influence of Sea Power upon History* (Boston: Little, Brown, 1890).

[18]Mackinder, *Democratic Ideals and Reality*, p. 150. The attempts of Napoleon and Hitler to establish large continental-based empires can be related to Mackinder's theory.

over the high seas and the strategic sea lanes. He ranked control of the oceans well above control of the large land masses.

Today, we find that the United States and the Soviet Union are heeding the advice, albeit contradictory, of both Mackinder and Mahan. The United States, a traditionally mobile and ocean-oriented power, has since World War II sought and managed to establish a near-permanent military presence adjacent to the so-called heartland of Eurasia. The Soviet Union, a traditionally continental power, has expanded its naval forces rapidly and now rivals the United States in naval tonnage, mobility, and presence in nearly all the seas of the world.

Natural Resources and Industrial Capacity. We need not belabor the topic of natural resources. It is clear that the possession of resources such as coal, iron, uranium, oil, rubber, bauxite, and manganese is essential to industrial production in nation-states. In recent years, for example, it has been demonstrated that the availability of petroleum at reasonable prices is essential to the good economic health of industrialized nation-states.

However, in evaluating the importance of natural resources, we must view them in relation to the ability of nation-states to process them industrially and to distribute the products economically. Let us suppose that a country has more than adequate natural resources. If that country does not possess the technology, industry, and markets to process and dispose of those resources adequately, it is reduced to the status of a weak raw-material–exporting nation-state. Conversely, a country with developed technology but without natural resources is greatly dependent on the importation of raw materials from foreign markets. In addition, it has no firm control over supply and price fluctuations. Placed in an economic perspective, the appearance of political power can often be deceptive, for even those nation-states leading in industrial capacity respond to pressure on the sensitive nerve of energy. To maintain a high level of production, the major industrial economies are all, to varying degrees, dependent upon the importation of petroleum. In late 1980, the delegates to the Supreme Soviet assembled in Moscow to learn from a government economic survey that the production of energy was not keeping pace with industrial requirements. When Mikhail Gorbachev became the general-secretary of the Communist Party in 1985, he initiated a program of *perestroika* (restructuring of the economy and the government) in an effort to bolster production. Condemning eighteen years of stagnation under his predecessor, Leonid Brezhnev, Gorbachev stated bluntly that during the 1970s, "The most important principle of socialism, distribution according to work, was violated."[19] A reform-minded Soviet leadership may remedy the shortfall in the production of petroleum, but many industrial countries have no choice but to import it. Japan, France, and the Federal Republic of Germany possess coal but must depend upon overseas sources of petroleum, despite the planned growth of their nuclear power industries. In this regard the political stability of states surrounding the Persian Gulf is critical.

---

[19]Mikhail S. Gorbachev, "Why 'Restructuring'," *Survey: A Journal of East-West Studies,* 29 (August 1987), 123.

Agricultural Capacity.   This is also a tangible element of power. Countries that can feed themselves, especially over the course of a long war, will be relatively more powerful than countries that are not self-sufficient. Note, however, that, even in the case of food production, intangibility and controversy arise. For instance, one can argue that in general, communist-ruled countries are less productive agriculturally than democratically ruled countries, but they distribute their produce more equitably. The obvious question then is: What contributes more to the power profile of a nation-state, superior agricultural production or more equitable distribution?

Military Strength and Mobility.   These elements of power are related most intimately to the traditional notion that power is backed by military force.[20] Both military strength and mobility can be considered quite tangible elements since they can be measured in a number of meaningful ways. For example, military strength can be measured in terms of funds expended for defense and security purposes. Mobility is a somewhat more elusive concept. Basically, it stands for the ability of a nation-state to deploy its armed might in locations at great distance from its territory. The traditional indicator of mobility is a nation-state's ability to transport and effectively support military operations on land, sea, and air. We should realize, however, that mere figures regarding military expenditures or the size of armed forces do not necessarily enable us to conclusively rank nation-states in terms of their military might. Factors such as readiness, training, leadership, morale, attitudes of military personnel toward their government, socioeconomic origins of the armed forces (especially the officer corps), quality, adaptability, and source of equipment should seriously affect the performance of armed forces in a given situation. All of these factors are more intangible than tangible.

Intangible Elements (Attributes) of Power

Leadership and Personality.   Undoubtedly, greatness or incompetence, wisdom or irrationality, effectiveness or impotence in leadership considerably affects the power that a country has. Leaders such as Napoleon, Adolf Hitler, Winston Churchill, Franklin D. Roosevelt, Joseph Stalin, Mao Zedong, Mahatma Gandhi, John F. Kennedy, Charles de Gaulle, Nikita Khrushchev, and Richard Nixon have made a deep impact on world history. We must content ourselves, however, with the inexact assessment that leadership is an important variable that affects the power potential of a nation-state. There are unfortunately no foolproof methods with which we can measure the positive or negative impact of personality or leadership upon the total capabilities of nation-states or upon specific power relationships. The question, for example, whether the post-1987 *rapprochement* between the United States and the Soviet Union is a product of

[20]Robert J. Art, "To What Ends Military Power?" *International Security,* 4, no. 4 (1980).

leadership of men such as Ronald Reagan and Mikhail Gorbachev or the outcome of a wider set of variables remains hard to answer.

Bureaucratic-Organization Efficiency. One of the hardest elements of power to measure is the efficiency of large and complex organizations, especially organizations designed to serve political purposes. Yet we should readily admit that prosperous, well-armed, and even wisely governed countries cannot function effectively unless they establish efficient bureaucracies with which to implement their policies. There are at least four philosophies regarding the proper role, method of operation, and adequate functioning of bureaucracies. First, communist countries emphasize large-scale bureaucratization not only in political but also in economic and social sectors. Second, democratic-competitive countries seek to enhance private initiative and limit the role of governmental bureaucracies to defense, taxation, and other regulatory functions. Third, there are those who argue for the strict separation of "politics" from professional bureaucracies. These people believe that bureaucracies best provide continuity by remaining outside the helter-skelter of political and partisan activity. Fourth, some people are eager to establish political control over the bureaucracies, plug leaks, and ensure that political decisions are carried out faithfully by the professional bureaucrats. Each of these four philosophies has its merits and its demerits, and we do not propose to consider them here. We should realize, though, that it is quite difficult to assess the precise impact of a given bureaucratic philosophy upon the power of a nation-state.

Type of Government. One of the hardest unanswered questions in political science deals with the relationship between type of government (or *polity*) and national power. Aristotle subdivided polities into aristocracies (political systems in which the wisest rule), democracies, tyrannies, and ochlocracies (political systems under mob rule). His implicit assumption was that aristocracies and democracies (the former more than the latter) provided good government, whereas tyrannies and ochlocracies (the former less than the latter) provided bad government. Contemporary experts in comparative government have supplied us with a more complicated array of models—variants of the Aristotelian types. We have at least three varieties of communist models—the Soviet, the Chinese, and the Yugoslav. We have democratic-competitive models ranging from the private-enterprise–oriented United States to socialist-oriented but democratic countries such as Sweden and Norway. We also have a large category of authoritarian polities, ranging from military regimes, such as those of Chile and Indonesia, to traditional monarchical rule, as Saudi Arabia and Morocco.

The intangible yet extremely important question remains: What is the effect of these different types of governance on national power in general and in specific situations? For example, we can argue that authoritarian regimes can make quick and flexible foreign-policy decisions because their decision makers are few and relatively unaccountable. On the other hand, we should consider whether quick decisions by unaccountable decision makers are necessarily wise decisions. The checks and balances characteristic of democratic regimes subject decisions to greater scrutiny and presumably guard against capricious and irrational politics. One can continue to argue such questions and remain firmly in the realm of intangibility.

Societal Cohesiveness. This is a multivariate and therefore highly intangible element of power. Many of us implicitly assume that internally unified nation-states are strong whereas divided ones are weak. The causes of disunity or unity can range from ethnic, linguistic, racial, and religious diversity all the way to economic, political, ideological, and foreign-inspired divisions. Certain phenomena can be used as crude indicators of disunity: terrorism, number of political prisoners, riots, demonstrations, paralyzing strikes, media censorship, insurgency, and even civil war. Given the state of the international-relations field today, it is still quite difficult to assess how varying degrees of national unity affect the power profile of a nation-state, in general as well as in specific situations.

Reputation. One of the hardest elements of power to measure and yet one of the most important ones is a nation-state's reputation. For example, it is often asserted that the Yugoslavs tend to fight and the Czechs tend to acquiesce.[21] So, whereas the Czechs are expected to succumb to Soviet penetration without a fight, the Yugoslavs, on the basis of their previous reputation, are expected to mount a desperate, even "irrational," fight to blunt a hypothetical Soviet invasion of their country. In the same vein, one can explain the strenuous opposition of America's "hawks" to a withdrawal from South Vietnam in the early 1970s. They were concerned that such a withdrawal and the resulting collapse of the American client regime in Saigon would make the United States look like a "pitiful, helpless giant."[22] Power, therefore, should be evaluated not only in terms of each country's ability and willingness to *use* its capabilities when challenged, but also in terms of its reputation for decisive action in response to previous challenges.

Foreign Support and Dependency. Many students of international politics who concern themselves with the elements of power merely enumerate tangible and intangible elements such as the ones described above. This tendency proceeds from an unwarranted assumption that nation-states are finite units of decision, organization, and action. Thus, one of the most important elements of power is usually left completely out of the picture. This element consists of international connections such as alliances, foreign economic and military aid, the leasing or granting of strategic bases to the great powers, and participation in regional and universal international organizations. To ignore such factors would

---

[21]Here it should be remembered, however, that the Yugoslavs possess a mountainous and hard-to-traverse terrain, but the Czechs and the Hungarians inhabit fertile valleys that are hard to defend and isolate.

[22]This was President Richard Nixon's graphic analogy of the type of reputation that the United States should avoid at all costs.

leave us measuring the power of Syria and Israel, for example, without considering Soviet and American aid and commitments to these two countries. Foreign support is not always a positive element of power. At times, foreign support may turn to outright foreign dependency. When this occurs, the sovereignty and the tactical and strategic flexibility of the dependent nation-state vis-à-vis its protector become seriously limited. In the last analysis, foreign support and dependency remains an extremely vital, albeit quite intangible, element of power.[23]

Accidents.   The sudden death of a great leader, an earthquake, a famine, an epidemic of a dread disease such as the plague, a misunderstanding or a breakdown in communications during a crisis, and many other unforeseen events may deeply affect the power relationships of nation-states. Since accidents cannot be predicted in any other but an aggregate statistical sense, they remain at the summit of the pyramid of intangibility. It is therefore appropriate that we close this discussion of the intangible elements of power by noting this factor.

CAN WE RETURN TO A SINGLE USEFUL CONCEPT OF POWER?

If you have followed us through this tortuous path among the tangibles and intangibles of power, you may be ready to give up and discard the elusive concept altogether. The logical question of those skeptical about the concept of power is this: If there are so many elements of power, many of which are nearly impossible to measure, how do we synthesize them all into a single useful concept? For example, if nation-state A had eight units of armed force, two units of leadership, and one unit of cohesiveness, and was confronted by nation-state B with three units of armed force, eight units of leadership, and three units of cohesiveness, which of the two should we consider more powerful? Our problem is that once we identify and quantify the various elements of power, we continue to have difficulty ranking their approximate contribution to the total concept. How important, for instance, are elements such as population, territory, GNP, and military expenditures in the total rating of power? Are the values of each of these elements to be considered as contributing equally to total power? Or should we weight, say, industrial capacity three times as much as population but somewhat less than military mobility?

If we wish to construct a single aggregate measure of power, we can easily but arbitrarily do so. All we need do is collapse a number of variables into a gargantuan and unified measure similar to the GNP calculated by economists. We could take the various measures of Deutsch's subconcepts (domain, range, and scope) and combine them into single composite values. Simultaneously, however, we would be robbing power of its intangible, psychological characteristics.

---

[23]For a review of the influence relationships involving a superpower and two medium-small–level states, see T. A. Couloumbis, *The United States, Greece and Turkey: The Troubled Triangle* (New York: Praeger, 1983).

Ray Cline's formula, discussed before, moves us a step further in the right direction, but we would continue to have great difficulty measuring will, strategic purpose, and "power fit," especially in specific issue-areas.

We conclude, therefore, that power as an aggregate concept is best portrayed by elusive qualities such as prestige, status, and reputation. American businesses, to view the concept in microcosm, could be considered organizational units wielding economic power. They have characteristics such as size, sales, physical plant, number and quality of personnel, effectiveness of management, morale, and organizational philosophy. The "power" of these businesses is a function of the confidence of a variety of stockholders in their health, durability, and profit potential. Thus, the Dow-Jones Industrial Average is a usable quantitative indicator of the collective, pluralistic, and ultimately *subjective* judgments of millions of shareholders and thousands of stockbrokers regarding the "power" of various businesses. Until we develop a stock market of the world, where shares of national power can be bought and sold according to the laws of supply and demand, we may have to settle for just a vague *concept* of power and do without generally acceptable measures of it.

In closing, we should remind our readers that we do not share the view that imprecise concepts—those that cannot be easily operationalized—have no place in political science. Admittedly, concepts such as power, love, hate, brotherhood, and envy are extremely hard to define, isolate, and measure. Yet they are also extremely important in motivating and explaining human behavior. Imprecision notwithstanding, power remains at the heart of the political process. Wars are fought to preserve power, to defend power, to increase power, and to balance power. Nation-states, through their diplomatic, military, and intelligence services, are constantly watching, charting, and analyzing one another's power profiles. The construction of new fortifications, the purchase of tanks and jets, the development of nuclear capabilities, the signing of treaties of mutual friendship and guarantees, and the discovery of new energy sources are frequently perceived as changing the power situation among nation-states and generating chain reactions of offensive, defensive, or preemptive military activity.

The British political philosopher Thomas Hobbes, writing well over three hundred years before Hans Morgenthau, summarized quite successfully the central relationship of power to politics:

> I put for a general inclination of all mankind, a perpetual and restless desire of power after power, that ceaseth only in death. And the cause of this is not always that a man hopes for a more intensive delight than he has already attained to; or that he cannot be content with a more moderate power; but because he cannot assure the power and means to live well, which he hath present, without the acquisition of more.[24]

---

[24]Quoted in George H. Sabine, *A History of Political Theory*, 3rd ed. rev. (New York: Holt, Rinehart & Winston, 1961), p. 463.

SUGGESTIONS FOR FURTHER STUDY

The dichotomy between multilateral and unilateral action in the assessment of power is a theme of Joseph S. Nye, Jr., "Understating U.S. Strength," *Foreign Policy,* 72 (Fall 1988), 105–29. Ronald A. Morse has considered the dynamics of power relationships in "Japan's Drive to Pre-eminence," *Foreign Policy,* 69 (Winter 1987–88), 3–21. The quest for a definition of *power* is the basis of a substantial literature in international relations. Power viewed as coercion is the theme of both Inis L. Claude, Jr., *Power and International Relations* (New York: Random House, 1962); and Bertrand de Jouvenel, *On Power: Its Nature and History of Growth,* trans. J. F. Huntington (New York: Viking Press, 1949). Michael P. Sullivan offered a broader interpretation including influence in *International Relations: Theories and Evidence* (Englewood Cliffs, N.J.: Prentice Hall, 1976). Power as a focus of national political analysis is the subject of Harold D. Lasswell and Abraham Kaplan, *Power and Society: A Framework for Political Inquiry* (New Haven: Yale University Press, 1950). The relationship of power to the legal position of the state is one of the topics discussed in Brian Barry, ed., *Power and Political Theory: Some European Perspectives* (London: John Wiley, 1976). Felix E. Oppenheim has analyzed power as a facet of a wide range of relationships in "'Power,' Revisited," *Journal of Politics,* 40 (August 1978), 589–608. The multidimensional character of the word *power* is the subject of Robert A. Dahl, "Power," *International Encyclopedia of the Social Sciences,* vol. XII (New York: Macmillan and Free Press, 1968), pp. 405–15; and William H. Riker, "Some Ambiguities in the Notion of Power," *American Political Science Review,* 58 (June 1964), 341–49. David A. Baldwin has treated power as clusters of *specific* relationships in "Power Analysis and World Politics: New Trends versus Old Tendencies," *World Politics,* 31 (January 1979), 161–94. For a perspective on state power in terms of such contextual variables as population and climate, see Katherine F. Organski and A. F. K. Organski, *Population and World Power* (New York: Knopf, 1961); and Ellsworth Huntington, *Mainsprings of Civilizations* (New York: John Wiley, 1945), respectively. The geographical basis of world politics is the subject of the provocative study by Paul Colinvaux, *The Fate of Nations* (New York: Simon & Schuster, 1980).

6

NATIONAL INTEREST AND OTHER INTERESTS

Despite its ambiguity, the concept of *national interest* remains of great importance in any attempt to describe, explain, predict, or prescribe international behavior. Students and practitioners of international relations agree almost unanimously that the primary justification of state action is national interest. The disagreements begin when one asks conceptual or substantive questions about the national interest: How do we arrive at a generally acceptable or standardized definition of national interest? What is specifically in the national interest of a given country and its people at a given time and in regard to a given issue? Who decides what the priorities of state action are going to be, and when and how they are to be implemented? How and by whom are enemies defined? How and by whom are friends designated? What is the role of the government when faced with serious internal disagreements regarding national goals and values?[1]

For each of these questions there are responses from proponents and opponents seeking to justify their views, in the name of the national interest. Alcibiades said he was acting in the interest of ancient Athens when he recommended so fervently that the Athenians launch what turned out to be the disastrous Sicilian expedition during the Peloponnesian War. Napoleon said he was acting in France's interest when he initiated the Russian campaign and when, later, he mounted a last desperate battle at Waterloo. President Abraham Lincoln argued that civil war would be less painful to America than the breakup of the Union. Adolf Hitler justified his expansionist policies, including a mindless mul-

[1]Stephen Krasner, *Defending the National Interest* (Princeton, N.J.: Princeton University Press, 1978).

tifront war, in the name of Germany's national interest. Joseph Stalin destroyed or displaced Russian farmers and other "anti-Soviet" elements by the millions in the name of the Soviet Union's interest. Lyndon B. Johnson was convinced that the interests of America and the Western world were at stake in the historic Indochina confrontation. In each of these and many other instances, we find leaders justifying their foreign policies in the name of national interest. But how can we evaluate the wisdom of these policies prior to the great tests of chance and history? The remainder of this chapter and much of what follows in this book will try to shed some light on this very difficult question.

DEFINING THE NATIONAL INTEREST: AN ART OR A SCIENCE?

There is a major division of opinion in the field of international relations between those who feel that national interest can be arrived at *objectively* and *rationally* and those who see the definition of national interest as a struggle among various *subjective* views and preferences, a struggle in which the national interest is the political outcome. For the first group, identifying national interests is a science; for the second group, it is an art.

The father of the first school of thought, which is usually viewed as elitist, is Plato. For him, the good of the *polis* (that is, the public good) could best be arrived at by a philosopher-king aided by a few highly learned, detached, and fair-minded advisors. These individuals could make wise and well-informed decisions regarding the common good without accounting for the yearnings of lesser minds or accommodating selfish and sectarian pressures. The basic assumptions of this school of thought are as follows:

1. Wise and well-informed decisions can be made by a few carefully selected individuals who have been expressly trained to think in terms of the collective good.
2. These few individuals, who possess awesome and unchecked power, will not be corrupted by this power.
3. Once socially optimal decisions have been made, they can be implemented effectively by loyal, well-trained, and obedient bureaucracies.

Plato's ideas have been used as the inspiration for dictatorial forms of government, both leftist and rightist. Paternalistic, authoritarian, or mass–single-party dictatorships usually assume that they should emphasize the *substance* and wisdom of policies rather than procedural niceties such as public debate, consultation, participation, and criticism. The defenders of authoritarianism believe that *one* person with strength, wisdom, knowledge, and, above all, power can make good decisions, whereas extremely complex and rule-bound collectivities usually produce a lot of rhetoric but very little substantial action.

The father of the second school of thought, which is usually viewed as democratic, is Aristotle. For him, the public good (i.e., the national interest) can best be defined through the democratic process. This process involves open and continual debate and the expression of various perceptions regarding the collective interest. Decisions—which are usually syntheses of conflicting interests—are shaped by the majority of the people (through their representatives), and at the same time, the rights and interests of minorities are protected. The major assumptions of this school of thought include the following:

1. The collective interest cannot be arrived at abstractly and scientifically. It involves individual and group *preferences,* which are normally subjective and pluralistic. Therefore, there are no *universally acceptable* standards for selecting useful, effective, wise, or prudent policies.

2. In such a world of subjective pluralism, the collective interest can best be equated with the will of the majority, fairly and freely arrived at, on an issue-by-issue basis.

3. Public-interest decisions, once made and implemented, are not sacred. They are subject to review, revision, or reversal on the basis of public dialogue.

Historically, the Aristotelian approach seems to have fared better than the Platonic one, for it has been difficult to find decisions that have been made with scientific precision and rationality. Let us look at a particular example in order to illustrate this point. President John F. Kennedy made two very important decisions in 1961 and 1962—the Bay of Pigs invasion and the Cuban quarantine, respectively. Both decisions involved the island of Cuba. Both required the partial use of American military forces. And both were designed to bring about political and strategic changes in Cuba. The Bay of Pigs invasion turned out to be a fiasco. However, the president's quarantine of Cuba during the Cuban missile crisis eventually resulted in the bloodless removal of Soviet intermediate-range missiles from the island. It would have been extremely hard to have gauged in advance the effectiveness of either of these decisions. After the fact, we can praise the 1962 decision because it succeeded within certain limits, and condemn the 1961 decision because it failed miserably. Because hard-to-gauge decisions have had to be made throughout history, national leaders have come to believe that they must carry out policies that *they think* are in the best interest of their country while letting chance and history be their ultimate judges. President Lincoln made a characteristic statement of this attitude:

> I do the very best I know how, the very best I can, and I mean to keep doing so until the end. If the end brings me out all right, what is said against me won't amount to anything. If the end brings me out wrong, ten angels swearing I was right would make no difference.[2]

In our opinion, national interest might best be seen as a synthesis of the objective and subjective approaches. We concede that in large political collectivities such as nation-states, regardless of their type of polity, governmental decisions are made by only a few men and women. These decisions are usually de-

[2]Quoted in Hans J. Morgenthau, *Politics among Nations: The Struggle for Power and Peace,* 5th ed. (New York: Knopf, 1973). p. 11.

signed to promote the national interest as this concept is perceived and defined by the decision makers; at the least, they are justified by being related to the national interest. A noted British theorist of international relations, Hugh Seton-Watson, has suggested that the expression *national interest* is unsatisfactory because governments, not nation-states, make foreign policy.[3] The expressions *state interest* and *government interest* are, therefore, closer to reality. But the latter terms are not frequently used by politicians or political scientists.

In order to determine intelligently and realistically how national interests are pursued by given polities, and which interests are being pursued, we must relate the formulation of interest to several variables, such as the qualities, personality, and ideals of decision makers; the types of philosophies of governmental structures and processes; the customs and cultural styles of different societies; the geopolitical location and the capabilities of various countries; and, finally, the types of challenges and pressures that each country faces from neighboring countries, great powers, and international organizations.

IDEOLOGIES: GUIDES FOR THE DEFINITION OF NATIONAL INTEREST? OR RATIONALIZATIONS FOR ITS BEAUTIFICATION?

Students of international relations and political science have debated a very interesting question for some time. Do ideological perspectives, adopted by ruling groups of nation-states, determine the definitions of national interest arrived at by these groups? Or, alternatively, are ideological frameworks general and abstract guidelines for action, which are flexible enough to justify and accommodate most choices made by ruling groups? Put another way, does ideology determine policy or is it merely a sugarcoating designed to justify whatever policy choices are made? To give concreteness to our question, we could ask whether the ideology of Marxism-Leninism helps us predict the policies made by the governments of China and the Soviet Union today. Alternatively, we could ask whether the precepts of Western-style liberal-democracy help us explain the policies made by the governments of Western industrial countries such as the United States, Canada, France, Great Britain, and Sweden.

Before proceeding to a full discussion, it might be useful to offer a definition or two for the concept of *ideology*,[4] for we should expect that the response we give to the question stated above will in large part depend on the definition we adopt for the concept in question. Formal ideologies such as Marxism-Leninism and fascism could be defined as elaborate and internally consistent systems of thought—usually supplied in written form by a small group of intellectuals—

[3]Hugh Seton-Watson, "The Impact of Ideology," in *The Aberystwyth Papers: International Politics, 1919–1969*, ed. Brian Ernest Porter (London: Oxford University Press, 1972), p. 209.

[4]A useful definition of ideology has been provided by Abdul Said and Charles O. Lerche: "An ideology may be simply defined as a self-contained and self-justifying belief system that incorporates an overall world view and provides a basis for explaining all of reality." *Concepts of International Politics*, 3rd ed. (Englewood Cliffs, N.J.: Prentice Hall, 1979), pp. 199–200.

that contain a characteristic world view and that offer tools for the analysis, explanation, prediction, and prescription of political and economic relations in societies.[5] In Western states, one finds fewer tendencies toward the adoption of formal doctrines in written form that would conform to the definition of an ideology. Rather, in the West one can speak of belief systems, generally shared outlooks, consensus of values and so forth. At best one can argue that in most Western societies the ruling elites tend to share a set of core values that function—albeit less formally—in a fashion analogous to that of ideologies.

It would be instructive for us to identify here some of the basic elements of Marxist-Leninist ideology and assess the degree to which they have influenced the shaping of policies and practices of the communist governments of the Soviet Union and the People's Republic of China since the time of their respective ascendancy to power in 1917 and 1949.

As we have already seen in Chapter 1, some of the basic elements of the Marxist-Leninist ideology involve the following:

1. The economic substructure of a society determines its political, social, cultural, and religious superstructures.
2. Class struggle (between the bourgeoisie and the proletariat) over the means of production is the central characteristic of national and international politics.
3. The state in bourgeois societies is an instrument of the capitalist class, which seeks to maintain itself in a position of permanent exploitation over the proletariat (working class).
4. After a socialist revolution, the state is run by the communist party (the workers' party) by dictatorial means. Once the means of production are taken over by the working classes, and the bourgeoisie disappears, the "state" as a mechanism of class repression is no longer needed. It should, thus, "wither away."
5. Working classes across national boundaries should unite in the name of a classless and stateless world society.
6. War is inevitable between the forces of socialism and the forces of capitalism.
7. Internal contradictions between and within capitalist societies will lead inevitably to proletarian revolutions and world communism.

Realist scholars of Soviet and Chinese foreign policy have tended to emphasize the factor of national interest more than the one of ideology in explaining Soviet and Chinese behavior. They have pointed out, for example, a number of quarrels involving communist regimes exclusively—USSR versus Yugoslavia (1948), USSR versus Hungary (1956), USSR versus China (1960 to 1985), USSR versus Czechoslovakia (1968), China versus Vietnam (1979 to present)—to support the view that the sharing of various interpretations of Marxist-Leninist ideology does not lead to conflict-free relationships, let alone to relations of solidarity and mutual support.

---

[5]For a useful set of distinctions between formal ideologies and less formal systems of thought, see Juan Linz, "An Authoritarian Regime: Spain," in *Mass Politics,* ed. E. Allardt and S. Rokkan (New York: Free Press, 1970), pp. 251–83.

Realists have argued that Soviet behavior can be better predicted by focusing on traditional national interests (that were pursued even by the Russian czars for centuries preceding the Bolshevik revolution). These interests include the strong desire to be accepted as a great power and continuous efforts to develop and maintain secure borders by ensuring that countries in the Soviet periphery become "buffer zones" ruled by elites friendly to Russia or, later, the Soviet Union itself. Other such interests are the need for access to warm-water ports in the Mediterranean and elsewhere, the construction of sizable naval and air forces to enable a global projection of Soviet power, a desire to deter or limit the damage resulting from war (especially nuclear), and the constant quest for allies that would accept at reasonable cost Soviet military bases, Soviet arms, military and technical advisors, and so forth.

In the case of China, too, it has been argued that Marxist-Leninist ideology has not been as potent in shaping Chinese foreign policies as the requisites of territorial integrity (protection of border areas) and regime security. Thus the post–Mao Zedong thaw in Sino-American relations (political, economic, and military) is a massive indication of interest-motivated as opposed to ideology-determined behavior.

Turning to the Western world's superpower, the United States, we can ask similar questions regarding the interplay between ideology and interests. Of course, we should realize that the term *ideology*, in its formal sense, may not apply to Western liberal and pluralistic societies where a number of ideological orientations tend to coexist or to compete for the public's approval. However, one could argue that certain core values (or belief systems, as discussed further in Chapter 7) are generally shared by American ruling elites.[6] These can be summarized as follows:

1. Individual freedom and dignity and the protection of human rights should be the paramount objective of a developed society.
2. Free enterprise and economic freedom in an atmosphere of political liberty offers incentives for the most efficient and rapid economic development of states. A safety net should be provided for members of society who for reasons of age or health are unable to provide for their subsistence.
3. All efforts to concentrate unlimited power over all facets of social activity in the hands of a large, bureaucratic state should be thwarted. Checks and balances among the various branches of government are the best insurance against the growth of centers of totalitarian authority.
4. In foreign affairs, it is fair to assume that tyrannies, especially those of communist/totalitarian variety, are by definition aggressive, while democracies are by nature peace loving and defensive.
5. The United States, as the major center of political, economic, military, and cul-

[6]In an important article in *World Politics*, James Rosenau and Ole Holsti argue that there is a breakdown of foreign policy consensus in the United States in the post-Vietnam era. They provide evidence on the emergence of conflicting "belief systems" in the United States, with "neoisolationism" assuming greater proportions than any time since 1945. See James N. Rosenau and Ole R. Holsti, "U.S. Leadership in a Shrinking World," *World Politics*, 35, no. 2 (April 1983), 368–92.

tural power, is the leader of the free world and has a special responsibility to contain the aggressive and expansionist international communist movement. This can best be achieved through effective defense preparedness to avoid a position of military inferiority in the face of real and present external threats.

As we have suggested in the case of the Soviet Union and China, the foreign policy behavior of the United States also has demonstrated some disparities between statements of value and principle on one hand and practical policies on the other. Realist students of foreign policy can point out that U.S. foreign policies in the twentieth century can best be explained by emphasizing national interest and objectives such as the overriding American concern with the maintenance of the balance of power in Europe. Presumably it is concern for the maintenance of the balance of power that explains America's belated entry in both world wars, each time on the side of the weaker (losing) side with the objective of averting single-power hegemony over the entire European continent. Other statements of practical interest would include the maintenance of vital spheres of influence, the guarding of freedom of commerce through open sea lanes, the support of governments committed to free market and free trade philosophies, the concern for deterrence and damage limitation in cases of war (especially nuclear), and on occasion, the willingness to maintain good and even friendly relations with ideologically incompatible regimes such as those of communist Yugoslavia, China, and Romania, or right-wing, authoritarian Chile and Argentina (prior to the collapse of military dictatorship in 1983). Nothing illustrates this trend better than a comparison of President Ronald Reagan's rhetoric about the nature of communism and the Soviet Union in the early 1980s and the reality of his pragmatic and compromising actions, especially during his second presidential term.

The discussion up to this point may lead the reader to assume that interests are dominant and that ideologies and value systems are merely *ex post facto* rationalizations for purposes of propaganda. We feel, however, that this position may be overstating the case of the realist school of thought at the expense of demonstrated behavior. Perhaps the best position to take is to accept that there is a mutual and feedback relationship between ideology and interests in which each affects and even shapes the formulations of the other. Schematically we could present the relationship as follows:

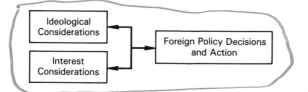

HANS MORGENTHAU ON NATIONAL INTEREST

Hans Morgenthau (1904–1980), a well-known proponent of the realist view of international relations, was a systematic supporter of the premise that diplomatic strategy should be motivated by national interest rather than by utopian and dangerous moralistic, legalistic, and ideological criteria. As we saw in Chapter 5, Morgenthau equated national interest with the pursuit of state power, where power stands for anything that establishes and maintains *control* by one state over another. This power-control relationship can be achieved by coercive as well as cooperative techniques. Morgenthau has been criticized, with some validity, for constructing two abstract and imprecise concepts—interest and power—which he used as the ends and the means of international political action. His critics, recruited mostly from the scientific school of thought, have demanded more precise operational definitions of these basic concepts in the field of international affairs. Morgenthau, however, remained firmly in support of his position that great abstractions such as power and interest cannot and should not be quantified.

Morgenthau believed that political action is not finite, precise, and clearly observable. Therefore, if political concepts are to reflect accurately the hazy reality of politics, they must also be vague and imprecise. He argued:

> The concept of national interest is similar in two respects to the "great generalities" of the [American] Constitution, such as the general welfare and due process. It contains a residual meaning which is inherent in the concept itself, but beyond these minimum requirements its content can run the whole gamut of meanings that are logically compatible with it. That content is determined by the political traditions and the total cultural context within which a nation formulates its foreign policy.[7]

The residual meaning inherent in the concept of national interest is *survival*. But whose survival? In Morgenthau's view, the minimum requirement of nation-states is to protect their physical, political, and cultural identity against encroachments by other nation-states. Translated into more specific objectives, the preservation of physical identity is equated with the maintenance of the territorial integrity of a nation-state. Preservation of political identity is equated with preservation of existing politico-economic regimes, such as democratic-competitive, communist, socialist, authoritarian, and totalitarian. Preservation of cultural identity is equated with ethnic, religious, linguistic, and historical norms in a nation-state. From these general objectives, argued Morgenthau, a country's leaders can derive specific cooperative and conflictive policies, such as competitive armaments, balance of power, foreign aid, alliances, subversion, and economic and psychological warfare.

Over the years, a number of challenging questions have been raised that emphasize the elusiveness of national interest as a political concept. It is on some of these questions that we shall now focus.

First, how do we differentiate national interest from group, class, elite-establishment, or foreign-inspired interest? The same question, asked specifically, might be: How, by whom, and on what basis are the national interests of the United States, the Soviet Union, China, Czechoslovakia, and Albania defined? Morgenthau's answer to this question is simple but not straightforward. The national interest is, he argued, a compromise of conflicting political interests; it is

---

[7]Hans J. Morgenthau, *Dilemmas of Politics* (Chicago: University of Chicago Press, 1958), p. 65.

not an *ideal* that is arrived at abstractly and scientifically, but a product of constant internal political competition. The government, through its various agencies, is ultimately responsible for defining and implementing national-interest–oriented policies.

Second, what should be the scope and range of a country's national interest? Morgenthau's response would be that a country's national interest should be proportionate to its capabilities. (See Chapter 5 for an examination of ways of assessing a country's power and capabilities.) He would argue, for example, that it is a mistake for countries such as France and Britain to aspire in the 1980s to superpower status—that is, to seek to have an impact on the resolution of disputes throughout the world. Further, Morgenthau would argue that nationalist universalism—aspiring to turn the whole world into the image of a single country—would be beyond the capabilities of any single state, including the United States and the USSR. So the legitimate exercise of state power should not be equated with the arrogance of power.

Third, how should a country's national interest be related to the interests of other countries? A good diplomat, according to Morgenthau, is a rational diplomat, and a rational diplomat is a *prudent* diplomat. Prudence is the ability to assess one's needs and aspirations while carefully balancing them against the needs and aspirations of others: "The national interest of a nation that is conscious not only of its own interest, but also of that of other nations, must be defined in terms compatible with the latter. In a multinational world this is a requirement of political morality; in an age of total war it is also a condition for survival."[8] This observation coincides with Morgenthau's assumption that the international system is neither naturally harmonious nor condemned to inevitable wars. Morgenthau assumes varying levels of continual conflict and threats of war, which can be minimized by the piecemeal and prudent adjustment of conflicting interests by diplomatic action.[9]

Finally, how should national interest be related to the requirements of collective (global) security or selective (regional) security? Morgenthau is opposed to state action that is founded on abstract and universal principles other than that of national interest. (Concepts and processes of collective and regional security are discussed in some detail in Chapters 14 and 15.) If the security of every nation-state of the world is equated with the security of every other nation-state (a major prerequisite of the theory of collective security), then conflict cannot be localized and disputes will quickly escalate and have dangerous consequences in this nuclear era. Morgenthau, as a result, was skeptical toward leaders who justify their policies on the basis of collective security rather than plain national interest. He would, for example, be systematically opposed to American intervention anywhere in the world in the name of principles such as democracy or collective security. He would be equally critical of Soviet intervention in the name of principles such as world communism and socialist solidarity.[10]

---

[8]*Ibid.,* pp. 74–75.

[9]*Ibid.*

[10]What Morgenthau fails to consider here is that leaders often find it useful to dress interest-motivated policies into a moral, legal, or ideological garb.

In regard to the relationship between national interests and regional or alliance interests, Morgenthau argued once more the precedence of national interests over regional interests. For Morgenthau, useful alliances are best supported by foundations of reciprocal advantage and mutual security of participating nation-states rather than by ideological or moralistic frameworks.[11] A regional alliance that does not genuinely serve the interests of the participating nation-states (as pursued by their governments) is not likely to survive or to be effective in the long run.

Viewing the realist school of thought as exemplified by Hans Morgenthau, we are left with one central question: In the struggle between realist and idealist motivations of the human conscience, how does one pursue national interests prudently? The answer for the realist is that decisions concerning national interest should always be made on the basis of concrete and demonstrable national advantage (within the limits of prudence) rather than on the basis of abstract and impersonal criteria of morality, law, and ideology. The most powerful example of a statesman acting on the basis of concrete national advantage rather than moralistic principles was provided by President Lincoln. On August 22, 1862, he wrote:

> If there be those who would not save the Union unless they could at the same time save slavery, I do not agree with them. If there be those who would not save the Union unless they could at the same time destroy slavery, I do not agree with them. My paramount object in this struggle *is* to save the Union and is *not* either to save or to destroy slavery. If I could save the Union without freeing *any* slave I would do it, and if I could save it by freeing *all* the slaves, I would do it; and if I could save it by freeing some and leaving others alone I would also do that. What I do about slavery, and the colored race, I do because I believe it helps to save the Union; and what I forbear, I forbear because I do not believe it would help to save the Union. I shall do *less* whenever I shall believe what I am doing hurts the cause, and I shall do *more* whenever I shall believe doing more will help the cause. I shall try to correct errors when shown to be errors; and I shall adopt new views so fast as they shall appear to be true views. I have here stated my purpose according to my view of *official* duty; and I intend no modification of my oft-expressed *personal* wish that all men everywhere could be free.[12]

This pungent and controversial passage contains the essence of the great debate between idealism and realism. The personal ideals of Lincoln clearly oppose slavery and favor freedom for all people everywhere. But his official duty (the national interest) is to safeguard the Union. When his personal ideals conflict with his official objectives, he feels that the ideals must give way to the duty—the perpetuation of the Union.

---

[11]Yet the *raison d'être* of both NATO and the Warsaw Treaty Organization involves more than the protection of the territorial security of the member nation-states. It includes the protection of the political, economic, and cultural identities of the states. Morgenthau's definition of *national interest* includes the preservation of the political identity of the nation-state, which is summarized (if not glorified) in the ideological superstructure of the state.

[12]See *The Collected Works of Abraham Lincoln,* ed. Roy P. Basler (New Brunswick, N.J.: Rutgers University Press).

At the global level of international relations, Morgenthau is opposed to dangerous flights of emotion, preferring instead the safer passageways of pedestrian reason. He would be opposed to a suicidal nuclear confrontation based on dubious objectives such as "the liberation of Poland from the Soviet Communist yoke" or "the saving of Taiwan and Chile from their imperialist overlord, the United States." Morgenthau consistently prefers containment and peaceful coexistence to great-power confrontation, which might raise the risk of nuclear annihilation. In taking such a stance, one may exhibit moral laxity—for instance, indifference to the plight of others. But, unfortunately, in a pluralistic world amorality may be the ticket to survival and prudence may be elevated to the peak of the pyramid of political morality. When someone strikes you, moral behavior is to turn the other cheek. Legal behavior is to seek fair punishment for the assailant in the courts or to engage in reprisals. But political behavior is to assess the size of the person who struck you and then respond prudently.

What are leaders to do when their own principles conflict with the dictates of the public interest? As individuals, human beings are free to give their lives in defense of their principles. But as leaders, whose task is to act in the collective interest, they are not free to make decisions that might endanger their country and people, even if these decisions are made in defense of their personal ideals. The realists believe that the highest collective morality is prudence, which in turn is equated with the need to preserve the collectivity. Morgenthau argues, for example, that "there can be no political morality without prudence, that is, without consideration of the political consequences of seemingly moral action."[13] A national leader may have to lie, cheat, steal, and deal with the devil, if necessary, in order to ensure the *survival* of his or her country.[14]

Morgenthau concluded that the debate between idealists and realists is not one of morality versus cynicism, but one of alternate conceptions of collective morality:

> The contest between utopianism [idealism] and realism is not tantamount to a contest between principle and expediency, morality and immorality, although some spokesmen for utopianism would like to have it that way. The contest is rather between one type of political morality and another type of political morality, one taking as its standard universal moral principles abstractly formulated, the other weighing these principles against the moral requirements of concrete political action, their relative merits to be decided by a *prudent* evaluation of the political consequences to which they are likely to lead.[15]

[13]Morgenthau, *Dilemmas of Politics,* p. 84.

[14]The Watergate affair effectively dramatized the problem of applying distinctly different standards to domestic and foreign policy. Domestic policies are supposed to be tempered by laws, rules of justice, fair play, and cooperative rather than conflictive behavior. In contrast, foreign policies are expected to be amoral, tricky, and conflictive, if necessary, in cases of vital interest. Watergate is a case where foreign-policy behavior was applied to domestic political competition. All other countries, to a lesser or greater extent, experience situations in which domestic-policy behavior becomes similar to foreign-policy behavior. In the long run, domestic politics thus waged results in civil war or revolution.

[15]Morgenthau, *Dilemmas of Politics,* p. 86.

THE FRAGMENTATION OF NATIONAL INTEREST

Despite its utility and challenge, Morgenthau's discussion of national interest has some flaws. By neatly separating moralistic and legalistic behavior from realistic and prudent behavior, Morgenthau creates the impression that these behaviors are mutually exclusive. Yet, one could argue that foreign policies that are (or appear to be) moralistic and legally restrained may prove in the long run to be the most prudent foreign policies. Countries and governments with consistently selfish and opportunistic outlooks tend to gradually develop "bad" reputations, which return to haunt them in subsequent situations. As smart businesspeople have learned, there is nothing more important for sound business relationships than a good reputation.

National interest, as defined by Morgenthau, is a grand abstraction. Diplomats and bureaucrats can be urged to act prudently and realistically and to avoid moralistic and legalistic decisions. But their main difficulty lies in the derivation of specific policies from general guidelines. Policies such as the formation of alliances, the declaration of war, U.N. votes, covert foreign intervention, and foreign aid can be justified on moralistic, legalistic, or realistic grounds. Public officials justifying important foreign-policy decisions tend to employ all three grounds. For example, American intervention in Vietnam in the 1960s was justified moralistically on the ground that the United States was honoring a commitment toward a friendly, noncommunist country. It was justified legalistically in the sense that it was a response to the South Vietnamese government's formal request for military assistance. Finally, intervention was justified realistically on the basis that it maintained the balance of power in Indochina and safeguarded a friendly government in a strategic area against unfriendly and aggressive elements.

To further complicate the problem of identifying national interest, foreign-policy decision making is not necessarily a clear-cut and rational process, as we shall see in Chapter 7. Policies are often generated through great internal political and bureaucratic debates. An abundance of conflicting criteria compete for priority in the minds of decision makers as they shape foreign policies. Official statements made for purposes of propaganda and public consumption cloud the picture and prevent the analyst from identifying the real motives of state action.

Criteria for the Definition of National Interest

Proceeding on the assumption that official decision makers are responsible for making decisions that define national interest, we invite you to step into the shoes of policy makers and policy implementers and to experience the multiple pressures that tend to affect their decisions and actions. Assume, if you will, that you have become the president, prime minister, foreign secretary, intelligence chief, defense secretary, or military chief of staff of a country. What criteria will you use to make or implement new policies or to modify or abandon old policies?

Operational-Philosophy Criteria. Depending on time, location, your outlook toward the world around you, and in particular the actions of your predecessors, you may choose one of two major styles of operation.

First, you may act in a bold and sweeping fashion. Upon taking office, introduce major new practices, policies, and institutions and discontinue others. This style is usually referred to as *synoptic* in the decision-making literature.[16] The decision maker with a synoptic orientation assumes that he or she has (or can obtain) enough information about an important issue to develop a major policy with some confidence that its consequences can be predicted or controlled. Examples of decisions made from a synoptic viewpoint would be declaring war, capitulating to a foreign ultimatum, instituting a social security system, abolishing taxation, entering or leaving a regional defense organization such as NATO or the Warsaw Treaty Organization (WTO), nationalizing private property and resources, and redistributing landholdings.

The second major style of operation is to act in a cautious, probing, and experimental fashion, following the trial-and-error approach. This style is called *incremental* in the decision-making literature.[17] The decision maker with an incremental orientation assumes that political and economic problems are too complex and imponderable for any statesperson or staff to be able to study them thoroughly and to proceed with bold initiatives without worrying about their consequences. The incrementalist prefers, instead, to make a series of small decisions, constantly watching for the effect that each decision has upon the environment and constantly taking corrective action in order to maintain some kind of social equilibrium. Thus, the incrementalist usually seeks to improve existing legislation, policies, institutions, and practices. Examples of decisions made from an incremental perspective would include gradually escalating or de-escalating an ongoing conflict (but not making a sudden withdrawal), marginally increasing or decreasing social security benefits, increasing or decreasing the rate of collectivization of agriculture in a socialist country, controlling but not altogether abolishing nuclear arsenals, and, finally, increasing or decreasing programs of economic and military aid to foreign countries.

Ideological Criteria. As we have seen earlier in this chapter, most governments employ various types of formal or informal ideologies. The day-to-day decisions of policy makers must be somewhat consistent with these doctrines. For example, if your country's prevalent ideology is Marxist-Leninist, your foreign policies should be designed so that you appear friendly to communist governments and leftist revolutionary movements in capitalist countries. If your ideology is liberal-democratic, you should appear to encourage free enterprise, support democratic governments and movements, and oppose totalitarian and authoritarian ones. Finally, if your ideology is traditional-authoritarian, you

---

[16]See David Braybrooke and Charles E. Lindblom, *A Strategy of Decision: Policy Evaluation as a Social Process* (New York: Free Press of Glencoe, 1963), pp. 37–57.

[17]*Ibid.,* pp. 81–110.

should side with those countries (or governments) that support your regime, or at least do not oppose it, and oppose those countries (or governments) that are unfriendly to you.

Moral and Legal Criteria. Acting morally is equated with acting honestly and making your public decisions accordingly. Thus, moral behavior, in international politics especially, involves keeping your promises (treaties), being true to your friends, living and letting others live, avoiding exploiting others, and generally standing up for the principles to which you are morally committed and that are widely accepted in your culture. Acting legally means abiding by the rules of international law to the extent that such rules are identified and accepted. If there are *lacunae* (areas where no international laws have been developed), then you act in a general spirit of global equity and prudence.

We should recognize at this point that although it appears easy in the abstract to urge decision makers to do good and avoid evil, it is quite difficult to decide what the moral or legal action in a specific situation is. Let us consider a hypothetical illustration involving what is referred to as *lifeboat ethics.*

Five shipwrecked men are on a raft in the middle of the ocean. They are slowly dying of starvation, and there is no sign of help. Do they throw lots to determine which one of their number will be killed to become food for the others so that their lives may be prolonged in the hope that help might eventually arrive? Do the stronger kill and eat the weaker ones? Do they all die together in brotherly love? What is the moral thing to do? The situation could be complicated by adding to the five passengers of the raft children, women, pacifists, warriors, and members of various races, nationalities, cultures, and political and ideological orientations, together with a large quantity of pistols, knives, ropes, powdered poisons, drugs, assorted nuclear devices, and other weapons.

Lynn Miller, in a lucidly written study, has offered excellent illustrations of dilemmas in politics involving conflicting political values.

> Is the loss of freedom in a highly centralized authoritarian state worth the greater security to a greater number of individuals that may come with it? Does wide participation in making political decisions in a liberal democracy compensate for a lessened efficiency in government? Does the so-called right of national self-determination have any limits as, for example, when those who identify themselves as a subject nation are scattered, or constitute a very small group, or are not educated for self-government? Can the desire to achieve political independence ever justify the use of force against innocent civilians?[18]

These and similar questions are very difficult to answer unequivocally. Usually they involve the clashing of preferences and interests within a larger collectivity. The clarification of ends versus the adequacy and permissibility of means to achieve those ends and the resolution of the central political dilemma

---

[18]Lynn H. Miller, *Global Order: Values and Power in International Politics* (Boulder, Colo.: Westview Press, 1985), p. 9.

between the need for freedom and the dictates of order will remain controvesial subjects of debate for many years to come. The synthesis, in the abstract, is freedom with self-restraint in a setting of legitimized and accountable order. It is, however, in the transformation of abstractions to reality that the stuff of politics, both conflictual and cooperative, intervenes.

>*Pragmatic Criteria.* As a pragmatist, your orientation is low-key, matter-of-fact, unemotional, and professional. You look at life in a dispassionate fashion, and you are not concerned with questions of good and evil, ideological compatibility, operational philosophy, or other general principles of action. As a pragmatist, you see life as an endless series of disjointed and finite problems. Your approach is to solve each problem, much as an engineer solves problems such as the building of bridges, hospitals, and weapons factories. Your motto is, "If it works, it's good." You defend yourself when you are attacked, take advantage of an opportunity if you have the resources to do so, and make short-term and even long-term friendships if they are useful. Utility rather than sentimentality is the criterion of action. As a pragmatist, you value human life because it is useful to do so and you obey laws and moral precepts if doing so helps you to improve your external image and to sell your policies. On occasion, you may have to lie and even cheat in order to protect your country's interests and to solve the problems confronting the governmental organization to which you belong.[19]

At this stage, you should be ready to ask a rather uncomfortable question: How can you differentiate a policy that is justified in ideological, legal, and moral terms (but only for pragmatic reasons) from a policy that is *genuinely* motivated by moral, legal, and ideological considerations? The answer, we suppose, is that it will be impossible to make this distinction unless decision makers allow us to subject them to psychoanalysis in order to reveal their true motivations.

>*Professional-Advancement Criteria.* Your actions must frequently be manipulated and adjusted in consideration of your professional survival and growth—in short, your success. Quite often, in large bureaucracies the trick to success is to "play the game" and not to "rock the boat." This attitude has been referred to cynically as the "go along to get along" effect. Bureaucratic behavior is frequently equated with conformist behavior, and so-called "whistle blowers" normally have to pay a heavy professional price. Even presidents and prime ministers have to conform, either to popular pressures or to powerful elites whose support they consider indispensable for their political survival.

>*Partisan Criteria.* Here you tend to equate the survival and the success of your political party or faction with the survival and success of your country. The problem is this: Will you support certain policies that you consider benefi-

---

[19]Often, these interests are equated subconsciously with your own political interests. This type of "dilemma" might help explain the behavior of persons (from both sides) involved in the so-called Iran-Contra affair.

cial for your country if doing so might cause you and your party to lose an election or to be removed from a position of power?

Bureaucratic-Interest Criteria.   Here you tend to equate the interest of your organization (the army, the navy, a foreign office, an intelligence service, a cabinet office, and so forth) with the national interest. Given limited budgetary resources, battles among security, welfare, education, and economic interests for scarce funds are fiercely waged within all governments. The normal outcome of this bureaucratic infighting is that each agency tends to exaggerate its specific funding requests and to argue in the name of the national interest rather than the bureaucratic interest.

Ethnic/Racial Criteria.   If you are recruited from an ethnic or racial minority group, you may tend to exaggerate the importance of projects that might benefit that group. By the same token, if you are recruited from the majority ethnic or racial group, you may tend to overestimate the needs of that group and be insensitive to the needs of the minorities.

Class-Status Criteria.   If you are recruited from the upper or middle class of your country (or if you reside in a communist country and are recruited from the bureaucratic, professional, or party circles), you may tend to support policies that benefit the class with which you identify yourself. If you are recruited from the lower (worker and farmer) classes into a Western bureaucracy, you may find yourself gradually becoming torn between your loyalty to the class of your origin and your opportunity to become an important upper-middle-class bureaucrat.

Foreign-Dependency Criteria.   These criteria usually apply to small or medium-sized countries whose governments find themselves highly dependent on one or more foreign "protectors" in order to remain in office. Among the many countries in this category are Afghanistan, El Salvador, and Chad, three countries that span the world's ideological spectrum. If you are a decision maker in one of these governments, you may find that the needs, guidelines, and dictates of the foreign protectors interfere with your assessments of what is in your country's national interest. Yet do you follow your conscience when doing so might lead to your abrupt removal from office?

Looking at the long array of conflicting guidelines discussed above, we should become modest in our support of the "objectivity" of national interests. It should be clear to us by now that decisions about the national interest are not purely scientific or mathematical formulations that result in optimal advantages for a nation-state. On the contrary, national-interest decisions appear to be products of conflicting wills, ambitions, motivations, needs, and demands.

Perhaps the best way to summarize our discussion of national interest is with the insightful words of Raymond Aron:

> The plurality of concrete objectives and ultimate objectives forbids a rational definition of "national interest," even if the latter did not involve, in itself, the

ambiguity that attaches to collective interest in economic science. Collectivities are composed of individuals and groups, each of which seeks its own objectives, seeks to maximize its resources, its share of the national income, or its position within the social hierarchy. The interests of these individuals or of these groups, as they express themselves in actual behavior, are not spontaneously in accord with each other, and added together they do not constitute a general interest.[20]

GLOBAL INTERESTS AND OBJECTIVES

If we accept the proposition that it is the business of governments to protect only their national interests, then whose business is it to protect global interests, and are such interests identifiable? Richard A. Falk and Saul H. Mendlovitz have ranked the major problems facing humankind and suggested global objectives that would control these problems:

World Problems

1. War
2. Poverty
3. Racial oppression and colonialism
4. Environmental decay
5. Alienation

Global Objectives

1. The minimization of violence
2. The maximization of social and economic welfare
3. The maximization of social and political justice
4. The maximization of ecological balance
5. The maximization of participation in authority processes [governmental decision-making][21]

Who is going to worry about global problems such as war, poverty, unemployment, discrimination, alienation, and environmental decay? Our answer is, given the quasi-anarchical structure of today's international system, *no one.* Global action will have to await the development of institutions led by officials whose mentality will parallel Lincoln's, but at the global level. In short, we cannot make legitimate and effective policies on the basis of global interests until we develop a global government with a global leadership whose official task will be to save the "Union of the Earth."

In the meantime, concern with global interests will probably continue at

[20]Raymond Aron, *Peace and War: A Theory of International Relations* (New York: Doubleday, 1966), pp. 91–92.
[21]Richard A. Falk and Saul H. Mendlovitz, eds., *Regional Politics and World Order* (San Francisco: W. H. Freeman, 1973), p. 1.

the level of private national and international organizations, and among well-meaning academic and business people, who are at times dismissed unfairly as utopians, do-gooders, and eggheads. Throughout history, necessity has been the mother of invention. Global problems such as nuclear war, ecological imbalance, depletion of resources, environmental pollution, and population growth call for the development of new institutions with global rather than national orientations. We shall discuss in some detail those new global challenges, and some responses to them, in Part V of this book.

SUGGESTIONS FOR FURTHER STUDY

The meaning of the *national interest* is the subject of a lively dialogue in the confirmation hearings held by the Senate Committee on Foreign Relations on the *Nomination of Henry A. Kissinger to Be Secretary of State*, 93rd Cong., 1st sess., 1973. Roy E. Jones argues that the national interest is a set of values that constitute the core of a community in *Principles of Foreign Policy: The Civil State in Its World Setting* (New York: St. Martin's Press, 1979). Case studies of contending views of the national interest are Cyrus R. Vance, *Hard Choices: Four Years in Managing America's Foreign Policy* (New York: Simon & Schuster, 1983); and Zbigniew K. Brzezinski, *Power and Principle: Memoirs of the National Security Advisor, 1977–1981* (New York: Farrar, Straus & Giroux, 1983). The ideal of a national interest transcending group demands is the subject of Walter Lippmann, *Essays in the Public Philosophy* (Boston: Little, Brown, 1955); and Hans J. Morgenthau, "Another 'Great Debate': The National Interest of the United States," *American Political Science Review*, 46 (December 1952), 961–88. William T. R. Fox has commented extensively on the imprecision of the term *national interest* in "The Uses of International Relations Theory," in *Theoretical Aspects of International Relations*, ed. William T. R. Fox (Notre Dame, Ind.: University of Notre Dame Press, 1959), pp. 29–49. Charles A. Beard, in collaboration with George H. E. Smith, has challenged the historical validity of the concept in *The Idea of the National Interest: An Analytical Study in American Foreign Policy* (New York: Macmillan, 1934; reprint ed., Ann Arbor, Mich.: University Microforms, 1962). Hugh Seton-Watson has expressed a preference for *state* rather than *national* interest in "The Impact of Ideology," in *The Aberystwyth Papers: International Politics, 1919–1969*, ed. Brian Ernest Porter (London: Oxford University Press, 1972), pp. 211–37.

7

FOREIGN-POLICY DECISION MAKING

In Chapters 5 and 6, we covered power (capabilities) and national interest (intentions) of states and were exposed to the problems and the ambiguities surrounding these concepts. In this chapter the uncertainty is compounded, since foreign policies are syntheses of the ends (national interests) and means (power and capabilities) of nation-states. We shall begin our survey with a standard definition of *foreign policy:*

> Reduced to its most fundamental ingredients, foreign policy consists of two elements: national *objectives* to be achieved and *means* for achieving them. The interaction between national goals and the resources for attaining them is the perennial subject of statecraft. In its ingredients the foreign policy of all nations, great and small, is the same.[1]

As you may suspect, we cannot easily get off the conceptual hook with this definition. It defines foreign policy in terms of objectives and means available for their implementation and leaves out foreign-policy actions and eventual outcomes that may or may not relate to stated intentions. So the question remains of exactly what foreign policy is. This question, in turn, embraces a panorama of subsidiary questions:

---

[1]Cecil V. Crabb, Jr., *American Foreign Policy in the Nuclear Age,* 3rd ed. (New York: Harper & Row, 1972), p. 1. For a comprehensive review of the state of the art in foreign-policy analysis, see Charles F. Hermann, Charles W. Kegley, Jr., and James N. Rosenau, *New Directions in the Study of Foreign Policy* (Boston: Allen & Unwin, 1987).

Is there such a thing as a *single, coherent, orchestrated,* and *rational* foreign policy? Or are we really dealing with a series of disjointed, finite, and often mutually conflicting policies emerging from different governmental levels and divisions that are responding piecemeal to their own narrow-focused problems? Can we separate foreign policies from domestic policies when we realize that so-called foreign policies (for instance, wars, military aid programs, and alliances) have important domestic consequences and that so-called domestic policies (for example, political-party platforms and economic reforms) have important international consequences?

Who makes foreign policies? Presidents, prime ministers, and kings? The various bureaucratic cadres serving in political, economic, and military ministries and in the field? Interest groups such as business, the media, political parties, ethnic lobbies, and academic associations? What is the importance of variables such as national character, political and economic structure, culture and ideology, geographic location, and external challenges (as perceived by national decision makers) in the determination of foreign policy by different nation-states?

Is it fair to generalize about foreign policies of nation-states as being offensive, defensive, revisionist, status quo, imperialist, internationalist, isolationist, interventionist, aligned, nonaligned, neutralist, or neutral? Or would it be more accurate to say that foreign policies vary with the type of issues, the specific threat or opportunity at hand, the type and quality of regime, the level of sophistication in technology, and the characteristics of the decision-making team responsible for handling the issue-area in question?[2] Above all, how important are the time frame and the special circumstances in which a certain policy is being developed?

Is it accurate to assume that as a rule democracies follow peace-loving foreign policies and that dictatorships, especially left-wing ones, are aggressive and expansionist? Are insular nation-states more or less likely to be involved in wars and alliances than continental nation-states? Is the foreign policy of a nation-state affected by the number and military potency of the countries that border it? Do poverty and underdevelopment—or, conversely, abundance and industrial might—correlate with cautious or adventurist foreign policies?

Most of these questions are extremely difficult to answer with any finality. We shall nonetheless address ourselves to these and other questions in the remainder of this chapter.

THEORIZING ABOUT FOREIGN POLICY

To ask what causes foreign policy—in other words, to seek an explanation of the foreign-policy–making processes and their outcomes—is to attempt to theorize. As we indicated in Chapter 2, a theory in the field of international relations

---

[2]*Issue-area* is a term frequently used by scholars of international relations to denote categories of foreign-policy issues. One common breakdown of issue areas involves four categories: military-security, political-diplomatic, economic-developmental, and cultural-status.

presupposes an ordering of national and international phenomena in a fashion that allows us to identify probable causes and effects and to describe, explain, and predict these phenomena with a reasonably acceptable degree of probability.

Students of foreign policy are divided into protheoretical and nontheoretical orientations. The theoretically oriented students prefer to talk in abstractions and generalizations, to classify, compare, and evaluate foreign policies of nation-states, and to search for deeper causes of foreign-policy phenomena. The nontheoreticians, on the other hand, are impatient with generalizations, find real life too complex to be categorized in abstract terms, and generally treat each issue and policy as a *unique* entity subject to its own rules and dynamics.

Alexis de Tocqueville (1805–1859), the French scholar-politician and keen observer of the American political process, brilliantly captured the essence of the debate between the theorists of foreign policy and the practitioners of it (most of whom tend to be nontheoreticians):

> I have come across men of letters who have written history without taking part in public affairs, and politicians who have concerned themselves with producing events without thinking about them. I have observed that the first are always inclined to find general causes, whereas the second, living in the midst of disconnected daily facts, are prone to imagine that everything is attributable to particular incidents and that the wires they pull are the same as those that move the world. It is to be presumed that both are equally deceived.[3]

With de Tocqueville's wise remarks in mind, we can proceed to examine the great variety of possible "causes" of foreign policy. To aid us in our search, we will consider foreign-policy decisions as *dependent variables* and all other factors that tend to affect those decisions as *independent variables*.[4]

Foreign-policy decisions, in turn, can be subdivided into categories. For instance, we can differentiate among critical, important, and routine decisions. We can also distinguish decisions in terms of issue-categories such as military, political, economic, environmental, resource (e.g., energy), technical, cultural, and humanitarian.[5] Decisions can also be subdivided by geographic criteria such as East-West, North-South, West-West, East-East, and South-South relations. Further, some decisions involve—to a lesser or greater degree—domestic interest

---

[3]Quoted in Graham T. Allison, *Essence of Decision: Explaining the Cuban Missile Crisis* (Boston: Little, Brown, 1971), p. i.

[4]*Variables,* as opposed to *constants,* are quantities or measurements (e.g., population, density, temperature, inflation, unemployment, type of government) that have the capacity and the tendency to *change* over time. We name *dependent variables* those quantities whose changes we wish to explain as derivable from the impact of variables external to them. We name *independent variables* those quantities whose behavior we wish to examine in order to determine the degree to which they account for changes exhibited by dependent variables. A simple example, we hope, will illustrate the difference: If we are interested in determining the *impact* of heat or pollution on human behavior, then "heat" and "pollution" will be independent variables and human behavior the dependent one. We may, however, decide to reverse roles and name human behavior (e.g., exploding nuclear devices) as the independent variable and heat and pollution as the dependent ones.

[5]In reality, of course, most decisions are *hybrid* in nature in the sense that they cut across a number of issue-categories.

groups, and must be made with concern for their domestic political impact upon the decision makers.

For the purposes of our discussion we will subdivide foreign policy decisions into three major categories: *programmatic decisions, crisis decisions,* and *tactical decisions.*

> *Programmatic decisions:* Major decisions with long-range consequences; made following detailed study, deliberation, and evaluation of a whole range of alternative options.
>
> *Crisis decisions:* Decisions made during periods of grave threat; limited time in which to respond; and a surprise element that requires an *ad hoc* response in the sense that no preplanned responses are available.
>
> *Tactical decisions:* Important decisions that usually are derivative from the programmatic level; subject to reevaluation, revision, and reversal.

James N. Rosenau, a prolific scholar with a scientific orientation, has offered us a handy guide designed to aid our search for variables that affect the making of foreign policy.[6] Rosenau has grouped these variables into five major categories: idiosyncratic, role, bureaucratic, national, and systemic.

Idiosyncratic (Individual) Variables

These variables are concerned with the perceptions, images, and personal characteristics of decision makers:[7] cautiousness versus rashness, anger versus prudence, pragmatism versus ideological crusadism, superiority versus inferiority, creativeness versus destructiveness, paranoia versus overconfidence, and so on. Undeniably, the psychological characteristics and the ideological predilections of leaders and other makers and implementers of policy have a certain bearing on policy outcomes. However, the variables that are related to these characteristics are very difficult to measure. For instance, do variables such as the marital status, type and quality of education, social origin of parents, financial status, and influential friends affect the decisions that a leader makes?

The psychiatrist Erich Fromm has concluded from a study of selected political leaders that wartime heads of government, such as Adolf Hitler or, to a lesser extent, Winston Churchill, are often fascinated by destruction.[8] One might ask: What would have been the impact on German-British relations (and on history in general) had Hitler become a successful architect and Churchill a fine journalist, novelist, or artist? A more direct version of this question is: What was the impact of each one's personality upon his or her country's foreign policies? Charismatic leaders such as Kemal Atatürk, V. I. Lenin, John F. Kennedy, Marshal Tito, Francisco Franco, Constantine Karamanlis, Indira Gandhi, Anwar Sadat,

---

[6]See James N. Rosenau, *The Scientific Study of Foreign Policy* (New York: Free Press, 1971), pp. 95–150.

[7]Margaret G. Hermann, "Explaining Foreign Policy Behavior Using the Personality Characteristics of Policy Leaders, "*International Studies Quarterly,* 24, 1 (1980), pp. 7–46.

[8]See Erich Fromm, *The Anatomy of Human Destructiveness* (New York: Holt, Rinehart & Winston, 1973).

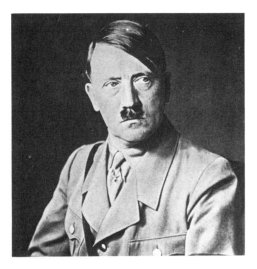

Adolf Hitler (1889–1945), leader of the Nazi party and dictator of Germany from 1933 to 1945. (Eugene Gordon)

Ayatollah Ruhollah Khomeini, Juan Peron, Archbishop Makarios, Jomo Kenyatta, Golda Meir, Charles de Gaulle, Ronald Reagan, and Mikhail Gorbachev offer us fascinating opportunities to study the impact of a single personality on domestic politics and foreign policies.

It would be fair to assume that the impact of idiosyncratic variables is greater in crisis than in programmatic decisions. During crisis, the time and threat constraints place most of the burden on the shoulders of a state's leader and a few advisors who can be hastily assembled. Similarly, one can argue that idiosyncratic variables help explain decisions more readily in authoritarian and totalitarian states than in democratic-competitive ones. A leader who is also a

Sir Winston Churchill (1874–1965), author, statesman, and prime minister of Great Britain from 1940 to 1945 and 1951 to 1955. (AP/ Wide World Photos)

dictator can reflect his or her own personal traits far more readily in all categories of decisions than a democratic leader subject to the scrutiny of governmental
checks and balances, as well as the free press, parliament or congress, public
opinion, pressure groups, and so on.

Role Variables

Role variables are somewhat more difficult to pinpoint. They are usually defined
as job descriptions or as expected rules of behavior for officeholders such as
presidents, cabinet officers, high-level bureaucrats, congressional representatives
and senators, journalists, educators, labor-union and other pressure-group leaders, and other elites who affect, formulate, and implement foreign policies.

Regardless of a person's psychological profile, when he or she takes on
a specific role, resultant behavior is modified considerably by the public's expectations of that role. A good example of the impact of role upon behavior is the
story of Thomas à Becket. As King Henry II's drinking, hunting, and lechering
buddy, Becket was a devil-may-care man whose main concern was to enjoy the
"deep" pleasures of life and to satisfy his friend, protector, and sovereign. However, once Becket was persuaded to accept the position of archbishop by his king,
a profound transformation occurred. Becket internalized the requirements of his
new role and decided to act in accordance with the dictates of his office. He
ceased being a yes-man and a sidekick of the king and proceeded to protect the
rights and to shoulder the responsibilities of the church. Had King Henry read
and understood role theory, he would not have had to consent to the murder of
his great personal friend, albeit political enemy, Becket. He would simply never
have offered him the job.

Another good illustration of the impact of role on foreign-policy attitudes is a comparison of foreign-policy statements made by political leaders when
they are in the role of the opposition with their statements following their assumption of governing responsibilities. As opposition leaders they tend to exaggerate their differences with the policies employed by those in power. They also
tend to make a number of promises designed to maximize the hopes and expectations (and the votes) of a given constituency. Once in power, however, they tend
to mute their rhetoric somewhat, and they come closer to assuming a role reminiscent of that of their predecessors.

The definition of a role affects larger political and societal variables, to
which we shall be turning shortly. For instance, the definition of the role of the
chairperson of the Chinese Communist Party is different from that of the British
prime minister. Whereas the chairperson has near monopoly in the conceptualization, definition, and handling of important foreign-policy issues, the British
prime minister is hampered by a great number of obstacles, such as the views of
important members of his or her own cabinet and party, the views of the opposition parties, the attitudes of the press, public opinion, and the constraints of
having to act in harmony with European, NATO, and Commonwealth colleagues.
It is safe, therefore, to hypothesize that given the less constrained role of the

Chinese chairperson, personality characteristics are much more likely to significantly affect his or her country's policy than are the personality characteristics of the British prime minister. This difference in definition between the role of the chairperson and the role of the prime minister allows us to visualize clearly the impact of role as a variable.

Unlike idiosyncratic variables, role variables are probably better suited to explain programmatic and tactical decisions in democratic-competitive societies. A justification for this assertion would include the following arguments: Programmatic decisions take much time and require multiple inputs into the decision-making process. Therefore, unlike crisis decisions, they permit a large number of individuals occupying a multiplicity of roles to enter into the decision-making process. Role variables, we could further argue, can be more operative in democratic-competitive systems because the behavior of the decision makers has to be much more visible and subject to criticism. Thus deviations from traditional expectations of the role in a given office (e.g., the Watergate events, 1972–74) may even lead to the removal of a leader from power.

Bureaucratic Variables

These variables are concerned with the structure and processes of a government and their effects upon foreign policies. Interesting studies by Graham Allison and Morton Halperin have detailed the complexities and nuances of bureaucratic politics.[9] These authors suggest that bureaucratic complexity is the normal characteristic in most countries, including those that are least developed. Allison and Halperin, and other authors as well,[10] argue with considerable merit that to view foreign policies as *rationally* derived plans designed to maximize the best interests of abstract and monolithic units called nation-states is to simplify if not openly distort reality. Instead, they argue, most policies reflect the conflicting interests of various government bureaus, military services, and subdivisions thereof, which constantly compete to maintain their narrow bureaucratic survival and growth and to maximize their involvement and influence in the policy-making process.

For example, the student of bureaucratic politics, rather than studying "American" policies toward Europe or the Soviet Union, should think in terms of Army, Navy, Air Force, CIA, and State Department views competing to influence the decisions of Presidents Lyndon Johnson, Richard Nixon, Gerald Ford, Jimmy Carter, Ronald Reagan, and George Bush on various issues. This picture of decisional nonrationality is further complicated when one realizes that each

[9]Allison, *Essence of Decision;* Morton Halperin, *Bureaucratic Politics and Foreign Policy* (Washington, D.C.: Brookings Institution, 1974).

[10]See, for example, Alexander L. George, "The Case for Multiple Advocacy in Making Foreign Policy," *American Political Science Review,* 66, no. 3 (September 1972), 751–85; Alexander L. George and Juliette L. George, *Woodrow Wilson and Colonel House: A Personality Study* (New York: Day, 1956); and Roger Hilsman, *The Politics of Policy Making in Defense and Foreign Affairs* (New York: Harper & Row, 1971).

of the major governmental agencies is subdivided into administrative, factional, and even personal domains. Moreover, between decisions at home and their implementation abroad there is a lot of room for misperceptions, disagreements, calculated distortions of orders from above, and even outright disobedience to them.

They argue, convincingly, that major powers (especially industrialized states) which possess large and complex bureaucracies are more likely to be subject to the impact of bureaucratic variables. They suggest, however, that political parties, pressure groups, independent mass media, and public opinion affect foreign policies much more in so-called democratic-competitive systems than they do in totalitarian or authoritarian countries.

To sum up, bureaucratic variables include the structure of governmental organizations, the standard operating procedures of major bureaucratic agencies, the decision-making processes at various levels of policy formulation, techniques for implementing policy decisions, and the attitudes of officials regarding the impact of foreign policies on domestic policies and on the general welfare of their country.

National Variables

This category embraces a vast number of national attributes that influence foreign-policy outcomes. We have already covered much of this category of variables in Chapter 5, in our discussion of tangible and intangible elements of power. We shall mention some of these variables here and leave it to your imagination and ingenuity to fill in the gaps.

Under the heading of national variables we include environmental variables, such as the size, geographic location, type of terrain, climate, and resources of nation-states. To illustrate, one would expect a continental nation-state with vulnerable boundaries and a strategic location either to develop an offensive strategy (such as seeking more secure boundaries or acquiring buffer zones) or to gain the protection of a more powerful and mobile nation-state. On the other hand, an insular nation-state or one bounded by nearly impermeable natural frontiers is more likely to develop a defensive strategy and avoid entangling alliances, which might limit its sovereignty.

We can also list under national variables, population attributes, such as the size and density of population of a country, and the vital statistics of a population, such as age distribution, literacy, and physical health. We could ask some interesting questions in regard to these variables: Do populous countries such as China, India, the Soviet Union, and the United States exhibit any similar characteristics in their foreign policies? Are countries with a high population density—such as China, Japan, and Indonesia—likely to follow expansionist policies? Are well-nourished and disease-free populations more prone to expansionist and adventurist policies than undernourished and disease-ridden ones? These questions await careful scientific research and analysis. The record of foreign-policy behavior to date is too mixed to allow firm answers to most such questions. We are likely, for example, to encounter as many instances of densely populated nation-states acting cautiously as instances of such states acting adventurously.

Gross national product, industrial and agricultural outputs, economic growth rate, military strength, and other attributes of a nation-state's capability should also be included in the category of national variables. What, for instance, would be the impact of an industrial, technological economy upon foreign policy? What would be the impact of a traditionally agrarian economy? One response would be that we cannot realistically predict an expansionist policy for an insular nation-state that is technologically backward and possesses no appreciable naval and air capabilities for overseas operations.

The political, economic, and social systems of a nation-state are still other attributes that seriously affect foreign-policy making. The theoretical questions in these areas are of central importance to students of political science. Let us consider political variables first. For example, does the type of political system in a given nation-state have an impact on foreign-policy decisions and their implementation? One could argue that dictatorships are so concerned with maintaining internal order in the face of a hostile domestic population that they are more likely to pursue cautious and compromising foreign policies and thereby avoid adding an external conflict to their internal one. This argument, naturally, can be reversed. For example, dictatorships have been accused of seeking foreign adventures in order to endow an oppressed domestic population with the type of solidarity that only serious external threats can produce. Both arguments sound logical and convincing, but a lot of empirical research over time would be called for before we could side with one or the other.

In the case of economic variables, questions could be asked about the effects of capitalist, market-oriented economies and communist, planned economies upon foreign policy. It has been argued, for instance, that communist countries, by virtue of their central control of their economies, are more effective in orchestrating their foreign economic policies in such a way as to advance their political objectives. The opposite would allegedly be true in capitalist countries, where powerful private economic actors, independent of governmental control, can shape the lines of foreign policy on the basis of corporate rather than national interests.

In regard to social variables, we would be interested in identifying the effects of class structure, distribution of income and status, and racial, linguistic, cultural, and religious homogeneity (or heterogeneity) upon different nation-states' foreign policies. We can argue that a nation-state with serious racial or ethnic cleavages will have to control these cleavages before embarking on offensive foreign policies. We can also argue that deep and uncompromising internal divisions in nation-state A can easily be exploited by nation-state B, which, wishing to gain new advantages, offers certain factions in nation-state A the external support they need in order to survive politically.

The last four categories of national variables we shall consider are national character, culture, shared images, and historical memories of nation-states.

National character is a very elusive concept. It can be described by both disparaging and complimentary generalizations. Both forms of generalization distort a complex reality that shifts with time. Disparaging stereotypes portray the Vietnamese and Germans as warlike and cruel, the French as arrogant and vacillating, the British as hypocritical and conniving, the Soviets as brutal and calculating, the Americans as blunt and exploitive, and so on. Complimentary images of national character are reflected in such terms as selfless, magnanimous, industrious, honest, and cooperative. The choice of words depends on who is doing the perceiving. A nation-state's self-image, as a rule, is more complimentary than images that are held by others. Despite the inexactness of the concept of national character, one could argue that national styles (another way of referring to national character) do indeed affect foreign policies. For example, one can detect a greater degree of caution in post–World War II Chinese and Soviet foreign policies than in United States foreign policies of the same period. Would it follow, then, that caution and gradualism are Russian characteristics, and that rashness and explosiveness are American characteristics? Perhaps we should wait one or two centuries before accepting such crude generalizations as useful propositions and only after submitting them to further testing.

In speaking of culture, shared images, and the historical memory of nation-states, we are referring to a collective state of mind—which emerges with the aid of educational institutions, the media, literature, and the fine arts—about the identity of a country. A nation-state's identity can be traced in its history, its great men and women, popular memories of crises and threats, historic battles for survival, and vital inventions and discoveries. Historical memories greatly affect the substance, direction, quality, and intensity of foreign policy. For example, traditional conflicts, such as the French-German, German-Russian, Chinese-Russian, Greek-Turkish, Chinese-Vietnamese, and Iranian-Iraqi, have been kept alive in the popular myths and the history texts of these peoples. The United States, in contrast, feels secure toward neighbors such as Canada and Mexico, whereas in periods of cold war tension its standard image of the Soviets is that they are aggressive, subversive, and expansionist.

An extremely important memory for most politicians and diplomats, a memory that emerged after World War II, is that of the Munich Agreement (1938).[11] Munich has been equated with the appeasement of aggressors, an action that serves merely to whet the aggressors' appetites for more territorial expansion. "No more Munichs" has been a conscious and in some instances subconscious aphorism in the minds of both Western and Eastern national leaders. Wars such as those in Korea and Vietnam have been fought allegedly to avoid another Munich. More recently, after the bloody and bitter Vietnamese experience, a new

---

[11]As a result of the Munich Agreement (signed in 1938 by Neville Chamberlain of England, Edouard Daladier of France, Benito Mussolini of Italy, and Adolf Hitler of Germany), Czechoslovakia lost a large portion of its most industrial territory, the Sudetenland, to Nazi Germany. At that time, Hitler declared that his sole objective was the reunification of German minorities with their homeland and that no future territorial claims would be made by Germany. However, Hitler soon broke his promises and thereby precipitated World War II.

memory has formed: "No more Vietnams!" What are the hapless leaders of the future to do when they are haunted by memories of both Munich and Vietnam? We can only suggest that in the future, both leaders and followers should ponder the dangers of thinking and acting on the basis of loose historical analogy.

Given the comprehensiveness and inclusiveness of national variables, one can assume that all these variables acting jointly have a very important impact on decisions of leaders in most categories of states. Once again, however, we may assert that national variables are more consciously and carefully taken into consideration in the making of programmatic and tactical rather than crisis decisions. In times of crisis, the pressure of the situation does not usually permit a systematic evaluation of capabilities prior to taking one or another type of corrective action.

Systemic Variables

Under this heading we can group the large number of variables that are *external* to the country whose foreign-policy decisions we are observing and analyzing. For instance, we can include in this category the structure and processes of the whole international system. An international system of balance of power—which we discussed in Chapter 3—is likely to have quite a different impact on foreign policies of nation-states than a cold-war bipolar system. Following the pioneering work of Morton Kaplan, for example, we can test the hypothesis that under the rules of the balance-of-power system foreign policies of great powers will be flexible, pragmatic, nonideological, and generally restrained.[12] In contrast, under the rules of cold-war bipolarity, we can test whether nation-states are pressured to enter into long-lived, mutually exclusive, well-organized and staffed, and ideologically oriented alliances. In a cold-war environment, pragmatism allegedly gives way to ideological and political orthodoxy, the suspicions of the global adversaries reach levels of political convulsion, and mutual urges to behave violently are restrained only by the knowledge of the mutual destructiveness of a total nuclear war.

Systemic variables also include the policies and actions of other nation-states, which can stimulate policy responses by the nation-state selected for study. In fact, the assumption of most traditionally as well as scientifically oriented theorists of international relations has been that foreign policy is a set of responses to external challenges and opportunities.[13] These theorists view foreign policies as rationally defined objectives of nation-states acting through their governments. These objectives are to defend existing possessions or accomplishments and to maximize opportunities, within prudent limits, for new possessions and

[12]See Morton A. Kaplan, *System and Process in International Politics* (New York: John Wiley, 1962).

[13]See, for example, Richard N. Rosecrance, *Action and Reaction in World Politics* (Boston: Little, Brown, 1963); Charles A. McClelland, *Theory and the International System* (New York: Macmillan, 1966); Hans J. Morgenthau, *Politics among Nations: The Struggle for Power and Peace,* 5th ed. rev. (New York: Knopf, 1978); and Raymond Aron, *Peace and War: A Theory of International Relations* (New York: Doubleday, 1966).

related accomplishments.[14] For example, the attack on South Vietnam by the North Vietnamese was viewed by U.S. policy makers as the attempt of a country supported by the Soviets and the Chinese to disturb the existing balance of power in Southeast Asia. In a more narrow setting, the South Vietnamese government, prior to its collapse in 1975, was considered "useful and friendly" by the U.S. government and therefore worthy of American support in its struggle with internal (Viet Cong) and external (North Vietnamese) opponents. This support lacking, these opponents were expected to overthrow the South Vietnamese government and to adversely affect American interests in Southeast Asia. The analysis of this situation was generally horizontal. That is, nation-states were viewed as cohesive and unified actors (in other words, nation-states were equated with their governments), and quarrels among states over territory or resources were considered to be the result of conflicting national interests in a turbulent international system.

The careful student might point out that systemic variables (such as structure of the international system, international law, international organizations, alliances, dependencies and interdependencies, and the actions and intentions of other states) affect a state's foreign-policy formulation both objectively and subjectively. The objective effect is that systemic variables provide constraints and opportunities that outline the general directions of foreign policies. In other words, there are objective limits to the actions of a nation-state. A country without landing craft, for example, cannot mount an amphibious invasion. The subjective effect is that systemic variables can be seen only through the eyes of foreign-policy makers. Let us consider just one illustration here. Soviet foreign policy toward China can be viewed as a reaction to Chinese behavior in concrete terms, or it can be viewed as a set of policies arising from Soviet leaders' *perceptions* of Chinese behavior. Traditionalist scholars usually employ the objective orientation; scientifically oriented scholars gravitate more often to the subjective orientation.

Before ending the discussion on international system variables, we must once more raise the question regarding the types of decisions and the types of states that these variables affect the most. This is a very important theoretical question that can hardly be disposed of in an introductory text. For our purposes, we can assume that systemic variables constrain more directly the decisions made by small and powerless states than they do the decisions made by leaders of great powers. For if we assume that the maintenance of the structure and processes of the international system can be affected by decisions made by the superpowers, then the "rules of the international game" will be set by the powerful, and they

---

[14]Much of the literature on foreign-policy bargaining adopts this attitude. See Thomas C. Schelling, *Arms and Influence* (New Haven: Yale University Press, 1966); Herman Kahn, *Thinking about the Unthinkable* (New York: Horizon Press, 1962); Anatol Rapoport and A. M. Gharmmah, *Prisoner's Dilemma: A Study in Conflict and Cooperation* (Ann Arbor, Mich.: University of Michigan Press, 1965); Bernard Brodie and Fawn M. Brodie, *From Crossbow to H-Bomb*, rev. ed. (Bloomington, Ind.: Indiana University Press, 1973); Harold Guetzkow et al., *Simulation in International Relations* (Englewood Cliffs, N.J.: Prentice Hall, 1963); André Beaufre, *Deterrence and Strategy*, trans. R. H. Barry (New York: Praeger, 1966); and Vo Nguyen Giap, *Banner of People's War: The Party's Military Line* (New York: Praeger, 1970).

will constrain the behavior of the powerless. In Thucydidean terms "the strong do what they can and the weak suffer what they must."

Viewing the whole bewildering array of variables that help shape foreign policy, we should feel considerably perplexed. Simplistic explanations of foreign policy will no longer suit us, and we will be more likely to reject the foreign-policy analyses of others without providing satisfactory analyses of our own. Despite the frustrating aspects of the enterprise, a consistent effort has been made—primarily by American political scientists—to focus on the decision-making process and on the decision makers themselves in order to reduce uncertainties and perhaps to reach some generalizations that could be subjected to further evaluation. Having reviewed variables that influence the foreign-policy–making process, we turn now to the study of this very process.

THE STUDY OF FOREIGN-POLICY DECISION MAKING

The traditional literature of international relations, which we reviewed in Chapter 6, has focused primarily on the subject of foreign-policy decision making in Washington. Numerous studies have been produced in the form of biography, diplomatic history, or analysis of strategic and diplomatic actions from the standpoint of power or national interest. Their authors have consistently attempted to describe and explain important decisions that they selected for intensive study. (Refer to Chapter 2 for a discussion of the differences between traditionalist and scientifically oriented scholars.) Some of this literature even attempted to predict decisions. Whether one reads the works of Stanley Hoffmann, Henry Kissinger, or Hans Morgenthau, one reads about decision making and its ups and downs.[15]

In this chapter we will review the work of scientifically or eclectically oriented political scientists who have addressed themselves to the same task. They too have sought to dissect the "belief systems" of individual decision makers and to assess the impact of idiosyncratic, role, bureaucratic, national, and systemic variables upon various types and levels of official decisions and actions. Scholars such as Graham Allison, Alexander George, Ole Holsti, Robert North, James Rosenau, Burton Sapin, and Richard Snyder have all sought to navigate in the murky waters of the decision-making swamp.[16]

---

[15]See Stanley Hoffmann, *Primacy or World Order: American Foreign Policy since the Cold War* (New York: McGraw-Hill, 1978); Henry A. Kissinger, *American Foreign Policy,* 3rd ed. (New York: Norton, 1977), and *White House Years* (Boston: Little, Brown, 1979); and Hans J. Morgenthau, *A New Foreign Policy for the United States* (New York: Praeger, 1969).

[16]See, for example, Richard C. Snyder, H. W. Bruck, and Burton Sapin, *Foreign Policy Decision-Making: An Approach to the Study of International Politics* (New York: Free Press, 1962); Robert C. North, "Perception and Action in the 1914 Crisis," in *Image and Reality in World Politics,* ed. John C. Farrell and Asa P. Smith (New York: Columbia University Press, 1967); David Braybrooke and Charles E. Lindblom, *A Strategy of Decision: Policy Evaluation as a Social Process* (New York: Free Press of Glencoe, 1963); Glenn D. Paige, *The Korean Decision, June 24–30, 1950* (New York: Free Press, 1968); John W. Spanier, *How American Foreign Policy Is Made* (New York: Praeger, 1974); Theodore C. Sorensen, *Decision-Making in the White House* (New York: Columbia University Press, 1963); and Harold Lasswell, *The Decision Process: Seven Categories of Functional Analysis* (College Park, Md.: University of Maryland Press, 1956). See also Steve Chan and Donald A. Sylvan, eds., *Describing Foreign Policy Behavior* (New York: Praeger, 1984).

We will begin our survey with the ground-breaking contribution made by Snyder, Bruck, and Sapin.[17] These scholars questioned the tendency of traditional foreign-policy textbooks to reify (personalize) the state.[18] Thus, in their work they sought to focus on specific decision makers who speak and act in the name of the state. As far as Snyder, Bruck, and Sapin were concerned, the so-called real and objective world did not matter! What mattered were the perceptions of decision makers, for these perceptions shaped the policy makers' views of reality and motivated their subsequent decisions.

Snyder, Bruck, and Sapin compared the team of high-level officials advising the chief executive to a massive filter that processes countless variables, including the decision makers' beliefs and roles, bureaucratic demands, political and societal interests, and the constraints on their policies that arise in the rest of the world. The analytical framework of Snyder, Bruck, and Sapin has been considerably discussed, refined, revised, and reviewed, but relatively few hard-data studies following its guidelines have been conducted. A major and well-known exception is Glenn Paige's voluminous study of the United States' decision to join the South Korean government in combatting North Korea's incursion.[19] Admittedly, there is considerable historical value in Paige's microanalytic treatment of President Truman's decision to commit American troops to the defense of South Korea in 1950. But the theoretical propositions about decision making emerging from Paige's study have not exactly caught fire. The size of a conference table determines the number of government officials invited to attend a decision-making session; crisis decisions tend to be reached by *ad hoc* decision-making units; participation in a crisis decision-making team reinforces friendships among decision makers—these and similar propositions appear to be too near the level of common sense to justify well over three hundred pages of microanalysis.

Another major contribution to decision-making theory has been made by James Rosenau, whom we have mentioned before.[20] His concept of issue area has helped us to internalize the notion that there is no such thing as a single, static decision-making team for all foreign policy; rather, such teams vary in composition with the issue area in question. Further, Rosenau's work with *linkage theory* has dramatized the interdependence of domestic and international politics. That is, no foreign policies are made without regard to their domestic consequences, and vice versa. Indeed, foreign and domestic policies are intimately linked; they can be separated only for the purpose of analysis and at the expense of some distortion of reality.

In Chapter 2 we mentioned Ole Holsti's study of John Foster Dulles's "belief system."[21] Holsti found that Dulles had a "closed mind" toward the Soviets

---

[17]Snyder, Bruck, and Sapin, *Foreign Policy Decision-Making*.

[18]To *reify* is to ascribe the characteristics of a single actor to a collective and heterogeneous entity, such as a crowd, a city, a nation-state, or the world.

[19]Paige, *Korean Decision*.

[20]See Rosenau, *Scientific Study of Foreign Policy*.

[21]Ole Holsti, "The Belief System and National Image: A Case Study," *Journal of Conflict Resolution*, 6 (1962), 244–52.

and that he tended to interpret all Soviet actions in a manner that reinforced his conception of Soviet leaders as international predators. Along similar lines are studies of the *operational code* of various leaders and elite groups. Such studies have been conducted by Nathan Leites, Alexander George, David McLellan, and Ole Holsti, among others.[22] George has defined *operational codes* as "general beliefs [of leaders] about fundamental issues of history and central questions of politics."[23] These beliefs affect policy making and implementation. Operational codes are like prisms through which information about external challenges and internal capabilities is constantly refracted.

Basing his insights on the earlier work of Leites, George reconstructed the operational code of Soviet Bolshevik leaders somewhat along the following lines. Prior to 1917, Bolsheviks formed their philosophical beliefs in a revolutionary environment in which they were hunted by czarist police and relied on violent struggle as the only means of political change. They saw the world as being in a state of continuous and deadly conflict between capitalists and socialists. The question was who would destroy whom. Once in power, the Bolsheviks maintained their revolutionary operational code, which contained a calculated mixture of rashness and caution. The Bolsheviks were quite optimistic about eventually attaining their long-range goal (world communism) but quite fearful of mistakes and other pitfalls in the short run. Thus, despite their belief in the "inevitable" victory of communism, they counseled that all credible opportunities to help realize this victory should be grasped. Bolshevik leaders rejected chance and accident as elements of the foreign policies of capitalist countries and came to believe firmly that such "chance events" were part of a major capitalist conspiracy to destroy communism.

Translating their philosophical beliefs into guidelines for action, the Bolsheviks embarked on a policy of struggle and adopted a set of escalating (but also realistic) policy objectives. When dealing with the capitalist enemy, one should push to the limit, engage in pursuit when the enemy retreats, but also know when to stop. Defensively, the Bolshevik should resist from the start even the slightest enemy provocations and trespasses, but should retreat when faced with superior force. In terms of style of operation, the Bolsheviks believed that it paid to be rude to their capitalist opponents. A combination of rude and violent language and cautious and inoffensive action would irritate the capitalists (who, it was usually assumed, possessed superior force) but would not lead them to counterattack.[24]

---

[22]Nathan Leites, *Study of Bolshevism* (Glencoe, Ill.: Free Press, 1953); Alexander L. George, "The Operational Code," *International Studies Quarterly*, 13, no. 2 (1969); David S. McLellan, "The 'Operational Code' Approach to the Study of Political Leaders: Dean Acheson's Philosophical and Instrumental Beliefs," *Canadian Journal of Political Science*, 4, no. 1 (March 1971), 52–75; and Ole Holsti, "The 'Operational Code' Approach to the Study of Political Leaders: John Foster Dulles' Philosophical and Instrumental Beliefs," *Canadian Journal of Political Science*, 3, no. 1 (March 1970), 123–57.

[23]George, *"Operational Code."*

[24]This philosophy is the exact opposite of Theodore Roosevelt's strong man's maxim, "Speak softly but carry a big stick!" The maxim now becomes "Speak loudly when all you carry is a small toothpick."

Lenin, Vladimir Ilich Ulyanov (1870–1924), founder of the Russian Communist (Bolshevik) party, leader of the Bolshevik revolution (1917), and head of the Soviet Union from 1917 to 1924. (Tass from Sovfoto)

George concluded that following the death of Stalin and the establishment of a greater sense of security among Soviet leaders, the Soviets' operational code changed perceptibly. They began to water down their policy of outright hostility toward capitalist nation-states, and the concept of peaceful coexistence rose to replace the concept of protracted struggle against the capitalists.

Operational code—as illustrated here—can be employed usefully as a framework for the comparison of the foreign-policy–making styles of various leaders, regimes, and even nation-states. The main problem with most studies of belief systems, operational codes, and other perceptual characteristics of policy makers is that their authors, by using variations of the content-analysis technique, survey published sources for traces of the images, ideologies, or idiosyncrasies of individual leaders or mass ideological movements.[25] But when one is studying political leaders who consciously cultivate a mystique of ambivalence, mystery, and maneuverability (as Charles de Gaulle and Mao Zedong did), one is hard-pressed to map their cognitive processes. Such leaders simply refuse to become questionnaire respondents or subjects of interviews, and they thereby frustrate systematic attempts by behavioral researchers to study them.

We referred in Chapter 6 to the work of David Braybrooke and Charles Lindblom.[26] These scholars argue that most political decisions fall into the category of "disjointed incrementalism." That is, most political decisions are *not* arrived at rationally and comprehensively, nor are they designed to promote socie-

---

[25]*Content analysis* is a quantitative technique for systematically classifying the content of documents, speeches, and other written materials. The messages are broken down into categories of meaning or attitude (such as conflict, cooperation, and threat), which are then coded for frequency and intensity.

[26]Braybrooke and Lindblom, *Strategy of Decision.*

ty's common good. Rather, these decisions are marginal steps taken by various branches and subbranches of government in order to "satisfice"—to bring about gradual change, to close political gaps, and to avert or control crises.[27] Braybrooke and Lindblom's framework is in a certain sense a theoretical glorification of the time-tested British approach to management—the art of muddling through. Disjointed incrementalism challenges rationalistic conceptions of decision making, which view domestic and foreign-policy decisions as being designed to maximize the benefits and minimize the risks of a nation-state. Thus, incrementalism is the antithesis of the rationalistic operational code of the Soviet Bolsheviks (at least in terms of their words if not their deeds).

Amitai Etzioni, a much-published sociologist, has tried to split the difference between the rationalists and the incrementalists by recommending the adoption of an intermediate decision-making approach that he calls "mixed scanning."[28] Decision makers are advised by Etzioni to proceed with an incremental philosophy but to simultaneously scan the global horizons for general trends and patterns that might have an impact on their country's destiny.

A large category of scholars straddle the scientific-traditionalist wall. We can call them "bureaucracy watchers." Scholars such as Graham Allison, I. M. Destler, Anthony Downs, Alexander George, Morton Halperin, and Thomas Schelling have studied the dynamics of bureaucratic imperatives. Their findings are quite useful but also difficult to summarize. To start with, bureaucracies do not blindly transform presidential decisions into specific actions. A saying circulating among bureaucrats is that when the president sneezes the bureaucracy catches a cold, if not pneumonia. It tends, in other words, to distort—usually, to magnify—presidential directives. We also know that there are bridgeless gaps between certain administration decisions and their implementation as well as follow-through by the bureaucracy. Messages constantly suffer intentional or accidental manipulation and distortion whether they travel up or down a governmental pyramid. This reminds us of the PFC-Wintergreen effect in the novel *Catch-22*.[29] Private First Class Wintergreen, an army communications clerk during World War II, read all the messages he was supposed to dispatch; he destroyed those he didn't like and forwarded those he approved of. Interestingly, Herbert Dienerstein has argued that because of the fragmentation of contemporary intelligence-gathering functions, decision makers' images in the sixteenth and seventeenth centuries were much less distorted, manipulated, garbled, and even ideologically predisposed than they are today.[30]

[27]The term *satisfice* has been attributed to Herbert Simon. See his *Administrative Behavior: A Study of Decision-Making Processes in Administrative Organization*, 2nd ed. (New York: Macmillan, 1958); and James G. March and Herbert A. Simon, *Organizations* (New York: John Wiley, 1958).

[28]See Amitai Etzioni, *The Active Society* (New York: Free Press, 1968).

[29]Joseph Heller, *Catch-22* (New York: Simon & Schuster, 1961).

[30]Herbert Dienerstein, "The Future of Ideology in Alliance Systems," in *Change and the Future International System*, ed. D. S. Sullivan and M. J. Sattler (New York: Columbia University Press, 1972), pp. 31–58.

Graham Allison is representative of the category of scholars we call bureaucracy watchers. In his much-quoted book explaining the Cuban missile crisis, Allison has summarized usefully the challenges and the opportunities confronting contemporary theorists of decision making.[31] He has outlined three models (or *paradigms*, as he calls them) that help us analyze the foreign policies of nation-states. Most traditionalist political scientists have employed the first or *rational-actor model*, according to Allison. Nation-states have been portrayed by traditionalist scholars as monolithic entities whose decision makers rationally maximize national interests. Allison cites Hans Morgenthau and George Kennan as typical examples of these scholars. He then argues that the rational-actor model cannot by itself explain foreign policy. Nation-states are not homogeneous "black boxes," and for this reason analysts should understand internal foreign-policy–making mechanisms.

This is where models II and III, which Allison prefers, enter the picture. Model II is called the *organizational-process model*. Looking at policy making under the guidelines of model II, the analyst realizes that different organizations (the Army, Navy, Air Force, State Department, Treasury, CIA, and so forth), acting with standardized capabilities and routines, considerably restrict the range of available options that lie before the president and presidential advisors. The national interest emerges in most instances as an outcome of interorganizational debates, differing perceptions, and maneuvers that confound attempts at rational explanation of policy.

Allison places the most weight in model III, the *bureaucratic-politics model*. Here he zooms his analytical lens to a close-up of the governmental nerve center, where in an atmosphere of crisis a few persons converge to make momentous decisions that have life-and-death consequences. This is very much in the Snyder, Bruck, and Sapin tradition that we discussed earlier. The Cuban missile crisis of 1962 was the case chosen by Allison to illustrate the intricacies of bureaucratic politics. He describes the arduous debates regarding the proper American reaction to the emplacement of Russian intermediate-range missiles in Cuba. Then he recreates in some detail the controversial internal debate following which President Kennedy declared a naval quarantine around Cuba. The main point that emerges from model-III analysis is that each member of the decision-making team is expected to take positions designed to protect and enhance the interests of the department or agency he or she heads. This has led Allison to summarize his views with the simple maxim, "Where you stand depends on where you sit." According to this logic, the secretary of defense, who sits atop the defense bureaucracy, will advocate policies that are designed to maximize the interests of the military services. The secretary of state will prefer protracted negotiations, the CIA will suggest the use of covert operations, and each of the military chiefs will suggest policies that are in keeping with the capabilities of his service.

---

[31]Allison, *Essence of Decision.*

It should be stated here that there is considerable criticism—from within and without the bureaucracy—of the Allison bureaucratic–self-interest approach. For instance, professional civil servants (career status) in agencies such as the Departments of State, Defense, Commerce, and Treasury, as well as the various intelligence agencies, resent the implication that their advice is purely self-serving and narrowly designed to promote careerist and organizational interests. On the contrary, they argue, they are trained to think and make recommendations meant to be in the "national interest" and to be understood in a rational, aggregate, and nonpolitical sense. The notion that the State Department, for example, recommends only what is good for that agency rather than what is good for the country appears misleading, insulting, and even ludicrous to them.[32] Even Henry A. Kissinger (Secretary of State, 1973–1977), who in the past had generated considerable criticism of bureaucratic politics and inertia, appears to have added his voice to the ranks of those supporting the utility and professional evenhandedness of the Foreign Service of the United States. The following quotation adequately reflects this spirit:

> This country and its leaders are fortunate to have a diplomatic service second to none in its professional competence and dedication to the public interest. For eight years, first as national security advisor and then as Secretary of State, I was privileged to work with the Foreign Service both in Washington and at our posts abroad. From that dual experience, I can attest to the heavy reliance of our political leadership on the expertise of our career diplomats for the successful conduct of foreign affairs. With the complexity and multiplicity of our international interests in the world today, there is no substitute for a strong Foreign Service. Presidents who fail to use fully the institutional strengths and loyalties of the service do so at risk.[33]

A "REVISIONIST" CRITIQUE OF DECISION-MAKING THEORY

Scholars with a Marxist-socialist orientation have been critical of much of the behavioralist and eclectic literature surveyed above. They have argued that behind the claims of scientifically oriented scholars that they are value-free lies a marked preference for the capitalist-dominated status quo. Gabriel Kolko's works are representative of this orientation.[34] Kolko has suggested in many of his works that it is a near waste of time to study bureaucratic structures, to trace informa-

---

[32]Interview with Professor Sidney Sober of the American University (retired State Department Foreign Service Officer) on August 11, 1980.

[33]Henry Kissinger testifying before House Committees of International Operations and Civil Service, *Department of State Newsletter* (Washington, D.C., October 1979), p. 4.

[34]See Gabriel Kolko, *Roots of American Foreign Policy: An Analysis of Power and Purpose* (Boston: Beacon Press, 1969), *The Politics of War: The World and United States Foreign Policy, 1943–1945* (New York: Random House, 1968), and *Wealth and Power in America: An Analysis of Social Class and Income Distribution* (New York: Praeger, 1962). See also Joyce Kolko and Gabriel Kolko, *The Limits of Power: The World and United States Foreign Policy, 1945–1954* (New York: Harper & Row, 1972).

tion flows, or to conduct social-origin studies in order to arrive at the sources or causes of bureaucratic decision behavior. At best, these are well-meaning, scholarly, but painfully accumulated superfluities. Kolko believes that there is a "power elite" in the United States and that this elite is virtually synonymous with big business (specifically, the three hundred largest corporations in the United States). This capitalist-oriented business elite, according to Kolko, has been responsible single-handedly for the definition of America's national interests.

A major premise of Kolko's is that big-business groups have achieved a near monopoly in their ability to equate America's foreign policies with the interests of large corporations. The post–World War II policies of the United States, Kolko argues, have been designed to secure cheaply priced raw materials from raw-material–producing developing countries, as well as to keep the markets of those countries open to the high-priced finished products of mammoth American industry. To realize these objectives, Kolko continues, the United States has adopted a systematic policy of opposing national liberation and socialist movements and supporting corrupt, reactionary, and oppressive regimes that can remain in power only with external economic and military support. In return, these usually militarist regimes satisfy the predatory needs and the gluttonous appetites of America's big-business establishment. To ensure the consistent application of this foreign-policy doctrine, the large business interests have supported the political fortunes of men and women in the Democratic and Republican parties who have adopted the capitalist world view. Once the top political positions are staffed by "business-minded" politicians, the staffing of the remaining key jobs in the bureaucracy and the military services is carried out with the aid of screening that permits or encourages the hiring of men and women who will not rock the business boat. Ironically, therefore, Kolko has implicitly changed Graham Allison's aphorism from "Where you stand depends on where you sit" to "Where you *sit* depends on where you *stand.*"

For Kolko, the Vietnam War (1965–75) was a normal, perhaps inevitable, outcome of America's policies as long as the United States continued to define its interests in terms of maintaining the dependencies of raw-material–producing nations in the Third World. From such goals, allegedly, flowed America's consistent postwar opposition to "national-independence" revolutions. Vietnam was considered worthwhile not for what it had to offer in terms of markets or raw materials, but because it was to serve as a gigantic demonstration of America's counterrevolutionary resolve toward all others who might be tempted to follow a course of "national liberation."

For revisionist scholars such as Kolko, the scientific study of foreign policy—conducted with the aid of modern quantitative techniques—is suspect because it buries in a mass of detail the "fact" that American policy makers are securely in the hands of big-business interests. Revisionists, therefore, may argue that no amount of change in idiosyncratic, role, and bureaucratic variables can have a significant impact on American policies as long as the power elite—which protects and is protected by America's capitalist system—is firmly entrenched.

Richard Barnet, William Appleman Williams, Harry Magdoff, and others have written a number of variations on the same theme.[35]

FORMAL ATTEMPTS TO COMPARE FOREIGN POLICIES

Before concluding this chapter, we shall take a brief look at some of the attempts that have been made to classify and compare countries in terms of the processes and outputs of their foreign-policy behavior.[36] The basic question here is whether one could or should fruitfully *compare* the foreign policies of different nation-states. Is, for instance, a comparison of foreign policies similar to a comparison of chemical elements, solar bodies, or various biological subsystems? One can respond safely by saying that some comparison is better than no comparison, for without a genuinely comparative perspective, one can hardly begin to develop a theoretical orientation. It is natural for us, therefore, to encourage studies, even marginal ones, that seek to compare the foreign policies of nation-states.

One of the most empirically oriented and hard-working scholars in the field of comparative foreign policy has been Rudolph J. Rummel. In time-consuming and expensive studies that focus on the dimensions of nation-states and that use a sophisticated statistical technique called *factor analysis*, Rummel has sought to correlate the behavior of eighty-two nation-states by means of an index of ninety-four variables. These variables have in turn been categorized according to military expenditures at home, conflictive behavior abroad, and various other cooperative or conflictive indicators in the bilateral and multilateral diplomacy of the eighty-two countries during the 1950s.[37]

One of the most significant findings of this scholar—a finding that at first blush may appear to be a truism—is that "nations generally act similarly to each other and . . . these similarities can be resolved into a few basic dimensions. In other words, international relations is structured behavior."[38] Assuming that there are no major problems with the data that support this generalization and

[35]See, for example, Richard J. Barnet, *Roots of War* (New York: Atheneum, 1972), and *Intervention and Revolution: The United States in the Third World* (New York: World Publishing, 1968); William Appleman Williams, ed., *From Colony to Empire: Essays in the History of American Foreign Relations* (New York: John Wiley, 1972), and *The Roots of the Modern American Empire: A Study of the Growth and Shaping of a Social Consciousness in a Market-Place Society* (New York: Random House, 1969); and Harry Magdoff, *The Age of Imperialism* (New York: Monthly Review Press, 1969).

[36]For a useful and representative sample of the work done in this area, see Wolfram F. Hanrieder, ed., *Comparative Foreign Policy: Theoretical Essays* (New York: McKay, 1971). For a more recent assessment of progress made in the field of comparative foreign policy, see James A. Caporaso et al., "The Comparative Study of Foreign Policy," *International Studies Notes*, 13, no. 2 (Spring 1987), 32–46.

[37]See R. J. Rummel, "The Dimensionality of Nations Project," in *Comparing Nations*, ed. Richard L. Merritt and Stein Rokkan (New Haven: Yale University Press, 1966), pp. 109–29. See also Rummel, *The Dimensions of Nations* (Beverly Hills, Calif.: Sage Publications, 1972), and *Applied Factor Analysis* (Evanston, Ill.: Northwestern University Press, 1970).

[38]R. J. Rummel, "Some Dimensions in the Foreign Behavior of Nations," in *Comparative Foreign Policy,* ed. Hanrieder, p. 139.

with its relevance over time (both past and future), Rummel's conclusion may have a great impact upon traditional and normative thinking regarding foreign policy. Traditionally, for instance, we have been taught to think in terms of aggressive (revisionist) versus defensive (status quo) states. We have been encouraged to view the world in terms of good and bad nation-states, or evil and virtuous leaders. Rummel's findings imply that such views are of sentimental, political, or journalistic value, but that they are not necessarily supportable by scientific research.

Another important effort of Rummel's has been to test the validity of traditional assumptions, such as the assertion that commercial expansion eventually leads to wars designed to protect the traders' interests. Rummel has sought to establish whether a relationship (positive or negative) exists between the external trading practices of nation-states and their conflictive behavior. The results are remarkably interesting. Rummel has found, on the basis of his processed data, that there is *no relationship* between trade and conflict variables. Thus, we may find that externally active nation-states (states that conclude many treaties, maintain numerous embassies abroad, and enjoy sizable exchanges of tourists and other visitors) are divided evenly between conflictive and peaceful behavioral profiles. This finding questions another major, even if conflicting, traditional assumption that the more active and externally involved a nation-state is, the more likely it is to become integrated with its neighbors and to live in peace with them.

The third and perhaps most thought-provoking finding of Rummel concerns the issue of internal and external conflict. Traditionally, external conflict has been related to internal conditions. For example, Marxist theorists posit that conflictive behavior is the product of capitalist sociopolitical systems. Other theorists, such as liberal president and scholar Woodrow Wilson, have sought to relate aggressive behavior to authoritarian and totalitarian political systems. Still others have argued that governments with difficult domestic problems seek to divert their population's attention by indulging in foreign adventures. However, these theorists are challenged by those who argue the exact opposite—that the more insecure domestically a government considers itself, the less likely it is to indulge in foreign adventures.

Rummel's findings in this area are, again, provocative. He found *no relationship* between domestic and foreign conflictive behavior. His studies indicated that the incidence of international conflict is accounted for by measures such as "economic and value distances, geographic distance, joint power to span distance, and power parity." In less esoteric language, this means that conflicts are the products of differences in ideological and nationalist orientation, of geographic proximity, and of power relationships of approximate equality between the antagonists. Rummel found that the nature of a country's regime does not alone predict the nature of the behavior of the country. Whether, therefore, a country is ruled by a democratic, totalitarian, or authoritarian government, its chances of being either aggressive or peace-loving at some point in time are quite even.[39] As we saw in Chapter 2, Rummel reversed himself on this important question in subsequent research. Some of his later findings, in fact, support the hypothesis that libertarian regimes (Rummel's version of Western democracies with a free-enterprise philosophy) indulge in considerably less external conflict than do totalitarian and authoritarian states.[40]

Dina Zinnes and Jonathan Wilkenfeld, two able quantitatively oriented scholars of comparative foreign policy, have attempted to qualify the general propositions of Rummel.[41] Studying the behavior of seventy-four states from 1955 to 1960, they divided these states into three categories: personalist, centrist, and polyarchic. These categories are approximately equivalent to the better-known polity categories of authoritarian, totalitarian, and democratic-competitive, respectively. The Zinnes-Wilkenfeld findings, although not definitive or conclusive by any means, are interesting, and suggestive of further fruitful research.[42] Zinnes and Wilkenfeld discovered that personalist (authoritarian) states tend to have *more* than their share of internal conflict but their fair share of external conflict. Centrist (totalitarian) states seem to have relatively low levels of internal conflict, but they exhibit more than their share of intense (violent) external conflict. Finally, polyarchic (democratic-competitive) states have exhibited a fair share of internal conflict and a somewhat lesser amount of intense external conflict. The student, however, should be warned that these results might at times be somewhat misleading. For example, Zinnes and Wilkenfeld found that some of their findings were reversed when they took into account the intermediate (nonviolent) level of external conflict rather than the intense level. They found that polyarchic states exhibited much more than their share of intermediate external conflict, whereas the centrist states exhibited much less than their share. Thus, the classification of a state's proneness to conflict depends heavily on arbitrary categorizations of the various intensities of conflict.

In the long run this type of research is likely to prove useful, for it will help students and practitioners of world politics to make clear connections between types of governments and profiles of external behavior. The development of definitive findings and theoretical propositions will give us the opportunity to make appropriate evaluations and recommendations on the basis of our different values or priorities.

---

[39]This general conclusion that domestic and foreign conflictive behavior are not related has been supported by the findings of Raymond Tanter, "Dimensions of Conflict Behavior within and between Nations, 1958–1960," *Journal of Conflict Resolution*, 10 (March 1966), 41–64; and Michael Haas, "Social Change and National Aggressiveness, 1900–1960," in *Quantitative International Politics*, ed. J. David Singer (New York: Free Press, 1968), pp. 215–44.

[40]R. J. Rummel, "Libertarianism and International Violence," *Journal of Conflict Resolution*, 27, no. 1 (March 1983), 27–71.

[41]Dina A. Zinnes and Jonathan Wilkenfeld, "An Analysis of Foreign Conflict Behavior of Nations," in *Comparative Foreign Policy*, ed. Hanrieder, pp. 167–213.

[42]Our own assumption is that once we use inclusive and representative data of the 1960s, 1970s, and 1980s, our findings in regard to the relationships discussed above are quite likely to differ considerably from previous findings.

A PARTING WORD

In this chapter, we have made a very wide and fast circle through various approaches and orientations to foreign-policy decision making. These approaches, whether traditionalist, scientific, or revisionist, help us to obtain a better focus on the elusive phenomena associated with foreign-policy making. Our own view is that the plurality of these approaches and methodologies is healthy. Thorny problems in the more practical sciences, such as cancer research, are not treated by a single, unified research institution or strategy. Attacking a problem or studying a phenomenon from many different angles and with many different methods increases our chances of coming closer to the truth. So whether we follow in the footsteps of a Rudolph Rummel, a Graham Allison, or a Gabriel Kolko, we are very much like the blind men in the Indian proverb who have gotten hold of various parts of the body of an elephant. The blind man who touches the leg thinks he has a tree; the blind man who touches the tusk thinks he has a spear; the blind man who touches the tail of the elephant thinks he has a rope; and the blind man who touches the side of the elephant thinks he has a mud hut. Yet their insights, once shared, are sure to bring them closer to precious reality.

SUGGESTIONS FOR FURTHER STUDY

Steven Smith has analyzed the problems of adjusting the goals of foreign policy to changes in the balance of power in *Foreign Policy Adaptation* (New York: Nichols Publishing, 1981). The role of perception and individual beliefs is the subject of Deborah Welch Larson, "Problems of Content Analysis in Foreign-Policy Research: Notes from the Study of the Origins of Cold War Belief Systems," *International Studies Quarterly*, 32 (June 1988), 241–55. Major works dealing with general problems of comparing foreign policy include Willam O. Chittick, *The Analysis of Foreign Policy Outputs* (Columbus, Ohio: Charles E. Merrill, 1975); Wolfram F. Hanrieder, ed., *Comparative Foreign Policy: Theoretical Essays* (New York: McKay, 1971); Howard H. Lentner, *Foreign Policy Analysis* (Columbus, Ohio: Charles E. Merrill, 1974); James N. Rosenau, ed., *Comparing Foreign Policies: Theories, Findings, and Methods* (Beverly Hills, Calif.: Sage Publications, 1974); Robert L. Wendzel, *International Relations: A Policy-Maker Focus*, 2nd ed. (New York: John Wiley & Sons, 1980); and David Wilkinson, *Comparative Foreign Relations: Framework and Methods* (Encino, Calif.: Dickenson, 1969). The relationship between structure and policy is the subject of Graham T. Allison, *Essence of Decision: Explaining the Cuban Missile Crisis* (Boston: Little, Brown, 1971); Morton H. Halperin, *Bureaucratic Politics and Foreign Policy* (Washington, D.C.: Brookings Institution, 1974); as well as Richard C. Snyder, H. W. Bruck, and Burton M. Sapin, eds., *Foreign Policy Decision-Making: An Approach to the Study of International Politics* (New York: Free Press, 1962). For a critical assessment of this literature, see Miriam Steiner, "The Elusive Essence of Decision," *International Studies Quarterly*, 21 (June 1977), 389–422. Richard W. Cottam has examined the setting of policy making in *Foreign Policy Motivation: A Gen-*

eral Theory and Case Study (Pittsburgh: University of Pittsburgh Press, 1977). For reflections of an academic-turned-practitioner, see Henry A. Kissinger, "Domestic Structure and Foreign Policy," *Daedalus,* 95 (Spring 1966), 503–29, and *American Foreign Policy,* 3rd ed. (New York: Norton, 1977). The distinction between image and reality of American foreign policy is the topic of William B. Husband, "Soviet Perceptions of U.S. 'Positions of Strength' Diplomacy in the 1970s," *World Politics,* 31 (July 1979), 495–517. The relationship between values and policy outputs is a major topic of G. Matthew Bonham and Michael S. Shapiro, eds., *Thought and Action in Foreign Policy* (Basel: Birkhäuser, 1977).

PART III: *International Political Processes: Civilized Actors in a Primitive System*

8

DIPLOMACY AND STATECRAFT

Diplomacy—official contacts among governments—is the foundation of state-craft.[1] The Persian minister of state Nizam al-Mulk (1018–92) wisely advised his sovereign to treat a foreign ambassador as if he were the king who sent him.[2] This advice remains as relevant today as it was then, for diplomacy is one of the few remaining devices shown to be effective in the often anarchical setting of modern world politics. Whether conducted at the summit by heads of government or at the ambassadorial level by their personal representatives, diplomacy offers hope for those endeavoring to build an orderly international community.

There is ample evidence of crude practices of diplomacy in the records of ancient China, India, and Egypt. These practices involved primarily the delivery of messages and warnings, the pleading of causes, and the transfer of gifts or tribute. These rudimentary diplomatic activities were considerably refined and institutionalized during the time of ancient Greece and Rome. Envoys became negotiators, not just messengers. But no system of permanent embassies was established during this era, so emissaries remained transient. The systematic use of

---

[1]For standard treatises on classical diplomacy, see John Watson Foster, *The Practice of Diplomacy as Illustrated in the Foreign Relations of the United States* (Boston: Houghton, Mifflin, 1906); Harold Nicolson, *Evolution of Diplomatic Method* (New York: Macmillan, 1962), and *Diplomacy,* 3rd ed. (London: Oxford University Press, 1964); Ernest Mason Satow, *A Guide to Diplomatic Practice,* ed. Nevile Bland, 4th ed. (London: Longmans, Green, 1957); and Graham Henry Stuart, *American Diplomatic and Consular Practice,* 2nd ed. (New York: Appleton-Century-Crofts, 1952).

[2]Nizam al-Mulk, *The Book of Government or Rules for Kings,* trans. Hubert Darke, 2nd ed. (London: Routledge & Kegan Paul, 1978), p. 95.

envoys declined substantially during the Middle Ages. It is not until the four-teenth century and the establishment of a system of independent city-states in Italy that we find the earliest persistent examples of resident embassies. Since that time, diplomatic activity has grown consistently.

By the seventeenth century there had arisen piecemeal in Europe an ex-tremely complex and disjointed code of diplomatic procedures, a code that re-sulted in confusion with respect to precedence and protocol. Frequent and vio-lent disputes over questions of diplomatic status, prestige, and power became the order of the times. It was not until the Congresses of Vienna (1815) and Aix-la-Chapelle (1818) that a serious effort was made to simplify the classification of diplomatic agents and formalize their functions. Finally, a century and a half later, at the Vienna Conference on Diplomatic Intercourse and Immunities (1961), attended by eighty-one states, a comprehensive agreement covering nearly all the aspects of diplomatic activity was signed.

The classical definition of *diplomacy* is "the application of intelligence and tact to the conduct of official relations between the governments of indepen-dent states."[3] But this definition is adequate only for the eras when both foreign-policy making and negotiations were functions reserved to a few powerful and competent practitioners of the diplomatic arts. Before World War I, the major powers permitted their foreign policies to be implemented and sometimes even framed by professional diplomats. After World War I, however, politicians took over not only the framing of policies, but at times even the conducting of negotia-tions.

In this chapter, we shall discuss the functions and processes of diplomacy at two separate levels. The higher level—statecraft—concerns the activities of na-tional leaders and other high-ranking officials and involves foreign-policy mak-ing. The lower level concerns the activities of professional diplomats and involves foreign-policy implementation through negotiations. Policy making and negotia-tions are in most instances interdependent processes. We separate them only for the purpose of analysis, and even then we do so arbitrarily. The separation must be made, however, because each level of diplomacy involves different assump-tions, calls for different methods of operation, and demands different skills of the diplomat.

DIPLOMATIC EXCHANGES AMONG NATION-STATES

The Vienna Convention on Diplomatic Relations (1961) divided the heads of diplomatic missions into three general categories. The first two categories com-

---

[3]Quoted in Harold Nicolson, "The 'Old' and the 'New' Diplomacy," in *Politics and the International System*, ed. Robert L. Pfaltzgraff, 2nd ed. (Philadelphia: Lippincott, 1972), p. 425. For more recent studies on the concept, substance, and process of diplomacy, consult Henry Giniger, *Diplomacy: How Nations Negotiate* (New York: Harper & Row, 1973); and Elmer Plischke, *Summit Diplomacy* (Westport, Conn.: Greenwood Press, 1958), and *Conduct of American Diplomacy*, 3rd ed. (Princeton, N.J.: Van Nos-trand, 1967).

prise ambassadors and ministers respectively. These diplomats are accredited (of-
ficially presented) to the head of the host state. The third category is made up of
chargés d'affaires. These lower-rank diplomats are accredited to the foreign minister (or secretary of state) of the host state. The establishment of diplomatic
relations between governments is not automatic. It can only take place subsequent to the *mutual consent* of the governments involved. Ambassadors and ministers represent the head of state of the sending state and are received by the head
of state of the host state.

There is a fundamental rule in diplomacy that high-ranking envoys must
be acceptable to the authorities of the host state. The host state issues a document
called the *agrément* (consent), which signifies the acceptability of a proposed chief
of mission. The host state may withhold the *agrément* without giving any formal
reasons for the unacceptability of a certain diplomat. Usually, the host state inves-
tigates the background of a designated diplomat to establish whether he or she
has been involved in any activities that are contrary to the interests of the host
state or that might otherwise create mutual embarrassment and friction. Upon
arrival at a new post, the ambassador-designate presents a *letter of credence* to the
head of state of the host country in a brief ceremony referred to as the *presentation
of credentials.* After this step is completed, the ambassador (the chief of the sending
state's diplomatic agencies in the host country) is now considered fully accredited
and is free to engage in formal diplomatic activities in the host country.

Over the centuries, a legal fiction has developed that the ambassador, his
or her premises, and the surrounding property are to be viewed as small islands
of sovereignty of the sending state in the capital of the host state. This status has
been supported by the principle of extraterritoriality. In recent years, however,
the practice of extraterritoriality has been weakened, and diplomatic premises
and personnel have returned to a status of relative dependency on the host state.
The turbulent and frustrating events (1979–81) surrounding the hostage-taking
of American embassy personnel in Teheran, Iran, have dramatized the need to
clarify the status of diplomatic missions throughout our planet, as well as protect
them more effectively.

All diplomats enjoy certain privileges and immunities, however. Duly accredited diplomats are exempt from the host state's criminal and civil jurisdiction, as well as from all host-state taxation. Embassies are supposed to be immune
from searches and other intrusive acts by the authorities of the host state. Diplomats are, however, expected to comply voluntarily with the host state's laws and
regulations. If they become involved in boisterous or violent behavior, they may
be restrained, temporarily detained, and eventually deported to the authorities
of the sending state, which are ultimately responsible for prosecuting them. Further, if diplomats become involved in private-business and investment activities
not related to their official duties, they are liable to taxation and legal suit under
the host state's laws.

Related to the diplomatic function is the consular function and derivative services. Consular functions (codified in the Vienna Convention on Consular
Relations, 1963) include processing and issuing entry and exit visas and certifi-

United States Embassy, Berne, Switzerland. (Berne Tourist Association)

cates of all types, facilitating commercial and other activities related to investment, processing ships' papers, and providing information about the sending
state to all interested parties. Consuls and their staffs are not exempted from
host-state jurisdiction as comprehensively as diplomats, but they too retain immu-
nity from taxation and are exempt from host-state jurisdiction in performing
their official duties.

The extent of the inviolability of the ambassador, staff, and embassy facilities is a function of the warmth or coolness of relations between countries and
the relative tension or détente that is prevalent in the international system at a
given time. For example, counterespionage policies may require that envoys from
an unfriendly nation-state be subject to travel restrictions (in order to prevent
them from visiting areas where there are strategic military and industrial installations) and even be followed, have their telephones tapped, and have their personal effects secretly searched.

THE FUNCTIONS OF DIPLOMATIC MISSIONS

The functions of diplomatic and consular missions range from routine activities
to difficult decisions—made usually with minimal instructions—during times of
crisis. Routine functions include registering the births, deaths, and marriages of
citizens of the sending state residing in the host state; issuing, validating, and
replacing passports; demanding the extradition of criminals claimed to be under
the jurisdiction of the sending state; and generally affording protection to the
person, property, and other interests of citizens of the sending state. A sizable
portion of routine activities consists of social and ceremonial affairs, such as

luncheons, benefits, cocktail parties, ground-breaking ceremonies, and parties hosted by important members of the local government as well as by other embassies in the diplomatic community.

The substantive functions of a diplomatic mission are *reporting* and *negotiating*. *Reporting* involves the observation of the political, economic, military, and social conditions of the host country and the accurate transmission of findings to the home office. Basically, what is reported home could be called *intelligence*. Economic attachés, for example, will send reports to their home offices containing general information on the balance of payments and trade, growth rates, inflation, and unemployment of the host state. If they represent Western trade- and investment-oriented countries, they will pay special attention to investment opportunities, contractual terms offered locally, and the possible development and stimulation of new markets for the sending state's export industries.

Political officers' reports focus on the structures, processes, and personalities of political parties and movements in the host country. Further, they assess the relative electoral strength (in Western-style democracies) or the political influence (in authoritarian systems) of various parties, personalities, and factions. Naturally, the attitudes and projected policies of each of these political parties or factions toward the sending state are of vital importance. In other words, reporting diplomats must assess the friendliness or hostility of the various political groupings toward their home state, and the power potential of each party or movement.

The nature and the intensity of military reporting depends on the strategic location of the host state and on whether its government is considered friendly, neutral, or potentially hostile to the interests of the sending state. Whatever the case, the diplomat attempts to develop relatively accurate assessments of the military intentions and capabilities as well as the strategic importance of the host state. Military attachés are usually involved in gathering information about the host state's military force; the quality of its military leadership; the nature, condition, and source of military equipment; and related information. One would expect military-intelligence reports to include photographs of new weapons systems exhibited in military parades, pictures of strategic military installations, and depictions of other tactical sites, such as bridges, factories, air and seaport facilities, shelter areas, and traffic-control points.

Social, cultural, and educational reporting is assuming increasing importance and is usually carried out to the extent that it relates to political, economic, and military affairs. For instance, reports about religious activities and youth affairs are sometimes of great potential importance to political analysis.[4] Information about class structures and statuses, vital statistics, and ethnic-, religious-, and social-group activities is of potential importance to political, economic, and military analysis.

---

[4]The impact of religion in countries such as Iran, Poland, and El Salvador has been self-evident. University students have also been a potent group in a number of Third World countries.

Diplomats of different nation-states engage one another frequently, at luncheons, at meetings, or even in casual conversations at cocktail parties and other social functions given by important personalities of the host state. As soon as possible after important discussions, they compose what is known as a *memorandum of conversation,* which is either filed or transmitted in cable form to the diplomat's home office. An effort is made in such documents to reflect the attitudes of one's conversational partner, his or her personal likes and dislikes, political allies and opponents, and noticeable mannerisms and idiosyncrasies. The result is a mountain of information—usually referred to as raw intelligence—which has to be sorted, verified, analyzed, evaluated, and synthesized into an estimate of the host country's political situation. Information gathering can be and is conducted both overtly and covertly. When it is conducted overtly, it is called diplomatic reporting. When it is conducted covertly, it is impolitely but accurately called spying—a subject that we shall discuss in the next chapter.

Negotiating is the second substantive function of diplomats. It involves, for the greatest part, the transmission of messages between the foreign ministries of the sending and the host states. Regardless of the nature of a given message, much depends on the manner and style in which it is delivered. A negative message, for example, can be variously interpreted, depending on the tone and medium of its delivery. Frequently, ambassadors or their subordinates do not adequately understand the acceptable manner and style of discussion and bargaining with agents of the host country. They thus arouse unnecessary hostility, which is more the result of their style of operation than the objectionable substance of their message. Often, badly briefed ambassadors fall into the trap of thinking about the host country in stereotypes. During periods of cold-war tension, for example, it is standard for both American and Soviet leaders and diplomats to assume that only tough talk is productive, that politeness will be interpreted as weakness, and that the only thing the other side understands and respects is force. Since the process of negotiations is central to both the policy and implementation levels of diplomacy, we shall return to it in greater detail in a later section of this chapter.

Customarily, a major restraint applies to all the activities of ambassadors and their staffs. This is the rule that envoys should not interfere in the internal affairs of host states. For example, diplomats are not supposed to pass judgment publicly on the internal policies of the host government or on the views of domestic opposition groups. In general, they are to avoid meddling in internal political, labor-management, church-state, student-professor, and other disputes. The principle of noninterference in internal affairs is easier stated, however, than defined or applied. It has often been bluntly violated, and in serious cases of interference a diplomat may be required by the host government to return to his or her country of origin within a few hours of being declared *persona non grata* (i.e., no longer acceptable as a diplomat by the host state).

The degree of real or apparent interference of a diplomatic mission in the internal affairs of the host country varies with the setting. The United States embassy in Moscow is relatively isolated from Soviet society, as is the Soviet Union's embassy in Beijing. In the instance of a client nation-state, however, an embassy may exert considerable local influence. The Soviet ambassador to the German Democratic Republic speaks for a major ally, and his or her views clearly receive careful consideration. A prudent diplomat will play a low-profile role and thereby avoid becoming the target of local politicians who seek to stigmatize a foreign embassy as the source of their country's problems.

In an international system consisting of states of diverse size and power, it is logical that the most powerful states will tend to interfere consciously in the affairs of smaller and dependent states. Further, as we shall see in the next chapter, the covert operations carried out by the various national intelligence agencies render claims of diplomatic noninterference in domestic affairs of host states quite inaccurate, if not hypocritical.

THE STRUCTURE AND INSTRUMENTS OF DIPLOMACY

Most nation-states carry out their formal diplomatic responsibilities through their foreign services. But with the industrial growth and technological complexity characteristic of the twentieth century, a progressively larger number of governmental agencies are becoming involved in the making and implementing of foreign policies. In the United States, for example, important foreign-policy decisions are made by the president after consultation with the National Security Council. The president weighs heavily the policy options presented by cabinet-level advisors, primarily those generated by the Departments of State and Defense. The information the president considers consists of integrated intelligence estimates prepared by intelligence-gathering agencies operating at home and abroad. The president must also be concerned with congressional advice and consent as well as with public opinion, as reflected in political parties, special-interest groups, and the mass media.

The responsibility for the implementation of United States foreign policy rests with the Department of State and the Foreign Service. Comparatively modest in size, the Department of State is organized in terms of both function (e.g., political-military, international-organization affairs) and geography. The department's representational activities are the mission of foreign-service officers (FSOs), of whom there are approximately three thousand. Most FSOs are assigned to one of the 141 embassies, 102 consular posts, or 10 missions, including the delegation to the United Nations. In addition to the Department of State, we should remember that other agencies, notably Agriculture, Commerce, Defense, Labor, and Treasury, offer extensive career opportunities in the field of foreign affairs.

Competition to enter the Foreign Service of the United States is keen, and annually an average of only two hundred new FSOs receive an appointment in the Department of State. Moreover, top posts often go to political appointees rather than to career officers. During the administration of President Ronald Reagan, one-third of the chiefs of mission were noncareer officers, a figure higher than in any administration for the past thirty years. This trend is unlikely to be reversed. As of 1979, 90 percent of all FSOs were men, and the Department of State is making a concerted effort to recruit women. At that time blacks constituted 3 percent of the FSOs, Hispanics 1 percent, and Asian-Americans one-half of 1 percent. Since 1979, the Foreign Service has improved on these percentages, but minority recruitment remains an area of concern in personnel policy.[5]

The staff of a United States embassy may vary in size from over a thousand in a world capital to a few individuals in a small state on the periphery of a zone of confrontation between major powers. A chief of a mission, usually with the rank of ambassador, serves as the personal representative of the president and as such is responsible for the administration of American foreign policy in the host country. The Department of State assigns to the embassy foreign-service officers who specialize in political and economic reporting, public affairs, and administration. The Departments of Agriculture, Commerce, Defense, Labor, and the Treasury augment the chief of mission's staff in their respective fields of expertise. The United States Information Agency (USIA) organizes cultural programs, disseminates news, administers educational exchanges, and usually maintains a library for the public. Finally, the responsibility for collecting and evaluating information affecting United States policy rests with the Central Intelligence Agency (CIA) and other members of the intelligence community.

The style, content, and instruments of the foreign policy of one state toward another are determined by its diplomatic relations with that state. If the relations between government A and government B are good, the diplomats of each adopt instruments of policy that reflect this atmosphere of cordiality. Positive instruments of diplomacy involve good-will gestures and propaganda emphasizing the strong relations between the two governments and their peoples. There are a number of economic rewards that government A can bestow upon a friendly government B, such as foreign aid (military and economic) through grants, loans, and low-priced sales; technical assistance; cooperative economic, social, and scientific projects; and exchanges of students, scientists, and other elites.

When relations between government A and government B worsen, diplomatic exchanges stiffen proportionately. Good-will gestures cease, and diplomatic speeches and actions begin to reflect disappointment with the "bad" government that is differentiated from the "good" people. Propaganda services now shift into high gear. A climate of suspicion—designed to influence the people and especially the opposition groups within the host state and to isolate and eventually remove its errant government—is methodically cultivated. Benign economic measures are discontinued. Government A, wishing to deter, punish, or isolate government B, may introduce a variety of economic and political sanc-

---

[5]For statistical references, see U.S., Congress, House, *The Foreign Service Act, Hearings before a Subcommittee of the Committee on Foreign Affairs and of the Committee on Post Office and Civil Service on H.R. 4674*, 96th Cong., 1st sess., 1979, pp. 246–47 and 738–45; and U.S., Department of State, *Key Officers of Foreign Service Posts*, Pubn. 7877 (May 1988). Sarah Booth Conroy has written a commentary on "Foreign Service Favors," in the *Washington Post*, July 24, 1988, pp. F1, F5.

tions. In the economic sphere, it may increase punitive tariffs, impose import and export quotas, institute selective or general trade embargoes and boycotts, freeze payments of outstanding loans, cancel planned investments, or induce other countries to join in an economic squeeze. (Chapter 9 is devoted to covert action organized by intelligence services, as well as economic and psychological warfare.)

The more the climate of hostility grows between government A and government B, the more their diplomats shed cooperative styles and adopt the roles of propagandists, agitators, plotters, and verbal warriors. Just before diplomacy yields to war, nation-states lower the profile of diplomatic relations, reduce the size of diplomatic missions, air their controversy before world organizations such as the United Nations, enter into offensive and defensive alliances against the hostile nation-state, and begin to mobilize economically and militarily for possible war. As we shall see in Chapters 10 and 11, negotiations continue even during times of war. But such negotiations are carried out—directly or through intermediaries—during truces or cease-fires, and their purpose is to arrange for short- and long-term peace settlements. There is, therefore, no single style characteristic of diplomats at all times. For the purposes of this chapter, we shall discuss diplomatic relations as they obtain during times of peace and relatively controlled levels of competition.

THE CHANGING SCOPE OF DIPLOMACY

The twentieth century has witnessed a technological revolution of unprecedented proportions. Rapid changes in transportation and communications have had, among other things, a deep impact on the scope and the process of diplomacy. In earlier centuries, when transportation and communications depended on the ship, the horse and carriage, and the carrier pigeon, ambassadors and their staffs might function for months without receiving instructions from their home offices. Understandably, they were afforded considerable leeway in reacting to host-state conditions and improvising from day to day the sending state's policies.

But it is sometimes argued that the telephone, telegraph, teletype, and computer, together with supersonic air transportation, have reduced the status of ambassadors to that of glorified clerks. Hot-line diplomacy—direct telephone or teletype links between heads of state—threatens to render ambassadors unnecessary, especially during times of great crisis. Further, the revolution in radio and television technology as well as in journalism has permitted an unprecedented degree of news exchange among nation-states. These developments have drastically affected the role of the diplomat in explaining the policies of his or her country before the audiences of another country.

Another phenomenon that has transformed the nature of traditional diplomacy is summit diplomacy and its variation, which became fashionable in the Nixon-Kissinger era, known as shuttle diplomacy. In summit diplomacy, broad agreements and important decisions are reached at the highest levels of government (between heads of state accompanied by their foreign ministers), and it remains for the ambassadors and their staffs to smooth out later the rough edges of the agreements. Further, in times of crisis, shuttle diplomacy (exemplified by Henry Kissinger's shuttling between the capitals of Egypt and Israel in the Middle East in the mid-1970s) is a rapid and effective alternative to the more cumbersome and formal traditional diplomatic process.

We might argue, then, that technological growth has reduced the importance of ambassadors and their staffs to practically marginal proportions. But a case can also be made to the contrary. In classical times, ambassadors acted as representatives of nation-states during ceremonial occasions and as transmitters of important messages in times of crisis. These messages usually involved threats, requests, or demands (or responses to demands) concerning territorial, commercial, and other disputes. Technology has added a vast array of new functions to the traditional responsibilities of diplomats. Now, ambassadors supervise a complex network of attachés, whose duties range from military and scientific operations to propaganda, cultural, educational, labor, commercial, financial, and political operations—not to mention covert intelligence operations. Consequently, we notice in diplomatic services a gradual shift from the hiring of generalists only toward the supplementary recruitment of specialists in areas such as economics, commerce, information management, and technology administration.

Much depends, even in our day, on the ability of ambassadors and on their managerial style in regard to their staff. Some ambassadors, for example, are *centralizers:* They insist that every report be brought to their evaluative attention. These ambassadors tend to minimize differences of opinion in the reports they receive, stifle staff initiatives, and discourage staff disagreements; they prefer a unified embassy line rather than majority and minority opinions. On the other hand, there are the *decentralizers*—ambassadors who prefer to delegate responsibilities widely and who encourage diversity of opinion in the reports they receive. Diplomats operating under such ambassadors are more likely to be involved in creative and self-satisfying activity than diplomats operating under the rigid supervision of the centralizers.

Some problems have arisen with respect to staffing embassies abroad. One of these is determining the utility of career foreign-service ambassadors versus the utility of political appointees.[6] A relatively large proportion (33 percent) of American ambassadors are politically appointed. In contrast, British ambassadors are drawn nearly uniformly from the ranks of career foreign-service officers. The primary advantage of political appointees (who are usually recruited from business, Congress, the government agencies, and academia) is their ready access to the chief executive who appointed them. The main disadvantage is their lack of firsthand experience regarding the operations of an embassy abroad. The rec-

---

[6]On the question of utilization of noncareer ambassadors in the American Foreign Service, see Bruce M. Lancaster, "Non-career Ambassadors: Their Antecedents, Service Abroad and Subsequent Professional Lives (1950–1969)" (unpublished Ph.D. dissertation, American University, 1974).

ord has thus far been inconclusive on this subject. Successful ambassadors have been drawn from career foreign service as well as from the ranks of the politically appointed.

Another difficult problem faced frequently is whether ambassadors and their senior advisors should possess deep and specialized knowledge about the host country or whether they should be "generalists," concerned about the global responsibilities of their home state. The specialists tend to "go native" and to exaggerate the importance of their host country without concern for global policy implications. The generalists, on the other hand, tend to understand rather superficially the conditions of their host country and to alienate local elites with their apparent ignorance of the country's language, history, and culture. The ideal appointee, of course, should combine intimate knowledge of the host country with a global orientation.

A very controversial problem relates to the utility of women serving in diplomatic posts overseas. As we indicated above, fewer than 10 percent of American diplomats are women. This figure compares favorably, however, with those of other countries. The standard arguments against the employment of women as diplomats—they tend to get married, become pregnant, and leave the service; or they tend to have marital troubles, since their husbands refuse to be considered their "dependents" and to bounce about the world from post to post—could easily be called sexist. A standard response to these arguments is that diplomats—whether men or women—can remain single, or they can marry highly mobile and employable individuals, such as doctors, journalists, writers, artists, secretaries, and fellow diplomats.

Finally, a developing problem is that the lives of diplomats are not entirely risk-free in contemporary times, notwithstanding the comprehensive system of immunities protecting them. The rise in the incidence of political terrorism has taken its toll among ambassadors and other diplomats, who have become targets of kidnappings, hijackings, assassination attempts, bombings, and other forms of intimidation practiced by various insurgent groups. The crisis that surrounded the hostage taking of United States diplomatic personnel in Teheran symbolizes the seriousness of the changing patterns in diplomatic intercourse.

SECRET VERSUS OPEN DIPLOMACY

Harold Nicolson, probably the most quoted student of diplomatic activity, divides diplomacy into two separate functions: foreign-policy making (statecraft) and negotiations.[7] He recommends that foreign-policy making is properly left to elected politicians and that it should reflect public needs and pressures. He is quite concerned, however, that the art of negotiation (that is, the effective implementation of established policies toward other states) be left to diplomatic professionals, who understand the peculiarities of international interaction and who have the

---

[7]See Nicolson, *Diplomacy.*

type of personality that contributes to successful negotiations. In short, policy making should ideally be subject to democratic controls, but the execution of policy should be left to trained and politically independent experts.

According to Nicolson, policy making should never be *secret*. Consider these durable remarks of his, which are over fifty years old but retain their freshness to our day:

> No system should ever again be tolerated which can commit men and women, without their knowledge or consent, to obligations which will entail upon them, either a breach of national good faith, or the sacrifice of their property and lives.[8]

There is considerable debate regarding the advantages and disadvantages of secretly formulated versus publicly debated foreign-policy making. The major advantage of public policy making is that the people can act as a check and balance to the whims or excesses of powerful individual policy makers. But the reverse may also be true: Public opinion, once excited, may prod otherwise prudent policy makers to adopt adventurist policies entailing great risks. Those arguing for policies arrived at secretly by experts point out that public debates tend to deprive nation-states of the advantages of swift decision making, thereby all but eliminating the important element of surprise in political and military action. Their critics respond that in the nuclear age, "advantages" such as secrecy, uncertainty, and surprise merely compound suspicion and thereby increase the probability of diplomatic miscalculation and nuclear holocaust. Making quick decisions, except in crisis situations involving defense against external attack, is not necessarily a virtue, argue these critics. Time affords decision makers the opportunity to balance the virtues and vices of different options and to predict as best they can the consequences of the preferred course of action, as well as the impact of policies pursued on the rest of the world.

A key criticism of publicly discussed and derived policies is that they tend to be imprecise rather than specific, and that when an attempt is made to cast them in a moralistic light (in order to satisfy public opinion) they end up being merely hypocritical. The resulting policies are umbrellalike slogans such as "Peace in our time," "Self-determination for peoples everywhere," and "Noninterference in the internal affairs of others." The response to this argument is that public debate helps sharpen and improve policies, and that the main purpose of publicly debated policies is to prevent the involvement of unchecked and unaccountable leaders in dubious foreign adventures that can have deadly consequences.

Most of the scholarly opinion in the United States supports Nicolson's preference for publicly debated policy making. In addition, however, the majority of scholars oppose publicly aired and scrutinized negotiations. Most observers argue that effective negotiations are not possible under the glaring light of press

---

[8]Nicolson, "The 'Old' and the 'New' Diplomacy," p. 426.

and television coverage or in conference-style settings such as the United Nations. The usual result of public confrontations among diplomatic representatives, they allege, is a maximum of posturing and a minimum of compromising. Negotiations can be compared to the situation of a small man who has the choice of being confronted by a heavyweight bully either in a crowded bar or in a deserted alley. In the bar, with other people watching, it would be difficult for the man to back down or to run away without being publicly shamed. In the alley, on the other hand, the weaker man's thoughts would revolve around how well and how quickly he could apologize or how effectively he could run, climb, or hide.

Nicolson recommends strongly that negotiations (as opposed to foreign-policy making) be carried out exclusively by seasoned professional diplomats rather than by politicians. Politicians, argues Nicolson, are frequently trained as trial lawyers; consequently, they exhibit an adversary and combative mentality. Politicians like to play the grandstand. They like to win cases, to score points, to trap and checkmate their opponents, to debate and outclass the other side, and to impress judges and juries. Frequently, politicians find themselves inadequately informed about foreign cultures and outlooks; their views are understandably parochial in that they are oriented to their constituency. Assuming that this portrait is accurate, we can assert that the characteristics of politicians and courtroom lawyers do not make for successful negotiations. The object of negotiations is not victory but a viable, acceptable, and preferably favorable compromise. The successful negotiator, therefore, is more likely to be the pliable diplomat than the adversary politician. Diplomats, by training and personality, are often indifferent if not opposed to public recognition and applause. They have studied and experienced foreign cultures closely. They tend to dislike controversy, avoid publicity, and take enough time to study policy options carefully before applying them to problem situations.

In summary, foreign-policy making should be an open and publicly accountable process carried out by politicians with the advice and support of seasoned diplomats. Negotiations, in contrast, should be carried out privately and discreetly by trained diplomats, and should promote the goals established by policy makers.

PROFILES OF THE EFFECTIVE DIPLOMAT

A late-sixteenth-century European conception of the successful ambassador would disqualify most diplomats of our day. An ambassador, according to this conception,

> should be a trained theologian, should be well versed in Aristotle and Plato, and should be able at a moment's notice to solve the most abstruse problems in correct dialectical form; he should also be expert in mathematics, architecture, music, physics, and civil and canon law. He should speak and write Latin fluently and must also be proficient in Greek, Spanish, French, German, and Turkish.

> While being a trained classical scholar, an historian, a geographer, and an expert in military science, he must also have a cultured taste for poetry. And above all he must be of excellent family, rich, and endowed with a fine physical presence.[9]

Times have changed considerably since the sixteenth century, and so have the requirements for the contemporary diplomat who represents and protects his or her country's interests overseas. According to Nicolson, seven qualities are indispensable for successful ambassadors: truthfulness, precision, calmness, good temper, patience, modesty, and loyalty.[10] Truthfulness is essential because it contributes to a good reputation, which enhances an ambassador's long-range credibility and subsequent effectiveness. Precision involves what Nicolson calls intellectual and moral accuracy. Intellectual accuracy is the faithful depiction of the reality perceived by the ambassador. Moral accuracy is the ability of ambassadors to express their views and interpretations boldly and to avoid providing the home office with equivocal, ambiguous, or politically agreeable reports. Calmness, good temper, and patience permit ambassadors to maintain the detachment and precision of true professionals. Nicolson argues that the worst kind of diplomats are those with fanatic or missionary temperaments; the best are reasonable and humane skeptics. Modesty is a central quality: All good diplomats should studiously avoid vanity and should not be flattered by or, worse, boast about their diplomatic victories and successes. In fact, they should try to play down even genuine successes and let them appear as fair compromises. Finally, ambassadors must be loyal to their governments, their ministries, their own staffs, their fellow ambassadors, and, to a certain degree, the host country. Their highest loyalty, naturally, should be reserved for their country's overall foreign-policy objectives.

In addition to these seven primary qualities, Nicolson takes for granted that effective ambassadors must possess qualities such as intelligence, imagination, knowledge, discernment, prudence, hospitality, charm, industry, courage, and, of course, tact.

By synthesizing these prerequisites, we can construct a set of guidelines for effective diplomats:

1. Suppress personal likes and dislikes; think only of national interests, as defined in the policy directives of your government.
2. Implement executive instructions faithfully, regardless of your personal assessment of the wisdom of these instructions. If you seriously disagree with your government's policy, seek reassignment or resign, if necessary, so that you can legitimately add your voice in public policy criticism.
3. Understand the needs and interests of the host country without losing sight of your own country's overall policy objectives.
4. Recognize and assess public opinion, but do not be entrapped by it.
5. Do not dramatize your reports merely to attract high-level attention at home and abroad—or just for the sake of good prose.

[9]This quotation is based on Ottaviano Maggi's formula for the preferred qualifications of an ambassador, contained in his *De Legato* (1596). Translated by and quoted in Nicolson, *Diplomacy*, p. 56.
[10]Nicolson, *Diplomacy*, pp. 55–67.

6. Do not be oversuspicious.
7. Do not act only for the time frame of your incumbency as ambassador; think also of your successors.
8. Do not be contemptuous of the host country's customs and traditions or of the constraints resulting from protocol.

Nicolson concludes much of his work with the optimistic assertion that diplomats of the twentieth century have improved considerably over the predatory diplomats of the sixteenth and seventeenth centuries. Back then, writes Nicolson, "they bribed courtiers; they stimulated and financed rebellions; they encouraged opposition parties; they intervened in the most subversive ways in the internal affairs of the countries to which they were accredited; they lied, they spied, they stole."[11] In the light of persistent revelations about the covert activities of various intelligence services that operate at times under diplomatic cover, Nicolson's conclusions appear to be overly hopeful, if not utopian. Convinced of the superiority in the long run of moral diplomacy over immoral practices, Nicolson may have been too eager in equating his own recommendations with reality.

Given their idiosyncrasies, styles, and methods, diplomats have not always escaped criticism. Critics argue, for example, that diplomats tend to acquire an excessively internationalist frame of mind. They become skeptical and even cynical about their own country and its culture, ideology, and values. They develop a special affinity for diplomats of other nation-states, and they invariably tend to be contemptuous of politicians and the press, who in their view thrive on sensationalizing situations they do not understand. To put it less elegantly, diplomats tend to be, by training and mentality, skeptical of democracy and its much-touted virtues.

Another frequent criticism of diplomats is lethargy—a tendency to avoid initiative and to let problems simmer on. Diplomats, according to this criticism, prefer to adopt a conservative and fatalistic mentality. They adopt the style of gardeners rather than that of engineers.[12] Gardeners are *organicists:* They assume the existence of a certain and *natural* way of things and merely try to affect it at its fringes. Engineers, in contrast, believe in finding finite solutions to finite problems. They want to move mountains, procure the building materials, cut the trees, pave the roads, and generally order things from above. For them, *nature* can be fundamentally controlled by the will of those who understand it.

In our opinion, the lethargy and organicism that allegedly characterize diplomats may at times be blessings in disguise. So-called drastic and final solutions in politics, whether domestic or international, frequently lead to different and sometimes greater problems. So the diplomatic style of slow and cautious activity, the attitude of seeing events in relative rather than absolute terms, the instinctive opposition to certainty and moral superiority of any kind—these may all be important and useful traits in successful negotiators.

[11]*Ibid.*, p. 20.
[12]This analogy is presented most eloquently in the works of George F. Kennan. See, for example, his *Realities of American Foreign Policy* (Princeton, N.J.: Princeton University Press, 1954), p. 92.

THE PREVALENT PROFILE OF EFFECTIVE STATECRAFT

As we have already suggested, the temperaments of diplomats tend to be quite different from those of politicians. We shall now turn to the latter, given the fact that they are primarily involved—backed by sizable diplomatic staffs—in the foreign-policy-making process.

If we are uncertain as to whether truthfulness or duplicity better serves a diplomat's professional objectives, this uncertainty usually vanishes at the higher levels of statecraft. For the statesman and stateswoman, the ultimate criterion for action is the survival and prosperity of the state. A national leader will employ truthfulness to the degree that it serves the state and duplicity to the degree that it serves the state. Niccolò Machiavelli prescribed long ago the formulas for the different mixtures of righteousness and deviousness that are appropriate responses to constantly shifting political fortunes. In a memorable passage that transcends all time, he advises rulers: "It is well *to seem* merciful, faithful, humane, sincere, religious, and also *to be* so; but you must have the mind so disposed that when it is needful to be otherwise you may be able to change to the opposite qualities."[13]

Machiavelli, the intellectual father of contemporary realism, believed that the highest objective of leadership should be the protection of the state. The ends of the state, therefore, justify its means, whether these means are moral or immoral. Many generations of leaders have since read and probably obeyed Machiavelli's aphorisms:

1. The "good" prince (i.e., leader) must avoid being despicable and hated.
2. The best fortress for a state and its prince is the love of the people.
3. It is safer to be feared than loved, but it is best to be feared as well as loved.
4. The "good" prince should abstain from taking the property of others, for men forget more easily the death of their father than the loss of their patrimony.
5. It is better to trust in your own power than in the good will of others.
6. Legislate good laws and back them with good arms.
7. Laws are the way of men and force is the way of beasts, but you cannot rely on law only.
8. Imitate the fox and the lion. The fox is shrewd and cunning, the lion is strong and brave. If you have to be one or the other, it is better to be a fox.
9. Do not put your trust in mercenaries, for they can easily be bought by your adversaries.
10. Be prudent. Prudence is the ability of knowing the nature of the difficulties and taking that which is least harmful as good.[14]

Over the centuries, Machiavelli's flexible and amoral outlook has been characteristic of rulers. A well-known leader in the Machiavellian mold is former

---

[13]Niccolò Machiavelli, *The Prince,* trans. Ricci-Vincent (Woodbury, N.Y.: Barron, 1975), p. 107 (emphasis supplied).

[14]This list is a synthesis of direct quotations and paraphrased material from the original text as translated by Ricci-Vincent in *ibid.*

Henry A. Kissinger (1923–   ), professor, political scientist, U.S. national security advisor (1969–1977), and secretary of state (1973–1977). (U.S. State Department)

U.S. Secretary of State Henry Kissinger. We could call Kissinger's career a study in *realpolitik*. The essence of a realpolitician's world view is measured pessimism. The world is seen as heading for catastrophe, and the task of diplomacy is to postpone it. Damage is almost inevitable, and the diplomat's major task is to limit it to tolerable proportions. Leaders must be pragmatic rather than idealistic; they must be secretive and flexible and must view themselves as mere catalysts rather than controllers of change. Above all, they must understand and accept "force" as the elemental ingredient of history. In Kissinger's own words, "Much as we deplore it, most major historical changes have been brought about to a greater or lesser degree by the threat or the use of *force*."[15] Applying this abstract principle to the Middle East crisis of October, 1973, Kissinger interpreted the situation something like this: "I hope we get a *military solution* quickly and then we can work on a *diplomatic solution*. You cannot have a diplomatic solution until you get a military solution."[16]

Kissinger believed that policy makers, unlike lower-level diplomats, should be completely free of the bureaucratic mentality. They should be imaginative and mentally agile and should possess a keen sense of timing and the "killer instinct." They should know, in other words, the exact location of their oppo-

[15]Henry Kissinger, *The Necessity for Choice: Prospects of American Foreign Policy* (New York: Harper & Row, 1961), p. 170. For a scholarly review of Kissinger's profile, see Harvey Starr, *Henry Kissinger: Perceptions of International Politics* (Lexington: University Press of Kentucky, 1984).

[16]Marvin Kalb and Bernard Kalb, in *Kissinger* (Boston: Little, Brown, 1974), p. 479 (emphasis supplied), have provided an interesting and generally favorable biography of the former secretary of state. The above quotation is presented in their book as Vice-President Gerald Ford's expression of Kissinger's outlook.

nents' political jugular vein. An opportunity to settle problems or to gain diplomatic points knocks only once. Once such opportunities are missed, they are lost forever.

The job of the policy maker (especially if he or she is in a position to define the interests of a great power) is to help the international system to attain a stable state of balance. To do this, according to Kissinger, leaders must be cunning and patient:

> They must be able to manipulate events and people. They must play the power game in total secrecy, unconstrained by parliaments which lack the temperament for diplomacy. They must connive with the largest possible number of allies. They must not be afraid to use force when necessary, to maintain order. They must avoid ironclad rules of conduct; an occasional show of "credible irrationality" may be instructive. They must not shy away from duplicity, cynicism, or unscrupulousness, all of which are acceptable tools for statecraft. They must never burn their bridges behind them. And if possible they must always be charming, clever, and visible.[17]

Zbigniew Brzezinski, who served as national security affairs advisor under President Jimmy Carter, echoed the sentiments of Henry Kissinger in testimony before the Senate Governmental Affairs Committee. He spoke of the need for "some degree" of "duplicity of intent" in diplomatic maneuvering. Explaining his view to some of the startled senators, Brzezinski added: "At some times when you are pursuing an objective . . . you cannot state openly what your objective is." For example, he added, "We may seek to improve relations with country A, as a means of putting pressure on country B, but it would be impossible to acknowledge that openly." The "awesome dangers of the nuclear age," according to Brzezinski, "have put a further premium on the rapidity of response, on the centrality of decision making, on the covertness of some needed actions, and even on some degree of duplicity in the area of publicly proclaimed intent." Brzezinski admitted that these characteristics of action clearly run into conflict with the traditional requisites of democracy. But, he concluded, "While duplicity in foreign affairs is publicly treated as out of bounds, it exists in the real world of diplomacy."[18]

Idealist critics consistently question the realpoliticians' credo of power without purpose, unrestrained by principle. They also object to the realists' artificial separation of prudence and morality. In fact, the idealists argue, principled rather than predatory behavior is the most prudent behavior. The realists respond that moral principles, as constraining rules of conduct, are and should be irrelevant to but not necessarily excluded by realist behavior. For the realist, the *only* operative principle is the survival and prosperity of the state and its people. Survival, in a system that is close to being an international jungle, is purpose

---

[17]Quoted in Kissinger's *The Necessity for Choice*, p. 47. Note that policy making in the Kissinger style is much more secretive than that advocated by Harold Nicolson and discussed earlier in this chapter.

[18]Testimony given on July 31, 1984. See "Duplicity Called Useful in Diplomacy," *Washington Post*, August 1, 1984, p. A 22.

enough. The method of attaining it is a pragmatic concoction of force, bribery, cooperation, and persuasion: The great leaders of the world cajole, pressure, urge, implore, warn, promise, threaten, and plead their way into yet one more day of "security" for their country.

This debate among realists and idealists will probably continue for some time, and basic questions about the purpose of statecraft will puzzle future generations. Is political survival as the sole purpose of statecraft adequate? Should survival not be qualified somewhat? Survival, after all, to what purpose and by what means? Should it be survival in honor or dishonor? Should it be survival with growth, with freedom, with justice, with glory, with humiliation, or what? Realpoliticians are content to stop at survival per se; the rest is a luxury. And for them, people who die for the sake of honor or in defense of a set of principles or ideals are no more than just plain dead.

The policy maker, according to Kissinger, must also exhibit a certain amount of arrogance—or, more politely, immense self-confidence. That person alone, sitting at the pinnacle of power, can make the momentous decisions that move masses of people and machines and account for the zigzags of destiny. Kissinger's semicontemptuous attitude toward America's foreign-policy bureaucracy is typical of this outlook. Kissinger is supposed to have voiced his sentiments toward bureaucrats as follows: "There are twenty thousand people in the State Department and fifty thousand in Defense. . . . They need each other's clearances in order to move . . . and they all want to do what I'm doing. So the problem becomes: How do you get them to push papers around, spin their wheels, so that you can get your work done?"[19]

In the last analysis, we must not forget that different leaders with radically different idiosyncrasies fulfill the duties of statecraft in radically different fashions. We must not, therefore, assume that the realpolitical profile sketched above is the exclusive method or model of operation for all policy makers. It would be safe to assume, however, that this profile probably suits the majority of foreign-policy makers.

DIPLOMACY: A SYNTHESIS OF REALISM AND IDEALISM?

In summary, it appears that the major functions of diplomacy have been to establish and maintain communications and to negotiate and bargain for tolerable agreements and other arrangements between sovereign centers of decision making in the international system. This system, as we point out throughout this book, is a political system in primitive form. In contrast, the process of govern-

---

[19]Quoted in Kalb and Kalb, *Kissinger,* p. 90. The reader should contrast this cynical view with Henry Kissinger's highly laudatory words regarding the professionals in the Foreign Service (see p. 132). The contrast provides a good illustration of the impact of *role variables* on one's manner and substance of expression. Then Henry Kissinger was praising foreign-service officers in his capacity of secretary of state. In this instance he was criticizing the bureaucracy while serving as a Harvard professor and prior to assuming a cabinet position.

ment within well-developed nation-states is highly institutionalized and rule-bound. Intragovernmental disagreements are therefore quite likely to be settled effectively and conclusively by legitimate high-level political and judicial organs. For example, in the Watergate affair in the United States, deep divisions and fundamental disputes between the chief executive (Richard Nixon) on the one hand and significant congressional groups, the press, and the public on the other hand had reached explosive proportions. The dispute was eventually resolved by a mix of executive, legislative, and judicial processes involving the U.S. Supreme Court and the relevant lower courts, congressional investigating and impeachment committees, and the Office of the Special Prosecutor (part of the Department of Justice).

Fortunately or unfortunately, depending on one's point of view, major disputes among nation-states can be settled only by diplomacy, an admittedly primitive political process relying on mixtures of threats and persuasion during negotiations and war. Diplomats perform the basic functions of regulation in the nearly anarchic international system.[20] Yet despite the primitiveness of this system, its agents (the diplomats of nation-states) are expected to abide by certain rules that promote the rational conduct of diplomacy.[21] Hans Morgenthau has offered us four such rules, which, in our view, help close the gap between ultra-realists and utopian idealists respectively.[22]

First, diplomacy must be divested of the crusading spirit. Diplomats who act as crusaders for higher causes (whether these be moralistic, legalistic, or ideological) cease to be pragmatic and flexible and may impede the process of negotiation and lock themselves into belligerent and uncompromising stances. It is nearly impossible for crusaders and other fighters for "truth" to compromise their principles without seriously embarrassing themselves.

Second, the objectives of foreign policy must be defined in terms of national interest and must be supported with adequate power. This rule qualifies and clarifies the previous one. If the diplomats are to avoid the crusading stance, what are they to do? The answer is that whether or not they are involved in the formulation or the implementation of policy, they must present their positions on the basis of the national interests (strategic, economic, and political) of their countries, and no more. They must, that is, avoid acting sentimentally, promoting the interests of a third nation-state or group, being motivated by hatred or spite, and, finally, seeking to promote the interests of a particular pressure group within their own

[20]Roger D. Masters refers to the present international system as a type of primitive political system involving independent units of decision making, the use of force as a means of bargaining and settling disputes, the lack of central and authoritative institutions of government, and in general a low level of institutionalization. See his "World Politics as a Primitive Political System," in *International Politics and Foreign Policy,* ed. James N. Rosenau, 2nd ed. rev. (New York: Free Press, 1969), pp. 104–18.

[21]The word *rational,* as used here, is nearly synonymous with prudent. In other words, rational behavior is behavior that maximizes the chances of survival of one's nation-state (or political collectivity), maximizes the servicing of one's national interests within tolerable limits of cost and risk, and minimizes the volume of tolerable damage to those interests.

[22]See Hans J. Morgenthau, *Politics among Nations: The Struggle for Power and Peace,* 5th ed. (New York: Knopf, 1973), pp. 540–48.

country. But defining objectives in terms of the national interest is not enough. One's diplomatic hand ought to be fortified with adequate power, which includes, perhaps primarily, military force and economic capability. To define national interests that are beyond one's country's power to achieve is to court either ridicule or defeat and destruction at the hands of more powerful opponents.

Third, diplomacy must look at the political scene from the point of view of other nations. Defining foreign-policy objectives in terms of one's own national interests is inadequate in diplomacy. Most of the time, one's interests can best be served only at the expense of the interests of someone else. It is important, then, for prudent diplomats to develop a very good understanding of the interests and perceptions of foreign nation-states. The threat of war is magnified when conflicting and vital interests of two nation-states intersect. It is the task of diplomats to defuse such situations and to avoid war by using techniques of bargaining and compromise. To return briefly to an analogy, when rats are involved in disputes they settle them with fierce violence, for they can accept only victory or death. Mice, on the other hand, allow themselves a third alternative between total victory and total defeat—compromise. Diplomats, as a minimum, should emulate mice in this respect and avoid the behavior of rats.

Fourth, nations must be willing to compromise on all issues that are not vital to them. We must look at this rule with great care, for much depends on what we mean by the word *vital.* For instance, we could arbitrarily call vital anything from defending one's territory and system of government to securing lucrative markets and military bases abroad to continuing one's imperial and semicolonial presence in distant territories. To offer an example, the deposed (in 1974) Portuguese government of Marcello Caetano considered the maintenance of the status quo in Portugal's African colonies vital. It therefore fought a protracted antiguerrilla war in order to maintain Portuguese control over these colonies. The revolutionary regime that assumed power in April 1974 decided, in contrast, that this war was counterproductive, that the maintenance of colonial control in places such as Guinea-Bissau, Angola, and Mozambique was anything but vital. This shift resulted in the granting of independence to the Portuguese colonies. Likewise, America's objectives and interests in South Vietnam were considered vital by the Johnson and early Nixon administrations, but not so vital in the later phases of the Nixon/Kissinger/Ford foreign-policy calculations. So the question remains: Who is going to define and interpret the word *vital* for us? A given government at a given time, wise men and women in academia, a computer (programmed by mortal human beings), or an abstract entity signifying the collective will and presumed to be public opinion?

We should also ponder the possible results of the use of Morgenthau's fourth rule by great powers confronting one another in this nuclear era. If, say, the Soviet Union and the United States were to find themselves locked in acute controversy over what both perceive to be vital interests, according to our interpretation of this rule they *must not* compromise. If they do not compromise, they may escalate into war. A conventional war might escalate further into nuclear war, which might entail mutual suicide and the destruction of our planet. We suggest, therefore, that Morgenthau's fourth rule be seriously reconsidered in this nuclear era. The option of "no compromise" might just be the luxury of a bygone era. After all, there is nothing more vital than life itself. In the end, it may take mutual compromise on vital issues to secure mutual survival.

SUGGESTIONS FOR FURTHER STUDY

Graham T. Allison, Jr., has speculated on the element of personality in summit diplomacy in "Testing Gorbachev," *Foreign Affairs,* 67 (Fall 1988), 18–32. For opposing views of American diplomacy, see Smith Simpson, *The Crisis in Diplomacy: Shots across the Bow of the State Department* (North Quincy, Mass.: Christopher Publishing, 1980); and Andrew L. Steigman, *The Foreign Service of the United States: First Line of Defense* (Boulder, Colo.: Westview Press, 1985). I. William Zartman and Maureen Berman have identified credibility as a key to success in the peaceful resolution of disputes in *The Practical Negotiator* (New Haven: Yale University Press, 1982). The multidimensional meaning of the word *diplomacy* is reflected in the extensive literature on the subject. In Charles Kingsley Webster, *The Art and Practice of Diplomacy* (New York: Barnes & Noble, 1962), the dominant theme is statecraft. Maureen R. Berman and Joseph E. Johnson extend the meaning of diplomacy to nonstate actors in their edited work *Unofficial Diplomats* (New York: Columbia University Press, 1977). The political accountability of diplomats receives careful attention in Thomas M. Franck and Edward Weisband, *Foreign Policy and Congress* (New York: Oxford University Press, 1979); and the suggestion that diplomacy should be open comes under scrutiny in Richard L. Merritt, "Public Perspective in Closed Societies," in *Foreign Policy Analysis,* ed. Richard L. Merritt (Lexington, Mass.: D. C. Heath, 1975). Elmer Plischke has provided an indispensable reference volume in the *Conduct of American Diplomacy,* 3rd ed. (Princeton, N.J.: Van Nostrand, 1967), and his anthology on *Modern Diplomacy: The Art and the Artisans* (Washington, D.C.: American Enterprise Institute, 1979) encompasses the insights of leading commentators on the American experience. Burton M. Sapin has written a classic study on the relationship of structure to the diplomatic process in *The Making of United States Foreign Policy* (New York: Praeger, 1966). In *Presidents, Secretaries of State, and Crisis Management in U.S. Foreign Relations: A Model and Predictive Analysis* (Boulder, Colo.: Westview Press, 1978), Lawrence S. Falkowski has developed a useful paradigm for the study of conflict resolution. In *How To Be a Delegate* (Washington, D.C.: Foreign Service Institute, U.S. Department of State, 1984), John W. McDonald, Jr., has collected maxims that enable the student to appreciate the practical side of diplomacy. Finally, a deep insight into the style and substance of diplomatic operations and dispatches may be gained in John O. Iatrides, ed., *Ambassador MacVeagh Reports: Greece, 1933–1947* (Princeton, N.J.: Princeton University Press, 1980).

9

INTELLIGENCE, COVERT ACTION, AND OTHER NONMILITARY INSTRUMENTS OF COERCION

Patterns of action and reaction among states invariably defy rigid categorization as peaceful or warlike. In the majority of cases, relations between governments are dynamic: They vary over time on a scale ranging from mutually advantageous cooperation all the way to hostility and declared war. The end of the scale leading to conflict contains a number of stages that are preliminary to war, during which one foreign-policy elite employs nonmilitary forms of pressure to influence the behavior of another. Under this heading we can include economic and psychological warfare, destabilizing schemes usually employed to weaken unfriendly governments, and, somewhat higher on the scale toward war, covert penetration through, among other things, bribery or blackmail of the target state's key decision makers. The decision to resort to conflict or to seek compromise is based on an assessment of the capabilities and intentions of other governments. Policy makers therefore place a premium on accurate (or "hard") intelligence in formulating such decisions.

THE ACTIVITIES OF INTELLIGENCE SERVICES

Let us imagine two football teams preparing to play a championship game. The players are in top physical and mental condition. They practice their formations to perfection and devise surprise plays designed to confound their opponents in the critical minutes just before the end of the game. But training itself is not enough, and wise coaches will endeavor to learn as much as possible beforehand about the opposing team. The characteristics of individual players and their performance will receive careful scrutiny. Coaches, too, will be studied to the last wince. The playing field, the weather, and crowd reactions also will enter into the overall estimate of the situation. Finally, the game will be played.

The extensive "intelligence" and "counterintelligence" operations conducted by both teams during their preseason preparations are limited by the traditions of the sport and the standards established by athletic conferences. But now let us picture football as it would be played in the far-less-regulated setting of international politics. In this environment, covert action, beginning with such pranks as greasing the football, would become part of a winning game plan. Secret agents from each team would endeavor to ferret out the opponent's formations and plays. The corruption of officials as well as opposing players would be common. Partisans of each team would be given false but agreeable information about the score, the time left to play, and often even the name of the other team. In the shrouded classrooms of the world, intelligence operatives learn to play just such a game, but in this game the outcomes can be much more serious: victory and the survival of one's country, or defeat and the fearsome prospect of national disaster.

The collection and evaluation of information is the first function of a foreign-intelligence service. A second function is the development of a counterintelligence system capable of frustrating the information-collecting efforts of similar services in other nation-states. Both active and passive intelligence operations are tacitly accepted dimensions of international relations. As the director of the Central Intelligence Agency (the ranking United States intelligence official) once commented to the general secretary of the Communist Party of the Soviet Union, "The more we know about each other the safer we will be."[1]

A third function of a foreign-intelligence service—a function that may at times overshadow the ongoing collection and counterintelligence efforts—is the conduct of covert operations designed to influence internal or external policies of other governments. Administratively and operationally, most governments separate intelligence and counterintelligence activity from what is referred to euphemistically as *covert action* or *unadmitted operations*. *Covert action* can be defined as any calculated and secretly applied effort to alter the course of events in the target state. Kautilya, an Indian statesman writing a "science" of statecraft in the fourth century B.C., revealed himself as a master of intrigue when he detailed the types of poisons suitable for the elimination of a hostile ruler, urged religious figures to include carefully fabricated "disinformation" in their prophecies, and repeatedly stressed the exploitation of human greed in any campaign to create disaffection among the ranks of the enemy. Over two millennia have passed since Kautilya set down his precepts of covert action, yet his seminal handbook for covert warriors continues to exert considerable influence.[2]

---

[1]"Rules for a Dirty Game," *Manchester Guardian Weekly,* January 25, 1976, p. 1.

[2]Kautilya, *Arthasastra,* trans. R. Shamasastry, 4th ed. (Mysore: Mysore Printing and Publishing, 1967).

Intelligence Collection and Counterintelligence

About 90 percent of all intelligence is collected overtly, through such means as diplomatic reporting, the content analysis of foreign news media, and a careful monitoring of scientific and technical journals. Even in a closed society, it is possible through the assembling of different pieces of publicly available information to compose a reasonable portrait of a political system's capabilities and the intentions of its policy-making elite.

Supplementing overt collection efforts are covert efforts, and of these, classical espionage is the oldest. Kautilya advised his prince to utilize vast numbers of spies as a first line of defense against foreign and domestic enemies. Subsequent princes have never failed to heed this advice. In the service of Elizabeth I, queen of England and Ireland from 1558 to 1603, Sir Francis Walsingham managed to place some fifty-three agents in the courts of Europe. He thereby established the legendary reputation of the all-knowing British secret service. During World War II, the Swiss banking center of Zurich became a focal point of espionage activity directed against the Axis powers. In the cold-war period, the attention of the secret services was directed toward Berlin, Vienna, and Hong Kong. The emergence of the Third World countries as an arena of confrontation has placed a high priority on the classification of their domestic political forces as friend or foe, and the rapid spread of intelligence activities throughout the southern regions of the planet has been a natural result.

To neutralize the collection efforts of foreign intelligence services, every government seeks to perfect a protective shield of counterintelligence. In the United States, the Federal Bureau of Investigation (FBI) has the statutory authority to carry out this mission. In Great Britain, the responsibility rests primarily with the Special Branch of Scotland Yard. In the Soviet Union, the KGB encompasses both domestic- and foreign-intelligence operations. Since counterintelligence techniques very often involve the penetration of enemy intelligence apparatuses, and therefore the deployment of agents in other countries, counterespionage operations cannot be classified as purely domestic. Consequently, jurisdictional controversies easily arise between the defensive and offensive components of a state's intelligence establishment. An obvious source of bureaucratic rivalry would be the handling of a double agent—a secret agent allegedly in the service of one government but in reality under the control of another.

Covert Action

While intelligence and counterintelligence activity can be likened to the eyes and ears of a government seeking to record and assess the capabilities and intentions of other governments, covert action involves highly secret and often conspiratorial operations designed to serve important but often unadmitted policy objectives. Because of the secrecy with which it is conducted and the security that is needed, covert action requires the compartmentalization of the action agencies involved. (That way, the penetration of one agency by a foreign agent will not compromise the work of the other agencies.) From that moment on, the effective coordination of operations in the field becomes exceedingly difficult. In these circumstances, bureaucratic rivalry may engender a deadlock that can be broken only by increasing the tempo of the interstate conflict. A scenario of covert action escalation might appear as follows:

> *Phase 1:* Political advice is extended to friendly politicians in another country, and their actions are supported. This support includes some payments to selected individuals in and out of government.
>
> *Phase 2:* Planned penetration of political parties, trade unions, student groups, commercial organizations, and the media begins. A campaign of propaganda from controlled sources is launched.
>
> *Phase 3:* Diplomatic pressure and economic sanctions in the form of a boycott and/or embargo are begun. Alert orders are issued to military forces in the area, and deep-cover intelligence agents start to carry out prearranged assignments.
>
> *Phase 4:* Paramilitary action (e.g., sabotage and staged demonstrations carried out by covert agents) designed to replace the incumbent government with another government more responsive to the policy needs of the intervening power takes place.

As we can see, covert action can be limited in its earliest phase. The subsequent stages become increasingly dangerous, however, for they involve such activities as inciting popular unrest, training and equipping native forces for a *coup d'état,* and even removing opposition leaders through kidnapping or assassination. The benefit of such efforts is far from certain. Public disclosure of covert operations tends to expose their sponsor to international and possibly domestic outcries. The result is a loss of credibility on the part of the government carrying out the campaign, and possibly its removal from power. The decision to wage covert action is fraught with peril, and the results are more often than not politically questionable.

Nevertheless, politicians and functionaries justify covert operations by pointing out that the international system remains a primitive one incapable of affording peace and security under a global rule of law. Hence, governments develop standing military forces to defend their frontiers and other vital security interests. The employment of military force in the cause of self-defense is guaranteed by Article 51 of the United Nations Charter, and the history of those states unable or unwilling to avail themselves of this right has been short. Moreover, international law recognizes war as legitimate under certain conditions. Indeed, a prevalent definition of sovereignty is the right of a state to defend its interests militarily.

Once war is accepted as an instrument of policy, the rationale for covert operations becomes evident. In its abstract form, war is the unrestrained use of violence. Given the destructiveness of modern weaponry, this conception of war blurs the traditional distinction between combatants and noncombatants. In contrast, covert action is a controlled form of physical and psychological violence, which is directed against specific foreign personalities or publics. Assuming that policy makers are confronted with a choice between indiscriminate war and selective covert action—an argument that is often made—which option should they exercise? The question dictates the answer and conveniently omits a third course: compromise through negotiation.

The Organization of the Intelligence Mission

The intelligence mission of a given state, as we have already indicated, has three components: collection and evaluation of information, counterintelligence, and covert action. Since each of these has its own purpose and set of operational principles, the typical intelligence organization tends to be divided into three distinct hierarchies of activity, which are joined administratively only at the top. For example, during World War II the Office of Strategic Services (OSS), the global American intelligence network, was divided into three major units. A Secret Intelligence Branch (SI) produced the strategic estimates necessary for the conduct of military operations; the Counter-Intelligence Branch (X–2) neutralized hostile infiltration efforts; and the Special Operations Branch (SO) engaged in sabotage in enemy territory.[3] These units paralleled their British models: the Secret Intelligence Service, mentioned above; the British Security Service (the fabled MI–5); and the Special Operations Executive (SOE), which during World War II worked closely with Marshal Tito's partisans in the mountains of Serbia. It appears that the basic organizational pattern established by the American and British services during World War II has remained unchanged.

Intelligence organizations present students of public administration with two problems that are unique to their type of activity. The first arises from the sensitive nature of intelligence work, which requires a rigid compartmentalization of the various intelligence offices. Presumably, coordination from the top will prevent the duplication of effort or, worse, the unwitting thwarting of one group's plans by another group. Unfortunately, the span of control exercised by the uppermost officials is often so limited that synchronized operations are nearly impossible. A well-known example of an intelligence defeat suffered because of a breakdown in internal communication and control occurred during World War II. American communications experts working for naval intelligence had succeeded in breaking the Japanese military code. The significance of this development was such that knowledge of it was restricted to a very few. Unaware of their colleagues' success, agents of the OSS surreptitiously entered the Japanese embassy in neutral Lisbon and stole the enemy codebook. Upon discovery of the theft, the Japanese quickly changed the code, thereby plugging a major leak in their security.[4]

The second problem is the dominant influence of the political environment on estimates presented by intelligence analysts. Is there a missile gap? Are the parties to an arms-control agreement abiding by their treaty commitments,

---

[3]See R. Harris Smith, *OSS: The Secret History of America's First Central Intelligence Agency* (Berkeley: University of California Press, 1972).

[4]*Ibid.*, p. 6.

or are they secretly expanding stores of forbidden weaponry? The answers to these questions are politically sensitive, and it is unrealistic to assume that the intelligence officers who provide these answers are not conscious of the cues provided by their political superiors.[5] The standards of bureaucratic behavior apply in intelligence work as in all other fields of governmental activity. Thus, it is unlikely that bureau chiefs would approve of deviation from "intelligence policy" by subordinates whose assessments vary with those on which national policy is founded.

The political predisposition with which information on the capabilities and intentions of other governments is evaluated greatly affects the nature of the intelligence forecast. Often, identical information is treated in widely varying fashions by different national intelligence agencies. A case in point is Operation Barbarossa, the German invasion of the Soviet Union in 1941.[6] In the weeks prior to the outbreak of German-Soviet hostilities, the governments of the United States and Great Britain warned the Soviet leadership that the German military buildup in Poland indicated a subsequent march eastward. But for reasons that remain unclear, Soviet Marshal Stalin disregarded these alert messages—an attitude that was apparently encouraged by his own intelligence service. A possible explanation is that the Soviet leader viewed the warnings from London and Washington as provocations designed to disrupt the pattern of Soviet-German collaboration begun by the Molotov-Ribbentrop Pact of 1939. For whatever reason, the Kremlin remained passive in the face of a mounting military threat to the survival of the Soviet state.

The organization of an intelligence service requires the application of principles other than the basic administrative theories of line and staff relationships and the criteria of efficient management that are concerned with program budgeting. This organization should achieve a balance between two needs:

1. The need to prevent subordinate units from competing with one another or deviating from national policy
2. The necessity to reduce the impact of the political environment on the analyst so that he or she can formulate the objective though not always agreeable estimates essential to a sound foreign policy

To meet the first need—adequate control of intelligence structures—policy makers and intelligence officers must interact continually. Accountability after the fact is insufficient to meet this requirement. In a constitutional democracy, responsible leadership must exercise its mandate from the electorate and involve itself in the formative stages of covert action so that decisions regarding covert action are outcomes of the political process and not the result of bureaucratic schemes. Only in this way can a democracy prevent the establishment of an invisible government and the resulting political decay.

[5]See Benno Wasserman, "The Failure of Intelligence Prediction," *Political Studies,* 8 (Spring 1960), 156–69; Richard K. Betts, "Analysis, War and Decision: Why Intelligence Failures Are Inevitable," *World Politics,* 31, no. 1 (October 1978), 61–89.
[6]See Barton Whaley, *Codeword BARBAROSSA* (Cambridge, Mass.: MIT Press, 1973), passim.

To meet the second need, the various agencies of government should possess an in-house intelligence capability so that they can utilize information collected by a central agency to produce their own interpretations of political, economic, and military situations. The cost of such diversification is a degree of duplication; the benefit is a pluralistic approach to the analysis of foreign-policy options. From the standpoint of managerial efficiency, the production by a single hierarchy of an estimate of the international situation, preferably an estimate whose major points can be summarized on a few sheets of paper, appears attractive. However, the successful operation of such a centralized system means that political, military, and economic intelligence services must continually bargain in order to achieve a uniformity of opinion. In the give and take of these negotiations, bureaucratic politics and institutional loyalties often replace the search for objectivity as the basis for action. The closer an agency is to that point in the fiscal year when it must defend its budgetary requests, the more concessions to its position it will demand. Although the encouragement of a diversity of interpretations of the same situation may strengthen parochialism in the intelligence community, it at least provides a channel for dissent to centrally controlled intelligence policies. The lesson of Operation Barbarossa is that in the nuclear age, challenges to the orthodox point of view may be the key to survival.

Profiles of Secret Agents

The rise of secret services throughout the world has given birth to a large, if not always scholarly, body of literature on intelligence and counterintelligence operations.[7] Many of these writings exaggerate the role of intelligence work in shaping national policy and emphasize the heroic and idealistic aspects of covert operations. The frustrations of bureaucratic routine and the inherent inconclusiveness of intelligence work receive little attention. In films and popular novels spies often emerge—like their cousins, private investigators—as people of extraordinary capabilities (such as the legendary James Bond) who defeat the system and live lives of derring-do. Employing a diametrically opposite perspective, John Le Carré, in *The Spy Who Came in from the Cold,* attempted to reduce the spy to "realistic" proportions and tilted his portrait perhaps toward the side of

---

[7]The following works are representative: Julian Amery, *Sons of the Eagle: A Study in Guerrilla Warfare* (London: Macmillan, 1948); Paul W. Blackstock, *The Strategy of Subversion: Manipulating the Politics of Other Nations* (Chicago: Quadrangle, 1964); Richard Deacon, *A History of the British Secret Service* (New York: Taplinger, 1970), and *A History of the Russian Secret Service* (New York: Taplinger, 1972); Allen W. Dulles, *The Craft of Intelligence* (New York: Harper & Row, 1962); Roger Hilsman, *Strategic Intelligence and National Decisions* (Glencoe, Ill.: Free Press, 1956); Ronald Hingley, *The Russian Secret Police: Muscovite, Imperial Russian and Soviet Political Security Operations* (New York: Simon & Schuster, 1970); Klaus Knorr, *Foreign Intelligence and the Social Sciences* (Princeton, N.J.: Princeton University Press, 1964); Paul Leverkühn, *German Military Intelligence* (New York: Praeger, 1954); E.C.W. Myers, *Greek Entanglement* (London: R. Hart-Davis, 1955); Harry Howe Ransom, *The Intelligence Establishment* (Cambridge, Mass.: Harvard University Press, 1970); Richard Rowan and Robert Deindorfer, *Secret Service: Thirty-Three Centuries of Espionage,* rev. ed. (New York: Hawthorn, 1967); and Thomas Powers, *The Man Who Kept the Secrets: Richard Helms and the CIA* (New York: Knopf, 1979). See also Stansfield Turner, *Secrecy and Democracy: The CIA in Transition* (Boston: Houghton Mifflin, 1985); and William E. Colby and Peter Forbath, *Honorable Men: My Life in the CIA* (New York: Simon & Schuster, 1978).

pessimism and cynicism.[8] Irrespective of their political allegiances, Le Carré's spies appear uniformly as petty technicians of espionage and sabotage; in the world of the undercover agent there exists a gray unity of method and mentality that transcends differences in political ideals and systems.

Allen W. Dulles, director of central intelligence from 1953 to 1961, summarized the attributes of professional intelligence officers as follows:

> To create an effective intelligence agency we must have in the key positions men who are prepared to make this a life work, not a mere casual occupation. Service in the agency should not be viewed merely as a stepping-stone to promotion in one of the armed services or other branches of government. The agency should be directed by a relatively small but *elite* corps of men with a passion for anonymity and a willingness to stick to that particular job. They must find their reward primarily in the work itself, and in the service they render the government, rather than in public acclaim.[9]

The standard recruit for an intelligence organization should be an educated individual who likes power but not publicity, who is a nationalist and an advocate of the norms that prevail in his or her social setting, and whose personality lends itself to the rigorous discipline that is characteristic of life in the secret service. The conviction that one is doing important work and is privileged to have access to state secrets must provide a continuing psychic reward to offset the sacrifices inherent in what Rudyard Kipling aptly dubbed "the great game."

A small nucleus of professional intelligence officers directs the information-collection efforts of a government and controls its covert operations. In the field, large numbers of nonnationals are recruited as the eyes and ears essential for adequate coverage of intelligence targets. Such auxiliary agents provide their services normally for the following overlapping reasons: ideological conviction, fulfillment of excessive personality needs, remuneration, or in response to blackmail. During the classic cold-war period, rival intelligence services succeeded in recruiting a large number of individuals on the basis of ideological appeals. In his introduction to the memoirs of Kim Philby, an Englishman who penetrated the British Secret Intelligence Service (SIS) as a deep-cover Soviet agent, Graham Greene probed the nature of Philby's ideological commitment and summarized it as "the logical fanaticism of a man who, having once found a faith, is not going to lose it because of the injustices or cruelties inflicted by erring human instruments."[10]

The type of personality that lends itself to recruitment as an agent of another country's interests is discussed in a book by R. Harris Smith, a former research analyst for the CIA. Smith observed that people who were willing to be recruited as agents of a foreign nation-state's intelligence agency tended to be neurotic individuals who were attracted to undercover work because "it involved

---

[8]John Le Carré, *The Spy Who Came in from the Cold* (New York: Coward-McCann, 1964).

[9]Quoted (from a 1947 memorandum) in E. H. Cookridge, *Gehlen: Spy of the Century* (New York: Random House, 1971), p. 1. Quoted with the permission of Random House, Inc.

[10]Kim Philby, *My Silent War* (London: MacGibbon & Kee, 1968), p. vii.

sensation, intrigue, the idea of being a mysterious man with secret knowledge."[11] Without question, most people with integrated personalities would have considerable difficulty in leading the double life required of secret agents serving the interests of a country other than their own. Yet for some it is precisely the need for deception that provides a sense of superiority and therefore security. The first duty of the double agent, Philby wrote with obvious pride, "is to perfect not only his cover story but also his cover personality."[12] In his memoirs, the former British intelligence officer J. C. Masterman profiled spies who served on two or more secret services as those "who have a natural predilection to live in that curious world of espionage and deceit, and who attach themselves with equal facility to one side or the other, so long as their craving for adventure of a rather macabre type is satisfied."[13]

Remuneration as a method of foreign agent recruitment most often takes the form of a direct monetary payment to the agent. But indirect methods of material reward may also be effective. In wartime, one of the most common of these methods is to promise prospective recruits political power after hostilities are ended. Governments-in-exile and revolutionary groups may be particularly responsive to these overtures, since the uncertainty of their domestic political base makes foreign support invaluable. Although intelligence officers should not necessarily avoid an alliance with such groups, they must bear in mind that the information they receive from such groups will carry a politically self-serving coloration.

In a divided world, blackmail frequently provides a means of enlisting the assistance of persons who would ordinarily never consider collaborating with a foreign secret service. For example agents who were originally recruited on the basis of ideological solidarity can be blackmailed into continuing their services—should they experience a change of heart—or else face exposure and humiliation in their own country. A threat to harm a close family member can also provide a powerful stimulus. Relatives separated by hostile frontiers are especially vulnerable in this respect. Counterintelligence agencies try to take the necessary precautions to ensure protection of their nationals in such contingencies.

In sum, the motives for becoming a secret agent are varied, and a prospective recruit will undoubtedly respond to a combination of inducements. It suffices to say that the extent of cultural and political disillusionment in postindustrial societies is sufficiently great to supply schools of espionage with a steady flow of students.

Intelligence in a Democracy

It has been argued that the intelligence apparatus of a totalitarian regime characteristically operates as a state within a state. It is an autonomous bureaucratic

---

[11]Smith, *OSS*, p. 7.

[12]Philby, *My Silent War*, p. 154.

[13]John C. Masterman, *The Double-Cross System in the War of 1939 to 1945* (New Haven: Yale University Press, 1972), p. 1.

empire that frequently constitutes a threat to the control enjoyed by the ruling elite, as witnessed by the unclarified circumstances surrounding the death of Lavrenti Beria, the chief of the Soviet secret service, in 1953. In contrast, in a constitutional democracy both legislative and executive authorities demand a comparatively greater degree of transparency in the conduct of intelligence operations. Balancing the need for democractic control with the requirements of security is difficult.

Beginning in the mid-1970s and resurfacing in the mid-1980s, a public debate developed in the United States over the compatibility of covert intelligence operations with constitutional government. In the media and in Congress questions were raised as to the legality, not to mention the political utility, of clandestine operations (e.g., plotting to assassinate foreign rulers or to precipitate the collapse of unfriendly governments) and of security-motivated surveillance at home (e.g., Watergate-related surveillance by the Nixon administration). Senator Frank Church chaired a select committee which investigated intelligence activities, and Congressman Otis G. Pike's committee on intelligence conducted a parallel inquiry in the House of Representatives. Responding to popular concern, Jimmy Carter expressed the sentiments of many when he observed during the 1976 presidential campaign:

> The moral heart of our international appeal—as a country which stands for self-determination and free choice—has been weakened. It is obviously un-American to interfere in the political processes of another nation.[14]

From the perspective of the oval office, President Carter was to learn some years later that no matter what he did—or did not do—his policies toward foreign countries' internal politics would be denounced as "interference" in at least some quarters.

Critics of covert action argue that a government's foreign policy should reflect the values of the society it serves. Covert action, they contend, spawns an "invisible government" capable of defying constitutional control. Indictments and trials of federal officials for unlawful actions in connection with intelligence operations provide both conservative and liberal critics with a palpable basis for concern. Supporters of covert action retort that espionage and counterespionage are essential if the Republic is to survive in a world where most other states—friendly or adversary—systematically employ covert action as part of their intelligence mission. In the 1980s, Congress has been seeking to implement a statutory charter that will provide effective legislative oversight of the intelligence community without hamstringing its vital national-security function.[15] In the final analysis, however, constitutional safeguards are less a matter of law than of personal

---

[14]Jimmy Carter, "Address to the Chicago Council on Foreign Relations," March 15, 1976.

[15]For an analysis of Congress and the intelligence community, see Cecil V. Crabb, Jr., and Pat M. Holt, *Invitation to Struggle: Congress, the President and Foreign Policy* (Washington, D.C.: Congressional Quarterly, 1980).

commitment and restraint on the part of men and women charged with the delicate task of intelligence in a democracy.

PROPAGANDA AND PSYCHOLOGICAL WARFARE

Propaganda has been effectively defined as a process involving a communicator whose intention is to *change the attitudes, opinions, and behavior* of a target population using spoken, written, and behavioral symbols and employing media such as books, pamphlets, films, lectures, and so forth.[16] If we employ this definition, we realize that propaganda—as is the case with diplomacy, intelligence operations, and war—becomes one of the standard methods used by states to secure power, to maintain power, and to apply power in their efforts to promote their national interest.[17]

States (and in many instances nonstate actors such as multinational corporations, nongovernmental and intergovernmental organizations, autonomist and terrorist movements, and religious organizations) employ in varying degree and effectiveness public information agencies and programs. The objective in each case is to project as positive and convincing an image as possible about themselves while seeking to influence foreign governments directly or through their populations about the rightness of their causes. The concept of propaganda, through the passage of time and the behavior of propagandists, has acquired a negative connotation. Propaganda, in a somewhat analogous fashion with commercials and advertising, is often assumed nowadays to be a mixture of exaggeration, selective reporting, emotional and sensational appeal, factual distortion all the way to premeditated falsehood and fabrication designed to "sell" the product of the propagandist.

The equation of propaganda with skillful disinformation campaigns is unfortunate. As we shall see below much of what occurs under the rubric of cultural, information, and education programs of the various governments is quite straightforward, benign, and generally constructive in nature. Most public information programs, in fact, strive to promote relations of understanding between peoples while seeking to activate further what are already friendly people-to-people relations.

In order to permit the disaggregation of the cooperative from the conflictful types of propaganda the terms *white, gray,* and *black* propaganda have been employed by students and practitioners of this challenging art.[18] Generally, the term *white* propaganda has been employed to denote cooperative and straight-

---

[16]See K. J. Holsti, *International Politics: A Framework for Analysis,* 3rd ed. (Englewood Cliffs, N.J.: Prentice-Hall, 1977), p. 221 (emphasis supplied).

[17]For a bibliography on propaganda and international relations, see Hamid Mowlana, *International Communication: A Selected Bibliography* (Dubuque, Iowa: Kendall/Hunt, 1971), pp. 57–67.

[18]These terms have been used by propaganda analysts for many years. We are fully conscious of the unfortunate, if not intentional, association of the color black with conflict and the color white with cooperation.

forward campaigns designed to explain a state's policies to audiences across its borders and over the seas. The "white propagandists" clearly identify themselves in each communication, and most of their activity in the cultural and educational domain is based on exchanges of artists, athletes, scholars, and other persons of note. Magazines, pamphlets, films, and lectures emphasize the positive aspects of the state orchestrating the messages as well as seek to point up and describe activities (bilateral or multilateral) that are dedicated to the cultivation of mutually beneficial friendship and cooperation.

Gray propaganda is employed when the relations between the communicator and the government of the target state begin to deteriorate. Propaganda materials still identify the true source of each communication, but now an effort is being made to report selectively and to differentiate the "good people" from the "bad government" of the target state. Exaggeration, even falsehood, creeps into the communications, which clearly become combative in tone and competitive in philosophy.

When war and actual hostilities break out, diplomacy and formal negotiations recede and warriors take over. It is at this level of tense relations that *black* propaganda and much that is described as psychological warfare is employed. In an effort to demoralize the population of a target state and to isolate the enemy government black propaganda is produced, and this product could best be equated with verbal and audiovisual weapons. In black propaganda, the communicators often hide their true identities and produce forged and fabricated documentation, attributed to enemy sources, which is designed to create confusion and chaos in the ranks of the enemy. Typical of such efforts are leaked documents alleging the intentions of a target state's leading figure to purge an important deputy and forecasts of dire economic developments including the prospect of large-scale unemployment, food scarcity, labor or ethnic unrest, and famine. Clearly, in the area of black propaganda, information and covert intelligence programs, which we have already discussed, are working hand in hand.

Governments usually carry out their propaganda functions (cultural, educational, and press relations) through agencies that act separately from but in coordination with foreign and defense ministries and intelligence services. In the United States propaganda activities are the responsibility assigned to the United States Information Agency (USIA), which was established in 1954 by President Dwight D. Eisenhower. This agency, which for some years had been renamed United States International Communication Agency (USICA) before reverting to its original title, runs Press and Information Offices and American Centers and Libraries in major cities of the world. The USIA also runs the multilingual radio programs of the Voice of America and Radio Free Europe as well as television, film and news services, and special programs such as scholar and student exchanges; speakers' tours; artistic, scholarly, and scientific conferences; and related activities.

The Soviet Union, Great Britain, West Germany, France, China, Japan, and most other countries also run expensive and elaborate culture, radio, and propaganda agencies that are designed to inform, reform, and at times even de-

form the opinions of target populations. The Soviet Union's radio broadcast services possess the world's most powerful and intensive facilities and ceaselessly
transmit in all directions radio programs in all the world's major languages and
dialects. The Soviet Union's primary propaganda aims include the reduction of
U.S. influence in the Third World by supporting nationalist and socialist liberation movements and the weakening of the Western defense establishment by encouraging the activities of peace and antinuclear movements (especially those
that target the United States) and supporting lobbies that for a variety of reasons
are opposed to high military expenditures in the West.

One of the functions of the propaganda business is the monitoring, classification, evaluation, and influencing of mass media. This is especially relevant
in countries of the West where the media are in private hands rather than under
governmental control. Press and information officers attached to embassies and
consulates throughout the world read, review, digest, evaluate, and report on
press and electronic media coverage in the host state regarding matters of interest to the sending state. Those journalists, columnists, commentators, and opinion makers whose attitudes are classified as friendly to the sending state are reinforced by receiving invitations to embassy functions being provided with
interesting and at times exclusive information, and if necessary being offered
remuneration to help them maintain their enthusiasm. Naturally among the most
important press and information activities is the identification of false and
biased reporting in various unfriendly newspapers and the sending of letters to
the editor signed by a press counselor or even the ambassador designed to correct the record and to rebut negative assertions.

In Western states where public opinion, pressure groups, and the media
are constantly involved in efforts to affect the policy formulation process through
lobbies and alternate forms of influence, the range of maneuver for foreign propaganda services is considerable. In the United States, for example, a number of
governments and movements (friendly or unfriendly to the United States) are
spending large sums of money to hire American public relations firms in order
to promote their images and interests among American influentials in the executive and congressional branches of government, business and ethnic groups, and
the general public.

As we have seen above, when relations between two or more states degenerate into hostilities and warfare, propaganda enters the phase of what is called
psychological warfare.[19] In time of war, the black and gray propagandists assume a
dominant role; censorship and other forms of manipulation of communications
become a way of life; and truth is among the first of the casualties. The objective
of psychological warfare, like all warfare, is to divide and demoralize the enemy
and break his will to resist. Typical psychological operations in time of war are

[19]John Barron, *KGB: The Secret Work of Soviet Secret Agents* (New York: Reader's Digest Press, 1974);
Ladislav Bittman, *The Deception Game: Czechoslovak Intelligence in Soviet Political Warfare* (Syracuse, N.Y.:
Syracuse University Research Corp., 1972). For allegations of disinformation campaigns conducted
by the CIA, see Victor Marchetti and John D. Marks, *The CIA and the Cult of Intelligence* (New York:
Knopf, 1974), pp. 155–81.

radio programs that are broadcast to soldiers fighting for the enemy side. Usually, a soft and appealing young woman's voice, speaking directly to the troops without an accent, warns them that while they are suffering and dying at the hell of the battlefield, privileged, old, and well-fed men back home are enjoying the pleasures of sex with their wives, girl friends, and sisters. Constant attempts are also being made to separate the evil government from the good people of the target state. In the meantime back home a series of films, books, articles, and pamphlets is being produced portraying the enemies as barbarians: brutal, arrogant, ruthless, as well as physically and psychologically deformed. It is most instructive to review after more than forty years the strongly one-sided films that had been produced during World War II and compare them with much more balanced and benign portrayals of later years. As passions subside and the calculus of interests shifts, the polar images of angels versus devils give way to scenarios that find heroes and villains on both sides of the fence and view the struggle as a tragic product of ignorance, misunderstanding, and the uncontrolled passions of the moment.

In closing we should point out that it is thankless to ask here whether processes such as covert action, propaganda, and psychological warfare are defensible or indefensible or, more plainly, good or bad. In a global political system where disputes are often settled through the threat or the use of force, these techniques are simply inevitable. They are different types of "weapons" in the hands of governments, as these governments seek to increase their leverage in their external affairs.

ECONOMIC WARFARE AND THE ROLE OF SANCTIONS

Since classical times, commercial relations among states have constituted one of the primary sources of conflict. Control of the Mediterranean trade routes was one of the key objectives of the Roman Republic's ultimately successful effort to destroy the Carthaginian maritime empire in the third century B.C. The clash of the two superpowers of that time led to the destruction of one and the transformation of an ancient prototype of the bipolar system (i.e., a system of states controlled by two conflicting superpowers) into a hierarchy of political communities under the leadership of Rome.

In contemporary world politics, the outcome of economic rivalry is rarely so drastic. The methods of statecraft that can be used for the pursuit of economic objectives are varied, and for the most part they fall short of violence. For example, nonviolent yet coercive means of self-help include the tactics of boycott and embargo. A boycott is the refusal to purchase goods and services from another state until specific political conditions have been met. In 1931, units of the Imperial Japanese Army occupied Manchuria, a territory of the Republic of China. The Chinese government responded by urging its citizens to boycott all Japanese goods, an economic reprisal whose effects were soon felt in the Japanese economy. Similarly, following the establishment in 1959 of the government of Fidel

Castro and the subsequent nationalization of properties owned by U.S. citizens in Cuba, the administration of President Eisenhower discontinued the United States' subsidized purchase of Cuban sugar in an effort to secure political concessions through the boycott of a vital Cuban export.

An embargo, in a broad sense, is the seizure of a foreign state's carriers and goods found within the territorial jurisdiction of another state, as well as the prohibition of the sale of specific commodities to nationals of the offending state. To frustrate the plans of the Imperial Japanese government, President Franklin D. Roosevelt established a series of embargoes in 1940 that prevented the overseas sale of aviation gasoline and scrap metal except to Great Britain and the countries of the Western hemisphere. The following year, the United States, Great Britain, and the Netherlands jointly froze all Japanese financial assets, thereby choking off the supply of oil to the Imperial Navy and its supporting industrial complex. Faced with the proverbial Hobson's choice of economic strangulation or political surrender, the cabinet of Premier Hideki Tojo made its decision to attack Pearl Harbor—an event that illustrates the dangers implicit in economic warfare.

Economic warfare (in the form of boycotts, embargoes, and blockades) usually is a means of goal attainment available to major actors in the international system. Consequently, great powers may succumb to the temptation to use this weapon indiscriminately against smaller states, on the assumption that the latter are defenseless. Historically, however, small states whose governing elites have been cohesive and committed to a policy of self-preservation have shown themselves quite resourceful in resisting attempts at economic coercion. The relations between the United States and Spain during World War II are a case in point. The German armaments industry required large quantities of wolfram (tungsten) for the manufacture of armor plate, and Spanish mines were the major source of this metal. The neutrality of Spain ruled out military action as a means of halting the flow of wolfram from Spain to Germany, so the United States initiated a program whereby it contracted to buy the amount of wolfram being produced at that time. The Spanish response was to mine more wolfram and to raise the price per ton. The cycle repeated itself until the cost of wolfram had risen almost tenfold, with no appreciable decrease in the amount being exported to Germany. Ultimately, Anglo-American armies advancing across France separated German industry from its Spanish suppliers, who by this time had reaped a handsome profit. The limits of economic warfare illustrated by this episode demonstrate the weakness of a foreign policy dependent solely upon the manipulation of trade and aid.[20]

Other historical experience with economic warfare is hardly more encouraging, for only in limited cases has it come close to achieving the objectives assigned to it. Examples often cited in this connection are the League of Nations action against Italy (1935–36) and a similar United Nations effort against Rhodesia (1965–68). (The League of Nations and the United Nations are discussed in

[20]Herbert Feis, *The Spanish Story: Franco and the Nations at War* (New York: Knopf, 1948), pp. 219–32.

some detail in Chapter 14.) As a global collective security organization, the League endeavored to stay Mussolini's aggression against Ethiopia by placing an embargo on the shipment of strategic materials to Italy. This embargo suffered from three major deficiencies. First, some twenty-seven states—over half the members of the world organization—refused to join in the sanctions. Second, the list of embargoed items omitted such vital war-supporting commodities as petroleum. Third, armies march faster than international organs deliberate, and by the time the League acted, the capital of Ethiopia had fallen. Of particular importance is the fact that the sanctions had the internal effect of unifying the Italian people in support of the fascist dictatorship and consequently encouraged Mussolini to think in terms of further conquests. An alliance of the Italian and German dictators followed, giving credence to the conclusion that the League sanctions set in motion a train of events that contributed to the outbreak of a general European war in 1939.[21]

In 1965, when the former British colony of Rhodesia (since 1980, the independent state of Zimbabwe) unilaterally declared its independence, London was quick to respond with selected economic sanctions, and within days the Security Council of the United Nations called for a voluntary oil embargo. These measures having proved ineffective, the Security Council voted in 1968 to impose a boycott on Rhodesian goods and to establish an embargo on all trade except medical and humanitarian supplies.[22] Not all the members of the world organization saw themselves as obligated to support these sanctions. Such neighboring states as Botswana, Malawi, Zambia, and the then Portuguese colony of Mozambique continued to carry on an active trade with Rhodesia. What limited amount of external economic pressure there was only motivated the Rhodesians to rationalize their systems of production and to develop new channels of trade. The outcome of this effort to bring about concessions by pressing on the economic jugular was counterproductive, and Rhodesia's economy gained a firmer basis than it had prior to the United Nations action. Guerrilla warfare and British diplomatic mediation, rather than an embargo, ultimately led to the capitulation of Rhodesia's white minority and to the adoption of a system of majority rule.

Although global international organizations, such as the League of Nations (1920–39) and the United Nations, have had great difficulty in bringing their member states to the point of joint action in choking off all sources of trade for a target state, governments acting individually or in alliance with others may have greater success in employing the weapons of economic warfare. In 1973 and 1974, the oil-producing Arab states, in support of their allies locked in armed conflict with Israel, embargoed the sale of petroleum to the United States and the Netherlands and set quotas on its production. The latter action was especially threatening to Japan, which must import almost all of its oil, as well as to Western

---

[21]For a very thoughtful treatment of the theory and practice of sanctions see Stefanie Ann Lenway, "Between War and Commerce: Economic Sanctions as a Tool of Statecraft," *International Organization,* 42, no. 2 (Spring 1988), pp. 394–426.

[22]Donald Losman, *International Economic Sanctions: The Cases of Cuba, Israel, and Rhodesia* (Albuquerque: University of New Mexico Press, 1979), pp. 94–95.

Europe. Lasting for five months, the oil embargo induced a crisis mentality, including speculation that the United States might even intervene militarily in the Persian Gulf in order to secure essential petroleum supplies. In terms of trade, however, the flow of oil, while restricted, was not halted. Tankers continued to arrive at American and European ports, suggesting a lack of political will on the part of those who called for the embargo. Nevertheless, the psychological impact, if not the economic reality, was profound.

The experience of the Carter administration in utilizing the techniques of economic coercion was uneven. On October 18, 1978, President Carter, reacting to repeated violations of human rights by the dictator Idi Amin, curtailed trade with Uganda and ordered the withdrawal of technical personnel. Although this action was unilateral—the British did not join the effort—and the difficulties of the Ugandan economy were not conclusively related to the American economic policy, foreign and domestic opponents of the dictatorship took heart because of the sanctions and were able to overthrow the regime some six months later.[23] In this instance the aftereffects of the trade restrictions were more important than the measures themselves.

As a partial response to the seizure and detention of American diplomatic and consular personnel in Teheran, President Carter sought in November 1979 to retaliate against the regime dominated by the Ayatollah Ruhollah Khomeini by first freezing Iranian assets in the United States and then calling upon allied governments to halt their trade with Iran. Although the major European industrial powers were initially supportive, one by one they resumed and eventually even expanded their commercial ties with the revolutionary state. In Iran the prospect of economic scarcity served to reinforce feelings of solidarity, which manifested itself in mass demonstrations against the "satanic" power of the West.

Also of questionable efficacy were the retaliatory steps taken against the Soviet Union in the wake of its December 1979 invasion of Afghanistan. The United States reacted by cutting back shipments of grain to the Soviet Union and compelling American firms to withdraw from contract negotiations with the Soviets. Immediately, competitors in the Federal Republic of Germany, France, Canada, and Argentina moved to fill the void. The Soviet army continued its advance in Afghanistan, and the effort to halt this movement with economic counterpressure succeeded only in creating a rift between the major NATO allies. Similarly, the Western alliance was divided over the question of whether or not to participate in the Moscow Olympic Games (1980). Although many governments and national Olympic committees did respond favorably to President Carter's call for a boycott, the reaction within the Atlantic community betrayed a serious disunity.

Shortly after his inauguration in 1981, President Ronald Reagan opted for the use of economic and covert warfare against Nicaragua in order to extract concessions from the Sandinista regime. The United States imposed an embargo on trade with Nicaragua and provided support for antigovernment guerrilla

---

[23]Judith Miller, "When Sanctions Worked," *Foreign Policy*, 39 (Summer 1980), 126.

forces battling the Sandinistas, who received assistance from the Soviet Union. The Nicaraguan government responded with a campaign of austerity at home and the mobilization of public opinion abroad. Ultimately, the approach taken by the Reagan administration proved ineffective.

The reasons for the inefficacy of the economic weapon against Iran, the Soviet Union, or Nicaragua were fourfold. First, many governments and commercial organizations saw in the embargoes only an opportunity to expand their trade with the target states. For example, both Iran and Pakistan have railroads equipped largely with American rolling stock. When the United States halted the shipment of spare parts for trains to Iran, the Pakistanis were eager to supply the needed materials at a price.

Second, if the country subjected to an embargo is experiencing the economic chaos associated with a revolutionary upheaval, the denial of trade has only a limited effect. In 1979, the Iranian gross national product (the sum of all the goods and services produced in one year) fell an estimated 20 percent. In view of the economic depression that had befallen the country, the American-sponsored embargo was hardly critical. The situation in Nicaragua was not very different.

Third, to be effective, economic sanctions must block both imports and exports. In the cases of Iran and the Soviet Union, their exports, such as oil or natural gas, remained in high demand. Both countries continued to acquire the capital needed to attract blockade breakers. In the case of Nicaragua, the lead of the United States was not followed by most of its Western European industrial partners, and Soviet aid proportionately increased.

Fourth, the collaboration of nonstate actors such as multinational corporations is indispensable. In Chapter 18 we will discuss the role of multinational corporations and banks, whose purposes and goals may vary markedly from those of national governments. In the Iranian instance many multinational banks declined to declare Teheran in default on its financial obligations and thereby mitigated the effect of the American sanctions. In sum, the international economy is sufficiently complex that it evades manipulation by any single center of power or even a combination thereof. While the economic weapon may appear deceptively simple, its application is complex and requires careful, extensive diplomatic preparation.

SUGGESTIONS FOR FURTHER STUDY

"Intelligence Services during the Second World War" is the theme of sequential issues of the *Journal of Contemporary History*, 22 (April and October, 1987). A case study on economic warfare is Roy Licklider, "The Power of Oil: The Arab Oil Weapon and the Netherlands, the United Kingdom, Canada, Japan, and the United States," *International Studies Quarterly*, 32 (June 1988), 205–26. An important memoir is William Colby, *Honorable Men: My Life in the CIA* (New York: Simon & Schuster, 1978). An opposing view is U.S. Congress, Senate, Select Committee on Intelligence Activities, *Covert Action in Chile, 1963–1973,* 94th Cong., 1st sess., 1975, one of a series of hearings and reports published under the same auspices. On the question of legality of covert activities, see Roland Stanger, ed., *Essays on Espionage and International Law* (Columbus, Ohio: Ohio State University Press, 1962). The issue of congressional oversight of intelligence agencies is analyzed by Cecil V. Crabb, Jr., and Pat M. Holt, in *Invitation to Struggle: Congress, the President and Foreign Policy* (Washington, D.C.: Congressional Quarterly, 1980); and by Peter Hackes et al. in *Foreign Intelligence: Legal and Democratic Controls* (Washington, D.C.: American Enterprise Institute, 1979). Commentaries on the role of economic warfare include Margaret Doxey, *Economic Sanctions and International Enforcement* (London: Oxford University Press, 1971); and Klaus Knorr and Frank N. Trager, eds., *Economic Issues and National Security* (Lawrence, Kans.: University Press of Kansas, 1977). The limits of economic influence are explored in Richard Stuart Olson, "Economic Coercion in World Politics: With a Focus on North-South Relations," *World Politics,* 31 (July 1979), 471–94; and Robert L. Paarlberg, "Lessons of the Grain Embargo," *Foreign Affairs,* 59 (Fall 1980), 144–62. Classic studies of the use of information to manipulate mass and elite behavior include William E. Daugherty and Morris Janowitz, *A Psychological Warfare Casebook,* 2 vols. (Baltimore: Johns Hopkins Press, 1952); and Harold D. Lasswell, *Propaganda Technique in the World War* (New York: Knopf, 1927). A useful historical study is Paul W. Blackstock, *The Secret Road to World War Two: Soviet versus Western Intelligence, 1921–1939* (Chicago: Quadrangle, 1969). Political warfare is the theme of Richard H. Shultz and Roy S. Godson, *Dezinformatsia: Active Measures in Soviet Strategy* (Elmsford, N.Y.: Pergamon Press, 1984).

10

WAR AND ITS CAUSES

"War is the exercise of the international right of action," wrote Sir Robert Phillimore in 1854.[1] He regarded war as a necessary tool of statecraft when it was waged for specific political objectives. By contrast, the Charter of the United Nations (1945) commits the organization's members to a renunciation of war by stipulating in Article 2(4) that: "All members shall refrain in their international relations from the threat or use of force against the territorial integrity or political independence of any other state."

Despite this appeal to reason, securing peace remains an elusive goal. Since the founding of the United Nations, it is difficult to identify a single year in which war, either international or internal, was not being waged. This observation does not include covert action by one government against another. Were that statistic to be added, the incidence of violence would significantly increase. In the 1980s, both revolutionary wars and armed struggles between states increased in frequency while diplomats struggled to find a solution. In an era of growing interdependence no war is an isolated event. For this reason the major powers must act in concert to limit war in an effort to maintain the international balance of power.

[1]Sir Robert Phillimore, *Commentaries upon International Law* (Philadelphia: T. & J. W. Johnson, 1854; reprint, Fred B. Rothman), vol. III, p. 99.

DIFFICULTIES IN DEFINING THE CONCEPT OF *WAR*

As we point out in various sections of this text, one of the central challenges to the study of international relations is conceptual imprecision and the multiplicity of competing definitions advanced for each major concept. The concept of *war* has not escaped this fate.[2]

The difficulty can be expressed in terms of a dichotomy between comprehensive definitions and narrowly focused ones. Possibly the most comprehensive definition would classify *war* as part of a more general phenomenon in human affairs called *conflict*. Conflict could include all explicitly and implicitly competitive/coercive relationships involving human beings interacting as individuals and as groups, regardless of whether the type of "violence" employed is physical or psychological, military or economic, actual or threatened and/or implied.

The problem with such a wide-ranging definition involves difficulties in the generation of data and in the testing of propositions. For example, if under the umbrella of *conflict/war* we included economic sanctions, propaganda, psychological warfare, covert action, suspension of diplomatic relations, and strong diplomatic protests in addition to violent and organized warfare, then it would be very hard to test propositions seeking to correlate "war-proneness" with particular leaders, regimes, national groups, and ideological orientations. It would be very difficult, for example, to differentiate between loud, provocative, but in practice war-shy rulers and those who "speak softly but carry a big stick." Therefore, for reasons of enhancing specificity and accuracy, we prefer a more narrowly focused definition of *war* that refers to a struggle among political units, within and between states, involving organized fighting forces, and resulting in a sizable number (e.g., over one thousand) of war-related casualties.

Lewis Fry Richardson (1881–1953) correctly identified the main conceptual problems that arise in the application of quantitative methods to the study of war.[3] First, the difficulty in selecting historical intervals as a basis of mathematical study may easily produce misleading results. The year 1815, marking as it does the final defeat of Napoleon at Waterloo, is an appropriate starting point for the organization of a history of European diplomacy extending, for instance, to the triggering of World War I at Sarajevo in 1914. However, the scope of an analysis founded on quantitative principles must be bounded by reference points other than those of historical importance to a particular nation-state or culture. This is not true of our proposed Waterloo-to-Sarajevo study, with its implicit Europe-centered bias. What the appropriate criteria are for a culturally unbiased and statistically founded study remains an object of continued discussion.

---

[2]In their definitions of such concepts as *war*, *violence*, and *conflict*, scholars differ widely. Some stress international norms, others the human cost in terms of combat-related casualties, and still others the degree of hostility in a government's actions. See Benjamin Most and Harvey Starr, "Conceptualizing 'War': Consequences for Theory and Research," *Journal of Conflict Resolution*, 27, no. 1 (March 1983), 137–59.

[3]Lewis Fry Richardson, *Statistics of Deadly Quarrels* (Chicago: Quadrangle, 1960), pp. 5–6.

A second question to which Richardson also refers is the controversy surrounding the definition of *war* and its correlate *casualty*. Even within the social sciences a uniform definition of *war* is often elusive. Because of their differing conceptual frameworks, social psychologists and political scientists tend to stress divergent approaches to the study of human conflict. The former emphasize feelings and attitudes of hostility, envy, and revenge, for example, while the latter frequently concentrate on evidence of battle and battle-related casualties. Quantitative precision in the measurement of hostility, as we have seen in Chapter 2, is subject to limitations. Similarly, the data of wartime casualties vary from one governmental source to another. This was true of the civil war in Nigeria (1966–70) and the Soviet intervention in Afghanistan (1979–1989) among other conflicts. Without these data, the problem of identifying trends in the intensity and scope of wars eludes statistical solution. Yet it is precisely in this area that quantitative research techniques should make their greatest contribution.

THE HISTORY OF WARFARE

The retention or expansion of control over a hunting territory was the reward in primitive warfare. As far as anthropologists have been able to ascertain, war at the dawn of history was waged in the pursuit of a few specific goals; the usual goal was the sustenance of the tribe. The harsh evidence of Tanzania's Olduvai Gorge—a crushed skull of a prehistoric hominid—reminds us of the human tendency to engage in violent conflict. The question of whether aggression and war derive from situational factors or from innate drives has generated a bitter de-

Siege of Jerusalem.
(Bibliotheque Nationale)

bate, one that we cannot hope to resolve in this discussion. Realists point to the persistence of war from the beginning of human history as a sign of its apparent inevitability, and idealists retort that a healthy social and political environment can reduce the incidence of war to the point at which it is no longer characteristic of the international system. The history of international relations since the end of World War II reveals, however, that war remains an instrument of statecraft acceptable to the overwhelming majority of governments.

Primitive war consisted of the pursuit by all members of the community of what was conceived to be a common good. In this respect, the wars of early humans strongly resemble the total warfare of today. In contrast, wars fought during the Middle Ages and the Renaissance tended to be waged on behalf of ruling dynasties that depended upon professional soldiers, who more often than not were mercenaries. The Italian city-states of the fifteenth century maintained an uncertain balance of power as a result of intermittent warfare conducted by *condottieri*—regiments of professional soldiers who sold their services to the highest bidder. The campaigning was of short duration and emphasized the gaining of tactical advantage rather than the total annihilation of opposing forces. The monetary investment in a mercenary corps was too great to permit the squandering of its "free companies" on the battlefield.[4] Machiavelli described a typical engagement: It decided the fate of a kingdom, but only one life was lost—and that because a luckless rider fell from his horse.[5]

The danger of a military system that relied primarily upon a professional and/or mercenary army was that an order of fanatic, intensely religious soldiers could arise and threaten the foundations of civil authority. The Janissaries of the Ottoman Empire are an example. Although they numbered only twelve thousand under Suleiman I (ruled 1520–66), they constituted a political force not to be taken lightly by the Ottoman administration. Historically, professional military elites have sought outlets for their energies, and intervention in politics is usually too tempting an alternative to resist.

The fifteenth century witnessed the beginning of the end of the limited wars of political and commercial rivalry among the city-states and principalities of Europe. Two developments were primarily responsible for this: the rise of standing armies, and the realization of the military potential of gunpowder. At the end of the Hundred Years' War between England and France (1338–1453), both sides found themselves burdened with a mass of impoverished, demobilized soldiers. In France, Charles VII (1422–61), with the backing of a wealthy merchant, recruited an elite military corps and had them forcibly disperse the remnants of the French army, which had turned to pillaging their own countryside. This corps was the first standing army in what was becoming a modern nation-state.

Until the siege of Constantinople (1453), the use of various infantry for-

[4]Stanton A. Coblentz, *From Arrow to Atom Bomb: The Psychological History of War* (New York: Beechhurst Press, 1953), p. 193; Keith L. Nelson and Spencer C. Olin, Jr., *Why War? Ideology, Theory, and History* (Berkeley: University of California Press, 1979).

[5]Niccoló Machiavelli, *History of Florence and of the Affairs of Italy* (New York: Harper & Brothers, 1960).

mations was the main tactic of European field commanders. A new strategy was introduced dramatically when the Turks surrounded Constantinople and deployed some fourteen primitive but effective batteries against the city's defenses. The Turkish success established the triumph of offense over defense and sounded the death knell of a feudal order based on impregnable fortresses.

Nation-building monarchs such as Louis XIV (1643–1715) laid the basis of the modern state by commanding a superior military force. By linking the institution of a standing army with the idea of the state as the dominant form of security community in international relations, the enlightened despots of the modern age also provided a political framework for the total warfare of the twentieth century.

In the aftermath of the French Revolution and the Napoleonic Wars, Henri Baron de Jomini (1779–1869), an experienced field commander, wrote a classical study of military strategy. In it, he identified three major types of war: national wars of a people against a foreign oppressor, civil wars, and "wars of opinion," a conflict between two ideologically opposed multinational blocs.[6] Aside from the Crusades and the Thirty Years' War (1618–48), "wars of opinion" were almost unknown until the Napoleonic Wars. Jomini was one of the first strategists perceptive enough to realize that the campaigns of Napoleon exemplified this new and dominant type of warfare.

Mass armies relying on conscription and on the ideological fervor engendered by the French Revolution transformed the old order of European dynastic international relations. In 1793, the Committee of Public Safety, the dictatorial government then existing in France, set a new style in the conduct of war by ordering a *levée en masse*, which mobilized women as well as men in the service of national defense. Later, Napoleon could boast to Prince Metternich, "I can spend 30,000 men a month." Despite its arrogance, this statement reveals that success in war had come to depend as much on a professional administrative system on the home front as on maneuvers on the battlefield.[7]

In the century between Waterloo (1815) and the general European mobilization during the summer of 1914, international politics were comparatively stable. Generally, armed conflict was of short duration and restricted to areas far removed from the European center. The diplomatic technique of international conferences, such as that held in Berlin in 1878, reinforced the notion of a community of interests among European elites and provided an institutional mechanism that inhibited the further evolution of warfare. But total war was to emerge in 1914. World War I and World War II involved not only a new type of warfare, but also an attempt to use total violence to achieve political ends.

Karl von Clausewitz (1780–1831), a Prussian general who distinguished himself first as a staff officer planning campaigns against Napoleon and later as the author of *On War*, summarized the inevitable relationship between war and

---

[6]Henri Baron de Jomini, *The Art of War*, trans. G. H. Mendell and W. P. Craighill (Westport, Conn.: Greenwood Press, 1971), pp. 25–36.
[7]Robert Leckie, *Warfare* (New York: Harper & Row, 1970), pp. 15–16.

Napoleon and Czar Alexander I. (New York Public Library)

politics—a relationship that is as valid today as when cholera ended his career a century and a half ago. The fundamental precept of von Clausewitz's doctrine was the strict subordination of war to a political object. The influence of the politician must predominate over that of the general. Von Clausewitz expressly limited the role of military representatives in the cabinet to that of advisor on technical matters; such representatives were to be denied major participation in the policy-making process. In short, for von Clausewitz military action could not be separated from politics.[8] Contemporary complaints about the presumably unwarranted intrusion of politicians into the conduct of war are, according to von Clausewitz's doctrine, thoroughly unjustified, for they reveal a failure to understand the nature of war.

During World War II, Prime Minister Winston Churchill and General Dwight D. Eisenhower debated at length the feasibility of an Allied invasion of the Balkans without ever directly confronting the only major question involved: What were the political objectives to be achieved by opening a front in southeastern Europe?[9] This failure to order priorities is an example of a clear violation of von Clausewitz's principle of the supremacy of political over military considerations.

Von Clausewitz's *On War* marked the beginning of a new phase in the use of armed conflict as an instrument of statecraft. Two features of this work stand out. First, unlike other writers of the period, von Clausewitz systematically

---

[8]Karl von Clausewitz, *On War*, trans. O. J. Matthijs Jolles (New York: Modern Library, 1943), pp. 595–99.

[9]Dwight D. Eisenhower, *Crusade in Europe* (Garden City, N.Y.: Doubleday, 1952), pp. 194, 281.

probed the psychological dimension of war. He correctly identified national morale as one of the major determinants of the outcome of a war. For von Clausewitz, the object of all war was to break the enemy's will to resist one's own political demands. A corollary to this proposition is that the degree to which the enemy's will to resist will bend or break depends upon the extent of the political demands imposed upon them: The less demanding the goals one proclaims in war, the easier it is to achieve a satisfactory negotiated settlement. Accordingly, such slogans as "unconditional surrender" and "total victory" have no place in von Clausewitz's thought.

To be sure, von Clausewitz introduced his work with an abstract definition of war as the unlimited use of violence in the service of the state. It is unfortunate, however, that many remember only these introductory remarks, for von Clausewitz quickly turned from speculative thought on the unlimited use of violence to the world of historical reality, in which he saw war as the servant and not the master of statecraft. Although von Clausewitz's death prevented him from completing his work, and although subsequent editing may not have done justice to the rigor of his theory, the dualism of his thought is clear. War as unrestrained use of force to attain a political goal is separate from war as an instrument of policy employed to protect the security of the state. After making this distinction, von Clausewitz turned from the role of the historical empiricist to conclude his study with a fundamentally normative proposition: Resorting to violence in the form of war is such an extreme step that it ought to be taken only on the advice of a civilian cabinet and in accordance with well-defined political objectives.

The governments engaged in World War I and World War II generally failed to subordinate their military purposes to precise political needs. Consequently, they did not observe the Clausewitzian maxim that the continuation of politics by other and often violent means does not entail the subordination of political reasoning to military action. The momentum of destructiveness in the world wars grew until the technical requirements of the confrontations replaced diplomatic efforts to create a stable international order. The grand strategy of winning the peace was forgotten in the struggle of carrying out the strategy designed to defeat enemy armed forces.

The two world wars represent not only a perfecting of the technique of fully mobilizing the human resources available to a society but also an effort to actualize the doctrine of the use of total violence to achieve ideological ends—an approach that von Clausewitz had rejected as being contrary to the nature of international politics. In its fury and relentless prosecution, the Albigensian Crusade, begun in 1209 for the purpose of suppressing the Catharist sect in southern France, offers a possible parallel to the total wars fought in the twentieth century. The ideologically motivated warriors of today, however, have at their disposal weaponry of an infinitely more destructive potential than their medieval forebears could have imagined. And the willingness of governments to employ these weapons rather than to compromise their declared vital interests is a matter of record.

CAUSES OF WAR

Any effort to identify a single cause of war relevant to all time is futile. Yet a series of causes can be singled out in an attempt to suggest the circumstances in which war is most likely to occur.[10] The explanations government officials offer for military action against opposing regimes vary greatly and are designed to appeal to the prevailing mood of mass opinion. Yet by looking at the past, it is possible to single out a set of causes of war that possess an explanatory value beyond the present era and outside the environment of the Western state system. A review of the literature on the origins of war reveals some seven primary factors or conditions that have precipitated armed conflict: human aggression, elite and popular fatalism regarding war, small-group conspiracy, economic imperialism, nationalist expansionism and irredentism, systemic inadequacy, and the general cycles of history. This list, as with all others, however ambitiously prepared, does not cover all wars. Yet most armed conflicts have been found to be rooted in a political environment characterized by the conditions listed above.

Human Aggression

Humans are thought by many (especially realist thinkers) to be innately aggressive beings. This assumption cannot be dismissed lightly by students of international relations. Our present obligation is not to establish conclusively whether or not there is an instinctive aggressive drive in humans; that question lies outside the scope of this discussion. Throughout international history, humans have frequently behaved as if aggression fulfilled a biological need, and it is this historical reality that should occupy our attention here.

The British social philosopher Thomas Hobbes (1588–1679) defined the basic political motivation in humans as a struggle for dominance over others. He called upon the sovereign to place a check upon the people's appetites and their capacity to do harm to each other.[11] Contemporary students of human behavior have also concluded that without a common restraining force, aggression and war will dominate relations among humans.

The English anthropologist Anthony Storr has suggested that humans have a physiochemical system that responds to threats or frustration by producing violent behavior. There is, then, a physiological basis for violence—a series of reactions that ready the body for combat.[12]

---

[10]In their comprehensive treatment of the war phenomenon, Richard Falk, Samuel Kim, and their associates review a large amount of literature devoted to the study of war, its causes, and strategies leading to its prevention and ultimately its cure. They subdivide the literature by method and discipline of each theorist as follows: (1) moral and philosophical, (2) ethological and psychological, (3) cultural and anthropological, (4) sociopsychological, (5) sociological, (6) socioeconomic, (7) decision making, (8) international systemic, (9) normative. See Richard A. Falk and Samuel S. Kim, eds., *The War System: An Interdisciplinary Approach* (Boulder, Colo.: Westview Press, 1980).

[11]Thomas Hobbes, *Leviathan* (Oxford: Basil Blackwell, 1947), pp. 80–84.

[12]Anthony Storr, *Human Aggression* (New York: Atheneum, 1968), pp. 11–14.

The international environment lacks the normative and political restraints of civil society and is therefore incapable of curbing, on a global scale, the human tendency toward violence. Or is it possible that the various control mechanisms in domestic society are so effective that humans turn to international war as a release for their suppressed aggressive drives? Thucydides observed, as have other historians, that the outbreak of the Peloponnesian War was greeted enthusiastically by the youth of Athens, who were eager to win glory on the field of battle. Observers of many other societies at the outbreak of war have noted the same phenomenon.

Ethology, the study of animal behavior, may offer us some suggestions for coping with the problem of human aggression and violence. Konrad Lorenz, an Austrian ethologist, has concluded that although humans do behave as if they were innately aggressive, there are ways other than wars to ritualize and even release this aggression. Indeed, the space race and international athletic events may serve as surrogate wars.[13] Interestingly, the Olympic Games of ancient Greece had a stabilizing influence on the Hellenic interstate system. Wars were simply suspended during the time period set out for the games every four years.[14]

Despite the record of human warfare, the issue of whether a tendency toward violence is innate in humans remains in vigorous dispute among anthropologists. On the one hand, Robert Ardrey has argued that humans satisfy their needs for identity, security, and a release from boredom by engaging in war.[15] On the other hand, the noted English anthropologist Geoffrey Gorer has criticized Ardrey's theory of innate human aggressiveness. Gorer points out that the experimental data underlying Ardrey's thesis derive from studies of animal behavior. These data, according to Gorer, cannot be transferred to the realm of international relations without doing serious damage to the logic of scientific inquiry.[16]

The debate as to whether or not war is an inevitable outgrowth of human nature will doubtless continue. Regardless of the outcome of this debate, it is important for students of international relations to realize that warfare is currently an avenue through which many governments seek to bring about changes in the international system. Optimistic statements about human nature are welcome, yet they should not delude national leaders or their publics into believing that social forces can easily succeed in sublimating human aggression and thereby remove one of the several sources of war.

The political sociologist Stewart G. Cole hypothesized that more contact among different peoples will lessen militant nationalism and the chances of war. Cole wrote that if only different groups would begin to consider each other *demo-*

---

[13]Konrad Lorenz, *On Aggression*, trans. Marjorie Kerr Wilson (New York: Harcourt, Brace & World, 1963), pp. 279–82.

[14]It is unfortunate that the Olympic Games of 1980 (Moscow) and 1984 (Los Angeles) were marred by the nonparticipation of the United States (in 1980) and the USSR (in 1984), which was justified on political and ideological grounds.

[15]Robert Ardrey, *The Territorial Imperative: A Personal Inquiry into the Animal Origins of Property and Nations* (New York: Atheneum, 1966), p. 333. Cf. Robert Bigelow, *The Dawn Warriors: Man's Evolution toward Peace* (Boston: Little, Brown, 1969), pp. 45–51, 57–59, 249.

[16]Geoffrey Gorer, "Ardrey on Human Nature," *Encounter*, 28 (June 1967), 70.

cratically, they would soon realize that their common bonds are greater than the divisive forces of ethnic and national interests.[17] But the operative word *democratically* defies a universally acceptable definition in a world of cultural pluralism and extremely unequal distribution of power and privilege.

Elite and Popular Fatalism and Misperceptions

The self-fulfilling prophecy regarding the inevitability of war is the subject of the second and possibly the most incisive theory on the causes of armed conflict.[18] According to this theory, a general feeling of resignation regarding this presumed inevitability characterizes foreign-policy makers and their publics. Consequently, a process of planning and organizing resources based solely on the presumption of the impending outbreak of hostilities is set in motion. An interview in 1911 between Czar Nicholas II of Russia and his newly appointed ambassador to the Ottoman Empire, A. Nekliukov, illustrates this point. Before departing for Constantinople the ambassador was told by his emperor that a general European war was coming and that every effort must be made to delay the call to arms until 1917.[19] The czar was not alone in his anticipation of war. Indeed, the adoption of the same point of view in other European capitals is a convincing example of the effect of a self-fulfilling prophecy in international relations. By the summer of 1914, the governing elites of Europe were so conditioned to the prospect of a general war that they were incapable of resisting the demand for mobilization that arose over an issue of Balkan politics. A generation earlier, this issue would have been resolved in an international congress.

Self-fulfilling prophecies about the inevitability of war are often fortified by the attitudes of elites and publics that conjure up distorting and hostile images of other states and ethnic groups. Robert Jervis, employing a political-psychological approach to the study of world politics, has argued that misperception, distorted images, selective attention to evidence supporting one's beliefs or misconceptions, thinking and reacting by historical analogy, imputing unity of purpose and policy cohesiveness to one's presumed adversaries, are all characteristic of the attitudes of decision makers in the history of the last two centuries.[20] He concluded, for example, that prior to World War II a number of Western decision makers, influenced by their experiences in World War I, underestimated Adolf Hitler's aggressive potential. After World War II, however, having been traumatized by the appeasing tactics of the interwar period, they tended to overestimate the aggressive potential of the Soviets.[21] For Jervis, and for other scholars in the

---

[17]Stewart G. Cole, "Europe's Conflict of Cultures," in *Group Relations and Group Antagonisms*, ed. R. M. MacIver (New York: Harper & Brothers, 1944), pp. 154–55.

[18]Robert Jervis, *Perception and Misperception in International Politics* (Princeton, N.J.: Princeton University Press, 1976).

[19]Sydney Bradshaw Fay, *The Origins of the World War*, 2nd ed. rev. (New York: Macmillan, 1928), vol. I, pp. 412–13.

[20]Robert Jervis, "Hypotheses on Misperception," in *The War System*, ed. Falk and Kim, pp. 465–90.

[21]Ibid., pp. 475–79.

same tradition, *misperception* (one-sided or mutual) is expected to be found at the bottom of every conflict.[22]

The sociologist Emory S. Bogardus developed the concept of *social distance* in order to measure the degree of affinity or aversion of persons toward members of other national, religious, or economic groups. In analyzing the responses to questionnaires concerning this concept, Bogardus found significant variations in popular attitudes toward different groups. Moreover, he determined that the responses he received on his surveys were reflections of natural attitudes rather than simply rationalizations contrived to satisfy the researcher.[23] Clearly, mass opinion in a particular society consists of a complex set of attitudes toward specific foreign groups and cultures. The efforts of foreign-policy makers to mobilize popular support for their objectives must therefore take into account the social distance that average citizens believe exists between their way of life and the society they are being asked to defend or oppose.

In the last analysis, the credibility of a government's foreign policy rests upon its ability to utilize force in a conflict of interest with foreign powers. "Credibility" in this context may depend upon the readiness with which members of a society will sacrifice personal interests in order to make war. If there is a biologically rooted pattern of behavior in humans that can be described as aggressive, then the way in which the mass of the population perceives another state may well determine whether a policy of appeasement or a firm stand is adopted in a crisis involving that state. The empirical evidence for this assertion derives partially from an exhaustive psychological study of the American soldier in World War II. A team of social psychologists examined combat attitudes and behavior in representative army companies. Of the soldiers interviewed, 38 to 48 percent stated that they "would really like to kill a Japanese soldier." In contrast, only 5 to 9 percent expressed the same spirit of hostility toward German soldiers.[24] Such differences in attitude reveal not only society's image of itself in relation to other societies, but also the degree to which a people and its government will resign themselves to a fatalistic belief in the "inevitability" of war with another power.

Small-Group Conspiracy

A third and somewhat controversial theory of the origins of war posits a governmental or quasi-governmental conspiracy to bring about an armed conflict. Borrowed from criminal law, the concept of a conspiracy suggests that two or more people come together for the purpose of secretly planning a crime. The essential element in the definition is the intention of the wrongdoers as opposed to the

[22]J. D. Steinbruner, *The Cybernetic Theory of Decision* (Princeton, N.J.: Princeton University Press, 1974); Robert Axelrod, ed., *Structure of Decision* (Princeton, N.J.: Princeton University Press, 1976).

[23]Emory S. Bogardus, "A Social Distance Scale," *Sociology and Social Research*, 17 (January-February, 1933), 265–71, and "Scales in Social Research," *Sociology and Social Research*, 24 (September-October 1939), 74.

[24]Samuel A. Stouffer et al., *The American Soldier*, vol. II: *Combat and Its Aftermath* (Princeton, N.J.: Princeton University Press, 1949), p. 34.

act itself. The conspiracy theory brings into play the idea of individual free will and emphasizes the variable of personality as the key to explaining the outbreak of war.[25]

The history of the foreign relations of the United States offers a typical example of the conspiracy theory. In 1935 and 1936, Congress passed the Neutrality Acts, which forbade the sale of arms or their transport to warring countries once the president acknowledged the outbreak of war.[26] This legislation resulted in part from a sensational congressional investigation conducted by Senator Gerald P. Nye. The well-publicized finding of this investigation was that the American involvement in World War I stemmed from the tight interweaving of American and Allied financial interests. This similarity of interest was manifested in the granting of large loans by Wall Street bankers to the British and French military establishments so that they could purchase munitions in the United States. The financial commitment to the Allied cause engendered a public campaign against neutrality and in favor of intervention. President Wilson's war message of April 2, 1917, was presumably the culmination of this effort at mass persuasion.[27] In the popular historical literature of the 1930s, the financial manipulations of unscrupulous bankers conspiring to bring on war for their own profit came to be viewed as the single major source of armed hostility in world affairs.

The English novelist and historian H. G. Wells (1866–1946) stressed the idiosyncratic behavior of heads of government in his interpretation of the origins of the two world wars.[28] To Wells, the institutionalization of the doctrine of power politics as a result of the development of professionalized diplomacy in the foreign offices of the great powers was the indispensable quality of the European balance-of-power system and the accompanying European imperialism in Africa and Asia. When one adds to the schemes of diplomats the militaristic fantasies of demagogic political leaders, war is to be expected. Wells concluded that war is not a historical necessity and that it can be prevented by curtailing the ambitions of paranoids in power. The trials of the major war criminals in Nuremberg and Tokyo (1945–48) gave legal sanction to this point of view, in the form of indictments for crimes against peace.

In an exhaustive study of the political background of the Imperial Japanese government's decision to wage war on the United states, David Bergamini developed an elaborate historical application of the conspiracy theory. Bergamini saw Emperor Hirohito not as a ceremonial chief of state but as an effective formulator of a policy whose explicit goal was the subduing of China and the conquering of Southeast Asia.[29] To achieve this end, an "imperial conspiracy," whose key members included the emperor and selected military figures, came

[25]For a historical case study of the conspiracy theory in World War II, see Richard E. Minear, *Victors' Justice: The Tokyo War Crimes Trial* (Princeton, N.J.: Princeton University Press, 1971).

[26]Thomas A. Bailey, *A Diplomatic History of the American People*, 9th ed. (Englewood Cliffs, N.J.: Prentice-Hall, 1974), pp. 700–701.

[27]Walter Millis, *Road to War: America, 1914–1917* (Boston: Houghton Mifflin, 1935), pp. 334–36.

[28]See H. G. Wells, *The Outline of History*, rev. ed. (Garden City, N.Y.: Garden City Books, 1949), vol. II, pp. 1059, 1074, 1171.

[29]David Bergamini, *Japan's Imperial Conspiracy* (New York: Morrow, 1971), pp. xxviii-xxxii.

The Japanese bombing of Pearl Harbor (December 7, 1941). (National Archives)

into being in the 1920s and successfully imposed a militaristic regime on Japan, the first of a series of steps leading to Pearl Harbor. Critics of Bergamini's thesis point out that much of his evidence is circumstantial. Nevertheless, his book has received serious attention. Its emphasis on the role of personality makes it a most impressive contemporary statement of the conspiracy theory. Bergamini's interpretation contrasts sharply with the prevailing thesis that the roots of Japan's war policy were impersonal historical and economic forces.

A classic and documented example of an effort to instigate a war against a foreign foe as an artificial means of fostering national unity occurred at the outbreak of the American Civil War. William H. Seward, President Abraham Lincoln's secretary of state, composed a memorandum euphemistically entitled "Some Thoughts for the President's Consideration," which reached the chief executive's desk on April 1, 1861. Seward described what he perceived as a lack of clarity and purpose in the federal government's response to the formation of the Confederacy. Accordingly, he advocated that the cabinet move to deemphasize the issue of slavery and to emphasize the goal of national unity. To accomplish this end, the secretary blandly proposed that the United States demand "explanations" from Great Britain and France for their interference in Mexico and from Spain for its activity in Santo Domingo. Simultaneously, American agents should be dispatched to Canada, Mexico, and Central America, where they would arouse in the populace a spirit of resistance to European influence.[30] These

[30]Bruce Catton, *The Centennial History of the Civil War*, vol. I: *The Coming Fury* (Garden City, N.Y.: Doubleday, 1961), pp. 288-90.

moves would constitute a prelude to war with a European enemy—a manufactured conflict against a traditional rival for the purpose of unifying a divided nation. President Lincoln wisely rejected the memorandum, but eleven days after its delivery the Confederate bombardment of Fort Sumter began.

Economic Imperialism

To the popular mind the fourth supposed cause of war, the economic motive, is the most persuasive.[31] Briefly stated, those who argue for this cause of war identify human greed as the root of war and the profit motive as the catalyst of war. The struggle to capture new markets or to control new sources of raw materials drives governments, acting at the bidding of captains of industry, to embark upon imperialist ventures that invariably result in armed conflict. In such situations, governments serve merely as agents of commercial interests and fail to represent recognized national interests. War becomes the handmaiden of a marriage of convenience among the financiers and industrialists of an imperialist state seeking to achieve a position of regional or global economic monopoly.[32]

The theorists who have identified economic forces as the main cause of war fall into two groups: the classical advocates of free trade and the Marxists. For different reasons, both groups have viewed the workings of monopolistic capital as the source of international violence. The English political economist Leonard Trelawney Hobhouse (1864–1929) wrote that the curtailment of free trade for the sake of protecting domestic economic interests results in governmental subsidization of overseas colonization. In turn, colonization engenders a policy of imperialism on the part of the mother country. Imperialism brings in its wake not only war against the peoples of prospective colonies, but also war against rival colonial powers. For Hobhouse, only a system of free trade would dissolve the symbiotic relationship between political authority and financial interests seeking overseas markets and sources of raw materials.[33] Free trade would also lead to the application of the economic law of comparative advantage to the distribution of goods and services in the world market. The resulting command of the market by the most efficient producers of a given commodity would benefit consumers uniformly and would also encourage stability and order in the world community. An equilibrium of economic and political forces would prevail, and sources of friction among governments would diminish, if not disappear completely. The chain of destruction beginning with government sponsorship of foreign commercial ventures, leading to colonization and imperialism, and ending ultimately in war, would thus be broken.

If free trade was the way to peace for Hobhouse, it was the way to war

---

[31]Charles Reynolds, *Modes of Imperialism* (Oxford: M. Robertson, 1981).

[32]Richard Lewinsohn, *The Profits of War through the Ages*, trans. Geoffrey Sainsburg (New York: Dutton, 1937), pp. 225-28; Lionel Robbins, *The Economic Causes of War* (London: Jonathan Cape, 1939), pp. 60–66.

[33]Leonard Trelawney Hobhouse, *Democracy and Reaction* (Brighton, Sussex: Harvester Press, 1972), pp. 6–7, 55–56.

for Vladimir Ilyich Lenin (1870–1924).[34] According to Lenin, to protect the fortune of the capitalist class meant more than merely merchandising one's surplus goods abroad. It involved a process of action and reaction whereby financial interests acquired captive markets and defended them against rival exporters. One's colonial possessions constituted the only safeguard against other monopolies. The result of this unrelenting process was that a cluster of capitalists divided the world into regional trade zones, which in turn gave birth to militaristic rivalries among the great powers for additional annexations.

In short, the presumed inevitable growth of manufactured surpluses at home demanded the creation of new outlets beyond the domestic market and led to imperialism in the form of overt colonialism. In the post–World War II era, neo-Marxists point out, colonialism has taken a more sophisticated form than the extension of direct governmental authority over one country by another. Nevertheless, the result is the same: The race by the industrialized states of the North for secure, accessible markets in the South generates frictions that result in conflict among the great powers as well as wars of self-determination waged by colonial peoples. According to this theory, the aggressive state is merely an agent of capitalist interests that it cannot begin to control. Presumably, these interests have grown desperate over the problem of disposing of accumulated goods that are unmarketable in a saturated domestic economy. Both Marxists and non-Marxists alike point to the multinational corporation as a new manifestation of organized capital's effort to structure the international economic system in a manner beyond the reach of political control.

Despite the popularity of the economic interpretation of the causes of imperialism and war, it is open to doubt for a number of reasons. First, modern capitalism is a product of the industrial revolution and cannot, therefore, account for all the wars of history. True, some economic determinists assert that commercial motives were the hidden causes of Athenian involvement in the Peloponnesian War, but the evidence in support of this hypothesis is contested by many historians. The history of violent conflict is too long to be explained by a single cause, especially one limited to a contemporary phenomenon of economic organization, however satisfying that explanation might appear. Nevertheless, we would do well to bear in mind the judgment of the British historian J.F.C. Fuller that British grand strategy in World War II aimed at the reduction of German trade and finance as well as military power.[35]

Without doubt, the record of modern imperialism does reveal that in selected cases the competition among great powers for colonies led to war. However, the colonial record also gives rise to the second reason challenging the economic thesis. It can be phrased in one question: Were the colonies commercially

---

[34]V. I. Lenin, *Imperialism: The Highest Stage of Capitalism*, rev. ed. (New York: International Publishers, 1933), pp. 75–81.

[35]J.F.C. Fuller, *The Second World War, 1939–45: A Strategical and Tactical History* (New York: Meredith Press, 1949), p. 26. For an evaluation of the economic thesis regarding the Peloponnesian War, see G.E.M. de St. Croix, *The Origins of the Peloponnesian War* (Ithaca, N.Y.: Cornell University Press, 1972), p. 216.

profitable? The answer is that in many cases they were an economic liability to the mother country. The German colonies in Africa prior to 1918 provide one such case. Ultimately, one might argue, the loss of those colonies to Great Britain served to strengthen the German economy. Similarly, the granting of independence to British and French colonial possessions in the 1950s and 1960s contributed to the creation of a stronger, inward-looking Europe, one capable of such experiments as the formation of the European Economic Community in 1958. Without this successful movement of decolonization, the major European powers would have been enmeshed in quashing an unending series of wars of national self-determination. Their withdrawal from Africa and Asia enabled the states of Western Europe to focus their attention on domestic problems and to undertake the most ambitious project in regionalism in modern times—the movement to bring about a political unification of Western Europe.

The third criticism of the economic imperialist interpretation is that the theory fails to explain wars between communist states exclusively, such as the Chinese-Vietnamese war of 1979. Wars between communist states serve notice that violence between territorially organized political collectivities can not be traced to a single cause such as the form of government or the economic philosophy professed by ruling elites.

Nationalist Expansionism and Irredentism

Related to the controversy over the economic interpretation of the origins of war is the theory that war arises from nationalistically motivated imperialistic ambitions manifested by one government toward others. In this sense, the word *imperialism* connotes more than the profit-motivated drive for markets and economic dependencies posited by the theorists of economic imperialism. It is rooted, rather, in a relentless quest for expansion to satisfy an amalgam of instinctive, psychological, and ideological needs that could be summarized with the single word *glory*.

Thucydides viewed the Peloponnesian War as having resulted in part from the unchecked rise of Athenian maritime power and the consequent growth of an empire capable of destroying the equilibrium existing among the Greek city-states. Historians may doubt that Athens was truly an expansionist power, but in Thucydides' day an observer of the diplomatic maneuvers of the city-states could not be sure that Athens was not a threat.[36] Then, as in most subsequent instances, the issue was decided on the basis of the perceptions of the parties involved. The threat of Athenian expansionism, whether real or imagined, readily justified Sparta's adoption of a policy of counterexpansionism and, ultimately, war. Mutual perceptions of aggressiveness in both Sparta and Athens merely increased the chances for war between them.

A prime example of the use of the charge of nationalistic expansionism to justify a war resulted from the utilization of the so-called Tanaka Memorial for

---

[36]See Donald Kagan, *The Outbreak of the Peloponnesian War* (Ithaca, N.Y.: Cornell University Press, 1969), pp. 345–56.

purposes of propaganda. In the late 1920s, the Japanese general and sometime prime minister Giichi Tanaka allegedly wrote a memorandum in which he outlined Japan's need to conquer China. The Chinese published the memorandum in 1929, claiming that it had been leaked by a Korean clerk employed by the Japanese government.[37] The text of the document laid bare Japan's nationalist dreams and aggressive ambitions toward China. Although scholars have expressed uncertainty regarding the authenticity of the Tanaka Memorial, its psychological impact on China and the United States cannot be doubted. Those who believed the document authentic regarded it as proof of Japan's nationalistic expansionism and of the need to check the growth of Japanese power. In retrospect, however, the argument of Japanese expansionism fails to explain fully the subsequent entry of the United States into war with Japan. Subsequent historical accounts indicate that the rise of the Japanese Empire was not a "clear and present danger" to the security of the United States and that the Japanese-American collision in the Pacific was not inevitable.[38]

Governments engaged in armed conflict seek to persuade their publics that war is the only alternative open to them. Often, the claim is of dubious validity. The 1962 war between India and the People's Republic of China is a case in point. Each side claimed that the other was an imperialist determined to pursue a policy of nationalist aggrandizement. The truth of the matter is that the disputed border that underlay the war was not clearly demarcated, and that each of the warring parties could advance only a vague claim to the contested region.

Aside from the problem of accurately labeling a war as *imperialist* and *aggressive* (as opposed to *defensive*) at the time of its occurrence, there is the historical question of establishing a valid time frame within which to make the normative judgment of who is an aggressor. Is a government seeking to regain lost national territory pursuing an aggressive policy? In 843, the Treaty of Verdun divided the empire of Charlemagne and in doing so placed the provinces of Alsace and Lorraine under French sovereignty. For centuries thereafter, this area was disputed by Germany and France. After the Franco-Prussian War (1870–71), the two provinces were ceded to Germany. In 1918 they were regained by France. In asserting a historical claim to Alsace-Lorraine, was France acting in an expansionist role? Or was it justifiably seeking to restore its national territory? The answer is judgmental, for it depends upon one's national allegiance and political perspective. In this instance, as in most other frontier disputes, the historical record is so unclear that international law cannot give a definitive answer. Instead, it is left to the manipulators of mass opinion to stigmatize one of the warring countries as the aggressor.

The key to popular nationalist feeling is often *irredentism*—the struggle to reunite lost provinces with the national state. In 1919, the Italian poet and war hero Gabriele D'Annunzio led his irregular forces into the Adriatic port of Fiume

---

[37]See Upton Close, *Behind the Face of Modern Japan* (New York: Appleton-Century, 1942), p. 105; Arthur E. Tiedemann, *Modern Japan: A Brief History* (Princeton, N.J.: Van Nostrand, 1955), pp. 127–33.

[38]Bruce M. Russett, *No Clear and Present Danger: A Skeptical View of the United States Entry in World War II* (New York: Harper & Row, 1972), pp. 55–58.

(Rijeka) and vainly sought to add his part of *Italia irredenta* (unredeemed Italy) to the motherland. Irredentist sentiment continues to inflame nationalist passions, often resulting in armed conflict. Recent examples include the Sino-Soviet clash on the Ussuri River in 1978, the Persian Gulf War (1980-88) begun by an Iraqi attempt to regain from Iran the Shatt-al-Arab waterway, and the British reconquest of the Falkland/Malvinas Islands after their seizure in 1982 by Argentine forces seeking to regain what they believed to be *Argentina irredenta*.[39]

We should keep in mind, however, the historical reality that an irredentist claim may, at times, provide a cloak for aggression. The slogan of "national liberation" may be abused by the propagandist to disguise a policy of expansionism.

Systemic Inadequacy

A predominantly idealist view among international relations scholars is that the international system, given the absence of centralized and effective institutions to regulate relations among sovereign states, is by its very structure condemned to gravitate to war as an instrument of state policy. This view, which we will explore in depth in Chapters 13–15, emphasizes the ineffectiveness of existing global peacekeeping mechanisms such as the United Nations and recommends the adoption of global federal institutions if war is to be some day abolished.

Among realist scholars, also, and despite their tendency to accept an anarchic international system as a fact of life, there is considerable debate regarding the type of global political structures that are more or less conducive to the maintenance of peace. Historically, as we have seen in Chapter 3, a balance-of-power system, whether bipolar or multipolar, has had to adjust to the tension between those governments supporting the existing global or regional distribution of power and those challenging it. Some theorists dispute the proposition that a stable balance-of-power system involves a condition of equilibrium between status-quo (satisfied) and revisionist (dissatisfied) governments. An increasing number of observers of international politics argue that a preponderance of power must exist on the side of status-quo forces. Otherwise, the temptation to resort to war is too great to be resisted by those who are unhappy with the existing system.[40]

In his history of World War II, Winston Churchill wrote that the failure of the victors of 1918 to halt German rearmament in the 1930s was the greatest single cause of the war.[41] The essence of this observation is that the European state system was based on a balance of power that was characterized by the success of the status quo powers in preventing revisionist opponents from shifting

---

[39]For an excellent study asserting that ethnic conflict has been responsible for heavy loss of life in primitive as well as in modern societies, see Cynthia H. Enloe, *Ethnic Soldiers: State Security in Divided Societies* (Athens, Ga.: University of Georgia Press, 1980).

[40]On this and similar questions, see Geoffrey Blainey, *The Causes of War* (New York: Free Press, 1973).

[41]Winston S. Churchill, *The Second World War*, vol. I: *The Gathering Storm* (Boston: Houghton Mifflin, 1948), pp. 15–18.

that balance in their favor. For Churchill, the preservation of peace in a balance-of-power system was due to the preponderance of actual or potential military power in the hands of the usually small number of governments who were satisfied with the prevailing global or regional order. Within their theoretical context, the balance-of-power system is scarcely distinguishable from a hierarchy of states.

In contrast with this theory is the argument that a stable balance of power can be maintained only by a third force. With consummate skill, this *balancer* shifts from one coalition of states to another in order to uphold a delicate equilibrium. An assumption of English diplomacy from the time of Henry VIII (1509–47) has been that the balance of power can be achieved only by a continuing readiness to shift from one continental alliance to another. This so-called tongue-in-the-scale approach remained a cardinal feature of British diplomacy until the end of World War II. Even today, some would argue that Great Britain continues to play the role of balancer among the most powerful members of the European Community.

Whether one interprets the balance of power as a preponderance of power on the part of the status-quo countries or as an equilibrium between those challenging the system and those satisfied with it, the reality of the situation is that the balance of power is both unreliable and unstable. Until the French Revolution, military power was two dimensional. That is, the strength of professional armies and navies could be estimated with a fair degree of accuracy. But the total mobilization of the Napoleonic Wars, combined with the emphasis of von Clausewitz on the role of national morale, completely altered this picture. Today, the ability of a foreign-policy elite to mobilize the varied national resources at its disposal in support of a war effort is crucial. This capability rests on such intangibles as leadership and public support of the government—factors nearly impossible to assess accurately.

The ruling elites of the twentieth century have been more prone to risk unlimited war than their counterparts a century ago. In 1941, the government of the Empire of Japan was well aware that in terms of resources it could not offer a prolonged challenge to the United States. Nevertheless, the cabinet in Tokyo hoped that the Japanese spirit of dedication to the imperial cause would enable Japan to win a quick victory, as it had in the Russo-Japanese War (1904–05). The balance-of-power system in the modern world has operated in an international setting where governments convinced of their widespread popular support—or of the effectiveness with which they have stilled domestic dissent—may chance a war even though their resources are limited.

The unpredictability of the international system itself intensifies the danger of armed conflict on a global scale. Consequently, architects of world order have sought, either through collective security or collective defense, to achieve some cohesiveness and stability in the international system. The avoidance of open warfare between the great powers since 1945 suggests that this goal has been partially realized. However, this record has been offset by the increasing frequency of war among and within the small powers.

General Cycles of History

The final theory we shall consider on the origins of war—cycles of history—is perhaps the most intriguing philosophically, but at the same time the most difficult to apply. The British historian Arnold J. Toynbee has perfected a cyclical theory of history. According to this theory, the decay of a civilization first becomes evident when the normative aspects of its culture begin to lose their unifying capability and civil disorder erupts. Ancient Greece (in the fourth century B.C.) and Renaissance Italy, two highly developed civilizations, fell victim to internal strife and consequently succumbed to superior political organizations—the Macedonian Empire and the dynastic French state, respectively.[42]

Writing nearly six centuries earlier, the Arab philosopher Ibn Khaldûn (1332–1406) proposed an early and non-Western version of the cyclical theory. He divided societies into sedentary and nomadic. The sedentary ones grew roots, and produced civilization and culture, but ultimately grew soft and became easy targets of vigorous and barbaric nomadic invasions. In Khaldûn's words, "The goal of civilization is sedentary culture and luxury. When civilization reaches that goal, it turns toward corruption and starts being senile, as happens in the natural life of living beings."[43]

Another cyclical theory of history was proposed by sociologist Pitirim A. Sorokin. Sorokin divided political cultures into the ideational and the sensate. Law in an ideational culture is of divine origin and of established universal moral standards, which bind together the members of society. The quest for pleasure, combined with internal distress, eventually replaces ideational with sensate law. This law is based on the utilitarian principle that law should be a means of producing the maximum amount of pleasure and the least amount of pain for the citizen. In the face of the demand for pragmatic legal standards, universal values give way to moral relativism. Domestically, this transition produces civil war; internationally, the frequency of war increases. An international system dominated by sensate political cultures is characterized by a perpetual state of war. This prolonged crisis becomes an unbearable ordeal, which produces a societal need for a moral revival. Historically, such revivals have usually taken the form of a charismatic movement. The political and social resurrection that follows restores the ideational character of law and with it peace in both the domestic and international spheres. Then a new transition from ideational to sensate values occurs, and the cycle repeats itself.[44]

An apparent linkage between imperialism and prosperity has led to a resurgence of interest in *long-cycle theory* as a means of explaining the outbreak of war. In 1925, the Russian economist N. D. Kondratieff theorized that boom-and-

---

[42]Arnold J. Toynbee, *Civilization on Trial* (New York: Oxford University Press, 1948), p. 120.

[43]Ibn Khaldûn, *The Muqaddimah: An Introduction to History*, trans. Franz Rosenthal (New York: Pantheon Books, 1958), vol. II, p. 296.

[44]Pitirim A. Sorokin, *The Crisis of Our Age: The Social and Cultural Outlook* (New York: Dutton, 1944), pp. 146–51, 205–24.

bust cycles of about fifty years in the world correlated with major wars. Building on this thesis, contemporary scholars postulate the existence of a global system dominated by one or more central powers possessing military and economic supremacy. Periodic economic crises gradually weaken the hegemonic states, making them vulnerable to successful challenges by revisionist forces, and a new cartel of international elites takes control, only to be replaced in forty to sixty years by still another group of challengers.[45]

Critics of the cyclical theory of history, and in particular of the argument that international war increases as civilizations move through a process of decay and dissolution, point out that the organization of human history into a rise-and-fall schema is to a great extent guesswork. Indeed, some historians question the existence of "patterns" in history, and they doubt that in the record of humanity there is a progression from one stage of interaction to another. Although these abstract arguments are interesting, at present they are unlikely to produce useful guidelines for action for the practitioners of statecraft.

AN ATTEMPT AT SYNTHESIS

The preceding interpretations of the causes of war illustrate the present state of infancy of international-relations theory. Each of the seven theories does offer some insight into the causes of organized violence among states; each calls for further study. Yet by themselves the theories are incomplete, and the gaps among them are sufficiently great to present a formidable barrier to the construction of a general model of the conditions under which war is most likely to occur. Is the ultimate cause of war the failure of the international system to organize and stabilize itself? The unleashing of the innate aggressive drive thought to exist in humans? The unchecked expansionism of great and smaller nationalistic powers? The dynamics of state-controlled or private capitalism? The resignation of decision makers and their publics to the presumed inevitability of war? The schemes of political-military conspiracies? Or the working out of recurring patterns of history?

Until a grand theory regarding the causes of war is developed, synthesizing elements of partial theories reviewed above, we have to settle for an understanding that each of these "theories," as well as others, helps only in part to explain war phenomena whenever and wherever they occur. Further, we should realize that some incidents of war can be better explained by using a Marxist explanatory framework, others using a realist one, and yet others using an idealist one.

Reviewing the seven theories about the causes of war, we can classify them philosophically and operationally by employing the framework displayed in Figure 10–1.

---

[45]Terence K. Hopkins and Immanuel Wallerstein, *World Systems Analysis: Theory and Methodology* (Beverly Hills, Calif.: Sage, 1982); George Modelski, ed., *Exploring Long Cycles* (Boulder, Colo.: L. Riemer, 1987).

REALISM MARXISM	IDEALISM MARXISM	
WAR VIEWED AS INEVITABLE *(Nonpreventable but manageable)*	WAR VIEWED AS ACCIDENTAL *(Subject to effective regulation or control)*	AGGRESSIVE WAR VIEWED AS PREMEDITATED CRIMINAL ACTIVITY *(Punishable and preventable by law)*
Human aggression Systemic inadequacy General cycles of history	Elite and popular fatalism Mutual misperception Overlapping irredentism	Small-group conspiracy Economic imperialism Nationalist expansionism

Figure 10-1   A Classification of the Theories of War

As Figure 10–1 attempts to demonstrate, the students of war can be classified as to their philosophical outlooks toward war (inevitable/preventable) and as to operational remedies they propose for its eradication or control. Realists tend to view warfare as inevitable, a product of human frailties, of tendencies of self-promotion, as well as the accidental result of a quasi-anarchic international system that does not possess effective central institutions which can contain the conflict. War, although not totally preventable, is nonetheless considered manageable. The reduction of global violence can be the result of the mutual self-restraint of great powers. Self-restraint and mutual toleration by great powers are the key prerequisite for an effective operation of the balance-of-power system.

Idealists, on the contrary, view war as the product of aggressive, ignorant, or criminal leaders as well as the consequence of sorely inadequate global institutions. Needed as a remedy to war are effective international organizations that can reorient warlike tendencies and provide procedures for the peaceful and just settlement of disputes. Marxists fall on both sides of the realist-idealist spectrum in the sense that they consider war inevitable in a system dominated by capitalist states. They also view it as preventable criminal activity perpetrated by imperialist leaders, and correctable through the revolutionary transformation of capitalist states into communism.

SUGGESTIONS FOR FURTHER STUDY

Amitai Etzioni and Martin Wenglinsky survey Western theory on armed conflict in their anthology on *War and Its Prevention* (New York: Harper & Row, 1970). The Marxist perspective is provided by N. I. Lebedev, *A New Stage in International Relations* (Elmsford, N.Y.: Pergamon Press, 1978). The rational premeditation of war is the theme of Bruce Bueno de Mesquita, *The War Trap* (New Haven: Yale University Press, 1981). Social and economic facets of war receive close attention in Richard A. Falk and Samuel S. Kim, eds., *The War System: An Interdisciplinary Approach* (Boulder, Colo.: Westview Press, 1980). The normative dimension of war is the guiding question of Hedley Bull, "Recapturing the Just War for Political

Theory," *World Politics*, 31 (July 1979), 588–99; and Michael Walzer, *Just and Unjust Wars: A Moral Argument with Historical Illustrations* (New York: Basic Books, 1977). The relevance of traditional theory is borne out in Peter R. Moody, "Clausewitz and the Fading Dialectic of War," *World Politics*, 31 (April 1979), 417–33. Comprehensive works include Richard Smoke, *War* (Cambridge, Mass.: Harvard University Press, 1978); and Quincy Wright, *A Study of War*, (Chicago: University of Chicago Press, 2nd ed., 1965). Lancelot L. Farrar, Jr., ed., *War: A Historical, Political, and Social Study* (Santa Barbara, Calif.: ABC-Clio Press, 1978) has drawn together analyses of the origins of war, which complement the case studies in John G. Stoessinger, *Why Nations Go to War*, 2nd ed. (New York: St. Martin's Press, 1978). Maurice L. Farber has applied the theory of aggression to the topic in "Psychoanalytic Hypotheses in the Study of War," *Journal of Social Issues*, 11 (1955), 29–35. By comparison Charles A. Beard has offered an idiosyncratic interpretation of war in *The Devil Theory of War* (New York: Vanguard Press, 1936; reprint ed., New York: Greenwood Press, 1969); and C. Wright Mills stressed socioeconomic factors in *The Causes of World War Three* (New York: Ballantine Books, 1958). J. William Fulbright explored the notion of *hubris* in *The Arrogance of Power* (New York: Random House, 1966).

11

MODES AND LEVELS OF WARFARE

Despite the indefinite results of contemporary research on war, the increase in intensity of armed conflict is all too apparent.[1] Undoubtedly, the problems of this growing intensity, if not frequency, will command a high priority in future statistical studies on war. It is also important to note that quantitative studies suggest that violence in international relations reaches a peak every twenty to forty years.[2] If this cyclical trend is historically sound, the prognosis for the near future is depressing.

Imprecise theories as to the origin of war should not blind one to the ever-present reality of armed conflict in international affairs. Effective means of eliminating war as a technique of political action continue to elude politicians and theorists alike. Organized violence among states and within states remains a basic component of international politics. At the opening of the United Nations in 1945, the participating governments entered into a solemn commitment to renounce war as an instrument of policy. Article 2 of the Charter of the United Nations embodies this pledge, which remains undisputed even if the most flexible legal interpretation is adopted. However, only aggressive warfare is prohibited.[3] The prerogative of determining who the aggressor is presumably falls

---

[1]B. Bueno de Mesquita, *The War Trap* (New Haven: Yale University Press, 1981).

[2]David Singer and Melvin Small, *The Wages of War, 1816–1965: A Statistical Handbook* (New York: John Wiley, 1972), p. 212.

[3]See William V. O'Brien, *The Law of Limited International Conflict* (Washington, D.C.: Institute for World Polity, Georgetown University, 1965), pp. 22–29.

to the governments concerned, in which event the deterrent effect of Article 2 is indeed limited.

It is important to note that not all forms of conflict among states in the modern world fall into the category of war. As we have seen in Chapter 9, governments may wage economic and psychological warfare against each other without ever approaching armed hostilities. Throughout history, war has taken on many forms. Today, however, international law, as codified in the Geneva Conventions of 1949, identifies war as a condition existing under any one of the following three circumstances:

1. Declared or undeclared armed conflict between two or more states
2. Civil or internal war
3. Occupation of territory of a state by another, even though the occupying power does not encounter armed resistance.[4]

Under the last definition, the military occupation of Czechoslovakia by the Soviet Union and four other Warsaw Pact powers in 1968 constituted an act of war.

For the purpose of political analysis, the foregoing definition may not be fully adequate, for it does not distinguish limited from general war. That is, it does not distinguish the use of violence to accomplish a short-range political goal from the use of violence to obtain the unconditional surrender of an opponent. A general war whose outcome is the elimination of one of the major actors in the international system is rare. Nevertheless, it remains a possibility and is therefore a necessary consideration in any attempt to determine the role of war in international relations. It is all too easy to develop a feeling of false security in observing that wars since World War II have been limited rather than general.[5]

Just as World War I and World War II marked a new stage in the history of warfare, the post-1945 trend toward the regionalization of warfare seemed to suggest that the era of global conflict had passed. The argument was advanced that the superpowers would condone limited wars in areas far removed from their geographic homelands and that such wars were not a threat to the stability of the international system. The Anglo-Argentine War over the Falkland/Malvinas Islands (1982) was presented as a case in point. Both belligerents had contained the conflict and by tacit agreement limited themselves to conventional weapons. The presumption was that such wars were not only tolerable but even helpful, for a British victory meant the end of a military dictatorship in Argentina. Conversely, the danger of such thinking is illustrated by the struggle between Iraq and Iran in the Persian Gulf War (1980–88). Although limited at first, the intro-

---

[4]U.S. Department of the Army, *Treaties Governing Land Warfare* (Washington, D.C.: Government Printing Office, 1965), p. 67.

[5]The term *limited* is clearly employed here from the vantage point of the great powers and from a global perspective. From the perspective of those involved in these wars, such as the tragic Lebanese conflict and the protracted Persian Gulf War, these experiences are hardly limited in ferocity and destructiveness.

duction of poison gas by Iraq led to a rapid escalation of the conflict. Both sides began in 1985 to bombard each other's cities with missiles armed with high-explosive warheads. In 1987 the United States intervened with naval force to keep open the sea lanes of the Persian Gulf. Rapid movement up the ladder of escalation in terms of weaponry and external involvement forced the international community to take action to end the conflict, which cost over one million lives. Assuming a spectator stance in the event of such a "local" war is both dangerous and self- defeating. The presumed regionalization of war is a myth.

Most limited wars have been predominantly internal, although external involvement has frequently played a significant role. Civil wars—arising out of ethnic or economic cleavages—form the base of a scale of armed conflict that progresses to conventional international wars and ultimately to thermo-nuclear war among the nuclear powers. If Karl von Clausewitz's maxim that war is a continuation of politics by other means holds true, the reliance of governments on military action to attain their ends must vary in direct proportion to those ends. For this reason, one type of war must be placed in clear contrast with another. Internal (civil) war must be distinguished from international conflicts and from a combination of the two types.

INTERNAL GUERRILLA WAR

Internal/civil war develops out of a failure of a national political system and its institutions to function effectively. In this condition of institutional collapse, significant sections of the population, including major factions of the elite, no longer accord those in power, or even the regime they represent, a sense of legitimacy. Although many social scientists have hypothesized about the causes of revolution, the theories advanced by Ted Robert Gurr appear to have considerable acceptability.[6] Gurr begins with the pivotal concept of *relative deprivation*, which he defines as the perceived discrepancy between one's abilities and the rewards one may realistically expect. If those rewards are limited to the very few and are based largely on family name and ties, then relative deprivation, in the form of individual discontent, will be high. It is vital to note that in this context, the psychological variable of perception is more important than the actual social and economic conditions. The perceived disparity between capability and reward in an impoverished and autocratically governed society may not be as great as in a rapidly developing social setting, due to the passivity and lack of interest in politics that are cultivated by the ruling groups of traditional autocracies. Moreover, societies on the verge of industrialization experience more political ferment than predominantly agrarian societies in which government is monopolized by a narrowly based traditional elite.

Revolutions frequently begin under the leadership of a frustrated middle

[6]Ted Robert Gurr, *Why Men Rebel* (Princeton, N.J.: Princeton University Press, 1970).

class that may have some of the characteristics of an academic proletariat (i.e., an educated but unemployed or alienated elite group). If the revolutionary movement gains some success, a moderate regime utilizing the experience of the existing bureaucracy tends to assume power. This condition will be a transitory one, however; once the momentum of revolution develops, the desire to compromise with the old order diminishes before the pressure for radical change. The resulting ascendancy of radical elements is accompanied by a wave of terror. Nominally directed against the adherents of the old order, this campaign is in reality aimed toward all who express or may express doubt about the new revolutionary order. Ultimately, the revolutionary flame begins to flicker and those who initiated the purges often fall victim to their own tribunals. The cycle is completed when a government pledged to the restoration of order and stability in a postrevolutionary social setting takes power.[7]

Social and economic causes dominate the literature on revolution. Yet one of the most profound analyses of the revolutionary syndrome in all its manifestations is that of Frantz Fanon, a West Indian physician educated in France, whose work centered on the psychological dimension of internal war in the modern colonial setting.[8] According to Fanon, the psychological relationship between European colonizers and native peoples was such that violent conflict between the two was inevitable. The Europeans were forced to renounce their humanist heritage in order to impose an autocratic regime on the native population. The natives reacted with a spontaneous campaign of passive resistance, often manifested in deliberate laziness and a rise in criminality. In order to meet this challenge, the colonial authorities became increasingly repressive, and in turn, popular unrest grew. Untimately, covert and unorganized resistance gave way to the overt, organized opposition typical of the anticolonialist wars of the 1950s and 1960s.

According to Fanon, this process was an inevitable result of colonization because the human need for dignity and self-respect could never be satisfied under colonial rule. Although Fanon focused his analysis on instances of formally established colonial domination by an external power, the same psychological responses he described would probably obtain in cases of indirect foreign control—for example, of satellite and puppet governments. Violent reactions by nation-states to indirect but nevertheless effective foreign influence have been a trait of international relations. The East German (1953) and Hungarian (1956) uprisings as well as Czech and Slovak popular resistance to the Soviet-led five-power occupation of Czechoslovak Socialist Republic (1968) are cases in point. Similarly, popular resentment against the interventionist policies of the United States remains a theme of Latin American and Third World domestic politics. Although economic and military indicators can be used to assess foreign penetration of a domestic political system, the popularly perceived degree of external

---

[7]Admittedly these are patterns of revolutionary behavior that are not necessarily applicable in every case. For example, some revolts may begin with radical declarations and intentions but soon pass into the hands of managers, whose primary aim is to stay in power.

[8]Frantz Fanon, *The Wretched of the Earth*, trans. Constance Farrington (New York: Grove Press, 1968).

influence, whether real or imagined, is the key to understanding anticolonialism as a force in world politics.

Since 1945, most wars have involved popular resistance to foreign domination or domestic oppression, and guerrilla warfare has been the primary mode of struggle in a majority of these conflicts.[9] We will analyze guerrilla warfare in terms of the writings of its major theorists and in terms of its effectiveness in attaining political objectives. Although military history is well supplied with instances of military operations carried out by irregular forces—for instance, the Boer War (1899–1902)—this discussion will focus on more recent examples, as they are better related to the current international political system.

Following the principles of von Clausewitz, proponents of guerrilla warfare stress the inevitable relationship between war and foreign policy. There is a profound difference between guerrilla leaders of an essentially conservative and nationalist ideological commitment and those of a Marxist-Leninist persuasion. The conservative nationalists tend to view guerrilla operations as a limited means of attaining political goals. On the other hand, the Marxist-Leninists rely heavily upon a combination of urban and rural guerrilla warfare to effect major social, economic, and political changes. Typical of these opposing points of view are General George Grivas, the commander of the Greek Cypriots in their struggle for independence from Great Britain (1955–60), and Ernesto "Che" Guevara (1928–67), the fiery revolutionary who fought with Fidel Castro in Cuba and was later killed following an ambush by government forces in Bolivia.

In 1953, Grivas outlined the plans for a guerrilla campaign to be conducted on Cyprus. The purpose of the campaign was to mobilize the effective support of the Greek Cypriot population, first for independence and ultimately for union with Greece.[10] Grivas foresaw that the guerrilla activity would compel British authorities to institute military countermeasures, which would place London in the position of suppressing a colonial people's demand for self-determination. World opinion, acting through the United Nations, would then presumably approve the independence movement.

Whereas guerrilla warfare was secondary to the psychological and diplomatic efforts of the Greek Cypriots, some communist guerrillas operating in Latin America, such as Ernesto "Che" Guevara and Régis Debray, viewed it as a primary means of revolutionary struggle. As early as 1906, Lenin had identified sabotage and armed combat by irregular forces as a principal means of highlighting the societal contradictions that led to proletarian revolutions.[11] In the 1960s, Guevara elaborated on this theme by placing the guerrilla at the center of his theory of revolution. He asserted that guerrillas were themselves capable of overthrowing the established political and social order. In short, Guevara attributed to the guerrilla a role of significantly broader scope and greater effectiveness

---

[9]See Baljit Singh and Ko-wang Mei, *Theory and Practice of Modern Guerrilla Warfare* (Bombay: Asia Publishing House, 1971), pp. 92–109.

[10]See *The Memoirs of General Grivas*, ed. Charles Foley (New York: Praeger, 1965), pp. 204–7.

[11]See V. I. Lenin, "Partisan Warfare," in *Marx-Engels-Marxism*, 4th ed. (Moscow: Foreign Languages Publishing, 1951), pp. 186–99.

than the role of Grivas's irregular soldier, who was mainly a catalyst of change and not the primary agent of it.

Guevara integrated guerrilla warfare into a broad political context, as can be seen from the three principles that form the basis of his doctrine:

1. Popular, irregular forces can defeat not only the regular army but also the policies of the government.
2. A disciplined nucleus of revolutionaries can create an internal war instead of waiting for it to develop through the interaction of social forces, in the classical Marxist sense.
3. Latin America offers the most promising opportunity for guerrilla warfare because the guerrilla is more effective in rural areas with underdeveloped systems of communication.[12]

Guerrilla warfare is therefore the touchstone of the revolutionary movement and not merely the outgrowth of internal conflict in a society.

The French journalist and intellectual Régis Debray was considerably less optimistic about the use of guerrilla warfare in Latin America. Debray pointed out that an examination of the Chinese revolutionary experience in the 1930s and 1940s reveals five preconditions of a militarily successful guerrilla campaign:

1. Extensive territory within which to maneuver
2. A relatively high percentage and density of rural population
3. A common frontier with a sympathetic state that will provide sanctuary whenever needed
4. The inability of enemy forces to launch counterattacks by air
5. An opposing army not large enough to protect vital lines of communication

Debray concluded that these essential conditions were absent from Latin American revolutionary movements. He observed, further, that these movements were weighted down by entrenched oligarchies too comfortable in their leadership roles to take to the field as guerrillas.[13] Debray's incisive analysis of the inherent difficulties in waging a successful campaign of hit-and-run warfare contrasts sharply with Guevara's thesis that the guerrilla is the architect of historical progress.

For the roots of contemporary insurgency theory in Latin America, one must examine the record of Chinese communists. In their protracted revolution, they sought to adapt Marxism-Leninism to contemporary world political processes. In the *Communist Manifesto* (1848), Marx had postulated that a proletarian revolution would occur only in a society in which the class struggle had fully matured, not in predominantly agrarian, feudal societies.[14] But the Chinese Civil

---

[12]Che Guevara, *Guerrilla Warfare*, ed. Harries-Clichy Peterson (New York: Praeger, 1961), p. 3.

[13]Régis Debray, "Revolution in the Revolution? Armed Struggle and Political Struggle in Latin America, *Monthly Review*, 19 (July-August 1967), 61, 120–21.

[14]See Karl Marx and Friedrich Engels, *The Communist Manifesto* (New York: International Publishers, 1948), pp. 18–21.

Mao Zedong (1893–1976), Chinese Marxist theorist, revolutionary, leader, soldier, and statesman; ruled the People's Republic of China from 1949 to 1976. (Michal Heron)

War, which ended in 1949 with a communist consolidation of power, showed that winning control of rural areas can lead to the conquest of cities as well. Lin Biao, once a leading Chinese communist strategist, summarized the issue on a global basis by likening Western Europe and North America to "cities" of the world that will be subjugated by revolutionary action originating in the "countryside" of Latin America, Asia, and Africa.[15] According to this thesis, guerrilla warfare should replace conventional and nuclear war as the primary mode of international conflict, and war will once again become a feasible instrument of policy.

The ascendancy of guerrilla warfare in the Third World is better understood with a knowledge of the writings of Mao Zedong (1893–1976).[16] Mao's theory of protracted conflict reforged the link between war and politics that was broken by the introduction of nuclear and bacteriological weapons. Mao's thought is a blend of oriental and occidental strains. Among other things, it runs parallel to the thinking of Sun Tzu (400–320 B.C.) and von Clausewitz. For Sun Tzu, the reputed author of the great Chinese classic *Ping-fa* (The Art of War), national morale, weather, terrain, command structure, and military doctrine were

---

[15]Lin Biao, *Long Live the Victory of the People's War* (Washington, D.C.: Department of Defense, 1965), p. 19. It should be pointed out that since the end of the cultural revolution and Mao's death in 1976, Lin Biao's ideas have fallen from grace in Chinese ruling circles.

[16]The modern Chinese names appearing in the text are spelled in the Pinyin system, which came into common usage in 1979. Mao Zedong and Lin Biao were formerly Mao Tse-tung and Lin Piao, respectively.

the five fundamental elements of war.[17] Mao's five criteria for successful guerrilla warfare are popular sympathy, a disciplined party organization, a credible military force, favorable terrain, and ample logistical support.[18] In addition to the obvious parallel between these two sets of criteria, we should note that both Mao and Sun Tzu emphasized the psychological dimension of war. That is, both viewed the primary object of war to be the garnering of popular support and the undermining of the enemy's will to resist specified political demands.[19] To this end, modern guerrilla warfare is well suited.

Although he attributed it to Lenin, Mao employed the Clausewitzian dictum that war is the implementation of policy by violent means.[20] And reminiscent of von Clausewitz's argument that policy concerning war and peace should be made by a government dominated by civilians is this famous aphorism of Mao's: "Political power grows out of the barrel of a gun. Our principle is that the Party commands the gun and the gun must never be allowed to command the Party."[21] Mao never deviated from the principle of civilian supremacy. Even during the period of incipient military rule growing out of the cultural revolution of the late 1960s, the Chinese People's Liberation Army was never allowed to supplant the Party; it functioned mainly as an agent of political socialization and mobilization.

Despite the effectiveness of guerrilla warfare in various struggles against feudalism and foreign influence, Mao counseled in 1938 that regular armed forces are eventually necessary if a defeat is to be inflicted upon the enemy. Mobile guerrilla campaigning is, therefore, only a prelude to the establishment of a war of position—that is, a temporary strategic stalemate that evolves into a crushing counteroffensive against central government forces.[22] It is notable that neither Guevara nor Debray acknowledged the need to establish positional warfare. Judging from recent military history, Mao's views are probably more realistic than those of Guevara and Debray.

The indirect influence of Sun Tzu and of von Clausewitz on Mao's thought appears to be pronounced. Yet it would be false to assume that Mao's thinking was merely a contemporary adaptation of military science. Throughout his life, Mao's commitment to dialectical materialism (i.e., Marxism) was an overriding prescriptive element in his view of world affairs. There is no conflict between the precepts of statecraft and those of Marxism-Leninism, for these two bodies of thought apply at different levels. The application of traditional theories of statecraft to specific problems of policy formulation does not rule out or even inhibit a world view that history moves unrelentingly in a given direction. Consequently, it is possible to make and implement policy empirically and to continue to interpret events in terms of an all-inclusive ideology. Proponents of realpolitik

---

[17]Sun Tzu, *The Art of War*, trans. Samuel B. Griffith (Oxford: Clarendon Press, 1963), p. 63.

[18]Mao Tse-tung, *Selected Works* (Peking: Foreign Languages Press, 1967), vol. I, p. 73.

[19]Mao Tse-tung, *Selected Military Writings* (Peking: Foreign Languages Press, 1963), p. 230.

[20]*Ibid.*, pp. 226–27.

[21]Mao, *Selected Works*, vol. II, p. 224.

[22]Mao, *Selected Military Writings*, p. 211.

persistently discount the role of ideology in international relations by pointing out that it does not provide a set of guidelines for coping with specific types of problems. However, ideology does not have to perform this function in order to be effective in setting the parameters within which policy will be made. Mao's theorizing is instructive on this point.

The Vietnamese revolutionary leader Ho Chi Minh (1890–1969) also incorporated the dualism of pragmatism and ideological commitment into his thinking. He emphasized that guerrilla warfare is aimed primarily at liberation, and he deemphasized the goal of establishing a dictatorship of the proletariat.[23] General Vo Nguyen Giap, a leading North Vietnamese military strategist, has postulated that a people's war is a struggle of the peasantry under the leadership of the working class against both feudalism and imperialism.[24] This notion is fully compatible with a Marxist-Leninist interpretation of history. Throughout the process of setting policy goals and then modifying them so that they meet the requirements of concrete situations, ideological compromises are unavoidable, yet these compromises are regarded as acceptable tactical adjustments and do not indicate a lessening of political fervor.

In summarizing our discussion of internal war, we should attend to one final question: How effective is the guerrilla? This question must be answered first from a political and then from a military perspective. Politically, guerrilla warfare has often been successful in weakening the opponent's will to resist. The campaign of General Grivas on Cyprus is an example. Another case in point is the North Vietnamese Tet offensive (1968), which combined guerrilla with positional warfare. Militarily, it fell short of the objectives set by General Giap, yet the political impact of the offensive was undeniable. In its aftermath, President Lyndon Johnson announced that he would not be a candidate for reelection, and the senior American commander in Vietnam was replaced.[25] A year earlier, Soviet Premier Alexei Kosygin had told British Prime Minister Harold Wilson that time was on the side of the North Vietnamese, to whom he counseled a policy of patience.[26] Implicit in this advice were two assumptions: The American government would find itself politically unable to sustain a prolonged conflict, and the primary purpose of the guerrilla war in Indochina was psychological rather than military.

Militarily, the record of the guerrilla has been unimpressive. Even assuming the optimum conditions of ideologically committed personnel, popular support, ample matériel, and a favorable geographic setting within which to operate,[27] it would be difficult to forecast with any degree of certainty a defeat of a professional army by irregular forces. And it must be noted that the four condi-

[23]Ho Chi Minh, *On Revolution: Selected Writings, 1920–66*, ed. Bernard B. Fall (New York: Praeger, 1967).

[24]Vo Nguyen Giap, *People's War, People's Army: The Viet Cong Insurrection Manual for Underdeveloped Countries* (New York: Praeger, 1962), pp. 27–31.

[25]See discussion in Robert J. O'Neill, *General Giap: Politician and Strategist* (New York: Praeger, 1969), pp. 198–99.

[26]Henry Brandon, *The Retreat of American Power* (Garden City, N.Y.: Doubleday, 1973), p. 286.

[27]N. I. Klonis, *Guerrilla Warfare* (New York: Robert Speller and Sons, 1972), p. 193.

tions enumerated above are rarely present in combination at the same time. The environment in which guerrillas function invariably imposes severe limitations on their operations. Historically, members of guerrilla units have been youthful idealists convinced that they are waging a just war against an unjust regime, that time is their ally, and that the superficially powerful enemy is on the verge of collapse because of internal corruption. The myths that hold a guerrilla movement together often cannot withstand the strain of prolonged conflict unless external assistance from a friendly foreign power is forthcoming. An open frontier leading to a sanctuary fulfills a vital psychological as well as logistical need for guerrillas. Without either direct or indirect intervention by other powers, the guerrilla effort will encounter almost insurmountable obstacles.

Nevertheless, the support of a guerrilla movement demands few resources. Thus, guerrilla activity persists, and the guerrilla continues to occupy a well-publicized and somewhat romanticized place in the literature of contemporary world politics. In September 1980, fifty-five heads of government and nearly as many top-level officials from other countries assembled in Havana for the triennial meeting of the nonaligned Third World movement and heard President Fidel Castro issue a call for solidarity against the "imperialism" of the West. True to this theme the delegate of the Nicaraguan junta, whose Sandinista guerrillas had overthrown the dictatorship of General Anastasio Somoza, identified partisan warfare not only as the military manifestation of popular discontent in developing countries but also as the historic means through which world imperialism would meet its defeat. At the highest stage of capitalism in the Leninist sense, the Sandinista leader insisted, the interventionist forces of imperialism are no match for the revolutionary zeal of the guerrilla.[28] Ironically enough, soon after the Sandinistas took control of the state, they themselves faced a sizable guerrilla challenge by the United States–supported Contras.

INTERNATIONAL WAR

The involvement of other countries in an internal war raises the specter of escalation—of both the geographic scope of military operations and the scale of weaponry being employed. General Matthew B. Ridgway recounts in his memoirs that as chief of staff of the U.S. Army, he sent a team of specialists to Indochina in 1954 for the purpose of assessing the military feasibility of American intervention on behalf of the French forces then battling the Viet Minh. The resulting report was negative: It stressed that a modern army could not fight guerrillas on the Indochinese terrain.[29] In other words, an effort to wage war on a limited scale would soon prove unsatisfactory and lead to a heightening of the conflict. An expanded war would inevitably involve the People's Republic of China and result

---

[28]Alan Riding, "Castro No Longer Frightens the Rest of Latin America," *New York Times*, September 9, 1979, sec. 4, p. E3. For a critical view of the role of the guerrilla, see J. Boyer Bell, *The Myth of the Guerrilla: Revolutionary Theory and Malpractice* (New York: Knopf, 1971), pp. 245–48.

[29]Matthew B. Ridgway, *Memoirs* (New York: Harper & Brothers, 1956), pp. 275–78.

in a major Asian conflict. Limited internal war and a general international war are not, therefore, easily separable categories of conflict, but often are extensions of the same problem.

The intensification of military ardor, psychological tension, governmental power, and social integration that takes place in time of war influences the members of a nation-state to react similarly to the war.[30] Once war has begun, the social and political processes involved attain a dynamic of their own, one that is virtually impossible to reverse in a contemporary mass society. In international relations, political power is manifested in the ability of a government to influence or force another government to accept its political will. Military power is effective not only when a country resorts to war but also when it makes a show of force or in some other way leads other countries to anticipate that force will be used against them.[31] Should threats—whether overt or subtle—fail to produce results, a government is confronted with the painful choice of abandoning its goals or taking the fateful step toward armed hostilities. In this sense, every government wants peace—but only under certain conditions.[32] Beyond a certain level of challenge to its perceived vital interests, a government will respond with force. Invariably, it will do so in the belief, frequently mistaken, that the conflict will be shorter and less devastating than initially expected by all participants. The protracted Persian Gulf War of the 1980s is an excellent case in point.

The rationality of war is obscure unless the anticipated political gains exceed the cost of human suffering, and such is likely to be the case only in the defense of one's homeland against an enemy bent on a genocidal conquest. In most other instances death and devastation far outweigh the presumed gains of a war. When World War I broke out in 1914, none of the belligerent governments anticipated that ten million soldiers and an equal number of civilians would die in the ensuing struggle, or that another twenty million would perish from famine and disease. At the outset of World War II, foreign-policy elites did not foresee that the conflict would result in the loss of seventeen million combatants and an estimated forty-three million noncombatants.[33] When President John F. Kennedy and his successor, Lyndon Johnson, escalated the American military presence in Vietnam (1961–68) they could have hardly predicted a 2.2 million death-toll in war-related casualties in the Indochina region.[34]

Increasing the intensity of conflict has been the most common form of escalation. However, escalation may also be accomplished by a widening of the geographic area of military operations or by the addition of new belligerents.[35] The history of strategic air bombardment offers the best examples of escalation. As a response to the German Zeppelin raids on London during World War I, the

[30]See Quincy Wright, *A Study of War* (Chicago: University of Chicago Press, 1942), vol. II, pp. 698–700.

[31]Klaus Knorr, *Military Power and Potential* (Lexington, Mass.: Heath, 1970), pp. 3–5.

[32]Geoffrey Blainey, *The Causes of War* (New York: Free Press, 1973), pp. 142–44.

[33]"War," *Encyclopaedia Britannica*, 23 (1971), 201–2.

[34]For these statistics see Ruth Leger Sivard, *World Military and Social Expenditures, 1983* (Washington, D.C.: World Priorities, 1983), p. 21.

[35]Herman Kahn, *On Escalation: Metaphors and Scenarios* (New York: Praeger, 1965), pp. 4–5.

British Independent Bombing Force planned to launch poison-gas attacks against Berlin in the spring of 1919.[36] In World War II, the same pattern of action and reaction was repeated. During the early stages of the conflict in Europe, both sides concentrated their air attacks on military targets and respected each other's civilian sanctuaries.[37] This unspoken agreement on targeting came to an end in 1940 with Prime Minister Winston Churchill's decision to bomb Berlin.[38] In this respect, the noted British strategist Basil Liddell-Hart has observed with considerable perception that peaceful states at times go to greater extremes than predatory ones when they are aroused to the point of war.[39]

The policy of strategic bombing for the purpose of destroying the national morale and economic structure of an enemy developed to its fullest extent during World War II. This development also exposed the limited degree of control that civilian leadership actually exerts over the evolution of military strategy during time of war. The Anglo-American bombing of Dresden in 1945 illustrates the weakness of the notion of civilian supremacy. Beginning with the fire bombing of Hamburg in 1943, the Allies undertook a campaign of air bombardment aimed at the destruction of major continental industrial and population centers. The raid on Dresden had been planned for February 4, 1945, so that it would occur immediately prior to the meeting of the Big Three at Yalta. The timing was important because Washington and London wished to demonstrate their support for the Soviet armies then preparing to advance into central Germany. However, the military significance of Dresden, a city filled with refugees and only lightly defended, was recognized as negligible. (Informed by the Allied Military Mission in Moscow of the impending attack, the Soviet government was unimpressed by either its military or its political significance.[40]) Ironically, because the moon and weather were unfavorable, field commanders postponed the attack. Before the operation could be rescheduled the Yalta Conference had concluded. Although the original political purpose of the raid no longer obtained, the wheels of military bureaucracy continued to turn, and the raid was carried out on February 13. The resulting loss of life, primarily among noncombatants of several nationalities, was greater than that of any single air raid of the war, except possibly the fire bombing of Tokyo the following month.

The bombing of Dresden shows that in war, considerations of military organization and planning are frequently so overwhelming that they tend to take precedence over political goals. Georges Clemenceau, French premier during World War I, summed up the matter most emphatically when he declared that war is too serious a business to be left to generals. All too often, the validity of this aphorism remains obscure to those entrusted with vital decisions.

---

[36]George H. Quester, *Deterrence before Hiroshima: The Airpower Background of Modern Strategy* (New York: John Wiley, 1966), pp. 44–45.

[37]See Kahn, *On Escalation*, p. 28.

[38]Quester, *Deterrence before Hiroshima*, p. 117.

[39]B. H. Liddell-Hart, *Strategy: The Indirect Approach*, 2nd ed. rev. (New York: Praeger, 1954), p. 372.

[40]David Irving, *The Destruction of Dresden* (London: William Kimber, 1963), pp. 93–95, 148.

Augsberg, Germany: The bitter product of Allied bombing during World War II. (U.S. Army photograph)

The basic problem illustrated by the Dresden raid is the inability of gov-ernments to synchronize political and military policies because of rapidly chang-ing conditions in both realms. The meshing of the two areas of policy enables a government to regulate the escalation of a conflict and possibly to induce the process of deescalation. The deescalation of armed hostilities may result from any or all of the following:

1. The intervention of a third party (a government or an international organiza-tion)
2. The historical experience the warring parties have had with each other in settling their disputes effectively through treaties
3. The realistic, if pessimistic, acceptance by the involved foreign-policy elites that total victory on the battlefield is not possible[41]

For example, all three factors, especially the good offices of the United States, combined to deescalate and ultimately end the Russo-Japanese War (1904–05).

[41]Richard E. Barringer, *War: Patterns of Conflict* (Cambridge, Mass.: MIT Press, 1972), pp. 112–15.

THE NUCLEAR DIMENSION: A DEADLY CALCULUS

The Hague Convention of 1907 established the requirement in international law that the outbreak of hostilities must be preceded by a formal declaration or war. In 1914, the belligerents in World War I did declare war before their armies marched. World War I was exceptional in this respect; most armed conflicts flare up without the protocol of a declaration. In the nuclear age this historical fact is of obvious significance, for a single nuclear missile can deliver on target more destructive force than has been released in conventional warfare since the invention of gunpowder. The Stockholm International Peace Research Institute (SIPRI) reported in its *Yearbook* for 1987 that the number of missile-deliverable nuclear warheads available to the United States was 8,340, and that the corresponding figure for the Soviet Union was between 9,300 and 17,100.[42] Notably, these figures do not include weapons carried by bombers or fired by artillery, nor do they reflect the nuclear inventory of third states. The prospect of an enemy resorting to a surprise nuclear attack and decimating with one blow the population centers of the target state is a contingency that heads of government can ignore only at their peril.

In 1945, the two atomic bombs dropped on Hiroshima and Nagasaki yielded only twenty kilotons (i.e., twenty thousand tons of TNT). The immediate casualties numbered one hundred thousand killed with an untold number of wounded, many of whom perished as a result of burns or radiation after-effects. By comparison, the devastation wrought by a nuclear war in the 1980s would be incalculable. A single one-megaton warhead—the equivalent of a million tons of TNT—would reduce a city of approximately one hundred fifty square miles to a state of blazing rubble and radiation contamination. Those few who survive would face an uncertain fate. The United Nations has estimated that in a nuclear war each of some four hundred metropolitan areas in the Northern Hemisphere would be attacked with a destructive force roughly equal to a thousand Hiroshima bombs.[43] The survival of civilization itself would be in question.

When compared with other pressing environmental and social problems, the possibility of a nuclear holocaust tends to lose some of its urgency. This is especially true in view of the restraints exercised by nuclear powers since the first atom bombs were dropped on Hiroshima and Nagasaki in 1945. Nevertheless, a nuclear arsenal remains an important projection of a nation-state's power. Even though the rattling of the atomic saber may be muted, its mere existence influences the behavior of other states. In order to exercise its influence, a government possessing nuclear weapons must leave its options open. Therefore, the possibility of a nuclear confrontation continues to be a major background factor in the planning and implementation of a foreign policy. Despite the 1973 agreement between President Richard Nixon and General-Secretary Leonid Brezhnev

[42]Stockholm International Peace Research Institute, *World Armaments and Disarmament: SIPRI Yearbook 1987* (London: Oxford University Press, 1987), pp. 6 and 18.

[43]United Nations, Department of Public Information, *Disarmament Fact Sheets*, no. 5: *Nuclear Disarmament* (New York: United Nations, 1979), p. 1.

The nuclear destruction of Hiroshima, Japan on August 6, 1945. (National Archives)

that they would voluntarily restrain themselves from being the first to strike with nuclear weapons on the battlefield, both governments have retained the nuclear alternative in the event their vital interests are imperiled. National objectives, a willingness to employ force, a readiness to accept the possibility of a general war, and domestic political considerations establish the parameters of nuclear policy.[44] As long as the formulation of nuclear strategy is dependent upon this complex of variables, the practice of nuclear restraint is not assured, despite statements to the contrary by the great powers.

The preoccupation of national leaders as well as social scientists with the specter of nuclear confrontation and proliferation has led to the growth of a specialized "nuclear jargon." In the 1980s the nuclear lexicon includes such terms as *first strike, second strike, preemptive strike, counterforce, countervalue, megatonnage, throwweight, circular error probable* (CEP), the *single integrated operational plan* (SIOP), *overkill,* and *hardening.*

First strike refers to a hypothetical attack by state A on military and industrial targets (avoiding major population centers) of state B.

Second strike presupposes that state B, having absorbed a first strike by the forces of state A, has retained enough retaliatory power (especially in well-

[44]See Morton H. Halperin, *Defense Strategies of the Seventies* (Boston: Little, Brown, 1971), pp. 87–94. See also Richard Betts, *Nuclear Blackmail and Nuclear Balance* (Washington, D.C.: Brookings Institution, 1987).

hidden underground missile sites or aboard airplanes and nuclear-powered submarines) with which it can bomb major population centers in state A. The retaliatory second strike by B on A's population is designed to *deter* a first strike to begin with. Naturally, the less vulnerable a nation's second-strike weapons are, the greater are the chances that it will deter a first strike.

A *preemptive strike* is a surprise attack by the nuclear forces of a given state against targets (logically military and industrial facilities rather than population centers) of another state. A *counterforce* strike designates as its targets military and industrial facilities, while a *countervalue* strike (also referred to as *countercity* strike) concentrates on major urban centers.

Megatonnage measures the destructive capacity of nuclear weapons with one megaton equivalent to one million tons of TNT and its subdivision, the kiloton, equivalent to one thousand tons of TNT. Thus, the twenty kiloton bombs dropped in 1945 in Hiroshima and Nagasaki were quite "small" by today's standards where monster bombs packing the power of fifty megatons are in uneasy storage.

Throwweight and the *circular error probable* are the principal elements in assessing the lethal potential of a nuclear weapon. The former is the weight of the missile after the booster stage, and the latter is the radius within which the weapon will effectively destroy its designated target. Related to these two mathematical concepts is the judgmental one of the *single integrated operational plan*, which establishes a list of targets ranked in order of priority according to national objectives, strategic concepts, and domestic political considerations.

Overkill is another bizarre late-twentieth-century term: It describes the capacity of the superpowers to destroy each other's military, industrial, and population targets a few times over, as if destroying the opponent once would not be sufficient to the gruesome task. Finally, *hardening* is a term that denotes the relative invulnerability of retaliatory weapons. For example, one can harden one's missiles by hiding them in concrete silos or, as in the case of the MX missile system, by developing underground systems of corridors and circles with multiple launching sites that allow missiles to be moving constantly, thus frustrating the chances of an effective first strike by adversary forces.

In the nuclear era, especially after the successful Soviet test of a nuclear device in 1949, the superpowers and other states possessing nuclear weapons (e.g., France, Great Britain, and the People's Republic of China) have operated with variations of what students of strategy term *deterrence* theory.[45] *Deterrence* is a concept that has assumed special meaning given the potential of mass destruction that nuclear weapons possess. In that context, deterrence is a relationship between adversaries in which the threat of unacceptable devastation caused by a

---

[45]On the theory and practice of deterrence in U.S. foreign policy, see Robert Jervis, *The Illogic of American Nuclear Strategy* (Ithaca, N.Y.: Cornell University Press, 1984); Alexander George and Richard Smoke, *Deterrence in American Foreign Policy* (New York: Columbia University Press, 1974); Leon Sigal, "The Logic of Deterrence in Theory and Practice," *International Organization*, 33, no. 4 (Autumn 1979), 567–579; and Paul Huth and Bruce Russett, "Deterrence Failure and Crisis Escalation," *International Studies Quarterly*, 32, no. 1, (March 1988), 22–45.

nuclear exchange prevents them from taking overt hostile actions, however tempted they may be to do so. Deterrence in its essential form is a theory of prevention rather than one of inducement.

Technological breakthroughs in the development of nuclear weaponry have brought about modifications in the deterrence strategies employed by the United States vis-a-vis the Soviet Union and vice versa. A summary of United States nuclear strategies since 1945 reveals that the interplay between policy and technology prevents the formulation of an enduring definition of deterrence, which in the final analysis is a matter of perception rather than scientific calculation.

The first period, 1945 to 1949, was one of American *nuclear monopoly* because the Soviets did not detonate a nuclear device until four years after the bombing of Hiroshima and Nagasaki. Despite mounting tensions of the early cold war, as exemplified by the East-West confrontation in Berlin, the United States did not use nuclear weapons against East European targets in order to force the Soviets into capitulation. The implicit expectation throughout these years was that an advance by Soviet armies into Central Europe would have been met, in all probability, with an American nuclear retaliation against the Soviet homeland. The interesting theoretical implication is that at a time when the United States enjoyed a monopoly of nuclear capability, it chose not to use nuclear weapons after the end of World War II. The reverse question would also be interesting for speculation: What would have happened if the Soviet Union instead of the United States enjoyed a nuclear monopoly?

The second period, which coincided with the presidency of Dwight D. Eisenhower (1953–61) could be characterized as one in which the United States employed a strategy of *massive retaliation*. Although the Soviets made impressive technological advances, such as the launching into orbit of the first space satellite, "Sputnik," in 1957, the United States maintained an overall lead in the number of available nuclear weapons and the means with which to deliver them. Based on *nuclear superiority*, the policy of massive retaliation outlined by Secretary of State John Foster Dulles sought to deter the Soviet Union from using its conventional superiority to gain advantages in Europe and Asia by reserving to the United States the option of retaliating, if necessary with nuclear weapons, at a time and place of its own choosing. To contain Soviet expansionism through overt conquest, Dulles sought to project the image that the United States might, under duress, resort to nuclear war. In terms of inhibiting a Soviet seizure of West Berlin, the policy was effective, but it was useless in counteracting the Soviet army's intervention in Hungary (1956).

The recognition that nuclear weapons would not be employed to halt the intervention by Soviet forces in the internal affairs of a client state, coupled with the introduction of intercontinental ballistic missiles (ICBMs), led President John F. Kennedy to initiate policies that brought about the third period in American nuclear strategy. The "missile gap" was a hard-fought issue in the election of 1960, when some analysts argued that the Soviet Union had a pronounced advantage over the United States in the development of powerful ICBMs. The issue

John Fitzgerald Kennedy (1917–1963), thirty-fifth president of the United States from January 20, 1961 to his tragic death on November 22, 1963. (Library of Congress)

was crucial because only with the existence of *nuclear parity*, and therefore the possibility of a powerful retaliatory blow, would either side refrain from a first strike. The credibility of massive retaliation had depended upon a perceived inequality of forces. Without clear American superiority the rationality of the policy was questionable.[46] Would an American president hazard Chicago or New York for Hamburg or Paris? was a question asked with increasing frequency by members of the North American alliance.

The Kennedy administration accordingly developed the strategy of a *flexible response*, which posited that the United States would augment and deploy its forces in such a manner that every Soviet probe, whether direct or indirect, would encounter a reaction of similar type and intensity. Through the strengthening of its conventional forces, the United States would not have to advance to the brink of nuclear war in order to check a Soviet effort, for example, to support a procommunist revoluntionary movement in a Third World country. *Counterinsurgency* came into vogue as a doctrine whereby American advisors would equip and train military forces of various Third World countries whose governments were battling Soviet-supported guerrillas. The priority attached to this new dimension of warfare led to the involvement of the United States in Indochina (1961–75).

In Central Europe the concept of a flexible response committed the United States and its allies to counter a Soviet conventional thrust with analogous nonnuclear forces as a means of gaining the necessary time in which to decide whether to cross the nuclear threshold. The strategy did not rule out, however, a possible nuclear response to an incursion by Soviet forces into Western Europe, and accordingly the notion of securing sectors of NATO's eastern perimeter with nuclear land mines received close attention before it was rejected on technical

[46]Thomas G. Schelling, *Arms and Influence* (New Haven: Yale University Press, 1966), pp. 36–43.

grounds. The theory of a flexible response gave the United States a set of options other than massive retaliation, and concurrently enhanced the credibility of the nuclear deterrent.

The flexible-response strategy remains the cornerstone of United States policy and leaves open the option of launching a nuclear strike. The circumstances under which this momentous decision might be made are deliberately left undefined. Caspar W. Weinberger, serving as secretary of defense, summarized this aspect of American policy in 1983 in a report to the Congress:

> To maintain a sound deterrent, we must make clear to our adversary that we would decisively and effectively answer his attack. To talk of actions that the U.S. Government could not, in good conscience, undertake tends to defeat the goal of deterrence.[47]

In order to guard against the contingency of a paralyzing first strike, both superpowers have sought to diversify and harden their nuclear weapons arsenals. Consequently, both have developed a strategic triad of ICBMs, long-range bombers, and submarines capable of launching missiles armed with nuclear warheads. A credible deterrence depends upon the rational assessment that enough of these various weapons systems would survive a preemptive attack to enable the target state to deliver a devastating second strike against the aggressor. The belief in mutual vulnerability is the basis of deterrence and serves to reduce the temptation of a foreign-policy elite to opt for a first strike. Population centers are held hostage in this deadly calculus. The fearsome strategy of balanced terror is appropriately named MAD for *mutually assured destruction* and relies upon the assumption that each of the two major nuclear powers would be able to retaliate massively against a first strike.

Nevertheless, the theory is subject to criticism because it applies primarily to the United States and the Soviet Union. Even assuming that the threat of MAD suffices to stay the nuclear hand of the superpowers, will this restraint hold true for middle-ranking states, which through great economic sacrifice acquire a nuclear capability? Will not a growing number of Third World governments be tempted to exploit the advantage of momentary nuclear superiority to attack a historic enemy? The carefully contrived scenario of MAD would scarcely apply in such situations.

Since the late 1970s the strategy of deterrence through mutual vulnerability of the superpowers has come under increasingly skeptical review.[48] Critics of MAD assert that the Soviet Union possesses sufficient nuclear capability to nullify United States strategic forces in a first strike and still retain plenty of missiles with which to threaten American cities. As improbable as a surprise attack might be, influential strategic thinkers insist that MAD leaves the president

---

[47]U.S. Department of Defense, *Report to Congress: Fiscal Year 1984* (Washington, D.C.: Government Printing Office, 1983), p. 55.

[48]Steven J. Brams and D. Mark Kilgour, "Deterrence versus Defense: A Game Theoretic Model of Star Wars," *International Studies Quarterly*, 32, no. 1 (March 1988), 3–28.

of the United States with the thankless choice of either ordering massive retalia-tion against Soviet cities in anticipation of an equally devastating counterstrike against American cities or, alternatively, capitulating to Soviet demands. There-fore, the critics argue for the development of a range of limited nuclear options enabling the United States to use its strategic forces without engaging in an all-out nuclear exchange. Representative of this orientation is a widely read account of a hypothetical third world war—a month-long conflict in which nuclear weapons play a "limited" role in a series of battles decided by conventional forces.[49]

The Carter administration's Presidential Directive 59 (1980) reflected some of the skepticism of MAD's critics and modified the countercity strategy to include command and communication centers as well as purely military targets in the Soviet Union, and the Reagan administration continued to develop this policy. No one suggests that the United States now regards a nuclear war as win-nable, but rather that enhanced missile accuracy may enable an attacker to para-lyze a target state by destroying its governmental nerve centers. Retaliation on the part of such a "decapitated" state would be difficult if not impossible, for its cities would still be open to a second strike. The makeshift remnants of leader-ship in such a state would presumably find strategic surrender the only available option.

To ward off a Soviet attempt to engage in nuclear blackmail of the gov-ernment of the United States, American defense strategy in the 1980s rests on the principle that should deterrence fail, the president ought to have several credible nuclear options. In 1984, a Department of Defense statement put the matter this way:

> If the Soviets recognize that our forces can and will deny them their objectives at whatever level of nuclear conflict they contemplate and, in addition, that such a conflict could lead to the destruction of those political, military, and economic assets that they value most highly, then deterrence is effective and the risk of war diminished.[50]

Ultimately, this new phase of nuclear strategy is open to disturbing criticism. Soviet strategists, too, may be concerned over the possibility of a United States effort to destroy their strategic forces in a preemptive first strike. Fear breeds fear, and the belief in the possibility of a limited nuclear war may disturb the balance of nuclear power and move the probability of actually waging a nuclear war one notch closer to reality.

In a world of continuing nuclear stalemate between superpowers, the threat of a preemptive (surprise) attack remains ever present. As each side paces the other in the development of new weapons and defense against them, the danger exists that one power might perceive itself on the disadvantaged side of a "missile gap" and be tempted to launch a preemptive attack while it still has

---

[49]General Sir John Hackett et al., *The Third World War: August 1985* (New York: Macmillan, 1978).
[50]Dov S. Zakheim, "Deterrence: Cornerstone of Our Strategic Policy," *Defense* (May 1984), p. 4.

the means to do so. The "balance of terror," as Winston Churchill so aptly phrased nuclear confrontation, is neither reliable nor stable. It is unreliable because each potential adversary views equilibrium as a dangerous state of affairs and accordingly seeks a margin of superiority for its own security. Continuing technological change destabilizes the "balance" in that it forces it to alternate constantly between phases of adjustment and readjustment. Nuclear confrontation can hardly be termed self-regulating in the classical sense of the balance of power (see Chapter 3). It is therefore a source of considerable peril for the survival of the international system.

Adding to the destabilization of the international system is the proliferation of nuclear weapons to other countries. This proliferation could culminate in a condition of international anarchy in which any of several states, great or small, could have a finger on the nuclear trigger. The legal and organizational bonds of international comity cannot long withstand the pressure imposed by an unlimited expansion of the nuclear club. George F. Kennan, former United States ambassador to the Soviet Union, has written that the destructive potential of a global nuclear war is so great that no political purpose could justify it.[51] Arnold J. Toynbee has suggested that the development of nuclear weapons may ultimately make war obsolete in the same way that the daily hunt for one's food has become unnecessary.[52] Finally, Liddell-Hart's maxim that the only valid object of war is a better state of peace implies that war in the nuclear era is losing its usefulness as an instrument of policy.[53]

SUGGESTIONS FOR FURTHER STUDY

The development of the Strategic Defense Initiative and its effect on the theory of nuclear deterrence is the subject of Congressional Office of Technology Assessment, *SDI: Technology, Survivability, and Software*, OTA-ISC-353 (Washington, D.C.: Government Printing Office, 1988). For a commentary oriented more toward policy, see Harold Brown, "Is SDI Technically Feasible?" *Foreign Affairs: America and the World, 1985*, 64 (1986), 435–54. The environmental effects of nuclear war are the theme of Carl Sagan, "Nuclear War and Climatic Catastrophe: Some Policy Implications," *Foreign Affairs*, 62 (Winter 1983–84), 257–92; and Andrei Sakharov, "The Danger of Nuclear War," *Foreign Affairs*, 62 (Summer 1983), 1001–16. The related problems of perception and escalation are discussed in Roman Kolkowicz, ed., *The Logic of Nuclear Terror* (Boston: Allen & Unwin, 1987). Kenneth Boulding has applied the tools of econometrics to the study of conflict among the superpowers in *Conflict and Balance: A General Theory* (New York: Harper & Row, 1962). The "balance of terror" provides a focus for Alexander George et al., *Deterrence in American Foreign Policy: Theory and Practice* (New York: Columbia University Press, 1973). Leslie H. Gelb has questioned the logic of some deter-

[51]George F. Kennan, *Russia and the West under Lenin and Stalin* (Boston: Little, Brown, 1960), p. 391.
[52]Arnold J. Toynbee, *War and Civilization* (New York: Oxford University Press, 1950), p. 15.
[53]Liddell-Hart, *Strategy*, p. 351.

rence theories in "Is the Nuclear Threat Manageable?" *New York Times Magazine,* March 4, 1984, pp. 26ff. While still useful, the discussion of credibility and rationality in Thomas C. Schelling, *Arms and Influence* (New Haven: Yale University Press, 1966) is subject to review because of the spread of nuclear weapons, as described by Stephen M. Meyer in *The Dynamics of Nuclear Proliferation* (Chicago, Ill.: University of Chicago Press, 1984); and by U.S. National Foreign Assessment Center, *International Political Effects of the Spread of Nuclear Weapons,* ed. John Kerry King (April 1979). For the theoretical foundations of Soviet military thought, see U.S. Department of the Air Force, *Selected Soviet Military Writing: 1970–75* (Washington, D.C.: Government Printing Office, 1977).

12

THE CONTROL OF CONFLICT
IN THE INTERNATIONAL SYSTEM

Weapons have been developed over time as artificial extensions of the human ability to fight. Traditionally, weaponry has fulfilled three functions:

(1) protection against other people (groups, tribes, or nation-states) as well as against wild animals;
(2) the improvement of one's economic condition, through hunting and the acquisition of goods; and
(3) the enhancement of prestige, through one's increased ability to intimidate others.

The industrial revolution and the contemporary global trend toward vast military-industrial complexes have increased the rewards for those involved in the production of armaments. The preparation for the possibility of war generates demands for services and commodities that would otherwise not be required. In many countries military-preparedness programs have led to industrialization, the mobilization of a national labor force, and the formation of the class of skilled managers that is indispensable to the administration of the modern state. The history of France and Germany in the nineteenth century reflects this pattern of development, one that is being repeated today in the Third World.

As industrialization, colonialism, and militarism grew in the last century, intellectual and religious groups in Europe and the United States responded by organizing peace societies. These societies called for either the elimination or the control of armaments. Essentially, their arguments were based on the assumption that through total or partial disarmament humans could attain better protection, a higher standard of living, and greater prestige. Society as a whole would profit if, in the words of George Bernard Shaw's fictitious munitions maker, nitrogen were to be used to manufacture fertilizer rather than explosives.

The advocates of arms control and disarmament (often reflecting the idealist orientation) normally support their case with some or all of the following arguments:

First, arms and arms races can themselves be causes of bloody and costly wars. The possession of arms definitely increases the probability that they will be used. Consequently, an arms race heightens the psychological insecurity of nation-states rather than providing them with a sense of security against attack.

Second, a reduction in a state's armaments releases sizable funds, which could be transferred to programs designed to improve the general welfare of that state's citizens. In the timeless dilemma of choosing between "guns and butter," the advocates of arms reduction opt for the latter.

Third, the unchecked growth of military-industrial complexes in the major nation-states may give rise to foreign-policy elites bound together by a common belief that their political and economic survival is synonymous with the national interest and that matters cannot be otherwise in an anarchic and warlike international system.

The so-called Frankenstein syndrome, wherein machines developed to augment human capabilities escape from control and run rampant, offers the advocates of arms control a fourth argument. The increasing technological sophistication of modern warfare may serve, for example, to insulate electronically controlled weaponry from political monitoring in a crisis situation. To achieve the condition of "fail-safe," systems analysts have developed a variety of safeguards. Nevertheless, the proponents of nuclear-arms control argue that grave dangers remain.

The fifth and philosophically most effective argument is that war is morally wrong and, by extrapolation, so is the preparation for war. One can cite numerous examples from history of war preparations and attendant arms races culminating in war. One major such example is the European arms race preceding World War I.

Opponents of the disarmament and/or arms-control movement, usually assuming the stance of political realists, sharply counter the arguments presented above. They point out that weapons are not the causes but rather the consequences of conflictive relationships. Moreover, a historical survey of arms races in the nineteenth and twentieth centuries indicates that this form of international competition frequently terminates peacefully with the recognition of the military superiority of one side or the other.[1]

---

[1]Patrick M. Morgan, *Theories and Approaches to International Politics: What Are We To Think?* (San Ramon, Calif.: Consensus Publishers, 1972), p. 255.

The advocates of a strong military posture argue that recurrent warfare is a part of international relations and that countries that cannot defend themselves effectively are a constant temptation to armed and covetous aggressors. Hence, the argument runs, the most effective method of avoiding a war is to prepare for one (*si vis pacem, para bellum*).[2]

Additional arguments favoring a strong military establishment stress that a war of self-defense is not only morally just but an obligation under natural law. Even if the dangers of a military-industrial complex are significant, as President Dwight D. Eisenhower warned in his farewell address, the advocates of prepared-ness agree that disarmament is not the answer. They stress that the need for a nation-state to absorb certain costs in order to provide for its security has been accepted by most societies over time. For, they ask, what benefit is derived from enriching a society domestically only to have it succumb to external aggression?

Alleging that a unilateral reduction in armaments is both utopian and dangerous, nuclear strategists rebut the "Frankenstein" argument by pointing to the perfected systems of administrative control. These systems, they argue, are preferable to the unilateral destruction of one's armaments—a step that is certain to create a power vacuum and consequently invite aggression. Accordingly, these observers regard military expenditures as justifiable means of preserving the peace, for armaments are indispensable to the maintenance of the balance of power.

Laying aside the merits and demerits of the arms-control and the mili-tary-preparedness positions, there can be little doubt that the preparedness school has usually carried the day. Many important nation-states devote from 5 to 20 percent of their gross national product to military programs, and the quali-tative advances in military technology are being matched only by the increasing quantities of arms available to all governments. Within nation-states, political parties rarely question the need for a large defense budget. Whenever political controversy about defense matters surfaces, the issues usually concern the type of armament and the sensitive question of whether air, ground, or naval forces should be favored in the allocation of resources. In other words, the debate ulti-mately hinges upon the amount and the programmatic thrust of expenditures rather than on the justification of the entire defense package being funded.

A WORD ON CONCEPTS

In its colloquial sense the term *disarmament* is quite inclusive. It can mean any-thing from the outlawing of all military arsenals and establishments, to the ban-ning of particular weapons in the interest of the "humanization" of war, to the implementation of specific agreements designed to prevent the accidental out-

---

[2]Of course the opposite principle is also found in Latin: *Si vis pacem, tolle bellum* (if you want peace, abolish war).

break of war. For purposes of clarification, it would be useful to distinguish between *disarmament* and *arms control* and between two categories of arms control.

Disarmament in its absolute sense requires the global destruction of weaponry and the disestablishment of all armed forces. *Arms control*, a relative concept,
entails the limitation of certain types of weaponry or the reduction of armament
levels. The chances of total disarmament are so minimal that its advocates are
often dismissed as utopians or propagandists. On the other hand, arms control
frequently becomes a goal of state policy and a subject of serious consideration
in the literature of international relations.

Arms control can be divided into two categories: *arms reduction* and *arms
limitation*. *Arms reduction* (or *partial disarmament*, as it is sometimes called) implies a
mutually agreed-upon set of arms levels for the nation-states involved. The arms-
reduction formula may apply either on a worldwide or on a regional basis. The
prototype of a regional arrangement is the Rush-Bagot Agreement (1817) between the United States and Great Britain, which led to the eventual demilitarization of the Great Lakes. Following World War II, Finland (1947) and Austria
(1955) committed themselves to a policy of neutrality and accepted restrictions
on their armaments. Perhaps the most ambitious of the regional understandings
is the Treaty for the Prohibition of Nuclear Weapons in Latin America (1967),
through which twenty-two governments of Central and South America strive to
ban nuclear weaponry from their homelands. Argentina, Brazil, and Chile have,
however, attached conditions, so far unfulfilled, to their implementation of the
treaty.

Arms limitation embraces the wide variety of international accords designed to limit the impact of war and to prevent its accidental outbreak. Thus,
under arms limitation we can list the installation of fail-safe devices designed to
detonate nuclear missiles in midair should they be fired accidentally, hot lines to
keep key decision makers in constant contact during crises, moratoriums on specific types of nuclear testing, and agreements between two or more countries
restricting the sale of arms and the transfer of military technology to third countries. Arms limitation also encompasses the conventional rules of international
law, whose purpose is to limit the scope and destructiveness of warfare within
the confines set by the doctrine of military necessity.

Examples of arms limitation are nearly infinite. They vary from the 1907
Hague Conference declaration forbidding the firing of projectiles from balloons
to the 1949 Geneva Conventions establishing certain protective guarantees for
prisoners of war and the wounded. Putting gloves on the fists of boxers in order
to reduce the injury inflicted by their punches is perhaps a suitable analogy to
arms limitation. The ancient Athenian playwright Aristophanes depicted one of
the earliest, most amusing, but ultimately unsuccessful attempts at arms limitation. In his play *Lysistrata* the Athenian women, who had had their fill of the
prolonged Peloponnesian War against Sparta, conspired to deny their husbands
the pleasure of conjugal relations in order to "limit" their bellicosity and persuade them to negotiate a peace.

A HISTORICAL OVERVIEW OF ARMS CONTROL

Leonid Brezhnev some years ago summed up a major difficulty in arms control negotiations when he observed,

> At talks on the reduction of armed forces and armaments in Central Europe we are told in effect: you should reduce more and we shall reduce less. This position certainly will not facilitate the progress of the talks.[3]

Normally negotiating teams tend to compare the quantity and quality of weapons available to their side with the weaponry estimated to be at the future disposal of their potential adversaries. Rival negotiators then define their positions accordingly. There is a tendency for each partner in the talks to justify the acquisition of new weapons in the name of a balance of military power, while charging that the opposing government is pursuing a destabilizing policy should it deploy the same type of weaponry.

Thucydides wrote of this problem when he described the decision of Athens to extend its walls.[4] The Athenians claimed that their policy was defensive. As leaders of an opposing bloc, the Spartans countered that the expanded fortifications were an effective countermeasure to Spartan infantry and therefore presented a threat to peace. For if the Athenians were able to secure themselves behind impregnable walls, they would be free to wage aggressive wars against their less fortunate neighbors without fear of retaliation. In this sense, the launching of the Peloponnesian War in 431 B.C. can be considered a preemptive strike by the enemies of Athens, who were alarmed at its growing imperial ambitions. The relative vulnerability to counterattack of the Greek city-state was in itself a deterrent to war, because political enemies were equally vulnerable, in modern parlance, to a second strike, or retaliatory blow. The insecurity of not having massive systems of walls was fundamental to the existence of the Hellenic city-state system. The strategic effect of the construction of fortifications in antiquity is comparable to that of the installation of antiballistic missile (ABM) systems around major cities today.[5]

A major obstacle to the institutionalization of stable arms-control ratios today is the seemingly insoluble problem of distinguishing between quality and quantity when comparing rival inventories of military hardware. Are the armored divisions, bomber squadrons, and naval task forces of one nation-state equivalent to those of another? Even a superficial analysis of this proposition suggests that

---

[3]L. I. Brezhnev, *To Stop the Arms Race, To Prevent Nuclear War, To Start Disarmament* (Moscow: Novosti Press Agency, 1978), p. 11.

[4]Thucydides, *The Peloponnesian War*, trans. Richard Crawley (New York: Modern Library, 1951), pp. 47–53.

[5]The Strategic Defense Initiative (SDI, or Star Wars), which raises images of the creation of a massive, impenetrable antimissile dome over the entire United States, would have—if ever developed—a similar effect, for it would neutralize the mutual vulnerability formula on which postwar deterrence doctrines have been based.

they are not. The diplomatic and scientific task becomes one of developing an acceptable conversion formula for equating different yet somewhat comparable military categories. As revealed by the long-drawn-out negotiations begun in 1973 by NATO and the Warsaw Pact nations on mutual and balanced force reduction, the bargaining undertaken to implement a fixed ratio of unconventional forces is invariably lengthy and often without conclusive results.

The Washington Naval Conference (1921–22) is an example of the tenuousness of efforts to freeze an arms race by establishing fixed force ratios. The naval-armaments agreement negotiated by the United States, Great Britain, Japan, France, and Italy prescribed a formula of 5:5:3:1.67:1.67 in regard to the tonnage of the capital ships of their respective fleets. Although the accord did have the immediate effect of forestalling a naval arms race between the Anglo-American powers and Japan, the 5:5:3 relationship that bound them included neither aircraft carriers nor submarines—the principal naval weapons of World War II. Technology, it seems, works relentlessly against designs for arms reduction and/or limitation.

Despite the difficulties encountered in past efforts to attain arms control, most governments today publicly proclaim their readiness to enter into negotiations toward this end. A successful precedent was the 1925 protocol prohibiting the use of poison gas and bacteriological agents in warfare, a proscription in international law that has been observed in subsequent armed conflicts.[6] Efforts to control the development and use of nuclear weapons, however, have not been as successful. In 1946, the United States proposed the Baruch Plan, which envisaged the creation of an Atomic Development Authority under the United Nations. The main function of this agency would be the international control of nuclear energy. The Soviet Union rejected the plan, responding that nuclear disarmament should take precedent over control (at the time the United States had a nuclear monopoly).[7]

In subsequent negotiations over nuclear-arms control, a recurrent problem was the verification of treaty compliance through on-site inspection. At the four-power Geneva Summit Conference of 1955, President Eisenhower presented his "Open Skies" proposal, which provided for reciprocal air inspection. The Soviet government countered with a plan for ground-control stations, and an unproductive dialogue followed.

The first major breakthrough was the Antarctic Treaty (1959), which committed the United States, the Soviet Union, and sixteen other states to a ban on the stationing of nuclear weapons in Antarctica. On-site inspections were also agreed to, and some have already taken place. This accord was the first arms-limitation treaty in the post-1945 era. Its implementation led to further agree-

---

[6]Hans Kelsen and Robert W. Tucker, *Principles of International Law*, 2nd ed. rev. (New York: Holt, Rinehart & Winston, 1966), p. 117.

[7]See Inis L. Claude, Jr., *Swords into Plowshares: The Problems and Progress of International Organization*, 4th ed. (New York: Random House, 1971), pp. 301–3.

ments, which prohibited the stationing of nuclear weapons in outer space (1967), in Latin America (1967), and on the seabed (1971).[8]

The institution of these arms-limitation treaties was paralleled by a diplomatic effort to cope with the dangers of radioactive fallout and to inhibit the spread of nuclear weaponry. The Limited Test Ban Treaty (1963) committed an overwhelming majority of the members of the United Nations to a prohibition of nuclear testing in the atmosphere, in outer space, or under water. Five years later, the Treaty on the Non-Proliferation of Nuclear Weapons was signed by ninety-eight governments who agreed to forbid the transfer of nuclear explosives to nonnuclear states and to oppose the development of nuclear weapons by those states. The International Atomic Energy Agency, a specialized agency of the United Nations, monitors this agreement. Unfortunately, France and the People's Republic of China—both armed with nuclear weapons—did not sign the treaty. Having successfully tested a nuclear device in 1974, India also withheld its approval. In 1976, the Central Intelligence Agency revealed that Israel's nuclear program possessed military features. Should other governments follow the example of these nonsignatory powers, efforts to halt nuclear proliferation may prove futile.

Arms-control negotiations between the United States and the Soviet Union centered on the Strategic Arms Limitation Talks (SALT).[9] SALT I, the initial phase, produced two major categories of agreements in 1972. One limited the establishment and hardening of antiballistic-missile systems (the so-called ABM Treaty), and the other imposed force levels on the nuclear weapons held operational by the superpowers. The original executive agreement signed by President Richard Nixon and General Secretary Leonid Brezhnev was due to expire at the end of five years, but President Jimmy Carter announced that the United States would continue to adhere to its terms as long as the Soviet Union did. Meanwhile the negotiations entered a new phase, which resulted in the Vienna Summit Conference of 1979. The Carter-Brezhnev draft treaty, known as SALT II, encountered determined opposition when submitted to the U.S. Senate for its approval, and the Soviet intervention in Afghanistan brought with it a suspension of the ratification process.

The SALT II agreement drew criticism for three reasons. First, the proposed treaty ignored the nuclear-strike capability of third powers, especially the People's Republic of China. Talk in the United States of playing the "China card" tended to make the Soviet leadership increasingly apprehensive over Chinese intermediate-range ballistic missiles (IRBMs). Second, the agreement limited the number of missile launchers available to each signatory, but the subject of war-

[8]For the texts of arms-control agreements, the authors have relied upon the U.S. Arms Control and Disarmament Agency's, *Arms Control and Disarmament Agreements: Texts and History of Negotiations*, Pub. 94 (Washington, D.C.: Government Printing Office, 1977).

[9]U.S. Department of State, Bureau of Public Affairs, *SALT II Agreement: Vienna, June 18, 1979*, Selected Documents No. 12B, Pub. 8986 (1979), and *SALT II: Senate Testimony, July 9–11, 1979*, Current Policy No. 72A, Pub. 8989 (1979).

heads received little attention. Technological breakthroughs enabling interconti-nental ballistic missiles (ICBMs) and submarine-launched ballistic missiles (SLBMs) to carry additional warheads would weaken the restraining power of the treaty. Third, SALT II failed to address the problem of growing numbers of IRBMs in Central Europe—an omission that strained the relations of the princi-pal members of the North Atlantic Treaty Organization.

Whatever its failings, SALT II represented a high point in the recent his-tory of arms-control negotiations. Confrontational relations between the United States and the Soviet Union impeded and ultimately disrupted diplomatic efforts to slow the nuclear-arms race. Starting in 1981, the Reagan administration initi-ated a two-track policy, which separated the framework of negotiations for strate-gic and for theater (or intermediate-range) weapons. At the first level United States representatives met in Geneva with their Soviet counterparts to discuss strategic intercontinental weapons under the optimistic acronym START (Strate-gic Arms Reduction Talks), and in the same city distinct Soviet-American negotia-tions focused on IRBMs, whose operational capability is limited to a single conti-nental theater.

In theory the decoupling of the two sets of negotiations would enable the diplomats to cope with the problem of arms control on an incremental and therefore tractable basis. Critics of this method urged the adoption of a unified format that would result in a comprehensive agreement covering major weapons systems. In particular, they pointed out that the conceptual distinction between strategic and theater nuclear weapons was indeed vague. Nevertheless, both gov-ernments accepted the view that simultaneous negotiations at two levels, each concentrating on a different class of nuclear missile, would be more productive than a single, complex set of talks.

In the mid-1970s, the Soviet Union had begun to deploy a new, faster, and considerably more accurate type of IRBM, the SS-20, in Eastern Europe. At the urging of Chancellor Helmut Schmidt of the Federal Republic of Germany, NATO's defense ministers decided in late 1979 to respond with a counterbalanc-ing deployment of Pershing II and cruise missiles, first in West Germany and Great Britain, and later in Belgium and Italy. The Western response to create an intermediate-nuclear force (INF) was, however, to take effect only if no agreement on theater weapons could be reached in Geneva. In 1981, President Ronald Rea-gan proposed the *zero option*, under which the United States would indefinitely postpone the INF if the Soviet Union would dismantle its SS-20s.

Former general-secretary of the Communist Party of the Soviet Union, Yuri Andropov, did not foreclose negotiations but stated that his government could not accept the zero option unless it included British and French as well as American missiles. For reasons of alliance policy, the United States could not deny an independent nuclear deterrent to Great Britain and France, and a Soviet counterproposal to withdraw some SS-20s from Eastern Europe in exchange for a deferral of the INF plan was deemed unacceptable.

Diplomacy had reached an impasse, and the United States moved to modernize the nuclear deterrent available to NATO. In Great Britain, the Nether-

Ronald Reagan and Mikhail Gorbachev signing the INF Treaty in Washington, D.C. on December 8, 1987. (AP/ Wide World Photos)

lands, and West Germany a widespread peace movement staged demonstrations, and a new party—the Greens—committed to a nuclear freeze, entered the West German parliament in 1983. Despite the threat of passive resistance, British Prime Minister Margaret Thatcher and West German Chancellor Helmut Kohl affirmed their governments' support of INF. At the end of 1983, cruise missiles were on station in Great Britain and Pershing IIs in West Germany. These events led the Soviet regime, by that time under the leadership of General-Secretary Konstantin Chernenko, to withdraw from both sets of negotiations in Geneva.

With the passage of time and the gradual improvement of Soviet-American relations during the second term of President Ronald Reagan, the field of arms control was boosted by the signing of the historic INF Treaty on the elimination of intermediate-range and shorter-range missiles. The product of long and hard negotiations, the treaty was signed by Ronald Reagan and Mikhail Gorbachev in Washington, D.C., on December 8, 1987. Within months it was ratified by both sides and put into force. The treaty covers ground-launched ballistic missiles (GLBMs) and ground-launched cruise missiles (GLCMs) of intermediate range (1,000–5,500 kilometers) and of shorter range (500–1,000 kilometers).[10]

As a result of this agreement, the two parties undertook the obligation to *eliminate* their intermediate-range and shorter-range missiles and their launchers (approximately 800 on the part of the United States and 1,800 on the part of the Soviet Union), which include the Soviet SS-20s and the U.S. Cruise and Pershing II missile systems.

Despite lack of dramatic movement in the nuclear field, the 1972 convention prohibiting the production and stockpiling of biological weapons and tox-

---

[10]Missile systems with range over 5,500 kilometers are normally considered *strategic* and those with ranges under 500 kilometers are referred to as *tactical*. Missile systems whose range falls between 500 and 5,500 kilometers are *intermediate*. For details on the INF Treaty, see United Nations Department of Disarmament Affairs, *Disarmament Fact Sheet*, no. 56 (New York: United Nations, March 1988).

ins, signed by 112 states, has been a most impressive step toward universal arms control. In 1969, President Nixon declared that the United States was unilaterally renouncing the use of such weapons. He subsequently instructed government agencies to destroy existing stocks of biological weapons—a precedent that contributed to the successful conclusion of the negotiations in the 1972 convention.

Related to the issue of arms control is the grave problem of the outbreak of an accidental war between the two superpowers. In 1963, the "hot line" linking the heads of government in Washington and Moscow was established. During the 1967 war in the Middle East, this channel of communication proved exceptionally important. A 1971 Soviet-American agreement strengthened the organizational and technical safeguards designed to prevent a nuclear disaster resulting from a failure of equipment or from human error.

The attempts to reduce international tension by limiting and reducing armaments have been many. Skeptics point to a long record of arms-control treaties broken in the name of expediency and the defense of vital interests. They argue that arms-control treaties do not seriously slow the arms race since they often deal with secondary problems and require signatories to make only nominal concessions, which are often rendered inoperative by subsequent advances in technology. For example, the United States and the Soviet Union have been competing to be the first to introduce laser weapons capable of destroying incoming missiles. The Strategic Defense Initiative (SDI) of President Reagan is at the end of the technological tunnel for the United States. Such defensive weapons systems would be technically lawful, yet they would have the result of invalidating part of the SALT I agreement. The labyrinth of disarmament negotiations since World War II and the charges of violations of SALT I appear to lend credence to a pessimistic view of arms control, yet the effort to control the proliferation of weapons of mass destruction must continue if humankind is to survive.

SYSTEMS OF ARMS-CONTROL VERIFICATION

As we have already suggested, meaningful steps against arms buildups and in favor of partial disarmament and arms limitation cannot be taken unless they are justified in the interest of a state's national security. In the past, arms-control agreements have been most effective when reached in an atmosphere of relative confidence that they would be respected by their signatories. In order to create such a feeling of confidence (and hence security), representatives of nation-states have insisted upon provisions of adequate verification.

Verification—in the language of arms controllers—is the assessment of compliance with the provisions of arms-control treaties and agreements. Its primary purposes are to detect violations of agreements, to discourage potential violations (especially through effective inspection and detection mechanisms), and to build confidence among the signatories of arms-control agreements that will pave the way for further progress in arms control.

Verification proposals have consistently had to face an important problem: Nation-states like to keep the numbers, quality, and variety of their military capabilities secret in order to enhance their national security. Yet effective verification can be based only on such sensitive information. The more advanced a country's intelligence capabilities are, therefore, the more likely that country will be confident enough to enter into agreements concerning the mutual limiting of military capabilities and defense expenditures.

Prior to World War II, there was no serious concern with verification in arms-control and disarmament arrangements. But with the rapid growth in the technological complexity of weaponry since the war, the issue of verification has assumed greater importance.

Reviewing the record of arms-control negotiations since 1945, we find a fundamental division in the approaches toward verification adopted by the United States and the Soviet Union. This division was certainly deepened by the attempts of each side to score propaganda points by offering the type of proposals that would obviously be unacceptable to the adversary. In general, America's arms-control proposals—whether providing for the transfer of all nuclear weapons to an international authority or calling for sizable reductions in conventional weapons and force levels—were invariably accompanied by verification proposals, such as demands for frequent on-site inspections of important military installations. The Soviet Union, in turn, steadfastly opposed any system of on-site inspections that would allegedly violate its sovereignty. In their view, such inspections would amount to legalized espionage. Instead, the Soviets made ponderous proposals for total and complete disarmament (but without any inspection procedures) or called for the creation of nuclear-weapons–free buffer zones—especially in Central Europe and including both German states.[11]

The two superpowers held firmly to their respective positions until the late 1950s, when some significant progress was registered in the arms-control field. The mellowing in both Soviet and American attitudes regarding inspection and verification was a function of a number of changes in the international system. First, there was a considerable thaw in the cold war that decreased somewhat the level of mutual suspicion. Second, and perhaps more important, there was a marked change in the attitudes toward military deterrence in both countries. In the prenuclear international system, secrecy about one's military capabilities had been considered an important strategic asset. But with the advent of nuclear weaponry, it became apparent to strategists of both sides that deterrence was more effective if the potential adversary knew quite specifically one's nuclear capabilities.

With the ratification of the Antarctic Treaty (1959), the Soviet Union accepted the procedure of on-site inspections of its scientific installations in the southern polar regions. Despite this concession, the Soviet government refused to permit such inspections in its national territory. The United States, for its part, retreated from its demands for verification by agreement to the 1963 Limited Test Ban Treaty. As a result of this treaty, the United States stopped insisting upon on-site inspections. Instead, it settled on the use of its own national-intelli-

---

[11]George F. Kennan, *Memoirs*, vol. II: *1950–1963* (Boston: Little, Brown, 1972), p. 241.

gence monitoring and detection services to evaluate compliance by the Soviet Union.

Verification techniques available to nation-states can range widely in complexity and obtrusiveness. The less obtrusive techniques, referred to as *national technical means*, involve intelligence practices such as photographic, radar, and electronic surveillance; seismic-detection instruments; high-sensitivity air-sampling techniques; and highly computerized data-processing and data-analysis systems. On the more obtrusive side, we should list *ad hoc* inspection facilities, fixed observation posts, mobile inspection teams, and unstaffed monitoring instruments.

Verification practices involving on-site inspection—despite the Soviet Union's longtime refusal to permit such inspections on its territory—have gained gradual acceptance. For example, the Sinai II disengagement agreement between Egypt and Israel (1975) involved buffer areas, demilitarized zones, U.N. observation teams, American communications specialists, and continuous monitoring and verification—all of which were designed to increase mutual confidence in the workability of the agreement. Also, signatories of the Nuclear Non-Proliferation Treaty have agreed, as we have seen, to periodic on-site inspections by the International Atomic Energy Agency.

The Soviet-American INF Treaty (1987) has been termed historic not only because it is the first nuclear–arms-control treaty to provide for the elimination (the actual destruction) of a specific category of nuclear weapons but also for pathbreaking progress in the field of verification. Indeed, the two states have agreed upon a *verification triad*, which consists of on-site inspection, inspection by challenge, and unobstructed use of verification satellites.

The Soviet Union, under Mikhail Gorbachev, has retreated from its traditional objection to on-site inspections. Thus the treaty calls for the stationing of an inspection team outside the main facility of each side where intermediate- and shorter-range missile components are being produced. This monitoring activity is to be carried out for a period of thirteen years from the signing of the treaty. The provisions for inspection by challenge provide that each side can request and carry out one inspection per year at any site suspected to be producing launchers for the weapons covered by the INF Treaty. On the third component of the triad, the unobstructed use of satellites, both sides have agreed not to hamper the use of each other's satellites in carrying out treaty-related verification activity. Finally, the treaty "institutionalizes" mutual verification by establishing a joint verification commission whose task is to resolve technical disputes, to facilitate plans and procedures for verification, and, more generally, to continue improving the viability and effectiveness of the INF Treaty.

SOCIAL COSTS OF ARMAMENTS

Excessive military expenditures, required by factors such as a spiraling arms race and fuel inflation, hinder economic growth and divert both human and material resources from such programs as public education and health. As of 1983, global military expenditures exceeded $600 billion annually. By 1987 this figure exceeded the $700 billion mark. Accounting for approximately 80 percent of all defense spending are, in rank order, the United States, the Soviet Union, Great Britain, France, and West Germany.[12] These states together with China are also the leading suppliers of arms to the developing countries of the Third World, as demonstrated by the Argentine Air Force's use of French-manufactured exocet missiles against British warships in the Anglo-Argentine War (1982). In 1983, an estimated twenty-five million men and women were under arms, and at least twice that number are engaged in military-related pursuits. The indirect costs in terms of labor and the dissipation of nonrenewable resources, such as petroleum, are difficult to calculate, yet they must be paid for at the expense of the civilian economy.

Depending upon the region of the world, the annual rate of growth in military spending varies from 3 to 5 percent. With the possible exception of the Soviet Union, the states of Eastern and Western Europe have made relatively moderate increases in their military programs, and the People's Republic of China had stabilized its program by 1983. Similarly, most African states have limited the yearly expansion of their military budgets. By contrast, Latin America, the Middle East, and Oceania experience a yearly expansion in military expenditures of about 5 percent. One-fourth of the developing countries already produce conventional weapons. Munitions industries in the Third World are invariably labor-intensive; as a result, they siphon off human resources from more socially beneficial endeavors. In addition, the purchase of costly aircraft and naval vessels by developing countries absorbs much of their limited reserves of foreign exchange and therefore creates a serious balance-of-payments problem. The resulting imbalance in the economies of developing societies leads to an ever-widening gap between them and the industrialized democracies of the West.

As of 1987, over $163 billion was spent globally to import sophisticated weapons systems. Among the top ten leading importers were developing countries such as India, Iraq, Egypt, Saudi Arabia, Syria, Turkey and Angola. It is fair to say that in the 1980s arms purchases accounted for a large proportion of the gigantic debt incurred by Third World countries.[13]

The following case study illustrates the problems caused by the transfer of arms from an industrialized to a modernizing nation-state. Until the overthrow of the Shah Mohammed Reza Pehlavi in 1979, the largest single arms-transfer program in the world was that between the United States and Iran. A congressional staff report had assessed this bilateral arrangement as follows: "Everyone seemed to be basically pleased. The Government of Iran was getting the equipment it wanted; the State Department was happy because U.S.-Iranian relations were good; DOD [Department of Defense] was actively selling in accord-

---

[12]Elisabeth Sköns and Rita Tullberg, "World Military Expenditures," in Stockholm International Peace Research Institute, *World Armaments and Disarmament: SIPRI Yearbook 1984* (London: Taylor & Francis, 1984), pp. 63–64, 118–20; and *World Armaments and Disarmament: SIPRI Yearbook 1988* (London: Oxford University Press, 1988), pp. 163–67.

[13]Ruth Leger Sivard, *World Military and Social Expenditures, 1983* (Washington, D.C.: World Priorities, 1983), p. 24; SIRPI Yearbook 1988, p. 179.

Ayatollah Ruhollah Khomeini (1901–1989), leader of the Islam Revolution and ruler of Iran from 1979 to 1989.

ance with policy; the contractors were pleased because they were making money."[14]

As satisfactory as this relationship might have appeared at first blush, its implementation not only created friction between Iran and the United States but also served to strengthen the ultra-conservative insurgent movement under the Ayatollah Ruhollah Khomeini. The revolutionary ideology stressed the need to return to the fundamental teachings of Islam and to reject negative Western influences, all of which ran counter to such policies as, for example, the shah's insistence that English rather than Farsi, the national language, be used in military activities involving advanced technical skills.[15] The power of an ideal—an Islamic political order—destroyed whatever political gains the United States might have anticipated by placing Iran in a position of military dependency.[16]

The justification of an arms-transfer program such as that of Iran and the United States often rests on the thesis that a modernization of the military provides the needed impetus for further economic development. That is, the technical and administrative skills taught to military trainees are readily convertible to civilian enterprises. To a degree, there is indeed a spill-over effect: The repairs to a tank can sometimes approximate those to a tractor. Nevertheless, for many military skills there is no civilian counterpart. In the end, the development

[14]U.S. Congress, Senate, Subcommittee on Foreign Assistance of the Committee on Foreign Relations, *U.S. Military Sales to Iran*, by Robert Mantel and Geoffrey Kemp (Washington, D.C.: Government Printing Office, 1976), p. 46.

[15]*Ibid.*, p. 37.

[16]For an analysis of the political implications of the Islamic revival, see Martin Kramer, *Political Islam*, Washington Papers, vol. 73, Georgetown University Center for Strategic and International Studies, (Beverly Hills, Calif.: Sage Publications, 1980).

of the kind of economic structure required to maintain advanced weaponry in a state of operational readiness means that other areas of public policy will be neglected.

For the United States, the outcome of the close alliance with the shah, as manifested in the arms transfers and other forms of penetration, has been equally serious. The establishment in 1979 of a new government under the Islamic Republican Party led to a cancellation of orders for arms, which signaled a cooling of relations between Washington and Teheran. In November of that year Revolutionary Guards stormed the United States embassy compound in Teheran and took hostage diplomatic and consular personnel stationed in Iran. The outbreak of the Persian Gulf War between Iraq and Iran in September 1980 required the United States to base its policy on Saudi Arabia and Kuwait in order to keep open the vital Strait of Hormuz. A painful epilogue to this sad story was written with the so-called Iran-Contra affair (1987–88). This well-publicized scandal involved an apparent attempt by high-ranking members of President Ronald Reagan's National Security Council staff to sell, clandestinely, sophisticated military equipment to the Khomeini regime and to divert the proceeds—also clandestinely—to the Contra guerrilla force fighting the Sandinista regime in Nicaragua. The policy of arms and influence followed so long in Iran had come to naught.

LEGAL AND HUMANITARIAN CONSTRAINTS ON WAR

As the history of warfare indicates, the development of the European balance-of-power system brought with it the concept of limited war. In 1625, the Dutch jurist Hugo Grotius published his monumental treatise, *Law of War and Peace*. Among other things, this work described restraints on the use of military and naval force.[17] The historical importance of this work lies in its emphasis on the volitional aspect of international law—that is, on the belief that governments consent to follow specified rules of conduct even in time of war. The decision to adhere to rules is a rational one designed to further the goal of maintaining the international system. Although chivalry and fair play remain one of the roots of the customary law of war, in its present-day form this code of law reflects a calculated acceptance on the part of most governments that unlimited war is synonymous with MAD—*mutually assured destruction*.

During the Mexican War (1846–48), General Winfield Scott, commanding an American expeditionary force marching inland from Vera Cruz, issued General Order 20, which directed his troops to take no action against "unoffending civilians" and therefore to respect the honor and welfare of the native population. The principle of distinguishing between combatants and noncombatants became a part of the laws of the United States with the issuance of General Order 100 in 1863. Francis Lieber, the author of this code and a founder of American political science, identified war as an act of violence perpetrated on behalf of the

---

[17]See Gerhard von Glahn, *Law among Nations* (New York: Macmillan, 1965), pp. 42ff.

state but also circumscribed by the law of nations.[18] If a state engages in war to achieve a stable peace, it follows that military operations should not be such that they make the return to peace unnecessarily difficult. Adherence to the rules of war, therefore, is based on political pragmatism as well as on humanitarianism.

Early steps to codify the law of war—and to maintain the balance-of-power system—took the form of international conferences, first in Brussels (1874) and later at The Hague (1899 and 1907). Although the Declaration of Brussels was never ratified by the fifteen participating governments, it introduced the principles of the Lieber code as a subject for international consideration. The subsequent conferences at The Hague resulted in agreements designed to lessen the effects of war on noncombatants. This was to be done by internationalizing the restraints on field armies outlined in the precedent-setting American instructions of 1863. Of particular importance in the 1907 Convention were provisions requiring a military command exercising governmental authority over a foreign population to respect family rights and honor, to refrain from imposing collective penalties, and to respect local laws and customs. In 1949, the Geneva Convention on the Protection of Civilian Persons in Time of War updated and reaffirmed many of these earlier acts.

The interpretation of the laws and customs of war is complicated by three unresolved questions: What are the limits of military necessity? What is the extent of command responsibility that senior civil and military officials bear for their own actions as well as for unlawful acts committed by their subordinates? And what is the personal responsibility of subordinates for unlawful acts committed while carrying out the orders of a superior?

The expression *military necessity* has been defined in two ways. According to legal scholars, it means a field commander may employ whatever weapons or schemes appear suitable as long as they are not expressly forbidden by domestic or international law. The second definition is more relevant to an understanding of the international system: A commander must defer to the political guidance of his government and not conduct operations in such a fashion that the enemy's current or potential leadership finds it impossible to consider a negotiated settlement.

We can distinguish between these two definitions by considering two war-crimes trials conducted in Germany after World War II. The first, convened before an American court, resulted in the acquittal of General Lothar Rendulic on a charge of illegal mass deportation of the civilian population of the Norwegian province of Finnmark. In anticipation of an attack by Soviet forces, General Rendulic had evacuated several communities, thus imposing considerable hardship on their inhabitants. Although the expected offensive never occurred, the military court was able to establish that the defendant's objective was to protect the civilian population. Therefore, his action was consistent with the law of land warfare.

---

[18]U.S. War Department, *Instructions for the Government of Armies of the United States in the Field*, drafted by Francis Lieber (Washington, D.C., 1863).

In a parallel case heard by a British military court, Field Marshal Erich von Manstein was convicted on a charge of ordering the illegal removal of civilians from their homes in the Ukraine. Making a distinction between military "advantage" and military "necessity," the court ruled that the defendant's objective had been to deny labor and recruits to the oncoming Soviet armies. In doing so, he hoped to gain an economic as well as military advantage over the enemy. His transfer of civilians was therefore motivated by other than strictly military and humanitarian considerations. Clearly, such behavior was inconsistent with the provisions of the 1907 Hague Convention. It also escalated the level of the Soviet-German conflict to a point at which neither side possessed a political option other than the extremes of total victory or total defeat.

The second question, that of command responsibility, can also be illustrated by specific cases. In 1902, President Theodore Roosevelt reviewed and upheld the conviction of General Jacob Smith before a military court. The defendant was found to have abused his authority in ordering an excessive reprisal against Filipino communities harboring insurgents on the island of Samar. An American unit had been ambushed, and in reprisal General Smith had dispatched an expedition with explicit orders to turn the interior of the island into a wilderness and to regard anyone over ten as an enemy. The president wrote that even though Smith's instructions were never implemented, they cast discredit upon the United States Army. He therefore ordered that the general be retired.

In 1945 an American military commission convened in Manila to try General T. Yamashita, the senior commander of Japanese ground forces in the Philippines at the end of World War II, for war crimes. Although the charges were varied, of particular concern for our discussion are two allegations: that General Yamashita had failed to exert proper control over his forces; and that he ignored his obligation to punish subordinates who had inflicted unlawful reprisals against civilians in order to suppress underground resistance activities. In this instance, the defendant was held responsible for an act of omission rather than of commission. The charge was not that he had personally ordered atrocities, but that he had fallen short of the standards of command responsibility established by the law of war. The commission rendered a verdict of guilty and imposed a sentence of death.

On the third question, the degree to which a plea of superior orders (*respondeat superior*) absolves civil or military officials of responsibility for their acts, national codes are usually explicit. During World War II, some governments considered superior orders an extenuating circumstance. However, war-crimes trials in Europe and East Asia have established the precedent of rejecting superior orders as a defense. The military legal code of the United States also incorporates this precedent.[19]

This discussion on the application of the law of war should not blind us

---

[19]U.S. Department of the Army, *The Law of Land Warfare*, FM-27-10 (Washington, D.C.: Government Printing Office, 1956).

to two major obstacles to the legal control of violence. The first is that although international conventions are regularly violated, only a small proportion of offenders are brought to trial. Moreover, the proportion of prosecutions to offenses varies significantly from country to country, and the trials that have been held are frequently examples of victors' justice. Nevertheless, the progressive codification of the law of war and the increasing number of judicial precedents are advances in the international system.

A second, unintended obstacle is the temptation to assume that the very existence of a law of war renders the use of organized violence permissible in the international system. The basis of this assumption is that what is not expressly prohibited is permitted. Such an interpretation may well lead decision makers to conclude that deadly force is preferable to prolonged diplomatic negotiations or a gradual escalation of conflict. For example, they might very well advocate a preemptive strike if they believe they hold a momentary military advantage and time is working against them. In the nuclear age, the dangers in this type of reasoning are obvious. These dangers are aggravated by the occasional rise to power of political leaders who are fixated on destruction and have an insatiable desire to punish those with opposing world views. Leaders who are fascinated with destructiveness, withdrawn from reality, and committed to a historic "mission" are not likely to be deterred by the often nebulous law of war.

The United Nations has sought since its founding to bolster international law with a meaningful definition of aggressive war. In 1974, the General Assembly approved a convention identifying the various forms of direct and indirect aggression, as defined by any one of the seven following acts committed by one nation-state against another: invasion, bombardment, naval blockade, attack upon foreign armed forces, unlawful use of military forces stationed abroad, allowing one's territory to be used as a base for aggression, and the sending of irregulars or mercenaries against a target government. The opening paragraphs, which condemn aggressive war in firm language, give way to a clause approving wars of "self-determination, freedom and independence."[20] The meaning of these value-laden concepts is then left to the perception of the foreign-policy elites weighing the question of war or peace.

SUGGESTIONS FOR FURTHER STUDY

Leonard S. Spector addressed the problem of nuclear proliferation in *The New Nuclear Nations* (New York: Random House, 1985). The compatibility of the Strategic Defense Initiative and the Antiballistic Missile Treaty was the subject of hearings held by the House Committee on Foreign Affairs under the heading *ABM Treaty Interpretation*, 99th Cong., 1st sess., 1986. Strobe Talbott has explored the intricacies of superpower arms-control negotiations in *Deadly Gambits* (New York:

---

[20]United Nations Office of Public Information, *Definition of Aggression* (New York: United Nations, 1975), pp. 9–10.

Vintage Books, 1985). The normative dimension of arms control is the focus of Morton A. Kaplan, ed., *Strategic Thinking and Its Moral Implications* (Chicago: University of Chicago Press, 1973). Official sources include U.S. Department of State, *Treaty between the United States of America and the Union of Soviet Socialist Republics on the Elimination of Their Intermediate-Range and Shorter-Range Missiles, December 1987*, Pub. 9555, and *SALT II Agreement: Vienna, 1979*, Pub. 8986. An additional documentary source is U.S. Arms Control and Disarmament Agency, *Arms Control and Disarmament Agreements: Texts and History of Negotiations*, Pub. 94 (Washington, D.C.: Government Printing Office, 1977). For an analysis of scenarios which could lead to nuclear war, see Joseph S. Nye, Jr., "Arms Control and the Prevention of War," *Washington Quarterly*, 7 (Fall 1984), 59–70. Herman Kahn has studied the possibility of a so-called winnable nuclear war in *Thinking about the Unthinkable in the 1980s* (New York: Simon & Schuster, 1984).

13

INTERNATIONAL LAW: FACT OR FICTION?

> The law of nations is a system of rules, deducible by natural reason, and established by universal consent among the civilized inhabitants of the world. . . . This general law is founded upon this principle, that different nations ought in time of peace to do one another all the good they can; and in time of war as little harm as possible, without prejudice to their own real interests.
>
> Sir William Blackstone,
Commentaries on the Laws of England (1765–69)

In this eighteenth-century description of international law, Sir William Blackstone postulated that in world politics law is based on consent given in response to right reason. Yet the debate continues as to the true nature of international law. Some argue that there is no such thing as international law; there is only positive international morality.[1] The other extreme argues that international law is at the very apex of all legal systems, that it is a source of legitimacy for municipal systems of law.[2] The stand one takes in this controversy depends on the definition of law he or she chooses to work with.[3] One could, for example, adopt the very crude and primitive definition that a system of laws is "a set of orders backed by threats." The problem with such a definition, however, is that it does not permit us to differentiate between legitimate and illegitimate orders backed by

---

[1]See John Austin, *Lectures on Jurisprudence: Or the Philosophy of Positive Law*, 5th ed., rev. and ed. Robert Campbell (London: John Murray, 1885).

[2]Hans Kelsen, *Principles of International Law*, 2nd ed. (New York: Holt, Rinehart & Winston, 1966).

[3]For a fine discussion of the great controversy regarding the various ways of defining law, see H.L.A. Hart, *The Concept of Law* (Oxford: Oxford University Press, 1961).

threats. Thus, we could consider as equally legal the orders of a police officer who controls traffic at a busy intersection and the order of a bank robber who passes a note to a terrified bank teller demanding the money or the teller's life. What is missing, obviously, from the above definition of law is the concept of recognition of the legitimacy of an order. Most societies recognize the right of the police to issue reasonable orders and to enforce them when necessary. In the case of the bank robber, no similar right is recognized, although the bank teller will most likely obey the robber's order to ensure his or her own survival.

We shall adopt, then, a more qualified concept of *law*, one that contains at least the following three prerequisites:

1. Lawmakers should be recognized by their subjects as having the right (i.e., the authority) to issue orders.
2. The orders (or laws) should reflect the habits, norms, or needs of those regulated by or subjected to them.
3. Lawmakers should be in a position to enforce laws with adequate sanctions.

Thus, the adequacy of law is a function of its acceptability, its just nature, and its enforceability. We can now restate our definition of a *system of laws* as a set of *legitimate* orders backed when necessary by adequate threats and/or rewards. *Legitimacy*, in turn, can be seen as a function of both the recognition of the authoritative source of law and the general acceptability of the provisions of law. In simpler words, laws are considered legitimate by their subjects if they are developed by effective and authoritative institutions and if they do not violate the vital interests, customs, and attitudes of their subjects.

Most municipal legal systems pass, to varying degrees, the threefold test of *legitimacy*, *acceptability*, and *enforceability*. In countries with popular systems of government, laws are obeyed more because of their acceptability and less because of their pure enforceability. In countries with tyrannical governments—for instance, those immediately following *coups d'état*—laws or decrees are applied primarily because they are enforceable rather than because they are acceptable. In the case of international law, as we shall elaborate below, we can identify with relative ease some of its legitimate sources. We can also observe that international law is usually obeyed to the degree to which it is acceptable among its disparate subjects. The major weakness of international law can be traced to the absence of adequate instruments for its development (legislation) and enforcement (implementation).

If one were to require an effective system of law enforcement as a prerequisite for the existence of law, one would conclude that there is no such thing as international law. On the other hand, one could posit the existence of law as a result of habitual observation of certain rules of behavior. In this case, and regardless of sanctions or systems of enforcement, the world community has developed a respectable, if not comprehensive system of international laws. For the purposes of this book, we shall operate with a less restrictive definition of international law, one that does not require effective enforcement machinery. On the other hand, we must insist on a minimal degree of customary and voluntary obedience of international rules of conduct before we can call them laws. To do less would be to consider as law any set of general principles, regardless of whether they were habitually obeyed or institutionally enforced. By not insisting on enforcement as a prerequisite of law, we can pronounce the existence of international law without exaggerating its effectiveness.

We believe that no system of laws that relies on force alone can remain viable over a prolonged period of time. In fact, most legal systems survive primarily because of the substantial degree of voluntary obedience to their laws. On the other hand, no system of laws that relies primarily on voluntary obedience and self-help—as is the case, we are afraid, with international law—can credibly carry out the function of legitimate, centralized institutions backed by adequate law enforcement agencies.

THE HISTORICAL DEVELOPMENT OF INTERNATIONAL LAW

International law, understood in terms of rules binding sovereign political collectivities, can be traced back to the fourth and third millenniums B.C. These early rules were at best rudimentary; they covered activities such as the sending of and safe conduct for heralds and emissaries, formalities involving the initiation and cessation of hostilities, and the arrangement of truces during holiday periods. These rules were further formalized by the customary practices of Greek and Roman city-states. The contributions of these city-states were primarily philosophical. Greece and Rome, for example, introduced the legal concept of a society of humankind, which was to be governed by natural law. Rome, acting through the medium of the Roman Empire, had an especially significant impact. It unified much of the world and facilitated the application of laws throughout the many nations under its control.

Medieval Europe, through its customary practices, contributed to the development of rules of commerce and clarified the rights and duties of merchants on land and sea. During the same period the laws of the sea for belligerents and neutrals were considerably elaborated, and the highly controversial concept of *just war* was advanced by religious scholars. Just war was initially studied and analyzed by St. Augustine (A.D. 345–430) and a series of other churchmen, referred to as the scholastics, who followed St. Augustine's path in the tradition of divine and natural law. A war was considered just by the scholastics if it were fought in self-defense—that is, against external attack—or if its purpose was to punish wrongdoers.[4] The latter provision offered policy makers a hunting license for conducting wars outside their own territory that could be justified on the grounds of defending or spreading the truth, or punishing transgressors (as defined by the policy makers).

---

[4]This is a huge loophole, for it assumes that in a decentralized international system there can be found an unimpeachable source to determine who the wrongdoer is. In the days of the scholastics, of course, that source was God, and his representative on earth—the pope.

Beginning in the sixteenth century, the writings of great scholars and publicists of international law became a major source of identification, propagation, and development of international law. Francisco de Vitoria wrote about the justice of Spanish conquests in America (his lectures were published in 1557). Alberico Gentili (1598) and Francisco Suarez (1612) elaborated on the doctrines of just and unjust war, and differentiated natural law (*jus naturale*) from the law practiced by nations (*jus gentium*). The Dutchman Hugo Grotius established himself as the "father of international law" with the publication of his famous book *De jure belli ac pacis* (Law of War and Peace) in 1625. Samuel Pufendorf, author of *De jure naturae et gentium* (The Law of Nature and of Nations) in 1672, became the leader of the naturalist school of legal thought. Cornelius van Bynkershoek, whose major works were *Forum of Ambassadors* (1721) and *Questions of Public Law* (1737), took a stance that was contrary to Pufendorf's naturalism. Van Bynkershoek became a leading exponent of what came to be known as the *positivist* school of thought. The gap between *positivism* and *naturalism* (to be discussed shortly) was bridged by the writings of Emmerich de Vattel, whose major work, *Le Droit des Gens* (The Law of Nations), was published in 1758. Vattel became known as the father of the eclectic school of thought. Our list of publicists would not be balanced if we did not include legal scholars such as John Jacob Moser and George Friedrich von Martens, whose works appeared in the middle and late eighteenth century. Finally, the nineteenth and early twentieth centuries saw the focus of international legal scholarship move to British and American institutions respectively.[5]

THE NATURALIST-POSITIVIST DEBATE

The proponents of natural law firmly rooted in the idealist tradition predated the positivist school. A prominent naturalist such as Samuel Pufendorf can trace his intellectual and philosophical roots to the works of religiously oriented scholars such as St. Augustine, Vitoria, and Suarez. These publicists argued that all law is derived from God, and they called God's superior law *divine law. Natural law*, in turn, was seen as a faithful application of divine law by human societies. The central assumption of proponents of divine law, and by extension natural law, was that there exist fundamental and unchangeable principles that transcend the will and the consent of the rulers.as well as the ruled in human societies. Thus, all laws developed by societies have to be tested for conformity with the precepts of divine and/or natural law. The problem with such a philosophical approach to law rests in the search for an acceptable method with which one can *identify* such things as divine principles and unchangeable laws of nature. If we assume merely that God or nature speaks through the media of sovereign rulers or through mystically inspired church leaders, then we manage to substitute for

[5]For a good overview of the history of international law, see Arthur Nussbaum, *A Concise History of the Law of Nations* (New York: Macmillan, 1954).

the will of God or nature the will of politically selected or church-appointed human interpreters of God and nature.

The *positivist* school of thought proceeded from the strongly realist assumption that there is no more to law than what its subjects *agree* to be bound by. Accordingly, the positivists rejected "higher" (divine or natural) legal principles and considered as law only those rules that were adopted by the consent (either through custom or treaties) of sovereign nation-states. The critics of the positivist approach to law have opposed, for their part, the amoral and socially disinterested aspects of positivism. States or individuals, freed from concern with higher principles, could advance to the status of law unjust and unnatural rules merely because these rules were adopted by mutual consent.

The *eclectic* school of thought sought to steer a middle course in the positivist-naturalist (realist-idealist) debate. Eclectics, such as Emmerich de Vattel, accepted the simultaneous existence of two tiers of law—one at the natural level and one at the positivist level. Natural law, referred to also as *necessary law*, transcends the practices of a given period and reflects the accumulated wisdom of all ages and times. Yet natural law becomes the subject of conflicting interpretations among sovereign political entities. So the eclectics identified a second (lower) tier of law, which they called *voluntary law*. This law reflects the consent of the governments of nation-states and is analogous to positivist international law. It is the voluntary rather than the necessary law that the subjects of the international system abide by.

This train of thought leads us into one of the central problems in political science. Specifically, in what ways can societies harmonize their laws with general principles of justice? As we have seen in our discussion of national interest (see Chapter 6), abstractions such as public welfare, due process, collective interest, and justice are extremely complex and difficult to pinpoint objectively. It is perhaps safer to assume that most legal systems reflect to a large extent the vital interests of their powerful and influential members or subgroups.[6] The question of justice, it seems, becomes in practice a political question. What is taken as just is what the lawmakers of a given society agree to consider as just. Once laws are made by legislators, the interpretation of these laws is a matter for the courts to determine and for executive authorities to enforce.

We shall assume in this textbook, joining after a fashion the positivist school of thought, that there is no ultimate and generally acceptable set of criteria with which to evaluate the "justice quotient" of different systems of laws, be they national or international. The definition of what is fair and just in a given society is the product of the combined attitudes of the rulers and the ruled of that society. A society's cultural background, historical experiences, and political structures, as well as its legislative processes and its interpretation, adjudication, and enforcement of laws, contribute significantly to the definition of its laws.

---

[6]This assumption is controversial. A critic could argue, for instance, that without any laws at all societies would resort to systems of vigilante justice where the "mighty" would be even less encumbered.

THE SOURCES OF INTERNATIONAL LAW

Article 38 of the Statute of the International Court of Justice identifies the sources of international law as follows:

1. International conventions [treaties], whether general or particular, establishing rules expressly recognized by the contesting states;
2. International custom, as evidence of a general practice accepted by law;
3. The general principles of law recognized by civilized nations;
4. Subject to the provisions of Article 59, judicial decisions and the teachings of the most highly qualified publicists of the various nations, as subsidiary means for the determination of the rules of law.[7]

As we noted above, the naturalist-positivist debate extends to the area of sources of law. The positivists hold *consent* to be an absolute prerequisite of international law. Thus, they recognise only treaties and custom as its authentic sources. The naturalists, on the other hand, emphasize supranational sources that they call general principles of law. Both naturalists and positivists concede that court precedents and the works of respected publicists are *subsidiary* sources of law.

The differences between the two schools of thought are more philosophical than practical. The naturalists tend to view the law in a hierarchical fashion. They are opposed to anarchy and the law of the jungle, as exemplified by the old adage that "might makes right." Under the influence of the Roman/Christian traditions, they assume the existence of universally acceptable and generally applicable laws. The positivists, on the other hand, are realists who claim that the basic ingredient—in fact, the *unique* characteristic—of the international system is the sovereignty and unaccountability of national governments. Thus they reach the paradoxical conclusion that international law consists only of law that legitimizes the right of its subjects not to be bound by any laws against their will. The eclectics, as we suggested above, concede the existence of general principles of law but stress the importance of voluntarism—the consent of the governments of nation-states—for practical purposes.

Stanley Hoffmann has brilliantly summarized this state of affairs. "International law," he argues, "like its Siamese twin and enemy, war, remains a crystallization of all that keeps world politics *sui generis*."[8] In other words, both international law and war are products of a political system of decentralized power based on the recognition of sovereign political units. In times of political harmony, international law is applicable. In times of dissonance, war takes over.

[7]Article 59 provides that "the decision of the [International] Court has no binding force except between the parties and in respect of that particular case." See "Statute of the International Court of Justice," Appendix III, in Herbert W. Briggs, *The Law of Nations*, 2nd ed. (New York: Appleton-Century-Crofts, 1952), pp. 1072–1080.

[8]Stanley Hoffmann, "International Systems and International Law," in *The Strategy of World Order*, vol. II: *International Law*, ed. Richard A. Falk and Saul H. Mendlovitz (New York: World Law Fund, 1966), p. 134.

If we were to compare international law with various municipal systems of law, which are taken as *standard legal models*, international law would be found seriously wanting. In most instances, municipal law is generated by well-developed legislative institutions, such as parliaments, congresses, presidiums, and soviets. International law, in contrast, has no institutionalized legislative sources. The United Nations General Assembly comes the closest to being a global legislature. But, as we shall see in the next chapter, General Assembly resolutions are no more than pious wishes reflecting the interests of the majority of the governments represented in the United Nations. These resolutions have neither legal nor substantive binding power. On the other hand, such resolutions are clearly previews of changing patterns and attitudes, which are subsequently reflected in treaty law and customary practices of states.

Municipal laws are usually implemented by well-developed executive branches of government that possess an overwhelming preponderance of power (in the form of institutional authority and adequate military and police forces) over their subjects. There are no such institutions at the global level. The United Nations Security Council, veto bound and security oriented, stands for the collective will of the great powers when they occasionally happen to be in reluctant agreement. The United Nations secretary-general and occasional United Nations peacekeeping forces can be considered—with much stretching of the imagination—to constitute a rudimentary form of world administration. But the secretary-general has a long way to go before achieving the role of global chief executive. Finally, and quite important, municipal systems of law are interpreted and applied to specific disputes by courts that enjoy compulsory jurisdiction (regardless of consent) over their subjects. The fifteen-member International Court of Justice (ICJ), meeting in The Hague, hears only those cases referred to it by consenting governments or international organizations, and no executive authority exists to enforce its decisions. In a 1980 opinion, for example, the ICJ ordered the release of United States diplomatic and consular personnel held hostage in Teheran as well as the payment of reparations. The Islamic Republic of Iran contested the jurisdiction of the court and ignored its ruling.[9]

In smoothly functioning societies, municipal law supplies credible and comprehensive legal procedures that replace or contain intersubject violence as a method of regulating disputes and bringing about change. International law, in contrast, implicitly legitimizes war as a technique of securing international change. At best, it seeks to control the means and styles of waging war. Stretching the analogy somewhat, international laws of war could be compared to municipal laws that would seek to regulate and civilize modes and styles of murder, arson, rape, and breaking and entering. For example, an international law requiring the humane treatment of prisoners of war would be analogous to a municipal law providing that burglars *should not* mistreat the occupants of a burglarized

---

[9]"Case concerning United States Diplomatic and Consular Staff in Teheran: Judgment of the International Court of Justice," *American Journal of International Law*, 72 (July 1980), 746–81.

residence too harshly and that in any case they should not shoot them unless they considered this measure absolutely necessary for the success of the burglary.[10]

Another major principle of international law, noninterference in the domestic affairs of sovereign states, can be compared to municipal laws that would ban police authorities from investigating instances of mistreatment, torture, and even murder that take place within a person's "sovereign" home. Extending this analogy one more notch, municipal authorities would be banned from instituting regulations such as maximum working hours, minimum wages, social security, and taxation. The purpose of such a ban would be to prevent municipal authorities from interfering in the domestic affairs of corporations, farms, churches, private universities, political parties, and other "sovereign" organizations.[11]

We can suggest, therefore, that when international law is compared with municipal law, it emerges as, at best, a loose and legitimizing set of rules designed to perpetuate a decentralized international system. On the other hand, one could shift orientations and look at international law as a crystallization and conscious reflection of a loosely bound society of autonomous nation-states that is referred to as the international community. From this perspective, each nation-state is seen as the best interventionary and regulatory unit of administration for interindividual and intergroup affairs. In this context, international law is a set of residual rules that regulate only the relations *between*—not *within*—nation-states.

Without worldwide consensus on vital international issues; without central global authorities; without a legislature; without effective courts; given the existence of large autonomous subjects with powerful military establishments; given further the permanent companion of human history called war—in these circumstances, all that international law can hope to accomplish is to limit violence, to substitute for it at times, and generally to use it for the mutual convenience of the various national units. After all, argue some of the proponents of the nation-state system, an effective system of world government could very likely result from the dominance of one or two powers over the rest of the world. This system would severely restrict the autonomy of most of the earth's inhabitants and would become the masked equivalent of world empire, which would gradually but surely degenerate into a technologically administered world tyranny.

---

[10]The international custom that a warring nation's destruction of an opponent's land, property, and population should not exceed the limits established by *military necessity* is another analogue to this hypothetical municipal law.

[11]There is considerable ambiguity surrounding the legal definition of *sovereignty*. Consider, for example, a definition employed by Judge Max Huber, who served as arbitrator in a dispute between the United States and Holland (1928) involving the Island of Palmas (Miangas): "Territorial sovereignty . . . involves the exclusive right to display the activities of State. This right has as corollary a duty: the obligation to protect within the territory the rights of other States, in particular their right to integrity and inviolability in peace and in war, together with the rights which each state may claim for its nationals in foreign territory." Given this definition, it is somewhat unrealistic to assume that all states have equal capacity to protect their sovereign rights in a world of superpowers, intermediate states, and weak states (e.g., mini-states). For a good discussion, see Briggs, *The Law of Nations*, pp. 239–40.

THE SUBJECTS OF INTERNATIONAL LAW

States, acting through their recognized governments, have been considered the primary subjects of international law. For certain issues (such as the privileges and immunities of their functionaries), international organizations have also been considered subjects of international law. In contrast, individual human beings have been treated only as the objects of international law. In other words, individuals have been represented, protected, and held accountable internationally only through the auspices of their governments. However, after World War I and, more formally, World War II, major efforts were made to hold individuals directly responsible for acts of state. Thus, during the Nuremberg and Tokyo trials, leaders of the Nazi and Imperial Japanese governments were tried for committing war crimes, crimes against humanity, and crimes against peace. (Most of these individuals were convicted and sentenced to death, life imprisonment, or long jail sentences.) Crimes against peace specifically involved the planning and waging of "aggressive war."[12] It could be said, therefore, that important but highly controversial precedents have been set for the trying of the leaders of the vanquished by the victor nation-states at the end of a future world war—assuming with unwarranted optimism that there would be victors and vanquished following a global and nuclear war.

Unlike the situation in global organizations (such as the International Court of Justice), the status of individuals, corporations, pressure groups, and other subnational actors has gained considerably in regional organizations, especially those developed within the context of post–World War II Western European integration. The status of individuals and other nongovernmental actors has been strengthened considerably before European institutions such as the European Court of Human Rights and the Court of Justice of the European Community. Individuals from Western European countries can be held accountable directly before these courts and can also initiate cases before them, even against their own national governments. We shall return to this topic in greater detail in Chapter 15.

RECOGNITION OF STATES AND GOVERNMENTS

The objective criteria for acceptance as a sovereign member—a state—by the international community are threefold: territory, population, and an autonomous and effective government. Once a state becomes a member of the international system, the related issues of government recognition or nonrecognition usually arise following revolutions, *coups d'état*, and other violent forms of sudden governmental change. In recognizing new governments, a number of states apply

---

[12]To this day, no unambiguous definition of *aggression* has been accepted by the world community. For a discussion of the attempts of global political organizations to deal with aggression, see the relevant discussion in Chapter 14.

such subjective (or political) tests as whether or not a new government reflects the freely expressed will of its people and is willing to fulfill its international obligations under the rule of law. Illustrative of the application of judgmental standards was the refusal of President Woodrow Wilson in 1913 to recognize the Mexican government of General Victoriano Huerta on the well-founded belief that it was a repressive dictatorship. Conversely, there are examples illustrating a rush to grant premature recognition. The new state of Guinea Bissau was recognized by eighty-one governments before it achieved substantive independence from Portugal in 1974.

Recognition is a reversible process. Should a government's capacity to meet the legal standards associated with sovereignty be questioned, it may forfeit the recognition of other governments. In 1979, for example, Congress passed the Taiwan Relations Act, which had the statutory effect of confirming the recognition of the Beijing (Peking) regime as the lawful government of the historic Chinese state and ending formally the recognition of the nationalist Chinese authorities in Taiwan.

There are two conflicting theories of recognition. The first, and the stricter theory from the legal viewpoint, is called the *constitutive theory* of recognition. According to this theory, a state or a new government of a previously recognized state does not exist legally until and unless it is duly recognized by the other states. One big problem with this theory is determining how many states (that is, what percentage of the total) are needed to bring about the legal birth of a new state, such as Bangladesh, or a new government, such as the postdictatorship government in Portugal or the postindependence government in Angola. The answer is usually that a "reasonable" number of states would be sufficient. A reasonable number, in turn, could mean the majority of states.

The second and more politically oriented theory is called the *declarative theory* of recognition. According to this theory, a state or a new government can be shown to exist by the application of "objective" tests (such as the ability of a government to maintain control over its population), regardless of other states' actions to recognize it or not. Recognition is viewed as a purely political act in which state or government A merely declares its intention to institute and maintain formal diplomatic contacts with state or government B. The declarative theory of recognition is more realistic and is probably better suited to explain most governments' current practices of recognition.

In the past, a distinction was frequently made between *de facto* and *de jure* recognition. *De facto* recognition was recognition in fact, without the formal trappings and ceremonies of full-scale diplomatic exchanges. *De facto* recognition usually took place in situations where governmental succession occurred through unconstitutional or irregular means but where the new government exercised firm control over all of the territory and inhabitants of the country. Thus, it was a provisional recognition of fact with the implication of international support or approval. *De jure* recognition, on the other hand, involved full and normal diplomatic relations and a showing of good will and even approval by the recognizing agent toward the recognized one. From the point of view of international law, there is no important difference between these two types of recognition. The distinction between them is made less frequently in contemporary times.

Some of the most difficult cases involving recognition arise immediately after revolutions, *coups d'état*, or wars that spawn new states, new governments, or both. Three schools of thought have developed in regard to such cases. One school argues that recognition should be purely a mechanical acceptance of legal fact. In other words, the moment a determination is made that a state or a new government exercises "effective control" over its inhabitants, then recognition should be extended automatically. The second school of thought argues that beyond the objective determination of control over inhabitants, a new state or government must pass certain qualitative tests. For example, there are those who argue that a government must be democratic, popular, anticommunist, and peace-loving in order to earn the right of entry into the international community. In short, the new applicant must pass an ideological eligibility test. Following a somewhat different tangent, there are those who prefer a political eligibility test. For them, recognition is a benefit to be granted to friendly and/or obedient governments in exchange for their good will and political affinity, regardless of their ideological orientation and the effectiveness of their internal control.

No state operates according to a single, standard set of rules for recognizing or not recognizing other states and governments. For example, a certain country may opt to alternate among primarily legal, political, or ideological approaches to recognition, depending on the specific circumstances at a given time. By and large, however, Great Britain and France have opted for the legal approach to recognition. The United States has vacillated among all three approaches in its relatively short history. Since World War II, the United States has used a mixture of the ideological and political tests of eligibility. The stubborn American nonrecognition of the government of the People's Republic of China until 1979 is an excellent case in point. The Soviet Union, with minor exceptions, has followed the British style of recognizing governments on the basis of an objective test free of qualitative considerations. This has not prevented the Soviet Communist Party's propaganda apparatus from vilifying unfriendly governments recognized by the Soviet regime.

JURISDICTION OF STATES AND GOVERNMENTS

Since international law represents a mutual attempt among governments to formalize and safeguard their sovereign control within their respective territorial boundaries, the rules regarding jurisdictional prerogatives of states have been developed rather carefully. For example, a state enjoys primary jurisdiction over the people, land, and property within its territorial limits. However, there often arise cases where conflicting claims of jurisdiction among states have to be painfully resolved. Think, for example, of the complications that would arise if a jealous gentleman from country A were to kill his girlfriend from country B and her temporary escort from country C at a Paris sidewalk cafe. In a hypothetical situation like this, at least four countries may make claims for jurisdiction in the case. France has the primary claim on the basis of the principle of *territoriality*, inasmuch as the crime was committed on French soil. Country A can also make a claim, on the grounds of the principle of *nationality* of the defendant, since the accused is a national of A. Countries B and C can also make claims for jurisdiction on the basis of the nationality of the victims. Of course, the country that has *custody* of the defendant has the upper hand with respect to the eventual disposition of the case. Anglo-American common-law nation-states adhere more to the principle of territoriality—of trying a person in the country where the offense was committed. Civil-code nation-states such as France, Italy, and Spain, on the other hand, insist on trying their own nationals no matter where the offense was committed.

If crimes are committed aboard ship on the high seas or in airplanes flying over the ocean, the jurisdiction belongs to the state whose flag is flown by the ship or the state that registers the airplane. If crimes are committed aboard a ship in port or within the territorial waters of a state, that state may seek custody and jurisdiction, especially if the crime has disturbed the "peace and tranquility" of the local residents. Otherwise, jurisdiction rests with the state whose flag the ship is flying.

At times, special provisions have been made under international law to partially or totally exempt citizens of one state from the jurisdiction of another. For example, from the Middle Ages until World War I, considerable use was made of the practice of extraterritoriality, especially by Western powers in places such as the Ottoman Empire, Egypt, Japan, and China. This practice was manifested on behalf of British, French, Russian, or American citizens residing or doing business in other countries. Instead of being held under the jurisdiction of those countries, these citizens were to be legally accountable to their own consular authorities and were to be considered as being technically outside the host state's territory.

With decolonization and the increasing assertion of at least the trappings of national sovereignty in most parts of the world, the practice of extraterritoriality has declined. However, its spirit has survived in a modified form. For example, great powers that maintain bases and armed forces overseas, such as the United States and Great Britain, usually conclude status-of-forces-agreements (SOFAs) with the states hosting these facilities. As a rule, SOFAs provide for primary jurisdiction to be reserved to the host states. However, specific provisions based on residual jurisdiction permit sending states to maintain custody of their nationals and even to claim jurisdiction over crimes committed either within a military base or in connection with official duties. Crimes committed by troops serving overseas normally involve traffic accidents, drunk and disorderly conduct, breaking and entering, and only occasionally manslaughter, murder, and rape. In the economic sector, also, there are often provisions for the special treatment of foreigners in host countries. For example, countries seeking to attract foreign capital often give preferential treatment to those foreigners willing to invest above certain sizable levels. These investors may be allowed to import items duty-free or to purchase local products at specially discounted prices. We must also not forget the privileges and immunities of diplomatic and consular personnel, which were discussed in Chapter 8.

Some of the most controversial cases of jurisdiction involve crimes committed in country A by persons who escape and seek asylum in country B. Extradition is a practice whereby a country returns an alleged criminal to the country where the offense was committed. There are no provisions binding all nation-states to extradite common criminals. As a rule, extradition arrangements are made through bilateral treaties. The most interesting cases arise when escapees are sought by a country for having committed "crimes" that are not considered as such by the country in which they have sought asylum, gambling offenses, for example. Finally, in most instances, extradition does not apply to political offenses (that is, offenses committed for public purposes—against a government—rather than for private enrichment). Persons wanted for so-called political crimes are usually offered political asylum in most other countries in return for a promise not to engage in subversive activities against the government of the country of their origin.

Controversial Problems of Jurisdiction

There are many controversial jurisdictional issues in international law. These stem in part from the great lag between the necessity for and the actual development of international laws. There is strong disagreement, for example, over the limits of nation-states' territorial waters; the rights of passage through straits, canals, and other narrow bodies of water; the limits of and the nature of control over economic and conservation zones that extend beyond the territorial waters of states; and the limits of national territorial air space. Further, despite some progress since World War II, no unequivocal guidelines exist as yet for jurisdictional issues involving continental shelves, the deep-seabed, the high seas, the polar regions, outer space, and celestial bodies.

It would be safe to say that states, whether large or small, developed or underdeveloped, have generally supported rules that have been designed to favor their own narrow economic, political, and strategic interests. A major controversy, for example, has been raging in post–World War II years over the limits of a nation-state's territorial waters. Traditionally, maritime nation-states such as Britain and the United States have opted for the narrow, historically derived zone known as the three-mile limit. Cornelius van Bynkershoek, the Dutch positivist publicist, writing in the early eighteenth century, asserted that a state's territorial limits extended as far as its coastal cannons could fire. The range of coastal batteries during Bynkershoek's days was about three nautical miles. This established a legal principle according to which the limit of a state's territorial waters was determined by its defensive capabilities. Given the great range of artillery, missiles, and other weapons today, the extension of Bynkershoek's principle to our times would be absurd.

The historic rule of three nautical miles runs counter to the needs of states such as Iceland, Peru, and Ecuador, whose economic survival depends upon fishing. Alternatively, major maritime powers seeking to retain the freedom to maneuver their fleets threateningly close to target states have systematically opposed all attempts at unilateral extension of territorial waters by smaller states. The requirements of seapower also clash with those of commercial interests demanding the establishment of *exclusive economic zones* (EEZs). In 1960 the Soviet Union extended its territorial waters to twelve miles, a limit which appears to have gained widespread acceptance or acquiescence. By 1971 eight Latin American republics had claimed a territorial sea of two hundred miles, and Indonesia and the Philippines similarly asserted their jurisdiction over extensive reaches of the high seas, including strategically important straits. The United States established an exclusive fishing zone of two hundred miles in 1977, thereby adding to the free-for-all for the wealth of the sea.

The difficulties accompanying the efforts of governments to produce a treaty on the law of the sea are a case in point. From 1973 to 1982, the Third United Nations Conference on the Law of the Sea (UNCLOS III) sought to write a constitution for the oceans. At the end of nearly a decade of diplomatic effort the representatives of 117 states signed the final act, a draft treaty updating and codifying existing international law of the seas. As of the end of 1988, only 36 governments had ratified the treaty, and the minimum number of ratifications necessary to put it into effect is 60. The United States did not sign the treaty; the Soviet Union signed but has so far not ratified. The leading powers appear determined to go their own way in dealing with the economic exploitation of the resources of the sea. Great Britain, Israel, the Federal Republic of Germany, Turkey, and Japan, among other states, have also withheld either their signatures or their ratifications.

The draft treaty has secured overwhelming agreement on previously controversial points such as the establishment of twelve miles as the generally acceptable width of states' territorial waters. Also, elaborate procedures defining rights of passage for commercial and military vessels have been established. The treaty has hit a major snag, however, on the question of defining an acceptable regime for the exploitation of the deep-seabed and the vast resources that are potentially available for extraction. The division reflects the impact of North versus South global politics in international law.

The technologically less-developed states of the South argue that the treaty rightly declares the deep-seabed a "common heritage of mankind" and establishes an international agency to issue licenses for deep-seabed exploitation and to provide for global redistribution of benefits derived from deep-sea mining.

The technologically advanced states of the North have argued that those who possess the technology and are also risking heavy capital investments to mine the oceans should have the right to unencumbered benefits of deep-sea mining and exploitation without being subjected to supranational limitations and controls.

There are many other controversial jurisdictional questions stemming from the issues mentioned above. For example, how far out can one exploit the seabed in one's continental shelf, given the steadily increasing technical ability of nation-states to drill and generally tap the ocean floor in depths much greater than two hundred meters?[13] What about antipollution safeguards or international compensation for damages by oil spills, nuclear waste, and leaks of other toxic substances? What is the upper limit of a state's territorial air space? Who has title and claim to various portions of the Antarctic continent?[14] How are conflicting claims concerning potential strategic and economic exploitation of the moon and other planets to be resolved? Who has title to deep-seabed resources, and how may one exploit them? Surprisingly, the answers to most of these questions cannot be given unequivocally by international law. Conflicting interests, real or assumed, preclude general accord. If this were the situation in municipal law, citizens and corporations could not be informed as to which areas were privately owned, which were common areas, what easements and transit rights were available to whom, whether building permits should be issued, and how and by whom the taxes should be collected.

Jurisdiction over Natural Resources: The Problem of Nationalization

Another heated debate has been going on over the expropriation of foreign-owned property by various socialist-oriented governments around the world. The right of national expropriation has generally been accepted in international law and has been reinforced politically by a number of United Nations General Assembly resolutions. All nation-states have an undisputed right to expropriate for "public" purposes any and all property on their soil, whether owned by domestic or foreign interests, provided that prompt and adequate compensation is paid to the property owners.

The controversy centers in questions of what is "reasonably" prompt and adequate compensation, and by whom and how it is to be determined. There are two important schools of thought on this issue. Roughly, one reflects the views of Western industrial nation-states and the other expresses the attitudes of poor, developing states. The view of developing nation-states is that the principle of *equality of treatment* should govern all expropriation policies. This principle pro-

---

[13]President Harry Truman proclaimed unilaterally on September 28, 1945, that coastal states had the right to "exercise . . . jurisdiction over natural resources of the subsoil and seabed of the continental shelf" and that this right was "reasonable and just." Subsequently, similar proclamations were made by a great number of other states. The issue eventually came up before the Geneva Conference on the Law of the Sea (1958), and a convention on the continental shelf was adopted. The continental shelf was defined in this convention as "the seabed and subsoil of the submarine areas adjacent to the coast but outside the area of the territorial sea, to a depth of two hundred meters, or, beyond that limit, to where the depth of the superadjacent waters admits of the exploitation of the natural resources of the said areas." For further discussion of the legal status of the continental shelf, see C. Fenwick, *Foreign Policy and International Law*, 4th ed. (New York: Appleton-Century-Crofts, 1965), pp. 447–50.

[14]The Antarctic Treaty signed in Washington, D.C., in December 1959 is a remarkable arrangement, one worth emulating in other areas. It provides for joint and free scientific exploration of the Antarctic area, demilitarization, free and open mutual inspection of national facilities, and the postponement (freezing) of the resolution of conflicting territorial claims for a period of thirty years.

vides that whenever foreign property is expropriated, compensation should be equal or proportional to that received by natives whose property has also been expropriated. The industrial nation-states are not as sanguine about this so-called equality-of-treatment guideline. They advance instead the principle of a *minimum standard of international justice*. In their view, it is quite probable that a state could treat foreign investors unjustly and then rationalize such an injustice by treating its own citizens in a similar fashion. For the industrial nation-states, a minimum standard of adequate and prompt compensation should therefore be set by international boards of arbitration. This is an area in which international legal controversy will remain high in the years to come.

THE LAW OF TREATIES

Considerable controversy has also arisen regarding the status and interpretation of treaties among nation-states. Treaties can be divided into two major categories: *specific* and *lawmaking*. *Specific treaties* are usually bilateral agreements that settle concrete issues or provide for unique arrangements between two states, with no global or regional consequences. They are analogous to contracts in municipal law. Bilateral treaties become part of international law, as it applies to the two signatory states. *Lawmaking treaties* (also referred to as *multilateral conventions*), such as the Hague Convention on the Laws of War (1907), the Geneva Convention on the Law of the Sea (1958), the Vienna Convention on Diplomatic Relations (1961), and the Vienna Convention on the Law of Treaties (1969), result from attempts by a number of states to agree on generally applicable codes of international behavior. Multilateral conventions are analogous to legislation in municipal legal systems, with the exception that they are applicable only to the states that have signed and ratified them. Lawmaking treaties—as drafted by United Nations agencies such as the International Law Commission—account for the increasing volume of international law that is being codified.

There is a basic difference between municipal and international laws with respect to contracts and treaties. Both systems provide that agreements must be arrived at by mutual *consent* of the signatories. However, in international law we encounter the peculiar phenomenon of legal recognition of peace treaties. These treaties are arrived at usually after long and bloody wars. If this were the practice in municipal law, the ownership of disputed homes, property, land, and capital would be determined by publicly waged duels, the winners of which would take most, if not all, of the disputed items. Thus, in consenting to treaties that are imposed by the victors on the vanquished, international law, unlike municipal law, implicitly recognizes and legitimizes the use of force as an instrument of arbitrating change.

Up to now, international law has been basically conservative in its orientation. For example, one of its most fundamental principles is that states should behave as they have customarily behaved. This principle provides for continuity, stability, and general predictability in the international system. But societies, whether national, regional, or global, cannot be assumed to be static. Changes inevitably occur with the passage of time. So the problem arises of finding peaceful means of accommodating such changes. International lawyers and the practices of nation-states, however, have not been very productive or useful in this respect. In fact, two of the most important principles in international law seem to work at cross-purposes. The first of these principles, *pacta sunt servanda* (agreements should be kept), holds that treaties are not to be violated. However, the second principle, *rebus sic stantibus* (things remain the same), offers an escape clause by positing that treaties can be revised when the conditions that led to their initiation and adoption have been substantially altered. Consequently, we encounter case after case where one party to a treaty is satisfied by the status quo and firmly supports *pacta sunt servanda*, whereas the second party feels slighted by existing arrangements and invokes *rebus sic stantibus*. A peaceful way out of such predicaments awaits the development of an authoritative international court. Such a court would enjoy compulsory jurisdiction over all international disputes, would be backed by a strong and cohesive international executive, and would pass definitive judgments on controversies about a treaty's interpretation. In addition to deciding which disputed treaties should be kept, the court would decide which should be revised, either to accommodate for previous injustices (those resulting from unequal or imposed treaties, for example) or to account for substantially changed conditions.

We can now ask a vital question: How can peaceful change under law become an international way of life? Answers seem simple, but they are difficult to apply in the real world. Adequate institutions for international legislation, interpretation, and implementation are needed. Any time there is a controversy over the provisions, interpretation, revision, or termination of a treaty (or future forms of international legislation), the International Court of Justice (ICJ) should be authorized to pass definitively on the issue, and its decisions should be respected and, when necessary, enforced by an effective global executive. Unfortunately for those who are proponents of world peace through world law, states are quite reluctant to form global legislative and executive bodies or to take their cases to the International Court of Justice. Most states, for example, have refused to accept the compulsory jurisdiction of the ICJ, even for carefully limited categories of disputes. As Table 13–1 on p. 262 illustrates, the docket of the ICJ is scarcely overcrowded. Not all cases submitted lead to a decision, and occasionally one of the parties to a dispute desregards the Court's ruling, as Iran in the case of the United States diplomatic and consular hostages or the United States in the Nicaragua mining case. Political rather than judicial methods continue to serve as the means of managing conflict in the international system.

THE "LAWS" OF WAR AND REPRISALS, AND OTHER METHODS OF SELF-HELP

It is hypocritical, if not outright irrational, to apply the term *laws* to rules that specify permissible methods and styles of killing and destroying adversaries. Yet this is what laws of war appear to be about. The reasoning behind them is some-

Table 13-1 Cases between States, International Court of Justice, 1967–87

1984–87	Paramilitary Activity (Nicaragua v. United States)
1986	Border Incident (Nicaragua v. Costa Rica)
1986	Border Incident (Nicaragua v. Honduras)
1986	Maritime Boundary (El Salvador v. Honduras)
1985	Frontier Dispute (Burkina Faso v. Mali)
1982	Continental Shelf (Libya v. Malta)
1981–84	Gulf of Maine (Canada v. United States)
1979–81	Hostage Case (United States v. Iran)
1978–82	Continental Shelf (Tunisia v. Libya)
1976–78	Aegean Continental Shelf (Greece v. Turkey)
1973	Prisoners of War (Pakistan v. India)
1973–74	Nuclear Tests (Australia and New Zealand v. France)
1972–74	Fisheries Jurisdiction (Great Britain and West Germany v. Iceland)
1971–72	International Air Transport (India v. Pakistan)
1967–69	North Sea Continental Shelf (West Germany v. Denmark and the Netherlands)

SOURCE: International Court of Justice, *Yearbook, 1987*, pp. 3–7.

thing like this: War is an unavoidable evil. We have it whether we want it or not. It is analogous to other natural disasters, such as plague, famine, earthquakes, floods, and drought. If, therefore, nation-states find it mutually advantageous to develop certain rules to humanize war, to limit its destructiveness, to ritualize its techniques, to control cruelty and deceit, and primarily to spare noncombatants from the effects of combat, then we should accept these rules, as the lesser among an array of evils.

Throughout the nineteenth century, and especially after the Congress of Vienna (1815), wars were fought at regular intervals with limited intensity and little popular involvement. Gradually, a series of customary war practices was developed. These practices were motivated principally by the desire of nation-states and their governments for reciprocity. It was as simple as this: "If you and I are at war, and if you don't kill and torture your prisoners of war, I will not kill and torture my prisoners of war either." Thus, war in the positivist-oriented nineteenth century was seen as an objective instrument of policy in an arsenal of alternative bargaining techniques available to policy makers. War was therefore waged in a controlled, predictable, and "civilized" manner.

Some of the major rules of war developed over time included the following: Wars ought to be declared prior to their initiation. Combatants ought to wear distinctive uniforms so as to be differentiated from noncombatants—in other words, the wider civilian population. Damage, killing, and destruction should be limited to what is required by *military necessity*. Only military targets should be marked for bombing and destruction. Prisoners of war should not be harmed or molested, should be fed and clothed, and should be kept in good physical condition throughout their captivity. Hospital crews and Red Cross and Red Crescent vehicles should be exempted from military attacks. Museums, historic edifices, and shrines should not be bombed or destroyed. Cities declared to be open (i.e., undefended) should be spared from bombing attacks. Populations in occupied territories should be properly administered and cared for. Women and children should not be raped or molested. Private property should not be looted. Private real estate should be requisitioned only with adequate compensation; it should not be seized permanently by the occupying armed forces. Most of these rules have been extended to sea and air warfare. Many rules specifying permissible types of weapons have also been developed. For example, extremely painful weapons, such as poison darts, dum-dum bullets, and various nerve and asphyxiating gases, are not to be used.

Most of the above rules were incorporated into voluminous codes of war during the Hague Conferences of 1899 and 1907 and the Geneva Conference of 1949, to mention the most important sources. These codes have also outlined the rights and duties of belligerents, as differentiated from those of neutral nation-states.

The twentieth century, with its revolutionary technological and political developments, has made a shambles of conventional laws of war. The invention and development of airplanes, missiles, and nuclear as well as conventional warheads of mass destructive capability have made it nearly impossible to separate combatants from noncombatants in a war. In this era of total war, an era in which the entire industrial structure of a nation-state is considered a legitimate military target, very little can be spared by bombing practices that are designed to paralyze the economic, logistical, and psychological capabilities of entire countries. The practice of declaring wars has been all but abandoned since World War II. The banning of dum-dum bullets and mustard gas in an era of mass-destructive nuclear and biological weapons is analogous to outlawing handguns but not dynamite in municipal systems.

Under the strategic stalemate of the post–World War II nuclear balance of terror, a whole series of unconventional war practices has taken root. The boundaries between civil and international wars are becoming increasingly blurred. In an age in which many wars are fought under cover by commandos, infiltrators, volunteers, guerrillas, terrorists, liberation fighters, mercenaries, subversives, fifth columnists, or other national surrogates, it is not realistic to expect that combatants be properly identified by their national uniforms so that they can be adequately protected if made prisoners of war.

In the nineteenth century, there was a clear-cut distinction between conditions of war and conditions of peace. The twentieth century has muddied the waters. As we suggested in Chapters 9 and 11, subversion, cold war, insurgency, externally supported wars of national liberation, revolutions, and *coups d'état* have all created a vast grey area that spills over the poles of peace and war. This gray area has been appropriately labeled *intermediacy* by Philip Jessup, an American judge and international-law scholar.[15] Jessup's argument is that international law provides rules for peaceful intercourse and rules that apply during conventional

---

[15]See Philip Jessup, "Should International Law Recognize an Intermediate Status between Peace and War?" *American Journal of International Law*, 48 (1954), 98–103; and Quincy Wright et al., *The International Law of Civil War*, ed. Richard A. Falk (Baltimore: Johns Hopkins University Press, 1971).

and classical wars, but is relatively silent on questions of intermediacy. It is within the range of intermediacy that much international law needs to be developed. However, it will be extremely difficult to arrive at uniformly acceptable rules and practices in the present era of political, ideological, cultural, and military fragmentation. And such fragmentation is likely to persist in the foreseeable future.

A few still unanswered questions will be brought up here just to illustrate how difficult issues of international law are going to remain. To begin with, what should be the status of terrorists or freedom fighters under international law? Who is responsible for the acts of these individuals if they do not formally fall under the authority of any one nation-state or government? Who will differentiate between hijacking an airplane for private gain and hijacking an airplane in order to bring about political change? How does one differentiate between a privileged sanctuary for guerrilla operations and political asylum for undesirable citizens?[16] Are governmentally administered reprisals legal, given the United Nations Charter's qualified prohibition of the use of force?[17] More recently, with a flood of refugees—popularly referred to as "boat people"—originating in countries of Indochina and the Caribbean, a new set of questions has been raised with increasing urgency. For example, how does one differentiate between political refugees (expelled by country A) and economic refugees (departing from country B in quest of a more viable future elsewhere)? Is there an international duty to accept a quota of homeless and stateless refugees? Do refugees have a fundamental right to compensation, and who is responsible for payment?

International law has no generally acceptable answers to these and many other questions. It merely advocates the doctrine of self-help, which is equivalent to vigilante justice in primitive communities. Under this doctrine, a state has the right to retaliate against acts of other states or their agents by engaging in economic sanctions, blockades, military reprisals, and even limited war. Once again, we clearly see the weakness of international law. There is no central police force available, and the subjects are asked to police themselves as best they can.

What is needed both at the municipal and international levels is a set of acceptable laws and enough impartial police officers and judges to enter into conflicts, separate the combatants, study the situation, assign blame to those breaking the law, and apply appropriate and effective sanctions. The basic prerequisite of international law is a consensus among states on the need to regulate international relations and to submit conflicts to peaceful means of resolution. International law can be developed in one of two ways. It can be imposed from above, as was the case with ancient Roman law. Or it can be legislated on the

---

[16]A *privileged sanctuary* is an area usually located in country A near its border with country B, where guerrillas from country B can train, organize, regroup, and launch guerrilla raids against the government of country B.

[17]We say "qualified prohibition" since the United Nations Charter prohibits war as an instrument of policy, except in individual or collective self-defense, as provided in Article 51 of the Charter. Further, the definition of *defensive use of force* is very difficult to pinpoint. Thus, states continue to resort to force and to consistently justify doing so in the name of self-defense. Incidentally, no state would dream of naming its war ministry a "Department of Offense" rather than a "Department of Defense."

basis of a uniform international acceptance of values and a compatibility among different national and sectional interests. Neither of the above conditions is particularly likely in our day or in the foreseeable future. This renders the chances for rapid growth of international law rather slim.

The positivist attitudes toward war that were characteristic of the nineteenth century seem to have survived the challenges posed by the twentieth century. Following two world wars, a number of attempts, albeit ineffective ones, have been made to outlaw war as an instrument of policy. The grand experiments in international organization, such as the League of Nations and the United Nations, have attempted to prohibit war and to provide the international community with an institutional and legal spine. Using the tactic of collective security, these institutions have sought to discourage aggressive warfare and to morally and materially isolate potential aggressors. (The theory of *collective security* is discussed in Chapter 14.) Unfortunately for humankind, the effectiveness of international organizations has so far proved marginal at best. We shall devote the next chapter to a detailed evaluation of experiments in international institutionalization, such as the League of Nations and the United Nations.

ALTERNATIVE PERCEPTIONS OF INTERNATIONAL LAW

We should ask one more important question before concluding this chapter: Can we gradually develop an effective and universally acceptable body of laws, given the great economic, ideological, cultural, religious, and racial divisions of our earth? The response depends upon one's philosophical orientation. Pessimists (usually positioned in the realist school) assume that international divisions are so deep and implacable that enforceable global law is impossible. Optimists (closer to the idealist orientation) assert that the acceptance of globally applicable legal principles is a matter of time and the outcome of competent and constructive liberal education.

Wolfgang Friedmann, one of the finest legal writers of contemporary times, offered some of the most definitive and balanced responses to our question.[18] He carefully reviewed representative cultural and legal systems, such as those of the ancient Chinese, the ancient Indians, the Muslims, contemporary socialists, and the Third World countries. He found a surprisingly high degree of symmetry in all these settings. For example, each of these societies or regions seems to have been operating simultaneously at two distinct and easily identifiable legal tiers. The *higher tier* encompasses abstract principles. The *lower tier* concerns practices that are empirically observable and pragmatically motivated. In all these diverse societies, one discerns consistently that the so-called higher principles oppose violence and favor justice, altruism, and kindness. In practice, how-

---

[18]For a discussion of two different views of the cultural dimension of international law, see Wolfgang Friedmann, *The Changing Structure of International Law* (New York: Columbia University Press, 1964); and Adda Bozeman, *The Future of Law in a Multicultural World* (Princeton, N.J.: Princeton University Press, 1971).

ever, one finds that such principles are usually sacrificed on the altar of tangible national, factional, and personal interests.

Friedmann concluded that we should not be blaming cultural heterogeneity as the obstacle to the creation of global law. Rather, we should be blaming the incompatibility among the various nation-state interests. Interests, in turn, according to Friedmann, reflect the economic status, development, and objectives of nation-states. Thus, he asserted, the greatest affinity among legal positions can be found within groups of industrialized nation-states and within clusters of developing nation-states. The greatest difficulty, therefore, is to harmonize the legal interests of rich, industrial nation-states with those of poor, developing nation-states.

A superficial review of the differences among various perceptions of international law may prove misleading. Soviet writers, for example, emphasize how much better a socialist system of international law is than a capitalist system. The latter, they argue, is the remnant of the decadent and elitist capitalist international system and is designed to perpetuate the control of the ruling classes over the world's proletariat. The Chinese, for their part, oppose all treaty and customary law in which they have not had an opportunity to participate, and they reject most nineteenth-century treaties as unequal. They contend that unequal treaties have been imposed by imperialistic Western countries upon the weak and dependent non-Western regions of the world. Thus, all unequal treaties, they stress, must be rejected. Finally, the developing nation-states reject a large portion of traditional international law as reflecting the purely selfish interests of European and American nation-states. They are bitterly opposed, for example, to the principle of noninterference in another country's domestic affairs if this principle is used merely to prevent the international community from punishing colonialism, economic exploitation, racial discrimination, and other such "crimes."

Yet, in their overall practices all nation-states, whether Western, socialist, or Third World, have found it in *their interest* to employ and to abide by many rules of so-called capitalist or Western international law. There are powerful incentives for voluntary compliance with international law. First among them is the desire for *orderly coordination* of international transactions, which benefits all the concerned parties. Second is the need for *reciprocity*. Good treatment begets good treatment just as bad begets bad. Third is the incentive for *participation*. By participating in regional or global organizations, nation-states can take advantage of political, economic, technical, and even informational benefits. A fourth, if somewhat weaker, incentive is *reputation*. Most nation-states wish to *appear* law abiding, even if they are not genuinely interested in being so. An extremely important incentive is missing from this list—the fear of negative sanctions administered by central authorities. The reason for this is simple: There are no central authorities in the international system. Hence, the long-range problem is this: How can we effect universal legitimacy, develop comprehensive laws, and construct workable institutions of enforcement, and at the same time avoid threatening entrenched national interests in a system in which territory, wealth, population, and power are distributed quite unevenly?

Will it take another war to centralize the international system? In an era of nuclear overkill, is such a war rational or feasible? The likely forecast is that we are bound to continue with our "imperfect" international legal order for some time to come. By using Friedmann's analysis, we may predict that the institution of more effective and more widely acceptable legal rules will depend on the rate with which the gaps between rich and poor countries close. (See Chapter 17 for a detailed discussion of the process and problems of development.) However, the prognosis in this area, as we shall see in Part V of this volume, is for increasing gaps between the rich and the poor, rather than for a genuine economic integration of the two through the redistribution of global income and resources. Consequently, the long-range outlook for the development of international law should not be overly optimistic.

Nevertheless, international law continues to provide a framework for the peaceful resolution of disputes between governments. Law and diplomacy remain the twin pillars of world order. It is, therefore, with concern that we note that a report on foreign-service recruitment by the Department of State found in 1982 that experts in international law are at a premium and that there is a growing need for their services as members of delegations to conferences on the seas, space, and international communications. Despite the demand, the supply of qualified personnel is so limited that the United States may have to hire foreign specialists to represent its interests in various international organizations.[19] If this assessment is accurate, the prospects for American multilateral diplomacy are not encouraging.

SUGGESTIONS FOR FURTHER STUDY

Larman C. Wilson has argued the case for international protection of individual freedom in "Human Rights in United States Foreign Policy," *Interaction: Foreign Policy and Public Policy*, ed. Don C. Piper and Ronald J. Terchek (Washington, D.C.: American Enterprise Institute, 1983). Political realists are rebutted in Tom J. Farer, "International Law: The Critics are Wrong," *Foreign Policy*, 71 (Summer 1988), 22–45. The future of international jurisprudence is the theme of Anthony D'Amato, *International Law: Process and Prospect* (Dobbs Ferry, N.Y.: Transnational Publishers, 1987). Antonio Cassese has studied the problem of small states in *International Law in a Divided World* (Oxford: Clarendon Press, 1986). The future of transnational law is a subject of Kenneth W. Thompson, ed., *The Moral Imperatives of Human Rights: A World Survey* (Washington, D.C.: University Press of America, 1980). Evan Luard has investigated the impact of a legal doctrine on statecraft in "Human Rights and Foreign Policy," *International Affairs*, 56 (London: Autumn 1980), 579–606. The role of the International Court of Justice emerges in Charles

---

[19]Donald J. Healey, *Beyond the In-Box: The Selection and Training of Personnel to Formulate and Implement Foreign Policy of the 21st Century* (Washington, D.C.: U.S. Department of State, Foreign Service Institute, 1982), pp. 22–32.

Maechling, Jr., "The Hollow Chamber of the International Court," *Foreign Policy*, 33 (Winter 1978–79), 101–20; and in "U.S. Presses Case in World Court on American Hostages in Iran," *Department of State Bulletin*, 80 (May 1980), 36–60. A. G. Noorani has studied the problem of aggression in "Afghanistan and International Law," *The Review: For a Rule of Law*, 24 (June 1980), 37–51, which should be read in conjunction with Y. Rybakov, "Aggression and International Law," *International Affairs*, 8 (Moscow), (1980), 38–46. The role of law in international crises is the theme of Richard B. Finnegan, Robert S. Junn, and Clifton E. Wilson, *Law and Politics in the International System: Case Studies in Conflict Resolution* (Washington, D.C.: University Press of America, 1979). The cause of social justice within the framework of the law of the sea is the thesis of Arvid Pardo, "Ocean Space and Mankind," *Third World Quarterly*, 6 (July 1984), 559–72. John King Gamble, Jr., has assessed the current status of treaty law in "Reservations to Multilateral Treaties: A Macroscopic View of State Practice," *American Journal of International Law*, 74 (April 1980), 372–94.

14

THE GREAT EXPERIMENTS IN GLOBAL ORGANIZATION

DEFINING INTERNATIONAL ORGANIZATION

What is *international organization*, and how can it be defined?[1] As with all complex and inclusive concepts, definitions at first appear elusive. For our needs, we have decided to approach this definitional problem at three different levels. First, international organization could be defined in terms of its intended purposes. Second, it could be defined in terms of existing international institutions or in terms of ideal models and blueprints for future institutions. Third, international organization could be defined as a process approximating government regulation of relations among nation-states and nonstate actors. (Nonstate actors are discussed in some detail in Chapter 18.)

Purposes

International organizations have generally been established in order to accomplish all or some of the following purposes:

---

[1]For an informed and comprehensive treatment of international organization, see Harold K. Jacobson, *Networks of Interdependence: International Organization and the Global Political System,* 2nd ed. (New York: Knopf, 1984). For a very competent review of international organization accurately pointing out its decline as a field of study in the United States, see J. Martin Rochester, "The Rise and Fall of International Organization as a Field of Study," *International Organization,* 40, no. 4 (Autumn 1986), 777–813.

1. Regulation of international relations primarily through techniques of peaceful settlement of disputes among nation-states.
2. Minimization, or, at the least, control of international conflict and war.
3. Promotion of cooperative, developmental activities among nation-states for the social and economic benefit of certain regions or of humankind in general.
4. Collective defense of a group of nation-states against external threat.

Institutions

There are two major categories of international institutions: intergovernmental organizations (IGOs) and nongovernmental organizations (NGOs). IGOs, as the name suggests, are institutions whose members are official government delegations of nation-states. The best-known IGO is the United Nations. NGOs, also known as private international associations, consist of private groups of religious, scientific, cultural, philanthropic, technical, or economic orientation. They do not involve direct government participation. Examples of NGOs are the International Chamber of Commerce, the Interparliamentary Union, the World Veterans Federation, and the International Red Cross. There has been a steady growth in the number and scope of both IGOs and NGOs. Most responsible projections call for continued increases in international institutionalization in the foreseeable future.

Despite their greater numbers, NGOs are by and large modest-sized and modestly funded organizations. The average yearly budget of NGOs is less than $1 million, and the average staff consists of ten professionals. IGOs, in comparison, have a larger budget, averaging just under $10 million yearly, and an average staff of two hundred professionals. The bulk of IGOs and NGOs are headquartered in major Western cities, such as Paris, Brussels, London, Geneva, Copenhagen, Washington, Rome, Zurich, Stockholm, and Vienna.

Most political-science literature on international organization has concentrated on the study of IGOs. Recently, the range of interest has increased considerably to include the activities of NGOs, which are treated under the heading of transnational politics.[2] In this chapter we shall focus on IGOs. (The discussion of transnational politics is left to Chapter 18.)

The institutional structure of IGOs exhibits a characteristic pattern. All IGOs, for example, have permanent offices staffed by full-time professionals. These permanent bureaucracies are called secretariats. Their employees are supposed to be international civil servants, and are expected to develop supranational or organizational rather than national loyalties. The long-range objectives of IGOs are usually defined by bodies called general assemblies or conferences. These assemblies, in which all member states are represented, meet in plenary session at periodic intervals and set the limits of the general policies and range

---

[2]See Robert O. Keohane and Joseph S. Nye, eds., *Transnational Relations and World Politics* (Cambridge, Mass.: Harvard University Press, 1972). See also, by the same authors, *Power and Interdependence: World Politics in Transition* (Boston: Little, Brown, 1977).

of action of each IGO. Finally, most IGOs are governed by executive councils. These councils are made up of a small elected or selected number of governmental delegations, some of which are permanent and some of which alternate. The councils come closest to assuming executive responsibility for the IGOs, and the secretariats carry out the administrative functions of implementing the specific decisions of the councils.

IGOs can be classified into four major categories on the basis of membership and purpose:

1. *General-membership and general-purpose organizations:* This category refers primarily to the United Nations and the League of Nations. Such organizations are global in scope and serve a variety of functions, such as security, socioeconomic cooperation, human-rights protection, and cultural growth and exchange.

2. *General-membership and limited-purpose organizations:* These are also known as *functional* organizations because they are devoted to a specific function. Typical examples are United Nations agencies such as the International Bank for Reconstruction and Development (the World Bank), the International Labor Organization (ILO), the World Health Organization (WHO), and the United Nations Educational, Scientific, and Cultural Organization (UNESCO).

3. *Limited-membership and general-purpose organizations:* These are regional organizations with a wide range of security, political, and socioeconomic functions and responsibilities. Examples include the Organization of American States (OAS), the Organization of African Unity (OAU), the Arab League, and the European Community (EC).[3]

4. *Limited-membership and limited-purpose organizations:* These are subdivided into socioeconomic and military/defense organizations. Examples of the former are the Latin American Free Trade Association (LAFTA) and the Soviet–Eastern European Common Market, which is named the Council for Mutual Economic Assistance (CMEA). Regional military/defense organizations are institutionalized alliances developed in conjunction with the cold war, such as the North Atlantic Treaty Organization (NATO) and the Warsaw Treaty Organization (the Warsaw Pact).

International organization can also be defined in terms of ideal or heuristic models of world government that are likely to be created sometime in the future.[4] Over the centuries, there have developed countless legal and institutional plans envisioning a transition to world government of one form or another.[5] Some of the alternative models of the structure and regulation of the international system, which we discussed in Chapter 3, would fit this role well.

[3]The European Community during the early phases of its development could be also classified as a regional, limited-purpose organization.

[4]*Heuristic* is a Greek word meaning "to discover." Heuristic models rest upon unproven (and often unprovable) assumptions. They are useful, however, in that they focus attention upon specific empirical questions.

[5]Among the legal and institutional plans developed over the centuries, one of the most carefully developed is that of Grenville Clark and Louis B. Sohn, *World Peace through World Law: Two Alternative Plans,* 3rd ed. (Cambridge, Mass.: Harvard University Press, 1966). See also the world constitution presented in Richard A. Falk and Saul H. Mendlovitz, eds. *Regional Politics and World Order* (San Francisco: W. H. Freeman, 1973).

Processes

The third and perhaps most elusive definitional approach to international organization is in terms of processes. One can ask, for example, what the process of international organization is, and how it differs from processes of national governments. Is international organization a rudimentary and ineffective form of global government? Is it an attempt by powerful and independent countries to institutionalize and legitimize the existing power distribution and thereby preserve their positions of privilege against the attempts of less privileged countries to redistribute territory, wealth, status, and other advantages? Or is it an experiment of the weaker and less-wealthy states to create institutional constraints that will limit unaccountable behavior of the most powerful states of our planet?

By posing these last three questions in an either/or fashion, we may be blurring somewhat the reality that should be reflected in the answer, which probably can be found through a synthesis of all three choices. The process of international organization may best be described as a rudimentary form of global regulation that is so fundamentally different from advanced forms of national government that it merits special classification.

There are vast differences between national governments and international organizations. The subjects of governments are, by and large, individuals, families, villages, social classes, corporations, cities, and other national groups. The "subjects" of international organizations, in contrast, are in most instances states, as represented by their governments. The functions of national governments are usually rather inclusive and penetrate deeply into the life and style of their subjects. On the other hand, international organizations maintain at best an indirect influence upon their members. Their functions, moreover, are limited to such activities as the resolution of security and political questions dividing small states, information gathering and reporting, and technical assistance—activities that are usually peripheral to the vital domestic interests of the great powers.

Yet, at least one parallel can be drawn between the processes of international organizations and those of national governments. National governments regulate the relations of their subjects and seek, ideally, to protect the integrity of each citizen. Nonetheless, through institutions and laws they tend to service the needs and interests of the more powerful groups and individuals in the society. Similarly, international organizations try to protect the integrity of their members by attempting to regulate their relations and to prevent them from engaging in armed conflict. Here, too, one could argue that powerful nation-states probably service their needs and interests through international institutions and laws better than the weaker nation-states do. One could easily reverse the above argument, however. For it could be pointed out, with some justification, that governments (as well as international organizations) usually serve to protect the interests of the weak against the excesses of the strong. In the absence of government or other institutions a society could degenerate into a jungle where the strong simply devour the weak.

THE HISTORICAL DEVELOPMENT
OF INTERNATIONAL ORGANIZATIONS

Although large, global international organizations are twentieth-century phenomena, one can trace their ancestors back to the early years of recorded history.
Looking into the past, we find, however, fewer examples of global institutions
and more examples of exhortations by philosophers urging the development of
"one world."

In our search for the ancestors of international organizations, we should
perhaps turn first to the city-state system of ancient Greece. This system reflected
in miniature most of the essential characteristics of contemporary international
politics. Reading through the pages of Thucydides, who has given us a fascinating
portrayal of the Peloponnesian War (431–404 B.C.) between Sparta and Athens,
we realize that the Greeks had become involved in the intricacies of international
bargaining, such as alliances, negotiations, dependencies, threats and bribes, and
cooling-off periods. It would not be too far-fetched to suggest that the alliance-
dependency systems of Athens and Sparta are the prototypes of regional military
and defense organizations such as NATO and the Warsaw Pact.

The Greek city-states also developed the first model of a universal
general-purpose international organization by conceiving the Amphictyonic
League. This league was originally a religious organization of twelve neighboring
tribes, established for the purpose of safeguarding the temple of Delphi. Its functions gradually increased to include the protection of its members from aggressive acts, both within and without the league. Each tribe sent two delegates to
league conferences and was allowed two votes of equal weight. Each tribe took an
oath pledging never to annihilate any of the other tribes during warfare. Those
considered guilty of acts of aggression were to be confronted collectively and
with all available means by the remaining tribes.[6]

Comparison-oriented students could also study global organizational patterns exhibited by the Persian, Macedonian, Roman, Byzantine, Arab, Ottoman,
and British empires. These students could, for example, learn a lot about international regulation and interdependency by studying the system of incentives and
rewards as well as sanctions and other threats that helped the powerful metropol-
ises maintain various forms of control over their dispersed and culturally heterogeneous subjects.

Certain fundamental problems have recurred throughout history's twists
and turns. For example, how does one regulate relations in societies of unequal
actors? Can there be justice among unequals? Should arbitrations and judgments
be left in the hands of a complex and crowded coalition of weaklings of the
world, or should they be left to a small but powerful directorate of giants? How
does one reconcile the inevitable clash between actual individual and group in-

---

[6]See William Smith, *A History of Greece,* rev. George W. Greene (New York: Harper & Brothers, 1854).

terests and abstract considerations such as determining the universal good of humankind?

Over time, the human genius has devised various forms of political institutions, both loose and tight, in order to prevent societies from descending into anarchy. Thus, from ancient times to the present, humankind has experimented with diverse styles of government, such as democracy and polity (participatory styles) and aristocracy and tyranny (elitist styles). Governmental structures have varied in their range and mode of political authority. They have included the band, the tribe, the city-state, the manor, the nation-state, the empire, the confederacy, and, finally, various forms of international and regional organizations. In each instance, the role of those in charge of political institutions has been balanced between service to their communities and attempts to stay in power. Political competition has hovered between the desire to curb the incidence of war and the need to promote and defend one's sectional and individual interests.

Throughout recorded history, the forces of conflict and bloodshed have been matched by the fervent desire of well-meaning people for peace, justice, and harmony. The Siamese twins of war and peace have coexisted in an uneasy and spotty truce. Concerned and wise individuals have urged fervently for a global attack on the apparently incurable problem of conflict and war. Thinkers such as the Italian poet Dante (thirteenth century); William Penn (seventeenth century); Abbé St. Pierre, Jean-Jacques Rousseau, Immanuel Kant, and Jeremy Bentham (eighteenth century); and Saint-Simon, William Ladd, William Jay, Gustave de Molinari, Johann Caspar Bluntschli, and James Lorimer (nineteenth century) have advocated various approaches with which to attain global government and perpetual peace.[7] Despite the politically disparaging labels that have been pinned to most of these individuals—labels such as "idealist" and "utopian"—most of them advocated only moderate transfers of national sovereignty to a central world authority. Many of these "utopian" suggestions have been gradually incorporated in the grand experiments of international organization of the twentieth century.

Most idealist blueprints for world organization have had certain characteristics in common: They have called for the peaceful settlement of disputes, the rule of law, adequate representation of the governed in the global government, and respect for the autonomy of member states' domestic affairs.[8] It is not surprising, therefore, that these principles have been reflected, to varying degrees, in the League of Nations and in the United Nations.

In addition to political and philosophical writings, an important precursor of international organization has been the practice of multinational conferences, which has paralleled the growth of the nation-state system since the Peace

---

[7]See Francis W. Hinsley, *Power and the Pursuit of Peace: Theory and Practice in the History of Relations between States* (Cambridge: Cambridge University Press, 1963).

[8]As long as *domestic affairs* remain off-limits to global authorities, one cannot make a case for the existence of effective world government. This outlook regarding domestic affairs, however, could be considered analogous to provisions in national constitutions regarding the sanctity of the individual and the home and related human rights.

of Westphalia (1648). In the closing phases of the bloody and destructive Thirty Years' War (1618–48), assemblies of victorious and vanquished nation-states met for over three years at Osnabrück and Münster (in the German province of West-phalia) in what came to be referred to as the First European Congress. The result of the war and the protracted negotiations was the establishment of the first inter-national balance-of-power system. (See Chapter 3 for a treatment of the concept and practice of *balance of power*.) The *balance-of-power* concept has since provided the political framework of the international system—except during the prime of Louis XIV, Napoleon Bonaparte, and Adolf Hitler.

Major conferences have been convened in every century since the West-phalia conference. Together with the gradual codification of international law, these conferences have contributed to the structuring and restructuring of Eu-rope. The Peace of Utrecht (1713), which ended the War of the Spanish Succes-sion, reaffirmed the principle of balance of power as the only key to peace. Then came the French Revolution (1789), which marked the birth of modern (mass-supported) nationalist movements. Among other principles, the French revolu-tionaries advocated nonintervention in the affairs of other countries, the renun-ciation of wars of conquest, and national self-determination in the form of plebi-scites.[9] Following Napoleon's imperial adventures, which were considered by some as an attempt to universalize the ideals of the French Revolution, the victor-ious anti-Napoleonic coalition met at the great Congress of Vienna (1815). There, it structured the nineteenth-century balance-of-power system and contributed to the existing body of international law. Among other rules, the congress estab-lished categories of diplomatic envoys, general principles for the navigation of international rivers, and provisions for the suppression of the slave trade.

The Monroe Doctrine (1823) of the United States was an early, if tooth-less, proclamation of regional independence against external (i.e., European) intervention and manipulation.[10] The Peace of Paris (1856), following the Cri-mean War, reaffirmed the principle of national self-determination and applied it to the disputed provinces of Wallachia and Moldavia. In the Declaration of Paris in 1856, laws of war and rights of neutrals were identified. This year marked the take-off point of international law. The Brussels Congress (1874) resulted in a code of land warfare approved by fifteen nation-states. The Berlin Conference (1884–85) continued earlier attempts to abolish the slave trade. It also sought to split the pie represented by European colonization of the Third World (which was then referred to contemptuously by the Europeans as *terra nullius*—"no man's land"), so as not to disrupt the stability of the balance-of-power system.

Simultaneously, public international unions such as the International Telegraphic Union (1865), the Universal Postal Union (1874), the Rhine River

---

[9]Napoleon, the stepchild of the French Revolution, did not hesitate to violate the principle of nonin-tervention in the name of allegedly higher principles.

[10]Small Latin American states often see the Monroe Doctrine as an early attempt by the United States to restrict intervention in Latin America to only the United States and to keep the Europeans out. Ironically, large parts of Latin America, which is often referred to as the backyard of the United States, are as far away from the United States as they are from parts of Western Europe.

Commission (1804), and the Danube River Commission (1857) became permanent international institutions. Their subdivisions—bureaus, councils, and conferences—served as institutional prototypes for the League of Nations and the United Nations. Beyond this, the public international unions contributed to the development of international administrative law in the so-called functional (that is, technical, economic, and social) areas.

With the Hague Conferences (1899 and 1907), an important threshold was crossed on the way to international institutionalization. These conferences, which were meant to occur every seven years, were convened in time of peace and enjoyed the nearly universal participation of the then-recognized nation-states. Unlike the great-power conferences of the nineteenth century, the Hague Conferences established rules that were designed to regulate the international system and to remove the causes of crisis and war. And whereas the great-power conferences had been designed to achieve settlements immediately after wars and crises, the Hague Conferences were preventive and regulatory in nature. Moreover, the great-power conferences had been the work of the few and powerful. In contrast, the Hague Conferences exhibited the legitimization process that only full participation—of small as well as great powers—can bring about. The 1899 Hague Conference produced major regulatory instruments, such as the convention for the pacific settlement of disputes (which established the Permanent Court of Arbitration), the convention on laws and customs of land warfare, and the convention on laws of naval warfare. The 1907 Hague Conference updated the 1899 conventions and produced ten more conventions on neutrality and land and sea warfare.

Inis Claude, a well-known scholar of international organization, has effectively summarized the ancestors of international organizations in terms of what he views as three "major streams of development" in the nineteenth century.[11] In the Concert of Europe system and the *ad hoc* great-power conferences that followed, Claude sees the precursor of the United Nations Security Council. The Concert of Europe was the product of a consensus among great powers that only they could define the grand security questions and the tolerable limits within which the balance-of-power system could shift.

The Hague Conferences have been portrayed by Claude as the precursors of the United Nations General Assembly. The egalitarian concept of "one nation, one vote" was clearly reflected in the Hague movement. Resolutions adopted by majority vote (rather than unanimously) gradually became an acceptable rule of international organization. Participation in the Hague Conferences reflected the decision of governments to limit their sovereignty voluntarily in order to aid in the development of rules of international law designed to minimize conflict in the international system and to maximize cooperation and conciliation.

The third and perhaps the most influential stream of development was

---

[11]Inis J. Claude, *Swords into Plowshares, The Problems and Progress of International Organization*, 4th ed. (New York: Random House, 1971).

the creation and expansion of public international unions, such as the Universal Postal Union and the Rhine and Danube river commissions. These unions were designed to carry out economic and social activities analogous to those of specialized agencies of the United Nations, such as the International Monetary Fund (IMF), the International Civil Aviation Organization (ICAO), the Food and Agriculture Organization (FAO), and the International Maritime Organization (IMO). A major contribution of these early public international unions was that their structure (conference, council, and secretariat) was subsequently adopted by the most advanced international organizations.

The public international unions stand for the process of functional cooperation. Functional activities, which are understood to be technical, scientific, and economic—in short, *nonpolitical*—activities, are presumably easier to organize than political activities. The incentives of collective functional projects are strong, and their success is mutually profitable. Nation-states have shown less reluctance to limit their sovereignty in functional than in political spheres of activity. Thus, the argument could be made that the public international unions are the precursors of such grand international institutional experiments as the European Community.

THE LEAGUE OF NATIONS

The historical developments reviewed above, together with the traumatic experience of World War I, contributed substantially to the founding of the League of Nations. World War I appeared to many observers to be the product of the balance-of-power system gone berserk. Secret alliances secretly arrived at, unsavory deals made in smoke-filled rooms, an atmosphere of mutual suspicion and amorality pervading the international system, and the virtual absence of international institutions that could provide cooling-off periods and objective information gathering—these and other factors led to a spiraling of threats and counterthreats that escalated the political assassination of Austria's Archduke Franz Ferdinand at Sarajevo to a four-and-a-half-year trench and attrition war that cost the earth twenty million souls.

The League of Nations, in large part the brainchild of President Woodrow Wilson, was designed to supply the necessary institutional structures and legal and ideological norms that would prevent another world war. The League's institutions included a ten-member Council (four major powers were named permanent members) that reflected the philosophy of the Concert of Europe and the needs and capabilities of major powers. It met four times a year and otherwise as needed. The League Assembly, which met once a year, was attended by all members of the organization. Both of these bodies made deep concessions to the principle of national sovereignty and required unanimous decisions on important issues. The day-to-day housekeeping, planning, and programming aspects of the League were assigned to the Secretariat, which was headed ably and quietly by Sir Eric Drummond, a respected British civil servant. Drummond's performance in office has been used as the model of an efficient, administrative, and nonpolitical style of international-organization leadership. Finally, the prestigious Permanent Court of International Justice (PCIJ) was established at The Hague. Although formally outside the League, it was designed to become the court of last resort of the international community.

The League consisted mostly of European nation-states. At its peak, its membership totaled fifty-nine. However, the League was designed to be a global organization, and it suffered a hard blow when the United States decided not to join. This decision was due in part to a fearful and isolationist Senate unwilling to accept the League's covenant, which it considered to be erosive of the sovereignty of the United States. The Senate was prepared to join the League only with reservations and only under certain stipulations, which were unacceptable to President Wilson but not necessarily to the other member states. Perhaps better communications and more flexibility between the president and the Senate would have brought the United States into the League.

The famous French marshal, Ferdinand Foch, referring in 1919 to the post–World War I settlement at Versailles, remarked prophetically: "This is not peace. It is an armistice for twenty years." The League of Nations was soon put to the peacekeeping test. In a period of twenty years, the new world organization became involved in over sixty political disputes. During the same period, approximately sixty more disputes were legally defined and eventually presented before the Permanent Court of International Justice.[12] Many other disputes were dealt with by reparations commissions, conferences of ambassadors, and other subsidiary bodies that remained in operation for a time as a result of World War I.

Despite the general reputation of the League as a dismal failure in maintaining peace, the statistical record tells a different story. According to scholars Jack Plano and Robert Riggs, the League was successful in solving more than half of the disputes that came to its attention.[13] The League failed decisively only in five major instances—the Japanese occupation of Manchuria, the Italian occupation of Ethiopia, the Chaco War (a destructive conflict between Bolivia and Paraguay), the Spanish Civil War, and the Soviet attack on Finland. Unfortunately for the League, however, the importance and magnitude of these few cases of failure gave it a bad reputation.

A meaningful discussion of success versus failure presupposes a definition of each of these terms. A definition of minimal success would be the settlement of a dispute by means short of war. Naturally, it would be much harder to achieve success if it were defined as the settlement of a dispute to the mutual satisfaction of parties involved in the dispute *and* on the basis of high standards of fairness and justice. Assessing the success or failure of an international organization in the role of mediator is extremely difficult. Although intermediaries often do play a role in settling a dispute, attributing success or failure to them

---

[12]See D. W. Bowett, *The Law of International Institutions* (London: Stevens & Sons, 1963); and Jack C. Plano and Robert E. Riggs, *Forging World Order: The Politics of International Organization* (New York: Macmillan, 1967).

[13]Plano and Riggs, *Forging World Order,* p. 28.

assumes that they are the *exclusive* variable affecting the outcome of the dispute. But conflict and its resolution involve too many other variables for such an assumption to hold.

An evaluation of the twenty-year peacekeeping record of the League of Nations leads the student to classify the first decade (1920 to 1930) as the successful years and the second decade (1930 to 1940) as the unsuccessful years. Typical disputes settled by the League of Nations in the 1920s involved marginal issues dividing small and intermediate-sized nation-states. Thus, the Aaland Islands dispute in 1920 pitted Finland against Sweden, and the Corfu case (1924) pitted Italy against Greece. These cases typified the gradually increasing use of force by a state to probe the intentions of or to sanction but not to destroy an opponent.[14] These and other instances of successful League conciliation are to be credited primarily to the harmonious state of the international political system during the 1920s. In turn, this state of harmony was due in large part to the relative economic prosperity and economic growth in the early 1920s. The principal powers that had joined the League were united in support of a policy of *rapprochement* with Germany. Further, the raw memories of the bloody and indecisive war, the "war to end war" in Woodrow Wilson's wishful words, cemented the will of nation-states to see disputes settled with words in conference rooms rather than with weapons on battlefields.

This euphoria, unfortunately, was short lived. The spirit and structure of the international environment took a sharp and drastic turn for the worse. The great American depression reverberated throughout Europe in the 1930s; fascism and populist authoritarian nationalism spread menacingly over the European continent; the victorious powers (especially Britain and France) were mistrusting one another and underestimating Nazi Germany's geometric growth of power. The world was moving once more on a potentially destructive collision course. These system-wide problems were inevitably reflected in the League's rear-view mirror. Against an early backdrop of hopefulness and success, the setbacks of the 1930s became all the more disheartening.

In its attempts to deal with relatively clear-cut cases of aggression by great powers, the League revealed the Achilles heel of a global international organization—its inability to sanction great powers.[15] To sanction great powers militarily in a decentralized balance-of-power system might necessitate a generalized war. To sanction them economically might create economic hardships within the

---

[14]For a good case history of the League of Nations, see Francis P. Walters, *A History of the League of Nations* (London: Oxford University Press, 1952).

[15]A universally acceptable and workable definition of *aggression* has not yet been reached. The Soviets prefer to emphasize *direct aggression*—that is, the sending of military forces to fight in another country without its invitation. The United States, on the other hand, emphasizes *indirect aggression*, such as inflammatory propaganda, economic warfare, subversion, support for guerrilla groups, and infiltration by volunteers. In April 1974, the United Nations Special Committee on the Question of Defining Aggression approved unanimously a draft resolution (subsequently adopted by the U.N. General Assembly in December 1974) defining *aggression* as "the use of armed force by a State against the sovereignty, territorial integrity or political independence of another State, or in any other manner inconsistent with the Charter of the United Nations." A/RES/3314. This definition would seem to share the Soviet emphasis on *direct aggression,* and it leaves the door wide open for multiple interpretations.

states applying the sanctions. If, in turn, these hardships were intolerable to influential commercial and investment elites, the effectiveness of the sanctions would be eroded. Finally, to sanction great powers only verbally is to leave them substantially unaffected or is merely to invite them to withdraw from the world organization, as was the case with some of the great powers during the late 1930s.[16]

The inability of the League of Nations to modify the activist and expansionist behavior of Japan in Manchuria, of Italy in Ethiopia, of Germany in Austria, Czechoslovakia, and Poland, and of the Soviet Union in Finland, coupled with the League's reluctance to become embroiled in the domestic affairs of Spain during the Spanish Civil War, confirmed the view that force was the final arbiter of a seriously disturbed and threatened international balance-of-power system.

In sum, the League failed in the 1930s because the international system itself, of which the League was a dependent part, had broken down. Depression, economic nationalism and exclusivism, xenophobia aggravated by mass nationalism, and the rise of exclusivist and expansionist ideologies (such as communism and fascism) together with American isolationism (seen by some as traditional indifference and by others as irresponsible opportunism)—all contributed to the great catastrophe that was World War II. The League, however, left us with an institutional legacy upon which the United Nations experiment has been elaborated.

THE UNITED NATIONS SYSTEM OF ORGANIZATIONS

While World War II was still raging, the Allied Powers—reflecting perhaps undue optimism regarding the outcome of the war—agreed through the Atlantic Charter (August 14, 1941) and the Moscow Conference of Foreign Ministers (October 30, 1943) that a new world organization should be established for the purpose of regulating the postwar international system.[17] Important preparatory conferences were held in Washington, D.C. (the Dumbarton Oaks Conference) on August 21, 1944, and at Yalta, Soviet Union, in February 1945. During these preparatory meetings, the victorious great powers established the foundations on which the future postwar world organization would be erected. Disagreements involving the scope and authority of the organization and questions on membership, voting, and great-power veto procedures were slowly and painfully settled.

These extensive preparations should make it clear that the great powers considered the development of multilateral and multifunctional world forums too important a task to be left to chance or to the whims and needs of smaller nation-states. The great powers had to guarantee their status of preeminence in the international setting—for instance, by demanding the power of veto—prior

[16]For example, Italy and Japan withdrew in anger from the League, and the USSR was expelled.

[17]The Atlantic Charter outlined principles of postwar cooperation among the Allies and was signed by Winston Churchill and Franklin D. Roosevelt. The eighth and final point of the charter provided for a "permanent system of general security" to be developed after the war.

to conceding to the drafting of a world political charter. Later, however, at the great (perhaps unprecedented) United Nations Conference at San Francisco, the smaller nation-states were given a genuine opportunity to affect the drafting of the United Nations Charter. Representatives from fifty countries deliberated hard for over two months (April and May 1945). In the end, they produced the United Nations Charter as well as the final version of the Statute of the International Court of Justice.[18]

Inis Claude, once again, has summarized very well the composite of forces and interactions that resulted in the United Nations Charter. According to Claude, the Charter

> was the product of past experience in the building and operation of international institutions, wartime planning, great power and particularly American leadership, intensive negotiation amid an intricate pattern of national disagreements and conflicts of interest, and popular pressures for realization of the desperate demand and noble aspiration for a just and durable peace.[19]

The drafters of the Charter were basically the representatives of nation-states that were victorious in World War II. They rushed the Charter through while the final, bloody phase of the war was still being fought in Europe and the Pacific. Their hope was that wartime unity and cooperation—both bonds that only peril and fear can create—would eliminate the obstacles that arise more easily in time of peace and security. Also, the framers of the new world forum were eager to disassociate the Charter of the United Nations from any postwar peace treaty, such as Versailles after World War I, that might hamper the smooth operation of the world organization in the long run. It was also necessary to disassociate the United Nations from its beleaguered predecessor, the League, whose unconvincing record and alienation from great powers such as the United States and the Soviet Union could at best inhibit the willing participation of these countries in the new world institution.

An overview of the structures and processes of the United Nations helps to clarify its goals. Of the six major organs (please refer to additional details in Figure 14-1), the first is the General Assembly, whose voting membership includes all governments that have ratified the Charter. In addition, selected non-state actors, such as the Palestine Liberation Organization (PLO), have a nonvoting observer status in the Assembly. Following the principle of one government, one vote, the Assembly passes resolutions dealing with the self-determination of nation-states, the new economic order, and a wide array of other vital issues of global concern. In its elective role, the Assembly collaborates with the Security Council to select the secretary-general and the judges of the International Court of Justice. Finally, approval of the United Nations budget is contingent upon favorable action by the Assembly.

[18]See Ruth B. Russell, *A History of the United Nations Charter: The Role of the United States, 1940–1945* (Washington, D.C.: Brookings Institution, 1958).

[19]Claude, *Swords into Plowshares*, pp. 64–65.

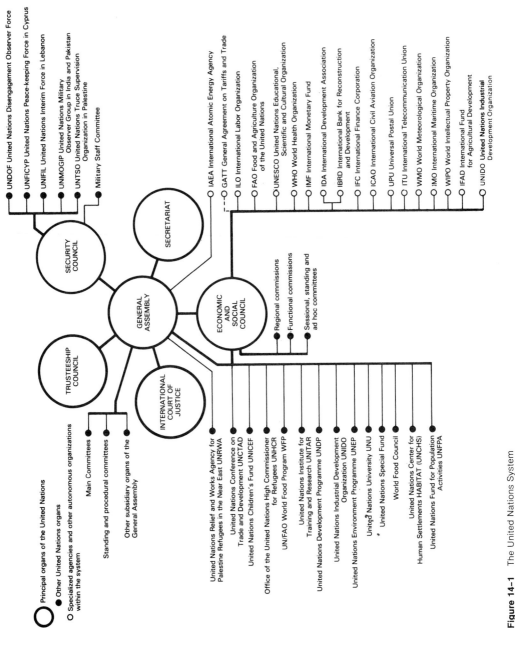

Figure 14–1 The United Nations System

SOURCE: *Basic Facts about the United Nations* (New York: United Nations, 1987).

282

The fifteen members of the Security Council, constituting the second major organ, have the authority under the Charter both to formulate and to implement policy. To take action on important questions, the five permanent members—China, France, Great Britain, the Soviet Union, and the United States—must concur and be supported by at least four of the ten nonpermanent members, whom the General Assembly elects for two-year terms. Should one of the permanent members cast a negative vote (a so-called veto), no decision is possible. The Security Council may set in motion the machinery of collective security, impose economic sanctions, or authorize the deployment of peacekeeping forces in such troubled areas as Cyprus, Lebanon, the Sinai, and Indonesia. The Council recommends a candidate for the post of secretary-general to the General Assembly and with that body elects the members of the International Court of Justice.

The third organ is the Economic and Social Council (ECOSOC), whose fifty-four members are elected by the General Assembly for three-year terms, one-third being replaced each year. Reaching decisions on the basis of a simple majority, ECOSOC focuses on human rights, world trade, the status of women, and related social and economic questions. Functional commissions, such as the one on human rights, implement its programs. ECOSOC has, among other functions, the responsibility of coordinating and lightly supervising the activities of the all-important specialized agencies listed in Figure 14–1.

Fourth among the major structures is the slowly disappearing Trusteeship Council, to which the Charter assigns the responsibility of monitoring the process of political development in those territories that have not yet attained

UN Headquarters in New York City. (United Nations/S. Lwin)

self-government or independence. Of the eleven original trust territories, only one remained under the administration of a foreign power in 1981: the Pacific Islands (Micronesia) of the United States.

The International Court of Justice (ICJ), which replaced the Permanent Court of International Justice (PCIJ), is the fifth deliberative organ. The General Assembly and the Security Council concurrently elect each of the fifteen judges for staggered terms of nine years. No two judges may be of the same nationality, and the composition of the Court reflects the world's principal legal systems. Members of the United Nations or the Security Council itself may refer a case to the Court, and the tribunal renders advisory opinions at the request of either the General Assembly or the Security Council. With a quorum of nine judges, decisions reflect the consensus of the majority.

Lastly, the Secretariat administers the world organization under the direction of the secretary-general, whom the Security Council recommends and the General Assembly appoints for a term of five years. Javier Pérez de Cuéllar of Peru assumed this office on January 1, 1982. The secretary-general provides good offices designed to help resolve international disputes and sometimes, as in the case of Cyprus and the Persian Gulf War, even serves as a mediator between contending parties. The staff of the Secretariat organizes conferences, collects data on social and economic trends, maintains peacekeeping operations, and supplies the media with information on the activities of the United Nations.

The United Nations was designed to be an organization of global membership, an organization whose functions were to spread well beyond the political and security areas, and an organization of realistic scope and activities.[20] The sovereignty of participating nation-states was generally to be respected, and the special rights and responsibilities of the great powers were to remain at the core of the world body. In sum, the United Nations would be a reflection of widely acceptable (especially to the great powers) international norms of behavior designed to reinforce cooperation and to moderate conflict.

Four and a half decades after the inception of the United Nations, one can clearly observe that the organization has evolved in ways the framers of the United Nations Charter could not have predicted. The political basis of operation of the United Nations (as had been the case with the League of Nations) was supposed to be *collective security*. Simply stated, *collective security* hypothesized a world of small-, medium-, and great-power nation-states operating independently of one another. Ideally, this balance-of-power environment, where alignments would be short-lived, flexible, and pragmatic, would deter future agressors (i.e., future Hitlers).

In practice, collective security meant that any nation-state aggressing or attempting to aggress against any other nation-state would immediately be faced

---

[20]The cold war prevented the rapid achievement of the goal of global membership. The Soviet Union blocked all American-supported applicants, and the United States replied in kind. The first breakthrough occurred in 1955, when a package deal resulted in the admission of both American- and Soviet-sponsored applicants. Since that time, the organization has achieved nearly complete representation, including the Chinese People's Republic and the two German states.

with collective economic and military sanctions imposed by all the remaining nation-states. Since a situation of all-against-one would drastically reduce the probability of success for the aspiring aggressor, collective security was expected to result in a world free of the scourge of war. "Details" such as defining *aggression,* pinpointing specific aggressors, and devising ways to impose collective economic and military sanctions were left for the organization to develop gradually with experience and time.

The cold war, however, dashed the hopes of the proponents of collective security. The growth of two major clusters of states, euphemistically referred to as the free world and the socialist camp, replaced the system of balance of power. The United States and the Soviet Union became the leaders (sometimes on the basis of coercion) of two strongly organized and fully armed coalitions of nation-states. These coalitions faced each other in a situation variously referred to as armed peace, balance of terror, cold war, and nuclear deterrence. This bipolar system, which pitted two "permanent" alliance systems against each other while the so-called nonaligned countries looked helplessly on, undermined the political environment of balanced and fragmented power that had been considered a basic prerequisite for collective security. In a global confrontation of uncompromising political, economic, and social systems, the problem of defining aggression became practically irrelevant. Half the world stood ready to denounce the other half as the aggressors, and vice versa. It is in this system of institutionalized

Symbol of an ideologically divided world—the Berlin Wall. (UPI/Bettmann Newsphotos)

suspicion and hatred that the United Nations has sought to develop itself since the early days of the cold war.

It is quite difficult to assess the record of the United Nations in the crucial areas of peaceful settlement of disputes and peacekeeping. As we have seen, the League enjoyed a fine record of peaceful settlement of disputes during its first decade of operation. During this time, the League successfully sponsored techniques such as good offices, mediation, conciliation, arbitration, and adjudication. This record has not been matched by the cold-war–torn United Nations. On the other hand, the United Nations has enjoyed, compared to the League, many more years without experiencing a global war. The skeptic, of course, could credit with good reason the balance of nuclear terror rather than the United Nations for the prevention of great wars in our day. In any case, we should admit that it is extremely difficult to *compare* with confidence the effectiveness of the United Nations and that of the League. Political environments have simply varied too greatly between the days of the League and those of the United Nations. (See Chapter 3 for a treatment of the evolution of the structures and processes of the international system.)

An important result of the cold-war years was the weakening of the effectiveness of the Security Council. The Soviet Union, finding itself frequently in the minority in the council, employed its veto right with near abandon, especially in regard to proposals to admit new members to the United Nations. In reaction, and sensing a favorable balance of political forces, the United States shifted the focus of United Nations activity to the General Assembly. The fundamental disagreements between the American and Soviet blocs had made it nearly impossible for the United Nations to smoothly implement the concept of collective security that was premised on collective great-power support. A genuine attempt by one bloc to apply collective military sanctions to the other bloc would have been tantamount to a collective declaration of world war in the nuclear era. Gradually, therefore, it became apparent that the United Nations could not act (especially through the Security Council) as an effective deterrent to great-power or great-power–sponsored aggression.

Following the disillusioning Korean War (1950–53), collective security was virtually abandoned as the dominant peacekeeping approach of the United Nations. North Korea had been pronounced an aggressor by the Security Council while the Soviet Union was absenting itself over the question of Chinese representation in the United Nations. It soon became clear, however, that the "U.N. police action" in Korea was no more than a polite term for American military support of the South Korean government. In the years following the Korean War, the United Nations has settled for the more realistic and less risky approach of *preventive diplomacy,* the brainchild of the second secretary-general of the United Nations, Dag Hammarskjöld (1953–61). In case after important case, such as the recurrent Middle East crisis (1956 to the present), the Congo crisis (1960–63), and the Cyprus crisis (1963 to the present), the United Nations has demonstrated this pragmatic and cautious style of diplomacy.

Preventive diplomacy attempts to prevent crises arising in the Third World from involving the great powers directly and thus endangering the earth with potentially explosive cold-war confrontations. Unlike collective security, preventive diplomacy does not seek to pinpoint the aggressor country, to apply sanctions against it, and to restore order. Rather, it accepts conflict as an objective condition of international relations. In this sense, preventive diplomacy is reminiscent of nineteenth-century realpolitik. Also, it is preoccupied with the control of conflict rather than with a legalistic and moralistic insistence on identifying the wrongdoers and punishing them effectively.

Preventive–diplomacy oriented peacekeeping forces have been relatively small, multilaterally staffed military contingents. Usually, they have been recruited from smaller and/or nonaligned nation-states. Their purpose has been to act as armed shields between combatants and as wartime mediators seeking to channel the conflict in streams of negotiation rather than streams of conflict.

With the gradual muting of the cold war, the painfully slow unveiling of détente, and the representation of the Chinese People's Republic in the Security Council, we witnessed a return of the political center of gravity from the United Nations General Assembly back to the Security Council. One indication of this trend was that the use of the veto in the Security Council was declining in the 1960s due in large part to the Soviet Union's dramatic decrease in veto employment. We notice, however, that the 1970s introduced a sizable increase in veto employment by Great Britain and the United States.

Following the assumption of power in the Soviet Union by a reformist and pragmatic leader, Mikhail Gorbachev, there has been a remarkable thaw in Soviet-American relations. President Ronald Reagan and General-Secretary Mikhail Gorbachev have initiated what may prove to be a long period of peaceful coexistence and even partial cooperation between the superpowers. The United Nations has profited considerably by the new détente, and trouble spots in various parts of the world (Afghanistan, Nicaragua, Iran-Iraq, Kampuchea, Cyprus, Angola–Namibia–South Africa) have been getting heavier doses of United Nations peacekeeping treatment. Some scholars are now predicting that the international system is moving away from bipolarity, as represented by the American and Soviet blocs, and toward a structure of five poles of power, as represented by the permanent members of the Security Council. We might even witness one day a "new concert of the world" system and the gradual resuscitation of a modified collective-security environment founded on great-power consensus.[21]

---

[21]Henry Kissinger's Ph.D. dissertation, "Peace, Legitimacy, and the Equilibrium: A Study of the Statesmanship of Castlereagh and Metternich" (Harvard University, 1954), is supposed to represent his grand design for a stable world of satisfied great powers seeking to maintain international legitimacy through a deft combination of bilateral, regional, and global organizational devices against relatively weak but revisionist centers of power in the Third World. It was published years later as *A World Restored: Metternich, Castlereagh, and the Problems of Peace, 1812–1822* (New York: Grosset and Dunlap, 1964).

BEYOND PEACEKEEPING

Up to this point, we have described the United Nations in terms of its theory and practice in the important area of peacekeeping. However, the bulk of the activities of the United Nations have not been in the realm of *high politics* (issues of war and peace), but in the area of *low politics* (economic development, technological regulation, and cultural and social coordination). The United Nations budget (see Table 14–1) is a convincing indicator of this focus of interest. As we can see in Table 14–1, the lion's share of the United Nations budget is devoted to economic, social, and humanitarian activities, common support services, and staff assessments. The amount devoted to peacekeeping activities, nearly $90 million, is meager by comparison. However, given the trend toward increasing United Nations peacekeeping activity—in an era of low superpower tension—the share of the United Nations budget devoted to political and security activities is expected to increase.

Despite its demonstrated concern for global socioeconomic problems, the United Nations has failed to solve many of them. For instance, disease and malnutrition, two central problems of underdevelopment, continue to plague over two-thirds of our globe's population. Disease control is improving, but the problems of inadequate food and energy, explosive population growth, environmental pollution, and resource exhaustion are reaching the proportions of gradual "ecocide." (Chapter 19 discusses these problems at some length.)

A useful way to summarize the socioeconomic record of the United Nations and its specialized agencies is to look at each of the major functions they have been performing. These functions include:

Table 14–1 United Nations Budget, 1986–89

	1986–87	*1988–89*
	In thousands of U.S. Dollars	*In thousands of U.S. Dollars*
Overall policy making, direction and coordination	46,149	44,932
Political and Security Council affairs; peacekeeping activities	94,625	89,893
Political affairs, trusteeship, and decolonization	30,678	31,825
Economic, social, and humanitarian activities	477,411	496,442
International justice and law	27,768	29,234
Public information	76,183	77,002
Common support services	649,546	710,929
United Nations bond issue	16,759	3,521
Staff assessment	261,260	266,606
Capital expenditures	30,823	19,203
Total	1,711,202	1,769,587

SOURCES: *Basic Facts about the United Nations* (New York: U.N. Department of Public Information, 1987); U.N., General Assembly, 42nd Session, September 15–December 21, 1987, *Biennium 1988–1989* (GA/7612).

1. Production of information—through research and publication carried on by nearly all organizations.
2. Regulation of international activities—through agencies such as the International Monetary Fund, the International Labor Organization, and the Universal Postal Union.
3. Redistribution of resources—through programs of technical assistance, loans, and development assistance.
4. Rudimentary legislation—through yearly conferences, meetings, symposiums, and publications directed toward the standardization and improvement of national legislation of member states.[22]

The United Nations has been quite successful in at least three of these four general functions. The weakest function, without doubt, is that of redistribution of resources. The United Nations, being at best a rudimentary form of global government, does not possess the means of taxation or other forms of revenue production that would allow it to undertake large-scale programs. Nor would most national governments find it advantageous to their vested interests, as these have been traditionally defined, to allow the United Nations system to grow to such proportions that it could begin competing with the national governments for the loyalty of their peoples.

Nonetheless, even the most superficial look at the record of the United Nations' socioeconomic activities reveals a steady and impressive growth pattern. For example, in 1952 only 1,733 United Nations experts of all types were sent to developing countries. By 1968, the figure had grown to an impressive 10,317. From 1946 to 1970, the World Bank and its affiliates loaned over $17 billion for reconstruction and development projects, a notable amount indeed. But one begins to realize the exponential growth in the World Bank's significance by contrasting earlier activities with its more recent $17.7 billion *annual* allocation in support projects to developing countries.[23] Concurrently, the constantly expanding activities of the World Bank have been matched by massive stabilization loans of the International Monetary Fund to financially troubled countries such as Pakistan, Turkey, Mexico, and Brazil.

THE UNITED NATIONS RECORD IN DECOLONIZATION

One is tempted to credit the United Nations with resounding success in decolonization. At the beginning of World War II there were well over 120 colonial territories, accounting for one-third of the world's land and population. In the 1980s, the number of dependent and non-self-governing territories had shrunk to about fifty, leaving less than ten million people (compared with the previous seven hun-

---

[22]Robert Gregg, "U.N. Economic, Social, and Technical Activities," in *The United Nations: Past, Present, and Future,* ed. James Barros (New York: Free Press, 1972), pp. 221–28.
[23]*The Europa Year Book 1988: A World Survey,* vol. 1 (London: Europa Publications, 1988), p. 61.

dred million) under external colonial rule.[24] However, crediting the United Nations for the birth of the new nation-states is like crediting the obstetrician for the conception as well as for the delivery of children. It is apparent that the United Nations was one of many factors, and not necessarily the most important one, that led to decolonization.

Perhaps the primary reason for decolonization has been the fatigue of colonialists. From the 1940s through the 1960s, colonial powers found it both economically costly and politically embarrassing to maintain control over dependent territories. They also found that less-direct means of external penetration (referred to disparagingly as neocolonialism) have secured economic advantages for them and have unburdened them of the political and psychological disadvantages of colonialism. Finally, the United Nations, perhaps as a result of the steady growth of its membership (51 at birth, 159 in 1989), has politically condemned colonial practices through the process of, to paraphrase Inis Claude, collective delegitimization.[25]

The success of decolonization has meant the atrophy of the Trusteeship Council as a major United Nations organ. Most United Nations trust territories, with the exception of strategic islands held in trust by the United States, have become independent.[26] Further, the excolonial nation-states have preferred to wage the struggle for decolonization in the General Assembly, where they can easily secure majorities with the help of Latin American and Soviet-bloc nation-states, rather than the Trusteeship Council, where voting power is divided evenly between colonial and noncolonial member states.[27]

THE INTERNATIONAL PROTECTION OF HUMAN RIGHTS

In a system in which individual human beings have been considered the objects rather than the subjects of international law, it is difficult to see how an acceptable standard of international justice can be applied across the globe. The earth is divided geographically, culturally, linguistically, politically, and legally. Sover-

[24]The data provided do not touch upon the problem of "internal colonialism," as exemplified by those multinational states in which an ethnic minority wields dominant economic and political power, nor do these statistics reveal that in some newly independent nation-states the ruling class continues to rely upon the former colonial power for support. For a historical and legal analysis of decolonization, see United Nations Department of Political Affairs, *Decolonization*, vol. II, no. 6: *Fifteen Years of the United Nations Declaration on the Granting of Independence to Colonial Countries and Peoples* (New York: United Nations, 1975).

[25]Notably 96 of the 159 members of the United Nations gained their independence since the end of World War II. See also Claude, *Swords into Plowshares*, pp. 349–77.

[26]The mandates of the League of Nations that had not gained independence, as well as colonies that were detached from the defeated Axis Powers after World War II, became United Nations trust territories.

[27]Excolonial nation-states have found another advantage in working through the General Assembly: In 1961, the Assembly established a special committee (popularly referred to as the Special Committee of 24) to assess the progress being made toward the self-determination of dependent populations. This committee, which was heavily dominated by anticolonial countries, gradually preempted many of the activities of the Trusteeship Council.

eignty presupposes that the internal affairs of nation-states, including the protection and control of their citizens, are not to be interfered with by other nation-states or by international organizations.

Even the most superficial look around the globe reveals that basic human rights are not respected in many countries.[28] We must not forget, however, that humankind took great steps forward in the nineteenth century by abolishing slavery and by gradually lifting women to equal status, psychologically if not occupationally, with men. The twentieth century, in addition to decolonization, sponsored the battle against racial, ethnic, sexual, religious, and linguistic discrimination. Human-rights advocates seek to provide minimum standards and freedoms for all the people of this earth.

Western Europe, which enjoys cultural and economic cohesiveness, appears to have progressed the fastest in the area of international protection of human rights. The Western Europeans have developed institutions such as the European Commission and the European Court of Human Rights. These are pioneer international organizations, in that they permit individual citizens, groups, or corporations to take complaints against their own governments before regional supranational authorities. However, such organizations have not had much success at the global level, as we shall see in Chapter 15.

In 1948, the General Assembly of the United Nations adopted overwhelmingly the Universal Declaration of Human Rights. A summary of the civil and political rights provided in the Declaration is as follows:

> The right to life, liberty, and security of person; the right to freedom of thought, speech, and communication of information and ideas; freedom of assembly and religion; the right to government through free elections; the right to free movement within the state and free exit from it; the right to asylum in another state; the right to nationality; freedom from arbitrary arrest and interference with the privacy of home and family; and the prohibition of slavery or torture.

Economic and social rights include the following:

> The right to work, to protection against unemployment, and to join trade unions; the right to a standard of living adequate for health and well-being; the right to education; and the right to rest and leisure.

The Declaration has moral but not legal authority. Basically, it is a "wish" of the human conscience for future good behavior at the national and local levels of government.

The controversies regarding the interpretation of the Declaration are endless. For example, do individuals have a *right to work?* Does their government have a duty to provide them with either employment or unemployment compensation? On the other side of the coin, does a government have the right to *require*

---

[28]See David P. Forsythe, "The United Nations and Human Rights, 1945–1985," *Political Science Quarterly,* 100 (Summer 1985), 249–270; and Jack Donnely, *The Concept of Human Rights* (London: Croom Helm, 1985).

Corpses at the Bergen-Belsen Nazi concentration camp, monument to the unrestrained human brutality of genocide. (U.S. Army photograph)

its citizens to accept a certain job rather than provide them with unemployment compensation? To move to the area of political freedoms, can a person advocate the overthrow of the government and be protected by the right of freedom of speech? Does a government have the right to punish what it considers antisocial or parasitic behavior? Is there a fundamental right of revolution? Do programs of cultural, racial, or sexual integration violate the right of individuals to be different? Does the freedom of movement extend to unlimited rights of emigration anywhere on our globe? This issue has been dramatized by waves of homeless refugees, referred to as *boat people*, from countries in Indochina and the Caribbean. In the area of human rights, as in many other areas, we are confronted with the perennial political paradox of having to harmonize freedom with order, individual and group needs with those of society.

Since 1948, the United Nations has tried hard to spearhead an effort to develop covenants (with treaty-binding powers) rather than declarations. They include Conventions on the Prevention and Punishment of the Crime of Genocide,[29] on Political Rights of Women, on the Non-Applicability of Statutory Limitations to War Crimes and Crimes against Humanity, and on the Suppression and Punishment of the Crime of Apartheid. There are also Covenants on Economic, Social and Cultural Rights and on Civil and Political Rights, as well as an Optional Protocol to International Covenant on Civil and Political Rights. The

---

[29]Barbara Harff and Ted Robert Gurr, "Toward an Empirical Theory of Genocides and Politicides: Identification and Measurement of Cases since 1945," Research Note, *International Studies Quarterly*, 32, No. 3 (1988), 359–371. This article presents a careful and complex examination of the post-World-War-II manifestations of a gruesome phenomenon that has beset humankind from ancient times to the present, reaching the zenith of destructiveness and brutality during the holocaust of the Jewish people in Nazi concentration camps during World War II. The Harff and Gurr estimate of deaths for which data is available in 40 cases of *genocide* (death of a national group) and *politicide* (death of political and class enemies) since World War II touches a staggering high of 16.2 million deaths.

reluctance of the United States to ratify treaties internationally guaranteeing human rights, with the sole exception of the treaty banning genocide, has stimulated extensive controversy. Many supporters of these conventions find it deplorable that a government committed at home and abroad to the defense of human rights should hesitate to ratify those instruments giving them legal force. Conversely, opponents of ratification contend that present-day constitutional guarantees are more than adequate, that many of the covenants cover subjects best left to states (within the United States), and finally that these treaties might imply a transfer of governmental authority to an international body.

Existing conventions and declarations point the way to future international legislation. But it is safe to say that until the international political system becomes considerably more integrated, human-rights standards will probably remain in the realm of pious but unenforceable wishes. Pragmatically oriented governments will consent to them primarily to appease their publics.

ASSESSMENT OF THE UNITED NATIONS SYSTEM

Depending on one's outlook, expectations, philosophical orientation, and even educational background, one can conclude that the United Nations is a dismal failure, a resounding success, or something in between. Those who harbor great expectations about the ability of humankind to live in good order, given enlightened leadership and strong global institutions have concluded by and large that the United Nations has been a failure. They have referred to it as a talk shop, a barroom of international diplomacy, and a toothless little institutional monster whose roar is much greater than its bite. On the other hand, those who have trusted in a multisovereign and quasi-anarchic international system have become seriously alarmed at the growth of what they consider supranational institutional cancers that are slowly undermining the health of sovereign nation-states.

Perhaps the middle position is a better one for us to take. The United Nations cannot be considered either a success or a failure, because effective standards for assessing its success or failure have not been devised. The United Nations has sought to peacefully mediate and reduce international conflict. How can we effectively measure the degree to which this peacekeeping has succeeded? Other variables, such as decisions of national leaders, changes in their perception of a given conflict situation, and changes in the nature and structure of the international system, do not make this task any easier. At best, we can only assume that the United Nations is a positive factor in the maintenance of peace and in the development of international cooperation. Verification of our assumption is impossible in the present prescientific state of our discipline.

We should perhaps conclude that the United Nations is an institution that reflects but does not shape the political realities of the international system. It evolves when political consensus and cooperation evolve, and it retrogresses when political disagreement and conflict arise. It is an especially good reflection of the extent to which the great powers in the international system consider themselves privileged senior partners in a great global enterprise. A political compromise appears to be emerging among the most important centers of power in the world. To the extent that this compromise is realized, we can predict that in a progressively technologically interdependent system, the United Nations system of organizations will continue to grow in size, scope, and importance. The stakes are high. In fact, they are tantamount to global survival. U Thant, former secretary-general of the United Nations (1961–71), eloquently summarized the issues we face:

> As we watch the sun go down, evening after evening, through the smog across the poisoned waters on our native earth, we must ask ourselves seriously whether we really wish some future universal historian on another planet to say about us, "With all their genius and with all their skill, they ran out of foresight and air and food and water and ideas . . ." or, "they went on playing politics until their world collapsed around them" or "when they looked up, it was already too late." If the United Nations does nothing else, it can at least serve a vital purpose in sounding the alarm.[30]

SUGGESTIONS FOR FURTHER STUDY

Javier Pérez de Cuéllar has argued that the United Nations finds itself in a crisis in his *Report of the Secretary-General on the Work of the Organization, 1987* (New York: U.N. Secretariat, 1987). For a comprehensive description of the world organization, see U.N. Department of Public Information, *Everyone's United Nations: A Handbook on the Work of the United Nations,* 10th ed. (New York: U.N. Secretariat, 1986). The Soviet analyst Ednan Agayev has concluded that a restructuring of socialism will eventually result in a strengthening of the General Assembly in "United Nations and Reality," *International Affairs* (Moscow), 4 (April 1988), 23–32. Institutional bias is the subject of Thomas M. Franck, "Of Gnats and Camels: Is There a Double Standard at the United Nations?" *American Journal of International Law,* 78 (October 1984), 811–33. The United Nations as a rule-making institution is the subject of Quincy Wright, *International Law and the United Nations* (London: Asia Publishing House, 1960; reprint ed. Westport, Conn.: Greenwood Press, 1976). Contrary to popular belief, Inis L. Claude, Jr., has suggested that negative votes in the Security Council have a stabilizing effect in *The Changing United Nations* (New York: Random House, 1967). For an overview of the organization, the following two anthologies are useful: James Barros, ed., *The United Nations: Past, Present, and Future* (New York: Free Press, 1972); and Leon Gordenker, ed., *The United Nations in International Politics* (Princeton, N.J.: Princeton University Press, 1971). Alvin Z. Rubinstein and George Ginsburg have assembled an anthology on the diplomacy of the superpowers at the world organization in their *Soviet*

---

[30]Closing Statement to the Commemorative Session of the United Nations, October 24, 1970, reported in the *New York Times,* October 25, 1970, p.18.

and American Policies in the United Nations: A Twenty-Five Year Perspective (New York: New York University Press, 1971). Specialized studies of United Nations activities include James M. Boyd, *United Nations Peace-keeping Operations: A Military and Political Appraisal* (New York: Praeger Publishers, Inc., 1971); and Robert S. Jordan, ed., *International Administration: Its Evolution and Contemporary Applications* (New York: Oxford University Press, 1971).

15

THE THEORY AND PRACTICE OF FUNCTIONALISM AND REGIONAL INTEGRATION

The attitudes of practitioners and students of international relations have been strongly criticized as being overly conflict- and defense-oriented. In the literature of international relations, the international system has traditionally been portrayed in terms of large and small billiard balls that move around constantly and often stumble into one another with destructive consequences. High politics has been equated with the activities of diplomats and soldiers, as we saw in Chapter 1, and so-called important questions have been considered to be only those questions involving governments and their capital cities. All else has been relegated to the domain of low politics. Some critics have begun to argue, with considerable justification, that state-centered, conflict-oriented, and defense-oriented conceptions of the international system not only distort reality but tend to become self-fulfilling.[1] In other words, if you perceive the world from the viewpoint of "kill or be killed," you are likely to act accordingly, thus reinforcing a junglelike behavioral norm in the next generation.

The most insightful critics of the security/conflict conception of interna-

---

[1]A persuasive argument against the state-centered model of the international system is that of John Burton et al., *The Study of World Society: A London Perspective,* International Studies Association, Occasional Paper 1 (Pittsburgh: University of Pittsburgh, University Center for International Studies, 1974). Burton et al. argue for a transnational model of considerable actor complexity resembling much more a huge cobweb than a simple set of billiard balls. They prefer to focus on the activities of people and groups across national borders (transnational politics) rather than on the foreign policies of nation-states. Another useful study recommending a transition to "post-Westphalian" world politics is Robert C. Johansen, *The National Interest and the Human Interest* (Princeton, N.J.: Princeton University Press, 1980).

tional politics have been referred to as *functionalists.*[2] Functionalism has been presented as an operative philosophy that would gradually lead to a peaceful, unified, and cooperative world. The functionalists begin their argument with the assumption that wars are the product of a crudely organized international system. This system, they maintain, is founded on suspicion and anarchy and considers war an accepted means of settling thorny international disputes. Sovereignty, national exclusivism, and other forms of arbitrary fragmentation of the globe are viewed by the functionalists as an anachronistic and dangerous heritage of the preindustrial age. The functionalists claim to be realists (in the sense that they recommend the employment of realistic means for the attainment of idealistic ends). They grant that governments have vested interests and that nation-states will not be dismantled voluntarily. Hence, they advocate a gradual approach toward regional or global unity, an approach designed to isolate and eventually render obsolete the stubborn but inadequate institutional structures called nation-states.[3]

The functionalist strategy urges the development of piecemeal nonpolitical cooperative organizations, which are established most effectively in the economic, technical, scientific, social, and cultural sectors. These sectors are referred to collectively as functional sectors. The functionalists assume that it is easier to establish narrow-in-scope functional organizations (in sectors such as energy production and distribution, transportation and communications control, health protection and improvement, labor standards and exchanges, and customs unions) than to try to develop grandiose political institutions that jeopardize the national sovereignty of member-states. Governments find it difficult to oppose the growth of functional organizations since these nonpolitical bodies are mutually advantageous for the participating states and do not appear to constrict national sovereignty.

The steady spread of functional organizations to greater and greater circles of activity is expected to trigger a *spillover* effect. *Spillover* is a concept similar to what economists call the demonstration effect. For example, if an international cooperative venture works to mutual advantage in the sector of coal and steel production, then it whets the appetite of and creates additional administrative requirements for participating governments to enter into cooperative ventures in related functional areas, such as transportation, pollution control, and labor legislation. It thus leads to increasing degrees of cooperation and eventually to political unification.

Spillover is a process characteristic of most human organizations, including private business. The classic illustration is the American drugstore, which diversifies its functions and becomes also a restaurant, a supermarket, and a

---

[2]One of the early and most influential proponents of functionalism is David Mitrany. See his seminal essay, *A Working Peace System* (Chicago: Quadrangle, 1966), which was first published in 1943. The best-known practitioner of functionalism was the European statesman Jean Monnet.

[3]Stanley Hoffmann, without labeling himself a *functionalist,* adopts a gradualistic, reformist approach with respect to the transformation of the international system. See his *Primacy or World Order: American Foreign Policy since the Cold War* (New York: McGraw-Hill, 1978).

clothing store. As large department stores can boast of one-stop shopping, international organizations may want to boast of one-stop solving. In national bureaucracies and big business, task expansion and functional diversification (which often leads to redundancy if not outright duplication) have been referred to as *Parkinson's law of bureaucratic growth*. International organizations, as we saw in Chapter 14, have not been exempt from Parkinson's law either. Spillover, more generally, involves the development of subsidiary and related organizations designed to complement the activities of and meet the needs created by existing organizations.

Functionalists, as a matter of strategy, tend to emphasize cooperative aspects of international behavior and sidestep conflictive aspects. They look at the globe in terms of the politics of cooperation and reason rather than the politics of conflict and irrationality. Gradually, they hope, with the accumulation of a large variety of functional organizations linking people and their interests across national boundaries, a transformation in both national attitudes and institutions will take place. Eventually, transnational and supranational attitudes and institutions will relegate the nation-states to the museum of institutional curiosities.

THE THEORY OF INTEGRATION

Taking their cue from functionalism, theorists of international relations have studied the recent experience of Western Europe in some detail and have used the term *integration* to denote either a *process* toward or an *end product* of political unification among separate national units. A large volume of scholarship during the early 1960s was devoted to regional integration.

There is some academic controversy, and even different schools of thought, regarding the preferred methods and approaches to international integration. The *federalist* school of thought (solidly positioned in the ranks of idealism) conceives of integration in legal and institutional terms.[4] For federalist scholars, integration is an end product rather than a process. It stands for a political union among previously sovereign and independent territories, such as was formed in the United States and Switzerland. They recommend the adoption of federalism on both a regional and a global scale, and they consider the anarchic nation-state system to be primarily responsible for war. They discount arguments that federalism on a global scale is impractical and utopian. They feel that with a reasonable amount of discussion and education, enough people will be convinced that a rational plan for the regulation and governance of humankind should be adopted. Transition to a mutually acceptable model of federalism, ac-

---

[4]For an excellent example of the federalist approach, see Grenville Clark and Louis B. Sohn, *World Peace through World Law: Two Alternative Plans*, 3rd ed. (Cambridge, Mass.: Harvard University Press, 1966). For a useful approach to the study of federalism and federations, see Carl J. Friedrich, *Trends of Federalism in Theory and Practice* (New York: Praeger, 1968); and Edith Wynner, *World Federal Government in Maximum Terms* (Afton, N.Y.: Fedonat Press, 1954). For a federalist perspective focusing on the European Community, see Altiero Spinelli, *The Eurocrats* (Baltimore: Johns Hopkins University Press, 1966).

cording to federalist scholars, should follow a large-scale world conference similar to the one that gave birth to the United Nations.

A second school of thought, which is identified with Karl W. Deutsch and his associates, employs the *communications approach.*[5] This approach (in the scientific tradition) seeks to measure the process of integration by watching the flow of international *transactions,* such as trade, tourists, letters, and immigrants. It expects, further, that such transactions will eventually lead to the development of "security communities" or integrated sociopolitical systems. Deutsch has identified two major subcategories of security communities—*amalgamated* and *pluralist.* Both are characterized by the absence of intracommunity wars.

The United States is a good example of an amalgamated security community for it has a single federal government exercising central political control over a continent-sized region. Pluralist security communities, on the other hand, have no central political authority, but the national units that make up these communities do not expect to fight one another and thus do not fortify their borders. Pluralist security communities are usually larger areas, such as the North American continent and Western Europe. For the communications school of thought, then, integration can be seen both as a process leading toward political unification and as the end product of that process—amalgamated and pluralist security communities.

The third school of thought is referred to as *neofunctionalism.*[6] Neofunctionalist scholars also view integration as both a process and an outcome, but they prefer to emphasize cooperative decision-making processes and elite attitudes in order to assess the progress toward integration. An able scholar whose work has been identified mainly with this area is Ernst Haas. Neofunctionalists have focused primarily on formal institutions in an attempt to determine the extent to which important functions are carried out by national as opposed to international (integrated) agencies. Further, they have sought to assess, using systematic survey techniques (questionnaires and interviews), the degree to which important elites in various countries exhibit nationalist or internationalist orientations.

From our point of view, one should not have to choose among these different approaches to the study of integration. The genesis of "political actors," whether at the national, regional, or global level, is too complex a phenomenon to be left to any one method or conceptual approach. The recommendations and findings of federalists, communications analysts, and neofunctionalists should therefore be considered as useful steps in the ladder of understanding. Further, we should keep in mind a very important warning about integration. Whether

[5]See Karl W. Deutsch et al., *Political Community and the North Atlantic Area* (Princeton, N.J.: Princeton University Press, 1957), and *France, Germany, and the Western Alliance: A Study of Elite Attitudes on European Integration and World Politics* (New York: Scribner's, 1967).
[6]See Ernst Haas, *Beyond the Nation-State: Functionalism and International Organization* (Stanford, Calif.: Stanford University Press, 1964), and *The Uniting of Europe: Political, Social, and Economic Forces, 1950–1957* (Stanford, Calif.: Stanford University Press, 1958); Leon Lindberg, *The Political Dynamics of European Economic Integration* (Stanford, Calif.: Stanford University Press, 1963); and Leon Lindberg and Stuart Scheingold, *Europe's Would-Be Polity: Patterns of Change in the European Community* (Englewood Cliffs, N.J.: Prentice-Hall, 1970).

process or outcome, it should be purely voluntary. We learn from history that the more prevalent way to political unification has been through the force of arms. But coercive political unification should certainly *not* be confused with integration. The concept of integration should be reserved only for *peaceful* political unification.

The study of functionalism—especially in its applied form—has gone hand in hand with the study of regionalism. Given that the functionalist experiment has proceeded most systematically in a Western European setting, scholars have assumed that the transition from the state system to a global society must go first through a phase of regional integration.

PROBLEMS OF DEFINING REGIONS

The common-sense way of defining *regions* is on the basis of distinct land masses, such as Africa, Asia, Europe, North and South America, and Oceania. Unfortunately, even with such a relatively simple task as the definition of regions, conceptual controversy creeps in. For example, should Eastern Europe be grouped with a cluster of nation-states called Europe or with a different cluster called socialist countries? Should Arab-speaking northern Africa be grouped in a region called the Middle East, the Mediterranean, or Africa? Is Turkey an Asian, a European, a Balkan, a Mediterranean, a developing, an Islamic, or a NATO state?

It soon becomes obvious that different criteria for identifying regions yield altogether different regional configurations.[7] The following are the most commonly used criteria for grouping nation-states into regions:

1. *Geographical criteria:* grouping nation-states on the basis of their location in continents, subcontinents, archipelagoes, etc.—for instance, Europe and Asia.
2. *Military/political criteria:* grouping nation-states on the basis of their participation in alliances, or on the basis of ideological and political orientation—for instance, the communist bloc, the capitalist bloc, NATO, the Warsaw Pact, and the Third World.
3. *Economic criteria:* grouping nation-states on the basis of selected criteria of economic development, such as gross national product and industrial output—for instance, industrialized versus transitional versus less-developed states.
4. *Transactional criteria:* grouping nation-states on the basis of volume and frequency of exchange of people, goods, and services, such as immigrants, tourists, trade, and messages—for instance, the United States and Canada, the Western European market area, the Eastern European–Soviet market area.

One can group countries into regions according to a number of other criteria as well—for example, language, religion, culture, population density, and climate.

It is best not to spend much time seeking to determine what the "best"

---

[7]See Bruce M. Russett, *International Regions and the International System: A Study in Political Ecology* (Chicago: Rand McNally, 1967); and Louis J. Cantori and Steven L. Spiegel, *The International Politics of Regions: A Comparative Approach* (Englewood Cliffs, N.J.: Prentice-Hall, 1970).

definition of regionalism is, or which all-purpose criteria should be selected for clustering nation-states into regions. Instead, one should adopt different definitions of regional clusters from the list above, and seek to identify and compare the characteristics of each of these clusters over time. Important theoretical questions with potential normative value for humankind can then be asked. Here are some examples:

> Is the incidence of war greater in certain regions than in others?
>
> Do nation-states tend to fight less within regions than between regions?
>
> Is the distribution of resources improved or hampered by participation in regional organizations?
>
> Is the economic and political performance of nation-states improved or hampered by participation in regional organizations?
>
> Does involvement in regional organizations affect one's civil and political rights, and in general the quality of life for the citizens of involved nation-states, positively or negatively?
>
> What is the impact of regional integration on the cultural identity of involved nation-states?

We shall return to these questions in some detail in a later section of this chapter.

Let us turn now to the regional organizations that have developed since World War II. Regional organizations can be conveniently divided into two major types and perhaps a third, hybrid type. The first type is regional defense organizations, such as the North Atlantic Treaty Organization (NATO) and the Warsaw Treaty Organization (Warsaw Pact).[8] The second type comprises economic organizations (also referred to in the literature as functional organizations), such as the European Community (EC) in its early years of formation, the Council for Mutual Economic Assistance (CMEA), and the Latin American Free Trade Association (LAFTA). Hybrid regional organizations carry out multifunctional activities. The observer is usually hard-pressed to determine whether these are primarily political, economic, military, or cultural. Examples of the hybrid type are general-purpose institutions such as the Organization of American States (OAS), the Organization of African Unity (OAU) the European Community in the 1980s, the Arab League, and the British Commonwealth of Nations. Hybrid organizations contain elements of political and economic and occasionally military and cultural cooperation.

REGIONAL DEFENSE ORGANIZATIONS

These organizations were developed primarily as a response to the post–World War II cold-war environment and the shattering of the dream of global collective security. Most regional defense organizations were the product of American "pac-

---

[8]Another appropriate term for these organizations would be *institutionalized alliances.* Also, we referred to them in the preceding chapter as *regional military/defense organizations.* The United Nations Charter has made provisions for the development of military/defense organizations in Articles 51 and 52.

tomania" during the Truman/Acheson and Eisenhower/Dulles administrations in the late 1940s and the 1950s. Thus, we have witnessed the establishment of the Inter-American Defense System (1948), NATO (1949), the Australia–New Zealand–United States (ANZUS) Pact (1952), and the Southeast Asia Treaty Organization (SEATO, 1954). These pacts bound the United States—the mobile global power—with the defense systems of noncommunist nation-states in Latin America, Europe, and Southeast Asia, respectively. In addition, the United States associated itself indirectly with the British-led Middle Eastern defense mechanism initially named the Baghdad Pact (1955) and later renamed CENTO (1959). The Soviet Union, the primary continental power, developed an elaborate regional defense organization, the Warsaw Treaty Organization (WTO), in 1955.

It is obviously a distortion to classify all of these near-global military alliances as regional organizations. For example, in the case of the now-defunct SEATO, the greatest distance between participating national capitals was 11,500 miles. The equivalent distances are 5,500 miles for NATO, 5,300 miles for the OAS, 3,900 miles for the WTO, and 3,700 miles for CENTO, which was disbanded in March 1979, shortly after the Iranian revolution. Given the circumference of the earth—about 25,000 miles—it would have been absurd to refer to an organization such as SEATO as regional. It is more accurate, rather, to view postwar collective defense arrangements as institutionalized alliances, which reflect ideological and power bipolarity as well as the willingness of strategically positioned intermediate and small nation-states to seek or accept United States or Soviet military protection.

Regional defense organizations have exhibited remarkable institutional persistence, even in times of détente among the superpowers. If one were to generalize about regional defense organizations, one could claim that they have succeeded in their primary objectives—mutual deterrence and the maintenance of the strategic status quo—without resorting to unlimited or even major wars involving the superpowers directly. What have often been considered major East-West conflicts in the postwar period (Greece, Korea, Vietnam, and Afghanistan) have been kept well below nuclear and strategic levels of confrontation. Other conflicts, such as the Arab-Israeli, Indo-Pakistani, Indo-Chinese and Iranian-Iraqi disputes, have been localized in Third World zones. The remaining conflicts have consisted primarily of coups, insurgencies, civil strife, and national-liberation or anticolonial wars. Regional defense organizations have faced major difficulties only when disputes have erupted between member states. The serious disputes between Honduras and El Salvador in OAS, Greece and Turkey in NATO, and Czechoslovakia and the Soviet Union in the Warsaw Pact, are typical of such conflicts.

Judging from recent developments in the international system—the muting of the cold war, collective arrangements for arms control and disarmament, and the increasing participation of the Chinese People's Republic in global bargaining—one could expect that regional defense organizations are likely to be gradually deemphasized. However, these organizations might not atrophy completely, because their institutions—especially the elaborate bureaucracies that have been established for administrative purposes—have remarkable durability. The life-preserving mechanism in such organizations is functional diversification. This asset allows a defense organization to be defended on economic, social, scientific, or even cultural grounds—once the military grounds have been seriously questioned.

This leads us to one of the major unsolved problems of organizations at all levels. Organizations are easily established when there is a need for them, but they are very difficult to dismantle once that need subsides. SEATO (disestablished in 1975–77) and CENTO (disestablished in 1979) provide two recent examples of international organizations being quietly put out of commission. We do not mean to suggest that there is no further need for organizations such as NATO and the Warsaw Pact. On the contrary, it could be argued that détente is essentially the product of mutual deterrence achieved through the employment of collective defense organizations such as NATO, the Warsaw Pact, and whatever security system the Chinese People's Republic may choose to develop in the future.

Before we leave the topic of regional defense organizations, we might suggest some questions that are worthy of study. Is participation in regional defense organizations mutually advantageous for all participants? Is the burden for defense distributed equitably among all members? Is participation voluntary, or is it imposed upon some of the smaller and weaker members? Does participation in an alliance increase or decrease the incidence of conflict for each participant? Are the alliances popularly supported, or is there substantial domestic sentiment in favor of policies such as neutralism and demilitarization? These questions are extremely difficult to answer on the basis of empirical data. Students of international affairs, however, will have to answer these and other questions if they wish to help future leaders make decisions on the basis of national, regional, and global interests.

REGIONAL FUNCTIONAL ORGANIZATIONS: THE WESTERN EUROPEAN EXPERIMENT

Regional functional organizations are limited-membership and limited-purpose organizations according to the typology we adopted in Chapter 14. They exemplify best the functionalist approach to regional integration that begins, as we noted above, with nonpolitical cooperative arrangements that, ideally, will spill over into political integration with the passage of time. Good examples of organizations in this category are the Central American Common Market (CACM), the Andean Group, the Latin American Free Trade Association (LAFTA), the Association of South East Asian Nations (ASEAN), the Council for Mutual Economic Assistance (CMEA), and the highly potent and publicized Organization of Petroleum Exporting Countries (OPEC).[9]

[9]Although Arab oil-producing states located in the Middle East provide the critical mass of OPEC, one can hardly refer to this organization as *regional* given globally dispersed members such as Nigeria and Venezuela.

The most advanced cluster of regional functional organizations, however, has been developed in Western Europe. Accordingly, we shall focus our attention on the European experience. We shall then offer some generalizations about regional integration and try to answer some interesting questions about the future of experiments in this area.

One of the first postwar organizations to be formed (August 1949) was the Council of Europe, headquartered in Strasbourg, France. It was the first timid step in the direction of creating a "United States of Europe." According to its statute, the Council's primary aim was to discuss questions of common concern to Western European states in order to reach agreements and take joint action in economic, social, cultural, scientific, legal, and administrative matters. The Council would promote an environment protecting human rights and fundamental freedoms. The Consultative Assembly of the Council of Europe became a rudimentary type of European parliament. Representation in it was determined in proportion to population; it ranged from eighteen seats for the United Kingdom, Italy, and France to three for Luxembourg. Most parliamentarians participating in the Consultative Assembly are elected by the parliaments of their home states, but they are encouraged to act and vote as individuals and Europeans rather than as national delegates. The major limitation of the Council of Europe is that it can only make recommendations. Consequently, its decisions have primarily moral rather than political weight.

In the spring of 1952, Belgium, France, Italy, Luxembourg, the Netherlands, and West Germany agreed to form the historic European Coal and Steel Community (ECSC). This organization was the brainchild of French Foreign Minister Robert Schuman. It placed under a single, supranational authority the coal-and steel-production facilities of Germany and France and removed distributive restrictions among the six participating countries. The institutional structure of the ECSC has served as a prototype for the European Community that has subsequently been formed.

In 1954, the Western European Union (WEU) was founded, mainly as a defense-oriented Western European agency designed to coordinate and standardize the equipment and the logistic structure of European armed establishments in close cooperation with NATO.

In 1958, the Six—as Belgium, France, Italy, Luxembourg, the Netherlands, and West Germany were referred to—launched an ambitious project named the Common Market—formally, the European Economic Community (EEC). Simultaneously, they formed the European Atomic Energy Community (Euratom or EAEC), whose primary purpose was to stimulate and safeguard the development of atomic energy for peaceful purposes.

Eventually, the ECSC, the EEC, and Euratom were consolidated into a single massive organization, the European Community (EC). The Six were joined in January 1973 by Britain, Denmark, and Ireland, early in 1981, by Greece, and in 1986 by Spain and Portugal. Thus was created the largest economic power on earth. The organization and powers of the European Community have made substantial inroads into the sovereignty of the participating nation-states.

The institutional structure of the European Community is roughly analogous to the various branches of national governments. The chief executive organ of the Community is the Council of Ministers, which is headed by the foreign ministers of the participating states and which can make binding decisions by unanimous vote.

The key administrative organ of the Community is the Commission, which is supported by a large professional staff (nearly nine thousand) headquartered in Brussels and referred to in the literature as the Eurocracy. The Commission is a powerful body of Europe-minded technocrats whose recommendations to the Council of Ministers are generally accepted without much difficulty. The Community has functioned under the legislative umbrella of a European parliament whose members are elected by popular vote in each member state. The European parliament can by a two-thirds vote compel Commission executives to resign, and it is seeking increasing legislative and budgetary functions.

The judicial core of the European Community is the European Court of Justice. Its task is to interpret the founding treaties and settle disputes as they arise. The pathbreaking feature of this court—as we have indicated in Chapter 13—is that besides having compulsory jurisdiction over member states, it can hear cases initiated by individuals, corporations, and other legal entities.

The purposes of the European Community were outlined in the Treaty of Rome (1958). In summary, the main task of the Community is to lay the groundwork for the eventual establishment of a bona fide European federation. Specifically, the European Community is to coordinate and standardize European policies for dealing with monopolies, fixing prices, regulating internal trade flows, subdelegating and rationalizing production, arriving at common standards for working conditions, and developing social security and effective bargaining methods between management and labor groups. In recent years common and coordinated EC policies have also covered matters of foreign affairs such as responding to Middle Eastern frictions, Eastern European tensions, and other questions.

The record so far, despite occasional friction, some setbacks, and intermittent crises, has been more than impressive. As early as the middle of 1968, eighteen months ahead of its target, the Community had abolished customs duties and quota restrictions for trade among member states. Relatively unimpeded mobility of labor has been achieved, and agricultural policies of the participating states have been harmonized. Common external tariffs have been agreed upon as a means of regulating trade with all external states, and the Community has amassed a multi-billion-dollar collective fund, which can be used to stabilize the economy of any member state experiencing severe balance-of-payments pressures. Starting in 1962, the Community began to put into operation structures designed to implement a common agricultural regime. The most important of these is the European Agricultural Guidance and Guarantee Fund (EAGGF), whose expenditures, primarily in price supports, reached $14.8 billion in 1983. Seeking to reduce regional disparities in economic growth, the European Regional Development Fund (ERDF) carries out capital investment projects within the twelve nation-states. In 1980, ERDF's assets amounted to nearly $2 billion and were employed in such priority regions as southern Italy and portions of Ireland. The pattern in the range and inclusiveness of Community activity has been one of growth ever since. By 1989 the EC budget amounted to $50.7 billion, while the EAGGF alone topped $30.8 billion.[10]

In spite of all this progress, Western Europe has not managed to amalgamate itself into a political unit. There is still no standard European currency, the sovereignty-conscious Council is still the key organ, and the European parliament, the Commission, and the Court can be short-circuited in times of acute crisis, such as that posed by the Arab oil boycott following the October 1973 Arab-Israeli war. Yet, the year 1992 marks a historical threshold in the Community's development given that a "single market" without any type of legal or administrative restrictions will have become a fact of life.

SOME GENERALIZATIONS ABOUT REGIONAL INTEGRATION

A number of questions confront the analyst of the post–World War II European setting: Is integration mutually beneficial to the economic interests of participating nation-states? Is integration a gradually upward-moving process leading to political unification, or are there cyclical phases of integration and disintegration? Does integration lessen the incidence of conflict within integrated regions as well as between integrated regions? What are the effects of integration on the cultural, legal, political, and economic systems of participants? Do certain categories of people—for example, the young, ethnic minorities, farmers, workers, the middle classes, the rich, the poor, women, the more educated, and the less educated—favor or oppose integration? Is integration more or less effective when it binds relatively equal (in terms of size, population, economic, and military capacity) national actors? How does one differentiate among processes involving integration, interdependence, dependency, penetration, and various forms of colonialism? Is it better to start integrating at the economic, social, political, or military sphere if one wishes to generate spillover effects and enhance the chances for unification? These questions are many and difficult, and their answers tentative, elusive, and at times unconvincing. We shall attempt, nonetheless, to respond to some of these questions by synthesizing briefly some of the findings of the literature on regional integration.[11]

First, nation-states participating in regional-integration organizations tend to exhibit strong economic growth rates. Hence, it could be argued that integration is mutually advantageous for participants. But this finding has been

[10]*General Report of the Commission of the European Communities,* no. 17 (Brussels, February 1984); and *European Communities Bulletin,* no. 6 (Brussels, 1988), pp. 122–3.

[11]For comprehensive review articles on the literature of integration, see Chadwick F. Alger, "Research on Research: A Decade of Quantitative and Field Research on International Organizations," *International Organization,* 24 (Summer 1970); Leon N. Lindberg and Stuart A. Scheingold, eds., "Regional Integration: Theory and Research," special issue of *International Organization,* 24 (Autumn 1970).

confounded by frequent instances of nonparticipants also experiencing dramatic economic growth rates during the same period. For example, both Japan and Canada experienced dramatic industrial and economic growth in the 1960s without formally integrating themselves with larger political and economic communities.

Second, European integration since World War II (defined in terms of volume of transactions and development of multinational and supranational institutions) appears to be following a pattern of growth that can be represented by the following curve:

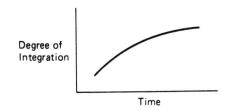

The most likely pattern for European integration in the next few years is one of slow growth leveling off at a given plateau, rather than one of sudden upward or downward fluctuations. We cannot, however, generalize with any degree of confidence from the European experience by projecting a similar pattern of integration onto other regions of the world.

Third, on the basis of the post–World War II European experience, it appears that integration correlates positively with decreasing conflict both within and between integrated units. For example, if one were to compare today's relatively peaceful environment with the conflict-ridden environment of Eastern and Western Europe prior to World War II, one would be tempted to attribute the current state of armed peace to the creation and operation of institutions such as the European Community and the Soviet-led CMEA. Naturally, the skeptic could argue that the European peace is the product of many other factors, such as the shifting of major military power away from Europe (to the United States and the Soviet Union), war fatigue, wiser leadership, bipolarity, the balance of terror, and even the historical cycles of war and peace.

Fourth, the effects of integration on the social, cultural, economic, and political systems and processes of participants are very difficult to assess. There is no question that integration has a long-range standardizing effect on the participants' political and cultural characteristics. In the EC, for example, the political standard appears to be one of pluralistic parliamentary democracies of the social interventionist (welfarist) variety, market- rather than budget-regulated economies, and secular and nonideological orientations. To mention two specific examples, considerable moral and material pressure was exerted by Western Europe on the authoritarian regimes of Portugal and Greece until they collapsed in 1974 and were replaced by functioning democracies. This pressure was designed to prompt the two regimes to abide by the human-rights norms prevalent throughout Western Europe.

Fifth, studies conducted indicate that the strongest proponents of European integration are to be found among the young, the affluent, and the highly educated. This does not mean, necessarily, that youth and "establishment" groups throughout the world are in favor of regional integration. It is clear, however, that integration does not benefit all sectors of the participating societies uniformly. Regional competition often threatens established groups, such as protectionist labor unions, small and subsidized national industries, farmers, nationalists, and privileged political, religious, and ethnic groups, who perceive that a larger and regionally defined community might threaten their traditional position in a narrow national setting.

Sixth, equality or inequality in the territorial size of participants is not a good predictor of the success or failure of integration. Geographically large France and geographically small Belgium seem to benefit mutually from their participation in European integration organizations. On the other hand, integration among territorial equals—for example, Belgium and Holland or West Germany and France—also seems to work quite well. However, integration between industrialized nation-states and less-developed nation-states frequently results in excessive economic dependence of the weak on the strong, which tends to perpetuate and even increase the gaps between the rich and the poor partners. So it might be argued that integration works best among economic equals and works worst among economic unequals. Further, political, ideological, and social affinity appears to enhance integration.

Seventh, a good way to differentiate among concepts such as integration, interdependence, domination, and dependency is to survey the attitudes of a society's government, its opposition elites, and various sectors of its general public. Different segments of a society will perceive differently the advantages and disadvantages of economic and political integration. The majority of Norwegians, for example, voted in 1972 to stay out of the European Community. What some groups or political parties will consider mutually beneficial integration, others will denounce as exploitation and undue dependency. Periodic surveys of various groups within a society should provide us with helpful assessments of shifting attitudes in that society regarding the merits and demerits of integration.

Eighth, it could be argued that economic activities enjoy the highest spillover rate and military activities have the lowest spillover rate. From this standpoint, one could predict that integration is more likely to be enhanced by the activities of the EC and CMEA than by those of NATO and the Warsaw Pact. This assertion, however, cannot be easily substantiated. There is considerable overlap in the memberships of NATO and EC on the one hand and Warsaw Pact and CMEA on the other. Therefore, we cannot easily credit economic organizations with greater amounts of spillover than military/defense organizations.

In retrospect, it appears that the Western European experience since World War II has proceeded under sets of rules and assumptions that are quite different from those that apply to other parts of the world. For example, in the Middle East, Southeast Asia, East Asia, and southern Africa, the incidence of internal and international conflict since World War II has been higher than the incidence of Western and Eastern European conflict. One could speculate that today's conflict-ridden regions are going through the preintegration stage that Europe experienced from the 1700s through the 1940s. Our hope is that these regions will not have to experience painful and disillusioning wars and accompanying privation and destruction in order to realize that they must find peaceful techniques for the resolution of territorial and ideological issues.

One could argue that it would be prudent for conflict-prone nation-states to recognize the global and regional status quo and thereby to attain the type of political and territorial legitimacy characteristic of nonconflict areas such as North America and Western and Eastern Europe. This simply means that nation-states in an integrated region do not fight wars over who controls what territory. So, nation-states, their publics, and especially their leaders must have cooperative attitudes in order to proceed with regional integration. Once this attitudinal take-off point is reached, a cycle is initiated that looks something like this:[12]

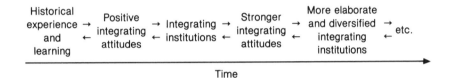

Time

THE DEBATE AMONG REGIONALISTS, UNIVERSALISTS, AND REGIME ANALYSTS

Students of international politics have debated the relative merits of regionalism and universalism as building blocs of world peace. The proponents of the regional approach to peace usually argue that regional integration is a halfway house between international anarchy (today's reality) and world integration (tomorrow's dream). They find that the relative cultural, economic, political, and geographic affinity within a region lends itself to more effective organization. Moreover, nation-states participating in schemes of regional integration can organize—politically and economically—in continent-sized operations, thus minimizing the erosive influence of the superpowers. Functionally oriented regionalists concede that integration works better in the economic sectors of societies but are convinced that with time, patience, and wisdom economic cooperation will spill over into the political sectors.[13]

---

[12]This *takeoff point* is an abstract point that is nearly impossible to specify empirically, and consequently it is open to several questions. For example, when are collective attitudes ripe for democracy, for peace, or for cooperation? Is it possible to measure attitudes that are conducive to integration or coercion? Is it not too risky to assume that once an attitudinal threshold has been crossed, attitudes will remain positive over time? Could not attitudes of cooperativeness degenerate to the attitudes of fear and suspicion that feed the fires of war and other conflicts?

[13]See for example Karl W. Deutsch et al., "Political Community and the North Atlantic Area," in *International Political Communities* (New York: Doubleday, 1966).

The proponents of universalism, for their part, argue that despite the appeal of the regionalist argument, the problem of attaining peace can best be faced at the global level. They point out that peace is indivisible and cannot readily be relegated to regional authorities. Great powers, in other words, will continue to reserve the right to influence world events heavily, regionalist rhetoric notwithstanding. Further, argue the universalists, the development of large, highly autonomous, and politically and economically integrated regions raises the specter of prolonged global wars among continent-sized regions reminiscent of George Orwell's *1984* scenario. So, the universalists concede advantages to economic-integration efforts at the regional level. But they feel that the question of global peace and security should best be left to global organizations, such as a concert of superpowers. Ideally, such organizations would reflect consensus on matters of mutual survival and would operate through the United Nations and other forms of global diplomacy.[14]

The battle against disease highlights the logic of the universalist position. Rita Süssmuth, West German minister for youth, family affairs, women and health, told an audience in Washington, D.C., on July 25, 1988, that only international cooperation can overcome the threat of acquired immune deficiency syndrome (AIDS) and endorsed the concept of a *world domestic policy.* Summarizing the universalist argument, she admonished that a commitment to "global thinking" meant respect for cultural diversity, not a demand for conformity.[15]

Regime analysts, producing theoretically oriented publications with increasing frequency in the 1980s, have sought to steer a middle course between the globalists and the regionalists. Extending their thought from premises found in functionalist and regional integration studies, influential authors such as Robert Keohane, Joseph Nye, Jr., and Gerard Ruggie focused their attention on complex transnational networks of political-economic interdependence in narrow sectors of international activity—e.g., trade, exchange rate regulation, deep-seabed exploitation, oil and energy production and distribution, nuclear proliferation—which they called *regimes.*[16] The concept of *regime,* despite its definitional ambiguity, permitted these authors to cluster the activities of governments, international organizations, multinational corporations, and other actors under a single conceptual roof. Thus one could describe the activities of regimes, such as mechanisms for a coordinated international effort to combat terrorism working at the subregional, regional, and global levels and involving the inputs of governmental as well as nongovernmental agencies.

The problem with this debate, as with many other academic debates, is

---

[14]Two good examples of what is referred to as a *neorealist/globalist* position are Kenneth Waltz, *Theory of International Politics* (Reading, Mass.: Addison-Wesley, 1979); and Robert G. Gilpin, *War and Change in World Politics* (Cambridge: Cambridge University Press, 1981).

[15]Based on notes taken by James H. Wolfe at lecture.

[16]Admittedly, *regime* is a hard concept to define specifically. The most widely accepted, if somewhat ambiguous, definition describes regimes as "implicit or explicit principles, norms, rules and decision-making procedures around which actors' expectations converge in a given area of international relations." The author of this definition is Stephen Krasner, "Structural Causes and Regime Consequences: Regimes as Intervening Variables," *International Organization,* 36 (Spring 1982), 185.

that it proceeds on a dichotomous basis. In other words, the debate seeks to resolve whether peace is better served by the regional, the global, or the regime approach. This implies that one approach is good for peace and the others are bad. In fact, all three approaches are good for peace, are greatly interdependent, and each is probably inevitable. People who are interested in working for peace will certainly find ways to do so, whether at the neighborhood, city, state, regional, functional, or global level. There is no single, magic formula for peace. If there were such a formula, humankind would have taken advantage of it long ago. So the search for peace will continue, and different antidotes will be used by governmental and private groups on a trial-and-error basis. Given the deadliness of the weaponry currently available, let us hope that there will be very little error in the years to come.

ASSESSING REGIONALISM

We can now conclude with some generalizations about regionalism as a whole. Regional defense organizations tend to be *macroregional*.[17] Macroregions have been defined as areas in which the maximum distance between participating capitals ranges from three thousand to eleven thousand miles. Of course, the term regional is quite inapplicable in such unwieldy and inclusive arrangements. Regional defense organizations are led, in most instances, by a superpower partner (either the United States or the USSR). So it would be fair to look at organizations such as NATO and the Warsaw Pact as manifestations of the global system of nation-states, rather than as regional systems. As we suggested earlier, defense organizations are global alliances of superpowers and are regional in name only.

Regional economic organizations could be referred to, on the other hand, as *microregional*. This means—once more, arbitrarily—that the maximum distance between participating capitals is 3,000 miles or less. Most economic communities conform to this criterion of size and inclusiveness. For example, maximum distances between capitals are 1,700 miles for the EC, 500 miles for the Central American Common Market (CACM), 1,100 miles for the Central African Customs Union (UDEAC), and only 200 miles for the Benelux arrangement. Exceptions in this category are the Latin American Free Trade Association (LAFTA)—4,700 miles—and the Eastern European Common Market (CMEA)—13,000 miles. It is also fair to say that the more well-integrated regional organizations are the economic microregional ones, since they are founded on geographic, economic, and, naturally, cultural interdependences rather than on great-power political and military control.

Historically, regional organizations have been growing faster, absolutely and relatively, than global organizations. Mere numbers of organizations do not, however, provide a clear indicator of the importance, utility, size, impact, or effi-

---

[17]Macroregional and microregional organizations are differentiated in Joseph S. Nye, "Regional Institutions," in *Regional Politics and World Order*, ed. Richard A. Falk and Saul H. Mendlovitz (San Francisco: W. H. Freeman, 1973), pp. 78–93.

cacy of these international actors. Not all organizations are of equal importance, and it would be absurd to weigh the United Nations equally with the Central American Common Market.

Regional affinity or participation in regional organizations does not necessarily predict political cohesiveness among the participants as manifested in their voting in the United Nations. Voting "cohesiveness"[18] in the United Nations varies dramatically among different regions and among different issue-categories.[19] The Soviet bloc demonstrates the greatest voting solidarity in nearly every issue-category. The Commonwealth of Nations exhibits the least solidarity on most issues. The Organization of American States is quite cohesive except in the issue-category of development. The Arab League is quite cohesive on the issues of Palestine and decolonization, but quite divided in other issue-categories. Western Europe is quite heterogeneous in most issue-categories; however, on East-West (cold-war) issues it exhibits considerable solidarity. Finally, the Afro-Asian nation-states are quite cohesive on the issues of decolonization and development, but are divided on East-West and intra–Third World issues. Groupings of states also exhibit varying degrees of distance from or voting coincidence with the United States voting record in the U.N. General Assembly. For example, during the Assembly's forty-second session (1987), the average voting coincidence of all the United Nations members with the United States was 18.6 percent, reflecting a downward shift compared to 1986. The highest records of voting agreement were registered by NATO allies and other states friendly to the United States (Israel scoring the highest, 80.0 percent, followed by Great Britain, 79.2 percent). The Arab group, the Warsaw Pact, and other countries closely associated with the Soviet Union registered the lowest levels of voting coincidence (e.g., Cuba, 5.8 percent, and Syria, 5.0 percent).[20]

Unquestionably, Western Europe is the most advanced region in the world in the development of international institutions. It has established organizations such as the Common Market and the European Court of Justice. As we noted before, individuals have the opportunity to appeal directly to this Court and thereby go over the heads of their national governments. On the other hand, if one were to view multinational, multicultural, and continent-sized countries such as the United States, the Soviet Union, India, and China as integrated regions, then Western Europe would appear to be lagging far behind in terms of regional integration. We could therefore increase our knowledge of the process of integration not only by studying the successful European institutional experiments since World War II but also by studying the formation of politically unified nation-states out of separate political units in the cases of Switzerland, Germany, Italy, the United States, the USSR, China, and others.

---

[18]The degree to which one can measure accurately cohesiveness, or solidarity, is debatable both conceptually and mathematically. We shall not enter into the controversy in this book.

[19]The term *issue-area* is fashionable in the literature of international relations as an equivalent to *issue-category.*

[20]For these and other statistics see U.S. Department of State, *Report to Congress on Voting Practices in the United Nations,* (Washington, D.C., March 14, 1988).

In retrospect, political unification has been served by coercion as well as it has been served by functional cooperation. But political unification through war and other coercive means is outside our definition of integration—as we strongly suggested above. The advantage of integration theory is that it offers peaceful and realistic techniques for the transformation of the international system from anarchy to a rational and just global order. The future, however, is likely to remain suspended between the poles of conflict and cooperation, war and peace, coercion and influence, might and law. Trends toward integration can reverse themselves and run into serious obstacles. We must not assume that regional or global integration is leading inevitably to global unity. As we saw in Chapter 4, Europe prior to the French Revolution was led by aristocratic elites whose manners and attitudes were quite homogeneous (i.e., European) and who could shift loyalties from one sovereign to the next without a sense of loss or shame. Jean-Jacques Rousseau (1712–78), the great French political theorist, vividly described the erosion of national and patriotic values of his times: "Today there are no longer Frenchmen, Germans, Spaniards, or even Englishmen; there are only Europeans. . . . They are at home wherever there is money to steal or women to seduce."[21]

Yet these early attitudes of European oneness did not prevent the continent from being plunged into two major nationalistic wars in the twentieth century. For the sake of regional and global peace, let us hope that the patterns of integration in operation since the end of World War II will continue undisturbed for some time to come.

SUGGESTIONS FOR FURTHER STUDY

The role of regional organizations in framing the interests of their members is the subject of Stephen D. Krasner, ed., "International Regimes," a thematic issue of *International Organization* 36 (Spring 1982). A case study of regime theory is *European Communities, Steps to European Unity* (Luxembourg: Office for Official Publications, 1980). Gayl D. Ness and Steven R. Brechin have investigated the relationship between administrative science and regional communities in "Bridging the Gap: International Organizations as Organizations," *International Organization,* 42 (Spring 1988), 245–73. The effect of the Organization of American States on its international subsystem is a topic of Harold Eugene Davis and Larman C. Wilson, *Latin American Foreign Policies: An Analysis* (Baltimore: Johns Hopkins University Press, 1975). William C. Cromwell has examined collective defense and regional organization in *The Eurogroup and NATO* (Lexington, Mass.: Lexington Books, 1974). Harold K. Jacobson has adopted a historical sociological framework for the study of international integration in *Networks of Interdependence: International Organizations and the Global Political System,* 2nd ed. (New York: Knopf, 1984). For theoretical insights into the formation of political communities, see

---

[21]Quoted in George H. Sabine, *A History of Political Theory* (New York: Holt, Rinehart & Winston, 1961), p. 593.

Amitai Etzioni, "A Paradigm for the Study of Political Unification," *World Politics,* 15 (October 1962), 44–74; and Arend Lijphart, "Cultural Diversity and Theories of Political Unification," *Canadian Journal of Political Science,* 4 (1971), 1–14. The word *community* itself is subject to diverse interpretations, as indicated in Philip E. Jacob and James V. Toscano, eds., *The Integration of Political Communities* (Philadelphia: Lippincott, 1964), and Elmer Plischke, ed., *Systems of Integrating the International Community* (Princeton, N.J.: Van Nostrand, 1964).

16

THE INTERNATIONAL ECONOMY: WIDENING THE POLITICAL NET?

Given our focus so far on the processes of international politics, the concepts of power, interest, nationalism, conflict, law, and diplomacy have dominated our discussion. In comparing the international system of the nineteenth century with that of today, it is apparent that a new and vital dimension has developed: *global economic interdependence.* Since World War II, dramatic advances in such technological fields as transportation and communication have promoted commercial and financial links among states, often irrespective of the differences among their social systems. The outcome of this course of events has been a multiplication of the opportunities for both conflict and cooperation among states and the entry of powerful, economically based nonstate actors onto the international scene.[1] In this chapter we seek to demonstrate that contemporary international politics cannot be effectively understood without focusing on vital processes such as international trade, international financial regulation, and the impact of imbalances in nation-states' balances of payments.

INTERNATIONAL TRADE: THE ARGUMENT BETWEEN FREE TRADERS AND PROTECTIONISTS

International trade has grown exponentially in the two decades between 1960 and 1980. Trade has been generally defended in the international relations litera-

[1]For a detailed discussion of nonstate actors, see Chapter 18. For an influential book pointing to the need of studying economic variables affecting international politics see Robert Keohane and Joseph S. Nye, Jr., *Power and Interdependence: World Politics in Transition* (Boston: Little, Brown, 1977).

ture because it fulfills a number of socially useful functions.[2] Through trade, countries rich in certain resources or efficient in the manufacture of certain products can exchange them for needed goods from other countries, with mutual benefit. Trends in the 1980s, however, suggest that trade growth may be leveling off and that a trade-reducing psychology of protectionism of "homegrown" products may be on the upswing.

Not all countries of the world rely upon trade equally. Some countries, such as Britain, the Netherlands, Belgium, Italy, and Japan, depend heavily on trade to maintain their economic well-being. Other countries, such as the United States, the Soviet Union, and the Peoples' Republic of China, are much less dependent. For example, about one-fourth of Britain's and about one-fifth of Canada's national income is derived from foreign trade. Foreign products amount to nearly half of the goods sold in the Netherlands. In contrast, exports and imports constitute only about 6 percent of the American gross national product (GNP).

Yet even the United States is trade dependent. It relies to a considerable extent upon foreign suppliers for the raw materials that are critical to its industries. For example, the United States imports large portions of its iron-ore, copper, and wood-pulp supplies. It also imports more than 90 percent of the bauxite and manganese needed, respectively, for aluminum and steel production. In the case of chrome, cobalt, nickel, tin, and platinum, it depends almost totally on imports. Further, the United States is becoming increasingly dependent on foreign markets for its vital supply of petroleum.[3] So-called luxury products, such as coffee, tea, chocolate, and bananas (which the affluent consider necessities), are grown primarily outside the United States. On the other side of the coin, the well-being of a number of export-oriented American industries, such as agriculture, mining, and manufacturing, depends substantially on the continuation of normal trade relationships with the outside world.

Looking at this brief analysis of America's trade profile, it should be obvious that the United States—despite its relative self-sufficiency—needs trade in order to complement and cultivate its complex production base. Other countries, such as Britain and Japan depend so heavily on trade that they might face extremely serious dislocations, if not utter chaos, if their trade relationships with the outside world were to stop altogether.

Economic and political considerations begin to merge when one asks the basic question of how the utilities and disutilities of trade are related to the power and security interests of various nation-states. With occasional exceptions,

---

[2]In this section, we are heavily indebted to the clear exposition of the subject of international economics presented by Robert L. Heilbroner and Lester C. Thurow, *The Economic Problem*, 4th ed. (Englewood Cliffs, N.J.: Prentice-Hall, 1975), especially pp. 551–69. For other useful discussions on the subject of international trade, see C. F. Bergsten et al., "International Economics and International Politics: A Framework for Analysis," *International Organization* (Winter 1975), 3–36; and Ernest Preeg, *Economic Blocs and U.S. Foreign Policy* (Washington, D.C.: National Planning Association, 1974). For a comprehensive work on the politics of economics, see Robert G. Gilpin, *The Political Economy of International Relations* (Princeton, N.J.: Princeton University Press, 1987).

[3]See Ernest J. Wilson, III, "World Politics and International Energy Markets," *International Organization*, 41 (Winter 1987), pp. 125–149.

economically oriented analysts tend to consider trade a positive force in international society. Such analysts argue in favor of free trade at the global level, which they believe results in planetary advantage. On the other hand, politically oriented analysts tend to emphasize the importance of economic autarchy (national self-sufficiency), which frees a country from external dependence and maximizes its autonomy—in short, protects its sovereignty and its power.

Stripped of political considerations, a rational and convincing case can be made for free international trade. This case is supported by the logic of what economists since the days of David Ricardo (1772–1823) have called the *law of comparative advantage.* This law asserts that the division of labor and the specialization of other factors of production (land, capital, and entrepreneurship) are best determined through the free operation of market forces. For example, this law would discourage the growth of bananas in Canadian hothouses or the development of a fishing and canning industry in a landlocked country. The goods produced in these industries would simply be too costly and not competitive in the free market. Therefore, each region specializes in what it can produce best, and everyone gains by the fair exchange of these most efficiently produced items. For the law of comparative advantage to work well, at least two conditions must hold: first and foremost, a truly unencumbered movement of goods across national boundaries; and second, competitive markets, an absence of monopolies and oligopolies, fair and informative advertising practices, and reasonable transportation costs. In short, the international economy should function in a manner that is free from political calculations and intrusions.

The advocates of national economic autarky are very dubious about what they consider to be "idealistic assumptions" made by the free traders. The prescriptions of the free traders may appear workable in the purified world of economic theory, they argue, but these prescriptions are rarely applicable to real international economic practices. The opponents of free trade therefore employ mostly para-economic or para-political rather than purely economic arguments. Chief among these arguments is that one's country must maintain a strong and self-sufficient national defense. The opponents of free trade also believe that the prolonged economic specialization prescribed by the advocates of comparative advantage tends to cultivate long-range and sometimes irreversible dependencies, thus rendering one's country vulnerable to external "blackmail" or lesser forms of diplomatic manipulation.

Other arguments are often heard against free trade and in favor of strong tariffs, quotas, and other forms of economic "protection." One such argument is that labor unions in advanced countries should be opposed to the importation of cheap products from backward and oppressive countries in which the workers are paid only "slave wages." These cheap imports, so the argument goes, tend to disestablish traditional domestic industries. Eventually, they force plants to close down, thereby creating unemployment, privation, and political unrest.

Anti–free-trade advocates in less-developed countries emphasize the need to protect infant domestic industries from the competition of more efficient industries in developed states. Further, they argue that small and poor states must

avoid the embrace of excolonialist states that kept their colonies externally dependent by discouraging all but extractive industries and preventing them from
diversifying their economies.

The proponents of free trade have advanced a number of rejoinders to
these arguments. They point out that tariffs, quotas, and other means of hinder-
ing free competition and the free flow of trade have tended to subsidize inefficient domestic industries by rendering them immune to the challenges of more
efficient foreign producers. The long-range result has been overstaffed, inefficient, unimaginative, antiquated, and underproductive domestic industries.

Further, the free traders point out that tariffs and quotas are not one-
way instruments. Rather, foreign countries tend to employ them in retaliation,
thereby creating unemployment and hardships for the workers in one's own
export-related industries.

The free traders grant the protectionists' argument that uncontrolled
economic competition among states dislocates noncompetitive domestic industries and leads to unemployment and its resulting hardships. They recommend
as a remedy that governments of nation-states affected by foreign competition
should employ programs such as unemployment compensation, labor retraining,
and labor relocation in more competitive enterprises.

Finally, in response to the argument relating trade dependency to national security, the free traders point out that policies of autarky and economic
warfare are highly contagious and tend to escalate into political disputes and
eventually into costly military confrontations. Free trade, on the other hand, sus-
tains interdependence, which in turn minimizes the incidence of war. Siamese
twins—probably the best analogy to economic interdependence—cannot afford
to stab and kill each other. Economic interdependence, the argument concludes,
shifts international conflicts and confrontations from the fields of battle to the
board rooms of large corporations and the staff rooms of governmental
economic-planning bureaus.

Before evaluating the merits of each side to this debate, we should note
that the volume of goods traded has increased steadily since World War II. This
trend is likely to continue, short of another worldwide conflagration, whose consequences upon trade (as well as upon other forms of international interaction)
would definitely be retrogressive. In the future, we are likely to continue seeing
peaks and valleys of international trade growth and decline that reflect periods
of free economic exchange and periods of competitive nationalist protectionism,
respectively.

Evaluating the arguments of the free traders (closer to idealist premises)
and the protectionists (closer to realist premises), we find that there is considerable merit in the logic of each side. The free traders have the edge, provided that
their assumptions about the free flow of goods based on purely economic criteria
obtain. The positive experience of large regional economic markets, such as the
United States and Western Europe seems to support the argument favoring specialization of production and maximization of welfare through effective and vigorous trade practices.

Unfortunately, free-trade principles have not been applied to international practice. As we saw in Chapter 9, trade and other economic activities have been employed at times as tools of diplomacy and even warfare. In a world where labor mobility is severely inhibited, where economic practices are subject to the unchecked decisions of sovereign governments, and where wage, price, and standard-of-living differentials are huge, countries cannot afford to be without at least the rudiments of diversified domestic production, which could sustain them during times of military and economic emergency.

As we observed in the previous chapter, international economic integration is often measured by the progress made in the volume and variety of goods traded among states. Economic integration, in turn, is expected to spill over into political integration. In this chapter, however, we cannot fail to point out that governmental decisions to lift artificial restrictions inhibiting the flow of goods and services cannot be made to stick, and that confidence in economic interdependence cannot be built unless a certain level of political integration is attained first. Free planetary trade may therefore have to await the development of planetary political integration. This may take a very long time—if, in fact, it is ever achieved.

THE REGULATION OF INTERNATIONAL TRANSACTIONS

The prices of goods that are imported and exported are strongly affected by the foreign-exchange rates of the currencies of the trading countries.[4] The foreign-exchange rate is a measure of equivalency between different national currencies. This equivalency is either the result of direct agreements between countries pegging the exchange rates of their respective currencies at a given ratio or the product of market forces of supply and demand, which determine the going exchange rate for these currencies. To illustrate, during the mid-1940s one British pound was equivalent to four American dollars. At that time, therefore, an English product selling in England for £10 could be imported into the United States for $40 plus packaging, transportation, and delivery costs. By the late 1940s, however, the value of the British pound had fallen substantially: The former ratio of £1 to $4 became a ratio of £1 to $2.75. As a result, the item that had previously been imported for $40 could now be procured for only $27.50. The impact of this particular fluctuation in exchange rates, understandably, was to increase American demand for British products (now relatively cheaper for dollar holders) and, correspondingly, to decrease British buyers' demand for American products.

[4]In this section, we are again indebted to Heilbroner and Thurow, *The Economic Problem*, especially pp. 570–600. For other useful readings on the subject of foreign-exchange regulation, see Gerald Meier, *Problems of a World Monetary Order* (New York: Oxford University Press, 1974); Preeg, *Economic Blocs and U.S. Foreign Policy;* Bruce Moon, "Exchange Rate System, Policy Distortion and the Maintenance of Trade Dependence," *International Organization,* 36 (Autumn 1982), 715–739; and Ulrich Pfister and Christian Suter, "International Financial Relations as Part of the World System," *International Studies Quarterly,* 31, no. 3 (September 1987), 239–72.

Thus, the direction and volume of trade is affected—apart from policies of protectionism—by the fluctuations in the exchange rate of currencies. In the sense that they largely determine the "price" of goods traded, devalued currencies tend to increase one's exports and decrease one's imports. Figure 16-1 reflects the fluctuations in the exchange rates of key currencies from 1978 to 1987.

Allowing market forces to determine the ratio of exchange among currencies has been considered by traditional economists to be the most effective way to regulate trade flows and to restore trade imbalances to equilibrium. For example, if two countries developed trade relationships in which one was doing the bulk of the exporting and the other the bulk of the importing, then freely fluctuating exchange rates would eventually adjust themselves to correct the trade imbalance. If, for the sake of illustration, we were to assume that many more goods were being imported from the United States by Italy than from Italy by the United States, then the Italians would consistently need more dollars (with which to pay for American goods), and the Americans would need fewer liras (with which to buy Italian goods). Thus, over time, the disproportionate demand for dollars would increase the "value" of the dollar and decrease that of the lira. Correspondingly, the exchange rate would shift in favor of the dollar. The gradual impact of this shift would be to increase the price of American goods for Italian buyers and to decrease the price of Italian goods for American buyers.

Figure 16-1 Exchange Rates of Key Currencies, 1978 to 1987

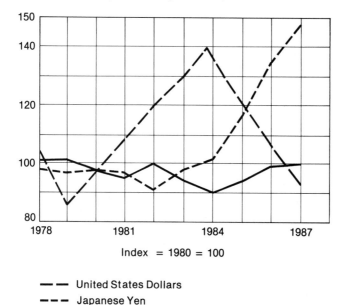

Index = 1980 = 100

— — United States Dollars
- - - Japanese Yen
——— German Marks

SOURCE: Adapted from *World Development Report, 1988* (Washington, D.C.: World Bank, 1988), p. 20. Used with the permission of Oxford University Press.

Eventually, this process would begin to reverse the original imbalance in Italian-American trade relationships.

Related to the debate between free traders and protectionists is the controversy (admittedly somewhat more esoteric) between the proponents of free-floating exchange rates and the proponents of rates that are fixed by governmental agreements. Usually, the proponents of free trade tend to favor floating exchange rates based on freely functioning market forces. They are opposed to fixed exchange rates because the rigidity of these rates invites long-term disequilibrium in the balance of payments, especially among countries that are heavy importers of goods and services.[5] Eventually import-dependent countries are forced to devaluate their currencies sharply in order to balance their payments, an act that disrupts their trade and investment relationships.

On the other hand, the proponents of fixed foreign-exchange rates usually exhibit a protectionist orientation toward international trade. They argue that only fixed exchange rates can assure long-range stability and predictability in international trade and investment relationships. Fixed rates also discourage private speculators from trying to take advantage of exchange-rate fluctuations by strategically buying and selling selected currencies.

Since World War II, the international economic system has operated on the basis of fixed foreign-exchange rates. The basic rules of the game were drawn up during a major international economic and monetary conference held at Bretton Woods, New Hampshire, in July 1944. It was agreed that most world currencies were to be valued in relation to gold as well as to the American dollar. The value of the dollar was in turn pegged at the rate of $35 per ounce of gold. Thus, after World War II, the dollar succeeded the British pound as the world's central currency—a role that had been played quite effectively by the pound throughout the nineteenth century and up to the end of World War II. The currencies of most remaining countries were then pegged in relationship to the dollar at reasonable exchange rates. No rate fluctuations above 1 percent were to be permitted without mutual consultation. To provide for such international consultation, those who assembled at Bretton Woods established the International Monetary Fund (IMF). The purpose of the IMF was to act as a monitor and as a clearing agency of monetary transactions among nation-states. If a country experienced a chronic unfavorable balance of payments in its trade relationships, it would be authorized to devaluate its currency following highly confidential negotiations within the IMF. Ideally, this devaluation would correct the imbalance by encouraging exports and discouraging imports by the deficit country.

[5]A country's *balance of payments* comprises its total exchange of payments with the rest of the world. These payments account for all the commodities exchanged through trade (the balance of trade); for the exchange of services rendered (for example, tourist, travel, and transportation expenditures and military transactions); for unilateral transfers of funds (such as immigrant remittances, foreign aid, and emergency relief); and for the exchange of long-term and short-term capital transactions (such as investments by private business in foreign enterprises, the purchase of foreign stocks and bonds, and the movements of private savings accounts in and out of the country). The *balance of payments* should be distinguished from its subconcept, the *balance of trade,* which accounts *only* for transactions involving exchange of commodities and excludes payments rendered for services and various other types of transfers of funds.

The international monetary system established at Bretton Woods seemed to work quite well until the late 1960s. The system had been described informally by economists as operating on a "gold and dollar standard." That meant that the U.S. Treasury was willing at any time to sell to foreign holders of dollar accounts the dollar equivalent in gold that was being stored in what appeared to be inexhaustible quantities at Fort Knox, Kentucky. Thus, foreign individuals, firms, and banks were expected to remain secure in holding large deposits of dollars. With these holdings they could procure imports from any country, because dollars were considered "as good as gold."

The early 1970s witnessed an acute crisis that threatened to destroy the very foundations of the postwar international economic structure. The American dollar was dealt a very severe blow by this crisis, and its position as the invulnerable reserve currency of the world was ended. The crisis was the result of a number of converging factors, chief among which was the decreasing competitiveness of American products in the face of extremely vigorous and imaginative industrial challengers from Western Europe and Japan. In 1971, the United States experienced the shock of a deficit in its balance of trade (that is, the total value of its imports was greater than the total value of its exports) for the first time since 1895. This deficit was a far cry from the trade surpluses of as much as $7 billion per year that the United States had enjoyed only a decade earlier. The Americans also suffered a deficit in their balance of payments, which was due primarily to skyrocketing military costs outside the continental United States. These costs were incurred in the long and stalemated war in Vietnam (1965–75). In 1972, the United States sustained a record deficit in its balance of payments—$10.3 billion. To add to this challenge, American multinational corporations, attracted by cheaper labor in Europe, Asia, and other continents, diverted an increasing amount of investment capital in those directions. (The role and significance of multinational corporations will be discussed in greater detail in Chapter 18.) This outflow of investment dollars was ultimately counterbalanced by increased amounts of corporate profit returned to the United States. But the reverse flow of profits was initially not large enough to offset the large balance-of-trade deficit and heavy overseas military expenditures.

In the late 1960s, Western European and Japanese business executives and government officials began watching the deterioration of America's economic condition with increasing concern. These businesses held huge reserves of American dollars, in American banks as well as in their own central banks. Gradually, speculation began to mount that the United States would soon be forced to devalue the dollar in order to arrest the mounting deficit in its balance of payments. Naturally, dollar holders everywhere, fearing that this devaluation would hurt them financially, wanted to exchange their dollar holdings for "harder" currencies, such as the German mark, the Swiss franc, and the Japanese yen, or for American gold. This mounting apprehension merely aggravated the condition of the hard-pressed dollar. By 1972, the run on American-stored gold reserves had begun to assume gigantic proportions. That year, the gold stock at Fort Knox fell to the low level of $12 billion, from a high of $24 billion in 1960.

Conversely, dollar holdings in European and other foreign central banks reached nearly $100 billion, as opposed to less than $13 billion in 1960. Theoretically, therefore, even if all of the American gold had been shipped overseas, huge amounts of foreign-held dollar reserves would still have been uncovered.

The world financial crisis was eventually contained by the Nixon administration, which took unprecedented actions between 1971 and 1973. First, it discontinued the sale of gold to foreign private holders of dollar accounts. Eventually, it discontinued the sale of gold altogether, even to the central banks of foreign countries. Consequently, the Nixon administration allowed the price of gold to fluctuate freely in the open market, where it eventually climbed to rates ranging between $300 and $875 per ounce (compared with the postwar pegged rate of $35 per ounce). The effect of these decisions was the virtual abandonment of the postwar gold and dollar standard.

The new financial arrangement involved the adoption of loosely managed floating exchange rates and the free fluctuation of the dollar in relation to European, Japanese, and other foreign currencies. The consequence was a substantial dollar devaluation, which amounted over time to nearly 20 percent. Shortly thereafter, the American balance-of-trade deficit was dramatically reduced and then eliminated. America's financial recovery was also a function of the conclusion of the Vietnam War and the inflationary impact upon European and Japanese industries of the 1973 oil embargo by the Organization of Petroleum Exporting Countries (OPEC). This embargo was followed by huge increases in the price of oil exported by OPEC countries. The inflationary pressures experienced by oil-dependent Western Europe and Japan in turn reduced their competitiveness in regard to American-made goods.

By the mid-1970s, the international system had settled upon an "interim" financial arrangement, which in actuality seems to be lasting a long time. Economists refer to this new international financial system, in which foreign-exchange rates are allowed to fluctuate freely but within certain implicit yet not clearly specified limits as a *dirty-float*. This system is somewhat of a compromise between the arguments of fixed-rate proponents and those of flexible-rate proponents. Since 1973, gold and the American dollar have lost their previous preeminence. There are now a number of currencies (among them, certainly, the dollar, the mark, the yen, and the French and Swiss francs) that can be considered hard-reserve currencies.

In the early 1970s, the International Monetary Fund began assuming an increasing role in international financial regulation. Since the foundation of the IMF in 1944, its range of responsibilities has been growing slowly but steadily. Western and less-developed countries have treated the IMF as an informal, global-scale central bank. (The Soviet Union and a number of communist countries have stayed out of the IMF and the World Bank, which they consider purely the product of capitalist economics. It should be noted, however, that other communist states—such as Afghanistan, the People's Republic of China, Kampuchea, Laos, Romania, Vietnam, and Yugoslavia—have accepted membership in the World Bank and the International Monetary Fund.) Member states of the IMF have agreed to deposit in the organization prearranged shares of gold and currency. In turn, they acquire the right to borrow gold and other countries' currencies from the fund as needed to ease periodic balance-of-payments deficits.

In 1971, the IMF began issuing a new and artificial global reserve currency, referred to as special drawing rights (SDR). The exchange value of SDRs is a function of the relative exchange status of a *basket* (i.e., a group) of hard currencies, such as the ones referred to above. The total amount of SDRs available in the IMF (July 31, 1987) has been estimated to have a dollar value of $116.3 billions.[6] (The value of the SDR on August 31, 1987, was $1.29313 U.S. dollars.) Countries can now transfer SDRs as well as gold and other currencies to their central banks as a stopgap measure for correcting their balance-of-payments deficits, while taking other necessary actions (such as devaluation and the controlling of inflation) to reverse the conditions causing those deficits. The SDRs have the potential to become a central world currency some day, a standard against which the currencies of all nation-states will be valued. It is in this vein that some analysts and journalists have referred to SDRs as "paper gold."

THE BALANCE OF PAYMENTS AS AN INGREDIENT OF NATIONAL POWER

In Chapter 5, we suggested that power is a function of many tangible variables—including a country's size, population, military strength, industrial and agricultural capacity, and general economic well-being—as well as a number of intangible variables. All these variables add up to a national reputation of strength, intermediate capability, or weakness. Balance-of-payments status is often considered a very important indicator of a country's economic health and durability. Hence, it reflects on a country's overall power.

It is, therefore, in regard to the relationship between balance of payments and national power that we witness the intersection and even competition of political and economic considerations during the determination of national policies. From a purely economic viewpoint, a country experiencing balance-of-payments "troubles" is actually better off than a country with a balance-of-payments surplus. A deficit in the balance of trade, for instance, means that a country imports more than it exports and that it is therefore a net gainer of goods and services. From the political viewpoint, however, a deficit country is seen as an externally dependent country, a country unable to secure reserve assets with which to pay for its imports, and in general a country whose products are not competitive in the international market. It is against this backdrop of economic and political considerations that governments faced with balance-of-payments deficits must select policies and programs designed to correct such imbalances. Let us consider six such measures that are available to governments.

[6]The "exchange rate" between the dollar and the SDR fluctuates. In late August 1987 the rate was 1 SDR = 1.293 dollars. For a comprehensive set of statistics regarding the activities of the IMF, see "International Monetary Fund—IMF," *The Europa Yearbook 1988: A World Survey*, Vol. 1 (London: Europa Publications, 1988), pp. 71–74.

First, the government can call for higher interest rates. This action would encourage domestic savings, limit monetary liquidity (availability of money in the market), and generally deflate the economy (in other words, lower prices), all of which would render the country's exports more competitive internationally. Although this measure would tend to improve a country's balance of payments, it would also contribute to domestic unemployment, lower incomes, and other forms of domestic hardship.

Second, the government can restrain the flow of domestic capital abroad. Means of doing this would include taxing the purchase of foreign securities, taxing citizens and firms who wish to invest in business enterprises abroad, and raising the rates of short-term interest at home in order to attract the funds of foreign savers and investors. The problem with this measure is that it invites retaliatory policies by other countries, and eventually limits overall international trade and investment and their benefits.

Third, the government can reduce its foreign aid and expenditures for military bases abroad. Or the government could insist that foreign aid be given only to countries that are willing to buy its national products. The political problem for a government (usually that of an advanced country) that reduces its foreign aid and military presence overseas is that in doing so it reduces its ability to influence the recipient governments and thereby reduces its domain, range, and scope of power. Understandably, the trade-offs between economic and political benefits in this area are very difficult to evaluate objectively. Much depends on the philosophy, tradition, and style of a given government, over time.

Fourth, the government can apply measures such as tariffs, quotas, commodity agreements, and special-purpose taxes—measures designed to discourage imports. Simultaneously, it can subsidize export industries or cultivate foreign-oriented service industries (especially tourism), which result in a considerable inflow of foreign currencies. Once more, the problem with such policies is that they tend to be contagious: Other governments adopt similar policies as defensive and retaliatory measures. Unchecked growth in tourism, although useful in producing foreign exchange, tends to distort and dilute a country's cultural and economic identity.

Fifth, the government can adopt flexible and freely fluctuating exchange rates for its currency. As we saw above, the most likely outcome of floating exchange rates is the devaluation of the currency of countries that experience chronic balance-of-payments deficits. This gradual devaluation helps correct imbalances in trade and other payments. Two problems are readily associated with this approach. First, it invites private and official speculation. Second, it leads to domestic unemployment, the dislocation of labor, increases in the prices of sorely needed imported consumer goods, and, in the longer run, domestic inflation, with all its unpleasant political consequences.

Sixth, the government can announce a sizable devaluation of its currency in order to reverse trade and payments deficits as quickly as possible. The advantage of a sizable one-step devaluation (if done without prior leakage of news of its planned implementation) is twofold. First, it discourages speculation. Second, its effects are more immediate than those of the gradual devaluations that occur during periods of freely floating exchange rates. The disadvantages of this approach are similar to, if not identical with, the disadvantages of the previous approach. Additionally, a sudden currency devaluation (unless carried out by joint consultation and agreement) may trigger retaliatory responses by other governments, which would all but eliminate the benefits—but not necessarily the liabilities—of the devaluations.

Let us synthesize our discussion so far. Economically oriented experts tend by and large to favor free trade and fluctuating exchange rates. On the other hand, politically oriented experts are intent upon securing political sovereignty by augmenting national economic self-sufficiency. Undoubtedly, if the earth today were a homogeneous political and economic unit, then the argument would have been won by proponents of free trade and of uniformly regulated, rational, and global production processes. But the earth has been and still is fragmented politically, and national economies must reflect this fragmentation. Therefore, until workable global political institutions are developed, national governments will probably continue to attempt to maintain a semblance of regulation in the international economic system without exposing themselves to the type of economic dependency that may tempt other countries to seek political advantages over them.

Much of what we have presented so far in this chapter is neither relevant nor applicable to the over 40 percent of the world's population that is governed by communist regimes. In their trade relationships with one another, as well as with the capitalist countries, communist countries prefer to conclude exchange-of-commodity agreements that specify in great detail the quantity and quality of a cluster of goods and services to be exchanged. This is no more than a sophisticated form of barter.

Through a series of interlocking bilateral trade agreements, the communist countries, whose governments exercise control over their industrial and agricultural production, seek to avoid large trade imbalances that could lead to chronic deficits in their balance of payments. Consequently, foreign-exchange rates among communist currencies are used more for accounting than for regulating purposes. Normally, they are fixed by intergovernmental agreements. They are changed periodically, only after consultation, and only for the purpose of achieving a workable measure of equivalency.

The proponents of Marxist economics consistently argue against capitalist conceptions of the free market, free trade, and fluctuating exchange rates based on market and speculative forces. They feel that these are anachronistic and inequitable practices of economic distribution that stem primarily from the capitalist credo, which sanctifies the private ownership of the means of production. On the contrary, the Marxist economists argue, public ownership of the means of production and economic systems that are centrally planned (rather than market-regulated) provide greater stability, predictability, and rationality in economic relationships. Therefore, phenomena such as large-scale unemployment and rapid inflation, which tend to beset laissez-faire capitalist systems, have been eliminated from the Marxist economies by means of arbitrary governmental policies. The great crises of inefficiency, unemployment, and underproduction that have surfaced in most communist countries in the late 1980s have induced the leadership in most of these countries (especially China and the Soviet Union) to abandon standard Marxist economic assumptions and to permit the partial return of market rules and mechanisms in order to provide higher productivity incentives and to permit the forces of supply and demand to lead to more rational patterns of exchange and consumption.[7]

INTERNATIONAL ECONOMIC INSTITUTIONS AND THE PLANETARY ECONOMY

There is a substantial and growing number of problems facing the planetary economy. Probably the biggest of these problems is the chasm in living standards between the countries of the industrialized Northern regions of our planet and the developing and often poverty-stricken countries of the Southern regions. Accordingly, Chapter 17 will be devoted to an analysis and discussion of development. Other economic problems that we have already alluded to include recession, depression, inflation, unemployment, and underemployment. All of these economic maladies are continually aggravated by disruptive cycles of economic boom and bust that have proved quite contagious, given the interdependence of the international economic system.

In addition to these problems, developing countries are faced with challenges peculiar to their location and level of socioeconomic development. These include overpopulation, famine, capricious weather conditions that seriously affect agricultural productivity, chronic balance-of-payments deficits, low economic productivity, poor labor efficiency, the absence of usable technology that can be imported from the industrialized countries, and the lack of trained specialists, many of whom are siphoned off to industrial countries by the so-called brain drain.

A major problem for developing countries is whether or not to nationalize private enterprises (both domestic and foreign). Nationalization measures without adequate compensation tend to discourage further domestic and foreign investments and technology transfers, which are so important to long-range developmental programs. Still another important problem is the need for formal processes and institutions that can regulate the economic relationships between communist and capitalist countries, whose economies and philosophies are so fundamentally different.

So, despite the increasing realization that all the states of our planet are dependent parts of a global economic system, the international economic institutions that have been developed so far to regulate the international economy are

---

[7]Ellen Comisso, "Introduction: State Structures, Political Processes, and Collective Choice in CMEA Countries," *International Organization*, 40, no. 2 (1986). 195–238.

not adequate to the task.[8] These institutions will need substantial augmentation in the future if they are to keep pace with increasing international interdependence.

As we have seen in Chapters 14 and 15, a steadily increasing number of public international organizations, at both the regional and global levels, provide regulatory services to the functional (nonpolitical) sectors of the international system. (For a detailed list of globally oriented functional organizations, see Figure 14–1). Most of these organizations are coordinated under the porous administrative umbrella of the United Nations Economic and Social Council (ECOSOC). The activities of these organizations are wide ranging: global food supply; health control; weather control; communications and transportation regulation and standardization; social, educational, and cultural improvement; regulation of labor-management relations; and international economic and developmental services.

Following World War II, the United Nations Economic and Social Council established four regional commissions—for Europe (1947), Asia and the Far East (1947), Latin America (1948), and Africa (1958). The purpose of these commissions was to help implement postwar reconstruction programs and to systematically promote economic cooperation and development in their respective regions.

The record of international organizations in the sector of international trade has been somewhat uneven. In 1947 and 1948, protectionist forces in many nation-states objected to the founding of the International Trade Organization (ITO), which would have been authorized to set standards regarding tariffs, subsidies, quotas, trade agreements, and general trade practices. Instead, a weaker agency was established. Inoffensively titled the General Agreement on Tariffs and Trade (GATT), it was headquartered in Geneva, Switzerland. GATT has grown to become a substitute for the stillborn ITO. In spite of many obstacles, GATT has contributed to significant reductions of tariffs and other trade barriers. For example, GATT strongly supported the ambitious tariff negotiations of the mid-1960s, known as the Kennedy Round, which gradually led to sizable tariff reductions and corresponding increases in trade among Western industrialized countries.

A number of communist nation-states did not join GATT, which they dismissed as a capitalist creation designed to perpetuate neocolonial relationships in the economic sphere. Less-developed countries felt that GATT denied them the type of forum in which they could make a strong case for the linking of trade directly to workable plans of economic development. Hence, in 1964 the less-developed countries gave birth to a new organization in Geneva—the United Nations Conference on Trade and Development (UNCTAD). The historic first meeting of this organization was attended by 119 countries and over two thou-

---

[8]For detailed descriptions of the structure and functions of international economic organizations, see the latest edition of the *Yearbook of International Organization* (Brussels: Union of International Associations).

sand delegates and observers. The newborn organization was authorized to report to the Third World–oriented United Nations General Assembly rather than to ECOSOC. Since 1964, UNCTAD has met in plenary session every four years. It maintains a permanent secretariat in Geneva, Switzerland, which enables it to coordinate its activities with the GATT Secretariat. Since its founding, UNCTAD has grown in membership, prestige, and importance. Its membership—comprising less-developed, capitalist, and communist countries—is nearly universal, and its influential forum is a place where have-not nation-states can air their problems and outline their expectations before the industrialized countries of the North.

In the sector of international finance and foreign exchange, the International Monetary Fund is the chief regulatory agency. Like most other functional international organizations, it has grown steadily in the magnitude and importance of its responsibilities. This growth has been especially noteworthy since the 1971–73 monetary crisis. Following that crisis, the IMF assumed the role of a central coordinating "bank" for noncommunist countries. The IMF's issuing of over $116 billion in SDRs represents a significant addition to its repertoire of short-term remedies for countries with balance-of-payments problems.

Finally, in the sector of development assistance, four important institutions should be mentioned. Chief among these is the International Bank for Reconstruction and Development (IBRD). The IBRD together with one of its affiliates—the International Finance Corporation—is referred to as the World Bank. Like the IMF, the IBRD was established in 1944 at Bretton Woods, New Hampshire. With headquarters in Washington, D.C., the Bank began operation in December 1945. Its original authorized capital was $10 billion, a figure that was increased to $20 billion in 1959. By the late 1970s, its membership had grown to over 140 nation-states, and in the late 1980s up to 151. Its financing power has also grown steadily. For the year 1980, for example, the World Bank approved $11.4 billion in development loans. By 1983 this figure had jumped to $13.5 billion, and by 1987 to $17.7 billion. Two institutions supplement the Bank's developmental activities in specialized areas: the International Finance Corporation (IFC), established in 1956, provides, unlike the IBRD, risk capital rather than fixed-interest loans, and it invests primarily in the field of industry with host-government guarantees. The International Development Association (IDA) was founded in 1960 and was designed primarily to meet the needs of the least-developed states by providing loans with the softest possible terms for basic projects dealing with irrigation, road construction, and economic infrastructure. Both of these affiliates are located in Washington, D.C., next to the complex of buildings occupied by the World Bank and the International Monetary Fund.[9]

Scores of other international economic institutions have been established. We shall mention only some of the more important ones. Twenty-four

[9]For more comprehensive figures, see "International Bank for Reconstruction and Development—IBRD (World Bank)," *The Europa Yearbook 1988: A World Survey,* Vol. 1 (London: Europa Publications, 1988), pp. 59–63.

Western industrial countries are serviced by, and their policies are coordinated through, the Organization for Economic Cooperation and Development (OECD). In response, 112 less-developed countries established an organization for the purpose of publicizing their interests. This body is known as the Group of 77, named after its original membership. Thirteen petroleum-producing countries accounting for two-thirds of the world oil exports established the extremely influential Organization of Petroleum Exporting Countries (OPEC). Among other things, OPEC has the power to affect significantly the world prices of oil. The Conference on International Economic Cooperation (CIEC) provides a forum in which major representatives of developed and less-developed countries can orchestrate the North-South economic relationships that are so crucial for the future. The CIEC membership comprises 7 developed countries and 19 less-developed countries. Finally, 10 communist countries closely coordinate their economic and financial activities through the Council for Mutual Economic Assistance (CMEA), also known as COMECON. The member-states of CMEA are Bulgaria, Cuba, Czechoslovakia, the German Democratic Republic (East Germany), Hungary, Mongolia, Poland, Romania, the Soviet Union, and Vietnam.

Despite the rapid growth and the complexity of the various global and regional economic institutions, the international system remains in a state of relative economic anarchy. As long as nation-states persist in being jealous of their political and economic sovereignty, as long as politics and economics continue to be closely interrelated, as long as the wealth of our planet is distributed unequally, and as long as the globe is divided ideologically, the planetary economic system will continue to hobble around without much regulation, stability, and predictability.

THE DEVELOPING-COUNTRY DEBTORS: A FINANCIAL TIME BOMB

The early and mid-1980s have served global notice that the international economic system is undergoing an extremely serious crisis. The crisis reflects the worldwide economic interdependence and helps us realize that no part of our earth is immune from economic developments that are taking place in its environment.

The crisis cannot be traced to single causes. It has been triggered by a number of factors. One of the major factors that set it off is that a number of rapidly developing countries—Brazil, Mexico, the Philippines, and Nigeria, among others (See Table 16-1)—increased their external borrowing exponentially. The capital was borrowed from Western private banks to finance what appeared to be profitable development projects (we will discuss development in depth in the following chapter). Western bankers, probably exercising poor judgment, assumed that the debtor-nations' economies would continue generating the necessary income to repay these rapidly multiplying loans, which jumped from a mere $31.2 billion in 1970 to a staggering $227.5 billion in 1981.

Table 16-1   Most Highly Indebted Countries

Latin America and Carribean	Africa
Argentina	Côte d'Ivoire
Bolivia	Nigeria
Brazil	
Chile	**East Asia**
Colombia	
Costa Rica	Philippines
Ecuador	
Jamaica	**Europe and North Africa**
Mexico	
Peru	Morocco
Uruguay	Yugoslavia
Venezuela	

SOURCE: *World Development Report 1988* (New York: Oxford University Press, 1988), p. 194.

There were other factors at work as well: A major recession in the global economy in 1981–82; higher interest rates in the United States triggered by the deficit-financing policies of the Reagan administration; and a sharp drop in oil prices that was a product of disarray in OPEC, a glut of demand in the oil market, and the corrosive financial impact of the Persian Gulf War. Added to all of this were worsening terms of trade in developing countries aggravated by extremely high inflation rates (300 percent in Argentina, 130 percent in Brazil, and 100 percent in Mexico in 1982) and unemployment rates of over 20 percent.

Mexico, overextended in debt by anticipation of great revenues from oil exports that did not fully materialize, announced in August 1982 its inability to repay on the principal portions of its external debts. This sent shivers down the spines of the world's financial community. What would happen, the question was asked, if most debtor states were to announce simultaneously a default in payments? Would the banking systems of the industrialized states collapse? What would be the impact on the economic and the political networks crisscrossing the planet?

By 1984 debtor countries such as Argentina, Brazil, Chile, Mexico, and the Philippines had found themselves required to use nearly 50 percent of their declining export earnings just to service existing debts. Further, high interest rates in the United States as well as cautious managerial policies by the lending institutions have dramatically reduced available credit in the world market.

As a consequence, a new cartel of debtor states appears to be emerging. Collectively, they can bargain more effectively with their lenders for some relief. Recommendations for relief measures include debt repayment rescheduling, lower interest payments with new long-term stabilization loans, and much more active participation by global economic institutions such as the World Bank and the IMF. The solutions will not come easily in a setting of microlevel decisions designed to maximize the interests of each actor concerned.

The Charter of Economic Rights and Duties of States, adopted in 1974 by the General Assembly of the United Nations, illustrates the difficulty in achieving a just international economic order. Article 26 expresses the ideal of justice by asserting:

> All States have the duty to coexist in tolerance and live together in peace, irrespective of differences in political, economic, social and cultural systems, and to facilitate trade between States having different economic and social systems.[10]

The appeal to divorce economics from politics in world affairs ignores the reality that trade and finance, like coercive power, are often reduced to instruments of state policy.

SUGGESTIONS FOR FURTHER STUDY

Comprehensive surveys of international political economy include David H. Blake and Robert S. Walters, *The Politics of Global Economic Relations,* 3rd ed. (Englewood Cliffs, N.J.: Prentice-Hall, 1987); and Joan Edelman Spero, *The Politics of International Economic Relations,* 3rd ed. (New York: St. Martin's Press, 1985). Richard E. Feinberg has analyzed the political influence of global financial institutions affiliated with the United Nations in "The Changing Relationship between the World Bank and the International Monetary Fund," *International Organization,* 42 (Summer 1988), 545–60. In the *World Bank: A Critical Analysis* (New York: Monthly Review Press, 1982) Cheryl Payer has argued that the Bank's structure makes it insensitive to the needs of the Third World. Michael Posner and others have examined the international debt crisis in *Problems of International Money, 1972–85* (Washington, D.C.: International Monetary Fund, 1986). The linkage between international tension and economic interdependence is the focus of Jagdish N. Bhagwati, ed., *Economics and World Order* (New York: Free Press, 1972); and Peter J. Katzenstein, *Between Power and Plenty: Foreign Economic Policies of Advanced Industrial States* (Madison: University of Wisconsin Press, 1978). For an overview of the world economy, see John S. Hodgson and Mark G. Herander, *International Economic Relations* (Englewood Cliffs, N.J.: Prentice-Hall, 1983). Official publications include *The World Bank and International Finance Corporation* (Washington, D.C.: World Bank, 1986); and *The Role and Function of the International Monetary Fund* (Washington, D.C.: International Monetary Fund, 1985).

---

[10]United Nations, *Resolutions of the General Assembly: 29th Session* (New York: United Nations, 1974), p. 134.

17

THE GAP BETWEEN RICH AND POOR: REASSESSING THE MEANING AND PROCESS OF DEVELOPMENT

In this chapter, we will examine some of the most vital questions in the field of international relations. Specifically, we will examine the problem of the great inequality in status and wealth among nation-states. In many instances, scholars of international relations have neglected the normative issue of inequality in the international system and have overlooked problems posed by patterns of uneven development among the 160 or so nation-states of our planet.

For example, the study of international law and international organization has for the most part focused on international norms, rules, resolutions, and debates—in short, on conflict and its settlement. It has not shown much concern for the issues of resource inequality, cultural diversity, and governmental variety. In this chapter, therefore, we shall assess the impact of the unequal distribution of the world's income and resources upon the maintenance of world peace.

The concepts of *development* and *modernization,* which are often used interchangeably, presuppose a certain philosophical orientation about our world.[1]

---

[1] The literature on development and modernization is voluminous. See, for example, Cyril E. Black, *The Dynamics of Modernization: A Study in Comparative History* (New York: Harper & Row, 1966); Frantz Fanon, *The Wretched of the Earth,* trans. Constance Farrington (New York: Grove Press, 1968); Denis Goulet, *The Cruel Choice: A New Concept in the Theory of Development* (New York: Atheneum, 1971); Barbara Jackson, *The Rich Nations and the Poor Nations* (New York: Norton, 1962); Gunnar Myrdal, *Asian Drama: An Inquiry into the Poverty of Nations* (New York: Twentieth Century Fund, 1968); Ernst F. Schumacher, *Small Is Beautiful: Economics As If People Mattered* (New York: Harper & Row, 1973); Fernando Cardoso and Enzo Faletto, *Dependency and Development in Latin America,* trans. M. M. Urquidi (Berkeley: University of California Press, 1979); and Johan Galtung, *The True Worlds: A Transnational Perspective* (New York: Free Press, 1980).

Scholars using such concepts often imply that they can identify differences among *developed, developing,* and *underdeveloped* countries, or, less politely, differences between *modern* and *backward* countries. They argue that progress can be observed and measured in human affairs (whether in the economic, political, or social sphere) and that countries can easily be classified somewhere in a spectrum ranging from the most backward to the most advanced countries.

THE MAGNITUDE OF INEQUALITY

In the twentieth century, our planet has crossed the *takeoff point* (i.e., reached a level of sustained growth) in such indexes as population, production, and exchange of goods and services. Taking 1950 as a base year, future students of international history will surely characterize our era as one of growth, inequality, and increasing interdependence. Statistics depict our planet's past economic performance and suggest future trends. The planetary product—the sum of the gross national products (GNPs) of all nation-states and other territorially organized political entities—was estimated for 1980 as $11.7 trillion and was distributed unevenly: The wealthy, developed states, accounting for 23 percent of the world's population, enjoyed 77 percent of the world's wealth. The developing states were left with 23 percent of the global wealth to divide among the remaining 77 percent of the global population. This situation has further deteriorated ever since.

However large and growing the planetary product may be, the wealth it represents continues to elude most of the world's population. Moreover, it is questionable whether continued growth will bring about a more equitable distribution of global goods and services. Until the onset of the industrial revolution (1770–1870), all countries presented a relatively static profile of production, consumption, and trade. Industrialization in the nineteenth century accelerated the economic growth of the countries of Western Europe at a rate of roughly 3 percent annually, a trend that was maintained until the Great Depression of the 1930s. The period after World War II witnessed a new takeoff, as global economic growth increased at an annual rate of 5 percent. As impressive as these percentages are, they ought not to obscure the fact that economic development centered on Western Europe and North America, thereby laying the basis for the present-day contrasts in standards of living between the Northern and Southern regions of our planet.[2]

For the five-year period beginning in 1973, the world economy grew, on the average, 3.8 percent annually, but this trend has leveled off in the 1980s. The slowdown in projected economic expansion will be accompanied by a doubling of the world's population within an estimated forty-one years. The need to bring global supply and demand into harmony implies a major increase in the volume and value of international trade. With only 9 percent of the world's population,

[2]For a discussion of the economic dimension of the North-South cleavage, see Willy Brandt et al., *North-South: A Program for Survival,* Independent Commission on International Development Issues (Cambridge, Mass.: MIT Press, 1980).

Extremes of the quality of life are contrasted in this Canadian street scene and the homeless sleeping in the streets of Calcutta. (United Nations/J. P. LaFonte)

the leading noncommunist industrial powers—the United States, Japan, and the Federal Republic of Germany—accounted in 1978 for 40 percent of the planetary product. The high level of trilateral trade among these states is indicative of the interdependence of the most technologically advanced economies, yet this relationship suggests an emphasis on regional groupings rather than on an authentic universal web of trade.

The transformation of the international economy from one based on regional subsystems to a global network of commerce requires a reorientation of the perceptions of foreign-policy elites. Assuming that interdependence means the maximum utilization of resources, it follows that a reduction in trade barriers is in order. The liberalization of trade through the lessening of protectionism appears unlikely at this time because, among other factors, the American economy is beset with a need for modernization in vital sectors.[3] For example, a fail-

[3]Depending upon their use, economic statistics may convey different messages. For example, American economists tend to rely on the gross national product (GNP) as the basic unit of comparison, while Europeans use the gross domestic product (GDP). The GNP measures the income of all nationals of

ure to introduce new methods of production has caused American steelmakers to fall behind their foreign competitors and to rely upon governmental intervention in the form of import controls as a means of protecting their domestic market. The outcome of the linkage between an organized economic interest group and United States foreign economic policy is a weakening rather than a strengthening of the ties that should bind—to mutual advantage—the national economies of the West with those of the developing world.

Reacting to inequitable economic conditions such as we have just described, the developing states have chosen a strategy designed to alter the structure of the international system. The strategy entails a systematic quest for the establishment of a New International Economic Order (NIEO) based on premises of economic justice and balanced planetary growth.[4] It is an understandable strategy for Third World nation-states to follow in that it is designed to redistribute the wealth of the world economy in the direction of have-not states. The strategy urges, optimistically, leaders of industrialized states to choose the path of "enlightened realism" by adopting policies that, in the short run, do not maximize the advantages of rich states but rather nurture and subsidize the struggling economies of the Third World.

The developing states justify their demands for a new economic order by sketching out with graphic regularity the statistics of global inequality. They point out, for example, that the mean per-capita income of industrialized countries was at least thirteen times larger than that of the developing countries in 1972. Since that time the situation, instead of improving, has been deteriorating, with the per-capita income of industrialized countries increasing by approximately $120 per year, while the analogous figure for developing countries was increasing by only $7 per year. Other complaints include the growing concentration of world trade (about one-third of the planetary total) in the hands of three hundred giant multinational corporations whose rates of profit have more than tripled in the past thirty years.

The primary demands for the fulfillment of NIEO objectives have been expressed repeatedly in meetings and conferences of Third World economic organizations such as the United Nations Conference on Trade and Development (UNCTAD) and the Group of 77. Third World economic demands can be summarized as follows:

1. The developed states should initiate a process for the drastic redistribution of international credit. It is unacceptable to continue a situation where over two-thirds of the world's population, living in developing countries, have been secur-

---

a state irrespective of where they are; the GDP measures the income produced within the territory of a given state. The GNP of the United States would include the income of American-owned overseas corporations, whereas the GDP would not. Using the GDP as a standard, the per-capita income in West Germany is higher than that in the United States. See *Der Spiegel*, 34 (August 11, 1980), 96.

[4]The discussion devoted to the subject of NIEO is heavily indebted to the work of James H. Weaver and Kenneth P. Jameson, *Economic Development: Competing Paradigms—Competing Parables*, Developmental Studies Program Occasional Paper 3 (Washington, DC.: Agency for International Development, 1978).

ing less than five percent of the finance credit created by the International Monetary Fund.

2. Technical and financial assistance should be directed to the building of raw-materials–processing facilities and transportation and insurance systems so that developing countries can process as well as distribute their products. It is unacceptable to continue with a situation where the developing countries receive $30 billion for exports that are sold yearly in the markets of industrial countries for a total of $200 billion. The $170 billion difference goes into the pockets of intermediaries (usually from industrial countries) who process, package, ship, transport, and distribute these products.

3. Industrial countries should drastically reduce tariffs and quotas on goods that are produced in the inexpensive, labor-intensive markets of Third World countries.

4. Industrial countries should greatly increase foreign assistance to developing states. This assistance should not be viewed as charity but as a duty and an obligation—a form of global progressive tax.

5. Developed countries should encourage and accept a more meaningful role for the developing ones in international economic decision making. It is not acceptable for over two-thirds of the world's population to have less than one-third of the voting power in international economic organizations such as the World Bank and the International Monetary Fund.

The foregoing summary highlights the magnitude of global inequality and interdependence and calls for the adoption of a global rather than a restricted regional view of our planet's economic environment. Unprecedented economic mobility, the inequality among different countries' rates of economic growth, and the deepening of patterns of interdependence are transforming the study of international relations. The post–World War II strategy designed to bridge the gap between the world's rich countries and the poor ones has been named *development*. Development has been divided by scholars into three components: economic, political, and social.

ECONOMIC DEVELOPMENT

Economic development has been equated with industrialization as well as with the attainment of GNP (gross national product) and GNP-per-capita levels equal to those attained by the United States, Canada, Japan, and advanced Western European countries.[5] The task for less-developed nation-states, according to this view, is to find ways to emulate the industrial West and to gradually close the gap between them and the advanced nation-states of the North. A nation-state would

---

[5]For useful studies dealing with economic development, see Irma Adelman, *Theories of Economic Growth and Development* (Stanford, Calif.: Stanford University Press, 1961); Milton Friedman, *Money and Economic Development: The Horowitz Lectures of 1972* (New York: Praeger, 1973); John K. Galbraith, *Economic Development* (Cambridge, Mass.: Harvard University Press, 1964); Robert L. Heilbroner, *The Great Ascent: The Struggle for Economic Development in Our Time* (New York: Harper & Row, 1963); and W. W. Rostow, *The Stages of Economic Growth* (New York: Cambridge University Press, 1960).

therefore receive good marks for its developmental performance if it managed to achieve a per-capita GNP of $2000 or more, or if it began to move away from agricultural dependency and toward urban-centered industrialization.[6] Other indicators of developmental performance would include high per-capita levels of road networks, electrical or mechanical tools and appliances, the progressive concentration of working forces in urban and capital-intensive (relying heavily on machinery and automated processes) production centers, and in general a high standard of living.

Using hard empirical criteria to measure development, political scientists and political economists can talk about *stages of development* or identify *transitional* stages between backwardness and development.[7] These stages have been referred to as *takeoff points*.[8] The 1960s cultivated a great sense of hope about development among the students and practitioners of international affairs. The United Nations designated this period as a development decade, and much brain power was dedicated to the study and recommendation of means of effective modernization.

However, euphoria was soon shattered upon the rocks of experience. It gradually became apparent that the gap between so-called advanced and backward nation-states was not closing. On the contrary, it was increasing with the passage of time. In fact, a number of studies have asserted pessimistically that the gap between the rich and the poor states will not be closed as long as the existing patterns of unequal international distribution of military power and mobility continue.[9]

The ecological, sociological, and psychological hazards in so-called post-industrial societies—pollution, traffic congestion, ghettos, alienation, crime-rate increases, governmental impotence or neglect, the fragmentation of the family and of the community—have made a number of authors aware of the perils as well as the limits of growth.[10] Thus, to some bewildered leaders of the Third World who have been trying systematically to industrialize their nation-states, the traffic jam, a burning sensation in the eyes, and the concentration of lonely crowds in large, congested, but impersonal urban centers have come to be self-defeating manifestations of progress.

Finally, the field of economic development has received an additional focus, from a "go-it-slow-but-distribute-it-fairly" school of political economy. This brand of political economists, applying a modified version of Marxist philosophy

---

[6]With the progressive fluctuations in the exchange rates of the dollar, a number of dollar-pegged indicators should be subject to continual review and updating.

[7]See A. F. K. Organski, *The Stages of Political Development* (New York: Knopf, 1965).

[8]The concept of *takeoff* was developed by Rostow, *Stages of Economic Growth;* see also W. W. Rostow, ed., *The Economics of Take-Off into Sustained Growth* (New York: St. Martin's Press, 1963).

[9]See, for example, Lester R. Brown, *World without Borders* (New York: Random House, 1972), and *The Interdependence of Nations* (New York: Foreign Policy Association, 1972).

[10]For a well-publicized work alerting us to the perils of uncontrolled growth, see Donella H. Meadows et al., *The Limits to Growth: A Report for the Club of Rome's Project on the Predicament of Mankind* (New York: Universe Books, 1972). See also Robert L. Heilbroner, *An Inquiry into the Human Prospect* (New York: Norton, 1974).

to their works, argue by and large that economic development has been mindlessly equated with aggregate national growth and that not much concern has been shown for fairness in the distribution of the yearly increases in wealth.[11] These economists insist that aggregate growth alone is not an adequate indicator of good performance by a given government. For them, happiness and welfare must be distributed widely and evenly in a nation-state before one can call its government efficient or successful. These political economists advise, with some justification, that a slower-developing nation-state that is concerned with fair income distribution, social security, and general welfare is preferable to a nation-state that achieves phenomenal development records at the expense of fair income distribution, justice, and humanity. As a consequence, the new political economists disapprove of the rapid industrialization programs advocated by Western as well as Soviet economic planners, for these programs entail great human costs.

POLITICAL DEVELOPMENT

In the study of political development, opportunities for disagreement increase dramatically.[12] For example, are we to consider Western parliamentary democracies and republics the most-advanced polities? Or do the socialist systems of the communist states provide better and more modern forms of governance? Should we consider the great variety of authoritarian and managerial regimes to be the most appropriate models of modernization for the developing countries of the Third World?[13] As could be expected, the Protagorean maxim that "man is the measure of all things" is operative here.[14] We tend to consider ourselves—our own systems, norms, and processes—as the measure against which to establish deviant cases. Someone who is like us is considered modern; someone who is not like us has to do quite a bit of catching up. Thus, it is not surprising that formida-

---

[11]For representative works relating to this category, see Paul A. Baran, *The Political Economy of Growth* (New York: Monthly Review Press, 1957); Pierre Jalee, *The Pillage of the Third World* (New York: Monthly Review Press, 1968); Andreas G. Papandreou, *Paternalistic Capitalism* (Minneapolis: University of Minnesota Press, 1972); and James H. Weaver, *Modern Political Economy of Development and Underdevelopment* (New York: Random House, 1973).

[12]There is an extensive literature in the field of political development. Some characteristic studies are David E. Apter, *Choice and the Politics of Allocation: A Developmental Theory* (New Haven: Yale University Press, 1971); Paulo Freire, *Pedagogy of the Oppressed* (New York: Herder & Herder, 1972); Celso Furtado, *Development and Underdevelopment*, trans. Ricardo W. de Aguiar and Eric Charles Drysdale (Berkeley: University of California Press, 1964), and *Obstacles to Development in Latin America*, trans. Charles Ekker (Garden City, N.Y.: Doubleday, Anchor Books, 1970); and Lucian W. Pye, *Aspects of Political Development: An Analytic Study* (Boston: Little, Brown, 1966).

[13]There is a certain degree of Western chauvinism in the employment of the term *Third World*. It presupposes that the First and Second Worlds are the Western states and the communist states, respectively. Yet the term is said to have been coined by a person who was hardly a First World chauvinist, Jawaharlal Nehru.

[14]Protagoras (ca. 485–410B.C.) was an ancient Greek sophist philosopher who is sometimes credited for being the Father of the behavioral, social-scientific school of thought.

ble amounts of literature in both the West and the East place democratic/competitive and socialist models of governance, respectively, at the top of the modernization pyramid.

Western scholars have consistently sought to equate modernization with the attainment of democratic/competitive political systems. Consequently, political modernization in the West has been measured most often by indicators of *political participation.* A polity is considered modern if its citizens are allowed to vote. The more people voting, the more they are informed, interested, and eligible to participate in public affairs. Freedom to vote, in turn, has been clearly associated with freedom to choose among different sets of candidates, programs, parties, and policies. Thus, the hallmark of democracy has been considered the freedom to establish political parties (two or more) that are allowed to compete for the confidence, loyalty, and approval of well-informed electorates.

By and large, Western scholars of political development have associated democracy with high levels of voluntary political participation,[15] the presence of two or more political parties competing for power; the safeguarding of human rights and freedoms (such as a free press, freedom of assembly, and freedom of expression), which provide for genuine competition among political parties; and a measure of political institutionalization.[16] Institutionalization, in turn, permits the growth and spread of strong, durable, and specialized institutions—political parties, pressure groups, bureaucracies, labor unions, professionally rather than politically oriented military establishments, and well-differentiated and independently operating branches of government. These institutions check and balance one another's power and prevent an inordinate concentration of power in any one individual or institution.

Gabriel Almond and G. Bingham Powell, Jr., who have produced some very influential literature in the field of political development, consider functional diversification and specialization among the various branches and agencies of government to be an all-important characteristic of modern (i.e., Western) polities.[17] They argue that the more primitive a society, the more multifunctional the power and authority of its ruler(s). The rulers in primitive societies tend to assume the combined functions of father, religious leader, lawmaker, law implementer, judge, jailer, and referee. The more advanced a society is, the more this composite role is fragmented into various specialized functions, which are distributed among a great number of persons and specialized institutions. This fragmentation and distribution limits the unaccountability of any single source of authority. In advanced societies, police stick to the role of policing, teachers to teaching, legislators to legislating, and judges to judging. Ideally, this specializa-

---

[15]Involuntary participation—which is fostered by laws that make voting absenteeism a punishable offense—is considered "undemocratic," since it interferes with one's freedom to abstain or to be politically indifferent.

[16]See Samuel Huntington, *Political Order in Changing Societies* (New Haven: Yale University Press, 1968).

[17]See especially Gabriel Almond and G. Bingham Powell, Jr., *Comparative Politics: System, Process and Policy,* 2nd ed. (Boston: Little, Brown, 1978).

tion affords ordinary citizens better protection of their rights from inordinately large concentrations of power and authority.

Communist scholars have questioned and rejected the capitalist conception of the developmental utopia described above. They prefer the models of socialist systems (present and ultimate) as the embodiment of modernization.[18] They reject the capitalist liberalism of the West as a massive charade performed at the expense of the majority of the working people (workers and peasants). They point out that big-business interests have permeated and corrupted Western political institutions—political parties, the bureaucracy, legislatures, the executive, the courts, and even the mass media. Although the Western people continue to harbor the illusion of freedom and unlimited participation in their political systems, the truth, according to the communist view, is that only those candidates who are backed by big-money interests are given a chance to play important political roles. Also, the communist argument goes, most Western legislation reflects the interests of the profit-making classes and neglects the demands and needs of the workers and other wage earners.

The communists maintain that revolutions in Western capitalist countries are necessary if workers are to expropriate their capitalist expropriators and to develop new societies based on principles such as "From each according to his ability, to each according to his needs."[19] Indeed, such revolutions are inevitable. After a revolution, the proletariat (i.e., the Communist Party, which exclusively represents the interest of the workers) assumes the dictatorial rule of a country in the short run. Eventually, the country becomes ripe for communism and the state apparatus withers away. In practice, however, the dictatorships of the communist parties have become permanent governmental institutions.[20] Rationalizing the obvious negation of civil rights and freedoms for their citizens and the steady growth of state-controlled bureaucracies, these parties have placed primary emphasis on industrialization and on the insulation of their governmental apparatuses from corrosive capitalist influences.

The standard critique of this socialist path to modernization has proceeded something like this: Collective ownership and policies of guaranteed income and employment have prevented economic forces from stimulating effi-

[18]For representative works presenting or reviewing communist scholarship, see Branko Horvat, *Towards a Theory of Planned Economy* (Belgrade: Yugoslav Institute of Economic Research, 1964); Michio Morishima, *Marx's Economics: A Dual Theory of Value and Growth* (Cambridge: Cambridge University Press, 1973); Viktor G. Rastiannikov, *Food for Developing Countries in Asia and North Africa: A Socio-Economic Approach,* trans. George S. Watts (Moscow: Nauka Publishing House, 1969); and E. L. Wheelwright and Bruce McFarlane, *The Chinese Road to Socialism: Economics of the Cultural Revolution* (New York: Monthly Review Press, 1970).

[19]The communists soon amended the last word of this slogan to read *work* instead of *needs*. This alteration was obviously designed to reintroduce incentives and to reduce the tendency to freeload in a society that guarantees one's needs in any case. Mikhail Gorbachev's *perestroika* (restructuring of the economy and government) has made the compensation for analogous work maxim an article of faith. See Mikhail Gorbachev, *Perestroika: New Thinking for Our Century and the World* (New York: Harper & Row, 1987).

[20]The USSR has celebrated well over seven decades of dictatorial conditions without visible signs of letting the state or its steadily growing bureaucratic apparatus wither away.

cient, quality production. Economies without profit incentives become sluggish and generate uneven economic growth, lower efficiency, poorer services, poor-quality consumer goods, and, eventually, lower rates of aggregate growth. The end result is the relatively equal distribution of scarcity. Thus, the greatest num-ber of people are reduced to a minimum standard of mediocrity. At the same time, new privileged bureaucratic and political classes find it advantageous to lengthen the temporary phase of the proletarian dictatorship into a permanent way of life. The critics of the communist way of modernization conclude, there-fore, that in return for dubious promises of socioeconomic equality, large popula-tions in Eastern Europe, the Soviet Union, China, Southeast Asia, and Cuba have been deprived of their standard political freedoms and on many occasions their fundamental human rights.

For its part, the so-called Third World, wishing to gain a unique identity and to limit both Western and Eastern cultural and political domination, has sought to develop a set of systems and styles of governance that are particularly suited to their poor economies and immobile societies.[21] So, with few exceptions, the pattern of governance in the Third World has hovered between rightist or leftist authoritarian regimes. Spain under Francisco Franco and Iran under the shah are now discarded models of rightist authoritarianism. Cuba, Bulgaria, and China are variants of leftist authoritarianism. Further, Chile and Libya exhibit, respectively, right-of-center and left-of-center variations of military regimes. In-dia, which had been considered the primary model for democracy in the Third World, experienced considerable political strain in the mid-1970s and mid-1980s and may still be courting authoritarianism.

The problem with the Third World countries, as we shall soon demon-strate, is that regardless of their type of government, they are being left behind economically in comparison with the advanced nation-states of the North, whether communist or capitalist. Overpopulation, underproduction, worsening terms of trade, pressures for emigration, the brain drain, and foreign penetration are becoming constant companions of Third World countries. So, the open-minded student of political development is left to drift into a stormy sea of confu-sion and indecision. Is there no universally accepted and acceptable standard for political development? The experience of nation-states, as discussed above, suggests that no such standard exists. The definition of national modernization seems to vary with factors such as the preferences of a nation-state's leaders and publics, size, location, economic well-being, predominant political ideology, and cultural traditions. Intellectuals in Western, communist, and Third World sys-tems are therefore busy penning laboriously documented rationalizations of the regimes prevailing in their respective portions of our earth.

Ultimately, most national cultures tend to define political modernization in accordance with their peculiar values and preferences, hoping to gain enough disciples and converts to make their definition universal. The optimal model of

---

[21]An important assumption here that could be challenged is that the developing states' political sys-tems are strictly "homegrown" and not the result of interference of external great-power "protectors."

political development, then, depends on one's philosophical orientation and value preferences. If one's highest values seem to be placed on safeguarding individual political freedoms and free economic competition, which is often attended with some inequalities among social groups and classes, one will opt for Western democratic/competitive systems. If one's highest values seem to be placed on the maintenance of certain laws, the protection of a certain order, and a somewhat more equal distribution of the economic products of society, one would opt for communist bureaucratic/regulative systems, with the attendant sacrifices in the areas of political and cultural civil rights and freedoms. Finally, if one prefers a system that guards the traditional distribution of property, status, and wealth in a pyramidal type of society, one would opt for conservative/authoritarian systems.

SOCIAL DEVELOPMENT

The controversies in this area are as great as, if not greater than, those in the sectors of political and economic development. After all, how do we differentiate between advanced and undeveloped societies?

Our conventional Western-culture–bound wisdom is ready to supply us with apparently definitive answers. Obviously, we could argue, primitive societies are backward and modern industrial societies are developed. Primitive societies are characterized by informal institutions, a concentration of power in the hands of a few chiefs and elders, the absence of political participation and self-government, low levels of literacy, subsistence agriculture, low levels of artisanship (not to mention industrialization), communitarian living, high birth and death rates, verbal rather than written agreements, and very low social and geographic mobility. On the other hand, modern societies are characterized by highly formalized, specialized, and growing institutions; power that is divided (by means of checks and balances) among a variety of elected and selected politicians and bureaucrats; high degrees of political participation (whether voluntary or required); regional and functional autonomy and specialization; high levels of literacy and multimedia communication; high levels of urbanization and industrialization; the development of numerous intermediaries in service professions; the fragmentation of extended families; complex and formalized contractual relationships; controlled rates of birth and death; and greatly fluctuating patterns of population location and status.

The students of social development have used terms such as urbanization, mobilization, social integration, and social adaptation to characterize developed social systems.[22] They have concluded that the industrially developed

---

[22]For illustrative works in the social development field, see Erik Allardt and Stein Rokkan, eds., *Mass Politics: Studies in Political Sociology* (New York: Free Press, 1970); Raymond Aron, *18 Lectures on Industrial Society,* trans. M. K. Bottomore (London: Weidenfeld & Nicolson, 1967); Daniel Bell, *The Coming Post-Industrial Society: A Venture in Social Forecasting* (New York: Basic Books, 1973); George Dalton, ed., *Economic Development and Social Change: The Modernization of Village Communities* (Garden City, N.Y.: Natural History Press, 1971); and Ivan D. Illich, *Tools for Conviviality* (New York: Harper & Row, 1973).

nation-states are nearer to the model of social advancement, whereas the agrarian nation-states are closer to the primitive social model. But here one could introduce some legitimate controversy. For instance, is cannibalism a more backward social characteristic than mass human killing caused by the employment of nuclear or other weapons of mass destruction? Is the loneliness and selfishness of the nuclear family (i.e., made up only of father, mother, and one or two children) to be preferred to large and cheerful extended families in which grandparents can serve as instant but loved baby sitters and in which members are provided with built-in entertainment, interdependency, and a strong sense of security? Further, what is it that makes a person prefer the pollution and alienation of the slums of an industrialized city to the open fields and the clean atmosphere of an agriculturally backward village? Finally, to pick yet one more controversial example, why should one consider endless mind-conditioning television programs a more advanced form of entertainment than happy chatter around the dinner table or the singing of songs around the campfire?

We do not wish to convey the impression that industrialized countries are socially backward and that agrarian countries are socially advanced. In fact, as there is a high cost of human suffering to rapid and enforced development programs, there is also a high cost of suffering in so-called traditional societies.[23] Chapter 19 highlights the tragedy and despair of hunger, disease, illiteracy, alienation, and stasis that have been plaguing more than half of the inhabitants of our earth. Here, we merely wish to urge the reader to avoid equating development only with industrialization and to avoid neglecting many other factors (such as literacy, political participation, public health, and other human rights) that affect the quality of a people's life.

A major question in the area of social development is cultural, religious, and linguistic—in short, ethnic—heterogeneity. Should advanced societies be ethnically homogeneous or heterogeneous? Is cultural pluralism a sign of social strength or weakness? Should governments encourage the development of uniform linguistic standards? How are socially advanced nation-states to deal with the problems of ethnic minorities who are seeking greater independence? Are these minorities to be crushed? Are they to be assimilated and integrated into the core culture? Are they to be kept in separate-but-equal chambers of nation-states? Are they to be allowed to opt for political autonomy—thus fragmenting the political structure of polyethnic countries? Clearly, there is no point to making choices between cultural homogeneity and heterogeneity. These are not matters of preference but conditions that are present in some countries and absent in others. Whether they are ethnically homogeneous or heterogeneous, countries should be considered enlightened and advanced if they genuinely safeguard the civil rights and liberties of all their inhabitants and permit their unhindered cultural and economic development.

---

[23]For a useful and provocative outline of the human costs of rapid industrialization and development programs, see Peter L. Berger, *Pyramids of Sacrifice: Political Ethics and Social Change* (New York: Basic Books, 1975).

Before leaving the subject of social development, we should introduce one important caveat. The divisions of the world in terms of developed and underdeveloped societies may be misleading in one very important way. One may be tempted to assume that all regions and all inhabitants of the developed societies share in a general affluence. Similarly, one may assume that all regions and all inhabitants of poor societies are affected by general conditions of scarcity. In reality, however, we find sizable geographic and human zones of poverty in advanced societies (such as ghettos and depressed areas in the United States), and pockets of great affluence and power in poor societies. The problem of development, therefore, is not only the gap between the rich societies and the poor ones, but also the gap between the rich and the poor zones within national societies.

In summary, we would submit that criteria for social development should be qualitative as well as quantitative and that social development could be viewed more as a collective state of mind than as merely a set of conditions that can be observed and measured. We would suggest, therefore, that socially developed people are happy people—realizing that happiness is an exceedingly elusive quality to assess and evaluate. One could perhaps assume with some confidence that genuinely developed societies are those in which material and spiritual values are relatively balanced. These are societies in which values such as freedom, friendship, beauty, work, leisure, learning, love, community, family, self-respect, and health are valued as much as, if not more than, commodities such as big homes, large gardens, flashy cars, foreign travel, calories, caviar, massage parlors, and other forms of conspicuous consumption.

We conclude, then, that it is extremely difficult to construct a widely accepted definition that permits the differentiation between backwardness and development. We are at times hard-pressed even to justify development measured purely in terms of growth patterns. Is "more" necessarily "better"? For example, if you don't eat at all you go to sleep hungry. If you eat one steak you are satisfied. If you eat two steaks you become satiated. If you eat three steaks you are nothing but a glutton. What about a fourth and a fifth steak? Where does development end and avarice begin? It appears to us that balanced, reasonably self-reliant, and equitably distributed growth rather than mere accumulation of development records is the preferable modernization policy for governments to follow.

This line of reasoning might help us accomplish one of the hardest tasks in political science—the evaluation of the performance of governments in the area of development. For example, does one give high marks to a government if it performs well in economic development but demonstrates retrogressive tendencies in the political sphere? Or, to reverse the argument, is one to evaluate highly a regime that guarantees political freedoms but is unconcerned with social and economic inequalities—the frequent outgrowths of freely functioning societies? The choices one makes betray one's political philosophy, social preferences, and economic strategy. Yet, choices must be made if governments are to determine priorities, rank objectives, and make decisions. Further, students of international affairs should not hesitate to pose questions regarding the evaluation of governmental performance merely because the evaluation process is difficult. Governments can be evaluated relatively easily in terms of their ability to accomplish their stated objectives. But the fundamental question is how to evaluate the soundness of the objectives themselves. And for this task there are precious few generally acceptable criteria.

THREE STRATEGIES FOR THE DEVELOPMENT OF THIRD WORLD COUNTRIES

Despite the imprecision surrounding the definition and attributes of development, there is remarkable consensus among Third World countries that their uppermost objective is to "develop." Problems begin, however, when choices must be made regarding appropriate policies to that end. Three modernization strategies have emerged since World War II. They offer drastically different options to competing elites in developing countries.[24]

The first and more widely applied strategy can be referred to as the *orthodox* (or conventional, or classical) approach to development. This strategy is premised on the operation of a free-enterprise system, private ownership and initiative, and a market functioning in an atmosphere of governmental stability. Countries such as Taiwan, South Korea, and Singapore are among those who have employed the orthodox development strategy to their best advantage.

Orthodox strategists consider the "vicious cycle of poverty" the major obstacle to development in the Third World. This cycle condemns poor countries to remain permanently at levels of economic subsistence. Poor countries do not have the capacity to generate adequate savings. Whatever little capital is generated tends to be invested in lucrative opportunities offered by industrialized countries. The flight of finance capital is coupled with the exodus of entrepreneurial and scientific talent, which compounds the problem. To break the vicious cycle, the less-developed countries are encouraged to install strong and stable governments that can provide the long-range planning necessary for rational growth patterns. Governmental stability is presumed to encourage the inflow of foreign investment as well as foreign technical and economic assistance. Industrially developed countries can thus provide the capital that less-developed countries must have to break the vicious cycle of poverty.

The application of the orthodox strategy, it is argued, in countries such as Singapore and South Korea has paid handsome dividends. These countries have consistently attained economic growth rates that are among the highest on earth. The heavy input of foreign aid, investments, technologies, and managerial talent has drastically transformed their economies. Inefficient, labor-intensive (relying mostly on labor rather than machinery), and small-scale enterprises have given way to larger, efficient, capital-intensive (employing automated labor-

---

[24]For the characteristics of the major approaches to development, see the incisive work of Weaver and Jameson, *Economic Development.*

Singapore's waterfront: the old and the new. (United Nations/R. Witlin)

saving machinery), and more economically productive units. Naturally, the influx of new production techniques and modern methods of management creates some problems, displaces part of the labor force, and generally entails some sacrifices. But eventually, the orthodox argument concludes, the developing country *takes off* toward modernization and the aggregate growth *trickles down* to all the levels of the population and contributes to the general welfare.

The second strategy has been termed the *radical* (or political-economy, or neo-Marxist) approach. This strategy is diametrically opposed to the prescriptions, tactics, and strategies of orthodox economists. Radical economists point out that the large-scale, heavy-industry, and high-automation economies of the industrial world do not provide models that the developing countries can emulate without incurring terrible social costs. The economies of the industrial West are capital-intensive and are geared to produce consumer goods (such as automobiles, electric appliances, and television sets) that satisfy the desires of a few rich citizens rather than the needs of multitudes of poor citizens. The influx of multinational corporations, furthermore, tends to drive out of business less-efficient but labor-intensive local firms, thus contributing to high unemployment rates and inflationary spirals.

The net result of the orthodox experiment is to depress rather than improve the standard of living of the bottom 40 percent of a society. The radical economists conclude that orthodox strategies of development increase inequality in the distribution of income, contribute to an alienating atmosphere of unemployment and inflation, and reduce developing countries to the status of Western political and economic dependencies. In short, the orthodox strategy of development leads inexorably to neocolonialism.

Using China as their primary model and to a lesser extent Cuba and Yugoslavia, the radical economists argue that developing countries should initially sever their ties with the Western capitalist system. They should not accept any investments and foreign aid from Western sources; rather, they should proceed to take control of their own economies. They should assert worker sovereignty over the means of production at home by nationalizing foreign and domestic industries. Then, they should adopt rational and equitable development programs through central-planning institutions. Their strategy should be geared to attain autarky (self-sufficiency) and to eliminate foreign economic (and, by extension, political) penetration. Autarky can best be accomplished by adopting programs of rural-based, medium-sized industries (which would continue to utilize human resources fully), and by mobilizing populations politically and economically.

The critics of the radical strategy argue that it is at best a quixotic vision that cannot be accomplished by most developing countries, which do not possess the vast land, labor, resources, and traditions of China. Instead, their argument continues, developing countries that adopt a Marxist model of development substitute their dependency on the West for dependency on the Soviet Union, adopt political structures that limit their individual liberties, and in the last analysis find it nearly impossible to pull themselves up by their own bootstraps.

Chinese billboards–an outburst of consumerism. (Ira Kirschenbaum/Stock, Boston)

The third strategy, one of *self-reliance,* has been popularized by E. F. Schumacher. In a thought-provoking and frequently quoted book entitled *Small Is Beautiful,* he recommends a "development strategy" for Third World states that cleanly departs from the rapid-growth philosophies inherent in both the orthodox and the radical models of development.[25] Assuming a finite resource base and limits to aggregate growth, Schumacher feels that Third World states should not emulate the industrial revolution, should not uncritically import capital-intensive industrial technologies, but rather should develop "appropriate technology" that would sustain the greatest number at the lowest economic, political, and social costs.

The key guidelines of the self-reliance strategy include the following:

1. Keep workplaces in the countryside to the extent possible to prevent mass urbanization and attendant poverty that result from classical patterns of industrialization.
2. Maintain a labor-intensive, subsistence-agriculture–oriented pattern of employment, designed to satisfy basic needs (food, shelter, health care, employment).
3. Minimize capital-intensive (skilled labor, labor-saving) production patterns.
4. Minimize foreign-trade and foreign-investment dependency by localizing production, processing, and consumption cycles.
5. Conserve values of traditional society that would be otherwise deeply disrupted by the rapid developmental models (orthodox or radical).[26]

Needless to say, this strategy, too, could be criticized for subtly recommending, in the name of conservation and world-order values, the perpetuation of stasis and underdevelopment in the backward global South.

Looking at the actual development experiences of Third World states, we see that choices between these three strategies have not been made on a take-it-or-leave-it basis. Leaders of developing countries undoubtedly found it attractive and convenient to borrow and synthesize the best and most transferable elements from each strategy. Such eclectic strategies employ, for example, hybrid systems of private management for public profit. Or they combine the best elements of the market mechanism (for price determination) and central planning (for rational, small-scale, self-reliant, and long-range growth). An eclectic strategy, further, does not close the door to foreign investments and foreign aid, but it insists on majority control over all foreign investments and examines foreign-aid packages in order to limit any strings that tend to erode national sovereignty and economic self-reliance. This economic strategy has been named Growth with Equity and has been actively employed, without spectacular results, by countries such as Tanzania and Sri Lanka.[27]

[25]Schumacher, *Small Is Beautiful.*

[26]*Ibid.,* p. 175.

[27]For a thorough exposition of the Growth with Equity approach, see Weaver and Jameson, *Economic Development.* See also Denis Goulet, "Development Strategy in Sri Lanka and a People's Alternative," in *Survival with Integrity: Sarvodaya at the Crossroads* (Colombo, Sri Lanka: Marga Institute, 1981).

OBJECTIVE INDICATORS OF DEVELOPMENT

Our discussion up to this point may have suggested that there are few observable variables that can be used as accurate indicators of development. If, however, we strip the concept of development of all empirical referents, we risk reducing it to meaningless rhetoric and pure subjectivity. A balanced approach to the study of development would therefore identify both *tangible* (quantitative) and *intangible* (qualitative) indicators of the concept.[28] *Intangible* indicators of development, whether economic, political, or social, can best be identified as the assessments by publics and elites of their well-being relative to the capabilities and limitations of their countries. *Tangible* aspects of economic development can be measured by variables such as export growth, import growth, balance of payments, per-capita income growth, regional income distribution, aggregate and regional infla-tion rates, level of unemployment, and relative size of industrial product. Tangi-ble indicators of social development would include literacy rates, death and birth rates, net protein supply per-capita, social and geographic mobility, divorce, crime, and suicide rates. Tangible indicators of political development would in-clude—depending on the analyst's orientation—relative income distribution, governmental stability, regular recourse to elections, number of political parties, number of political prisoners, status of human rights, strikes, political assassina-tions, and protest demonstrations.

For the purpose of illustration, we have selected some variables that have been used to measure economic, social, and political development. Table 17–1 illustrates the huge gaps in economic capabilities between the industrialized and the developing regions of the world. Well over two billion of the planet's inhabi-tants from 35 countries are below the poverty line with per capita incomes of $400 or less, compared with only 776 million people in 48 countries that enjoy comfortable incomes of $4,300 or more.

Table 17–2 presents school enrollment as a social indicator of develop-ment. It lists privileged countries with over 90 percent school enrollment and nonprivileged ones with less than 50 percent. Contrast, for example, the United States (99 percent) and Spain (97 percent) with countries such as Bhutan (14 percent) and Mali (17 percent). Unfortunately, other social indicators of relative levels of social development (such as infant mortality, life expectancy, and urban-ization) correlate strongly with the sampling of statistics above.

We have chosen structure of income distribution as a meaningful indica-tor of political development (see Table 17–3) on the assumption that income inequality (which denotes the nonparticipation of large portions of the popula-tion in the social and economic life of a nation-state) correlates directly with political instability that is manifested in popular unrest, revolution, and/or fre-quent military intervention in politics.

[28]Ted Robert Gurr, in *Why Men Rebel* (Princeton, N.J.: Princeton University Press, 1970), employed the concept of *relative deprivation* to explain and predict the likelihood of revolution. For our purposes here we could employ the term *relative satisfaction* to explain why people participate and integrate in well-governed societies, maintaining their political systems in a state of equilibrium.

Table 17-1   Global Distribution of GNP per Capita

GNP per capita, 1985	Number of countries	GNP (US$000,000) 1985	Population (000) 1985	GNP per capita (US$) 1985
$400 and less	35	639,210	2,318,153	280
$401 to $1,635	47	524,960	672,211	780
$1,636 to $4,300	21	967,480	472,325	2,050
$4,300 and more	48	9,025,880	776,071	11,630
No data	33	n.a.	549,961	n.a.

SOURCE: *The World Bank Atlas–1987* (Washington, D.C.: The World Bank, 1988), p.16.

The stark picture of inequality that emerges from these tables may very well contain the fundamental reasons why the human species has not managed to eradicate international war and internal conflict as means of settling disputes and venting individual and collective frustrations. The statistics of inequality that we have supplied, and others that could be provided, lead to one conclusion: There is a vast unevenness of development both within and among nation-states. It follows, almost as an automatic rule of politics, that the more advanced and privileged groups want to defend and hold onto their accomplishments, whereas

Table 17-2   School Enrollment (World Bank Statistics on 184 Countries and Territories)

Countries and Territories with School Enrollment over 90% (1984)		Countries and Territories with School Enrollment under 50% (1984)	
Barbados	Jamaica	Bangladesh	Mauritania
Belgium	Japan	Benin	Morocco
Brunei	Malta	Bhutan	Mozambique
Canada	Martinique	Burkina Faso	Nepal
Chile	Netherlands	Burundi	Niger
Cuba	New Caledonia	Central African	Oman
Denmark	New Zealand	Republic	Pakistan
Dominica	Norway	Chad	Papua New Guinea
France	Poland	Djibouti	Rwanda
Finland	Reunion	Ethiopia	Senegal
Gabon	Romania	Gambia	Sierra Leone
German Democratic	Seychelles	Guatemala	Solomon Islands
Republic	Spain	Guinea	Somalia
Greece	Sweden	Guinea-Bissau	Sudan
Hong Kong	United Kingdom	Haiti	Uganda
Hungary	United States	Libya	Yemen Arab Republic
Iceland	Zimbabwe	Malawi	Yemen, PDR
Israel		Mali	
Italy			

SOURCE: *The World Bank Atlas–1987* (Washington, D.C.: The World Bank, 1988), pp. 6–9.

School enrollment is the number of primary and secondary school pupils (regardless of age) divided by the number of people between ages 6 and 17 in the total population.

Table 17-3 Income Distribution[a]

Countries	Reported year	Percentage Share of Household Income, by Percentile Groups of Households[b]					
		Lowest 20% of population	Second quintile	Third quintile	Fourth quintile	Highest 20% of population	Highest 10% of population
Low Income Economies							
Bangladesh	1981–82	6.6	10.7	15.3	22.1	45.3	29.5
India	1975–76	7.0	9.2	13.9	20.5	49.4	33.6
Kenya	1976	2.6	6.3	11.5	19.2	60.4	45.8
Zambia	1976	3.4	7.4	11.2	16.9	61.1	46.4
Sri Lanka	1980–81	5.8	10.1	14.1	20.3	49.8	34.7
Lower Middle Income Economies							
Indonesia	1976	6.6	7.8	12.6	23.6	49.4	34.0
Philippines	1985	5.2	8.9	13.2	20.2	52.5	37.0
Cote d'Ivoire	1985–86	2.4	6.2	10.9	19.1	61.4	43.7
Egypt	1974	5.8	10.7	14.7	20.8	48.0	33.2
Thailand	1975–76	5.6	9.6	13.9	21.1	49.8	34.1
El Salvador	1976–77	5.6	10.0	14.8	22.4	47.3	29.5
Peru	1972	1.9	5.1	11.0	21.0	61.0	42.9
Turkey	1973	3.5	8.0	12.5	19.5	56.5	40.7
Mauritius	1980–81	4.0	7.5	11.0	17.0	60.5	46.7
Costa Rica	1971	3.3	8.7	13.3	19.8	54.8	39.5
Upper Middle Income Economics							
Brazil	1972	2.0	5.0	9.4	17.0	66.6	50.6
Malaysia	1973	3.5	7.7	12.4	20.3	56.1	39.8
Mexico	1977	2.9	7.0	12.0	20.4	57.7	40.6
Hungary	1982	6.9	13.6	19.2	24.5	35.8	20.5
Portugal	1973–74	5.2	10.0	14.4	21.3	49.1	33.4
Yugoslavia	1978	6.6	12.1	18.7	23.9	38.7	22.9
Panama	1973	2.0	5.2	11.0	20.0	61.8	44.2
Argentina	1970	4.4	9.7	14.1	21.5	50.3	35.2
Republic of Korea	1976	5.7	11.2	15.4	22.4	45.3	27.5
Venezuela	1970	3.0	7.3	12.9	22.8	54.0	35.7
Trinidad and Tobago	1975–76	4.2	9.1	13.9	22.8	50.0	31.8
Israel	1979–80	6.0	12.0	17.7	24.4	39.9	22.6
Hong Kong	1980	5.4	10.8	15.2	21.6	47.0	31.3

Industrial Market Economies

Spain	1980–81	6.9	12.5	17.3	23.2	40.0	24.0
Ireland	1973	7.2	13.1	16.6	23.7	39.4	25.1
New Zealand	1981–82	5.1	10.8	16.2	23.2	44.7	28.7
Italy	1977	6.2	11.3	15.9	22.7	43.9	28.1
United Kingdom	1979	7.0	11.5	17.0	24.8	39.7	23.4
Belgium	1978–79	7.9	13.7	18.6	23.8	36.0	21.5
Netherlands	1981	8.3	14.1	18.2	23.2	36.2	21.5
France	1975	5.5	11.5	17.1	23.7	42.2	26.4
Australia	1975–76	5.4	10.0	15.0	22.5	47.1	30.5
Federal Republic of Germany	1978	7.9	12.5	17.0	23.1	39.5	24.0
Finland	1981	6.3	12.1	18.4	25.5	37.6	21.7
Denmark	1981	5.4	12.0	18.4	25.6	38.6	22.3
Japan	1979	8.7	13.2	17.5	23.1	37.5	22.4
Sweden	1981	7.4	13.1	16.8	21.0	41.7	28.1
Canada	1981	5.3	11.8	18.0	24.9	40.0	23.8
Norway	1982	6.0	12.9	18.3	24.6	38.2	23.8
United States	1980	5.3	11.9	17.9	25.0	39.9	23.3
Switzerland	1978	6.6	13.5	18.5	23.4	38.0	23.7

SOURCE: *World Development Report–1988* (New York: Oxford University Press, 1988), pp. 272–73.

[a]The table contains the countries reporting to the World Bank for which figures are available. Nonreporting nonmembers of the World Bank are Albania, Angola, Bulgaria, Cuba, Czechoslovakia, German Democratic Republic, Korean Democratic Republic, Mongolia, and the Soviet Union.

[b]According to the World Bank, these estimates should be treated with caution.

the disadvantaged want to redress the balance, to narrow the gaps, and to redistribute the wealth, status, and military power in a more equitable fashion.

As a result, one can argue that conflict becomes the Siamese twin of inequality. Within states, conflict remains somewhat controlled—leaving aside frequent civil wars—because of the relatively convincing and occasionally overwhelming concentration of power in the hands of the central governments. Globally, however, power is divided among nation-states. Consequently, the institutions that approximate central authorities (for example, the United Nations and its specialized agencies) are unable to control and regulate international conflict. Thus, wars break out. In the nineteenth and twentieth centuries, war has been considered an undesirable, albeit a practical and sometimes inevitable, means of settling disputes. When the politics of persuasion and bargaining fail, wars become the final arbiters.

We shall conclude this chapter after posing four difficult questions:

First, if one could make a case that inequality contributes to conflict, should we expect certain types of nation-states in the developmental scale to exhibit more conflictive or less conflictive patterns of international behavior? Would it not make sense to suppose, for example, that developed and satisfied nation-states tend to be defensive, whereas developing and revisionist nation-states tend to be aggressive?[29]

Second, if one were to establish conclusively that the politically and economically developed nation-states are more conflict-prone than less-developed nation-states, should one recommend that the advanced nation-states subtly impede all developmental efforts by the have-not countries? Further, to approach an absurd level, should one recommend that we undertake *undevelopment*—that is, a calculated rollback to precivilized levels—so as to remove the globe from the danger of sophisticated weapons of mass destruction?

Third, can one establish causal links and feedbacks among the political, economic, and social sectors of development? Is political development, for example, a prerequisite for or an outcome of economic development? Should a country change its political system *before* undertaking rapid advances in its economic and social sectors? This is very much a "chicken-and-egg" type of question. Yet it addresses the heart of the problem of identifying the processes through which economic, political, and social changes take place. In countries experiencing revolutions, one can safely assume that political changes predict social and economic changes. In countries that are operating with stable political systems, one should probably assume that social and economic changes predict political ones.

Fourth, finally, will it be possible some day to develop a genuinely integrated and unified world state, given the patterns of uneven development among and within nation-states? Would it, for example, be to the advantage of rich Americans to integrate their destinies with poor Africans and to share responsi-

---

[29]We must not lose sight of the fact that many poor and backward states are ruled by small (but privileged and satisfied) minorities who do not, therefore, feel particularly prone to rock the political and economic boat.

bilities for growth and income distribution at the global level? What would be the reaction of people in underpopulated countries, such as France, Canada, and Australia, if they were suddenly faced with the prospect of mass immigration from overpopulated countries, such as India, Indonesia, and China? How would labor unions throughout the world react to the flow of "cheap labor" from neighboring or distant countries? Obviously, one should expect strong opposition to genuine global integration (especially the free flow of labor) that would threaten the vested interests of the powerful, wealthy, and satisfied regions.[30]

The prospects for the quick transformation of the international system into a world state are quite slim, as we suggested in Part IV of this book. On the other hand, it would be wrong to assume that gradual world federation is impossible because of the world's diversity and inequality. Countries already exist—prime among them, the United States and the Soviet Union—in which different races, various ethnic and linguistic groups, and economically advanced and depressed regions are administered effectively by federal, state, and local authorities. If experiments in federal government such as those of the United States and the Soviet Union can continue with some success, then there is no reason why global federal arrangements may not some day have the opportunity to develop.

The dilemmas in the area of development, whether economic, political, or social, are indeed many. Central among these dilemmas is the question of whether the more-advanced countries have a duty to help the less-developed ones progress. Are there such norms as global responsibility and global civic duty? In short, is there a common conscience for humanity? If the answer is yes, then in what fashion should the advanced countries help those that are developing, given the disagreements among the supporters of orthodox, radical, and self-reliance strategies of development? Third World nation-states, jealous of their freshly won independence, are understandably fearful of new dependencies, such as those imposed by the operations of multinational corporations and by the intervention of foreign sponsors, advisors, or technicians in their internal affairs. They are not eager to exchange the overt bonds of colonialism with more subtle ties of economic, political, military, and even cultural dependency.

Ironically, it seems that the alternative to dependency is isolation and neglect. If advanced nation-states are not engaged in foreign aid and investment in developing regions of the world, they are accused of callously neglecting those who are less fortunate. According to one scholar, these neglectful nation-states are slowly building a time bomb of frustration and resentment that will one day explode in our faces.[31]

Is there no other way out? Are neocolonialism and calculated neglect the only choices? Our answer is that there are more than two choices. Advanced nation-states, for instance, may help their less fortunate brethren by channeling

---

[30]For a discussion of refugee and mass displacement problems, see Kathleen Newland, *Refugees: The New International Politics of Displacement*, Worldwatch Paper 43 (Washington, D.C.: Worldwatch Institute, 1981).

[31]This is the major theme of Jackson, *Rich Nations and Poor Nations*.

aid through international organizations, such as the United Nations, and regional organizations, such as the European Community. Multilaterally generated and administered aid, as well as better terms of trade, may be the way around the Scylla of neocolonialism and the Charybdis of calculated and benign neglect.

We will close this chapter with what might appear a provocative thought. The field of international studies should include in its research and teaching agendas not only studies on development but also studies on *decline*—especially graceful and relatively painless decline.[32] Whether we remember the rise and fall of the Roman Empire or the rise and decline of the British Empire, we must realize that those who move up ultimately must take the downward road. In an era of overpopulation, environmental risks, and rapid exhaustion of finite resources, a field of rational, programmed, and equitable *decline management* must be developed.

SUGGESTIONS FOR FURTHER STUDY

In *Common Crisis: North-South Cooperation for World Recovery* (Cambridge, Mass.: MIT Press, 1983), Willy Brandt et al. argued that the development of the Third World is an obligation incumbent upon the industrialized states of the West. Radical development models are the subject of Sam Cole and Ian Miles, eds., *Worlds Apart: Technology and North-South Relations in the Global Economy* (Totowa, N.J.: Rowman & Allanheld, 1984). An optimistic view is the theme of Robert Repetto, ed., *The Global Possible: Resources, Development and the New Century* (New Haven: Yale University Press, 1985). National development comparisons are the focus of Ilpyong Kim, ed., *Development and Cultural Change* (New York: Paragon House, 1986). In *Harambee!: The Prime Minister of Kenya's Speeches, 1963–1964* (Nairobi: Oxford University Press, 1964), Jomo Kenyatta advocated free trade as an incentive for development. By comparison Kwame Nkrumah espoused a planned economy in *Neo-Colonialism: The Last Stage of Imperialism* (New York: International Publishers, 1965). Peter L. Berger has taken to task both capitalist and socialist theories of development in *Pyramids of Sacrifice: Political Elites and Social Change* (Garden City, N.Y.: Anchor Books, 1976). Irving Louis Horowitz has examined the consequences of political fragmentation following decolonization in *Beyond Empire and Revolution: Militarization and Consolidation in the Third World* (New York: Oxford University Press, 1982).

---

[32]See Paul Kennedy, *The Rise and Fall of British Naval Mastery* (London: Macmillan, 1983) and *The Rise and Fall of the Great Powers* (New York: Random House, 1987). See also Mancur Olson, *The Rise and Decline of Nations: Economic Growth, Stagflation, and Social Rigidities* (New Haven: Yale University Press, 1982).

18

NEW AND NEGLECTED ACTORS IN THE INTERNATIONAL SYSTEM

So far, this book has projected the nation-state as the most important unit of political action, as other texts on international relations have done. Whether we discussed concepts such as power, national interest, foreign policy, intelligence, and war, or whether we discussed arms control, the balance of power, international law, international organization, international economics, and development, we have explicitly or implicitly treated the nation-state as our major unit of analysis.

In recent years, however, a considerable body of literature has challenged the predominance of the nation-state. This literature argues that nation-states are nearing obsolescence and that new focuses of analysis in international relations should be developed. These focuses should include, for example, rapidly growing *nonstate actors* such as terrorist organizations, religious movements, and important regional international organizations. The thrust of the literature on these new international political actors highlights the "retribalization" and fragmentation of world politics and suggests that people-to-people relationships are becoming as important as government-to-government relationships. The whole field of literature on various types of nongovernmental or para-governmental activity has been named *transnational politics*.[1]

---

[1]See the fine anthology on this subject edited by Robert O. Keohane and Joseph S. Nye, Jr., eds., *Transnational Relations and World Politics* (Cambridge, Mass.: Harvard University Press, 1972). See also Keohane and Nye's more influential book, *Power and Interdependence: World Politics in Transition* (Boston: Little, Brown, 1977); and Lynn H. Miller, *Global Order: Values and Powers in International Politics* (Boulder, Colo.: Westview Press, 1985).

An eclectically oriented study has sought to demonstrate the phenomenon of new actors using scientific as well as traditionalist techniques.[2] Employing the *New York Times* as reflector of important international events, the authors of this study calculated that over one-third of all international activity takes place exclusively among nonstate actors, such as multinational corporations and terrorist organizations. Further, well over 50 percent of all international activity involves interactions among nonstate actors and nation-states. The conclusion of the authors follows quite logically: An analysis of international relations on the basis of a traditional model that does not include nonstate actors seriously distorts reality, for it neglects a considerable and increasing amount of important transnational activity.

A well-known theorist of international relations, John Burton, has summarized the conceptual dimensions of this problem quite well.[3] He has likened the international system—as traditionally viewed by political scientists—to the game of billiards. The billiard balls stand for homogeneous nation-states. Like the billiard player watching the balls in motion, the political scientist watches the movements, maneuvers, and collisions of nation-states without much concern for their internal processes and components. Thus, interactions among nonstate actors such as political parties, ethnic groups, and multinational corporations, which at times elude the control of their governments, are conveniently ignored. Burton and his colleagues have concluded that as a result of the exponential growth of technology, especially in the fields of communication, transportation, and weaponry, the classical European balance-of-power model is grossly inadequate for contemporary analytical purposes.

Burton argues that a cobweb or a series of superimposed and intermeshing cobwebs would be much better than a set of unevenly sized billiard balls as a model of the highly complex contemporary international reality. Such a model, admittedly considerably harder to theorize about, would reflect with less distortion the actual political and economic processes that crisscross our planet. The cobweb model would take into account, for example, the activities of giant multinational corporations, such as General Motors, IBM, Hitachi, and Unilever. These and other corporations are acting more and more on the basis of profit maximization and corporate growth and are virtually unregulated by any national or international authority. The cobweb model would also account for the activities of separatist ethnic organizations and movements such as the Irish Republican Army in Ulster; the Turkish Cypriot community in Cyprus; Ibos in Nigeria; Basques in Spain; Kurds in Iran, Iraq, and Turkey; and Québécois in Canada. The cobweb model would also leave room for individuals and nongovernmental organizations (NGOs) having a powerful transnational impact, such as Pope John Paul II and Amnesty International, respectively.

---

[2]See Richard W. Mansbach et al., *The Web of World Politics: Non-State Actors in the Global System* (Englewood Cliffs, N.J.: Prentice-Hall, 1976).

[3]John W. Burton et al., *The Study of World Society: A London Perspective*, Occasional Paper 1 (Pittsburgh: International Studies Association, 1974).

In the context of the cobweb model, governments of the various recognized nation-states, especially the governments of the great powers, would still be treated as extremely important international actors, but no longer as the *only* actors. Once the cobweb model for the international system is adopted, models such as the balance-of-power, bipolar, and unit-veto system are rendered inoperative and largely irrelevant. (See our discussion of these models in Chapter 3.)

We believe that the case for the obsolescence, let alone the demise, of the nation-state has been overstated. This overstatement is perhaps designed to accommodate contemporary international political trends and to attract scholarly and popular attention to new or important issues. Nevertheless, we cannot ignore nonstate actors altogether without seriously distorting contemporary international political reality. We shall therefore devote this chapter to the examination of four sets of nonstate actors: multinational corporations, ethnic groups, terrorist organizations, and religious movements.[4] Much of the discussion that follows applies primarily to noncommunist countries and their interrelations. The trend among communist states, which account for over one-third of the world's population, is toward increasing concentration of power in the hands of central governments and increasing monitoring and control of the activities of nonstate actors such as universities, farmer and worker cooperatives, plants, and joint companies, by the state authorities.[5] Similarly, the contemporary trend in both the Third World and the industrialized, noncommunist First World is to increase the power of the central government to control large-scale social problems such as unemployment, inflation, population growth, mass hunger, environmental pollution, and growing crime rates.

MULTINATIONAL CORPORATIONS

Multinational enterprises have been defined in various ways.[6] One leading scholar considers a *multinational enterprise* to be a "cluster of corporations of diverse nationality joined together by ties of common management strategy."[7] Two other

---

[4]We realize that the term *terrorist* is implicitly derogatory. Euphemistically, a terrorist could also be referred to as a *freedom fighter*. We call our enemies terrorists, and our friends freedom fighters. A more detached description would be "nonstate actors employing standard and unorthodox forms of violence in pursuit of certain political objectives." We would like to employ the term *terrorist* in a clinical sense, without suggesting blanket approval or disapproval of terrorist activities and objectives.

[5]Throughout the 1980s, especially after the assumption of power in the Soviet Union by Mikhail Gorbachev, there has been a liberalizing trend—economically as well as politically—in the Soviet Union, China, and a number of other communist states in Eastern Europe and Southern Asia. It is difficult to forecast whether this will be a short phase or a longer-range cycle in the evolution of communist societies.

[6]Our discussion of multinational corporations is heavily indebted to three works: Richard J. Barnet and Ronald E. Müller, *Global Reach* (New York: Simon & Schuster, 1974); Lester R. Brown, *World without Borders* (New York: Random House, 1972); and Abdul A. Said and Luiz R. Simmons, eds., *The New Sovereigns* (Englewood Cliffs, N.J.: Prentice-Hall, 1975).

[7]Raymond Vernon, "Economic Sovereignty at Bay," *Foreign Affairs*, 47 (1968), 114.

analysts define multinational corporations as "companies that control production facilities in two or more countries."[8] Most of the informed literature emphasizes the awesome proportions of the multinational corporation. For example, the Exxon Corporation stations three times as many employees overseas as the U.S. State Department. Exxon's tanker fleet, estimated at six million tons, is half the size of that of the Soviet Union. The annual sales of General Motors Corporation exceed the gross national products of Indonesia, Turkey, and Yugoslavia. Further, the average annual growth rate of successful multinational corporations is two or three times that of the United States.

Table 18–1 is an eloquent comparison of the economic power of multinational corporations and that of nation-states. As the table clearly indicates, multinational corporations are assuming gigantic proportions. The first twenty-four entries in the table are the twenty-four richest nation-states in the world. The twenty-fifth largest entry, however, is not a nation-state but General Motors. Finland and Exxon are tied for thirty-first place, and the thirty-third entry is Royal Dutch/Shell.

These and other statistics lead us to the following conclusion: The size and wealth of multinational corporations are too large to be ignored by students of international relations. But although most analysts agree about the vast scope and volume of these corporations, they disagree strongly about their impact on and their utility for the international system in general and for specific types of nation-states in particular.

We could arbitrarily refer to the supporters of multinational corporations (MNCs) as MNC-optimists, and to their detractors as MNC-pessimists. The MNC-optimists[9] view the multinational corporation as "the most powerful agent for the internationalization of human society."[10] In a sense, MNC-optimists have extended the functionalist argument (which we presented in Chapter 15) one step further. They view multinational corporations as huge economic combines that have the capacity, know-how, and wisdom to treat the world as a single economic unit and to combine the factors of production (labor, land, capital, and management) for maximum efficiency and productivity, in accordance with the rules of the resuscitated *law of comparative advantage.*[11] Thus, the optimist argument

---

[8]Bernard Mennis and Karl P. Sauvant, "Multinational Corporations, Managers and the Development of Regional Identifications in Western Europe," *Annals of the American Academy of Political and Social Science,* 403 (September 1972), 23, n. 2.

[9]MNC-optimists would include Raymond Vernon, *Sovereignty at Bay* (New York: Basic Books, 1971); Howard V. Perlmutter, "The Multinational Corporation: Decade One of the Emerging Global Industrial System," in *New Sovereigns,* ed. Said and Simmons, pp. 167–86; and Brown, *World without Borders.*

[10]This statement has been attributed to Italian industrialist Aurelio Peccei. Quoted in Barnet and Müller, *Global Reach,* p. 13.

[11]The *law of comparative advantage* was articulated by British economists David Ricardo (1772–1823) and John Stuart Mill (1806–73), both followers of Adam Smith (1723–90). The law holds that under conditions of free trade and open markets, each nation-state or region should specialize in the production of those products that it can produce most efficiently and competitively and should import at the lowest available price those products that it cannot produce or can produce only at comparatively higher cost.

Table 18-1 Comparative Ranking of National Economies and the Largest Industrial Companies of the World

Rank (1987)	Unit of Analysis*	Billions of Dollars	Rank (1987)	Unit of Analysis*	Billions of Dollars
1	United States	4,486	31	Finland and EXXON	70
2	Japan	2,664	32	Austria	66
3	Soviet Union	2,357	33	ROYAL DUTCH/SHELL GROUP	65
4	West Germany	908	34	FORD	63
5	Italy	743	35	Bulgaria	61
6	France	724	36	Norway and South Africa	60
7	Great Britain	557	37	Algeria and Indonesia	59
8	Canada	413	38	Turkey	58
9	China	286	39	Nigeria and Venezuela	53
10	Spain	282	40	IBM	51
11	Brazil	270	41	MOBIL	45
12	Poland	260	42	Thailand	42
13	India	200	43	Greece, Iraq, and BRITISH PETROLEUM	40
14	Australia	196	44	Portugal and GENERAL ELECTRIC	35
15	East Germany	188	45	Columbia and AT&T	34
16	Netherlands	175	46	Pakistan and Philippines	33
17	Yugoslavia	145	47	I.R.I. (Rome), TEXACO, and TOYOTA	32
18	Czechoslovakia	144	48	DAIMLER BENZ	30
19	Romania	138	49	E.I. DUPONT	27
20	Mexico	127	50	Malaysia and MATSUHITA ELECTRIC	26
21	Switzerland	126	51	UNILEVER (Rotterdam)	25
22	South Korea	118	52	New Zealand, CHEVRON, and VOLKSWAGEN	24
23	Belgium	115	53	E.N.I. (Rome), HITACHI, and CHRYSLER	23
24	Sweden	106	54	PHILIPS' ELECTRIC	22
25	GENERAL MOTORS	102			
26	Saudi Arabia	85			
27	Hungary	84			
28	Denmark	79			
29	Argentina	77			
30	Taiwan	71			

SOURCES: Based on data from "The World's 50 Biggest Industrial Corporations," *Fortune*, 116 (August 3, 1987), and *The World Factbook, 1988* (Washington, D.C.: Central Intelligence Agency, 1988).

*Data used are the gross national product (GNP) for national economies and annual sales for companies.

continues, multinational corporations can produce more and better products at lower prices, thereby satisfying the progressively rising global demand for these products. The multinational corporations are able to do this because, operating with a global or regional perspective, they locate their plants, draw their resources, and select their management staffs from countries that can provide each factor of production at cost-efficient terms.

The multinational corporations, according to the optimists, are also powerful agents of world modernization, especially among the less-developed countries. In the various regions they enter, they create new jobs, introduce advanced technologies, and train local citizens in the arts and sciences of modern manage-

General Motors headquarters. (Courtesy of General Motors)

ment. One of the most important by-products, therefore, of multinational corporate activity is the internationalization of the production and distribution processes. Working side by side and owing their professional loyalties to rational economic-planning structures (rather than to chauvinistic or jingoistic nation-states), the managers and employees of multinational corporations become better citizens of the world, oppose anachronistic nationalism and war, and prepare the way for the development of world peace through world law and government.

Indeed, the most powerful argument of the MNC-optimists is that multinational corporations, by spreading and intermingling their facilities and products globally, will render the practice of international war obsolete. Observing correctly that the growth of multinational corporate activity has taken place primarily in the geographic area of the Atlantic community—where, simultaneously, the most visible growth in regional integration has taken place—they argue that this area has finally been transformed into a zone of peace after two bloody and destructive world wars. It is unthinkable in our days to predict a war between the United States and Canada, or between France and Germany. These hypothetical belligerents would be hard-pressed to find any industrial targets in which there were no joint ownership, interest, or interdependence.

Thus, the MNC-optimists conclude that the rise of globally oriented companies and world-minded managers is ushering in a new golden age of peace and plenty and that the global corporation will be humanity's best hope for producing and distributing the riches of the earth. What is needed, they contend, is better international regulation of multinational corporate activities; the standardization of different national legal systems, which would permit the effective transfer of capital, management, technology, and economic products; and the prevention of multinational corporations from taking advantage of loopholes in various national legal systems. Naturally, the bonus of a standardization of the international legal system will be the progressive transformation of the world into a homogeneous legal community, a "world village," or a "global shopping center."

The critics of multinational corporations—the MNC-pessimists—spring from at least four major social groupings:[12]

1. Nationalist and protectionist labor unions in the Western world.
2. Cautious governmental bureaucracies, which fear the unchecked concentration of wealth and power by the MNCs.
3. Governments or opposition movements of less-developed countries, which have become alarmed by the ability of multinational corporations to control the structures and styles of their polities, economies, and societies.
4. Elements of the academic and research communities that are watching with alarm the dislocations and disequilibria caused by giant, profit-minded institutions.

Organized labor is opposed to the growth of multinational corporations because as a result of "global-scale rational decisions," the managers and owners of industry are moving their plants to areas of "cheap labor." This movement creates unemployment in the United States, Britain, and other industrial countries that possess effective labor unions. Also, since multinational labor unions have not kept pace with multinational management, the MNCs can become much more resistant to strikes, at the expense of general working conditions and compensation. Finally, the unions insist that governments should provide protection to national industries against cutthroat foreign competition, which floods the markets with goods produced by "slave labor" in "banana republics," "tax havens," and "export platforms"—the new bases of operation of multinational corporations.

The argument of the remaining MNC-pessimists has been presented succinctly by Barnet and Müller in their *Global Reach*. Barnet and Müller view the multinational corporation as "the most powerful human organization yet devised for . . . colonizing . . . the future."[13] They take to task the central thesis of the MNC-optimists—namely, that multinational corporations are fundamentally agents of world peace and progress. On the contrary, Barnet and Müller argue, "present and projected strategies of global corporations offer little hope for solving the problems of mass starvation, mass unemployment, and gross inequality."[14]

The heart of the argument of the MNC-pessimists is that globally ori-

---

[12]The literature outlining the arguments of the critics of the multinational corporations is also very diverse—qualitatively, politically, and ideologically. See, for example, Barnet and Müller, *Global Reach;* Harry Magdoff, *The Age of Imperialism* (New York: Monthly Review Press, 1969); Gabriel Kolko, *The Roots of American Foreign Policy: The World and United States Foreign Policy, 1943–1945* (Boston: Beacon Press, 1969); and Kenneth E. Boulding and Tapan Mukerjee, eds., *Economic Imperialism* (Ann Arbor, Mich.: University of Michigan Press, 1972).

[13]Barnet and Müller, *Global Reach,* p. 363.

[14]*Ibid.,* p. 364.

ented corporations are like absentee landlords, who are concerned primarily with increasing their profits and are insensitive to the living conditions of those condemned to serve them on location. Barnet and Müller assert that multinational corporations have violated three fundamental human needs. These violations have disastrous consequences for the bottom 60 percent of humankind, which is finding itself progressively impoverished and alienated. These human needs are social balance, ecological balance, and psychological balance. The multinational corporations are allegedly destabilizing all three balances by breeding economic inequality, environmental pollution, and psychological alienation.

The Barnet-Müller argument is relatively simple: Multinational corporations are colonizing poor countries and progressively weakening and destabilizing rich countries while becoming gargantuan themselves. In this chapter, we can only summarize some of the justifications for these pessimistic assertions. According to Müller and Barnet, the multinational corporations tend to employ management and know-how from the industrial nation-states, especially the United States. They then locate plants in cheap-labor areas, such as Hong Kong, where wages are low and working hours long. And contrary to popular assumptions, the multinational corporations secure most of their finance capital in the host countries rather than bringing it with them.[15] Once established on location, the multinational corporation appears, at least at first, to create new jobs and to stimulate the economy. What is not taken into account, however, is that multinational corporations begin to buy up or drive out through uneven competition smaller local businesses. Since most Western multinational corporations are capital-intensive (that is, they employ automated, labor-saving equipment to accommodate the industrial standards of the West, where labor is expensive) and the smaller local businesses are labor-intensive, the net effect of the multinational corporate invasion over time is to increase local unemployment and to impoverish the unemployed masses.[16]

By means of massive and seductive advertising campaigns, the multinational corporations are distorting the tastes and styles of Third World inhabitants and transforming luxuries into necessities. At the same time, they are neglecting socially vital issues, such as nutrition, clean air, and public health. Since profit maximization at the global rather than the national level is their main concern, multinational corporations tend to be oblivious to environmental pollution and the living standards of the working class. In fact, the MNCs tend to promote and protect (sometimes through underhanded and corrupt practices) reactionary governments that will safeguard the MNCs' interests against the efforts of local labor to obtain better wages, antipollution controls, and the institution of socialization or nationalization practices recommended by the more radical local polit-

---

[15]Barnet and Müller point out that American MNCs operating in Latin America financed 83 percent of their activities with local funds and took 79 percent of their profits out of Latin America. *Ibid.,* p. 152.

[16]Estimates of unemployment in the Third World during the development decade of the 1960s ranged between 27 and 30 percent of the work force—and these figures may be understated, since they are collected by governments that are conscious of their own prestige.

ical elements. As the experiences of Chile, Brazil, Honduras, and other parts of the world suggest, multinational corporations are tempted to defend and collaborate with authoritarian governments. Such governments contribute the most to the global profit-maximizing formula because they offer the least demanding terms to multinational corporations. This situation led Emilio Medici, the military ruler of Brazil from 1969 to 1974, to remark with some bitterness that "Brazil is doing well but the people are not."[17]

The future for poor countries, according to the pessimists, remains grim as long as the activities of multinational corporations remain uncontrolled. One should expect greater inequality, greater unemployment, greater malnutrition, increasing population, exhaustion of natural resources, and neglect for the environment reaching the proportions of ecocide. (These and other problems will be discussed in some detail in Chapter 19.) Furthermore, this fate is not reserved for poor countries alone, according to Barnet and Müller. The United States, Japan, and other industrial countries are in for similar, albeit less harsh, treatment. With the increasing migration of factory and even company headquarters away from the United States, the problem of unemployment and the attendant maldistribution of incomes becomes more acute in the industrial West. Simultaneously, as less-developed countries band together into cartels of energy and raw-materials producers (such as the Organization of Petroleum Exporting Countries, in the case of oil) and manage to increase their prices for energy and raw materials, the multinational corporations will continue tacking the cost differences onto the backs of consumers in the United States and other industrial countries. Thus, Western countries will be hit simultaneously by increasing unemployment and inflation. In the meantime, the profits of the multinational corporations will continue to rise, and wealth will be divided among fewer and fewer pockets. Barnet and Müller conclude pessimistically that governments in the Third World as well as in the industrialized West will prove unable to stop this process of the concentration of wealth in the hands of a few multinational corporations while everyone else becomes impoverished. The multinational corporations have already become so rich and so powerful that they can influence, through campaign contributions and even outright bribes, the makeup of executive and legislative bodies throughout the noncommunist world.

Summarizing the Cases for and against
Multinational Corporations

Both MNC-optimists and MNC-pessimists agree on one basic assessment: The multinational corporations are too powerful to be ignored by analysts of international relations. These huge new actors must therefore be carefully studied and must be regulated for the advantage of all. The disagreements between the pessimists and the optimists concern the nature of the necessary regulation. MNC-optimists, employing a variant of idealist thinking, view the growth of multina-

---

[17]Quoted in Barnet and Müller, *Global Reach,* p. 149.

tional corporations as a creative internationalizing phenomenon in a world that has grown weary of narrow-minded chauvinism; they prefer loose regulation by an international body within or without the United Nations organization. The purpose of this body would be to set standards, harmonize national legislative processes, call for good working conditions, and restrict the repatriation of profits. The MNC-pessimists, on the other hand, employing a mixture of realist and Marxist premises, argue for strong national and even subnational regulation and for carefully designed intergovernmental coordination. They believe that international regulation through the United Nations is equivalent to little or no interference in the activities of multinational corporations. National and local regulation, they argue, will prove considerably stronger and will diminish the ability of global corporations to act as absentee landlords and not be concerned about local conditions.

In the future, the analysis of international politics will benefit considerably if more emphasis is placed on the activities and links of multinational corporations with governments, international organizations, and other nonstate actors, which we are about to discuss. However, we are reluctant to write off the nation-state, if for no other reason than the factor of territoriality. Nation-states exercise military and political control over clearly demarcated territories and their inhabitants. Multinational corporations, on the other hand, are networks of technology, finance capital, management, and labor spread over a number of nation-states. It is hard for multinational corporations to threaten the prerogatives of states without the latter retaliating by curbing the corporate "power."

ETHNICITY AND ETHNIC GROUPS: NEGLECTED ACTORS IN THE ANALYSIS OF INTERNATIONAL RELATIONS

Certain ethnic groups wish to break away from existing political entities and become sovereign. Others wish to join another state with which they feel more ethnically compatible. To classify these ethnic groups as "new actors" in international politics is an exaggeration. (This section should best be read in conjunction with our discussion of nation-states and nationalism presented in Chapter 4.) A review of the last two centuries of history reveals that the urge for national (and ethnic) independence has been one of the primary reasons for political activity and armed conflict. For example, the efforts of southern European and Balkan ethnic groups (such as the Bulgars, Greeks, Romanians, Serbs, and eventually the Turks) to gain their independence from the multinational Ottoman Empire took up much of the nineteenth and early twentieth centuries. The revolutionary wars in China (1911–49) were fundamentally nationalist. World War I was triggered by an ethnic incident[18] and ended with, among other things, the

---

[18]On June 28, 1914, in the Bosnian town of Sarajevo, a young Serbian activist named Gavrilo Princip assassinated the Austrian heir apparent, Archduke Franz Ferdinand, and his consort, in an act of patriotic defiance. This incident provided an occasion for the Austro-Hungarian government to mobilize its forces against the Kingdom of Serbia—an action that triggered a sequence of events culminating in World War I.

victorious nation-states proclaiming their acceptance of the principle of national self-determination. In the interwar period, Hitler's Germany based some of its initial offensive probes into neighboring countries on arguments of irredentism (that is, ethnic reintegration). The forced unification of Austria and Germany and the German attack on Czechoslovakia are the two most obvious results of such probes. Since the end of World War II, what could be called ethnic conflict has continued, if not intensified. The partition of the Indian subcontinent into India and Pakistan after India gained independence from the British; the Palestine dispute pitting various Arab nation-states and movements against the Israelis; the historic struggle of a host of colonies to gain national independence; the attempt of the province of Katanga to secede from the Congo (now known as Zaire); the Cyprus dispute between two potent ethnic groups, the Greek Cypriots and the Turkish Cypriots; the slow-burning disputes between Catholics and Protestants in Northern Ireland, French- and English-speaking people in Canada, Serbs, Croats, and Slovenes in Yugoslavia, and Flemish and Walloon peoples in Belgium; the Basque separatist movement in Spain; the Biafran civil conflict in Nigeria; the secession of Bangladesh from Pakistan; and the great racial and tribal convulsions of southern Africa—these are all examples of the powerful forces that underlie strong ethnic identification.

Ethnic groups are neither new phenomena nor new actors in international politics. However, the traditional field of international relations (especially the theory of international relations) has tended to deemphasize actors other than governments and by so doing to oversimplify and distort the reality it purports to explain. It is in this sense that we include the literature and cases of ethnic activity under the heading of "new actors" in international politics.[19]

What to Do with Ethnic Problems

A fundamental question confronts all students of the problems of ethnicity: Should ethnic boundaries coincide with nation-state boundaries?[20] Answering this question in the abstract, one is tempted to respond positively. In an ideal environment, it would be good if national boundaries coincided with ethnic boundaries. But what, then, should one do with polyethnic states such as India, the United States, the Soviet Union, Yugoslavia, and Spain? We posed this question in Chapter 4. We saw that a great majority of nation-states are composed of two or more ethnic groups. Should all these states be broken up into smaller and ethnically homogeneous entities? Would that not cause a global upheaval of unprecedented magnitude? What would happen if the different ethnic groups were territorially interspersed and economically interdependent? In such cases, should the various ethnic populations be moved arbitrarily, even forcefully, to

---

[19]For reference to useful studies on the subject of ethnicity and ethnic conflict, see Cynthia Enloe, *Ethnic Conflict and Political Development* (Boston: Little, Brown, 1972); R. A. Schermerhorn, *Comparative Ethnic Relations* (New York: Random House, 1970); and Alvin Rabushka and Kenneth A. Shepsle, *Politics in Plural Societies* (Columbus, Ohio: Charles E. Merrill, 1972).

[20]For a useful study on ethnicity, see Abdul A. Said and Luis R. Simmons, eds., *Ethnicity in an International Context* (New Brunswick, N.J.: Transaction Books, 1976).

separate territorial compartments merely to assure ethnic homogeneity? Once more, the answer to most of these questions is easy to give in the abstract: One should apply the principle of national self-determination, the best means to which are freely conducted *plebiscites*. A question remains, however: What is the smallest amount of population (computed as a percentage of total population of a polyethnic state, or in absolute terms, or in terms of territory inhabited) that should be permitted to exercise the right of self-determination? For instance, should one poll the wishes of all Yugoslav ethnic groups together, or each one separately? To proceed to even more controversial examples, should the various racial and ethnic groups in the United States and the Soviet Union be given a choice of adopting alternate institutions for their social, economic, and political development?[21]

All of these questions suggest that a strict application of the principle of national self-determination (here viewed as *ethnic* self-determination) would result in considerable fragmentation of ethnically pluralistic states and drastic redistribution of existing political power and influence. On the other hand, we should not be so simplistic as to assume that all members of a given ethnic group want the same thing. They, too, would be divided as to the degree of ethnic separateness they wish to exercise. Our guess is that if one were to strive for a system of ethnic self-determination—a quite unlikely development given the great-power–oriented international system of today—one would be opening a Pandora's box of potential conflicts. A movement to transform the international system into one with over three thousand ethnically homogeneous ministates would run squarely into the vigorous and violent opposition of existing governments around our planet.[22]

It appears to us that the way to manage ethnic problems is not through separation and insulation of ethnic groups but rather through their economic mobilization and the protection of their human and civil rights (which include the protection and promotion of their ethnic and religious identities). We know from previous experience that central governments of polyethnic states do not take kindly to separatist movements. Witness, for example, the experiences of the Katangese, Ibo, Québécois, Irish Republican, Basque, Croat, and Turkish Cypriot movements. Continued trends toward ethnic separatism are likely to intensify civil conflicts as well as invite intervention by outside powers. Such conflicts would have extremely dangerous consequences in our present nuclear era.

Perhaps the attention of those concerned with ethnic problems should focus on means of welfare protection and improvement rather than on secession by ethnic groups. The repression often encountered by ethnic minorities in the past does not dictate the partitioning of a state, but rather the adoption of legal standards that protect the rights of all citizens living in multinational political

---

[21]Another eloquent indication of the durability of ethnic divisions has been the unrest that surfaced in the 1980s in the Armenian and Baltic republics of the Soviet Union following the liberalization measures implemented by the Gorbachev government.

[22]For elaboration on this subject, see Elmer Plischke, *Microstates in World Affairs: Policy Problems and Options* (Washington, D.C.: American Enterprise Institute, 1977).

Latvians demonstrate in Mikhail Gorbachev's Soviet Union. (Novosti from Sovfoto)

communities. The model of Martin Luther King, Jr.'s campaign of nonviolence and passive resistance to obtain human rights and improve the economic and political status of the black community in the United States may well serve the needs of ethnic minorities in other heterogeneous states.

International law and international organization can perform very useful roles in the resolution of ethnic conflict. It would be helpful, for example, if ethnically heterogeneous nation-states agreed to convene a conference and produce a treaty outlining the minimum acceptable rights of ethnic groups as well as establishing institutions for monitoring the status and well-being of ethnic groups. Arguments regarding sovereignty and noninterference in domestic affairs are at best fig leaves behind which one attempts to hide the ill treatment of ethnic minorities or majorities. Unless effective rules and institutions are devised for the adequate regulation of ethnic disputes, it is fair to predict that such disputes will intensify in the years to come.

TERRORIST MOVEMENTS AND ORGANIZATIONS

In employing the term *terrorist*, we are conscious that it raises clearly pejorative connotations. As we indicated above, a more detached, value-free definition of terrorist organizations would describe them as nonstate actors employing unconventional as well as orthodox techniques of violence in order to attain certain political objectives.[23] Terrorism, like war, involves the use of organized violence in pursuit of political objectives. As a political instrument, terror has been used

---

[23]For a discussion of the political forms of terrorism, see Baljit Singh, "Values and Social Issues in Political Terrorism," *Ohio Northern University Law Review,* 6 (1979), 82–88. We should keep in mind, however, that terrorists are not always nonstate actors. A number of governments around our planet employ or encourage the use of terrorist activities as a means of maintaining themselves in power against the popular will or as indirect "weapons" to be used against unfriendly states.

by both oppressors and oppressed. One generally calls one's friends who employ terror *freedom fighters* or *unconventional warriors* and calls one's enemies *terrorists* or *saboteurs.*

Well-publicized terrorist organizations include Middle-East related groups such as *the Popular Front for the Liberation of Palestine* (PFLP), *Hizballah* (the Party of God), *the Abu Nidal Organization* (ANO); *the Armenian Secret Army for the Liberation of Armenia* (ASALA), which targets Turkey; *Action Directe* (AD), operating in France; *the Basque Fatherland and Liberty* (ETA/M), operating in Spain; the *Provisional Irish Republican Army* (PIRA, the Provos), operating in Ulster; the *Red Army Faction* (RAF-Baader-Meinhof gang), operating mainly in the Federal Republic of Germany; the *Red Brigades* (BR), operating in Italy; *Seventeenth November,* operating in Greece; *the Japanese Red Army,* operating in Japan and elsewhere in the world; *the African National Congress,* operating in Zambia, Angola, and South Africa; and many other terrorist groups and organizations in Central and South America and elsewhere on the planet. The methods of these groups encompass bombings in such crowded places as commercial centers, subways, military installations, and communications centers; hijackings of aircraft or ships; and abductions or assassinations of prominent figures in government or business. The short-term objective of most terrorist groups is to gain the attention of the mass media and through them the public. In this respect, they have been quite successful.

The 1980 bombings of the Bologna railway station and the Munich "October-Fest" attracted extensive media coverage. As Figure 18–1 indicates, the frequency of international terrorist acts has been increasing at a relatively slow pace. These figures do not reflect, however, the magnitude of terrorism in terms of total casualties. While the number of individual incidents has remained low, there has been an alarming increase in the number of casualties caused by these acts of indiscriminate violence.[24]

The destructiveness of terrorism is low in comparison with that of other people-killers, such as disease, starvation, war, and industrial or automobile accidents. How can we account, then, for the political notoriety and even popular fascination of some of these groups (especially the PFLP and the IRA-Provos)? The answer to this question is complex. The most obvious, but not necessarily accurate, response is that newspapers and other media tend to play up terrorist activity because it is considered newsworthy. This trend helps the terrorist organizations to accomplish easily and with relatively few acts their primary tactical objective, which is to focus world attention on their political problems. Another response is that unconventional violence is very difficult for regular military forces to detect and combat, but relatively cheap to carry out. It creates disproportionate feelings of insecurity and generally psychological malaise among the opponents of the terrorist organizations. A third response is that the use of terror *per se* is of secondary importance. The liberation organizations that succeed are

---

[24]For a detailed report on terrorist activity over time containing statistical information on terrorist groups, methods of operation, types of targets, and areas of activity, see *Patterns of Global Terrorism: 1987* U.S. Department of State Publication No. 9661 (Washington, D.C.: Government Printing Office, August 1988), pp. 1–70.

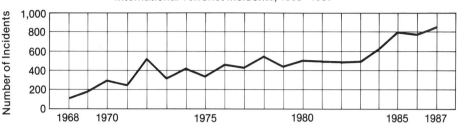

Figure 18-1 International Terrorist Incidents, 1968–87

SOURCE: *Patterns of Global Terrorism: 1987*, U.S. Department of State Publication No. 9661 (Washington, D.C.: Government Printing Office, 1988), p. 2.

those with well-organized political structures, a just cause, effective leadership, and the support of the masses.

Attempts to Regulate Terrorist Activity

A series of hijackings, letter-bomb explosions, and bloody airport incidents involving scores of casualties has mobilized many governments—in particular, the government of the United States—to seek international regulation of terrorist activity. According to concerned government officials, what has been perpetrated so far by various terrorists is not the real problem. What is at stake is the awesome and terrifying potential for terrorist activity in the decades to come. Terrorists could have a profoundly negative effect if in the future they were to shift from rifles and explosives to nerve gas, crude nuclear devices, heat-seeking missiles, and other dreadful weapons. Terrible scenarios project how nuclear waste material scattered widely by conventional explosions could result in very serious damage. Even more worrisome are scenarios of plots to pollute a city's air or its water supply with toxic chemicals or to disrupt urban transportation and communications systems by blowing up bridges and power stations.

All of this activity, incidentally, does not have to be restricted to politically motivated terrorist organizations. After all, most politically motivated organizations, conscious of their public image, will tend to limit the magnitude and nature of the destruction they will permit themselves to cause. A particular source of worry for government officials is the prospect of common criminals (especially members of organized crime) shifting to terrorist tactics. For example, they could hijack a nuclear bomber and its crew for the purpose of massive extortion for private profit. Thus, in this area as well, new measures and new national and international institutions will have to be devised if present and potential terrorist capabilities are to be controlled.

The effect of national and international measures that will be taken to combat terrorism will undoubtedly result in added inconvenience and deeper intrusions into the privacy and the freedom of movement of the general public. Any of us who have tried to use an airplane for domestic and international flights

Masked hijackers broadcasting their demands. (AP/Wide World photos)

have already had a taste of things to come: Metal-detection machines, personal searches, searches of carry-on luggage, armed guards, and other monitoring devices have been justified in the effort to reduce the probability of successful skyjackings. Paradoxically, we find that technological growth and complexity has invited terrorist activity—or so-called monkey-wrench politics—but has also armed the various security apparatuses with effective and unavoidably intrusive devices that limit personal freedom and cause considerable inconvenience. Ultimately, innocent bystanders are at the receiving end in both instances. First, they suffer the inconvenience of personal searches and other intrusions of privacy. Then, they must suffer the fear of a skyjacking or a midair explosion while they travel. Philosophically oriented commentators will probably dismiss this situation as an unavoidable evil, an inevitable manifestation of industrialized societies, or the price of being part of a human collectivity. Those concerned with practical politics will turn their attention to the development of institutions designed to eliminate the causes as well as the effects of terrorism.

RELIGIOUS GROUPS AND MOVEMENTS

Whether one is visualizing the Roman Catholic pope addressing adoring throngs numbering in the millions during visits throughout the world, or the Ayatollah Ruhollah Khomeini exercising religious and secular power astride Iran's post-shah revolution, or the impact of the "moral majority" in the 1984 American presidential election—one gets a clear impression of religious assertiveness in social and political affairs.

If we survey the political record of religion throughout history, we may advance the proposition that organized religion's direct role in political affairs has steadily diminished since 1648 (the Treaty of Westphalia). In the West the principle of separation of church from state is used as a clear symbol of this proposition. On the other hand, we can argue that history reflects a cyclical pattern of peaks and valleys, of waxing and waning religious influence alternating over time. In the pre-Christian period, for example, religious authority was relegated to a relatively secondary status, and kings, politicians, or generals had undisputed control of affairs of state.

With the advent of Christianity, however, in both the eastern and western sections of the Roman Empire the world witnessed the synthesis of religious and secular authority in what came to be referred to as *caesaropapism*. By combining religious and secular authority in their hands, kings or emperors were seeking to maximize their legitimacy and to maintain authority patterns with unquestioning obedience over long periods of time. Whether we study the record of Byzantine Emperor Justinian (ruled in Constantinople A.D. 527–65) or Pope Innocent III (ruled in Rome 1198–1216), we have clear examples of the comfortable fusion of the sword and the cassock, or of political with religious authority.

Like Christianity, a younger and equally politically assertive faith was that of Islam. Founded by the prophet of Islam, Mohammed (A.D. 570?–632), this faith and its major branches (Sunni and Shi'ite Islam) joined its proselytizing ardor with the secular expansionism of the venturesome Arabic and Ottoman Empires, which, in turn, served to spread the Islamic faith to most corners of the then-known world. In countries where the Islamic faith is today predominant, religious inputs to political life have remained relatively important. The impact of Islamic fundamentalism has been pervasive, for example, in countries such as Libya under Muammar al-Qaddafi and Iran under Shi'ite revolutionary rule.

Assessing the role and political impact of religious groups in the late twentieth century, we find a wave of revitalization, revival, assertiveness, and activism. An example is the Iranian revolution, in which the clergy exercised power directly as well as indirectly. Few, also, can dispute the great impact and political consequences that a pope's charismatic and authoritative pronouncements can have on important and controversial (hence political) issues such as population control, human rights, poverty, peace, and political liberalization. Further, the financial and political activities of American religious fundamentalists (operating under the rubric "moral majority") appear to have had a measurable impact in the 1980 American elections in support of conservative candidates.

We should keep in mind that, as in the case of multinational corporations, ethnic groups, or terrorist organizations, we cannot make facile generalizations about religious groups and movements. For example, we find some priests of the Roman Catholic faith in Latin America who have made their peace with military managerial regimes regardless of the latter's human-rights record, while many others have spearheaded revolutionary and populist liberalization movements.

At the risk of being challenged, we will venture some generalizations about the role and impact of religious activities in national and international politics. For example, in a number of countries that are characterized by considerable religious homogeneity, faith becomes one of the primary modifiers if not shapers of nationalism. Further, given the general orientation of religious groups in support of peace, order, love, and harmony, religious establishments by and large tend to become identified with the social, political, and economic status

Pope John Paul II on a visit to the Philippines. (UPI/Bettmann Newsphotos)

quo in many states. Occasionally following revolutionary transformations—as in the case of socialist states of Eastern Europe—religious authorities tend to adjust to the postrevolutionary status quo and to achieve working accommodations with postrevolutionary ruling groups in return for a measure of autonomy in the pursuit of their religious, philanthropic, and social functions.

It will remain a subject of debate for some time as to whether religious groups with antiwar, pro–human-rights, antipoverty, or anti-abortion ("pro-life") objectives technically cross the line separating the religious from secular and political affairs. There will be those—let us call them *religious minimalists*—who would like to see religions limited to purely ritualistic and humanitarian activities, who want them to remain politically neutral, not endorse candidates and planks, not fund advertising activities, and not pass judgment on the decisions and actions of domestic and foreign leaders. On the other side, those that we might dub *religious maximalists* would press the argument that religious leaders and groups have a right (in fact, a duty) to promote policies and practices that are designed to maximize ethical values, human welfare, human freedom, maintenance of cultural identity, and so forth.

Whether the action of self-immolation by a Buddhist monk in the early stages of the Vietnam War was an act of faith, an act of passive resistance, or a powerful and poignant revolutionary act of defiance will remain a matter of speculation, if not controversy. But regardless of where one stands on the proper role and activities of religious groups in organized societies, one must agree that the careful study of world politics cannot afford to leave religious activities outside the purview of international-relations phenomena.

A WORD OF CAUTION

In this chapter, we have sought to demonstrate that the discipline of international relations has tended to overlook the activities of nongovernmental actors and to emphasize mainly intergovernmental activities. By incorporating the analysis of the new and neglected actors of international politics, the discipline of international relations will become much more reflective of contemporary reality.

In addition to multinational corporations, ethnic groups, terrorist organizations, and religious movements, one could study a great variety of nongovernmental actors. Such actors include exile groups, underground opposition movements, nongovernmental international organizations (NGOs), "supranational" intergovernmental organizations (such as the European Community), internationally interlocking political parties, labor movements, and student movements.

Before closing this chapter we should offer a word of caution. In the late 1960s, in response to the groundswell of student demonstrations in many parts of the world, an assortment of new books eagerly asserted that a "new phenomenon," one of significant international consequences, had appeared! However, student demonstrations were not a new phenomenon. Further, when in the early 1970s the student movements began to subside, the searchers of new phenomena agilely transferred their attention to "newer" and more potent actors, such as multinational corporations, international religions, and terrorist organizations. We should alert the student, therefore, to the dangers of faddism and occasional academic sensationalism. In a field where publications in the form of books, monographs, and journal articles have often been equated with professional survival, talent and energy have at times been needlessly tapped in search of a new angle of vision or of the first Einstein of international relations.

We should also point out in closing that the focus on nonstate actors is not itself a new phenomenon in the social sciences and political philosophy. The theory of Marxism, for instance, treats the concept of *class* (certainly a nonstate actor) as the most important tool or unit of political analysis. The Marxist slogan "Proletarians of the world unite" was, among other things, a call for the intensification of transnational politics among nonstate actors. Further, many analyses of international politics have focused on a single actor, such as the manufacturers of armaments (the "merchants of death"), bureaucratic cliques, or ecology and women's movements. Admittedly, some of this literature is polemical. Yet it does open up a level of analysis of international politics beyond that of the impervious state. It is fitting, therefore, that new and/or neglected actors become the legitimate (but not the only) subjects of courses in international politics, and that we abandon "billiard balls" in favor of "cobwebs."

SUGGESTIONS FOR FURTHER STUDY

Louis W. Goodman has analyzed the social and political impact of multinational corporations, especially in Latin America, in *Small Nations and Giant Firms* (New York: Holmes & Meier, 1987). For earlier studies, see Forest L. Grieves, *Transnationalism in World Politics and Business* (Elmsford, N.Y.: Pergamon Press, 1979); and Raymond Vernon, *Storm over Multinationals: The Real Issues* (Cambridge, Mass.: Harvard University Press, 1977). Dependency is the theme of R. Harrison Wagner, "Economic Interdependence, Bargaining Power, and Political Influence," *International Organization,* 42 (Summer 1988), 461–83. The media as an international actor is the subject of Hamid Mowlana, *Global Information and World Communication* (White Plains, N.Y.: Longman, 1985). Abdul A. Said et al. have investigated the transnational role of ethnic groups in *Ethnicity and U.S. Foreign Policy,* rev. ed. (New York: Praeger, 1981). Charles Foster has balanced theoretical articles and case studies in his anthology on *Nations without a State: Ethnic Minorities in Western Europe* (New York: Praeger, 1980). The significance of transnational religious movements is the theme of Martin Kramer, *Political Islam,* Georgetown University, Center for Strategic and International Studies (Beverly Hills, Calif.: Sage Publications, 1980). An assessment of left- and right-wing terrorism is the subject of "Forum: Terrorism and Political Violence," *Orbis,* 28 (Spring 1984), 5–52. Yonah Alexander and Tunde Adeniran have drawn together the views of authorities on terrorism in *International Violence* (New York: Praeger, 1983), which complements Yonah Alexander, *International Terrorism: National, Regional and Global Perspectives,* rev. ed. (New York: Praeger, 1981). In the *Web of World Politics: Nonstate Actors in the Global System* (Englewood Cliffs, N.J.: Prentice-Hall, 1976), Richard W. Mansbach, Yale H. Ferguson, and Donald E. Lampers have successfully offered an alternative to the theory of international politics centered on the national interest.

19

THREATS FACING HUMANKIND

Can the international system, with its substandard regulatory institutions, survive the multiple challenges it is facing in our time? To ask an even more basic question, can the human race itself survive without drastically changing its global and regional institutional structures? We shall conclude this book by attempting to answer these two important questions and address some of their implications.

The way we respond to these and similar questions depends heavily on our assumptions regarding the processes that characteristically attend the genesis, growth, maintenance, and even death of political and social institutions such as governments, political parties, pressure groups, international organizations, and multinational corporations. Are social and political institutions spontaneous and even accidental phenomena, or are they conscious human inventions aiming to serve concrete human needs and to facilitate collective living? Our view is that social and political institutions reflect, for the most part, conscious efforts of individuals and groups to provide collective security and satisfaction and to facilitate through various regulatory mechanisms the challenge of collective living. The fundamental problem of politics, as we have stressed throughout this text, is to find ways of harmonizing the needs and wants of human individuals with the needs and the wants of collectivities, whether subnational, national, regional, or global. Since individual and collective needs often conflict, governments, laws, courts, police, and judges have been invented to regulate the resulting conflicts. Unfortunately, we sometimes witness situations in which governments become the servants of the few against the interests of the many—oppressing their citizens at times and neglecting them at others.

The oldest enemies of humankind have been hunger, war, disease, and alienation, discussed more fully later in this chapter. In this century—and primarily as a result of technological growth—we have added new and purely human-produced challenges to our existence. Collective dangers from environmental pollution, high noise levels, climate alterations, opinion control, and nuclear holocaust are twentieth-century phenomena. Scientists are warning us against destabilizing important equilibriums in the biosphere that might expose our planet to acute if not ultimate dangers. The limits of finite resources of food, energy, and production are within sight. And population growth—if unchecked—is certain to aggravate all of these challenges.

Following the decolonization of large portions of the earth, the nation-state became clearly the predominant form of political organization on the international scene. By and large, national governments have sought to redistribute income through taxation and public expenditures; to provide for public needs such as roads, canals, dams, and fortifications; to regulate transportation and communications; to stimulate and finance education; to ensure that crime is controlled; and in general to see that public order is kept. Above all, national governments have assumed the responsibility for defense against external threats.

Regardless of the relative effectiveness of governments in combatting purely *national* problems, one thing remains clear: National governments are not institutionally equipped to face a number of challenges that transcend national boundaries. Environmental pollution, natural-resource exhaustion, multinational corporate growth, international terrorism, international economic complexity, and accidental nuclear confrontation are the types of problems that lend themselves to international and supranational regulatory practices. The international institutions that have been developed so far do not have the authority and capability to legislate and enforce the necessary regulatory measures for combating such problems. But as we shall see shortly, the challenges will continue to increase in gravity. Eventually, if past practices offer any guidance, the people of this earth will be forced to develop appropriate supranational and subnational institutions to ensure at least the minimum goal of global survival. The international system—as we know it today—is likely to change, and traditional concepts, such as national sovereignty, nonintervention, and noninterference in domestic affairs, are likely to be watered down considerably, if not eventually abandoned.

THE THREAT OF WAR

As we saw in Chapters 10 and 11, war and various gradations of armed conflict have been our constant and destructive companions from the beginning of recorded history. We have traced "causes" of war to the very nature of human beings, to the imperfection of human institutions, and to the greed and ambition of specific leaders or interest groups. But whatever its causes, the phenomenon of politically motivated violence has persisted through history and is not, as is frequently assumed, merely a by-product of the existence of unaccountable nation-states operating in an anarchic international environment.

Since August 6, 1945, the date of the awesome nuclear explosion in Hiroshima, war has assumed a new and ominous dimension. Technological growth has managed to increase the destructive capacity of nuclear weapons to self-defeating levels. When the capacity to destroy becomes so total that war entails the mutual annihilation of the belligerent populations, then war as an instrument of policy in a Clausewitzian sense ceases to be a rational tool of statecraft. Regrettably, however, the history of diplomacy is replete with decisions that defy rational explanation. The doctrine of *mutually assured destruction* (MAD), which characterized U.S. strategy in the 1970s, pointedly made clear the futility of a total nuclear war. But MAD rested on the premise that heads of government of the nuclear powers would employ weapons of mass destruction only as the ultimate form of retaliation available to them. In the 1980s, theorists of strategy, both public and private, began to speculate about scenarios of limited nuclear war to achieve—in Clausewitzian terms—rational political ends. The speculation ceased to be theoretical when a debate in the British House of Commons in August 1984 revealed that two years earlier the Royal Navy had positioned a missile-firing submarine in the South Atlantic and thereby demonstrated an advanced state of readiness to use a nuclear weapon against an Argentine target in the Anglo-Argentine War.

The war record since World War II has been quite active in limited warfare, but relatively modest in head-on strategic confrontations between the United States and the Soviet Union. Despite the deep ideological rift between the globe's Eastern and Western camps, we have been spared a third (nuclear) world war for nearly fifty years. But as time passes, we know that through accident, plan, madness, or miscalculation we may find ourselves in the midst of a nuclear holocaust. The fact that our global house has not caught fire does not mean that it is fireproof. We know that universal and regional international organizations are grossly inadequate for keeping the nuclear genie in its brittle bottle. Our safety so far is based on a system of mutual vulnerability to nuclear destruction. The East and the West (and potentially the developing South) are like deadly scorpions trapped in a bottle. Obviously, this is not the time to rely for security on imperfect "institutions" such as the balance of power, mutual deterrence, conflict management, and a veto-blocked United Nations.

If we assume that war is mainly the product of inadequate global institutions, then the way to prevent it is to develop the needed institutions. The most obvious effective institution for the prevention of war is a form of federal government of the world that possesses adequate centralized power to enforce the United Nations Charter as well as other provisions for the peaceful settlement of international disputes. But although excellent legal minds from various parts of the world have constructed thoughtful plans and principles for world government, no practical way has yet been found to convince nation-states to transfer sovereignty and power to what they consider an ill-defined, alien, and suspect global authority.

Nuclear explosion: "The survivors will envy the dead." (Joint Task Force Three)

But even if we were to assume that an effective global governmental apparatus will be developed some day, we cannot assure ourselves that people would maintain themselves in a conflict-free environment. There would always remain the dangers of global "civil conflict," of terrorism against the global authorities, of takeovers of nuclear installations, and of other acts of insurrection. More alarmingly, if we were to assume that war and armed conflict are only products of human nature and that conflict is just another instinct—and, as such, no different from hunger, lust, fear, love, and suspicion—then to eliminate the "conflict instinct" we would have to change human nature. But changing human nature, whether through brainwashing, chemical, and surgical means or through techniques of "behavior technology," is in many ways interfering with the freedom and dignity of the individuals and groups whose "nature" is about to be artificially and arbitrarily changed.[1] In other words, if we attain a human universe that is harmonious at the expense of reducing human beings to conformist robots, that too is an intolerable future state of affairs.

Perhaps we will never attain a perfectly conflict-free planet. But we can still try to reduce the incidence of conflict as much as we can, and we must certainly reduce the probability of total nuclear destruction to microscopic levels. To do this, we shall need institutions capable of transcending national boundaries. So far, schemes for jointly authorized arms control and disarmament have not proved effective because they are based on assumptions of sovereignty—

[1]On this controversial subject, see the work of B. F. Skinner, *Beyond Freedom and Dignity* (New York: Knopf, 1971).

which disallow credible methods of supranational inspection and thereby multiply mutual national suspicions.

How, then, will humankind make the leap beyond the sovereign nation-state? Shall we have to undergo a nuclear catastrophe *before* we develop global institutions? We cannot afford such an option. After a nuclear spasm there may be no need for institutions of any kind, other than those necessary to police a scorched and then frozen earth.

In closing, war can be viewed as a terrible disease of the global political system for which we already know the cure—effective global institutions for the peaceful settlement of disputes. Our only problem, but a nearly insurmountable one, is that we do not know how to make the patients (national governments) take the medicine. There exists, unfortunately, no trusted and authoritative supranational doctor to prescribe and administer it.

ECOCIDE

Ecocide is a recently coined word that denotes the multiple capacity that humans have developed to destroy the earth—or at least to make it unfit for human life. By and large, until our own times, we have assumed that growth in human productivity has been good. We have judged the "power" of countries by watching for increases in indexes such as population, productivity, exports and imports, and national wealth. We have admired governments that have generated rapid economic development, and we have criticized others for letting their people stagnate and even regress.

But recently, as we enter what is often referred to as the postindustrial era, we are beginning to realize that growth and productivity involve some negative and dangerous by-products. Most industrial nation-states have become concerned about environmental pollution caused by automobile exhaust fumes, airplanes, factories, and waste products that are emitted into the atmosphere and into our rivers and seas. We are rapidly reaching the time when *air* may become unfit to breathe and *water* unfit to drink. Oil spills and dangerous chemical waste products are turning lakes, rivers, and beaches into vast disease-infested sewers. Toxic by-products of industrial processes are threatening certain animal species with extinction and are slowly undermining the health and integrity of the human species.[2]

Other serious dangers are being posed by attempts to control the earth's climate and to deflect natural waterways for purposes of irrigation and agricultural growth. For example, according to climatological data, the average temperature of the earth increased about one degree Fahrenheit between 1880 and 1940 and since 1940 has dropped about one-half degree Fahrenheit.[3] Recent evalua-

---

[2]See Lester R. Brown's excellent book, *World without Borders* (New York: Random House, 1972), pp. 15–40.

[3]*Ibid.*, p. 25.

The Chernobyl nuclear plant disaster in the Soviet Union in 1986–an early warning, or is it already too late? (Tass from Sovfoto)

tions have, however, forecast the so-called greenhouse effect (a dome of gaseous pollution trapping solar heat within the earth's atmosphere), which will dramatically raise the earth's average temperatures. By year 2035 much of the United States will have turned into a desert, while the population of "warm and friendly" Canada will swell to over two hundred million people.[4] Although no one can say whether these trends are cyclical or are triggered in part by industrial activity on earth, there is a consensus among students of these phenomena that humans have the capacity to destabilize the earth's climate. Another frequently cited example of climate control involves the Soviet Union. If the Soviets were to reverse the direction of four warm-water rivers that now flow from the USSR into the Arctic Sea, the North Pole would cool off further, with unpredictable consequences for the climate of countries that are near the Arctic region.

A basic concern of ecologists is that we on earth are rapidly running out of natural resources, especially food and energy. At the present level of extraction and consumption and with the projected exponential growth in the world's population, it is predicted that sometime in the twenty-first century we will run out of seafood, energy fuels, forest products, fresh water, arable land, and several industrial raw materials. The problem, therefore, is both absolute and relative. It is absolute in the sense that we can calculate today the earth's capacity to support

[4]See Jeremy Rifkin, "The Greenhouse Doomsday Scenario," *Washington Post,* July 31, 1988, p. C3.

about 4.3 billion people at a tolerable $2,700-per-capita income.[5] But as we shall soon see, unless drastic measures are taken, the earth's population will over-whelmingly exceed the current 5 billion mark. The problem of finite resources is relative in the sense that privation will not affect all nation-states equally and simultaneously. It will hit first and hardest in the countries of the Third World. The unequal distribution of income and population between the Northern and Southern regions of the earth, as well as within nation-states, is likely to become aggravated rather than improved with time. Consequently, the roots of conflict will be strengthened at a time when the destructiveness of weaponry is becoming prohibitive.

The challenges of controlling pollution and conserving natural resources extend well beyond the capabilities of national governments acting separately. Once more, as in the case of war, it is clear that new supranational, transnational, and subnational institutions are needed to regulate industrial production and pollution and to provide for the relatively equitable distribution of global income and resources. For example, wishing to control the problem of environmental pollution, social scientists recommend that the growth rate of global industrial production slow down considerably, if not begin decreasing on a programmed basis. However, the less-developed countries (LDCs) raise important objections. They argue that they have not been responsible for global pollution, which up to now has been spread by the industrial nation-states. LDCs also wish to industri-alize, and they have a right to do so. So, they argue, industrial slowdowns should apply only to advanced countries until the gap that separates the world's rich from the world's poor is narrowed. The LDCs have vigorously advanced this view since the World's Environmental Conference, which was held in Stockholm in 1972.

With 120 delegations voting in favor, 6 in opposition, and 10 abstaining, the General Assembly of the United Nations adopted the Charter of Economic Rights and Duties of States in 1974. In terms of both the liberalization of trade and the protection of the environment, the Charter is an appeal for justice for the less-developed countries. For example, Article 30 opens with the following exhortation:

> The protection, preservation and enhancement of the environment for the pres-ent and future generations is the responsibility of all States. . . . All States should co-operate in evolving international norms and regulations in the fields of the environment.[6]

[5]John P. Lewis and Valeriana Kallab, eds., *U.S. Foreign Policy and the Third World—Agenda 1983* (New York: Praeger/Overseas Development Council, 1983), p. 220.

[6]United Nations, *Resolutions of the General Assembly: 29th Session* (New York: United Nations, 1974), p. 134. This is the thrust of a growing body of literature that questions the planet's capability to continue developing and that proclaims resources to be scarce, finite, and limited and encourages their collec-tive exploitation in a strategy of conservation. For good examples of studies suggesting strategies of global conservation, see Richard A. Falk, *This Endangered Planet: Prospects and Proposals for Human Sur-vival* (New York: Vintage, 1971); Garrett Hardin, *Exploring New Ethics for Survival* (New York: Penguin, 1972); and Dennis C. Pirages and Paul R. Ehrlich, *Ark II* (San Francisco: W. H. Freeman, 1974).

In theory such a statement is a contribution to international law, but the reality is that the leading developed states of the West voted in opposition to the Charter. Consequently, the prospects for the fulfillment of this goal of international cooperation are not encouraging.

In retrospect, the decentralized nature of the international system and the continued competitiveness among national governments do not offer us much room for optimism. In a world system that considers industrial output a heavy ingredient of national political power, we should not expect that governments would voluntarily curb their countries' productivity unless their citizens were imminently threatened with mass poisoning and their territories with resource exhaustion. If global problems indeed stimulate the development of global institutions, then the trend may be toward more international (possibly supranational) regulation and the attendant weakening of national sovereignty and independence.

THE POPULATION EXPLOSION

Thomas Malthus,[7] writing at the end of the eighteenth century, sounded an alarm for humankind.[8] The British political economist warned that although the world's food supply would continue growing at an arithmetic rate, its population would grow at a much faster geometric or exponential rate. This disparity between the two growth rates would soon threaten humanity with famine, pestilence, and war. It might even court the destruction of the human species. Malthus's dire predictions did not materialize, and this has led scientists to dismiss similar warnings as Malthusian overstatements. However, we find that late in the twentieth century there is much room for the resurrection and application of the Malthusian theory. The so-called population explosion thesis is being taken seriously throughout the world. Population controllers are conjuring up frightful projections of an earth with "standing room only."

Our task today is not only to slow down the growth of the earth's population, but also to stabilize the number of human inhabitants at a fixed and ideally optimal standard of living. Fear of the population explosion, which has mobilized the neo-Malthusians, is essentially a post–World War II phenomenon. Rapid population growth has been caused primarily by a decisive reduction of death rates (as a result of an impressive performance by public health programs throughout the world) and the maintenance of previously existing birth rates. Currently, it is estimated that the earth's population is growing at an annual rate of 3.6 percent.

---

[7]Thomas Robert Malthus (1766–1834) was a British professor of political economy whose major work, *An Essay on the Principle of Population* (1798), had a major impact on the social sciences and contributed to the development of the discipline of demography.

[8]Much of the discussion in the remainder of this chapter is heavily indebted to Brown, *World without Borders*, pp. 132–54; and Fred A. Sondermann, "Implications of Population Growth," *Theory and Practice of International Relations,* ed. Fred A. Sondermann, William C. Olson, David S. McLellan, 3rd ed. (Englewood Cliffs, N.J.: Prentice-Hall, 1970), pp. 112–18.

This means that it will double every thirty-five years or so. Figure 19–1 looks at the problem another way. According to some estimates, it took two million years for the earth to house one billion inhabitants (1820). It took only a hundred more years for the second billion to be added (1920). The third billion came in thirty years (1960). The fourth billion arrived in fourteen years (1974). Two more billions are expected—unless the trends begin to shift drastically—by 1999.

But are there finite limits to the number of people the earth can resonably support? Is there an optimum number of people, a number that will permit an orderly and relatively harmonious coexistence among nation-states? What is this number, and who will determine it? Different demographic studies make different recommendations. For example, demographers argue that the United States, with a relatively sparsely populated territory, has already reached a post-

Figure 19–1   Growth of World Population

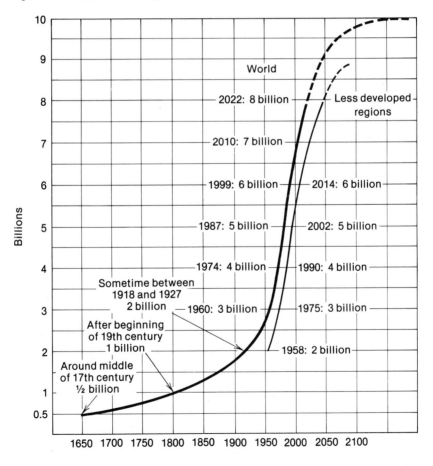

SOURCE: Nafis Sadik, *The State of World Population, 1988* (New York, United Nations Population Fund, 1988), p. 17

optimal population level and should now stop growing in order to maintain a constant standard of living.

Certain countries are especially responsible for the alarming post–World War II population expansion. India, China, Brazil, and Indonesia account for over 50 percent of the total (approximately 70 million per year) population increase. The obvious conclusion is that any coordinated attempt to stabilize global population should include the development of fair and equitable "quotas" of yearly population increases or decreases, as appropriate. A situation in which the world's poor continue to multiply at alarming rates, while the population of developed states has just about stabilized, may be a slow-fuse time bomb designed to explode during the twenty-first century.

Once more, basic questions arise: Who will determine population quotas? Who will monitor, evaluate, and control local, national, and regional population trends? Here again, we are confronted with institutional gaps that can be filled only if population pressures raise a sense of imminent collective danger. The challenges that will face future institutions of population control are many. In our decade, birth rates and death rates have been in a 5:2 ratio. In order to stabilize the globe's population, we need a 1:1 ratio. We cannot rationally argue for increasing death rates by such means as medical negligence, war, and famine. Therefore, our response must concentrate on reducing birth rates.

Birth-control techniques, whether natural or artificial, are well known, and medical science continues to make advances in this field. Few governments are prepared, however, to give serious consideration to a legislative approach to population control. This approach would entail the passage of laws providing for rewards and penalties designed to keep potential parents from exceeding the optimal limit of two children. For example, families having more than their quota

A Paraguayan family.
(United Nations/UNICEF/
D. Mangurian)

of two children would have to pay higher rather than lower taxes—unlike the current practice in most countries. Another suggestion along these lines would be to issue two child-bearing licenses per couple (or one license per individual), which could be bought or sold in the open market. Thus those who wished to remain childless could sell their reproduction licenses to those who wished to have larger families. Needless to say, these and other institutional control techniques would enroach upon the personal freedoms of action and preference. But given the multiplying dangers of collective living, perhaps we shall learn to obey more and more restrictions. After all, we have learned to stop at red lights and go on greens, to be searched and X-rayed at airports, to pay taxes, to secure licenses, and to wait our turn in line.

National and global institutions will continue to face major obstacles in their efforts to control population growth. First, there will be those who will keep faith in the infinite ability of science and human ingenuity to continue indefinitely to feed, clothe, and protect whatever number of inhabitants God and the collective human will choose to put on this earth. Of course, artificial birth control will remain a question of conscience or religious norm for many. Yet in most cultures natural control through abstinence or rhythm is permissible. Another major obstacle will be nationalists who argue that efforts to curb the growth of ethnic communities, especially in the Southern regions of our planet, are merely an outgrowth of the neocolonialist mentality.

But unless the current trends of population expansion change, and in the absence of effective institutions of population stabilization, the growth of humankind may be regulated by "invisible-hand" or "Darwinian" controls. These are old, familiar, and destructive standbys, such as famine, pestilence, and war. Philosophers at this stage might lift their hands and say, "Let the fittest survive." The choices, we feel, will range between conscious, rational, and coordinated techniques of population control and the historically self-defeating techniques of the "invisible hand." We opt for the way of human institutions and would like to leave the law of the jungle to the animals.

FAMINE AND EPIDEMIC DISEASES

The challenge of providing adequate food for humans is two-pronged. First, given the best projections of aggregate food supply and demand, a serious global scarcity is likely. Second, the severe inequality in production and consumption patterns that separates the rich nation-states from the more populous developing ones is expected to cause great material and psychological disturbances, ranging from mass starvation of the poor and guilt for the rich to violent domestic and international conflicts resulting from the elemental struggle for survival.

Until recently, there was little cause for alarm on the ability of humankind to feed itself. After World War II, the food supply increased steadily at a healthy rate of 2.5 percent per year. But in 1972 the global food supply declined, for the first time in twenty years. Cereal production (wheat, grains, and rice) fell by thirty-three million tons at the same time that an increase of twenty-five million tons was needed in order to keep up with world demand. The immediate cause of this decline was bad weather, which accounted for lower food production in the Soviet Union, China, India, Australia, Saharan Africa, and Southeast Asia. The disquieting result of this production setback was that wheat reserves of the principal exporting countries fell from sixty million tons in 1970 to twenty-two million tons in 1974. The inability of global supply to keep pace with global demand, coupled with price increases in petroleum products needed for the processing of chemical fertilizers, led to substantial increases in the price of food. Expectedly, these increases have hit hardest the poor and import-dependent countries, which often spend from 70 to 80 percent of their income to buy food. The consequence of the decline in the global food supply is that over half a billion people in developing countries are suffering either from outright starvation or from serious nutritional deficiencies that can have lasting consequences on human physical and mental development.[9]

The long-range outlook for food production is alarming.[10] We seem to be moving into a period of chronic scarcity with steadily increasing prices. The problem is fourfold. First, there is a scarcity of water needed for irrigation. Techniques for the desalinization of sea water are extremely expensive, and those for the artificial production of rainfall are both costly and unreliable. Second, there is a projection for a greater scarcity of nitrogen fertilizer. Third, there is land scarcity: Only relatively arid lands remain open to future cultivation. Fourth, there is a scarcity of energy, which is vitally needed for the functioning of modern agricultural techniques.

There is still no doubt that we theoretically have the capacity—through the effective use of energy and fertilizers—to increase current volumes of food production many times over. But this will be done only at high cost, and will deny food to those who need it the most but who cannot afford it. To begin with, food is already distributed inequitably among the world's population. This inequity will become more apparent with the improvement of statistical methods and reporting techniques. We should consider the consequences of prolonged and worsening inequality in the distribution of such a basic commodity as food. For example, in the developing countries the per-capita availability of grain is about 400 pounds per year (or little over a pound per day). Most of this grain is consumed directly, in the form of bread, pastries, and breakfast cereals. The comparable figure for the average North American is five times as much, or one ton of grain per year. Of this, only 200 pounds per year are consumed directly; 1,800 pounds are consumed indirectly, in the form of meat, milk, and eggs. Thus, the average American is five times better fed than the average Indian.[11] The food-

---

[9]For more detail, see *Crisis in Food,* U.S. Department of State Publication 8808, General Foreign Policy Series 293 (Washington, D.C.: Department of State, Bureau of Public Affairs, 1975). See also Lester Brown, "The Browning of the Green Revolution," *Washington Post,* July 3, 1988, Outlook Section.

[10]See Lester R. Brown, *Our Daily Bread,* Headline Series 225 (New York: Foreign Policy Association, 1975). The remainder of this section is based on this source.

[11]For an elaboration of the food shortage problem, see *ibid.,* pp. 12–15.

Starving children in Nigeria. (UNICEF photo by P. Larsen)

consumption gap is not increased further only because the North American stomach has apparently been stretched to its physical limits. The consumption of livestock products is even less equitable. The average American, Argentinian, and Australian consumes 250 pounds of meat per year. The French, Canadian, and West Germans require 200 pounds each. The English make do with 170 pounds. The average Russian, Swede, and Spaniard consumes 100 pounds. Yet the inhabitants of the developing world consume, on the average, less than 20 pounds of meat per year.[12] One does not need to be a statistical genius to realize that "something is rotten in the state of Denmark."

Current global grain production is about 1.6 billion tons per year, and is being used to feed an estimated world population of 4.5 billion. If everyone were to eat at the American level (one ton of grain per person per year), the grain production would have to be 4.5 billion tons. The United Nations has estimated that by the end of the twentieth century, the world's population will be 6.5 billion. This will require about 3 billion tons of grain annually, or about two times today's output. The challenge is therefore clear. The food problem can be controlled if population growth in developing countries is also controlled, if the price of food is kept within the reach of poor countries or poor social classes, and if the world's wealthy nation-states limit their consumption of food—which is currently three times higher than their fair share.

---

[12]These "average" figures can be quite misleading. As we know, there are great pockets of poverty in most countries. A per-capita figure suggests equitable distribution, which in reality does not exist.

Again, we find that this challenge cannot be met unless we abandon competitive and state-centered foreign policies and adopt attitudes and institutions that look upon our earth as a single, highly interdependent, and vulnerable society. We have already talked about the difficulties of controlling world population. With respect to food-price controls, it has been suggested that we need an internationally managed food-reserve organization to operate within the framework of the United Nations Food and Agriculture Organization (FAO). Under the direction of such an organization, nation-states (producers as well as consumers) would agree to hold certain minimum levels of food in stock in order to meet the needs of a "dry day." This food reserve would be let into the market during periods of scarcity and would help to limit sharp and sudden price fluctuations. Also, the proposed organization could provide for an emergency food reserve to alleviate famine in highly vulnerable areas such as India and Saharan Africa.

The United Nations Food Conference, which took place in Rome in November 1974, did much toward laying the informational groundwork for meeting the future challenge of food-or-famine. It remains to be seen whether we have the foresight and the wisdom to follow through with practical and effective measures. This question is both a moral and a pragmatic one for the generations to come. As Willy Brandt, chancellor of the Federal Republic of Germany from 1969 to 1974, remarked, "Morally it makes no difference whether a man is killed in war or is condemned to starve to death by the indifference of others."[13] Morality converges with pragmatism when we realize that human indifference breeds inequalities and social problems that feed the fires of war.

The Specter of AIDS

With increasing urgency in the second half of the 1980s a "new" enemy of humankind has been spreading its ominous wings: AIDS—the acquired immune deficiency syndrome.[14] We have used quotation marks around the word *new* because pestilence—e.g., the plague—has been one of the oldest enemies of the human species. AIDS has been spreading at an alarming rate since 1983 and, despite a massive mobilization of research programs involving well over two billion dollars, no effective treatment or preventive (immunization) techniques have been developed.

The disease, at first, afflicted special vulnerability groups such as male homosexuals, intravenous drug addicts, and persons needing frequent blood transfusions for medical purposes. Since the mid-1980s, however, accurate statistical studies indicate that all segments of the population, regardless of their sexual preferences, are becoming afflicted with increasing frequency. Accurate counts in 1988 show 67,000 persons suffering from the disease in the United

[13]Quoted in Brown, *World without Borders*, p. 59. This remark was made to the United Nations General Assembly in the fall of 1973.

[14]The discussion on AIDS here is based on the highly informed essay by Diane Johnson and John F. Murray, M.D., "AIDS without End," *New York Review of Books*, August 18, 1988, pp. 57–63.

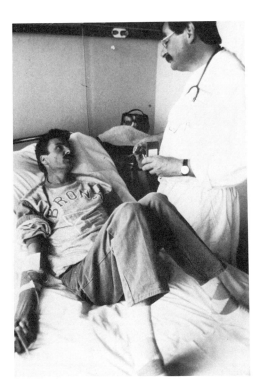

An AIDS patient. (D. Gutekinst/Gamma-Liaison)

States and 33,000 in Europe, and the World Health Organization estimates over 200,000 cases of the disease globally.[15] The projection is that there will be 450,000 cases of AIDS in the United States alone in 1993, with the number of people being infected by the AIDS virus (HIV) running between five and ten million.[16]

With no breakthrough in sight in the combatting of the disease, a number of difficult dilemmas are already apparent: Given that viruses and diseases recognize no boundaries, should the strategy to confront the treacherous new threat be national, regional, global, or all of the above? Within societies, do mandatory testing procedures, to identify those who are carriers of the disease, violate the civil rights of those to be tested? How does one confront myths, misconceptions, and collective hysteria (vigilantism) that might result from the projected malignancy of the problem? Will countries require AIDS tests prior to issuing immigration and tourist visas? How does one react to governments that might set up isolation centers and initiate formal or informal deportation practices against the victims of the disease? Ultimately, is AIDS becoming a sophisticated Malthusian revenge targeting postindustrial societies and eventually the total population of our planet?

All of the above are not rhetorical questions, and answers will be pro-

---

[15]The statistics, from the Centers for Disease Control, are cited in *ibid.*, p. 59.

[16]*Ibid.*, p. 61.

vided according to the cultural practices, political systems, and legislative proce-dures available in each nation-state. Clearly, the pooling of research and preven-tion resources internationally, under the coordination of the World Health Organization, will be called forward to act and react at an accelerated pace.

ALIENATION

Alienation is a very difficult concept to define. It could be described as a state of mind of people who feel no affinity for their social and work environments, per-ceive society as being hostile or indifferent to their existence, and are convinced that no matter what they say or do no one else cares.[17] The causes of alienation are multiple and complex. We shall assume that alienation is rooted primarily in poverty, backwardness, illiteracy, ill health, and in general in conscious percep-tions of social, economic, and political inequality. Of course, it is also possible (but less likely) for people to be alienated by life-styles of freedom, drabness, and a lack of challenge not necessarily accompanied by material privation. We shall concentrate, nonetheless, on inequality, unemployment, and rootlessness as three major ingredients of alienation.

Inequality

Inequality is a problem among as well as within countries. We talk about the gap between the rich countries of the North and the poor countries in the South. But we also know that there are zones of poverty and neglect in nearly every country of our earth. It is safe to assume that members of a society (whether individuals, groups, classes, countries, or regions) tend to become alienated if they perceive that an obviously unequal distribution of income in their society is being main-tained at their own expense. No matter how one seeks to rationalize it, a ratio of 1:40 between a poor person's income and that of a well-to-do person can result in extreme resentment, utter frustration, and resignation.

In Chapter 17, we presented and discussed statistics concerning the un-equal distribution of income. Here, we shall merely propose that income inequi-ties are certainly, if only partially, sources of alienation. However, we must still attempt to answer a crucial question: Given today's decentralized international system, what can be done to remedy a situation in which over half of our earth's inhabitants are living near or below the subsistence level?[18]

The most direct approach to effective redistribution would be through the installation of a world government with the power of progressive taxation and public spending at the global level. But how many of the governments of advanced industrial nation-states, and of any other states for that matter, would survive politically if they adopted policies of massive redistribution of income

---

[17]See Erich Fromm, *Marx's Concept of Man* (New York: F. Ungar, 1966).
[18]See Brown, *World without Borders*, p. 43.

and wealth that would transfer resources away from their own citizenry and toward the underprivileged people of the earth? It is probable that no government could survive such altruistic but politically unpopular policies. And even if a government managed to adopt self-sacrificing policies and to secure popular support for them at home, the recipient governments might, for a number of reasons (such as political sensitivity, prestige, and the perceived stigma of external penetration), reject such altruistic offers. Indeed, we can identify the dimensions of the problem of inequality, but we cannot identify easily any timely or acceptable remedies. In the meantime, statistics show that the gap between the rich and the poor of the world continues to increase. It is more than likely that institutions developed in the future (whether at the national or international levels) will seek only to treat the effects rather than attack the causes of inequality.

Unemployment

The 1970s have ushered in a pattern of unemployment that has assumed dangerous proportions in the less-developed countries and is progressively besetting the modern, industrialized ones. Ultimately, the primary cause of unemployment is technological progress. Advanced technology, by employing labor-saving techniques (such as automation) in both the industrial and agricultural sectors, has accounted for greater efficiency, increased labor productivity, and serious unemployment. In Latin America, for example, unemployment nearly tripled in fifteen years, jumping from 2.9 million in 1950 to 8.8 million in 1965, and the rate of unemployment nearly doubled—from a tolerably 6 percent to a prohibitive 11 percent—during the same period. India, Pakistan, Sri Lanka, Malaysia, the Philippines, and Indonesia have been experiencing unemployment rates of 15 percent or more. The middle and late 1970s have also shown that an industrial giant such as the united States can suffer unemployment rates ranging from 8 to 10 percent.

Unemployment, together with inflation and inadequate measures of social security, certainly contributes to alienation. There is nothing more demoralizing for human beings who are capable of and eager to work than being unable to find employment, or even to perform the most menial and low-paying tasks. Proposals for social and political remedies of unemployment continue to generate heated debate. Within some countries, only the government has resources sufficient to fund programs that require massive employment of labor but offer little or no capital profit. Similarly, only governments can bear the cost of the social legislation necessary to protect the individual citizen from the negative impact of global shifts in the supply and demand of key commodities and services. Nevertheless, the increasingly interventionist role played everywhere by governments remains controversial for both ideological and economic reasons.

The proponents of laissez-faire economics argue that a free market is indispensable to a free society, and taxpayers in North America and Western Europe are often vocal in their concern over the high cost of social-welfare programs. Ultimately, the question of government intervention becomes one of polit-

An unemployment line in the United States. (Charles Gatewood)

ical philosophy rather than economics: How does one reconcile individual liberty with the increasing authority of the state? If the state has an obligation to provide employment, can it not in turn require that the individual accept the particular employment opportunity provided? Taxation, military service, and economic controls are but a few of the devices that have been used by governments to meet their responsibilities, and all of them impinge upon individual liberty. The modern world is unlikely to be different in this respect. Perhaps, then, the meaning of liberty is the opportunity to do what is right, in contrast with license, which is the freedom to do what is wrong. Within this guideline, government can still play an interventionist role in the economy and simultaneously preserve civil liberties. Overcoming the global problems of today necessitates the adoption of such a balanced approach.

Internationally, the unrestricted flow of labor (in other words, uncontrolled immigration), which has been suggested as a logical remedy to curbing world unemployment problems, is also an extremely controversial if not impractical alternative. By and large, labor unions are opposed to the influx of "cheap labor" into countries of high employment. Also, there is an abundance of nationalist, political, religious, cultural, racial, and generally social arguments against large-scale movements of populations that would upset the delicate social and demographic balances existing in various parts of the world. Resistance to the settlement of immigrants and refugees in Great Britain, France, the United States, and the Soviet Union is just the tip of an iceberg of violent reactions that would be unleashed if a program of unrestricted labor movements were launched on a global scale. In fact, any plan to develop one government for our earth must carefully evaluate the difficulties that would arise in the vital area of unrestricted population movement.

Rootlessness

Allied to the problem of unemployment and immigration is the problem of rootlessness. Rootlessness is part of the larger and perhaps inevitable phenomenon of urbanization, which has grown constantly since the onset of the industrial revolution. Accompanying technological growth, automation in agriculture, and the concentration of industries in a handful of urban and transportation centers, has been a trend of population movement away from small towns and villages and toward bustling and crowded "primate cities," such as New York, Tokyo, Calcutta, Rio de Janeiro, and Mexico City. According to Lester Brown, urbanization is proceeding at a galloping pace in Asia, Africa, and Latin America.[19] In these continents, the yearly increase in the amount of urban population living in cities of one hundred thousand or more ranges from 5 to 8 percent. At 5 percent annual growth, the urban population doubles every fifteen years. At 8 percent growth, it doubles every nine years.

However, urbanization coupled with unemployment and the creation of sprawling slums in both the heart and the periphery of large cities is a sure road to rootlessness and despair. It is probably easier to accept poverty in a rural than in an urban environment. In a rural setting, one usually has a piece of earth with which to associate. The struggle is against the forces of nature, such as drought, flood, cold winds, barren land, and distance from fellow human beings. But poverty in the "lonely crowd" of large urban centers is probably worse. In the urban setting, one can compare one's desperate condition with that of privileged but apparently indifferent city dwellers who live in large homes, employ servants, drive flashy automobiles, feed their pets sumptuously, and take long pleasure trips. Radio and television programs constantly portray the kind of easy life that is mistakenly equated with the American dream, the Brazilian dream, the Indian dream, and other national dreams. People who live in crowded slums, or even in hovels, tents, boats under bridges, or in the streets; who are cut off from their villages and from their relatives; who face large, impersonal, impenetrable, and seemingly self-satisfied bureaucracies; who feel the pain of hunger, smell the stench of poverty, and suffer the aches of disease and premature old age—these people cannot help becoming alienated. Their reaction will most likely continue to be apathy, acceptance of their condition as the will of God, or a turn to crime, hooliganism, and prostitution as forms of escape from a social deadlock. Other forms of "escape" from alienation are drugs, alcohol, and suicide. Furthermore, people who have "nothing to lose" can be convinced that the status quo should be changed by any means, whether peaceful or violent. Alienation can thus become the mother of revolution and war. That a city like Calcutta, with a projected population of forty to fifty million souls by the end of the twentieth century, may be a standard "model" for the urbanization of the Third World is a dreary prospect by anyone's standards. It is obvious, then, that planning, control, and im-

---

[19]*Ibid.*, p. 77.

proved urban services must become central focuses of future governmental as well as supranational policies. These measures inevitably call for "big government," and thus conflict with the Jeffersonian principle that government should be both wise and frugal.

TRANSITION FROM INTERNATIONAL TO PLANETARY POLITICS

After reviewing our admittedly dismal planetary state of affairs, we should firmly keep in mind that the quasi-anarchic nation-state system (whether understood in terms of balance of power, bipolarity, or multipolarity) is hardly equipped to respond to some fundamental challenges facing humankind as a whole. A proliferating body of literature (referred to as peace research and as world-order studies) advances a basic proposition that is consistently stated and restated.[20]

Peace researchers and world-order specialists argue that the nation-state system—wherein each nation-state fends for itself and maximizes only its own benefits as defined by its governmental structures—cannot provide for the maximization (not even the mere protection) of at least four fundamental sets of human values. (We referred briefly to these values in terms of the *five* major world problems and the *five* resultant global objectives at the end of Chapter 6.)

1. Avoidance of global catastrophe as a result of international war, especially the type involving the unlimited use of nuclear weapons.
2. Provision of basic human needs in terms of food, shelter, and vital services for all human beings, especially the one billion—or 20 percent—of earthly inhabitants that are hovering around the gates of starvation and pestilence.
3. Protection of the ecological balance of our planet and coordination of the rational conservation and consumption of finite resources in a world vitally in need of population-management plans and policies.
4. Active promotion and protection of basic human needs and economic, political, and cultural human rights designed to minimize the causes of alienation and to reduce the sources of terrorism and counterterrorism and civil conflicts.

The biologist Garrett Hardin, in a much-quoted essay entitled "The Tragedy of the Commons," graphically offered us some of the key reasons why an anarchic international system cannot solve collective (global) problems.[21] Hardin made reference to nineteenth-century cattle-grazing practices in the "commons"

---

[20]See for example, Richard A. Falk, *A Study of Future Worlds* (New York: Free Press, 1975); Mihajlo D. Mesarovic and Edward Pestel, *Mankind at the Turning Point* (New York: Dutton, 1974); Johan Galtung, *The True Worlds: A Transnational Perspective* (New York: Free Press, 1980); Kenneth E. Boulding, *Stable Peace* (Austin: University of Texas Press, 1978); Robert C. Johansen, *The National Interest and the Human Interest: An Analysis of U.S. Foreign Policy* (Princeton, N.J.: Princeton University Press, 1980); and Lester R. Brown et al., *State of the World*. A World Watch Institute Report on Progress toward a Sustainable Society, (New York: W. W. Norton, 1988).

[21]Garrett Hardin, "The Tragedy of the Commons," *Science*, 162 (December 13, 1968), 1243–48. Hardin tells us that the story of the tragedy of the commons was first written in 1833 by an obscure British amateur mathematician whose name was William Forster Lloyd.

(the grazing areas) of Great Britain. Each cattle farmer seeking to maximize his well-being kept adding to the number of cattle under his ownership and therefore adding to the total number that had to be fed by the finite grazing capacity of the commons. Ultimately, a series of uncoordinated individual decisions by each cattle owner (justifiable by individual standards) led to an irrational collective result: the devastation and permanent destruction of the common grazing areas and the demise of all cattle farmers. Hardin extended the concept of *commons* to include the open seas, ocean floors, the earth's atmosphere, and the surrounding space. His suggestion was that interest-maximizing decisions by nation-states regarding issue-areas such as the production of armaments, industrialization, environmental pollution, climatic alteration, population growth, and resource consumption need to be subjected to global coordination and control. Short of developing global-level controls, we will certainly permit humankind to move toward its ultimate and tragic conclusion.

Whether recruited from the ranks of realism or idealism, scholars are currently stressing the need for the overhauling of the international system so that it can meet new and enormous global challenges. Realist scholars still emphasize the proclivity of people (as individuals or in groups) to seek power, to protect interests, to resort to violence in order to secure important values, and to act selfishly, despite the occasional employment of altruistic rhetoric. For the realists, a safer future world can best be based on institutions reflecting the collective needs of the globe's few powerful nation-states. In a system approximating a global concert of great powers, the threat of nuclear holocaust through accident or miscalculation may be diminished. In a concert of great powers, new institutions can be developed providing for arms control and even gradual disarmament, especially for nuclear and other weapons of mass destruction. The realists simultaneously posit that inequities in status, power, and welfare between and within nation-states are unfortunately likely to continue in the indefinite future. The future system, in short, will be based more on premises of power and less on those of justice. But, minimally, they argue, it will be a system that will provide strategic stability and buy us time—without a major nuclear confrontation—until some day a genuine global authority can be developed.[22]

Idealists look at the problem of transforming the present international system with much greater urgency. They cite reports that humankind—as presently organized—is marching toward its demise through nuclear holocaust before the year 2000.[23] They recommend in a variety of books and monographs what they consider to be realistic schemes toward a global structural transformation that protects human values while minimizing war, poverty, and injustice.[24] This calls for a multitiered strategy that encourages economic interdependence

---

[22]Kenneth Waltz, *Theory of International Politics* (Reading, Mass.: Addison-Wesley, 1979).

[23]See the report of the Harvard-MIT arms-control seminar by Paul Doty, Richard Garwin, George Kistiakowsky, George Rathjens, and Thomas Schelling, "Nuclear War by 1999?" *Current,* January 1976, pp. 32–43.

[24]The discussion that follows is heavily indebted to Johansen, *National Interest and Human Interest.*

(but not one-sided dependence); further development of nonmonopolistic, non-state actors such as intermediate-sized multinational corporations; and the growth of global, regional, national, state, local, and neighborhood organizations. The ultimate objective is to move away from competing state sovereignties, away from nationalist and ideological exclusivism, away from arms races and war, and toward systems of equity, cooperation, and interdependence. In this ideal future world there should be self-reliance, psychological equality, and a sense of dignity and self-actualization for all human beings. The transition—as was the case with the functionalist model we discussed in Chapter 15—is expected to take a long time (over thirty years) and is based on values such as positive education, populist political action, and other nonviolent means of opposing existing poles of power. Nation-states and their governments during the transition period will not disappear. Their power, however, will be gradually checked and balanced by the development of a plethora of additional political and functional institutions of the intergovernmental as well as nongovernmental variety.

Centralization at the global level will be limited to a relatively few but major functions. They will include the planning, coordination, and control of nuclear weaponry, the protection of the global common areas, and the gradual redistribution of our earth's unequally distributed resources. Most human affairs, however, will continue to be handled at subnational levels and by organizations whose primary range of action will be at the local and provincial levels. Thus these new organizations will be able to deal with relatively small numbers of human beings and—as a result—will not become depersonalized and undemocratic.

A PARTING WORD

We have argued throughout this textbook that politics can be viewed from at least two distinct perspectives. The first perspective considers the nation-state to be the ultimate political entity. Politics, from this perspective, is the struggle for national power and the maximization of interest. The world is seen as an alien and hostile chamber in which political collectivities must struggle to protect their own interests because no one else will care for them. The second perspective looks beyond the nation-state and emphasizes global rather than national interest. Politics, from the second perspective, is the quest for the good life for all.

More and more, the distinction between these two perspectives is losing its relevance. With growing interdependence at the global level, the suffering or the happiness of some can no longer be insulated from the quality of life of others on our planet. Hunger, disease, pollution, and alienation can no longer be confined to certain areas of our earth. Unless they are treated as problems that can affect the well-being of all humankind, they will not be cured. But if they are not cured, they will aggravate human relationships and degenerate into civil and international wars at the expense of us all.

Our hope and our recommendation is that the coming generations of leaders of national societies, as well as other important political actors around

View of our earth from the moon. (NASA)

our earth, will face rather than evade these global issues and that they will develop both private and public institutions designed to regulate and, ideally, eliminate humankind's major maladies. The development of new institutions will not necessarily solve the great problems, and it will surely lead to greater organized intervention (at local, national, regional, and global levels) in our daily lives. Governmental or other forms of organized interventionism should not be allowed to become oppressive. It should be generated and regulated through systems of government that are democratic on a global scale. Perhaps the days of the open frontier, of inexhaustible opportunities, of rugged individualism, of unlimited and uninhibited competition are gone forever. Whether we happen to be inhabitants of democracies, of communist countries, or of authoritarian nation-states, the future will probably bring increased institutional intervention in our daily lives. In the interest of preserving our freedoms and of reflecting our own attitudes and interests in the institutional structures of the future, we must actively seek to *participate* in new as well as in existing institutions. *Participatory interventionism* will have much more of a human face than authoritarian, dictatorial, scientific, and generally *elitist* interventionism.

SUGGESTIONS FOR FURTHER STUDY

The cycle of poverty is the theme of the United Nations Conference on Trade and Development (UNCTAD), *The Least Developed Countries: 1987 Report* (New York: United Nations, 1987). Carl Friedrich von Weizsäcker combines physics and social science in *The Politics of Peril: Economics, Society and the Prevention of War* (New York: Seabury Press, 1978). Behavioral psychology is a theme of Linus Pauling, *No More War* (New York: Dodd, Mead, 1983). The vulnerability of the territorial state in the nuclear age is the subject of Paul Kecskemeti, *Strategic Surrender: The Politics of Victory and Defeat* (Stanford, Calif.: Stanford University Press, 1958). Richard L. Rubenstein has argued for a global response to the problem of resource allocation in *The Age of Triage: Fear and Hope in an Overcrowded World* (Boston: Beacon Press, 1983). The greenhouse effect and ozone loss are discussed in "To Save Our Environment," *U.N. Chronicle,* 25 (June 1988), 40–49. For a depiction of social and economic crises, see *The Human Suffering Index* (Washington, D.C.: Population Crisis Committee, 1987). Data on the rate of population increase by country are available in the *World Population Data Sheet* (Washington, D.C.: Population Reference Bureau, 1987). Robert S. McNamara described the international ramifications of the growth of the world's population in "Time Bomb or Myth: The Population Problem," *Foreign Affairs,* 62 (Summer 1984), 1113–31. Opposing points of view on the issue of population and resources are Garrett Hardin, "The Tragedy of the Commons," *Science,* 162 (December 13, 1968), 1243–48; and Julian L. Simon, "Resources, Population, Environment: An Oversupply of False Bad News," *Science,* 208 (June 27, 1980), 1431–37.

INDEX

Note: page numbers in italics refer to illustrations or figures.

401